Including Exceptional Students

A PRACTICAL GUIDE FOR CLASSROOM TEACHERS

Canadian Edition

Marilyn Friend
Indiana University–Purdue University at Indianapolis

William D. Bursuck
Northern Illinois University

Nancy L. Hutchinson
Queen's University

ALLYN AND BACON CANADA
SCARBOROUGH, ONTARIO

Canadian Cataloguing in Publication Data

Friend, Marilyn Penovich, 1953-
   Including exceptional students : a practical guide for classroom teachers

Canadian ed.
ISBN 0-205-28381-0

1. Special education - Canada.   2. Mainstreaming in education - Canada.
3. Handicapped children - Education - Canada.   I. Bursuck, William D.
II. Hutchinson, Nancy Lynn.   III. Title.

LC3984.F74 1998   371.9'046   C97-932208-1

© 1998 Prentice-Hall Canada Inc., Scarborough, Ontario
Pearson Education

ISBN 0-205-28381-0

Vice President, Editorial Director: Laura Pearson
Acquisitions Editor: Dawn Lee
Marketing Manager: Christine Cozens
Associate Developmental Editor: Carol Steven
Production Editor: Andrew Winton
Copy Editor: Dianne Broad
Editorial Assistant: Sharon Loeb
Production Coordinator: Sharon Houston
Permissions/Photo Research: Susan Wallace-Cox
Cover Design: Sarah Battersby
Cover Image: José Ortega
Page Layout: Hermia Chung

Original English Language edition published by Allyn and Bacon, Inc.,
Needham Heights, MA. Copyright © 1996.

6 7 8   06 05 04 03 02

Printed and bound in the United States of America.

Table of Contents

▶ *Chapter 4*   Students with Low-Incidence Exceptionalities   104

▶ *Chapter 5*   Students with High-Incidence Exceptionalities   140

◤ *Chapter 10*   Strategies for Independent Learning   306

◤ *Chapter 11*   Adapting Assessment for Exceptional Students   342

� *Chapter 12*   Responding to Student Behaviour   378

Preface

Educators in other countries, including the United States, look to Canada's commitment to inclusive education as a model and an inspiration. This was driven home for me during my recent sabbatical leave when I visited two large American universities. In both settings, I was inundated with questions from preservice teachers, graduate students, and classroom teachers. They wanted to know how we included exceptional students, why I thought Canadians were so enthusiastic about inclusion, and what recent developments were in inclusive education in Canada. I attended conferences for teachers that were held near both universities. In each case, graduate students proudly introduced me as a Canadian and teachers told me about Canadian schools they had visited, read about, or heard about. I am proud of the teaching I see in classrooms where teachers are doing everything they can to support and meet the needs of exceptional children and adolescents. But I am also aware of teachers' frustrations at not having the time, energy, and resources to do the job the way they think it should be done. I did not know if I should simply accept the accolades on behalf of Canadian teachers or if I should also tell people about the challenges that remain in inclusive education in Canada.

My sabbatical conversations with American teachers and researchers reminded me of the great cultural differences between Canada and the United States and firmed my resolve in using Canadian texts in my teaching with teacher candidates. For about the past eight years, I have used only texts written by Canadians that describe Canadian context, legislation, and classrooms. For a moment in fall 1996, I was tempted by a new text with the subtitle, "A Practical Handbook for Teachers," to break my own rule. This book was practical; it spoke to teachers instead of speaking about teachers, that is, it said, "when you teach ..." I wished I had written this book. When I told Prentice Hall that I loved the book by Friend and Bursuck, but would not adopt it because it was American, they asked me to prepare a Canadian edition.

New to the Canadian Edition

This edition contains many references to Canadian educators and Canadian educational researchers, including their locations in the country. The first three chapters have been rewritten extensively to describe the importance of the Charter of Rights and Freedoms to inclusion in Canada and the current state of inclusive education in each province and territory. There are timelines showing early developments in exceptional education and recent examples of how Canada is becoming an increasingly inclusive society. I drew representative definitions of the exceptionalities from provincial policy manuals and examples from provincial handbooks—ranging from a sample IEP to a list of the responsibilities of paraprofessionals. The prereferral process within a school is described in detail along with the role of in-school teams. This edition includes examples from Canadian instructional programs, reading programs, and research papers. I have increased the number of references to gifted and developmentally advanced students throughout the book and provided more examples of adapting teaching, assessment, and classroom organization to accommodate their needs in inclusive classrooms. Whereas the previous edition organized exceptionalities according to American legislation, across Chapter 4, 5, and 6, this edition contains a chapter on high incidence exceptionalities, a chapter on low-incidence exceptionalities, and a chapter on students who may be at-risk for a variety of reasons. Both multicultural and anti-racist education are described within the chapter on at-risk students.

Perspective

For many years, I organized my preservice teaching about exceptional children and adolescents around topics like planning, adapting teaching, and assessment. I can remember a time when each class session was focused on one area of exceptionality, but the approach I take now is often described as *non-categorical*. Every year as I supervise the practicum experiences of preservice teacher candidates, I am reminded of how much is expected of beginning classroom teachers in the education of exceptional youth. It is most effective to think about the teaching—and adapting of teaching—for exceptional students right from the start of planning for the whole class. You can adjust for individual needs and troubleshoot for potential challenges by keeping all students in mind when you begin selecting themes, teaching approaches, and materials. This is the time to decide if using reading materials written at a lower comprehension level will enable students like Derek Clark, who are weak readers, to take part in the classroom activities and discussions about transportation and Canadian geography. In some cases, it may be necessary to make plans so Derek and other students can work on a parallel, less complex curriculum topic like transportation in the community. Early planning for the grade 10 science class means taking action because Fan Wang, who has visual impairments, will need the text in an alternate format. You must decide whether to order the text on audiotape, in large-print format, or in Braille, or in more than one format for home and classroom learning. Examples like these show how in preparing this book, I have tried to focus on the kinds of information, skills, and strategies that recent teacher candidates have considered both thought-provoking and practical.

Organization

The textbook is divided into three main sections. **Section one** provides fundamental background knowledge in the field of exceptional education in Canada as well as current knowledge of how exceptional students are served within inclusive school environments. Chapter 1 describes the current situation in Canada and provides a brief history of how we came to where we are. This first chapter also introduces a step-by-step strategy for adapting instruction, called INCLUDE, that will help teachers accommodate students with special needs more effectively. Chapter 2 describes the people who specialize in working with exceptional students. Readers will learn about their role in working with other professionals and parents to meet students' needs. In Chapter 3, the principles of collaboration and the school situations that call for collaboration are discussed. The partnerships that teachers form with paraprofessionals and parents are also considered.

Section two examines the characteristics of students with disabilities and other exceptionalities. Although the various categories of exceptionality are addressed, the emphasis is on major physical, psychological, learning, and behaviour characteristics and the implications of these characteristics for instruction. In Chapter 4, readers will learn about the characteristics and educational needs of students with low-incidence exceptionalities, that is students with developmental delay, hearing loss, visual disabilities, health or physical disabilities, as well as students with traumatic brain injury, fetal alcohol syndrome, and autism. Chapter 5 describes the characteristics and needs of students with high-incidence disabilities: students who are gifted, students with learning disabilities, communication disorders, attention deficit disorders, and behaviour disabilities. In Chapter 6, readers will be introduced to students who are at risk for cultural and social reasons, including students whose first language and culture are not English, and students who are at risk due to poverty, neglect, and abuse.

Section three represents the heart of any course on inclusive practices: instructional approaches that emphasize teaching students effectively, regardless of disability or special need. In Chapter 7, the relationship between classroom environment and the diverse needs of learners is discussed. The key features of classrooms discussed include classroom organization, classroom grouping, instructional materials, and instructional methods. Chapter 8 explores both formal and informal assessment strategies that will help teachers contribute to the process of decision making for students with disabilities. Chapter 9 provides strategies for adapting curriculum materials, teacher instruction, and student practice activities for both basic-skills and content-area instruction. The emphasis is on adaptations that are relatively easy to make and that may also be helpful for students not identified as disabled. Chapter 10 focuses on ways to help students with and without special needs become more independent learners. Specific strategies are described, such as encouraging student self-awareness and self-advocacy skills, developing and teaching learning strategies directly in class, and instructing students on how to use these strategies on their own.

One of a teacher's major jobs is to assess students' educational progress, through grading and tests as well as through performance-based assessments and portfolios. Chapter 11 describes many ways of adapting classroom assessment to ensure that accurate information is gathered that is helpful in guiding instruction. In Chapter 12, readers will learn procedures for group behaviour management, strategies for responding to individual student behaviours, and a problem-solving approach for changing student behaviour. With this foundation for effective classroom management, teachers can establish a positive classroom community and influence the learning of all students. Finally, inclusive practices are most effective when exceptional students are included as full participants in the social and academic life of the classroom and the school. Chapter 13 explores effective approaches for building positive relations among students with and without exceptionalities. These include collaborative learning, peer tutoring, and social-skills training. The chapter includes the perspectives of exceptional youth on the importance of social relations. The concluding section of the book includes reflections on the roles of teachers, inclusive schools, and social relations in Canadian classrooms in our efforts to create an inclusive society as we move into the next century.

Features

This textbook has the following features designed to help readers learn more effectively:

- *Vignettes* that serve as introductory cases help readers think about how the content of chapters relates to teachers and students.
- *Key terms* throughout the text are clarified through the use of boldface type and easy-to-understand definitions provided both in context and in a glossary at the back of the book.
- *Chapter summaries* highlight key information covered in the chapter.
- *Application activities* at the end of each chapter are designed to encourage students to apply text content to real-life classroom situations.
- *Marginal annotations* are designed to stimulate higher-level thinking.
- *Case in Practice* features clarify key course principles by providing mini case studies of course content in action and teaching scripts as models.
- *Professional Edge* features provide many practical teaching ideas.
- *Technology Notes* show the impact of the current technology explosion on key aspects of special and general education programming.

- *Weblinks* give students a list of useful Web sites relating to each chapter. The sites have been researched and tested for quality and relevance.

Supplements

An Instructor's Resource Manual and a Test Item File are available to instructors, as well as Prentice Hall Allyn and Bacon Canada custom tests in Windows and Macintosh formats.

For each chapter, the Instructor's Resource Manual contains an overview, outline, activities, discussion questions, transparency masters, handout masters, and test items, including multiple choice, true-false, and case-based application items. Answer feedback and guidelines are provided.

Acknowledgments

Many people have contributed to the completion of this project. First, a huge thank you to Hugh Munby for his support and encouragement. And then to Nicole Levesque for her persistence in locating elusive resources and for her positive outlook in the face of setbacks and looming deadlines. To Marilyn Friend and William Bursuck for writing a text that truly can be subtitled "A Practical Handbook for Teachers." Many thanks to the professionals at Prentice Hall Canada—Cliff Newman, Carol Steven, Sharon Loeb, Andrew Winton—and to Dianne Broad. You nudged me to take on this project and then worked with me every step of the way. Special thanks to instructors in the field who provided valuable feedback: Deborah Butler, University of British Columbia; Noel Williams, University of Windsor; Karen Bain, University of Alberta; Elizabeth Jordan, University of British Columbia; Len Haines, University of Saskatchewan; Don Dworet, Brock University; Margaret Brown, Acadia University. Finally, to thousands of preservice and inservice teachers and their students who have taught me more than they'll ever realize—I hope this book does justice to your fine practice and your high ideals for including exceptional children in Canadian society and in Canadian classrooms.

Nancy Hutchinson

Chapter 1

The Foundation for Educating Exceptional Students

Learner Objectives

After you read this chapter, you will be able to

1. Explain basic concepts and terms that describe inclusive education for exceptional learners in Canada.

2. Trace events in the early history of education for exceptional populations in Canada, and describe recent events that reflect a growing awareness of and commitment to an inclusive society in Canada.

3. Describe the current state of inclusive education across Canada.

4. Analyze alternative points of view on inclusion as the philosophical and instructional basis for educating exceptional students.

5. Describe the categories of exceptionality used across Canada and the other special needs your students may have.

6. Explain what it means to accommodate exceptional learners, and describe the steps of a decision-making process for accommodating exceptional students in your classroom.

AARON *has a learning disability that was identified when he was in grade two at Terry Fox Elementary School. Now in grade five, Aaron continues to learn how to compensate for the academic difficulties he experiences. Although he is a bright and personable young man, he reads at about a grade two level and struggles to transfer his thoughts and ideas into written form. He doesn't like to discuss his learning disabilities (LD); he doesn't want other students to tease him or treat him differently because he's "LD." In his social studies class, he is most successful when his tests are read aloud; he understands the concepts even if he sometimes cannot read the test items. Because he doesn't like to be singled out, however, he sometimes refuses test-reading assistance. Aaron is an excellent soccer player, and on the field he feels equal to his friends; but his parents are concerned that his interest in sports is distracting him from his schoolwork. They are considering whether he should continue on the team. How likely are you to teach a student such as Aaron? What is a learning disability? What are other disabilities that students you teach might have?*

NICKI *is 17 years old and a grade eleven student at Atlantic Secondary School. She has a serious emotional disability that often manifests itself through aggressive, acting-out behaviour. Last year, Nicki broke her wrist when she punched a wall after being reprimanded for using foul language. Nicki was hospitalized for four weeks earlier this term after she assaulted a classmate. The purpose of the hospital stay was to help her understand her emotions and to learn to express them without hurting herself or others. Although Nicki is very intelligent, her grades in most classes are nearly failing. Why is Nicki considered disabled? What assistance does her school need to provide for her?*

Students such as Aaron and Nicki are not unusual. They are among the nearly 10 percent of students in Canadian schools who are exceptional learners. But their exceptionalities do not tell you who they are: They are children or young adults and students first. Like all students, they have both positive and negative characteristics, they have great days and some that are not so great, and they have likes and dislikes about school and learning.

As a teacher, you will probably instruct students such as Aaron and Nicki as well as other students with disabilities and students who are gifted. The purpose of this book is to help you understand students with disabilities and students who are gifted and to learn strategies for addressing their learning needs and social needs at school. You might be the teacher who makes a profound positive difference in a student's life. With the knowledge and skills you learn for teaching exceptional learners, you will be prepared for both the challenges and rewards of helping exceptional students achieve their potential.

▶ What Basic Concepts and Terms Define Exceptional Education in Canada?

FYI: Canada was the first country to constitutionally guarantee the rights of persons with a disability to legal equality.

Looking at the education system in Canada tells us some things about ourselves and what we aspire to be. First, we must look at all education systems rather than at one education system. Since the Confederation of Canada in 1867, each province has had the authority to make laws about education. Every provincial and territorial government has an Education Act or School Act governing education in its elementary and secondary schools, including the education of exceptional students. This means that as a teacher, you will become familiar with the regulations of your own province and of your school board or school division. Unlike other Western countries, such as Britain and the United States, Canada does not have a national office of education. However, when Canada adopted the Constitution Act containing the Canadian Charter of Rights and Freedoms (1982), the federal government assumed a greater role in the education of exceptional students than it had held at any time in the past. The equality rights that apply to education are contained in section 15.(1):

> Every individual is equal before and under the law and has a right to the equal protection and equal benefit of the law without discrimination and, in particular, without discrimination based on race, national or ethnic origin, colour, religion, sex, age, or mental or physical disability.

When Canadian educators talk about students with special needs or **exceptional students**, generally, they are referring to students who are gifted as well as students with disabilities, and may include students who are at risk due to poverty and other social conditions. For example, British Columbia uses the following definition: "Students with special needs have disabilities of an intellectual, physical, sensory, emotional or behavioural nature or have a learning disability or have exceptional gifts or talents" (British Columbia Special Education Branch, 1995, section A, p. 1).

These needs mean that the student requires an **adapted education program** or **special education**. In Alberta, this specially designed program is described this way:

> Education program for a student with special needs means a program based on the results of ongoing assessment and evaluation, and includes an Individualized Program Plan (IPP) with specific goals and objectives and recommendations for educational services that meet the student's needs (Alberta Education, 1996, p. 1).

Students may receive **related services;** that is, assistance that helps them to benefit from adapted education (e.g., transportation, physical therapy, and so on). When you met Nicki at the beginning of the chapter, you read that she has an emotional disability. An adapted program for Nicki might include alternative curriculum goals that she can meet without excessive frustration and related services might include regular counselling sessions with a psychologist. Descriptions of exceptional students and adapted programs vary among provinces. For example, the Northwest Territories' *Education Act* (1995) and *Departmental Directive on Inclusive Schooling* (1996) contain no references to exceptional children or to special education. Rather they focus on the rights of all students to inclusive education in a regular classroom setting with support services and modifications to the school program, and, if necessary, individual assessment and an individual education plan.

Inclusive Education Within an Inclusive Society

Our education systems across the country reveal much about what we are and about what we aspire to be. We aspire to be an **inclusive society**. There are many signs of the growing movement to ensure access and full participation in all aspects of Canadian society for persons with disabilities. As we have seen, the Canadian Charter of Rights and Freedoms guarantees rights for minorities in Canada and specifically includes persons with mental or physical disabilities. Supplementary legislation, Bill 62, addressed employment equity, and specifically includes persons with disabilities. Other indicators include public libraries ensuring that their collections are accessible; for example, the Metropolitan Toronto Reference Library includes a centre for people with disabilities that contains specialized equipment as well as information on services for people with disabilities. A 1994 issue of *University Affairs* included an article on ways in which professors and administrators in Canadian universities can make campuses and courses more accessible for students with disabilities (Careless, 1994). Schools are also changing, to include students with disabilities in their neighbourhood schools; that is, to provide inclusive education.

As early as 1989, a group of Canadian researchers wrote that **inclusion** or **inclusive education** represents the belief or philosophy that students with disabilities should be integrated into regular education classrooms, regardless of

FYI: *Inclusion* is the integration of most students with disabilities into general education classes. *Full inclusion* is the integration of students with disabilities in the general education classrooms at all times regardless of the nature or severity of the disability.

whether they can meet traditional curricular standards (O'Brien, Snow, Forest, & Hasbury, 1989). Advocates of inclusion believe that if students cannot meet traditional academic expectations, then those expectations should be changed. Throughout this text, the terms *inclusion* and *inclusive education* will refer to students' participation in regular education settings as full members of the classroom learning community, with their special needs met there. We generally agree that inclusion maximizes the potential of most students and ensures their rights and is the preferred option whenever possible. Inclusion, sometimes called attendance at neighbourhood schools, is the current policy of the departments of education of all 10 provinces and both territories in Canada.

Least Restrictive Environment

The concept of **least restrictive environment (LRE)** entered discussions about educating exceptional children when it was enshrined in U.S. federal law during the 1970s. Least restrictive environment refers to a student's right to be educated in the setting most like the educational setting for non-disabled peers in which the student can be successful, with appropriate supports provided (Tucker, 1989; Vergason & Anderegg, 1992). Before this time, many if not most exceptional students had received much of their education in segregated settings with other exceptional students. They participated in small classes with different, usually less academic, curricula. While the concept of LRE may have become embodied in Canadian special education policies and practices, the term is used much less frequently than in the United States. However, some Canadian provinces, such as Prince Edward Island (1995), use the term "most enabling environment." For many exceptional students, the least restrictive environment or most enabling environment is a regular education classroom. For example, when you met Aaron at the beginning of this chapter, you learned that he succeeds in a regular class when his tests are read aloud. His LRE or most enabling environment is the classroom; the testing procedure is an appropriate support. Current Canadian policies require schools to consider regular classroom placement first and to ensure that the supports are provided so that each student's education is inclusive and as much as possible occurs in the least restrictive and most enabling environment.

Mainstreaming

Mainstreaming referred to the practices that brought exceptional students from segregated settings back into mainstream or regular classrooms. Two Canadian researchers, Robichaud and Enns (1980), defined mainstreaming as the "trend toward integrating the mildly handicapped as much as possible into the regular classroom" (p. 202). This concept can be thought of as placing students with disabilities in regular classrooms only when they can meet traditional academic expectations, or when these academic expectations are not relevant (for example, when participation in recess or school assemblies provides opportunities for social interaction).

Services for students with disabilities and other exceptional learners are changing rapidly. In your school, teachers might use the words *inclusion, integration,* and *mainstreaming* interchangeably, and they might use other terms to describe special education services. To assist you with the vocabulary used in special education programs and instructional approaches, a glossary is provided in the back of this textbook. Although learning the terms used in special education is important, your main task will be to learn about special education services in your school and to clarify your role in teaching students with disabilities.

✓ **Your Learning:** How do mainstreaming and inclusion differ?

◤ How Did Exceptional Education Services Come to Exist?

Exceptional or special education as it exists today has been influenced by several different factors. Although people with disabilities have been identified and treated for centuries (Kanner, 1964), special education evolved rapidly only in the twentieth century. As special education has grown, it has been shaped by provincial law, the Charter of Rights and Freedoms, and related court cases, and changing social and political beliefs. Figure 1.1 illustrates some of the factors that have influenced the development of exceptional education.

The Early Development of Education for Exceptional Students

Exceptional education in Canada has had a long history and many influences. Children and adolescents with disabilities have received special services since

FYI: One example of very early treatment of children with disabilities occurred in

◤ **FIGURE 1.1**

Influences on Current Special Education Practices

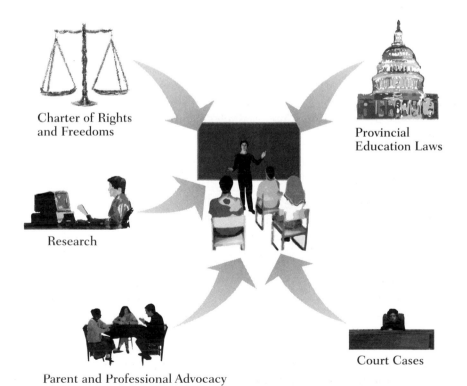

Charter of Rights and Freedoms

Research

Parent and Professional Advocacy

Provincial Education Laws

Court Cases

the case of Victor, a "wild" child who was deaf and mute and living in the woods of France. He was captured by authorities in 1799 and treated by Dr. Itard. Dr. Itard believed Victor was capable of learning and spent several years trying to teach him basic skills. Although Itard considered his work a failure, it was widely acclaimed (Scheerenberger, 1983).

before Confederation. The events highlighted in Figure 1.2 illustrate that most services from the early 1800s until the end of World War I were offered in residential settings and segregated classes (Winzer, Rogow, & David, 1987). However, with the return of veterans who had been disabled during World War I came questions about the wisdom of these practices and the resolve to provide services that would integrate persons with disabilities into Canadian society. For example, Colonel Edwin Baker, who lost his sight at Flanders Fields on October 10, 1915, was a founder of the Canadian National Institute for the Blind (CNIB) in 1918 and the World Council for the Welfare of the Blind in 1951. He is remembered as someone who brought to Canadian society the idea "that the disabled and handicapped can perform serious and demanding work" (Turner, 1996,

FIGURE 1.2

Highlights in the Early Development of Exceptional Education

From 30 years before Confederation until after World War I, Canadians accepted that individuals with disabilities were likely to live and learn apart from their families and peers.

1830-1860 Establishment of orphanages in Halifax, Montreal, Kingston, and Toronto to care for children in need.

1831 The first Canadian facility for exceptional children (a school for deaf students) was opened in Champlain, Québec.

1831-1886 Schools were opened for children who were deaf and children who were blind in Québec, Ontario, Nova Scotia, and Manitoba.

1851 The Toronto Asylum was opened to care for the insane.

1867 Confederation. The British North America Act made education a provincial responsibility when Canada was founded.

1876 In Orillia, Ontario, the first Canadian institution for the mentally retarded opened. A school was opened in 1888.

1886 Near Toronto the first industrial school opened for delinquent and vagrant boys.

1893 Children's Aid Societies were established in Ontario, with the model being followed in other parts of Canada and the United States.

1898 Woodlands was opened in British Columbia to serve the mentally retarded.

1906 In Montréal the Children's Memorial Hospital started day classes for children who were crippled.

1910 The passing of the Special Classes Act made existing special classes in Ontario board of education schools legal.

1916 At Wellesley School in Toronto, the first course for teachers of special classes was offered.

1918 Establishment of the Canadian National Institute for the Blind.

p. 49). The resolve that was evident by 1920 set exceptional education in Canada on a course that has taken decades to traverse and has contributed to our current commitment to inclusion.

By the 1920s special education classes were part of the general education system in urban elementary schools, while residential institutions (located in towns such as Weyburn, Saskatchewan and Smiths Falls, Ontario) were still "home" to many people with disabilities. Although questioned, this pattern continued until after the Second World War when the return of veterans with disabilities combined with an affluent society's focus on education to bring about change. In the 1950s and 1960s, parents and educators joined forces to establish national organizations such as the Canadian Association for the Mentally Retarded (now the Canadian Association for Community Living) and the Canadian Association for Children with Learning Disabilities lobbied for and, in some cases operated, special education classes. Provincial departments of education responded with increased testing and identification of exceptional learners. Services developed during this period often fell short of expectations.

FYI: The Council for Exceptional Children (CEC), founded in 1922 by Elizabeth Farrell, is a professional organization for teachers, administrators, parents, and other advocates for the rights of students with disabilities.

American Influences

During this period, the civil rights movement in the United States experienced the landmark case of *Brown v. Board of Education* (1954), which established that segregation denied some students equal educational opportunity. This early case contributed to the development, in Canada and the United States, of the perspective that fighting for the rights of the minority with disabilities parallels fighting for the rights of racial minorities (Smith, 1994). The education of gifted students was also thrown into the foreground in 1957 when the Soviet Union launched Sputnik into orbit around the Earth and beat the United States in that lap of the Space Race.

✔ **Your Learning:** Why would the launching of an unmanned space craft by the Soviet Union influence educational policy in North America in 1957? What events on the other side of the world influence our educational policies 40 years later?

Progressive Inclusion

By the early 1970s, there was considerable pressure throughout North America to change the categorical and segregated education experienced by most exceptional students. Dunn (1968) published an influential paper that questioned the effectiveness of segregated classes and suggested that exceptional students learned no more in special classes than in regular classes. In Canada, the CELDIC report, *One Million Children* (Roberts & Lazure, 1970), recommended integration, rights to free public education, and instruction based on individual learning characteristics, not category of exceptionality, for exceptional children. Wolfensberger's work on normalization at the National Institute of Mental Retardation in Toronto (e.g., Wolfensberger, Nirge, Olshansky, Perske, & Roos, 1972) promoted that all persons should live and learn in environments as close to normal as possible. A 1971 report, *Standards for Education of Exceptional Children in Canada* (Hardy, McLeod, Minto, Perkins, & Quance, 1971), led to the inclusion of courses about exceptional children in teacher education programs at many Canadian universities.

The 1970s saw extensive change in exceptional education in the United States with the passage of P.L. 94-142, the Education for the Handicapped Act.

Do It! Invite a veteran teacher to your class to discuss special education prior to current laws. What questions will you ask your guest about the way students were educated and the responsibilities teachers had?

This law, which set federal guidelines for special education services, remains the foundation of current practices there. In Canada, the period since the 1970s has been characterized by rapid change in the development of an inclusive society, as shown in Figure 1.3. People with disabilities have raised their own profiles and the awareness of their peers by winning major awards (such as Marjorie Woods, Jean Little, Henry Enns, and Chantal Petitclerc), and becoming Canadian heroes, such as Terry Fox and Rick Hansen. Canadians have also been proud hosts for two ground-breaking athletic events in recent years. In 1994 we gained the admiration of athletes from around the world by hosting the first completely inclusive Commonwealth Games. Again, in 1997, the Special Olympics World Winter Games brought athletes with disabilities to the Canadian headlines and provided Canadians with an opportunity to put our belief in inclusion into action. As discussed earlier, the repatriation of the Canadian Constitution, the adoption of the Charter of Rights and Freedoms, and subsequent court challenges have helped to focus the attention of Canadians on the rights of people with disabilities.

Probably the timing of the discussions about repatriating our constitution and adopting our Charter influenced the choice of groups that were included. In the early 1970s the United Nations had made a number of Declarations of Rights of people with disabilities. Then, 1981 was International Year of Disabled Persons. In Canada this brought people with disabilities to Parliament Hill to protest the possible exclusion of rights for people with disabilities from the Charter. The result was that when the Charter came into force, Canada became the first country in the world to guarantee rights to people with disabilities in its Constitution. While some countries, such as the United States and United Kingdom, have legislation that deals exclusively with exceptional students and their right to education, we have enshrined the rights of people with disabilities in our Constitution alongside the rights of other groups whose rights were seen to require protection. Additionally, rights to education are guaranteed in the same breath with other rights governed by law. Whereas some countries, such as the United States, must reauthorize periodically the legislation ensuring education for exceptional students, we have enshrined these rights in our Constitution where it would be extremely difficult to remove or diminish them. What does this tell us about ourselves? We have taken the rights of exceptional students to education very seriously, and these rights are part of our overall guarantee of rights to people with disabilities and to other minorities.

FIGURE 1.3

Highlights in the Recent Growth of Inclusive Society in Canada

1975 United Nations proclaimed the Declaration on the Rights of Disabled Persons, which included the rights to community living, to education, to work, to vote, to marry, to become a parent, to enter into contracts, and to have representation in court.

1976 Marjorie Wood was awarded the Order of Canada. This deaf-blind woman started the Canadian League for the Deaf-Blind and founded Canada's first Braille magazine for the deaf-blind, *Dots and Taps*.

1977 Canadian Human Rights Act stated that no one should be discriminated against for reasons of physical or mental disability.

1978 An Alberta Supreme Court decision ordered Lamont County school board to widen doors, build a ramp, and educate Shelly Carrière, a student with cerebral palsy, in her community school.

April 12, 1980 Terry Fox set off on his "Marathon of Hope," after losing his right leg to cancer in 1977. He ran 40 kilometres each day from St. John's, Newfoundland until lung cancer forced him to stop in Thunder Bay. He captured the imagination of Canadians and raised awareness about the abilities of people with disabilities, as well as raising money for cancer research.

December 12, 1980 Ontario's Education Amendment Act (Bill 82) became law, guaranteeing all exceptional pupils the right to an appropriate education.

1981 Declared International Year of Disabled Persons by the United Nations General Assembly.

1981 Canadians with disabilities lobbied on Parliament Hill to ensure the inclusion of rights for persons with disabilities in the Canadian Charter of Rights and Freedoms, which was being written and debated.

April 17, 1982 Canada received a new Constitution Act. Section 15 of the Canadian Charter of Rights and Freedoms came into effect. Canada became the first country to constitutionally guarantee the rights to legal equality for persons with a disability.

March 21, 1985 Wheelchair athlete Rick Hansen left Vancouver on a round-the-world "Man in Motion" tour to raise money for spinal-cord research and wheelchair sports.

1988 Jean Little won the Horne "Honour Book" award in the United States and her book, *Little by Little,* was shortlisted for the Governor-General's Award for Children's Literature. The book is the blind author's autobiography written for children.

September 1989 Yvonne Peters, a lawyer who is blind, became the national co-ordinator of the Canadian Disability Rights Council based in Winnipeg.

November 1989 Signing of United Nations Convention on the Rights of the Child, which contains 54 articles including children's right to an education, and right to learn to be useful members of society and develop individual abilities.

May 1992 Henry Enns, director of Disabled Peoples' International based in Winnipeg, became the first non-American to win the President's Award for Humanitarian Service for his work on behalf of people with disabilities around the world.

August 1994 Victoria, British Columbia hosted the first completely inclusive Commonwealth Games.

February 1995 Ontario Court of Appeal ruled that Emily Eaton, a student with severe, multiple disabilities, had a constitutional right to inclusion in a classroom with peers without disabilities.

July 1996 Ability OnLine, a free e-mail link for children who are chronically ill and children with disabilities logged its millionth call. The program was started by Dr. Arlette Lefebvre of Toronto's Hospital for Sick Children.

October 10, 1996 The Supreme Court of Canada overturned the decision of the Ontario Court of Appeal involving the case of Emily Eaton, ruling that she could receive an appropriate education in a segregated setting.

December 1996 Chantal Petitclerc was named Montreal's outstanding athlete of 1996, chosen over diver and Olympic medallist Annie Pelletier. Chantal won five medals in wheelchair races in the Paralympics at Atlanta.

February 1-8, 1997 The Special Olympics World Winter Games were held in Toronto and Collingwood, Ontario for 2,000 athletes from more than 80 countries. The motto of the Games was "Let me win. But if I cannot win, let me be brave in the attempt."

◤ What Is the Current State of Education for Exceptional Students in Canada?

Do It! Look in libraries for Canadian magazines and newspapers published in 1981. Read stories about International Year of Disabled Persons, protests on Parliament Hill by people with disabilities, and the debates surrounding the rights to be enshrined in the Charter.

In Canada the provision of equal educational opportunity to exceptional students is intended to allow every exceptional student to maximize his or her potential. In some cases, equality is fostered by providing students with disabilities with the same rights and benefits as provided to other students. In other instances, equality is fostered by providing different treatment. This is called "the dilemma of difference" (Minow, 1985). Throughout this book, you will learn about this dilemma and the demands it makes on teachers for professional judgment in their daily work meeting the needs of exceptional students. The current state in Canada can be understood by looking across the provinces and territories and focusing on the themes or long threads that make the pattern of exceptional education. Two dominant themes are change and inclusion.

Change

✓ **Your Learning:** What is a dilemma?

The first theme that is apparent in looking across the country is change—in education, generally, and in the policies for education of exceptional children. In the late 1990s, many of the provinces and territories have recently revised or are currently revising their education acts and their regulations and policies governing special education. The dominant movement in these changes is increasing inclusion of exceptional learners in neighbourhood schools and regular classrooms as the first choice of placement.

Alberta, British Columbia, and Nova Scotia have recently completed reforms in all aspects of education. All have released new policy manuals for special education services (Alberta Education, 1996; British Columbia Special Education Branch, 1995; Nova Scotia Department of Education and Culture, 1996). The Yukon and Northwest Territories have also completed recent overhauls of all aspects of education including education for exceptional students (see Northwest Territories Department of Education, Culture and Employment, 1996; Yukon Special Programs Branch, 1995).

Revision is ongoing in Saskatchewan, Ontario, Newfoundland, and Manitoba. Saskatchewan has a draft Special Education Policy Manual (Saskatchewan Education, 1996), which is unpublished awaiting changes to the regulations of the Education Act. Ontario consulted widely on changes to Regulation 305, which governs special education and on the changes recommended in the Royal Commission report (Ontario Ministry of Education and Training, 1995a, 1995b), but as of 1997 has not made the changes law. In Newfoundland, the Report of the Review of Special Education has been received (Canning, 1996) along with reports for revising all aspects of education in the province (e.g., Newfoundland Classroom Issues Committee, 1995). Manitoba began a special education review in 1996 that is expected to take up to two years. Prince Edward Island also has a draft document *A Model of Special Education Service Delivery* (Prince Edward Island Department of Education, 1995) and Quebec updated its special education policy in 1992 (Ministère de l'Education, Gouvernement du Québec, 1992). In 1994, New Brunswick released *Best Practices for Inclusion*, following its *Position Statement on Inclusive, Quality Education* (1991). Change in education for exceptional learners is under way or recently completed in every jurisdiction in Canada.

Inclusion

Although each jurisdiction sets its own policies, there is considerable consistency in the movement toward inclusion, the second dominant theme. Across Canada, most provinces and territories have adopted or are adopting the term inclusive to describe their approach to providing services for exceptional children. An inclusive approach is described in recent policy draft documents of British Columbia, New Brunswick, Nova Scotia, the Northwest Territories, Prince Edward Island, Saskatchewan, and the Yukon. In British Columbia, inclusion "supports equitable access to learning by all students and the opportunity for all students to pursue their goals in all aspects of their education" (1995, section A, p.2). Nova Scotia describes an inclusive school as "a school where every child is respected as part of the school community, and where each child is encouraged to learn and achieve as much as possible" (1996, p. 13). In its draft policy manual, Saskatchewan includes the guiding principle that "students with exceptional needs should experience education in settings that allow them to achieve their individual goals in *inclusive settings*; other arrangements are to be used only when compelling reasons necessitate using such alternatives" (1996, p. 7). The other five provinces also emphasize the regular classroom or the neighbourhood school as the placement of first choice (Alberta, Manitoba, Newfoundland, Ontario, and Québec). For example, Manitoba's policy is "to support the education of students with learning needs in regular classroom settings whenever this is in the best interests of the students" (Manitoba Education and Training, 1989, p. 1). Alberta states:

"Educating students with special needs in regular classrooms in neighbourhood or local schools shall be the first placement option considered by school boards, in consultation with students, parents/guardians, and school staff" (1996, p. 1). Ontario's draft document advises schools that the first placement option to be considered for an exceptional student is in a regular classroom with appropriate special education services (1995b). You may be asking what exceptional students in Canada are entitled to during the current period of change when inclusion is the dominant approach to their education.

What Are Exceptional Students Entitled To?

Do It! Examine the most recent documents available in your province or territory and learn what expressions are used when referring to inclusion, inclusive education, regular classroom, and neighbourhood school.

In the broadest terms, exceptional students are entitled to equal educational opportunity; that is, free and appropriate public education. This means "young people with disabilities have an equal right to be in school and to have something meaningful happen once they are inside" (Smith, 1994, p. 7). Smith has used several concepts to describe the rights of exceptional students in Canada. These include non-discrimination, access to schooling, identification, placement, parental participation, and service delivery, as discussed in Figure 1.4.

FIGURE 1.4

What Exceptional Students Are Entitled To

Non-Discrimination

Non-discrimination refers to the equal benefit of law without discrimination on the basis of disability. For example, many provincial Human Rights Codes include the right to be free to access buildings and services, to enter a school. As a teacher, you will become familiar with the procedures that would be followed in your province in the event of a parent lodging a complaint of discrimination against the school district.

Access to Schooling

Access to schooling means attending elementary or secondary school at public expense. The Education Acts assert that all children are entitled to a public education. In Canada, access to schooling has been called a platform right on which other more specific rights are constructed (Smith, 1994). These more specific rights include identification, placement, appropriate instruction and services, and parent participation.

Identification

Identification refers to actions to understand a student's exceptionality and the implications for learning; in the past this has led to labelling. However, Ontario suggests that a parent may request that the exceptionality be omitted from the decision. Most provinces still include definitions for categories of exceptionality (e.g., Ontario, Saskatchewan, Alberta, and British Columbia); however, New Brunswick and Prince Edward Island have described their approach as non-categorical, providing programs based on individual needs. The Nova Scotia manual cautions that labels should not be applied to individual students, only used for administrative purposes. In the Northwest Territories, programs are to build on student strengths. Increasingly, we are attempting to guarantee exceptional students the advantages of identification (appropriate services) without the disadvantages (labels).

Placement

In the past, placement referred to the settings for a pupil's educational program. With inclusion, the regular classroom in the neighbourhood school has become the first choice unless this has proven unsuccessful in the individual case. Writers have argued that what is important is that students are accepted and participate as full members of regular classrooms. We now describe programs in terms of the needs they meet rather than their locations. Meeting needs and full acceptance have begun to replace the previous emphasis on placement.

Participation of Parents

Parents are viewed as partners in the education of exceptional students. Nova Scotia describes parents as knowledgeable about the exceptionalities of their children and their primary advocates. Decisions are to be reached by mutual agreement among team members, including parents. One of Saskatchewan's Guiding Principles is that parent/guardian involvement is critical to planning appropriate educational programs, and Quebec requires parental participation. You will learn the expectations for parental participation in your province and find ways to involve parents as partners.

Service Delivery

Service delivery refers to the provision of appropriate educational and disability-related services. To describe an individual planning process, most provinces use the term "Individual Education Plan" (IEP) (Prince Edward Island, Manitoba, the Yukon, Ontario, British Columbia, the Northwest Territories, and Quebec). Three provinces (Nova Scotia, Alberta, and Newfoundland) use the expression, "Individual Program Plan" (IPP). New Brunswick refers to a "Special Education Plan" and Saskatchewan to a "Personal Program Plan." Each consists of a plan to adapt materials, instruction, assessment, and, perhaps, the curriculum. You may feel apprehensive when you first develop an IEP. However, an IEP is not necessarily long and most can be documented in one page.

What Is Inclusive Education and Why Is It Controversial?

There are many signs of the growing movement to ensure access and full participation in all aspects of Canadian society for persons with disabilities. On one hand, the development of inclusive schools reflects a movement that is evident

Do It! Review your local newspaper for articles on inclusion. What viewpoints are expressed? Does your local school district have a written set of guidelines on inclusion? How could you find out?

Do It! Participate in a class debate that presents alternative views on inclusion. What are your own beliefs about your responsibility to teach students who may not be able to meet traditional classroom expectations?

FYI: In *pullout* or *withdrawal programs*, students leave the regular classroom to receive specialized services. Resource teachers often offer pullout programs, but so do speech therapists, occupational and physical therapists, counsellors, and even remedial teachers.

in all parts of Canadian society. On the other hand, schools play a unique role in educating individuals with disabilities so they can take roles as educated adults, and in educating people without disabilities to accept and foster inclusion. A recent publication by the federal Office for Disability Issues suggests, "Attitudes can be the most difficult barrier persons with disabilities must face in gaining full integration, acceptance and participation in society" (1997, p. 1).

Many have argued that inclusion is a value judgment. Fullwood (1990), an Australian educator, makes a persuasive case that inclusion is about people with disabilities having the same chances and choices in life as other people to participate in activities and become members of communities. She focuses on both physical and social relationships, where physical refers to people being in the same places, participating in the same activities, and social refers to people interacting and being interdependent. Canadian writers have argued, "A major goal of inclusive education is to integrate all children and ensure that they have fair and equal access to normal school experiences. This type of educational system regards all children as equally accepted members of heterogeneous classrooms" (Andrews & Lupart, 1993, p. 9). The emphasis on acceptance is also evident in American writing on inclusive education. Stainback and Stainback (1992) wrote that the goal in inclusive schools is that

> all students, including those who have been labeled severely and profoundly mentally and physically disabled, chronically disruptive, typical, gifted, or at risk, are accepted as equal members, recognized for what they have to offer to the school community, and provided an appropriate educational program and any necessary supports (p. xi).

Inclusive education is a relatively new term, replacing terms such as mainstreaming from the 1970s and integration from the 1980s. The two earlier terms emphasized returning students from segregated and marginal settings to classrooms in the mainstream. The emphasis in inclusive society is not on the placement, but on participation. The intent is not that people are returned to inclusive settings, but that they are always included; as preschoolers, they attend daycare and preschool with the other children in their community; they play in the neighbourhood, and join community activities; at all ages they are preparing for full adult participation in employment and all other aspects of a democratic society. In Canada, the context for discussions about inclusion is society.

The practice of inclusive education has thus far proved an elusive goal in schools. This may be because our social values precede our knowledge about how best to accomplish these goals. Some wonder if we have found inclusion so challenging because we haven't put adequate human and financial resources into our efforts so far. Others suggest inclusive education may be harder to realize in large, departmentalized secondary schools than in neighbourhood elementary schools. Controversies abound about inclusive schooling. Two American critiques of inclusive education are the book called *The Illusion of Full Inclusion* (Kauffman & Hallahan, 1995) and the article, "Inclusive Schools Movement and the Radicalization of Special Education Reform" (Fuchs & Fuchs, 1994). Both argue against what they call "full inclusion." They acknowledge that the inclusive classroom may meet the needs of students with severe disabilities for social development. However, they argue that full inclusion does not provide instruction that is intense enough to meet the needs of students with high-incidence mild disabilities,

▼▼▼▼▼▼▼▼▼▼▼▼

Case in Practice

Problem Solving in Inclusive Schools: The Classroom Teacher's Role

A_T Highland Elementary School, staff members are meeting to discuss David, a grade three student with autism. Ms. Dowley is David's teacher; Ms. Jackson is the special educator who provides needed support. Ms. Janes, the school psychologist, is also present.

MS. DOWLEY: David is really a puzzle and a challenge. He is doing so much better at being in class than he was at the beginning of the year, but he can still disrupt the entire class when he tantrums. One of the parents called yesterday to complain about David taking time away from her daughter and the rest of the class. I'm starting to feel the same way. I hope we can come up with some ideas to improve the whole situation.

MS. JACKSON: What kinds of things seem to trigger the tantrums?

MS. DOWLEY: That's part of the problem. I'm still pretty new at teaching and I have my hands full with the whole class. I don't even have time to think carefully about what's happening with David. I just deal with him when a problem occurs.

MS. JANES: The tantrums seem like a serious problem, but before we start addressing them, are there other things we should be discussing, too?

MS. DOWLEY: No. Right now, it's the tantrums— and I want to be clear that I really can see all the other gains David has made. I *want* this to work for David. I know inclusion is right for him if we can just deal with this problem.

MS. JANES: It seems like we need more information. One question I have is this: What happens with you and the other students when David has a tantrum?

MS. DOWLEY: Well, I try to ignore him, but that usually makes it worse. A few of the other students laugh, and that's not helping, either.

MS. JACKSON: Maybe we should focus for a minute or two on when David doesn't tantrum. What are the times of the day or the activities that David does without having behaviour problems?

MS. DOWLEY: Let's see . . . He's usually fine and makes a good contribution when we're talking about science concepts. He loves science. If math is activity-based, he's fine there, too.

MS. JANES: Our meeting time is nearly up. I'd be happy to make time in my schedule to observe David, and perhaps Ms. Jackson could, too. I know you need answers right away, but I hope we can get a clearer sense of the pattern to David's behaviour so we can find the right strategy for addressing it. If we can get in to observe this week, could we meet next Tuesday to try to generate some strategies?

MS. DOWLEY: Sure. That would be great. Let's just work out the details on observing.

Reflections

Why was this meeting a positive example of teachers addressing a student problem in an inclusive school? What did they do that has set them up for success? If you were trying to understand David better, what other questions would you ask about him? What do you think will happen at the next meeting? On the basis of this case, how would you describe the role of classroom teachers in addressing the challenges of inclusion?

such as learning disabilities. Recent research suggests that approaches such as collaborative learning are effective strategies for inclusion (e.g., Putnam, 1993), and there are many accounts of exceptional learners achieving acceptance and learning successfully in inclusive classrooms (e.g., Harris, 1994; Hutchinson, in press).

An Analysis of the Inclusion Debate

✓ **Your Learning:** What impact have provincial policies had on exceptional education? How has the teaching of students with disabilities changed over the years?

As you read professionals' views on inclusion, you might notice that several related themes run through them. These themes include inclusion as a philosophical issue, as a social value issue, as an economic issue, and as an instructional issue. We believe that services for exceptional students will continue to change rapidly and that past programs have been valuable steps in the evolution of effective education, but they are quickly becoming obsolete because of issues in the inclusion debate. Given appropriate supports, most exceptional students can receive much or all of their education in the regular classroom. The Case in Practice illustrates how classroom teachers, special educators, and other school staff members can make inclusion successful by working together. However, a few students, because of the nature of their individual needs, require occasional or ongoing separate programming. And what is most clear is that we must continue to commit financial and other resources to ensure that exceptional students receive quality education.

Who are Exceptional Students?

Connections: More complete descriptions of the characteristics and needs of students with disabilities and other exceptionalities are found in Chapters 4, 5, and 6.

At this point you may be wondering who are these exceptional students that we have discussed throughout this chapter. Here we will introduce you to some specific types or categories of exceptionality. As we have seen, with the ascendance of inclusion, many provinces and territories are downplaying the identification of the particular type of exceptionality, avoiding labelling, and focusing on the individual needs of students. While reading the following generic descriptions, it is important to remember that we are discussing children and adolescents, but they *are* children and adolescents with characteristics that require us to adapt our teaching and other aspects of our classroom interactions with them. They *are not* their exceptionalities, but sometimes using the accepted expressions to describe their characteristics and learning will make it easier for us to communicate. For example, when we read that Nicki, described in the opening of the chapter, has an emotional disability, we know that the ways we can expect to adjust our teaching will most likely have to do with her self-control, which sets different expectations for us than if we were teaching Amber, who is blind and needs adaptations that replace all printed material with Braille and auditory or hearing formats. It is also important to remember that the specific definitions vary across jurisdictions, and when you begin teaching you will be introduced to the definitions used in your province or territory.

Categories of Exceptionalities

Students who are gifted or developmentally advanced.   Students who demonstrate ability far above average in one or several areas including specific academic subjects, overall intellectual ability, leadership, creativity, athletics, or the visual or performing arts are considered gifted. Erin is included in this group; she seems to learn anything new without effort, and she is also eager to learn about almost everything. Evan is also gifted; still in elementary school, he has participated in national piano recitals, and his parents have requested that he have access to the music room during recess so he can practise.

Learning disabilities (LD).   Students with **learning disabilities (LD)** have dysfunctions in processing information typically found in language-based activities. They have average or above-average intelligence, but they often have significant problems learning how to read, write, and compute. They may reverse letters and words, and they may take longer to process a question or comment directed to them. They may also have difficulty following directions, attending to tasks, organizing their assignments, and managing time. Sometimes these students appear to be unmotivated or lazy when, in fact, they are trying to the best of their ability. Aaron, whom you met at the beginning of this chapter, has a learning disability, but many types of learning disabilities exist, and no single description characterizes students who have one. It is estimated that approximately half of all exceptional students in Canada have LD.

Students with attention-deficit/hyperactive disorder (ADHD).   Students with ADHD have an inability to attend to complex tasks for long periods of time, excessive motor activity, and impulsivity. The impact of this disorder on students' schoolwork can be significant. Identification of ADHD requires input from a physician. Students with ADHD may take medication, such as Ritalin, that helps them focus their attention.

Communication disorders.   When a student has extraordinary difficulties in communicating with others because of causes other than maturation, a **communication disorder or speech or language impairment** is involved. Students with this disability may have difficulty with articulation, or the production of speech sounds. They may omit words when they speak, or mispronounce common words. They may also experience difficulty in fluency, as in a significant stuttering problem. Some students have far-reaching communication disorders in which they have extreme problems receiving and producing language. They may communicate through pictures or sign language. Some students have a speech or language disorder as their primary disability and receive services for this. For other students with disabilities, speech and language services supplement their education. For example, a student with a learning disability might also receive speech/language services, as might a student with autism or traumatic brain injury.

Emotional disability or behaviour disability.   When a student has significant difficulty in the social/emotional domain that is serious enough to interfere with the student's learning, an emotional disability exists. Students with this disability may have difficulty with interpersonal relationships and may respond inappropriately in emotional situations; that is, they may have trouble making and keeping friends, and they may get extremely angry when a peer teases or plays a joke on them, or show little or no emotion when the family pet dies. Some students with an emotional disability are depressed; others are aggressive. Students display these impairments over a long period, across different settings, and to a degree significantly different from their peers. Like Nicki, whom you met at the beginning of the chapter, students with this disability have chronic and serious emotional problems. Sometimes this is called a **behaviour disability**.

FYI: ADHD is a source of considerable debate among professional educators. Some questions asked are these: Should ADHD be considered a separate disability? How many students have ADHD? What proportion of students with learning disabilities also have ADHD?

FYI: Depression is more common among children than previously thought. More information on this serious disorder can be found in Chapter 5.

Developmental disabilities.   Students with **developmental disabilities** have significant limitations in cognitive ability and adaptive behaviours. They learn at a far slower pace than do other students, and they may reach a point at which their learning plateaus. Despite the degree of developmental delay, most individuals with this disability can lead independent or semi-independent lives as adults and can hold an appropriate job. The term **cognitive disability** is sometimes used instead of developmental disabilities. In this text, we use the two terms interchangeably.

Autism.   Children with **autism** usually lack social responsiveness from a very early age. They generally avoid physical contact (for example, cuddling and holding), and they may not make eye contact. Problems with social interactions persist as these children grow; they appear unaware of others' feelings and may not seek interactions with peers or adults. They may have unusual language patterns, including spoken language without intonation; echolalia, or repetition of others' speech; or little or no language. They may display repetitive body movements, such as rocking, and may need highly routinized behaviour, such as in how they put on their clothes or eat their meals, to feel comfortable. The causes of autism are not well understood, and the best approaches for working with students with autism are still under considerable debate.

Hearing impairments.   Disabilities that concern the inability or limited ability to receive auditory signals are called **hearing impairments.** When students are **hard of hearing,** they have a significant hearing loss but can capitalize on residual hearing by using hearing aids and other amplifying systems. Students who are **deaf** have little or no residual hearing and therefore do not benefit from devices to aid hearing. Depending on the extent of the disability, students with hearing impairments may use sign language, speech reading, and other ways to help them communicate.

Visual impairments.   Disabilities that concern the inability or limited ability to receive information visually are called **visual impairments.** Some students are **partially sighted** and can learn successfully using magnification devices or other adaptive materials; students who are **blind** do not use vision as a means of learning and instead rely primarily on touch and hearing. Depending on need, students with visual impairments may use Braille, specialized computers, and other aids to assist in learning. Some students need specialized training to help them learn to move around in their environment successfully.

Deaf-blindness.   Students who have both significant vision and hearing impairments have unique learning needs, particularly in the communication areas, and require highly specialized services. The severity of the vision or hearing loss may vary from moderate to severe and may be accompanied by other disabilities.

Orthopedic impairments.   Students with **orthopedic impairments** have physical conditions that seriously impair their ability to move about or to complete motor activities. Students who have cerebral palsy are included in this group, as are those with other diseases that affect the skeleton or muscles. Students with physical limitations resulting from accidents may also be in this group. Some students with physical disabilities will be unable to move about without a wheelchair and may need special transportation to get to school and a ramp to enter the school building. Others may lack the fine motor skills needed to write and will require extra time or adapted equipment to complete assignments.

Traumatic brain injury (TBI). Students with **traumatic brain injury (TBI)** have a wide range of characteristics and special needs, including limited strength or alertness, developmental delays, short-term memory problems, hearing or vision losses that may be temporary, irritability, and sudden mood swings. Their characteristics and needs depend on the specific injury they experienced, and these needs often change across time. Because TBI is a medical condition that affects education, diagnosis by a physician is required along with assessment of learning and adaptive behaviour. Students with TBI experienced serious head trauma from automobile accidents, falls, and sports injuries.

Health impairments. Some students have a disease or disorder so significant that it affects their ability to learn in school; these are called **health impairments.** This includes students with severe asthma who require an adapted physical education program, and those who have chronic heart conditions necessitating frequent and prolonged absences from school. Students with diseases such as AIDS, sickle-cell anemia, and diabetes may be described as health impaired, depending on the impact of their illness on learning.

Students with **fetal alcohol syndrome (FAS)** have a distinctive pattern of delayed growth, intellectual and behavioural disabilities, and facial characteristics caused by alcohol abuse during pregnancy. This neurological disorder can be difficult to recognize and is a medical condition that must be diagnosed by a physician. Other exceptionalities and learning difficulties commonly observed in children with FAS include learning disabilities (LD), attention-deficit/hyperactive disorder (ADHD), difficulty with sequencing, memory, generalizing, and understanding cause-effect relationships. Usually **fetal alcohol effects** (FAE) is the term used to describe a case where prenatal alcohol exposure has been confirmed, but only some of the other diagnostic criteria are present. It is not necessarily a milder case than FAS.

Multiple disabilities. The description used when students have two or more disabilities is **multiple disabilities.** Students in this group often have developmental disabilities as well as a physical disability, but this category may be used to describe any student with two or more disability areas. However, this classification is normally used only when the student's disabilities are so serious and so interrelated that none can be identified as a primary disability.

FYI: A *primary disability* is the one that most significantly influences the student's education. A *secondary disability* is an additional disability that affects education, but to a lesser degree.

Students at risk. Often, the general term **at risk** refers to students who have characteristics, live in an environment, or have experiences that make them more likely than others to fail in school. Students whose primary language is any other than English are sometimes considered at risk, and they may need assistance in school learning. They may attend bilingual education programs or classes for

English as a second language (ESL) for opportunities to learn English while also learning the standard curriculum. However, some students in this group may also have disabilities.

A second group of at-risk students are those who have been called **slow learners,** or described as having general disabilities or general learning disabilities. Their educational progress is below average but they do not have a learning disability or developmental disability. These students are learning to the best of their ability, but they cannot keep up with the pace of instruction in most general education classrooms without assistance. They are sometimes referred to as "falling between the cracks" of the educational system because most professionals agree they need special assistance, but they are not usually labelled exceptional. They sometimes, however, receive assistance in remedial reading or tutorial programs.

Other students who might be considered at risk include those who are homeless or live in poverty, who are drug or alcohol abusers, or who are abused. Students in these groups are at risk for school failure because of the environments or circumstances in which they live.

You may find that students who need adapted teaching but have not been identified as exceptional are particularly troubling because no single group of professionals is responsible for educating them. As inclusion becomes the dominant approach, resource teachers more often informally assist teachers in planning and adapting educational activities for these students. Thus, other students often benefit from the trend toward inclusive education for exceptional students.

When you discuss exceptional students, keep in mind that their disabilities do not define them or tell you who they really are. To stay aware of this important consideration, as the Professional Edge explains, you should always use "person-first" language with and when referring to all students, regardless of what disability category pertains to them.

Cross-Categorical Approaches to Special Education

Provinces, territories, and local school districts may use the categories of exceptionalities just described for counting the number of students in special or exceptional education and for allocating funding to educate them. When you prepare to teach a student, however, you will probably find that the specific category of exceptionality often does not guide you in finding appropriate teaching strategies. In some provinces and territories, some of the categories are combined to permit more flexibility for planning educational services. Also, students with different exceptionalities often benefit from the same instructional adaptations. Throughout this book, students will sometimes be discussed in terms of only two categories: high-incidence and low-incidence exceptionalities. **High-incidence exceptionalities** are those that are most common, including gifted, learning disabilities, speech or language impairments, and emotional disturbances. **Low-incidence exceptionalities** are those that are rare and include all the other exceptionalities: developmental disabilities, multiple disabilities, hearing impairments, orthopedic impairments, other health impairments, visual impairments, deaf-blindness, autism, fetal alcohol syndrome and fetal alcohol effects, and traumatic brain injury.

Cultural Awareness: Students whose language at home is not English are sometimes assigned to special education inappropriately because of academic difficulties that are actually caused by lack of proficiency in English.

✓ **Your Learning:** What are the high-incidence exceptionalities? What are the low-incidence exceptionalities? Why are these terms used?

▼▼▼▼▼▼▼▼▼▼▼▼▼▼▼▼▼▼▼▼▼▼▼▼▼

Professional Edge
Finding the Right Words

Lᴀɴɢᴜᴀɢᴇ *does* make a difference. "Person-first" language is the appropriate way to refer to anyone who has a disability. For example, you should say "a student who has a learning disability" or "my student with a cognitive disability" or "I teach four students who have learning disabilities" instead of "the LD student" or "I have four LDs."

- Language is a powerful and important tool in shaping ideas, perceptions, and ultimately, public attitudes.

- Words are a mirror of society's attitudes and perceptions. Attitudes can be the most difficult barrier that persons with disabilities must face in gaining full integration, acceptance, and participation in society.

- Demeaning, belittling, or negative words are a barrier to greater understanding and can trivialize genuine support given by a community to persons with disabilities.

- Language use is changing as persons with disabilities claim their individual and collective right to participate fully in society.

- Dated and disparaging words are being replaced with precise, descriptive terms that have specific meanings that are not interchangeable.

- Individuals with disabilities are working to achieve equality, independence and full participation in our society. The ways in which issues are reported [and discussed] and the use of proper terminology can help persons with disabilities reach these goals.

Source: From *A Way With Words: Guidelines and Appropriate Terminology for the Portrayal of Persons with Disabilities* by Office for Disability Issues, Human Resources Development Canada, 1997, Copyright ©1997 by Human Resources Development Canada. Reprinted by permission.

Consistent with a **cross-categorical approach,** when the characteristics of students with exceptionalities are discussed in more detail in Chapters 4 and 5, we pay more attention to students' learning needs than to their labels. In addition, although some strategies specific to categorical groups (for example, the use of large-print books for students with vision impairments) are outlined in those chapters, most of the strategies presented throughout the text can be adapted for most students. If you adopt a cross-categorical approach in your own thinking about teaching exceptional students, you will see that myriad options are available for helping students succeed.

Connections: Additional information on specific exceptionalities is included in Chapters 4 and 5.

▶ How Can the INCLUDE Strategy Help You Make Reasonable Accommodations for Exceptional Students?

At a recent conference presentation that included both classroom teachers and special education teachers, one of the authors asked the audience how many of those present worked with students with disabilities. A music teacher at the back of the room called out, "*Everyone* in schools works with students with disabilities!" He is right. Although the professionals who have specialized in meeting the needs of students with disabilities are valuable and provide critical instructional and support systems for students, you and your peers will be the primary teachers for many exceptional students, and you will form partnerships with special educators to meet the needs of others. That makes it critical for you to feel comfortable making accommodations for students.

✓ **Your Learning:** What is a reasonable accommodation?

This chapter introduces you to a systematic approach to adapting instruction for students with special needs, called INCLUDE. This approach is expanded and elaborated throughout the text, especially in Chapters 7 through 13, where specific strategies are presented. It is based on two key assumptions. First, student performance in school is the result of an interaction between the student and the instructional environment (Ysseldyke & Christensen, 1987). In other words, students do have problems, but sometimes the task or the setting causes or magnifies the problems. Second, by carefully analyzing students' learning needs and the specific demands of the classroom environment, teachers can *reasonably* accommodate most exceptional students in their classrooms. You can maximize student success without taking a disproportionate amount of teacher time or diminishing the education of the other students in the class. For example, Mr. Chin provided Royce, a student with a mild hearing impairment, an outline of lecture notes to help him keep up with the lesson. Soon, other students who struggled to recognize the important lecture points were also requesting and benefitting from the outlines. This type of reasonable accommodation assists many students in the class.

The **INCLUDE** strategy for accommodating exceptional students in the general education classroom has the following seven steps:

Step 1   **I**dentify classroom environmental, curricular, and instructional demands.
Step 2   **N**ote student learning strengths and needs.
Step 3   **C**heck for potential areas of student success.
Step 4   **L**ook for potential problem areas.
Step 5   **U**se information gathered to brainstorm instructional adaptations.
Step 6   **D**ecide which adaptations to implement.
Step 7   **E**valuate student progress.

These steps are designed to apply to a broad range of special needs and classroom environments.

Step 1: Identify Classroom Demands

Because the classroom environment significantly influences what students learn, analyzing classroom requirements allows teachers to anticipate or explain problems a student might experience. Then by modifying the environment, teachers can solve or lessen the impact of these learning problems. Common classroom demands may relate to classroom organization, classroom grouping, instructional materials, and instructional methods.

Classroom organization.   The ways in which a teacher establishes and maintains order in a classroom are referred to as classroom organization (Doyle, 1986). Classroom organization includes a number of factors: physical organization, such as the use of wall and floor space and lighting; classroom routines for academic and non-academic activities; classroom climate, or attitudes toward individual differences; behaviour management, such as classroom rules and reward systems; and the use of time for instructional and non-instructional activities. Oni is a student who needs adaptations in physical organization; she uses a wheelchair and requires wide aisles in the classroom and a ramp for the step leading to her classroom. Heinrich would benefit from a behaviour management system; he might move from class to class prior to the end of each period to eliminate many potential opportunities to fight with classmates. He would also benefit from an efficient use of time; minimizing transition times or the amount of time between activities would eliminate further opportunities to engage in inappropriate interactions with his classmates.

Classroom grouping.   Teachers use a variety of **classroom grouping** arrangements. Sometimes they teach the whole class at once, as when they lecture in a content area such as social studies. Other times teachers may employ small-group instruction. For example, they may teach a small group of students who have similar instructional needs, such as a group of students who all require extra help on their multiplication facts. They may also group together students of differing interests and abilities in an effort to foster cooperative problem solving and/or peer tutoring. Finally, classroom groups may be either teacher centred, in which the teacher is primarily responsible for instruction, or peer mediated, in which much of the instruction is carried out by students. Mike needs adaptations in classroom grouping to succeed; for example, he might do better in a small group in which other students read assignments aloud so that he can participate in responding to them. The three students in the class who are developmentally advanced in language arts and reading chapter books, while you are teaching the class beginning literacy, also need adaptations (Keating, 1991); for example, they might do better reading and discussing an adventure book chapter by chapter while the rest of the class learns to analyze and synthesize sounds.

Instructional materials.   The types of **instructional materials** teachers use can have a major impact on the academic success of students with special needs. Although many teachers are choosing to develop or collect their own materials, pre-published textbooks are still the norm. Pre-published textbooks include basic-skills texts called basals and texts that stress academic content in areas such as history and science. Other materials commonly used by teachers include concrete representational items, such as manipulative devices and technological devices, including audiovisual aids, telecommunications systems, and microcomputers. Roberta's use of large-print materials to assist her in seeing her work and Carmen's use of a study guide to help her identify important information in her history text are both examples of adaptations in instructional materials.

Instructional methods.   The ways in which teachers teach content or skills to students and evaluate whether learning has occurred are the essence of teaching and are crucial for accommodating exceptional students. Teachers use a number of different approaches to teach content or skills. Sometimes they teach skills directly, whereas other times they assume the role of a facilitator and encourage students to learn on their own. Instructional methods also involve student practice that occurs in class, through independent seatwork activities, or out of class, through homework. Ms. Correli's decision to use the overhead projector and then give Lon a copy of the transparency to help his learning is an example of an adaptation in presentation of subject matter. A paraprofessional who writes a student's words is an example of an adaptation in student practice.

Finally, **student evaluation,** or determining the extent to which students have mastered academic skills or instructional content, is an important aspect of instructional methods. Grades on report cards are frequently used to communicate student evaluation. When evaluating students with disabilities, teachers must focus on measuring what a student knows rather than the extent of his or her disability. For example, Alex, who has a severe learning disability in writing, may need to speak aloud the answers to a test to convey all he knows; if he writes the answers, you may only be measuring his writing disability. For some students, grading is an appropriate evaluation strategy. But for others, such as Mara, a student who has a moderate developmental or cognitive disability and is learning to recognize her name in her grade five class, a narrative report might be a better evaluation tool.

Step 2: Note Student Learning Strengths and Needs

Once instructional demands are specified, the *N* step of INCLUDE calls for identifying student strengths and needs. Remember that students with disabilities are a very heterogeneous group; a label cannot communicate a student's learning profile. For example, some students with developmental disabilities will learn many life skills and live independently, whereas others will always need daily assistance. Also keep in mind that students with disabilities are more like their peers without disabilities than different. Like their non-disabled peers, they have patterns of learning strengths and weaknesses. Focusing on strengths is essential (Aune, 1991; Bursuck & Jayanthi, 1993).

Three areas describe student learning strengths and needs: academics, social-emotional development, and physical development. Problems in any one area may prevent students from meeting classroom requirements.

Academics.   The first part of academics is basic skills, including reading, math, and oral and written language. Although these skills might sometimes be bypassed (for example, through the use of a calculator in math), their importance in both elementary and secondary education suggests you should consider them carefully. For example, a student with a severe reading problem will likely have trouble in any subject area that requires reading, including math, social studies, and science, and on any assignment with written directions.

Cognitive and learning strategies comprise the second part of academics. These strategies involve "learning how to learn" skills such as memorization, textbook reading, note-taking, test-taking, and general problem solving. Such skills give students independence that will help them in adult life. Students with prob-

Do It! Visit your university's study skills lab or learning centre to find out how beginning university students are helped to learn academic skills.

lems in these areas will experience increasing difficulty as they proceed through the grades. For example, students who have difficulty memorizing basic facts will have trouble learning to multiply fractions, and students who cannot take notes will probably fall behind in a history course based on a lecture format.

Survival skills, the third area of academics, are skills practised by successful students, such as attending school regularly, being organized, completing tasks in and out of school, being independent, taking an interest in school, and displaying positive interpersonal skills (Brown, Kerr, Zigmond, & Harris, 1984). Students lacking in these areas usually have difficulty at school. For example, disorganized students are unlikely to have work done on time, or unlikely to take home or return parent permission forms for field trips. Survival skills also help some students compensate for their other problems. For example, given two students with identical reading problems, teachers sometimes offer more help to the student who always attends school and tries hard. Students who are gifted but have difficulty completing tasks and working independently risk being excluded from mentorships and other programs designed to meet their needs for stimulation and challenge (Matthews, in press).

Social-emotional development.   Students' social-emotional development involves classroom conduct, interpersonal skills, and personal/psychological adjustment. Classroom conduct problems include a number of aggressive or disruptive behaviours, such as hitting, fighting, teasing, hyperactivity, yelling, refusing to comply with requests, crying, and destructiveness. Although most of these behaviours may be exhibited by all children at one time or another, exceptional students may engage in them more frequently and with greater intensity. Conduct problems seriously interfere with student learning and can lead to problems in interpersonal relations and personal psychological adjustment. For example, students who are disruptive in class are less likely to learn academic skills and content; their outbursts may also be resented by their peers and lead to peer rejection, social isolation, and a poor self-image.

▶ *What are the special needs of the students in this photograph? Would knowing the label given to them help you know how to teach them? How are the lives of students with disabilities and those without disabilities changed because of their interactions with one another?*

Interpersonal skills include but are not limited to initiating and carrying on conversations, coping with conflict, and establishing and maintaining friendships. Although these skills are not ordinarily part of the explicit school curriculum, their overall impact on school adjustment makes them important. For example, students lacking in peer support may have difficulty completing group projects (an example of student practice) or finding someone to help with a difficult assignment (an example of homework).

Personal/psychological adjustment involves the key motivational areas of self-image, frustration tolerance, and proactive learning. For example, students with poor self-image and low tolerance for frustration may do poorly on tests (an example of student evaluation); students who are inactive learners may have difficulty pursuing an independent science project (an example of student practice).

Physical development.   Physical development includes vision and hearing levels, motor skills, and neurological functioning. Students with vision problems will need adapted educational materials. Students with poor fine motor skills may need a computer to do their homework—an adaptation for student practice.

Professional Edge
Selecting Appropriate Instructional Adaptations

Here are some general guidelines to help you make reasonable accommodations in instruction.

- Employ an adaptation only when a mismatch occurs. Your time and energy as a teacher are limited; make changes only when necessary.

- Be certain that the student's problems are not physical in origin before you make any adaptations. This concern relates particularly to students with no obvious physical or sensory needs. Before adapting your class for a student with an attentional problem, ensure that the problem is not the result of a hearing loss, seizure disorder, or other physical problem.

- Determine whether you are dealing with a "can't" or a "won't" problem. Blankenship and Lilly (1981) describe a "can't" problem as one in which the student, no matter how highly motivated, is unable to do what is expected. A "won't" problem implies that the student could do what is expected but is not motivated to do so. Each type of problem may require a different adaptation. A student who is unable to do what is expected might need a bypass strategy; a student unwilling to do the work might need a behaviour management strategy. This distinction can also save you time. For example, if a student failed a test because she didn't feel like working on the day of the test, a teacher's attempt to provide extra tutorial assistance would likely be wasted effort. The "can't" and "won't" problems are particularly relevant for adolescents, who are often less likely than younger students to work to please their teachers.

- Keep the changes as simple as possible. A good general rule is to try the intervention that requires the least time and effort on your part that is likely to positively affect the student. Try a more involved adaptation only if needed.

Finally, students with attention deficits may need a wider range of approaches for presenting instruction, including lecture, discussion, small group work, and independent work.

Step 3: Check Potential Areas of Student Success

The next INCLUDE step is C, analyzing student strengths in view of the instructional demands identified in Step 1 and checking for activities or tasks that students can do successfully. Success enhances student self-image and motivation. For example, Jerry doesn't read but can draw skilfully. In social studies, his teacher asks him to be the class cartographer, drawing maps for each province and territory in Canada as it is studied. Kurt has a moderate developmental disability and learns very slowly, but he always comes to school on time. His second-grade teacher appoints him attendance monitor.

Step 4: Look for Potential Problem Areas

In the L step of the INCLUDE strategy, student learning needs are reviewed within a particular instructional context, and potential mismatches are identified. For example, Mika has a learning need in the area of expressive writing; she is unable to identify spelling errors in her work. She has an academic learning need. One student evaluation classroom demand is that her history teacher deducts one mark from her papers for each spelling error. For Mika to succeed in writing, this mismatch needs to be addressed. Similarly, Sam has a severe problem in speaking fluently—a physical problem that is a learning need. His grade four teacher requires that students present book reports to the class, a demand for student practice. Again, a potential mismatch exists that could prevent Sam from succeeding.

Step 5: Use Information to Brainstorm Adaptations

Once potential mismatches have been identified, the U step of INCLUDE is to use this information to identify possible ways to eliminate or minimize the effects of them. Adaptations could include bypassing the student's learning need by allowing the student to employ compensatory learning strategies, making a modification in classroom teaching or organization, and teaching the student basic or independent learning skills. The Professional Edge on page 28 summarizes points to keep in mind when making instructional adaptations for students.

Bypass strategies.   Bypass strategies allow students to gain access to or demonstrate mastery of the school curriculum in alternative ways. For example, a bypass strategy for Claire, who has a serious problem with spelling, would be a computerized spell checker. Alternatively, a peer could help her proofread her work. However, bypassing cannot be used on a primary area of instruction: Claire cannot spell check her spelling test. Also, bypassing a skill does not necessarily mean that the skill should not be remediated. Claire may need spelling instruction as part of her language arts class. Finally, bypass strategies should encourage student independence. For example, Claire might be better off learning to use a spell checker rather than relying on a peer proofreader.

FYI: *Bypass strategies* are techniques that exceptional students use to learn or demonstrate mastery of curriculum in a way that minimizes the impact of their disability.

Technology Notes

Using Multimedia for Students At Risk

COMPUTERS are one of the most readily available and helpful tools you will have for meeting the needs of students with disabilities in your classroom. Here are a few of the ways they can assist you.

1. **Computers as instructional assistants.** With the vast and ever-increasing array of computer software available for students of all ages, individualizing in classrooms and labs has become straightforward. You can provide a simpler math program to students not ready for your lesson on adding fractions; you can offer problem-solving practice at various levels. Computers can also enrich gifted and talented students' education and assist all students in maximizing their interests.

2. **Computers as a motivational tool.** For some students, opportunities to work on a computer can be tremendously rewarding. Students who have difficulty completing assignments might earn computer time as part of their instructional program.

3. **Computers as a means for adaptive communication.** Computers can help students communicate their ideas. Voice synthesizers can "read" for students with vision impairments, and specialized printers can translate Braille into print or print into Braille. For students with disabilities that prevent them from speaking, the computer offers a means to reach others. Computers fitted with picture boards help students with severe cognitive disabilities state their preferences and make their needs known.

4. **Computers as a data collection tool.** Using software that tracks the user's progress within the program, you can monitor students' learning. For example, most computer writing programs can count the number of words written at different intervals, which can provide you with a rough measure of students' writing fluency. Likewise, many programs can track the number of math problems completed and the problem-solving level reached, which can give you a general sense of students' strengths and trouble spots.

5. **Computers for teacher record keeping.** Spending five or 10 minutes at the end of the

The Technology Notes examines some of the ways in which students with disabilities can use computers for bypass and other strategies. It also illustrates how computers can help you in planning and managing students' instruction.

Classroom teaching and organization.   Teachers can make adaptations in their classroom organization, grouping, materials, and instruction to help students succeed. For example, if Ramos has attention problems, he might be seated near the front of the room, and he might benefit from a special system of rewards and consequences and a classroom in which "busy" bulletin board displays are removed. All of these are classroom organization adaptations. A change in classroom instruction would be to call on Ramos frequently during class discussions and to allow him to earn points toward his mark for appropriate participation.

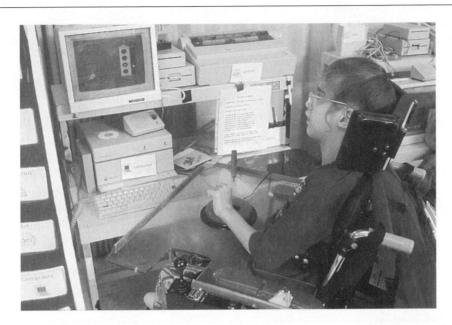

▼ *Student using assistive technology*

school day entering attendance, permission forms returned, student scores, and student behaviour data is a systematic and efficient way to keep professional records. Grading software can help you track student progress, as can spreadsheets. Simple files kept in word processing are appropriate for anecdotal records on students you are concerned about.

6. **Computers for teacher communication.** Teachers can also use computers to manage their many communication responsibilities. For example, you can prepare the class newsletter more easily on a computer than by hand. Letters sent to parents, schedules for and notes on meetings, and your news can all be stored on the computer for future reference. By keeping such files, you can maintain a chronology of your correspondence, and you can also create certain types of letters and notes just once and then copy them for future use.

Intensive instruction on basic skills and learning strategies.   A third option for including exceptional students is to provide intensive instruction designed to address basic skills or learning strategies in which the student is deficient. Often a special education teacher carries out this instruction in a resource room. This approach assumes that basic skills and learning strategies are prerequisites for successful general education experiences. Unfortunately, research indicates that such skills taught in pullout programs often do not transfer to the general education classroom (Wang, Reynolds, & Walberg, 1988). An alternative is to provide this type of instruction yourself. This option is feasible when many students have similar instructional needs and when you can easily monitor skill development. For example, Mr. Higgins, a grade seven science teacher, lectures frequently. As a result, students must be proficient note-takers. At the beginning of the school year, Mr. Higgins noticed during a routine check of student notebooks that many students were not taking adequate notes. With assistance from the special education teacher, he taught note-taking as part of science. Three students for whom note-taking was especially difficult handed in their notes each day so Mr. Higgins could monitor their progress.

Step 6: Decide Which Accommodations to Implement

After you have brainstormed possible bypass strategies or instructional adaptations, you will implement the *D* step in INCLUDE, which involves selecting strategies to try. A number of guidelines are suggested here to help you decide which accommodations best suit your students' needs.

✓ **Your Learning:** What are three examples of age-appropriate interventions? Why is age-appropriateness a key concept for thinking about exceptional students in general education classes?

Select age-appropriate adaptations.   Students' adaptations should match their age. For example, using a grade three book as a supplement for a grade eight science student reading at the grade three level would embarrass the student. In such a situation, a bypass strategy such as a taped textbook would be preferable if the student has the necessary background and cognitive skills to listen to the book with understanding. A good general rule is to remember that *no* students, whether in grade one or grade twelve and regardless of their exceptionality, want to use what they perceive as "baby" books or materials.

Select the easiest accommodations first.   Accommodations must be feasible. Although making adaptations will often mean some additional work for you, they should not require so much time and effort that they interfere with teaching the entire class. For example, it is easier to circle the six out of 12 math problems you want Maria to complete than to create a separate worksheet just for her.

Select adaptations you agree with.   You are more likely to implement an approach successfully if you believe in it, especially in the area of behaviour management. For example, in selecting rewards for students, if you are uncomfortable with candy, try activities such as time on the computer. However, adaptations should not be considered only in light of teacher beliefs. Legislation and policies in every province and territory are clear that the unique needs of students take precedence over the convenience of schools. With imagination and some input from special educators, you will undoubtedly find strategies that match your teaching approach while maximizing your students' learning.

Select adaptations with demonstrated effectiveness.   Over the past 25 years, a massive body of professional literature on effective teaching practices has accumulated. This research will help you avoid fads and other unvalidated practices. The strategies suggested throughout this text are based in research and form a starting point for your understanding of validated practices. Another means of staying professionally current is to read relevant professional journals. You will find a list of general education and special education publications in the Professional Edge.

▼▼▼▼▼▼▼▼▼▼▼▼▼▼▼▼▼▼▼▼▼▼▼▼▼▼▼

Professional Edge

Keeping Up to Date

J UST as physicians and scientists keep abreast of the developments in their fields, so, too, do teachers keep up with the latest research in education. Listed below are some special and general education professional journals that might interest you as you work to include exceptional students in your class.

Special Education Journals

B.C. Journal of Special Education
Canadian Journal of Special Education
Education and Training in Mental Retardation
    and Developmental Disabilities
Exceptional Children
Exceptionality Education Canada
Focus on Exceptional Children
Intervention in School and Clinic
Journal of Learning Disabilities

Journal of Special Education
Learning Disabilities Forum
Learning Disabilities Research and Practice
Learning Disability Quarterly
Remedial and Special Education
Teaching Exceptional Children

General Education Journals

Canadian Journal of Education
Education Canada
Educational Leadership
Instructor
Journal of Kappa Delta Pi
Journal of Reading
Phi Delta Kappan
Reading Research Quarterly
Reading Teacher
Review of Educational Research

Step 7: Evaluate Student Progress

Although many effective teaching practices exist, it is impossible to predict which ones will be effective for a particular student. As a result, once an adaptation is implemented, the *E* step of INCLUDE is essential: evaluate strategy effectiveness. You can track effectiveness through marks on assignments and tests; observations; analysis of student work; portfolios; performance assessments; and teacher, parent, and student ratings. Gathering this information will let you know whether to continue, to change, or to discontinue an intervention.

✓ **Your Learning:** What are all the steps in INCLUDE? What is an example of each?

◤ *Summary*

Exceptional education or special education refers to the specialized services received by thousands of exceptional students in Canada. Current practices have evolved from a combination of factors, including the inception of compulsory public education early in the twentieth century, research questioning instructional practices for exceptional students, the Charter of Rights and Freedoms, and provincial education legislation.

Special Needs Education Network

schoolnet2.carleton.ca/sne/

The Integrated Network of Disability Information and Education

indie.ca/

Special Olympics International

www.specialolympics.org/

The present trend is toward inclusion. Some professionals fully support inclusion, whereas others caution that it might not be the best option for some exceptional students. Many types or categories of exceptionalities are recognized across Canada including learning disabilities, students who are gifted, sensory impairments, and students who are at risk. As a classroom teacher, you will make reasonable accommodations for exceptional students. The INCLUDE strategy is a way to help you think through how you can successfully plan and provide these accommodations; it will also guide you through the strategies presented in later chapters of this book.

Applications in Teaching Practice

Using the INCLUDE Model

Carol Martinez, a special education teacher, talks to Jim Gentle, a grade six social studies teacher. They are conferring about Alex, a boy with a severe reading disability, who will be included in Mr. Gentle's class next fall.

MS. MARTINEZ: Jim, as we agreed to several weeks ago, Alex Bass will be included in your social studies class next year. Alex can read fluently and answer comprehension questions at the grade two level. How do you think he'll be able to handle your class, especially the textbook?

MR. GENTLE: Well, the book is written at about a grade seven reading level. But it's fairly well organized; the key vocabulary words are highlighted and spelled phonetically, and there are questions embedded throughout the chapter to help the kids figure out what is important.

MS. MARTINEZ: What do you do to get the class ready to read each chapter?

MR. GENTLE: I go over the highlighted vocabulary plus other important words on the board before they read. I also spend some time giving them background information to help them understand the text as well as tie the new material into earlier chapters in the book.

MS. MARTINEZ: That will help Alex, too, though he may need more practice on the vocabulary. Could you somehow provide him with extra practice?

MR. GENTLE: I don't have time during class to do it myself, but I could send the words home with Alex the night before we discuss them in class. I could also spend a few minutes with Alex before or after school.

MS. MARTINEZ: Jim, how are students evaluated in your class?

MR. GENTLE: Homework is worth 30 percent of their grade; multiple-choice tests on the textbook and lectures are worth the remaining 70 percent. The tests might pose a problem for Alex because of his reading difficulties.

MS. MARTINEZ: We could arrange for him to take his tests orally in the resource room, at least for the first term.

MR. GENTLE: I'm not completely comfortable with that. I usually don't let tests leave the classroom. But I guess it's okay as long as you can be sure there's no possibility of cheating. Besides, how would Alex react to that kind of special treatment? You had mentioned that he really worries about what his friends think—about being "dumb" because he's an exceptional learner.

Ms. MARTINEZ: We have really clear procedures for tests, so I can assure you that cheating won't be an issue. As for Alex, we can arrange for him to take the test in your room and then take it at another time in the resource room.

MR. GENTLE: It's okay with me. Will you talk with Alex? You already know him.

Questions

1. According to the description in this chapter, what exceptionality does Alex have?
2. What is Alex's least restrictive or most enabling environment? What are the appropriate supports being offered to him?
3. If Alex had been a student in the 1950s, what might his education have been like?
4. What parts of the INCLUDE strategy did Ms. Martinez and Mr. Gentle use to plan for Alex's education? How effectively did they use each step?
5. What type of strategy is used when Alex takes his tests orally? What other reasonable accommodations could Mr. Gentle use to help Alex succeed in class?
6. Mr. Gentle said that homework counted for 30 percent of students' grades. If the homework consisted of answering short-answer questions at the end of the chapter, what homework adaptations might be made for Alex?

Chapter 2

Procedures and Services for Exceptional Students

Learner Objectives

After you read this chapter, you will be able to

1. Describe the professionals who may be involved in instructing students with disabilities and explain their responsibilities.

2. Explain the process through which a student obtains school-based interventions and special education services.

3. Name the components of an individual education plan (IEP) and provide examples of these components.

4. Describe the types of services that students with disabilities may receive and the settings in which they may receive them.

5. Discuss what occurs if parents and school district representatives disagree about a student's special education.

6. Outline the role of the regular education teacher in the procedures and services of special education.

MR. PETERSON *is concerned. He teaches grade five, and one of his students, Leon, is having increasing difficulty mastering skills. Leon reads at about a grade two level, has learned about half of his math facts, and reacts to other children's teasing by shouting and hitting. Mr. Peterson isn't sure what to do next; the strategies he has used in the past have not had an impact, and he fears Leon is giving up on learning. He has met with Leon's mother and stepfather. They report that they are having more and more difficulty getting Leon to mind them. Leon's parents are concerned that he doesn't seem to care about school and that he is spending much of his time hanging out with older boys. They are worried about gangs and drugs. What steps should Mr. Peterson take next? Whom might Mr. Peterson contact to help him decide whether Leon's difficulties are serious enough to consider recommending assessment by the school-based team?*

TIM, *a grade eleven student in high school, has a learning disability. He is on schedule to graduate with his classmates. However, Tim is unsure about what he will do when he leaves school. He thinks he would like to go to university but is concerned about whether he can succeed there. He has also considered enlisting in the army, but his parents are discouraging that. He knows he could get a job at the local paper factory, but that prospect seems, in his words, "too boring." What is the responsibility of school professionals in helping Tim decide on a suitable career activity to pursue following graduation? Who can help Tim make his decisions?*

As a teacher, you will encounter students who are struggling. Some may appear to be doing everything they can to *not* learn. Others will be trying their best to learn and still not be successful. You might even have students whom you suspect have a vision or hearing problem so serious that it prevents them from learning. You may find yourself wondering whether some of these students should be identified as exceptional learners and receiving school-based interventions and who will provide them. This chapter introduces you to the people who specialize in working with exceptional students and the procedures involved in deciding if a student should be identified as exceptional and receive school-based intervention. You will also learn how students' instructional programs are designed and monitored, and which services exceptional students receive. You will discover that when parents or students disagree with school professionals about special services, procedures exist to help them resolve these problems. Most important, you will learn about your role in working with other professionals and parents to determine student eligibility for school-based interventions, carrying out students' educational programs, and monitoring student learning.

▶ Who Are the Professionals Who Work Together to Meet the Needs of Exceptional Students?

A school district or board's success in responding to the educational needs of all of its students depends primarily on the actions and beliefs of the teachers and administrators of each school. Effective school staff members work as a team with parents and other professionals to assume responsibility for all students in the school. They believe that all students can learn and that it is their responsibility to teach all students, with the assistance of a wide range of professionals. These beliefs and actions of schools that are effective in meeting the needs of exceptional learners were described by Napier (1995) in a report and handbook based on his experiences in one school district in British Columbia and described by Beveridge (1997) in a study in a school board in Ontario.

Exceptional students receive a wide range of school-based interventions and special services. Not surprisingly, many different individuals can be involved in the delivery of these services. You will probably interact with some of these professionals, such as resource teachers, every day. Others might not be so available; they serve students indirectly, or work only with the few students with the most challenging disabilities.

Regular Classroom Teachers

You, the **regular classroom teacher,** are the first professional included in this section because for many students with suspected or documented exceptionalities, you will be the person who has the most detailed knowledge of the students' day-to-day needs in your classroom. Your responsibilities span several areas. You are the person most likely to bring to the attention of other professionals a student whom you suspect may need school-based intervention; that is, you may

Do It! Talk to an experienced regular classroom teacher about his or her range of responsibilities for students with exceptionalities. Compare findings with your classmates.

encounter a student who is reading significantly and persistently below grade level; a student whose behaviour is so different from other students' that you suspect an emotional or behaviour disorder; or a student who has extraordinary difficulty focusing on learning. When you suspect a student needs intervention, you will document the student's characteristics and behaviours that led to your concern, often by gathering samples of the student's work, compiling descriptions of the student's behaviour, and keeping notes of how you have addressed the student's problem (Davidson & Wiener, 1991). You will work with special education colleagues to attempt accommodations in your classroom to clarify whether the student's problems need further exploration. If the student is referred for assessment, you will contribute information about the student's academic and social functioning in your classroom, and you will help identify the student's strengths, needs, and educational program components. For example, you might help others to understand the curricular expectations in your classroom and the types of adaptations that may be necessary for the student to succeed there. You might assist in updating parents on their child's progress annually. Most important, as Kamann and Perry (1994) reported in a study conducted in British Columbia, you will be expected to work with other professionals to provide appropriate instruction within your classroom. Responsibilities of a regular classroom teacher are presented in Figure 2.1.

When all your responsibilities are listed, your role in planning and providing services to exceptional students may appear overwhelming. However, studies conducted in Ontario, Alberta, and Nova Scotia of regular classroom teachers' perceptions of their roles in working with students with disabilities generally

FYI: Regular classroom teachers' roles in relation to exceptional education are especially critical given the changes occurring throughout education as part of school reform. Many professionals hope that we will soon have one integrated, inclusive education system that serves all students well.

Identifier of possible exceptional students

Member of prereferral or intervention assistance team

Member of multidisciplinary

Provider of day-to-day instruction

Communication link with colleagues

Liaison to parents

FIGURE 2.1

Regular Classroom Teacher Responsibilities in Special Education

report that the teachers are able and willing to contribute to students' education as long as some conditions are met. The most important conditions seem to be making time available for teacher planning and ensuring adequate funding for programs (Bunch, Lupart, & Brown, 1997).

Resource Teachers

FYI: An *individual educa-tion plan* (IEP) is the docu-ment that guides profession-als in the delivery of exceptional education and related services. Details on the usual components of IEPs are provided later in this chapter.

The professionals with whom you are most likely to have ongoing contact in teaching exceptional students are **resource teachers.** They are usually respon-sible for managing and coordinating the services a student receives, including the writing and implementation of the student's **individual education plan (IEP).** They may also provide direct instruction to exceptional students (Kamann & Perry, 1994). In addition, they may consult with you regarding the teaching of an exceptional student or a student suspected of having an exceptionality. In the lat-ter case they would be working with you to determine whether a referral for assessment is warranted (Heron & Harris, 1993).

Depending on the province in which you teach and the students in your classroom, you may work with different types of resource teachers. Sometimes, resource or learning assistance teachers are assigned to work with a specific cat-egory of students. For example, your school district may have a teacher for stu-dents with vision or hearing impairments. In provinces and territories that do not use categorical labels, some teachers teach students with high-incidence disabil-ities (such as learning disabilities) or low-incidence disabilities (such as autism). You may work with a **consulting teacher** or consultant (Jordan, 1994). This pro-fessional might meet with you regularly to monitor student progress and address your concerns but might not directly teach the students.

▶ *What are this teacher's roles and responsibilities in helping identify stu-dents who may be excep-tional and in assisting the exceptional learners in his class?*

Another type of special educator designated by type of services is an **inclu-sion specialist** or **support facilitator** (Beveridge, 1997; Stainback & Stainback, 1992). In inclusive schools, inclusion specialists are responsible for providing some student instruction, problem solving with teachers, and coordinating the services the student receives. As schools become more inclusive, this role is likely to increase in prominence. In an interview study conducted in the Toronto area, Beveridge (1997) found that support facilitators played an important role in schools and classrooms that were commended for a high level of inclusion of exceptional learners.

If you work in a school district where each school has only a few students with disabilities, the special educator you interact with might be an **itinerant teacher.** Itinerant teachers travel between two or more school sites to provide services to students. Teachers for students with vision or hearing disabilities are sometimes itinerant, too.

One other type of special educator is a **transition specialist** or career counsellor. This professional typically works in a secondary school and helps prepare students to leave school for vocational training, employment, or post-secondary education. A transition specialist may also work with community busi-nesses to arrange student placements for cooperative education (White & Bond, 1992) and can serve as a **job coach,** accompanying an exceptional student to a job site and helping the student learn and apply the skills needed to do the job successfully.

Specialists and Related Service Providers

In addition to working with school-based special educators, you will have contact with a variety of other service providers. These individuals also play important roles in educating exceptional students.

School psychologists. These professionals offer at least two types of expertise related to educating students with disabilities. First, **school psychologists** often have a major responsibility for assessing a student's cognitive, academic, social, emotional, and/or behavioural functioning. They may contribute a detailed written analysis of the student's strengths and areas of need; in many school districts, this document is referred to as a "psych. report"—that is, a psychological report.

A second major task for school psychologists is designing strategies with teachers to address students' academic and social behaviour problems (Rosenfield, 1987). Sometimes, school psychologists serve as behaviour consultants. Occasionally, they assist a teacher by working with an entire class group on social skills. They might also provide individual assistance to students with emotional or behavioural problems.

Counsellors. Although they most often advise high school students, **counsellors** sometimes work at other school levels and contribute to the education of exceptional students. For example, counsellors in some school boards assess students' social and emotional functioning, including areas such as self-concept; motivation; attitude toward school, peers, and teachers; and social skills. For teachers, they might suggest ways to draw out a student who is excessively shy, and ways to create an emotionally safe classroom environment. For students, counsellors might arrange group sessions with students from several classes who share specific needs; or, for example, counsellors can lead groups of gifted students to consider a wider range of careers than they might have observed in their own community.

Speech and language therapists. Many exceptional students have communication needs. Some have mild problems in pronouncing words or speaking clearly. Others have extremely limited vocabulary. Yet others can make only a few sounds and rely on alternative means of communication, such as communication boards. The professionals who specialize in meeting students' communication needs are **speech and language therapists.** At the elementary level, they might work with entire classes on language development or with individual students on pronouncing sounds. At the secondary level, they might focus on functional vocabulary and might help a student with a developmental disability learn to read common signs and complete tasks such as ordering in a restaurant or asking for assistance.

Social workers. Social workers' expertise is similar to that of a counsellor in terms of helping teachers and students address social and emotional issues. Thus, they may serve as consultants to teachers and also may provide individual or group assistance to students. However, **social workers** have additional expertise. They are often the liaison between the school and the family. For example,

✓ **Your Learning:** What are the typical responsibilities of special educators? Why do they have different job titles?

✓ **Your Learning:** Based on the grade and subject area you plan to teach, which special educators are you most likely to work with?

FYI: *Functional skills* are those students need for adult independence. They include the ability to shop, ride a bus, ask for help, and so on. Functional vocabulary words are terms that many adults need, words such as *sale, restroom, exit,* and *stop.*

they can create a family history by interviewing parents and visiting a student's home. The school social worker often follows up on teacher reports about the suspected abuse or neglect of students.

Physiotherapists and occupational therapists. For some students to benefit from education, they require assistance for problems with gross and fine motor skills. Physiotherapists and occupational therapists are the professionals who have expertise in these areas.

Physiotherapists assess students' needs and provide interventions related to gross motor skills. They might participate on a multidisciplinary team by assessing such areas as the obviously awkward gait of a student. They interpret information about a student's physical needs that has been provided by a physician. They might also monitor student needs related to how they should be positioned—whether in a wheelchair, standing with assistance, or on the floor—and how classroom settings can be adapted to accommodate their needs.

Occupational therapists are concerned with fine motor skills; they often are responsible for assessing students' use of their hands and fingers and developing and implementing plans for improving related motor skills. For example, an occupational therapist may assess whether a student with cerebral palsy can appropriately grip and use a pencil. This professional might help students with severe disabilities learn skills for feeding or dressing themselves.

Nurses. **Nurses** provide a link between students' medical and educational needs. As required, they develop student medical histories, and they may screen students for vision and hearing problems. They also provide the team with information about a student's specific medical conditions and the possible impact of a student's medication on educational performance as well as monitor student medical needs (for example, whether a change in medication is causing drowsiness or hyperactivity).

Administrators. The school's principal, assistant principal, or sometimes a special education department chairperson or team leader are the **administrators** most likely to participate actively in the education of students with disabilities. Their role is to offer knowledge about the entire school community and provide perspective on school district policies regarding in-school interventions. Administrators assist the multidisciplinary team in deciding students' need for services and exploring strategies for meeting their needs. They also play an important role in addressing parent concerns.

In some locales, especially in large urban and suburban districts, a **special services coordinator** plays an administrative role. Special services coordinators specialize in exceptional education procedural information. They also explain services and options to parents, problem solve with teachers when issues arise, and assist in monitoring to ensure that exceptional students receive needed supports.

Paraprofessionals. Individuals who assist teachers and others in the provision of services to exceptional students are called **paraprofessionals** or teachers' assistants. Although paraprofessionals may be certified teachers, they are considered non-certified staff according to the terms of their employment; that is, their

---

FYI: *Gross motor skills* refer to students' ability to use their large muscles effectively for walking, hopping, running, skipping, and so on. *Fine motor skills* refer to students' proficiency in using their small muscles for tasks such as writing, buttoning, or grasping a spoon.

Do It! Make a chart that lists all the professionals likely to provide services to students. With classmates, create a one- or two-page job description for each professional based on information you find in the library and from your local school district.

FYI: Although research does not yet clearly support the effectiveness of paraprofessionals in delivering special education services, the move toward inclusion has led to an increase in their use (Jones & Bender, 1993).

What is the role of paraprofessionals in inclusive classrooms? How do itinerant and other special education teachers carry out their responsibilities toward students with disabilities?

responsibilities for decision making about students are limited. Paraprofessionals might also be called instructional assistants, teaching assistants, aides, or other titles, depending on local practices.

School boards use paraprofessionals in many different ways (Jones & Bender, 1993). These are two of the most common: First, some paraprofessionals are assigned to a specific student who needs ongoing individual assistance. For example, students who lack the ability to move their arms may have a paraprofessional who takes notes for them and completes other tasks such as feeding. A few students have medical conditions requiring that a specially trained paraprofessional be present to monitor their status. Paraprofessionals in this role may be referred to as **personal assistants.**

The second and more common type of paraprofessional is one who assists in the delivery of services for many exceptional students. These paraprofessionals often work in both inclusive classrooms and special education classrooms and resource rooms as well as on the playground, at assemblies, and during bus duty. They have primary responsibility for working with exceptional students, but they sometimes also help other students and the teacher as the need arises and time permits.

Other specialists. Depending on student needs and provincial and local practice, other professionals may also participate in the education of exceptional students. For example, in some provinces a **psychometrist** completes much of the individual assessment of exceptional students. Sometimes, school districts have **consultants** who are used only when a need exists in their specific area of expertise (for example, severe behaviour problems, autism, or traumatic brain injury). If you work in a school district in which many students are non-native English speakers, you may also work with **English as a second language (ESL) teachers.** Although ESL teachers are not special educators, they sometimes help in decision making related to exceptional students who have limited English skills. One other type of specialist is a **mobility specialist.** These professionals are

Connections: Additional information about working with paraprofessionals is included in Chapter 3.

FYI: *Psychometrists* are experts in administering, scoring, and interpreting the results of individual assessment instruments.

FYI: In large schools with many students whose native language is not English, bilingual translators might be available to assist in communication with students and parents.

specially trained to help students with vision impairments learn how to become familiar with their environments and how to travel from place to place safely.

Another important service provider is a **sign language interpreter.** Interpreters are the communication link for students with significant hearing impairments. Interpreters listen to the instruction in a classroom and relay it to students with hearing impairments using sign language. The Technology Notes explains another strategy, captioned television and video, that helps to bridge the communication gap for students with hearing impairments.

Professionals from agencies outside the school are also part of the specialist group. If a student has been receiving services through a hospital or residential program, a physician, nurse, social worker, or other representative from there may work with school personnel to ensure that the student has a smooth transition back to school. Individuals from the medical community might also be involved when students are being assessed for attentional problems or when they have been injured or ill. Professionals from agencies might also be included if a student is receiving assistance from a community agency or has contact with the juvenile justice system. Finally, if parents wish to obtain expert opinion from a specialist who is not associated with the school, those individuals may attend team meetings or submit written reports for team consideration.

Parents, students, and advocates.   Whenever decisions are being made concerning an exceptional student, the best interests of the student and his or her family must be represented. Parents have the right to participate in virtually all aspects of their child's educational program, with slight variations across provinces and territories. Parent involvement spans the following areas:

1. Requesting assessment for special services.
2. Providing input on their child's strengths and needs.
3. Bringing to the team independent professionals' opinions about their child's needs.
4. Helping to decide if their child is exceptional and if the child will receive school-based intervention (e.g., Ontario Ministry of Education and Training, 1995b).
5. Assisting in the writing of goals and objectives for their child's individual educational program (e.g., Yukon, 1995, Section B, p. 5).
6. Participating in delivering instruction to their child.
7. Monitoring their child's progress.
8. Seeking assistance in resolving disagreements with school professionals.

Often, parents are a strong ally for regular classroom teachers. They can assist teachers by reviewing at home what is taught in school, rewarding their child for school accomplishments, and working with school professionals to resolve behaviour and academic problems.

Whenever appropriate, students with disabilities are also active participants in their own education. Increasingly, educators are involving students so that they can state directly their needs and goals and can learn to advocate for themselves. The extent of student participation on the team depends on the age of the student and the type and impact of the disability. The older the student and the greater his or her cognitive functioning, the greater the participation. If you teach secondary school science, it is quite likely that your students with disabilities will

FYI: The list of professionals included in this chapter is by no means complete. Your instructor might provide additional descriptions of professionals who contribute to the design and delivery of special education services in your province.

Do It! Consult the policy manuals for your school and province to identify parents' rights.

Connections: Additional information on parent roles in working with teachers and other school professionals is included in Chapter 3.

Connections: The topics of student self-advocacy and student self-evaluation are addressed in depth in Chapter 10.

Technology Notes

Teaching and Learning through Captioned Television

CAPTIONING for television was developed primarily to assist individuals with hearing impairments. However, educators have discovered and research supports the fact that captioned television can be a powerful tool for helping many students, including those who are bilingual and those who have reading disabilities, learn reading and vocabulary skills. Many television programs and movies are available in closed-caption format, and a TeleCaption can be purchased for under $300. Further, since 1993, many new television sets have built-in decoders and this can be selected as a special feature on others.

Here are some suggestions for using captioned television and other captioned video.

- Get to know your equipment. The decoder is easily attached to a television, and you can learn to use it in just a few minutes.

- Select a high-interest captioned video. Many hours of captioned video are available each week. You can select programs appropriate for your students by reviewing a weekly television guide. One example of such a program you may be able to access is *Reading Rainbow*. This type of show has few viewing restrictions since it is intended for widespread educational use.

- Preview the video. You are unlikely to need to use an entire video. By previewing, you can select the most relevant segments and plan your lessons accordingly.

- Locate related texts. By gathering books and magazines that relate to the video, you create a supply of print materials for students to use that complement the programs you have selected.

- Introduce the video. Captioned video is no different from other teaching: It should be clearly introduced to students. Some students will need to become accustomed to reading the captions. Once they do, you can use the mute button on the television remote control to challenge students to read the screen.

Likewise, you can have students read along with the video and retell the video after it has been watched and read.

- Create a video library. If you keep a record of the video activities you have used and enjoyed, you will be able to share them with your colleagues. You might also check to see if your school district has a video library. Remember that video materials are copyrighted and their use is restricted; your collection should not violate copyright laws.

If you would like more information on TeleCaption decoders, contact

Caption Resource Centre
890 Yonge Street, Suite 501
Toronto, ON M4W 3P4
Tel. 416-961-5336
Web www.captions.org

Source: Adapted from "Captioned Video and Vocabulary Learning: An Innovative Practice in Literacy Instruction," by P. S. Koskinen, R. M. Wilson, L. B. Gambrell, and S. B. Neuman, 1993, *Reading Teacher, 47* (1), pp. 36–43, by permission of the International Reading Association.

▶ *Closed-caption television*

DO YOU LIKE MILK?

attend and participate in team meetings that discuss them and request adaptations to help them learn. These students might also monitor their learning and behaviour and assess their progress toward their educational goals.

A final team member is an **advocate.** Sometimes, parents sense that they are not knowledgeable enough about the policies and procedures that govern special education to represent themselves. In other instances, they are not sure school board personnel are acting in the best interests of their children. In some situations, parents may be uncomfortable interacting with school personnel because of language or cultural differences. In many jurisdictions across the country, parents have the right to bring an advocate to meetings concerning their children. This person serves as their advisor and sometimes their spokesperson. Although advocates are sometimes professionals, more often they are volunteers provided through a professional organization or parent support group, such as the local Association for Community Living, or friends or relatives.

How Can You Decide If a Student Might Need School-Based Intervention or Special Services?

You will play a key role in deciding if a student in your class should be assessed for the identification of an exceptionality, school-based intervention, and perhaps special services. Although students with obvious cognitive, sensory, or physical impairments probably have been identified before reaching school age, learning, language, attention, and behaviour disabilities often are not identified until children start school. Because you are the professional in daily contact with the student, you are the person most likely to notice an unmet need. Your judgment often initiates a referral for assessment and an IEP.

Analyze the Unmet Needs

As you teach, you will sometimes discover that you have a nagging concern about a student. This concern might begin early in the school year, or it might take several months to emerge. When you review student records and your own impressions of the student and your concern, you decide that the student's achievement is not within your classroom's typical range, given the standards of your school board and community expectations. Should you ask other professionals to assess the student to possibly identify an exceptionality? Perhaps. But first, you need to ask yourself some questions. These questions are summarized in Figure 2.2.

Do It! List vague phrases sometimes used to describe students. Then write examples of student actions or behaviours that more clearly characterize teachers' concerns.

What are specific examples of the unmet needs?   Having a nebulous concern about a student is far different from stating specifically what your concerns are. For example, sensing that a student is unmotivated is not a clear concern. What does the student do that leads you to conclude that motivation is a problem? Is it that the student doesn't make eye contact when speaking to you, or that the rewards and consequences that affect other students seem to have no effect—positive or negative—on this student? Vague concerns and hunches

FIGURE 2.2

Teachers' Concern about Student Needs

should be supported by specific information. Phrases such as "slow learning," "poor attitude toward school," "doesn't pay attention," and "never gets work completed" might have very different meanings to different professionals. To prepare to share your concern with others, then, your first step is to ask yourself, "When I say the student . . . , what are examples that clarify what I mean?"

Is there a chronic pattern negatively affecting learning?   Nearly all students will go through periods in which they struggle to learn, behave inappropriately, or otherwise cause you concern. Sometimes, a situation outside of school may affect students. For example, parents divorcing, a parent losing his or her job, or an illness or death occurring in the family might all negatively affect student learning or behaviour. However, the impact of these traumatic events should not be permanent, and the student should gradually return to previous levels of functioning.

Students with disabilities may also be affected by specific situations or events, but their learning and behaviour needs form a chronic pattern. They struggle over a long period regardless of the circumstances. For example, Jared, a high school student with an emotional disability, is withdrawn whether sitting in a large class or interacting in a small group. Using the INCLUDE model to identify student strengths and weaknesses can help you pick up on students' patterns of need.

Is the unmet need becoming more serious as time passes?   Sometimes, a student's needs appear to become greater over time. For example, Ben, who seemed to see well at the beginning of the school year, now holds books closer

Connections: Using the INCLUDE model can help you analyze the patterns in a student's needs.

and closer to his face, squints when he tries to read, and complains about headaches. In another example, Karen, who began the school year fairly close in achievement to her peers, by November lags significantly. Indications that needs are increasing are a signal to ask for input from others.

Is the student's functioning significantly different from that of class-mates?   As you think about your concerns about a student, you should ask yourself how the student compares with other students. For example, in urban settings it has been demonstrated that students at risk are less involved in the classroom and receive less verbal feedback from their teachers (Bay & Bryan, 1992). If you have six students who are all struggling, it might be that the information or skills are beyond the reach of the entire group or that your teaching approach is not accomplishing what you had planned. Even though self-reflection is sometimes difficult, when many students are experiencing problems, it is important to analyze how the curriculum or teaching might be contributing to the situation. In such instances, you should make changes in those two areas before seeking other assistance.

✓ **Your Learning:** What questions should you explore to determine if your concern about a student warrants referral for assessment and possible special education services?

Do you discover that you cannot find a pattern?   In some instances, the absence of a pattern to student needs is as much an indicator that you should request assistance as is a distinct pattern. Perhaps Curtis has tremendous mood swings, and you arrive at school each day wondering whether it will be a "good day" or a "bad day" for him. However, you are unable to accurately predict his mood. Or consider Becka, who learns science with ease but cannot seem to master even basic reading skills. You are unsure why her learning is so different in the two subjects.

Communicate Your Observations and Try Your Own Interventions

Your analysis of your students' unmet needs is the basis for further action. Although your analysis can help you decide to seek assistance from special education professionals for one of your students, as part of your attempts to help the student, you are initially responsible for gathering other information and trying to resolve the problem.

Contact parents.   One of your first strategies should be to contact the family (Shea & Bauer, 1991). Parents or other family members can often inform you about changes in the student's life that could be affecting school performance. Family members can also help you understand the student's activities outside of school that might influence his or her schoolwork, including clubs, gang involvement, employment, and responsibilities at home. Furthermore, by contacting the family, you might learn that what you perceive as a problem is mostly a reflection of a cultural difference. For example, a student whose family emigrated from Thailand is extremely quiet in class because silence signals respect in her native culture, not because she is unable to participate.

Parents can also be your partners in working to resolve some student learning problems. They can assist you in monitoring if homework is completed and

Professional Edge
Communicating with Family Members

ONE of your most important responsibilities as a teacher working with parents of exceptional students is to maintain effective communication with them. The strategies you use to communicate with them are similar to those you would use to communicate with any parent; but you might also find that because this communication is so vital, you want to use some additional strategies.

Passport

A passport is a system of communication that can be valuable when daily communication is needed

▶ **FIGURE 2.3**   Sample Page from a Passport

TO: Ms. Dolores   9:00 a.m.

Good day on the bus. Tom sat in his assigned seat and waited his turn to leave the bus. I praised his behaviour and gave him two points.

Mr. Parker, Bus Driver

TO: Ms. Dolores   10:30 A.M.

During PE today the group played kickball. Tom was well behaved but had difficulty participating effectively. I awarded him six points and praised his behaviour. Can we meet to discuss some means of increasing his participation?

Ms. Minton, Physical Education

TO: Mr. and Mrs. Hogerty   2:30 P.M.

As you can see from the notes above, Tom had a good day at school.

He received 89 percent on his reading test this morning. That's real progress. Please praise him for this accomplishment.

This evening, Tom is to read pp. 1–5 in his new reading book.

Even better news! Tom remembered to walk in the hallways today. He is very proud of himself.

I shall talk to Ms. Minton today about increasing Tom's participation in PE. I'll let you know what we decide at tomorrow night's parent meeting.

Ms. Dolores

TO: Ms. Dolores   9:00 P.M.

We praised and rewarded Tom for his hard work on the reading test, the bus, and the hallways. You're right; he feels good about himself today.

Tom read pp. 1–5 in the new book with his father. The words he had trouble with are underlined.

We will see you at the parent meeting tomorrow night.

Mary Hogerty

or when the student is unable to convey information to the parent (Runge, Walker, & Shea, 1975). A *passport* is a spiral notebook or paper-filled binder in which the teacher writes a few essential comments at the end of each school day. The students take the passport home so the parent can read the teacher's notes. The parent then either responds with additional notes or acknowledges having read the passport by signing the day's information. Figure 2.3 shows a sample page in a passport.

Checklist

Another type of communication you can use when you and the parents are monitoring the behaviour of a student who has several behaviour problems is a *daily reporting system*. This reporting form is a brief list of critical behaviours and a checkmark assessment of the student's performance on these for the day. The parent signs the report and returns it to school. In some cases, an entire week's record can be kept on a single form, and the daily report is kept as a log of progress for the student. Figure 2.4 provides an example of a checklist report.

Class Updates or Newsletters

A third type of communication form to use with parents is an *informational sheet*. Typically, this one-page weekly update notifies parents about important class activities and identifies the types of supports you need from them for the coming week. Updates are most common at the elementary level. For example, you might use a newsletter to inform parents that the next science unit is on meteorology and includes a field trip to the planetarium. This advance notice enables you and the parents to work together to make any special necessary arrangements for the field trip. This type of communication is particularly important if you have students with disabilities that affect their ability to communicate with their parents. Without an update from you, the parents of these children might not be aware of what is occurring in their children's class.

Source: From *Parents and Teachers of Children with Exceptionalities: A Handbook for Collaboration* by T. M. Shea and A. M. Bauer, 1991, Copyright © 1991 by Allyn and Bacon. Reprinted by permission.

▶ **FIGURE 2.4   Sample Checklist Reporting System**

Name _____   Date _____

	Great	Okay	With Prompt	Needs Work
Brought homework to class.				X
Had all school supplies (pencils, paper, notebook).	X			
Arrived in class on time.	X			
Began assigned work promptly and without arguing.			X	

Teacher comments:

All supplies brought today—homework is the next goal.

Parent comments:

I would like to meet with you to discuss homework issues. Next Monday when I pick Milton up? Please let me know if this is ok.

Parent signature _____*Vivian Boerger*_____

Milton 2/6/97

returned to school, if behaviour problems are occurring on the walk home, or if a physician is concerned about a child's medical condition. If you work with students whose homes do not have telephones and whose parents do not have transportation to come to school, your social worker or principal can help you make needed contact. The Professional Edge on pages 49–50 also provides some strategies you can use to communicate effectively with students' families.

Contact colleagues. Especially as a new teacher, you will want to discuss your concerns with other professionals to gain an additional perspective on the student's needs. In most schools, a resource teacher will arrange to observe the student in your class and then to discuss the observation. In schools where school-based teams meet, you can raise your concerns in that context.

Try interventions. Part of your responsibility as a teacher is to create a classroom where students can succeed. To cultivate such a setting, you will make adaptations as part of your attempts to address students' unmet needs. For example, have you tried moving the student's seat? Have you changed from writing your tests by hand to inputting them on a computer to make them more legible? Do you give some students only part of their assignment at one time because they become overwhelmed otherwise? These are just a few alterations that many teachers make without even thinking of them as adaptations. Sometimes, these small accommodations will be sufficient to help a student learn. In any case, you should try common interventions before deciding a student might need larger interventions. The Professional Edge suggests several strategies you can use to help you stay current on classroom interventions.

Do It! Review the INCLUDE model. Which steps can help you decide the types of interventions to try?

Document the unmet need. If you anticipate requesting assistance for a student, you will need to demonstrate the seriousness of your concern and your attempts to help meet the student's needs. If you have implemented a behaviour contract with the student, you can keep a record of how effective it has been. If you have contacted parents several times, you can keep a log of your conversations. If you have tried to decrease the number of times the student misses your first-hour class, you can summarize your attendance data. Strategies to document student needs serve two main purposes. First, they help you to do a "reality check" on whether the problem is as serious as you think it is. Especially if you gather data from other students as a comparison, you can judge whether the unmet needs of one student are significantly different from those of typical students. Second, the information you collect helps you communicate with other professionals.

Connections: How does the concept of reasonable accommodations relate to your responsibility for trying interventions before requesting additional assistance?

How Do Students Obtain School-Based Interventions and Special Services?

In light of the neighborhood schools and inclusion policies adopted in provinces and territories across Canada that were discussed in Chapter 1, school districts are adopting a school-based team process for implementing and monitoring plans and special services to meet the needs of exceptional students.

▼▼▼▼▼▼▼▼▼▼▼▼▼▼▼▼▼▼▼▼▼▼▼▼▼▼▼

Professional Edge
Developing Alternative Interventions

MANY teachers are constantly on the lookout for innovative ideas for helping students with exceptionalities in their classrooms succeed. Here are a few strategies for keeping your idea file up to date.

- Join a professional organization that provides journals to its members. An examples of such a group is the Council for Exceptional Children (CEC). Most major disciplines also have professional organizations (for example, the National Council for Teachers of Mathematics and the National Council for Teachers of English). The publications distributed by such organizations often provide many new and practical ideas for working with exceptional students. Some of these organizations have student chapters; most have discounted student membership fees.

- Attend local or provincial meetings of professional organizations. Most boards have an annual special education conference and welcome participation by regular classroom teachers and teachers-to-be. Provincial organizations also have annual conventions. Participating in such meetings is a wonderful opportunity to build professional networks, find other professionals who share your interests, and learn about new happenings.

- Check on the availability of professional journals and books in the teacher centre of your school board or a faculty of education in a nearby university.

- Form a teacher support group. If you and three friends agree to meet monthly and each of you shares one new idea, you will soon have lots of strategies in your repertoire.

- Visit your local teacher materials and supply store that carries materials for helping students learn. These stores are particularly valuable for locating educational games and supplemental teaching materials.

Most students who are identified as exceptional students and receive school-based services have high-incidence exceptionalities that you may be the first to recognize. If you teach at the elementary level, you will probably have students every year whom you refer to the school-based team. If you teach in junior high or high school, you will find that many exceptional students have already been identified before they reach your class. However, there are exceptions; students may be identified as exceptional learners at any time during their school careers.

When you think a student appears to need services beyond those you can provide as a classroom teacher, and you can say you have a serious and documented concern, then you will bring the student to the attention of other school professionals on the school-based team so that further information can be gathered and decisions made. Figure 2.5 illustrates the steps in a school-based process.

A School-Based Team Process

Regular education teachers, principals, resource teachers, parents, physicians, and social service agency personnel may all initiate a school-based team process

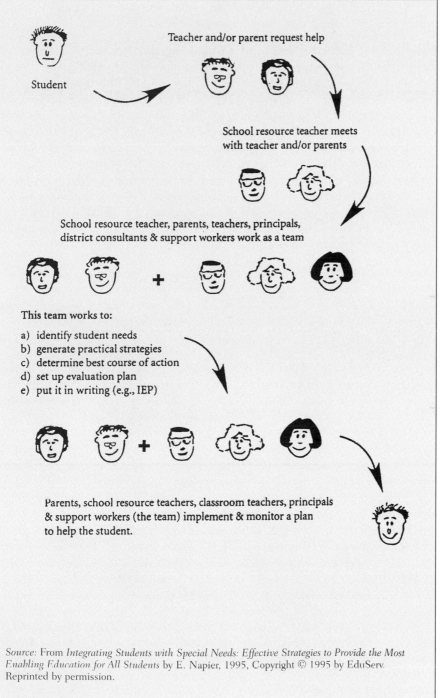

Source: From *Integrating Students with Special Needs: Effective Strategies to Provide the Most Enabling Education for All Students* by E. Napier, 1995, Copyright © 1995 by EduServ. Reprinted by permission.

FIGURE 2.5
Steps in a school-based team process

for a student. Typically, however, a student's classroom teacher will notice a pattern of academic underachievement, inconsistent learning, serious behaviour problems, difficulties in social skills, or a persistent physical or sensory problem.

FYI: Teams that meet to problem solve about students before consideration of an IEP might be called school-based teams, teacher assistance teams, intervention assistance teams, student-teacher assistance teams, or mainstream assistance teams. What are such teams called in your school district?

Connections: Chapter 3 discusses professional collaboration, including how teams can work effectively.

Cultural Awareness: Over the past two decades, efforts have been made to reduce the racial and cultural bias in assessment instruments and procedures.

Do It! Most communities have special education parent support and advocacy groups. Identify one in your area and attend a meeting. Who did you meet? What did you learn?

Connections: Information on psychological and other standardized tests is provided in Chapter 8.

When such problems occur, the teacher brings the student to the attention of others who will help decide if school-based or other services are warranted.

Pre-Referral Interventions and Consulting the Resource Teacher. In many schools, the first level of intervention is consultation with the resource teacher or learning assistance teacher in the school. Together, you and the resource teacher will probably identify which of the student's needs are being met and which are not. This consultation can lead to cooperative teaching or consultation that focuses more on helping you to use different teaching strategies and instructional materials than on the resource teacher helping the student. Chapter 3 describes ways that teachers can work well together to meet student needs. Parents should be informed and may wish to participate. Regular meetings are held and records are usually kept of the interventions planned and implemented. These interventions are assessed and this step may be repeated several times. Such collaborative planning and the resulting interventions will successfully address many students' needs.

Consulting the School-Based Team. If you and the resource teacher believe that the first level of intervention has been ineffective, then you will approach the school-based team for further assistance. The school-based team has been described as "a school-based, solution-finding group, the purpose of which is to provide a forum for dialogue on specific needs of students, by parents, teachers, and other professionals" (Napier, 1995). Typically, there is a core of team members, including a classroom teacher, the principal, and the resource or learning assistance teacher. On a case-by-case basis, the referring teacher, parent, and student (when appropriate) are members. Parental consent should always be given for critical decisions that significantly alter the educational program of an exceptional student.

Not all school districts within all provinces have school-based teams. However, they are growing in importance with the increase in inclusive policies across Canada. School-based teams make the best use possible of the resources within a school and bring other relevant professionals, who were described earlier in this chapter, into the school to become members of the team when they can support the teacher and the student.

You might ask what the school-based team does. According to British Columbia's *Manual of Policies, Procedures, and Guidelines*, "It provides support through extended consultation on possible classroom strategies, and may become a central focus for case management, referrals and resource decisions" (British Columbia, 1995, Section C, p. 4). It usually appoints a case coordinator and problem solves informally. Student data from the initial level of classroom intervention are presented, and decisions are made about what assessment data to collect, who will do the collecting, and what kind of intervention will proceed during this process. Interventions are carried out, based on the data collected, and, if they meet with success, the school-based team continues to monitor the child's progress and support the teacher.

Referral for an Extended Assessment and IEP

This kind of working group is the "cornerstone of the process of identification, assessment, and planning" for exceptional students and identifies whether a

It is 3:15 P.M. and Ms. Jacob's last-hour students have just left. She gathers a stack of information from her desk and heads toward the conference room for a School-Based Team meeting. Ms. Jacobs is the grade six representative on the team this year. Along with a grade seven and a grade eight representative, a special education teacher, and the assistant principal, Ms. Jacobs meets weekly to problem solve about students and to consider if any of their needs warrant making a referral for individual assessment.

The first student to be discussed today is grade eight student Toby. Reviewing her information sheets, Ms. Jacobs sees that Toby is chronically late to school, has what his teacher describes as a sullen attitude, is failing in math and English, and has a D in science. Toby's teacher, Mr. Petrovich, is worried that Toby is headed toward failure, especially as he nears high school age. According to Mr. Petrovich, reward systems have not been successful; Toby's dad seems cooperative but forgets to follow through on homework monitoring and other requests; and other teachers on the grade eight team share concern about Toby's future.

As the meeting begins and preliminaries are completed, Ms. Jacobs asks Mr. Petrovich several questions.

Ms. JACOBS: Mr. Petrovich, you've spent a great deal of time working with Toby. If you were to summarize your greatest concern for him, what would it be?

MR. PETROVICH: Probably his "I don't care and you can't make me" attitude. It seems to be getting worse as the year goes by. Toby is really a good kid; I don't know what's causing his problems—unless it's peer pressure—and I really want to get to the bottom of this.

Ms. JACOBS: Of all the things you've tried with Toby, what seems to have the biggest positive impact on him?

MR. PETROVICH: Right now, what's keeping him going is sports and the computer lab. But if his grades don't improve, sports isn't going to last long.

Ms. JACOBS: If you think about Toby's strengths, what might we start with to try to come up with some ideas for him?

MR. PETROVICH: I'd really like to see us work on something that takes advantage of Toby's computer skills. I only see him in math and we have very limited computer time, but I've seen some of his projects, and he's really good. He seems to like the structure and logic of the computer and the fact that it doesn't "get in his face."

Ms. JACOBS: It sounds as though you have an idea in mind.

MR. PETROVICH: I do. I'm hoping all of you can work with me to design some kind of very structured program that combines getting work done and getting to use computer equipment as a privilege. I think we have all the necessary components, we just need to put them together . . . and I think that's a concrete area to work in. I don't think a direct confrontation on attitude is going to have any effect.

The meeting continues with all the team members contributing. After 30 minutes, Mr. Petrovich leaves with commitment from others to try a structured work-for-computer-privileges plan and an agreement to review its effectiveness in three weeks. Ms. Jacobs stays as the team discusses another student and recommends an individual assessment for this student.

Reflections

Why was this team meeting constructive and productive? How did Mr. Petrovich help make the meeting a success? Besides the work-for-computer-privileges idea, what other strategies might the team try? What might happen when the team members review the intervention they planned? Given what you have learned about students with exceptionalities, do you think Toby is the type of student who might be referred for an individual assessment?

Strengths	Needs
Artistic talents Average academic potential Leadership qualities Strong peer relationships	To develop on task and work completion skills To increase appropriate responses to teacher direction To develop intrinsic motivation To develop positive attention seeking behaviours

Goals for the year (term) November, 1995 to March, 1996

Brian will increase the number of drill and practice assignments he completes.

Brian will increase his motivation to complete longer assignments by exercising choices between formats.

Brian will decrease disruption of class.

Brian will improve the organization of written assignments.

Brian will further develop his artistic talents by integrating them into his work in other subjects.

Adaptations	Resources/Assessment
– Reduce visual and auditory distractions by selective seating – Reduce volume of assignments and emphasize completion rather than amount – Give choice of assignment format that offers artistic flavour (posters, cartoons, charts, murals, etc.) – Provide instruction on computer and have Brian construct attractive planner and method for reinforcing its use – Set up consequences for uncooperative or disruptive behaviour – Provide weekly counselling sessions with the school counsellor	Use of study carrel and walkman with headset/Brian will choose to use compensatory strategies to help himself stay on task. Self-charting and positive social reinforcement by attention from art teacher when assignments are handed in complete. Learning assistance computer lab / Brian will independently use his planner to record assignments and their completion. Brian will leave his class and sit at the back of the grade five class across the hall until he completes the assignment and records his own inappropriate behaviour on his daily log.

Year (term) end review summary, transition plans, and goals for next year:

After the March reports, the school-based team will meet to discuss Brian's progress and make plans for his move to secondary school. The March-June term will need to focus on behaviours appropriate to these transition issues.

Date of review meeting: <u>March 10, 1996</u>

IEP Team: <u>Sarah Spell, principal, Theresa Villeneuve, grade seven teacher; Jack Evens, learning assistance teacher; Mr. Jake and Mrs. Rachel Levie; and Susan Cook, school counsellor.</u>

Source: From *Individual Education Planning for Students with Special Needs* by British Columbia Special Education Branch, 1996, Copyright ©1996 by British Columbia Special Education Branch. Reprinted by permission.

instructional strategies and materials; (5) dates for review; (6) identification of case co-ordinator and program participants (including parents), and their responsibilities; and (7) evaluation procedure.

Description of present level of functioning.   Information about the student including relevant medical, social, and educational background should be included. Students' records often include previous IEPs, progress reports, and anecdotal records of teachers' concerns. Derek, a new student at Hillside High, was experiencing difficulty in grade nine. When his records arrived, they revealed that he had previously attended 13 schools, and Derek had always moved before an IEP was completed. Information about the student's current learning strengths and needs is usually provided by the teacher, based on classroom assessment. "If there is sufficient information to plan for and implement programming, no further assessment is necessary" (Alberta Education, 1995, p. 6). If there is insufficient information, this may be supplemented by results of an individual assessment carried out by other professionals including psychologists, resource teachers, and speech therapists. As the classroom teacher, you will also be expected to describe the student's degree of participation in the regular program. The present level of functioning can serve as a baseline for judging student progress.

Long-term goals.   These may include learning goals, independence goals, and career goals. In planning for students with severe disabilities, these goals often focus on functional skills that will increase the student's independence. For students with mild exceptionalities, these are frequently annual goals referring to growth in academic areas such as reading; for example, a student with learning disabilities may have an annual goal to read and comprehend books at a particular grade level. Annual goals can also include desired changes in classroom behaviour or social skills. Long-term or annual goals should have realistic expectations and help set priorities. They should also consider parents' and students' values and goals, and age appropriateness.

Short-term goals.   These are usually descriptions of the goals the student will achieve on the way to annual or long-term goals; for example, Bess will use money accurately as a form of exchange, or Chen will reduce avoidance behaviour in the classroom and begin work as soon as it is assigned. Individual education plans may be written in various forms, but typically these goals are set for the next six to eight weeks or a typical reporting period. Then they are broken down into short-term objectives or outcomes so that a student with a short-term goal of using money might have short-term objectives: recognize and name the value of coins, of paper currency; create sets of coins up to $1.00 in value; create sets of paper currency up to $100 in value; create accurate combinations of coins and paper currency for values up to $200; or practise using money in the classroom store.

Instructional strategies, materials, and services.   Team members implementing the various objectives should identify the strategies they will use and the resources needed for the student to reach the objectives. As a classroom teacher, you play a central role in describing what you need to implement the strategies that you and the rest of the team are identifying. This may mean adapting teaching by assigning fewer questions or simpler reading materials, teaching phonological processing, compacting the curriculum for a student who is gifted, enabling the student to gain more practice with coins and paper currency than his or her peers, or enabling the student to take oral tests. However, it could require modifying the curriculum so that the learning outcomes are substantially different from the prescribed curriculum. Lisa, who has developmental disabilities, may be learning to print the letters in her name and dictating a sentence to a volunteer or teaching assistant while her peers in grade two are writing in their journals about their experiences of the day. Lisa is learning to communicate like her peers, but the specific curricular goal within communication is substantially modified. Teaching strategies can be determined according to the student's strengths, needs, and ways of learning successfully. Use all your creativity to help the student have a positive experience and reach the agreed-upon goals. Services such as transportation and speech therapy are typically also recorded on the IEP.

Evaluation or assessment procedures.   At the time the IEP is developed, decisions are usually made about how to monitor student progress toward the objectives and short-term goals. Responsibility for monitoring progress toward specific goals is assigned and criteria are set. "If the student is progressing slowly toward the objectives, alternate instructional strategies should be employed before revisions to the goals and objectives are made" (British Columbia, 1996). If changing the teaching approach does not result in satisfactory progress, then the goals and objectives set for the student may have to be reconsidered. Probably the most important thing to keep in mind, as a teacher, is that you will want to find assessment strategies that are simple and that occur naturally in the context of learning in the classroom.

Dates for review.   Some schools hold regular mini-reviews to monitor progress, while most provinces require annual reviews of the progress toward annual goals. To supplement the customary annual reviews, the most efficient and inclusive approach is to hold reviews at the same time you are preparing general report cards and holding conferences with parents. When students are experiencing adaptations in teaching and assessment, letter grades or marks are usually appropriate; these may have an asterisk and a note that explains the adaptations. Usually brief anecdotal comments can keep parents informed of specific progress. If you are making substantial modifications to the curricular goals, such as in the case of Lisa described above, you will probably choose to use anecdotal comments on effort and progress, but letter grades on the usual report card may be meaningless without considerable explanation. Consult with your principal, or department head in secondary school, to make yourself familiar with local and provincial requirements for monitoring, reviewing, and reporting on IEPs.

Identification of case co-ordinator and program participants (including parents), and their responsibilities. The case co-ordinator is typically a resource teacher in elementary schools, and may be a guidance counsellor in secondary schools. Regardless of who co-ordinates, it is important that an IEP contain clear delineation of responsibilities. As a classroom teacher, you will be responsible for implementing much of the IEP. This means that it will be especially important for you to speak up and clarify what role you can realistically play in the context of your current class of students (the numbers, other exceptional students) and the program you are committed to teaching (curriculum, split-grade). In Chapter 3 you will learn about working with other educators in a team, about co-teaching, and about working closely with a consultant. That chapter should help you prepare to ask questions about what is expected and to suggest ways you might work with other educators and professionals to ensure that the needs of exceptional students are met.

Other Aspects of IEPs. In addition to the seven basic components described, IEPs have other features. Usually they are signed by all the participants, including the student's parent or guardian. Sometimes they discuss placement of the exceptional student. Individual education plans for older students are increasingly including transition plans for employment preparation such as interview skills and anger management, or improvement of study skills and self-advocacy for youth who are continuing on to university or community college. Review the IEP in Figure 2.6 to find all the components just discussed.

Some educators dwell on the time and paperwork spent preparing IEPs (Smith, 1990). However, this should be a working document that guides daily expectations, teaching, and assessment. Ensure that you receive a copy of the IEP. Any confidential information can be removed from your working copy or stroked out with a black marker. Keep the working copy at hand when planning and teaching. An IEP should help you to understand and meet the student's needs.

Appealing IEPs. Parents and, in some provinces, students have the right to appeal the decisions that are made in IEP meetings. The Saskatchewan policy manual explains that students and parents are entitled to fair treatment in assessment, programming, and placement decisions. "Fair treatment implies that parents or guardians be consulted at all stages of educational planning and that they have their views taken into consideration before final decisions are made" (1996, p. 25). Each province or territory has a review or appeal process. The written appeal submitted by the parent or student is usually considered at the local school board or district level. If disagreements remain unsolved, either party may appeal to the provincial or territorial level. The specific process at this stage varies across jurisdictions; for example, in Manitoba, such appeals are heard by the Manitoba Education and Training, Child Care and Development Branch (Manitoba Education and Training, 1989). In the Yukon, appeals are heard by the Educational Appeal Tribunal, which is appointed by the minister of education, and considers the educational interests of the student, the impact of the decision on the total population of students served, and any other issues relevant to the case (Yukon Education, 1996, pp. 39-41). A recent case in Ontario, of a student named Emily Eaton, progressed through the Ontario Court of Appeals and was finally decided by the Supreme Court of Canada (for details of the Emily Eaton case, see Mandell, 1996). Although school districts work closely with parents to avoid appeals, if there was a hearing about one of your students, you could be called to testify about the student's level of functioning in your classroom and the supports you provide. You would receive support from your school administrator and school district staff involved in the provision of services to exceptional students.

Your job is to make a good-faith effort to accomplish the short-term objectives on the IEP. If you do that, you have carried out your responsibility; if you do not do that, you could be held accountable. For example, suppose an IEP indicates that a student should learn about coins and make change for up to a dollar. If you can demonstrate that you are helping the student learn this by providing play money and opportunities to learn, you are carrying out your responsibility, even if the student does not learn to apply this skill. If you state that your students are no longer working on money skills and refuse to create opportunities for practice in this area, you are violating the IEP.

◤ Where Are Exceptional Students Placed?

✔ **Your Learning:** When might it be appropriate for a few students with disabilities to receive services away from their classmates?

As schools become more inclusive, most exceptional students are learning in the regular classroom. A few students receive some teaching in a resource room with a resource teacher or learning assistance teacher, although increasingly resource teachers are co-teaching in regular classrooms. In the resource room, small groups are usually taught in a specific curriculum area such as reading. Some exceptional learners are placed in a separate class where a special education teacher has the primary instructional responsibility for the students. Children are usually grouped by age and exceptionality. Some separate schools exist for students with severe developmental disabilities. Residential facilities exist in Canada, primarily for students who are blind or deaf. Students who are medically fragile or undergoing surgeries or medical treatment may be educated in a home or hospital setting. However, for most exceptional students in Canada, "home" is the same classroom in the same neighbourhood school that they would attend if they did not have exceptionalities. As a classroom teacher, you will play a major role in the education of exceptional students.

Summary

Many individuals work to ensure that students with disabilities receive an appropriate education. These people include regular classroom teachers; resource teachers; other specialists and related service providers such as school psychologists, counsellors, speech and language therapists, social workers, physiotherapists and occupational therapists, nurses, administrators, paraprofessionals, and other specialists; and parents, students, and advocates. Depending on need, an exceptional student may receive instruction from just one or two of these professionals, or from many of them.

To determine whether special services are needed, regular classroom teachers begin a process of deciding whether to request that a student be assessed. They carry out this process by analyzing the nature and extent of a student's unmet needs, clarifying those needs by describing them through examples, determining that the need is chronic and possibly worsening across time, comparing the student's needs to those of others in the class, recognizing that no pattern seems to exist for the student's performance, and intervening to address the unmet needs and documenting those efforts. Based on these early strategies, the student's needs may be assessed by a school-based team, and if warranted, referral and assessment steps are followed. This process includes completing an individualized assessment with parental permission, making decisions about the need for interventions and special services, developing an individual education plan (IEP), and monitoring the child's progress.

When an IEP is developed, it includes the student's present level of functioning, long- and short-term goals, instructional strategies and materials, identification of procedure, and the person(s) responsible for the services, and dates for review. The IEP is usually reviewed at least annually.

The Council for Exceptional Children
www.cec.sped.org/

Inclusive Education Website
www.quasar.ualberta.ca/ddc/incl/intro.htm#resource

Virtual Assistive Technology Center
www.sped.ukans.edu/~dlance/atech.html

Applications in Teaching Practice

A Visit to an IEP Meeting

REGULAR EDUCATION (GRADE FOUR) TEACHER:	Ms. Richards
RESOURCE TEACHER:	Ms. Hill
PRINCIPAL:	Ms. Hubbert
PSYCHOLOGIST:	Ms. Freund
SPEECH AND LANGUAGE THERAPIST:	Mr. Colt
PARENT:	Ms. Wright

MS. HUBBERT: Our next task is to develop goals and objectives for Natasha. I'd like to suggest that we discuss academics first, then social areas, and wrap up with related services needed. Let's look at Natasha's strengths first.

MR. COLT: Natasha has a very strong speaking vocabulary. She is considerably above average in that realm.

MS. FREUND: Along with that, Natasha's general knowledge is very good. She also is near grade level in basic math skills.

MS. RICHARDS: It's not really academics, but one strength Natasha has that I see is her willingness to help classmates. She really wants to help everyone in class learn.

MS. HILL: As we write academic goals and objectives, then, we need to remember that Natasha has high vocabulary and common knowledge and that she does not need help in math. Perhaps we can use her social skills to help in the academic area. Ms. Wright, what strengths do you see in Natasha?

MS. WRIGHT: Hmmm. She minds me, that's for sure. And she helps out around the house with chores. She likes to help me watch her baby brother.

MS. HILL: Helping really seems to be Natasha's thing—let's keep that in mind.

MS. HUBBERT: Let's focus for a minute on academic areas of need.

MS. FREUND: Reading comprehension is by far the area that needs the most work. Natasha's comprehension is just at a beginning first-grade level.

MS. WRIGHT: She says she doesn't like reading because the other kids make fun of her when she can't read the words and they tease her when Ms. Richards gives her a baby book.

MS. RICHARDS: I didn't realize that was a problem. Let's be sure that before we finish today we talk about that some more.

MS. FREUND: Ms. Richards and Ms. Hill, given what you know about Natasha, what might be an appropriate goal?

MS. HILL: I agree that comprehension is the key. I think the goal should be for her to improve her comprehension on reading tasks that include stories, textbooks, and other materials such as children's magazines.

MS. RICHARDS: I agree. Natasha has a lot going for her, but we have to work on the comprehension.

MS. HUBBERT: Ms. Wright, how does that sound to you? [Ms. Wright nods.]

MS. HUBBERT: How about you, Mr. Colt?

MR. COLT: That's fine.

MS. FREUND: What are the objectives we need to include?

MS. RICHARDS: We definitely need something about fluency. Natasha reads one word at a time.

The others agree. They write an objective that says Natasha will read aloud at a rate of 50 words per minute with fewer than three errors in a grade two novel. Before the meeting ends, the MDT has generated these additional goals in reading comprehension using materials at her instructional level: Natasha will identify the main characters and the problem and solution in stories that she reads at a grade two level. She will comprehend 80 percent on stories she reads aloud with the teachers; 80 percent on stories she reads aloud to herself; and 80 percent on stories she reads silently.

Questions

1. What are the responsibilities of the professionals represented at the meeting?
2. What role was Ms. Richards taking at the meeting? Why was her presence so helpful in creating an educational program for Natasha?
3. What steps do you think had occurred prior to the point at which this vignette began? What had the regular classroom teacher done?
4. What part of the IEP was the team addressing? What other components would be completed before the meeting ends?
5. If you were at this IEP meeting, what services would you recommend for Natasha? In what setting would they be likely to occur? Did you find any evidence that she needs related services?

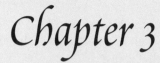

Chapter 3

Professional Partnerships

Learner Objectives

After you read this chapter, you will be able to

1. Define the term *collaboration* and describe the role of collaboration in providing services to exceptional students, including your role in making collaboration effective.

2. Describe inclusive programs and services in which collaboration is important, including shared problem solving, co-teaching, teaming, and consulting.

3. Identify ways in which you can work effectively with parents to educate exceptional students successfully.

4. Outline your responsibilities in working with paraprofessionals and ways in which you can enhance collaboration with them.

IN MS. MIKLOS' *biology class, five of her 42 students have been identified as exceptional students. April, who has a mild learning disability, does not need assistance in the course. Pierre and Austen, both of whom receive services for emotional disabilities, are capable of completing the work but need a great deal of structure and support to do so. Carl, a student with a mild cognitive or developmental disability, does part of the course work, but he is not expected to master the extensive vocabulary nor to write lengthy lab reports. Janet, who has a physical disability that requires her to use a motorized wheelchair and who has limited stamina, often needs encouragement to keep up with the work. Twice each week, Ms. Miklos is joined during biology by Mr. MacLean, a special education teacher. During these class periods, the two teachers share teaching responsibilities and group the students for instruction in various ways— by skill needs, by interest, and by random assignment, among others. On two of the days that Mr. MacLean is not in class, Ms. Hugo, a teaching assistant, is available to help Ms. Miklos and individual students. What happens when two teachers share instructional responsibilities in a classroom? What topics might Ms. Miklos and Mr. MacLean need to discuss to ensure their shared teaching is effective?*

THE *three grade four teachers are having a grade-level team meeting; Ms. Chiang, the resource teacher, is also present. They have discussed a curriculum issue related to social studies, and now the conversation has turned to a common problem. Mr. Balen states that the students with disabilities are taking a disproportionate amount of his time, especially in the morning.*

He explains that this group of students does not seem to be able to come into the classroom, put away their belongings, and settle into work without his close and constant supervision. Mrs. Dyer agrees but adds that many students without disabilities are having the same problem. After a few minutes of general conversation about this problem, the teachers begin generating ideas for dealing with it. Included in the list of ideas is letting students choose their own morning work, assigning all students a "morning study buddy," and reviewing expectations with all the classes. Even though Ms. Chiang does not teach grade four, she is in the classrooms to assist students, observe, or take part in lessons so often that she has several excellent ideas to contribute to the discussion. What is Ms. Chiang's role on the team? How can the team ensure that all the members feel committed to the team and valued as team members?

CHRISTINE'S *parents, Mr. and Mrs. Werner, arrived promptly for their after-school meeting with Ms. MacDougal, the junior high school inclusion facilitator, and Mr. Saunders, the grade seven team leader. Mrs. Werner began by declaring that the school was discriminating against Christine because of her learning disability. Mr. Werner asserted that Christine was not to be singled out in any way because of her exceptionalities and that he had learned that she was receiving tutoring during the lunch hour. He strongly expressed that the family provides tutoring for Christine so that this type of discrimination does not occur at school. Further, Mr. and Mrs. Werner showed the teachers examples of modified assignment sheets, another example of discrimination. When Mr. Saunders started to explain that he was modifying Chris's work so she could learn more in his class, Mr. Werner cut him off, stating that a teacher's poor instructional practice was no excuse to destroy a child's self-concept through public humiliation. If you were Mr. Saunders, what type of assistance would you want from Ms. MacDougal during this difficult interaction? How can you prevent miscommunication in your work with parents of students with disabilities?*

IN the past, becoming a teacher—whether in general education or in special education—meant entering a profession frequently characterized by isolation and sometimes loneliness (Little, 1982; Lortie, 1975). Teachers typically spent most of the day alone in a classroom with students. They learned that they were expected to have all the skills to manage student learning and discipline issues, and they rarely had opportunities to discuss their questions, concerns, and misgivings with anyone, especially not their colleagues at school.

That atmosphere of isolation is changing. Elementary school teachers are meeting on grade-level teams to share ideas and problem solve, and junior high school and high school teachers are creating interdisciplinary teams to redesign curriculum and share instructional responsibility for smaller groups of students. As Barth (1990) comments, "The success of a school, I believe, depends above all on the quality of interactions between teacher and teacher, and teacher and administrator" (p. 15).

As the scenes that open this chapter illustrate, these emerging partnerships also extend to special education and other support staff. Particularly as schools move toward increased inclusion, the working relationships among all the adults involved in the education of students with disabilities have become critical (Evans, 1991). For example, as a classroom teacher, you may find that you have questions about a student's behaviour in class. A consultant might come to your class, observe the student and the overall classroom setting, and then meet with you to discuss how to address your concerns. Similarly, you might find that some of your students cannot complete the grade-level work you are accustomed to assigning. To assist you, a special education or resource teacher might meet with you to design the necessary modifications.

At first glance, these interactions seem like logical and straightforward approaches to optimizing education. However, because of the strong tradition in education of professionals working alone and the limited availability of preparation for teachers in how to work effectively with other adults, problems sometimes occur (Friend & Cook, 1992a; Jordan, 1994). In some instances, support personnel are reluctant to make suggestions for fear that they will sound as if they are interfering with the classroom teacher's instruction. In other cases, the classroom teacher insists that no change in classroom activities is possible, even though a resource teacher is available for co-teaching. And often, when professionals in schools disagree, they are very uncomfortable discussing the issues.

Many school personnel in inclusive schools assert that collaboration is the key to their success in meeting the needs of all students (Kamann & Perry, 1994; Wiener & Davidson, 1990). The purpose of this chapter is to introduce you to the principles of collaboration and the school situations in which professionals are most likely to collaborate to meet the needs of students with disabilities. The special partnerships that are formed when teachers work with paraprofessionals and parents are also considered.

What Are the Basics of Collaboration?

As a teacher, you will hear many colleagues refer to many of their activities as collaboration. Sometimes they will be referring to a team meeting to propose ideas to help a student; sometimes they will mean sharing a classroom to teach a particular subject; and sometimes they will even use the term as a synonym for inclusion. How can all these things be collaboration? Actually, they are not. Collaboration is *how* people work together, not *what* they do. **Collaboration** is a style that professionals choose to use in order to accomplish a shared goal (Friend & Cook, 1992b; Jordan, 1994). Professionals often use the term *collaboration* to describe any activity in which they work with someone else. But just the fact of working in the same room with another person does not ensure that collaboration will occur. For example, in some team meetings, one or two members tend to monopolize the conversation and insist that others agree with their opinions. Although the team is in proximity, it is not collaborative. Only on teams where all members feel their contributions are valued and the goal is clear, where they share decision making, and where they sense they are respected, does true collaboration exist.

Connections: Students experience many of the elements of adult collaboration through cooperative learning, a topic discussed in Chapter 13. This chapter's focus is adult interactions.

Characteristics of Collaboration

Collaboration for schools has a number of defining characteristics that clarify its requirements. Cook and Friend (1993) have outlined these key attributes, which are summarized in Figure 3.1.

✓ **Your Learning:** If you are *required* to work with special education teachers and other colleagues, how can collaboration be voluntary?

Collaboration is voluntary.   Teachers may be assigned to work in close proximity, but they cannot be required to collaborate. Each teacher must choose to work collaboratively in such situations. You and another teacher could be told that you are expected to be part of a pre-referral intervention team. You could choose to keep your ideas to yourself instead of participating. Or, you could conclude that as long as you are a team member, you will contribute like a team player and collaborate. Your principal assigned the activity; you decided to collaborate. Because collaboration is voluntary, teachers often form close but informal collaborative partnerships with colleagues regardless of whether collaboration is a schoolwide ethic.

Collaboration is based on parity.   Teachers who collaborate must believe that all individuals' contributions are valued equally. The amount and nature of particular teachers' contributions may vary greatly, but teachers must recognize that what they offer is integral to the collaborative effort. If you are at a meeting concerning highly complex student needs, you might believe you have nothing to offer. However, you have important information about how the student responds in your class and the progress the student has made in developing peer relationships. The technical discussion of the student's disabilities is not your area of expertise, nor should it be; your ideas are valued because of your expertise in your classroom.

Collaboration requires a shared goal.   Teachers collaborate only when they share a goal. For example, if two grade three teachers or two grade nine teachers

FIGURE 3.1
Characteristics of Collaboration

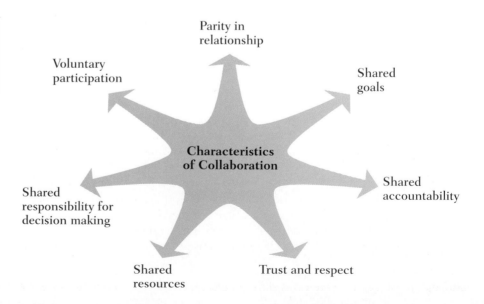

want to plan an integrated unit on the environment, their goal is clear. They will pool their knowledge and resources and jointly plan the instruction. However, if one wants to work on an environmental unit whereas the other prefers to stress weather, they will not develop their units collaboratively. Teachers sometimes perceive that they share a goal when in fact their goals differ. For example, if the two teachers agree to work on an environmental unit but one intends to address global issues whereas the other refers to the pragmatic aspect of recycling, either the content of the unit will have to be negotiated or the collaborative planning might not be possible.

Collaboration includes shared responsibility for key decisions. Although teachers may divide the work necessary to complete a collaborative teaching or teaming project, they should share as equal partners the fundamental decision making about the activities they are undertaking. This shared responsibility reinforces the sense of parity that exists among the teachers. In the environmental unit example, the teachers share decisions about the topics to address within the unit, perhaps the order of them, the learning objectives for students, and accommodations for exceptional students. However, they are likely to assign many tasks to just one person. One will contact the nearest zoo for information on tropical rain forests and arrange for a videotape on recycling. The other will duplicate the logbooks that students will use to record information they find in the newspaper about the environment and will contact a local conservation authority or environmental group to arrange for a guest speaker.

FYI: Sharing key decision making helps give all participants in a collaborative activity a sense of ownership in it.

Collaboration includes shared accountability for outcomes. This characteristic follows directly from shared responsibility; that is, if teachers share key decisions, they must also share accountability for the results of the decisions, whether those results are positive or negative. If both the grade three teachers carry out their assigned tasks, their unit will have a high probability of success. If one fails to contact a guest speaker, however, their shared unit is less effective. If something positive happens (the classes begin a school recycling project that receives local and then national press attention), the teachers share the success. If something negative happens (the experiment to measure the impact of pollutants on climate fizzles and students become bored with it), they share the need to change their plans.

Collaboration is based on shared resources. Each teacher participating in a collaborative effort contributes some type of resource. This contribution increases commitment and reinforces each professional's sense of parity. Resources may include time, expertise, space, equipment, or other assets. The teachers working on the environmental unit contribute the time needed to make necessary plans, but they also pool their knowledge on teaching about the environment, share information on local resources to access for the unit, and share the equipment needed to show the recycling video.

Collaboration is emergent. Collaboration is based on belief in the value of shared decision making, trust, and respect among participants. However, although these qualities are needed to some degree at the outset of collaborative

✓ **Your Learning:** What is an example of each of the defining characteristics of collaboration?

activities, they are not mature in a new collaborative relationship. As teachers become more experienced at collaboration, their relationships will be characterized by the trust and respect that grow within successful collaborative relationships. If the grade three or grade nine teachers have worked together for several years, they may share freely, including offering constructive criticism to each other. If this is their first collaborative effort, they are much more likely to be somewhat guarded and polite, hesitant about sounding critical, since they are unsure how the other person might respond.

Prerequisites for Collaboration

Cultural Awareness: How might cultural awareness affect collaboration? When people from very different cultures collaborate, what could you do to ensure that their collaboration is successful?

Creating collaborative relationships requires effort on everyone's part. Most professionals who have close collaborative working relationships note that collaboration involves hard work—but it is worth every minute of the effort. They also emphasize that collaboration gets better with experience; when colleagues are novices at co-teaching or working on teams, their work seems to take longer and everyone must be especially careful to respect others' views. However, with additional collaboration, everyone's comfort level increases, honesty and trust grow, and a sense of community develops. Here are some essential ingredients that foster the growth of collaboration.

Do It! Write a statement of your beliefs about working with school colleagues and about collaborating on behalf of exceptional students. Compare your views with those of classmates.

Reflecting on your personal belief system.   The first ingredient for collaboration is your personal beliefs. How much do you value sharing ideas with others? Would you prefer to work with someone to complete a project, even if it takes more time that way, or do you prefer to work alone? If your professor in this course offered the option of a small-group exam or group project, would you be willing to receive a shared grade with your classmates? If your responses to these questions suggest that you prefer working with others, you will probably find professional collaboration exciting and rewarding. If your responses are just the opposite, you might prefer to work alone, and might find collaboration somewhat frustrating. For collaboration to occur, all those participating need to feel that their shared effort will result in an outcome that is better than could be accomplished by any one participant (Dettmer, Thurston, & Dyck, 1993). They must also believe that a shared effort has value, even if the result is somewhat different from what each person envisioned at the outset (Phillips & McCullough, 1990).

Part of examining your belief system also concerns your understanding of and respect for others' belief systems. This tolerance is especially important for your collaborative efforts with resource teachers and with special educators in inclusive programs. For example, what are your beliefs about changing the standards in your classroom in order to help a student succeed? You might initially say that changing your standards is no problem, but when you reflect on the consequence of that belief, you might have second thoughts. For example, it means that you will give alternative assignments to students needing them, that you will teach *students* not *subject matter,* and that you will grade on the basis of student effort and progress instead of according to a single standard. The resource teachers or special educators with whom you work are likely to believe strongly that alternative standards are not only helpful in inclusive settings, but that they are a requirement. How will you respond if you meet a colleague with this belief? Similarly, what if three of the teachers in your department or on your primary team strongly oppose alternative standards for students with disabilities? Will you debate the matter with them and hold your beliefs, or will you feel pressured to compromise? Teachers have faced these issues in the past. However, in schools in which collaboration is stressed, issues such as these tend to become more apparent and the need to resolve them more intense. Further, as collaboration becomes more integral to public schools, learning to value others' opinions and to disagree respectfully with them while maintaining a positive working relationship becomes more essential.

Refining your interaction skills.   The second ingredient you can contribute to school collaboration is effective skills for interacting. In many ways, interaction skills are the fundamental building blocks on which collaboration is based since it is through our interactions with others that collaboration occurs. There are two major types of interaction skills. The first are communication skills. These skills include listening, attending to non-verbal signals, and asking questions and making statements in clear and non-threatening ways. They also include paralanguage, which refers to your tone of voice and your use of comments such as "uh-huh" and "okay." Examples of these communication skills are included in the Professional Edge.

The other type of interaction skill describes the steps that make interactions productive. Have you ever been in a meeting and felt that the same topic was being discussed repeatedly? Perhaps you wished someone would say, "I think we've covered this; let's move on." Or have you ever been trying to problem solve with classmates or friends only to realize that every time someone generated an idea, someone else began explaining why the idea could not work? In both instances, the frustration occurred because of a problem in the interaction process, that is, the steps that characterize an interaction. The most needed interaction process for you as a teacher is shared problem solving. Other interaction-process skills include conducting effective meetings, responding to resistance, resolving conflict, and persuading others.

> **Connections:** Additional information on shared problem solving is included later in this chapter.

You need both types of interaction skills for collaboration to occur. If you are highly skilled in communicating effectively but cannot help to get an interaction from its beginning to its end, others will be frustrated. Likewise, even though you know the steps in shared problem solving, if you speak to others as though you know all the answers, others will withdraw from the interaction.

Contributing to a supportive environment.   The third ingredient for successful collaboration is a supportive environment (Little, 1982). As a teacher, you will contribute to this atmosphere by your personal belief system and interaction skills, but this ingredient includes other items as well. For example, most professionals working in schools that value collaboration comment on the importance of administrative support. In his research in Ontario schools, Fullan (1982; Fullan & Stiegelbauer, 1991) of the University of Toronto has shown that principals play an important role in fostering collaboration. They can raise staff awareness of collaboration by making it a school goal and distributing information on it to staff. They can reward teachers for their collaborative efforts. They can urge

> **FYI:** *Communication skills* are the words, paralanguage, and non-verbal signals you use to convey meaning to others. *Interaction processes* are the steps for using communication skills to accomplish a goal.

teachers who are uncomfortable with collaboration to learn more about it and to experiment in small-scale collaborative projects, and they can include collaboration as part of staff evaluation procedures. When principals do not actively nurture collaboration among staff, collaborative activities are more limited and more informal and less a part of the school culture. If you work in this type of school, you may find that you collaborate with specific teachers but that your efforts are considered a luxury or frill and are not rewarded or otherwise fostered.

Another component of a supportive environment is the availability of time for collaboration (Greenburg, 1987; Johnson, Pugach, & Hammitte, 1988). It is not enough that each teacher have a preparation period; shared planning time also needs to be arranged. Jordan (1994) described the way some elementary schools in the Toronto area grouped together two classes and assigned a paraprofessional or educational assistant to work with one teacher while the other teacher attended shared planning meetings. Kamann and Perry (1994) described a school in British Columbia where one member of the special education team taught in a classroom while the classroom teacher met with another member of the special education team to do shared planning. One of the authors taught in an elementary school near Montreal where the children were released early one day each week to participate in activities organized by community volunteers and senior students from the school. Teachers used the time to plan instructional units, confer about students, and attend professional development activities. Secondary and junior high schools often use common lunch periods and common preparation periods to do shared planning.

As a teacher, time will be an important issue for you (Adams & Cessna, 1991). The number of tasks you need to complete during your preparation period will be greater than the time available. The time before and after school will be filled with staff meetings, meetings with parents, preparation, and supervision of extra-curricular activities. You can help yourself maximize time for collaboration if you remember the following points: First, it may be tempting to spend the beginning of a shared planning time discussing the day's events. But if you engage in lengthy socializing, you are taking away time from your planning. Teachers in collaborative schools have learned to finish the business at hand first and then to "chat" if time remains. Second, since you will never have enough time to accomplish all that you would like to as a teacher, you must learn to prioritize. You must choose whether collaborating about a certain student or teaching a certain lesson is justified based on the needs of students and the time available. Not everything can be collaborative; but when collaboration seems appropriate, time should be made available for it.

FYI: In our fieldwork with thousands of experienced teachers each year, lack of time is consistently noted as the most serious obstacle to collaboration.

FYI: As constraints on collaboration, general education teachers mention time, financial resources for needed supplies, the perceptions of other teachers, fears about sharing traditionally isolated classrooms, and the difficulty of maintaining communication.

How Can You Use Collaboration to Meet Student Needs in Inclusive Schools?

The basic principles of collaboration are your guides to meeting student needs through partnerships. These partnerships may involve other classroom teachers, special education teachers, support staff such as speech therapists or counsellors, paraprofessionals, parents, and others. Four of the most common activities are shared problem solving, co-teaching, teaming, and consultation.

▼▼▼▼▼▼▼▼▼▼▼▼▼▼▼▼▼▼▼▼▼▼

Professional Edge
Communication for Effective Collaboration

STRONG interaction skills are the basis of effective collaboration. Your recognition of your own frame of reference, your willingness to consider others' points of view, and your being a good listener are among the communication skills described here that foster successful interactions.

1. You have a frame of reference that influences your interactions. Others might have a frame of reference that is very different from yours. Whereas you view a student's use of "bad" language as very inappropriate, the special education teacher and consultant are delighted that the student has transferred his expressions of anger from physical to verbal aggression. They view this change as progress.

2. When you problem solve with others, you might have an idea you think is just right. Recognize that there are almost always many "right" answers regarding how to teach students best. Someone else's view that a student would be best served by spending more time in your class for the social interactions and modelling may be as valid as your conviction that the student would best learn social skills by participating in an intensive, separate program.

3. Communication relies on strong listening skills. You can ensure that you have accurately heard others' messages by paraphrasing the information and requesting confirmation that you have correctly received it. A colleague says, "I feel pulled in 20 directions at once. I don't know if I can keep up with this new inclusive education!" If you respond by commenting that you agree that the teacher is being given too much responsibility in the new program, you may have just made a huge error in listening. Perhaps the teacher is just tired after a hectic day; you should have checked your selective listening and interpretation for accuracy.

4. When someone shares a concern with you, avoid the temptation to offer advice immediately. Perhaps that person just wanted to vent a frustration or to share a new idea. When a colleague says, "I have a student who just won't work alone. I have to help her every minute," it is tempting to respond by saying something like, "When I had a student like that last year, it helped if I assigned another student to assist." Although this comment may be appropriate later in the interaction, you should first find out more information about what the teacher is saying.

5. As much as possible, focus your interactions on observable information. The more you rely on opinions or inferences, the more likely miscommunication will occur. Noting that a student threw a book on the floor and left a classroom is more accurate than discussing a student's "tantrum" and "serious attitude problem."

6. Use collaborative language; that is, ask questions that encourage others to speak (for example, avoid saying "What are the goals for Marcus in math this year?" and instead say "Does Marcus need to learn long division in my classroom?"). Avoid comments that guide (for example, avoid saying "You should give me adapted worksheets for Marcus for math" and instead say "I'd like Marcus's math worksheets adapted. How can we accomplish that?").

7. Monitor how much you talk. If you tend to monopolize, invite others to speak. If you tend not to contribute, offer some comments.

8. If you have a disagreement with a colleague, address it as soon as possible and in a straightforward manner. Avoid discussing the issue with others, especially if you have not shared your concern with the colleague. For example, if you are co-teaching and you believe that your partner is spending too much time on drill of basic information, you should discuss this issue with your teaching partner, not with your best teacher friend from another school.

Shared Problem Solving

Shared problem solving is the basis for many of the collaborative activities that school professionals undertake on behalf of students with disabilities (Jayanthi & Friend, 1992). Figure 3.2 shows a generic model for shared problem solving that has been applied to classroom collaboration by Jordan (1994) who has conducted research using this model in schools in Canada and England. Although shared problem solving sometimes occurs when a classroom teacher and a special education teacher meet to decide on appropriate modifications or other interventions for a student, it occurs in many other contexts, too. For example, as you read the following applications, you will find that some variation of shared problem solving exists in each. This happens because one way of thinking about co-teaching, teaming, and consultation is as specialized problem-solving approaches.

You might be wondering why problem solving is such a critical topic for professional partnerships. The reason the topic is critical is because most of the problem-solving that professionals learn is completed in isolation. However, as many authors have noted (for example, Dettmer et al., 1993; Schein, 1988), when professionals problem solve together, the process is much more complex since the needs, expectations, and ideas of each participant must be blended into shared understandings and mutually agreed upon solutions. This is not a simple task!

Discover a shared need.   As shown in Figure 3.2, the starting point for problem solving is discovering a shared need, which demonstrates the point about the

Connections: Problem solving you might engage in related to individual students is represented in the INCLUDE model and also in Chapter 12, on strategies for responding to student behaviour.

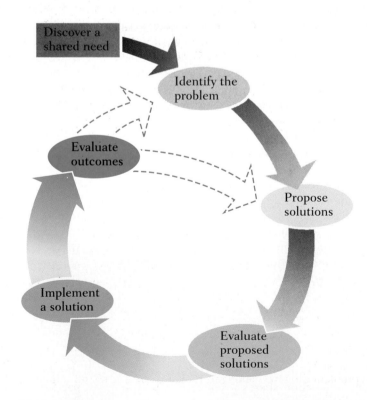

FIGURE 3.2
A Model for Shared Problem Solving

complexity of shared problem solving. If you face a problem that concerns only you, you try to resolve it alone. When you problem solve with colleagues and parents, all participants need to perceive that a problem exists. Further, it is important that all participants have a sense that they can have an impact on the problem, that they feel accountable for the results of problem solving, and that they can constructively contribute to resolving the problem. When these conditions exist, shared problem solving results in a high level of commitment. When these conditions do not exist, "shared" problem solving is not shared at all and may appear one-sided, with some participants trying to convince others to contribute. For example, many teachers report that they have been unsuccessful in convincing parents to help school staff resolve discipline problems. They then go on to describe meetings with parents in which school personnel describe the problem and the parents respond that they do not see such behaviour occurring at home. Too often, instead of working to come to a shared understanding of the problem behaviour, this type of meeting ends with the parents superficially agreeing to assist in a problem that they do not believe exists and the school professionals perceiving the parents as only marginally supportive. The dilemma could have been avoided if more effort had been made to identify a shared need to problem solve.

Identify the problem.   Research on problem solving suggests that the most critical step in the process is problem identification (Rodgers-Rhyme & Volpiansky, 1991). However, when educators meet to share problem solving, they often feel pressured because of time constraints to resolve the problem; hence, they rush through this essential stage. Problem-solving experts suggest that up to half of the time available for problem solving should be devoted to this step (Bergan & Tombari, 1975). The INCLUDE model described in Chapter 1, especially information gathered in steps 1, 2, 3, and 4, can assist in identifying problems about students.

In a shared problem-solving situation, you can help emphasize the importance of problem identification by asking whether everyone has agreed on the problem, by asking someone else to restate the problem to check your understanding of it, and by encouraging participants who have not spoken to share their opinions. Consider the following situation, which shows what can happen when problem identification is not done correctly. A teacher in a shared problem-solving session says to the parent of a student whose attendance is irregular and who consistently comes to school without assignments or basic supplies, "We really need your help in making sure Rickie gets up when his alarm goes off so he can catch the bus. And we'd like to establish a system in which you sign off on his written assignments." The parent replies, "It's so hard. I work until midnight and I don't get up when it's time for the kids to go to school. I don't think he sees any point in the homework he's getting—that's why he doesn't bring it back." In this situation, the educator has identified the problem before the meeting has even started: Rickie needs to assume responsibility, and his parents need to provide more guidance for school activities. The teacher is further proposing a solution to the problem and not exploring the problem itself. The parent's response suggests that the parent does not see the same problem; in fact, the parent is implying that perhaps the problem does not belong to Rickie at all, but to the school staff!

Do It! Practise problem identification by participating in a mock pre-referral team meeting with classmates. Who in the group helps keep others focused on problem identification? Who keeps offering solutions instead of focusing on understanding the problem?

✓ **Your Learning:** What makes the second parent interaction so much more constructive than the first?

Consider how this interaction could have been handled instead: The teacher says to the parent, "Ms. Trenton, thanks so much for taking time off work to meet with us. We appreciate your concern for Rickie. Lately, we've seen a problem with Rickie's attendance. We asked you to come to school so we can learn about your perspective on this situation and to let Rickie know that we're working together to help him." When the parent replies with the comment about her working hours and Rickie's perception of the homework, the teacher replies, "That's important information for us. We're hoping we can find ways to motivate Rickie to come to school—and that includes assignments that he sees as valuable." In this situation, the school professionals are working *with* the parent to identify the problem, not against her.

Propose solutions. Once a problem has been clearly identified, the next step is to create a wide range of options that might be tried to solve the problem. One of the most common ways to come up with solutions is to **brainstorm.** VanGundy (1988) clarifies brainstorming as being based on two important principles. First, judgment is deferred; that is, in order to free the mind to be creative, we must suspend our predisposition to judge ideas. Second, quantity leads to quality; that is, the more ideas that are generated for solving a problem, the more likely it is that novel and effective solutions will be found. Brainstorming requires openness and creativity. The grade four team you met at the beginning of this chapter was engaged in proposing solutions. What other solutions might they have generated if they had stressed brainstorming principles?

Evaluate ideas. With a list of ideas, the next step in shared problem solving is to evaluate the ideas by considering whether they seem likely to resolve the problem and whether they are feasible. Information gathered using the INCLUDE model can be particularly helpful at this step. One way to evaluate ideas is to use a decision sheet as illustrated in Figure 3.3. On this decision sheet, the participants have listed the problem—helping Angela to work independently on classroom tasks—and generated ideas for achieving this goal. They then selected criteria by which to judge the merits of each idea. They considered (1) how well the idea will do for increasing the amount of time Angela works on her independent assignments; (2) the extent to which the idea has a low time cost; and (3) the extent to which the idea preserves classroom routines. Ideas not seriously considered were crossed out, and the criteria for decision making were applied to those remaining, with each idea being rated against each criterion. In Figure 3.3, the two ideas with the highest rating were assigning a study buddy and using picture directions.

Plan specifics. Once one or two ideas are decided upon using a process such as the one just described, more detailed planning must occur. For example, you and others may have decided that you would like to try having students in a secondary school course in Personal Life Management provide volunteer tutoring in an after-school program. Some of the tasks to assign include asking the students about their interest, arranging a place for the program, ensuring that needed supplies are available, obtaining permission to operate the program, establishing a schedule for students, determining who will provide adult supervision and sched-

Problem Statement: How can we help Angela to work independently on assigned classroom tasks?

Ideas:

Tape-record instructions	~~Don't give independent work~~
Have an assigned "study buddy"	Let her choose the assignment
Make the work easier	~~Make her stay in from recess to~~
Use pictures for directions	~~complete~~
Ask a parent volunteer to help	

Decision Making: (3 = high, 2 = medium, 1 = low)

Criteria

Idea	Angela will work for at least 5 min.	Low time commitment for teacher	Doesn't disrupt class routine	Total	Rank
1. Taped instructions	3	1	2	6	
2. Study buddy	3	3	3	9	1
3. Easier work	2	2	2	6	
4. Picture directions	3	2	3	8	2
5. Parent volunteer	1	3	2	6	
6. Choose assignment	1	2	1	4	

FIGURE 3.3

A Sample Decision-Making Chart for Problem Solving

uling it, advertising the program, and creating training sessions for the tutors and delivering them.

Typically, at this step of shared problem solving, participants not only list the major tasks that need to be completed to implement the solution, but they also decide who will take responsibility for each task. They also specify a timeline for completing all the tasks and usually decide how long to implement the solution before meeting to evaluate its effectiveness.

Implement the solution. If all the steps in the shared problem-solving process have been followed carefully, implementing the idea(s) decided upon

Do It! Role-play a shared problem-solving interaction in class. Complete all the steps through implementation and then discuss what occurred.

may be the most straightforward part of the process. When problem solving occurs concerning a student with a disability in an inclusive school, each team member may have some responsibility for implementing the solution. Occasionally, you will have much of the immediate responsibility. In other cases, parents will play a major role. What is critical is that each person involved does his or her part so that the solution has a high probability of success. During implementation, it is helpful to keep some type of record documenting your efforts and the impact of the intervention on the student.

Your Learning: What are the steps in problem solving? As you observe others problem solve, can you recognize each step?

Evaluate outcomes.   After a period of time—anywhere from a few days to a few weeks—the professionals who are implementing the solution meet to evaluate its effectiveness. At this time, three possibilities exist. First, if the solution has been especially effective, it may be judged a success. It will then either be continued in order to maintain the results, discontinued if no longer needed, or gradually phased out. Second, if the solution seems to be having a positive effect but is not ideal for some other reason, it may be modified. For example, a behaviour management plan may be helping a student attend class rather than skip it, but the classroom teacher notes that the system is too time-consuming. The problem-solving group may then try to streamline the plan to make it more feasible. Finally, even when the steps in problem solving are carefully completed, a solution is occasionally judged ineffective. The team then must decide what to do next: Should a different solution be selected from the list already generated? Should additional solutions be proposed? Is the problem accurately identified? The team needs to consider all these possibilities before additional problem solving occurs.

Wiener and Davidson (1990) of the Ontario Institute for Studies in Education found that professionals who regularly use the strategies of shared problem solving acknowledge that the steps do not automatically lead to simple solutions that always work. They report, however, that when they problem solve in this fashion, they feel that their professional time is well spent and that the problem-solving process is truly a collaborative endeavour.

Co-Teaching

Co-teaching occurs when two or more teachers share the instruction for a single group of students, typically in a single classroom setting (Bauwens & Hourcade, 1994). Although any two teachers can co-teach, we focus here on the co-teaching that occurs between a classroom teacher and a resource teacher or special education support staff.

FYI: *Co-teaching* is an instructional arrangement in which two or more teachers share responsibility for a group of students. In an inclusive setting, one of the co-teachers is often a resource teacher or other special service provider.

In a classroom with several students with disabilities, combining the strengths of the general education teacher and a special educator can create options for all students (Friend & Cook, 1992b). Co-teaching typically occurs for a set period of time either every day (for example, every morning from 9:30 until 10:15) or on certain days of the week (for example, on Mondays and Wednesdays during third hour). Occasionally, especially in secondary schools, a group of students with disabilities who used to attend a separate class for a specific subject will join a general education class permanently. In such cases, the special education teacher may be available every day. For example, if a school used to have basic science for students with disabilities, the group of eight students from that class and their teacher may become members of a general education biology class of 25 students. One other strategy for co-teaching is to have a resource teacher and a classroom teacher share instruction for a particular unit, often one that many students find difficult (for example, changing decimals to fractions). After the unit is completed, the co-teaching is stopped until another specific need arises.

Effective as it is, co-teaching is only one option for meeting the needs of students in inclusive schools (Harris et al., 1987). Further, it is relatively expensive (that is, the cost of two teachers with one group of students) and should be reserved for situations in which the number of students with disabilities in a class justifies the presence of two teachers.

Many approaches are available to teachers who decide to co-teach (Gelzheiser & Meyers, 1990; White & White, 1992). Cook and Friend (1993) have outlined some of the common ones, three of which are described below.

One teach, one support.   In this approach, one teacher leads the lesson and the other takes an assisting role. For example, while the special education teacher leads a lesson on listening strategies or a test review, the classroom teacher gathers observational data on target students. Alternatively, while the classroom teacher leads a lesson on the causes of the War of 1812, the special education teacher helps keep students on task, checks written work as it is being completed, and responds quietly to student questions. The key to using this approach successfully is to make it only one of many approaches you use. With overuse, one of the teachers, often the special educator, may feel that he or she has no legitimate role in the class.

Alternative teaching.   In most classrooms, dividing the class into one large and one small group is sometimes appropriate. This co-teaching option is referred to as **alternative teaching.** Traditionally, a small group has been used primarily for remediation, but many other options are recommended. For example, some students may benefit from pre-teaching. In pre-teaching, one teacher works with a small group of students. Information to be presented the next day or later in the same day or class is taught to these students so that when questions are asked or vocabulary is introduced, the students have a "jump start" on learning. Enrichment also works well in smaller groups. Occasionally, grouping students for remediation is appropriate, but only if it is one among many grouping options. Otherwise, such an arrangement becomes the equivalent of running a special education program in the back of a general education classroom, an arrangement that completely belies the purpose and principles of inclusion.

Team teaching.   In the co-teaching option of **team teaching,** the teachers share leadership in the classroom; both are equally engaged in the instructional activities. For example, one teacher may begin a lesson by introducing vocabulary while the other provides examples to place the words in context. Two teachers may role-play an important event from history or a science concept. Two teachers may model how to address conflict by staging a debate about a current event. One teacher may lecture while the other models note-taking strategies on the

FYI: When you work with a special educator to select a co-teaching approach, you should base your decision on student needs, curricular demands, teacher preference, and pragmatic issues such as the availability of space.

Teachers experienced in collaboration say it is well worth the effort. What does it take to make collaboration work? How might you approach co-teaching if it becomes an option for you?

chalkboard. You reach the limits of team teaching only when you run out of exciting ideas for creating instruction with two teachers instead of one.

Do It! Review lesson plans you have made in other classes. How could you adapt them for co-teaching? Create an example for each co-teaching approach.

Co-teaching pragmatics.   As you consider these co-teaching approaches, you might notice that many considerations must be taken into account (Bauwens, Hourcade, & Friend, 1989; Brandenberger & Womack, 1982). First, in a co-taught class, students are heterogeneously grouped so exceptional students are appropriately integrated with their peers without disabilities. When alternative teaching occurs, the smaller group may or may not contain students with disabilities. Second, both teachers take on teaching and supportive roles. This principle is critical if students are to view both teachers as credible. Third, which approach is best depends on student needs, the subject being taught, the teachers' experience, and practical considerations such as space and time for planning. Sometimes, the type of curriculum dictates the approach. Curriculum that is hierarchical might be best presented in a format of one teach, one support. The Professional Edge provides some additional guidelines for successful co-teaching.

Teaming

Do It! Think about a team that is unrelated to education (for example, a professional sports team). List the strategies that help the team succeed. How would these strategies help a school team?

In Chapter 2, you learned that you have responsibility as a member of an intervention assistance team, sometimes called an in-school team or a school-based team, to problem solve about students before they are considered for formal assessment and, possibly, special education. You also learned that you may be a member of the multidisciplinary team that determines whether a student is eligible to receive special education services and that writes the student's IEP. Now you need to understand the concepts and procedures that make those teams and other school teams effective.

▼▼▼▼▼▼▼▼▼▼▼▼▼▼▼▼▼▼▼▼▼▼▼▼

Professional Edge
Tips for Successful Co-Teaching

CO-TEACHING is one approach that facilitates the inclusion of students who have disabilities in general education classrooms. The two teachers involved, often a classroom teacher and a special educator, can together offer instructional options for all students. Keep in mind the following tips to make your co-teaching efforts successful.

1. **Planning is the key.** Make time to plan lessons and to discuss exactly how you will work together throughout your co-teaching experience.

2. **Discuss your views on teaching and learning with your co-teacher.** Experienced co-teachers agree that both teachers should share basic beliefs about teaching.

3. **Attend to details.** Clarify classroom rules and procedures, such as class routines for leaving the room, using free time, discipline, grading, and so on.

4. **Prepare parents.** If parents have questions, explain to them that having two teachers in the class gives every child the opportunity to receive more attention than before; it does not change the curriculum except to enrich it.

5. **Avoid the "paraprofessional trap."** The most common concern about co-teaching is that the special education teacher becomes a classroom helper, which quickly becomes boring for the special education teacher and awkward for the general education teacher. Using various co-teaching approaches can help teachers avoid this situation.

6. **When disagreements occur, talk them out.** To have some disagreements in co-teaching is normal. But be sure to raise your concerns while they are still minor and to recognize that both of you may have to compromise to resolve your differences.

7. **Go slowly.** If you begin with co-teaching approaches that require less reliance on one another, you have an opportunity to learn each other's styles. As your comfort level increases, you can try more complex co-teaching approaches.

Source: Adapted from "The New Mainstreaming" by M. Friend and L. Cook, 1992b, *Instructor, 101*(7), pp. 30–32, 34, 36. Reprinted by permission of Scholastic, Inc.

When you think about highly successful teams, what comes to mind? Your favourite athletic team—the Saskatchewan Roughriders or the Calgary Flames? A surgical team? An orchestra? What is it about these teams that makes them noteworthy? **Teams** are formal work groups that have certain characteristics. They have clear goals, active and committed members, and leaders; they practise to achieve their results; and they do not let personal issues interfere with achieving their goals. Can you think of other characteristics of effective teams?

The teams you will be part of at school have many of the same characteristics as other teams (Abelson & Woodman, 1983). Their success depends on the commitment of every member and the clarity of their goals (Westby & Ford, 1993). On effective school teams, members keep in mind why they are a team, setting aside personal differences in order to reach a goal, often designing the best educational strategies possible for students with disabilities or other special needs. Figure 3.4 summarizes team characteristics typically associated with effectiveness.

Team participant roles. Team members must assume multiple roles (Morsink, Thomas, & Correa, 1991; Wiener & Davidson, 1990). First, you have a **professional role**. In your role as a classroom teacher, you bring a particular perspective to a team interaction, as do the resource teacher, special education teacher, counsellor, principal, and other team members. You contribute an understanding of what students without disabilities are accomplishing in your grade or course, knowledge of curriculum and its pace, and a sense of the prerequisites of what you are teaching and the expectations likely to follow the next segment of instruction.

The second contribution you make is through your **personal role.** The characteristics that define you as a person shape this role. For example, are you an eternal optimist, a person who sees the positive aspects of almost any situation? You will probably be the person who keeps up the team's morale. Are you a detail person who is skilled at organizing? You will probably be the team member who ensures that all the tasks are completed and all the paperwork is filed.

Third, you have a **team role** to fulfil as well. You may be the individual who ensures that the agenda is being followed or who watches the time so that team meetings do not last too long. Or, you may have the role of summarizing and clarifying others' comments or suggesting ways to combine what seem to be contradictory points of view into integrated solutions to student problems. As an effective member, you will recognize your strengths and offer them to the team; you

✓ **Your Learning:** What are the differences among professional, personal, and team roles? What team roles are you most likely to take?

FIGURE 3.4

Characteristics of Effective Teams

1. All participants understand, agree to, and identify the primary goal for the team.

2. The team is characterized by open communication that includes ideas, opinions, and feelings.

3. Team members trust one another; that is, they know that no one will deliberately take advantage of another team member.

4. Team members support each other by demonstrating care and concern.

5. Team members manage their human differences. They clarify how they are different from one another and use these differences as strengths for creative problem solving rather than as hindrances to problem resolution.

6. Teams meet and work together only when necessary.

7. Team members have fundamental team skills, including those for communication, those for addressing task goals, and those for maintaining effective team functioning.

8. Teams have leaders but recognize that all team members share leadership.

Source: Adapted with permission from NTL Institute, "Team Building" by W. W. Burke, 1988, in W. B. Reddy and K. Jamison (Eds.), *Team Building: Blueprints for Productivity and Satisfaction*, pp. 3–14, copyright 1988.]

will also be vigilant so that your weaknesses do not interfere with the team accomplishing its tasks. Common formal team roles include team facilitator, recorder, and timekeeper. These roles might rotate so that every team member has the opportunity to experience each one. Informal team roles include being a compromiser, an information seeker, and a reality checker. These informal roles are not usually assigned, but team members ensure that they are being fulfilled as the need arises.

Team goals.   One of the keys to effective teams is attention to goals (Morsink et al., 1991). Being clear and explicit about goals is particularly important in educational settings since team goals are often assumed or too limited. For example, on some intervention assistance teams, teachers perceive the team goal to be to document pre-referral interventions already attempted in the classroom so that the special education assessment and identification procedures can begin. Others believe the team functions to help teachers problem solve so that the entire referral process can be avoided. Note how crucial this difference is! With the former, a team may function as a sort of "confirmation hearing" process for students with learning and behaviour problems. In the latter, it may be a resource and idea support group. Without clear and specific goals, teams often flounder.

Another aspect of team goals is especially important. The goals just discussed are commonly referred to as **task goals;** that is, they are the business of the team. But teams also have another set of goals, known as maintenance goals. **Maintenance goals** refer to the team's status and functioning as a team. Maintenance goals may include beginning and ending meetings on time, finishing all agenda items during a single meeting, taking time to check on team members' perceptions of team effectiveness, improving team communication both during meetings and outside of them, and so on. These and other maintenance goals enable effective teams to accomplish the task goals they set.

One maintenance goal that many teams struggle with concerns how their meetings are scheduled, structured, and operated. Complaints frequently heard include some members' failure to arrive on time, the tendency of the group to wander off topic, some members' habit of monopolizing the conversation while others seldom say anything, and the pattern of hurrying to finish meetings and in the process making hasty decisions. All of these problems can be addressed and often alleviated through team attention to them.

The following example from an elementary school problem-solving meeting shows how each team member plays a vital role. The team included the principal, two classroom teachers, a special education teacher, a speech and language therapist, a reading/resource teacher, and a social worker. The reading teacher often spoke a great deal more than other team members, talking until others simply nodded their heads in agreement with whatever she wanted. At one team meeting, the reading teacher left early, just after the team had decided to assess a student for possible special education services. No sooner had the reading/resource teacher left than the team members confronted the principal, explaining that they did not believe the referral for assessment was appropriate and asking the principal to make the reading teacher stop pushing through ideas that other team members did not want. The principal made a wise reply. He said, "Wait a minute. If there's a problem it's a team problem. If a poor decision was

FYI: *Task goals* relate to the "business" of the team, such as meeting student needs in a pre-referral team or discussion curriculum at a grade-level or department meeting. *Maintenance goals* help the team monitor its own effectiveness, including how the team resolves conflict, whether leadership is clear, how communication occurs, and how others view the team.

What types of teams might you find at your school? How do teams use shared problem solving to meet student needs?

made, it was a team decision. It's not what am *I* going to do, it's what are *we* going to do." In the conversation that followed, team members recognized that each person was responsible for speaking out if he or she idea that was presented. They also acknowledged that they were uncomfortable confronting the reading teacher about her interactions during team meetings. However, with the help of the principal, the team spent part of their next meeting discussing each team member's verbal contributions and establishing procedures for checking all team members' perceptions prior to making a decision. Although their actions did not completely change the reading teacher's style, they did bring the team closer together and dramatically increased the team's effectiveness.

The Case in Practice lets you listen in on another team meeting, this time an annual review that includes a parent. Notice how each team member collaborates to make the meeting successful.

Consulting

FYI: Although special education teachers sometimes act as consultants, school psychologists, counsellors, and specialists in areas such as student behaviour management more often function in this role.

In some cases, you may find that although a student in your class does not receive direct support, you will receive the assistance of a consultant. Perhaps your school has adopted an inclusive approach to educating exceptional learners, and the student's needs can be met with occasional supports. You may learn that for the next school year you will have a student who has a significant hearing impairment; you would like to know how to assist the student and whether you should enrol in a sign language class. If you have in your class a student with autism, you might find that both you and the resource teacher need assistance from someone else to help the student transition from activity to activity. These are the types of situations in which you might seek support through consultation.

▼▼▼▼▼▼▼▼▼

Case in Practice

Collaboration at an Annual Review Team Meeting

Aᴛ Bill's annual review, his mother, Ms. Ippawa, is present, along with Ms. Dolbec, Bill's resource teacher; Mr. Dirk, his grade one teacher; and Ms. Bird, the principal. Here is how the meeting begins.

Ms. Dolbec: Thanks for joining us, Ms. Ippawa. How are you doing? I saw you at the community center the other day, but you were too far away to say "Hi" to.

Ms. Ippawa: Oh. I'm usually there every Wednesday. You should've come over.

Ms. Dolbec: As usual, I was in a hurry. And unfortunately, I'm going to have to hurry us now. I know you have to be back at work in less than an hour.

Ms. Ippawa: Yeah, I do.

Ms. Dolbec: Did you receive the annual review planning form I sent home with Bill?

Ms. Ippawa: Yeah.

Ms. Dolbec: We sent that home to give you a chance to think a little bit about what you've seen happen with Bill this year and what you would like to see happen at school for him next year. Before we get too far into this, is there anything from the form or anything else about Bill's schooling this year that you have questions about?

Ms. Ippawa: No, I don't think so. Except that I wondered what happened after he had that fight with that other little girl.

Ms. Dolbec: There really hasn't been anything else that happened. Bill spent part of his recess for a week in the time-out box on the playground thinking about what he had done. He hasn't fought again.

Ms. Ippawa: Okay. I was just worried about that. Him hitting a girl and all.

Ms. Bird: I'm glad you thought to ask. Maybe we could have Mr. Dirk talk a little bit about Bill's learning this year.

Mr. Dirk: Well, Bill's actually doing fairly well in language arts....

Reflections

What occurred at the beginning of this annual review that promotes positive interactions with parents and helps them feel part of the team? What strategy was Ms. Dolbec using in how she addressed Ms. Ippawa? Why do you think Ms. Bird waited to refocus the meeting on Bill's learning? What does this interaction demonstrate about the importance of the early part of team meetings setting the tone for the entire meeting?

Consultation is a specialized problem-solving process in which one professional who has particular expertise assists another professional (or parent) who needs the benefit of that expertise (Idol, Nevin, & Paolucci-Whitcomb, 1994; Jordan, 1994). You may contact a behaviour consultant for assistance when a student in your class is aggressive. You might meet with a vision or hearing consultant when students with those disabilities are included in your class. If you have a student who has received medical or other services outside of school, you may consult with someone from the agency that has been providing those services.

Although consultation is most effective when it is based on the principles of collaboration presented earlier in this chapter, it has a different purpose than collaboration. Even though the consultant working with you may learn from you and benefit from the interaction, the goal of the interaction is to help *you* resolve a

FYI: The detail of the information you provide for a consultant is important. If you are sketchy in describing the student's needs, the consultant will have to spend valuable time backtracking to learn necessary basic information.

problem or deal with a concern, not to foster shared problem solving, in which both or all participants share the problem. In consulting, the assumption is that you are experiencing a problem and that the consultant's expertise will enable you to solve the problem more effectively.

The process of consulting generally begins when you complete a request form or otherwise indicate that you have a concern about a student (Heron & Harris, 1993; Witt & Martens, 1988). Jordan (1994) has described the steps in this process. The consultant then contacts you to arrange an initial meeting. At that meeting, the problem is further clarified, the teacher's expectations are discussed, and often, arrangements are made for the consultant to observe in the teacher's room. After the observation phase, the consultant and teacher meet again to finalize their understanding of the problem, generate and select options for addressing it, and plan how to implement whatever strategies seem needed. A timeline is also established. Typically, the teacher then carries out the strategies. Following this phase, the consultant and teacher meet once again to determine whether the problem has been resolved. If it has, the strategy will either be continued to maintain the success or eliminated as no longer needed. If a problem continues to exist, the consultant and teacher may begin a new consulting process, or they may decide that some other action is needed. When appropriate, the consultant "closes" the case.

✓ **Your Learning:** What are the steps in consultation? How are they similar to the steps in shared problem solving? What are some differences between these two collaborative activities?

For consulting to be effective, both the consultant and the consultee (that is, you as the teacher) need to participate responsibly. Your role includes preparing for meetings, being open to the consultant's suggestions, using the consultant's strategies systematically, and documenting the effectiveness of ideas you try. The Professional Edge includes specific ideas for preparing for and collaborating successfully with consultants.

How Can You Work Effectively with Parents?

The partnerships presented thus far in this chapter have focused primarily on your interactions with special education teachers and other professionals who will support you in meeting the needs of students with disabilities in your classroom. In this section, we will emphasize your working relationship with parents.

The quality of your interactions with the parents of all your students is important, but it is vital for your students with disabilities (Waggoner & Wilgosh, 1990). Parents may be able to help you better understand the strengths and needs of their child in your classroom. They also act as advocates for their children, so they can help you ensure that adequate supports are provided for the child's needs. Parents often view their child's experiences in your classroom in a way that you cannot; when they share this information, it helps both you and the student experience more success. Finally, parents are your ally in educating students; when you enlist their assistance to practise skills at home, to reward a student for accomplishments at school, to communicate to the child messages consistent with yours, you and the parents are multiplying the student's educational opportunities and providing a consistency that is essential to maximize student learning.

Professional Edge
Working with a Consultant

SOME teachers have a cynical view of consultants. They roll their eyes and discuss experiences in which consultants' suggestions were unrealistic. Although these types of issues may arise because some consultants might be lacking in skills to assist teachers, they can also occur because the consultant did not understand the information the teacher provided and the expectations for the specific classroom and teacher. Here are some suggestions for ensuring that you get the maximum benefit from your interactions with consultants.

1. **Do your homework.** Working with a consultant should be an intervention you seek only after you have attempted to identify and resolve the problem by analyzing the situation yourself, talking about it with parents, presenting it at a grade-level meeting, and so on. By asking others for input, you will clarify your own thinking about the problem and your expectations for its resolution.

2. **Demonstrate your concern with documentation.** At your initial meeting with a consultant, bring samples of student work, notes recounting specific incidents in the classroom, records of correspondence with parents, and other concrete information. Chapter 12 includes strategies for collecting information about students having difficulty.

3. **Participate actively.** If you clearly describe the problem, contribute specific information about your expectations for how the situation should change, offer your ideas on how best to intervene to resolve the problem, imple-

ment the selected strategy carefully, and provide your perception of the effectiveness of the strategy, you will find consultation very helpful.

4. **Carry out the consultant's suggestions carefully and systematically.** Consultants often lament that teachers do not implement their suggestions but then complain about ineffective consultation. If you are asked to record certain behaviours for a student every day, then skipping an occasional day may reduce the effectiveness of the strategy. Likewise, if you agree to send a communication home each afternoon with the student, just calling the parents once in a while is inadequate. If you carry out a suggestion faithfully and it is not effective, you will be better prepared to discuss the matter with the consultant. Only agree to the consultant's suggestions if you believe them to be feasible for you to carry out in the realities of your classroom. If you do not think the suggestions are feasible, you and the consultant should seek other solutions.

5. **Contact the consultant if problems occur.** Because the consultant is unlikely to have direct contact with the student and will be able to spend only a very limited amount of time in your classroom, you will need to monitor carefully the effect of the strategies you are implementing. If you find they are ineffective or the student's problem is worsening, you should contact the consultant immediately rather than waiting for your next scheduled meeting.

Understanding the Perspective of Family Members

Imagine a boy who, despite his learning disabilities, always tried to do his homework and always brought a respectable effort to school the next day, regardless of

Cultural Awareness: Many parents, but especially those from minority groups, can find school an intimidating place. You can promote participation by encouraging parents to come to school meetings with a friend or another family member, by providing translation if necessary, and by asking them positive questions early during meetings (for example, "What does your child say about school at home?"

Do It! Talk to the parents of a child with a disability. What would they like you to do to educate their child? What do they wish all teachers know about working with their child?

the assignment. In Edmonton, the mother of an adolescent boy with learning disabilities described her feelings about her efforts to help her son keep up with his school work during his years in elementary school. "Doing homework at night was incredibly difficult; my husband and I took turns and it was screaming, fighting ... he hated homework. And we hated working with him" (Waggoner & Wilgosh, 1990, p. 97).

You might be tempted to assume that because you work with a student with a disability in your classroom on a daily basis you understand what it would be like to be the student's parent. This assumption could not be further from the truth. For example, the parent of a high school student with a moderate cognitive disability as well as multiple physical disorders made this comment at a meeting of parents and teachers:

> You see my child in a wheelchair and worry about getting her around the building and keeping her changed. But remember, before you ever see her in the morning, I have gotten her out of bed, bathed her, cleaned her, washed her hair and fixed it, fed her, and dressed her. When she's at school I worry about whether she is safe, about whether kids fighting in the hall will care for her or injure her, and whether they are kind. And when she comes home... And I wonder what will be the best option for her when she graduates in three years. You can't possibly know what it's like to be the parent of a child like my daughter.

As a teacher, you need to realize what this parent so eloquently demonstrated: that you do not understand what it is like to be the parent of a child with a disability unless you are the parent of one. That means that you should strive to recognize that the range of interactions you have with parents will be influenced in part by the stresses they are experiencing, their prior dealings with school personnel, and their own beliefs about their child's future. Apply this concept to Chris's parents, Mr. and Mrs. Werner, whom you met at the beginning of the chapter. What might be influencing their interactions with the school professionals? How would knowing about their reluctance to have Chris identified as needing special education and their concerns about the stigma of the "learning disability" label help the teachers to respond appropriately to them?

Parent Reactions to Their Child's Disability

Parents of children with disabilities have many reactions to their children. For some, the reactions may be minor and their approach pragmatic. For others, the child's disability might affect their entire family structure and life. Part of your work with parents includes recognizing that how parents respond to you may be influenced by these responses to their children's disabilities.

1. **Grief.** Some parents feel grief about their child's disability. Sometimes this is a sorrow for the pain or discomfort that their child may have to experience; sometimes it is sadness for themselves because of the added stress on the family when a child has a disability; and sometimes it is a sense of loss for what the child may not be able to become. Parents have a right to grieve about their child (Turnbull & Turnbull, 1990), a right educators that should respect.

2. **Ambivalence.** Parents may also feel ambivalent about their child's disability. This feeling may occur as parents attempt to confirm that the child's disability is not temporary or "fixable," as they try to identify the best educational options for their child, and as they ponder how their child will live as an adult. The decisions that parents of children with disabilities must make are often difficult, and these decisions continue throughout the child's childhood and adolescence, and sometimes through their adulthood. Parents often attend meetings at which tremendous amounts of information are shared with little time for explanations, and they often meet with representatives from many different disciplines (Schmid & Hutchinson, 1994). It is no wonder that they may feel ambivalent!

3. **Optimism.** One of our students was once interviewing the parent of a student with a mild cognitive disability. When asked what it was like having a child with a cognitive disability in the family, the parent replied, "Mary is my child. Just like any other child. I love her as my child. She is sometimes funny and sometimes clever and sometimes naughty. She can really get into trouble. She's just like my other children, except she's Mary." For this parent, her child's exceptionalities are just part of the configuration of needs that the children in any family may have. In this family, the emphasis is on the person, not the disability. There are many families like this one. In these families, the special needs of the child are met without extraordinary reactions. Parents may work diligently to optimize their child's education, but they are hopeful about their child's future. They work closely with educators and others to ensure that the child's life, whatever it may be, is the best one possible.

How parents respond when they have a child with a disability depends on many factors. One such factor is the intensity and complexity of the disability. The reaction of a parent of a child with a learning disability diagnosed in grade three is likely to be somewhat different from that of parents who learned two months after their child was born that she could not see.

In interviews with parents of preschoolers with disabilities in Kingston, Ontario, Schmid and Hutchinson (1994) found that when information about a child's disability is presented in a coldly clinical manner or when too little information is provided, parents' responses can be quite negative. A mother of a child born with Down syndrome described her frustration:

> No one in the hospital steered us in any direction at all. No one even came in and talked to us about anything. I was working with a woman at the time who has a child who is developmentally delayed. And she came and visited me, and said, "You've got to call this person and do this." That's what steered me in the right direction. (p. 14)

At a meeting when a parent was told about her son's learning disability, the parent said,

> "Wait a minute. Stop and let me think. Do you realize what you've just said? You've just unravelled my whole way of thinking about my son. What do you mean a learning disability? What does that mean? Will it ever change? How can you sit there and keep talking as though it's no big thing?"

✓ **Your Learning:** What kinds of reactions might parents have toward their child with a disability?

One other factor that affects parent response concerns family relationships and supports. Dyson (1993) of the University of Toronto, found that in families of children with disabilities, parental stress was lower when a family had a cohesive and supportive relationship that allowed free expressions of personal feelings with little personal conflict. Researchers in Alberta (Kysela, McDonald, & Brenton-Haden, 1992) have begun to study how in large families, families with many supportive relatives living in the same community, or families with a strong network of neighbours and friends, the stresses of having a child with a disability are greatly reduced. When parents are isolated or when friends and family are uncomfortable with the child, it is far more likely that the parents will experience difficulties.

Collaborating with Parents

Your working relationship with parents will depend on the student's particular needs, the parents' desire to be actively involved in their child's education, and your efforts to make parents feel like your partnership with them is important. In some cases, collaboration may be too ambitious a goal. For example, if you interact with a parent only three or four times during the school year, you may simply not have adequate opportunity for collaboration to occur. Still, for some parents, collaboration is not only appropriate, but recommended. Your first goal in working with parents, however, is to help them to participate in meetings, conferences, and other interactions. In this way, you will have the opportunity to learn whether collaboration is an appropriate next step.

Your attitude toward parents and their perceptions of their children will greatly affect how you interact with them. If you communicate through your choice of words and your body posture that the parents are limited participants

What are your responsibilities for working with parents of students in your class who have disabilities? How will your interactions with these parents be similar to and different from your other parent interactions?

in their children's education, you will probably find that parents do not communicate with you and may, in fact, perceive you as an ineffective teacher. However, if you make parents feel welcome in your classroom, listen carefully to their perceptions and concerns, treat them as important, and work with them to address student needs, you will find many benefits for the student, for the family, and for you. With a positive approach, students learn more and your time is spent in creating opportunities, not responding to parent complaints.

Parent Conferences

In addition to various types of communication systems, you will also collaborate with parents through conferences. Preparing effectively for parent conferences will help ensure successful conferences with the parents of all your students, including students with disabilities.

Prior to a conference.   Before parent conferences, you should take several steps to prepare. First, you should clarify the purpose of the conference, both for yourself and for parents. If the purpose is to explain briefly a class or course and parents understand this, they will be less likely to be disappointed when you do not share specific information about their child. If the purpose is to spend a specific amount of time discussing a child's progress and parents know this, they can come to school prepared for such a discussion. You can help parents prepare for a conference by sending home a list of questions and suggestions in advance. A sample of tips for parents, from Alberta, is presented in Figure 3.5.

You should also prepare for conferences by arranging details to maximize the time available and create a comfortable atmosphere. Specifically, you should plan to meet with parents at a conference table, since your desk may be perceived as a symbol of power. If your classroom is equipped for young children, you should also arrange to have adult-sized furniture available for the meeting. A box of tissues should be within easy reach, and you should make sure that the conference will be private, perhaps by posting a sign at your door that instructs parents to knock to indicate they have arrived and then to wait until you come to the door to greet them. Another part of planning a conference is preparing the questions and topics you wish to discuss with parents. These might include specific questions regarding how a student behaves at home and how rewards are given, or a list of academic strengths and concerns. Having samples of student work, the student's portfolio, your grade and plan books, and other pertinent student records easily available is also important.

If you are meeting with the parents of an exceptional secondary student, you may want to ensure that the adolescent accompanies the parents. That way everyone has a shared understanding of expectations, especially about the adolescent's responsibilities for being self-directed and seeking your assistance when it is necessary.

During a conference.   During the conference, your goal is to create a two-way exchange of information. To do this, greet parents positively, set a purpose for the conference, and actively involve parents in discussions. You should use all the collaboration skills you employ with colleagues in working with parents. In addition,

FIGURE 3.5

Tips to Help
Parents Prepare
for Conferences
About Individual
Program Plans

Individual Program Plans

General Tips

Parents are valuable members of the Individual Program Plan (IPP) team. The following tips may enhance your participation in your child's educational program:

____   maintain ongoing contact with the school

____   take an active role in decision making

____   ask about other parents who may be in a similar situation; they can be a valuable resource

____   ask about the services and resources available.

Tips for participating in the IPP Process

Before the meeting:

____   find out the agenda in advance

____   discuss your child's involvement in the process

____   jot down your comments and questions in advance

____   think about your goals and expectations for your child.

At the meeting:

____   make time limits known if you have other commitments

____   provide samples of your child's work done at home if you think they could be useful

____   ask questions if anything is unclear to you

____   ask how you can help achieve some of these goals at home.

Source: From *Partners During Changing Times: An Information Booklet for Parents of Children with Special Needs* by Alberta Education, Special Education Branch, 1996,Copyright ©1996 by Alberta Education. Reprinted by permission.]

you should use language respectful of the parents, their child, and their culture. Parents should be addressed as "Mr." or "Ms.," not as "Dad" or "Mom." Students should be referred to by name. Avoid using jargon. In addition, teachers should work to understand that parents might interpret the meaning of disability and educators' response to it in ways different from the meanings given by educators. For parents who are not confident in their understanding of English, it may be necessary to arrange for a translator. Sometimes your principal may assume responsibility for finding a translator. In some cases, it may be appropriate to ask the exceptional child, a sibling, another family member, or a family friend to translate. When you are new to a school, ask the teachers what has been done in the past. Parents may be seeking information about programs outside of the school for their exceptional child. In research conducted in Edmonton, Chan-Marples (1993) found that immigrant mothers of exceptional children identified their lack of knowledge about community programs as a problem. Lupart (1990) also described preparing information for parents of gifted children about extracurricular programs available in Calgary. Effective conferences with parents enable teachers to both provide and obtain information.

During a conference, you might be meeting with both parents and a resource or special education teacher. As teachers, you share the responsibility for creating a collaborative environment as well as for ensuring that all critical information is presented to parents, that parents have ample opportunities to share information with you, and that any needed strategies are developed and follow-up planned.

After a conference.   After a parent conference, you have several additional responsibilities to complete. First, you should write a few notes to remind yourself of the important points discussed. These notes will help you to be accurate in your recollections. Second, if you have made any major decisions regarding strategies that you and the parents will be implementing, you might want to write a brief note to the parents to confirm the decisions you made. Third, if you agreed to any action (for example, sending information to parents, asking a counsellor to call parents), it is best to carry it out as soon as possible. Finally, if the special education teacher did not attend the conference, he or she may appreciate a brief note from you with an update on the conference outcomes.

Of course, you will communicate with parents on many occasions besides conferences, using strategies such as those introduced in Chapter 2. The Technology Notes describes some additional ways to communicate effectively with parents.

Connections: Participants in meetings required by special education legislation and policies are discussed in Chapter 2. How does that material relate to the information about teams presented in this chapter?

How Can You Work Effectively with Paraprofessionals?

Throughout this chapter, in our discussion of forming partnerships with others in schools an assumption has been made that everyone involved has equal status; that is, a general education teacher has approximately the same level of authority and equivalent responsibilities as a special education teacher, speech and language therapist, school psychologist, reading teacher, and so on. In many school boards or school districts, individuals in these types of positions are referred to as certified staff.

One other partnership you may form involves another type of staff. As mentioned in Chapter 2, paraprofessionals are non-certified staff members who are employed to assist certified staff in carrying out the educational programs and otherwise helping in the instruction of students with disabilities. (Although some school districts also employ other types of paraprofessionals, for our discussion, we are referring only to paraprofessionals who are part of special education services.) In various parts of Canada, these paraprofessionals are referred to as teacher assistants, teaching assistants, and educational assistants. When students with disabilities are members of your class, a special educator may not have adequate time or opportunity to assist them frequently, or the student might not need the direct services of that professional. Instead, a paraprofessional might be assigned to you for a class period or subject, or, depending on the intensity of

FYI: A *paraprofessional* is a non-certified school employee with limited direct responsibilities for making decisions about students and delivering instruction. In special education, paraprofessionals give students personal assistance, assist in inclusive classrooms, and otherwise support programs for exceptional students.

▼▼

Technology Notes   Enhancing Communication

READILY available and simple-to-use technology can enhance your communication with parents and your colleagues. Here are some examples.

Videotape

If parents are unable to attend school meetings or have questions about their children's behaviour or developing skills, or if special educators want to get a better understanding of a student's functioning in your class, videotape may provide a tool for communication. Because many households now have videocassette recorders, you could tape children's plays, reports, or projects and make copies for parents who request them. You could focus the camera on a student who acts out frequently and record the occurrences for a behaviour consultant. Keep in mind these tips if you want to use videotape to communicate with parents or other teachers:

1. Check local policies on videotaping students. You may need to obtain parental permission.

2. If you are taping behaviours, you might need a few days for students to become accustomed to the camera before you get "realistic" results.

3. Consider asking a parent volunteer or older student to help operate the camera; even with help, a tripod is essential.

4. If you are taping a school event, check to see whether your school district has equipment to copy tapes easily.

Videotape can also enable parents to communicate with teachers. Hutchinson and Schmid (1996) interviewed a resource teacher in an inclusive preschool in eastern Ontario. She described encouraging parents of a medically fragile child to make a videotape to inform educators about their child's condition. "What I did was I took the video camera out to the home and videotaped [the father] explaining how this machine worked. We let him explain it in his terms. I took the video back to the staff" (p. 77). This strategy not only enabled teachers to learn about the needs of a child who relied on computerized medical equipment for digestion, but it also empowered the parents.

Audiotape

Audiotapes offer many of the advantages of videotapes but with less need for expensive equipment and less intrusion into your classroom. Audiotapes can be used to record student reports and to share with parents how their children read in school. For the latter use, students can use a reading station to record their own tapes.

student needs, for much of the school day (Jones & Bender, 1993; Lam & McQuarrie, 1989).

Understanding Your Working Relationship with Paraprofessionals

The partnerships you form with paraprofessionals are slightly different from those with certified staff since you have some supervisory responsibility for the para-

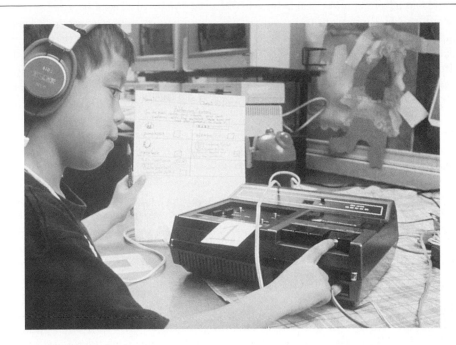

Students can tape-record themselves reading or giving a report. These tapes can then be shared with parents.]

Telephone

The telephone is a powerful communication tool, and not just for periodic phone calls to let parents know how their child is doing in your class. For example, if you have a phone in your classroom or can access one for evening calls, you could set up a weekly hot line through the use of voice mail. You record highlights of the week's activities and let parents know which night and which phone number to call to listen to the message. If you want parents to have the opportunity to leave a message, invite them to leave a brief one. You might try a telephone tree with your parents: You make three phone calls, and each parent you call relays information by calling three other parents. Obviously, this strategy requires conscientious parents who listen carefully.

Computer

Depending on your school and community technology use level, you might be able to communicate within your school on a local area network and with parents through an on-line service.

professional's work, a situation that would not exist in your work with colleagues (Reisberg & Gerlach, 1992). For example, you may be expected to prepare materials that the paraprofessional will use to work with a group of students, you may have the responsibility of assigning tasks to this person on a daily basis, and you may need to provide informal training to the paraprofessional regarding your classroom expectations.

Many classroom teachers have never been supervisors, and they worry about what types of tasks to assign to a paraprofessional and how to set expectations.

Adding to the complexity is the fact that some paraprofessionals have extensive professional preparation, a teaching licence, and years of classroom experience, which makes them want to do nearly everything you do, whereas others have a high school diploma and little training or experience in working with students (Morehouse & Albright, 1991). Cripps (1991), a New Brunswick teacher of children with visual disabilities, describes how some educational assistants have worked with the same exceptional child for many years and know the child better than the teacher, especially at the beginning of the school year or term. This is especially true when an educational assistant and an exceptional adolescent have worked together for many years and the secondary teacher only teaches the student for an hour each day. Figure 3.6 outlines some typical paraprofessional responsibilities. If you will be working with a paraprofessional, you will probably receive a written description of that person's job responsibilities that specifies the activities that he or she will complete. You can also arrange to meet with the special education teacher and the principal who have overall responsibility for the paraprofessional's job performance. The general guidelines for working effectively with paraprofessionals are these: First, paraprofessionals generally enjoy working with students and want to participate actively in that process, and they should have the opportunity to do so. However, they are also appropriately expected to help teachers accomplish some of the "chores" of teaching, such as record keeping and instructional preparation tasks. Second, paraprofessionals always complete their assignments under the direction of a teacher who has either already taught the information or decided what basic work needs to be completed; that is, paraprofessionals should not do initial teaching, nor should they make instructional decisions without input from a certified staff member.

Collaborating with Paraprofessionals

Do It! Think about working with a paraprofessional. List the questions you as a new teacher would ask an experienced teacher about working with paraprofessionals. If possible, invite a paraprofessional to your class to learn more about the paraprofessional's role.

An often-asked teacher question regarding paraprofessionals is, "Given the supervisory nature of teacher-paraprofessional work, is it possible to collaborate with this group of staff members?" The answer is "Yes!" Paraprofessionals can collaboratively participate in shared problem solving about student needs, in planning field trip details, and in making decisions regarding how to best adapt information for a specific student. Your responsibility as a teacher is to encourage this type of collaboration. At the same time, you should clearly inform the paraprofessional when a matter being discussed is *not* one in which the principles of collaboration are appropriate.

In a study conducted in five school districts in British Columbia, Lamont and Hill (1991) found that classroom teachers and educational assistants generally held similar views about the roles and responsibilities of paraprofessionals in regular elementary classrooms. However, the paraprofessionals were more willing to initiate taking responsibility for instructional support, diagnostic support, and classroom organization than the teachers believed was appropriate. This demonstrates the importance of establishing clear communication and a good working relationship with each paraprofessional who works with exceptional students in your classes.

To help get your work with paraprofessionals off to a positive start, it might be helpful to arrange a meeting that includes you, the special education teacher

FIGURE 3.6

Teacher Assistant Guidelines: Instructional Support

Instructional Support

A. Helps students with assigned tasks and classwork, reinforcing concepts presented by the teacher.

B. Monitors independent or small-group work.

C. Listens to students read.

D. Reads to students.

E. Demonstrates a sense of when either the teacher or a student needs assistance.

F. Adapts materials as planned and directed by the teacher.

G. Acts as a note-taker or scribe, if required.

H. Assists students in meeting their assigned goals within community settings.

I. Records required information on student activities as directed by the teacher.

J. Provides for a safe and comfortable environment.

Non-Instructional Support

A. Makes instructional materials (e.g., games, posters, booklets).

B. Makes displays and bulletin boards.

C. Locates and displays instructional materials.

D. Performs teacher-directed clerical duties (e.g., typing, photocopying, correcting, recording).

E. Assists with school supervision duties (e.g., bussing, yard, lunch, work site).

F. Assists individual students with physical needs (e.g., feeding, lifting, mobility, exercising, cleaning, dressing, toileting, etc.).

G. Gives medication and records appropriately according to school district policy.

H. After appropriate training, performs specific medical procedures (e.g., catheterization, taking blood pressure, administering hypodermic needles, etc.).

Source: From *Teacher Assistant Guidelines for Standards and Evaluation* by New Brunswick Department of Education Student Services Branch (Anglophone), 1994. Copyright © 1994 by New Brunswick Department of Education. Reprinted by permission.

and principal under whom the paraprofessional works, and the paraprofessional. At this meeting, some of the important topics to address might include these: Is the paraprofessional's role in the classroom to assist only a targeted student or group of students, or is it permissible for the paraprofessional to support the students by assisting throughout the class? Who is the individual who is specifically responsible for evaluating the paraprofessional's job performance? What limits exist regarding the types of tasks the paraprofessional may be assigned to do?

What are the paraprofessional's expectations for working in the classroom? What are the other job components for the paraprofessional (for example, other duties, times for breaks)? Stringer (1984) suggested, after studying the roles and training programs of First Nations teaching assistants in British Columbia, that they may have a role in infusing Native culture into the classroom and into the curriculum. What type of communication should be used to ensure that small matters are resolved before they become serious problems and that all parties feel valued and informed? The time that this type of meeting takes at the beginning of the school year is well worth the payoff of a strong, yearlong partnership. Both you and the paraprofessional will be more informed about expectations and more comfortable with your roles and responsibilities (Frith, 1982).

Summary

The Canadian Association of Family Resource Programs

www.cfc-efc.ca/frpc/

SchoolNet Homepage

www.schoolnet.ca

Teachers Helping Teachers

www.pacificnet.net/~mandel/

Collaboration has become an important job responsibility for all educators and is especially important in educating exceptional students. Collaboration is the style that professionals use in interacting with others, and it includes key characteristics such as voluntary participation, parity, shared goals, shared responsibility for key decisions, shared accountability for outcomes, shared resources, and the emergence of a collaborative belief system, trust, and respect. You help make your school's collaborative efforts more successful by identifying and clarifying your personal beliefs about collaboration, refining your interaction skills, and contributing to a supportive environment.

The collaboration you participate in can occur in many applications, but for exceptional students its most common ones include shared problem solving, co-teaching, teaming, and consulting. Each of these applications has its own set of guidelines and its own use in educating students.

Yet another collaborative responsibility teachers have relates to parents. You need to understand parents' perspectives on having a child with a disability, to work collaboratively with parents on the basis of your respect for their perspective, to communicate effectively with parents in conferences and in other ways, and to respond professionally to parents in team meetings, annual reviews, and other interactions at which you and they might be present.

A final group with whom general education teachers collaborate is paraprofessionals. Understanding your roles and responsibilities and those of the paraprofessional and basing your collaboration on these leads to positive working relationships with these individuals.

Applications in Teaching Practice

Collaboration Comes to St. Lawrence Elementary School

Although the 23 teachers at St. Lawrence Elementary School have always worked together informally, when they began emphasizing inclusive programs for students with disabilities, they realized that they needed more than ever to work collaboratively. Dr.

Tompkins, the principal, strongly agreed. Last spring, the teachers met on committees to decide what it would mean for them to be collaborative, what their collaborative priorities would be, and who would be involved in their first-year efforts.

First, the teachers reviewed their school mission statement as a starting point for their discussions about their beliefs about how students learn, how teachers teach, and how schools can be learning communities. They quickly realized that their mission statement, although not bad, did not explicitly say that teachers in the school are expected to work together to meet the needs of all their students. With another after-school meeting, the mission statement was revised.

Next, the teachers began to discuss forms their collaboration might take. Carole, a grade one teacher anticipating a class group with many special needs, argued strongly for co-teaching. She stated that she needed someone to help her for at least a couple of hours each day. Peggy reminded her that with only two special education teachers and one paraprofessional for everyone, kindergarten through grade seven, she was asking for far too much, especially since they also have other responsibilities. Jim, the special education teacher who works with students with moderate and severe disabilities, agreed. He noted that he had to reserve time to work individually with some of his students in a special education setting. Carole's reply to these comments was that she knew that when it really got down to it, there would not be enough resources to make their collaborative approach to meeting student needs work. She said little during the rest of the meeting.

For the first year, the teachers agreed that co-teaching should occur in four classrooms with particularly high needs. Jim would co-teach with a grade four teacher and a grade five teacher since most of his assigned students were in those grade levels. Marta, the teacher for students with high-incidence disabilities, would co-teach in grades one and three because of the needs of her assigned students and other students in those grade levels. Kindergarten would not have co-teaching since parent volunteers seemed to provide all the assistance needed. Grade two would have the services of Stu, the paraprofessional, for an hour four times each week.

The teachers also decided to begin one more collaborative approach. They agreed to meet in grade-level teams at least once every other week. These separate teams would function as pre-referral intervention teams for each grade level. They negotiated a schedule so that some grade levels met before school and others after school, and they staggered the meeting days so that Jim or Marta could attend all the team meetings. The teachers' goal for these teams was to renew their efforts to meet students' needs without relying on special education services, except when students clearly needed that extra assistance.

With much excitement and a little anxiety, the teachers finished their detailed planning. For example, they were a little concerned because grade four would have two new teachers who have not had the opportunity to participate in the planning. In the meantime, Dr. Tompkins lobbied for a few extra resources for the school's innovative plan so that the school could release the teachers for half a school day twice during the next year for evaluation of their efforts and problem solving.

Questions

1. Which characteristics of collaboration can you identify from the teachers' interactions and plans? Which are not evident?

2. How were the teachers working to ensure that their collaborative efforts would be successful? What was Dr. Tompkins's role?

3. How would you respond to Carole? What do you recommend that she do? What do you recommend that her colleagues do in their interactions with her?

4. What forms of collaboration did the teachers plan to try? What are key concepts the teachers should keep in mind related to each form?

5. How could the teachers communicate with parents about their plans? What reactions might they expect from parents? Why? How could they involve parents in their programs?

6. How should the second-grade teachers plan for the year with Stu? What are some responsibilities Stu should have? What are some responsibilities that should not be given to Stu?

Chapter 4

Students with Low-Incidence Exceptionalities

After you read this chapter, you will be able to

1. Describe adaptations that regular classroom teachers can make for students with moderate to severe developmental disabilities, and multiple disabilities.

2. Explain how regular classroom teachers can make accommodations for students with sensory impairments.

3. Outline adaptations that regular classroom teachers can make for students with physical or health disabilities.

4. Describe adaptations that students with autism might need in a regular classroom.

JESSE *is a kindergarten student who has multiple disabilities. He has a moderate developmental disability and mild cerebral palsy. Intellectually, he is functioning at about a three-year-old level. He is learning some basic colours and shapes but is not yet ready to learn letters and sounds. He especially likes the simplified colour-matching game he plays with classmates and the furry puppets sometimes used for storytelling. Jesse uses a wheelchair; he also needs help feeding himself and using the bathroom. His personal assistant or educational assistant ensures that he is moved whenever needed and also attends to his personal care. Jesse's limited speech is difficult to understand, especially when he is excited, and sometimes the other children in the class explain to the teacher, Ms. Cutter, what he is saying since they seem to understand it easily. In fact, the other students have welcomed Jesse and interact with him as with any other classmate, especially after Ms. Cutter explained that Jesse can do many things for himself and does not always need help. When the class is working at learning stations, Jesse participates as much as possible. His puzzles have larger and simpler pieces than the ones other children use, and sometimes he matches shapes instead of learning words; but those and many other adaptations are just part of Jesse being in class. What are the learning characteristics and needs of students such as Jesse? What adaptations does Jesse need to succeed in kindergarten? If Ms. Cutter has a question about Jesse, how can she find an answer?*

TIMOTHY *has a moderate developmental disability. He can read stories written at a grade one level and recognizes many words he sees daily (for example, exit, men, women, sale); socially, he wants to be friends and interact with his peers, but he often does not understand their conversations. In his grade eight science class, he is responsible for only a very small part of the vocabulary and concepts taught. For example, in the unit on chemistry, he learned what oxygen is. His other goal for that unit was related to fire safety: stopping fires by depriving them of oxygen and rules to follow in case of a fire. He did not learn the chemical formulas that other students learned, nor did he write the chemical equations. Although he listens to some of the presentations on topics meaningful to him, since one of his IEP goals is to sit quietly during explanations, he works with a paraprofessional on his objectives for at least part of the class. When other students are completing assignments, he does, too, but his assignments have been specially prepared for him by the resource teacher with input from his science teacher. How are decisions made about what Timothy should be learning in each of his classes? What can Timothy's teacher do to include Timothy in classroom activities?*

MARTINA is in her final year of secondary school. She plans to become a special education teacher some day, and she is studying hard to improve her chances of succeeding at university. Martina has had a profound hearing loss since she was three months old. At that time, she had an extremely high fever that the doctor believes caused her hearing problem. Martina's speaking voice is somewhat difficult to understand, and she receives speech therapy, as she has since she was two years old. Martina did not learn sign language until she began high school. She now prefers signing as a communication approach, and she has an interpreter who accompanies her to core academic classes. Martina's most difficult subject is English. She has problems writing down her ideas logically and elaborating on them. She becomes frustrated and occasionally says maybe she won't try to go to university after all. Her learning assistance teacher is working with her on developing work habits and attitudes that will assist her in university. How do hearing impairments affect learning for students such as Martina? What are Martina's responsibilities for self-advocacy? How can her teachers help her prepare for university?

STUDENTS such as Jesse, Timothy, and Martina have the same rights as other students to be part of the classroom community with non-disabled peers. For Jesse, attending kindergarten with peers prepares him for the demands of school and also of the real world. For Martina, success in university depends on her receiving the strong academic background available in regular education classes. Because of their exceptionalities, however, these and other students in inclusive schools might need specialized equipment or assistance.

Connections: In Chapter 1, all of the categories of exceptionalities are listed and the concept of high- and low-incidence exceptionalities is explained.

Canadian educators are moving away from emphasizing the labels and categories of exceptionality. However, in order to communicate about characteristics and meet student needs it is necessary to name these student characteristics and needs. The *Special Education Policy Manual* of Nova Scotia (1996) asserts that "descriptors should not be used as labels for individual students. Student strengths and needs must be the basis for developing appropriate programs" (p. 20). The *Guide to Education for Students with Special Needs* (Alberta Education, 1995) asserts "The following categories are generally accepted and used for administrative and funding purposes" (p. 24). Keep these cautions in mind while reading and learning about the most common characteristics of students with low-incidence exceptionalities. For our purposes, we usually use the term "cognitive disabilities" when we are referring to people with mild disabilities, and "developmental disabilities" when referring to people with severe disabilities. Definitional characteristics are summarized in Table 4.1.

TABLE 4.1   Students with Low-Incidence Disabilities (About 10 to 15% of Exceptional Students)

Exceptionality	*Definitional Characteristics*
Developmental disabilities	Significant below-average general intellectual functioning with deficits in adaptive behaviour
	Identified between birth and 18 years of age
	Adversely affects educational performance
Multiple disabilities	Two or more disabilities so interwoven that none can be identified as the primary disability
	Adversely affects educational performance
Hearing impairments	Hearing loss is permanent or fluctuating, mild to profound in nature, in one or both ears
	Loss may be referred to as hard of hearing or deaf
	Adversely affects educational performance
Orthopedic impairments	Physically disabling conditions that affect locomotion or motor functions
	May be the result of a congenital anomaly, a disease, an accident, or other causes
	Adversely affects educational performance
Other health impairments	Condition resulting in limited strength, vitality or alertness and caused by chronic or acute health problems
	Adversely affects educational performance
Visual impairments	Vision loss in which student cannot successfully use vision as a primary channel for learning or has such reduced acuity or visual field that processing information visually is significantly inhibited and specialized materials or modifications are needed
	Adversely affects educational performance
Deaf-blindness	Presence of both a vision and a hearing disability that causes severe communication and related problems
	Adversely affects educational performance
Autism	Developmental disability characterized by impairments in communication, learning, and reciprocal social interactions
	Usually identified in infancy or early childhood
	Adversely affects educational performance
Traumatic brain injury	Impairments manifested by limited strength, vitality, alertness, or other impaired development resulting from a traumatic brain injury
	Adversely affects educational performance
Fetal alcohol syndrome	Impairments manifested by delayed growth, neurological limitations (shown in developmental disabilities or learning disabilities), and characteristic facial features (including a flat midface and small eye slits) resulting from prenatal alcohol exposure

What Are Low-Incidence Exceptionalities?

When you work with students with low-incidence exceptionalities, you will be struck by the diversity of their needs, the range of educational services they access, and the variety of specialists who ensure they receive an appropriate education. Typically, individuals within any of the categories of exceptionality do not exhibit all of the characteristics of that exceptionality, but they display them much more than other students do. The following points can help you keep students' needs and your role in their education in perspective.

First, students with low-incidence exceptionalities together comprise only about 10 to 15 percent of all the students with disabilities in most schools. That means that you probably will teach students with these needs some years but not others, and will make the accommodations described in this chapter for a small number of students.

Second, students with low-incidence exceptionalities have often received some type of special education services from birth or shortly thereafter. They might come to kindergarten already having been in an infant-stimulation program or a preschool program in which their special needs were addressed. You will find that many supports and extensive technical assistance are available for some students with low-incidence exceptionalities.

Third, students with low-incidence exceptionalities need the same basic attention from you that other students do. If you are unsure about a student's needs, rely on the same professional judgment you would use in working with other students. If you encounter difficulty, you can access the technical support that special education professionals offer. Students with some disabilities, especially severe or complex ones, are often accompanied by a paraprofessional, teaching assistant, or personal assistant who might be able to offer insight about responding to the student.

If you learn you will have a student with a low-incidence exceptionality in your classroom, you might have many concerns about meeting that student's needs. The Professional Edge on page 109 features questions you can use to prepare for a student with a low-incidence disability to join your class. The questions address the student's strengths and needs. They also cover domains in which accommodations might be needed. What other questions would you add to these lists?

FYI: One valuable source of information about students with exceptionalities and related topics is your provincial or territorial department or ministry of education.

Connections: The INCLUDE strategy (see Chapter 1) can also guide you through the process of providing appropriate instruction for students with moderate or severe disabilities.

What Adaptations Can You Make for Students with Moderate, Severe, or Multiple Disabilities?

Students with moderate, severe, or multiple disabilities include those with developmental disabilities whose cognitive impairments and adaptive behaviour are so significant and pervasive that considerable support is needed for them to learn. This group also includes students with multiple disabilities; that is, students who have more than one disabling condition. These students typically have a curriculum significantly different from that of other students in your class, but many can still learn in a regular classroom setting and benefit from the social interactions with classmates that occur there.

▼▼▼▼▼▼▼▼▼▼▼▼▼▼▼▼▼▼▼▼▼▼▼▼▼▼

Professional Edge

Questions to Ask When Working with Students with Low-Incidence Exceptionalities

IF you will be teaching a student with a low-incidence exceptionality, you will probably have questions about the student's needs and your responsibilities for helping the student succeed. Here are some key questions you might ask in your conversation with a resource teacher, consultant, or administrator to help both you and the student feel more comfortable.

Student Needs

1. What is the student's area of greatest strength?

2. What activities or rewards does the student most enjoy?

3. What is the student's level of functioning academically, socially/emotionally, behaviourally, and in other domains?

4. Does the student have physical or health needs that require my attention? For example, does the student need to take medication? Does the student tire easily? Does the student need assistance in moving from place to place?

Student Goals

1. What are the three or four most important instructional goals for this student in my class? What are the academic, social/emotional, or other goals?

2. What are the goals for this student in each subject (for elementary teachers)?

3. What are the goals that this student is working on all day long?

Student Supports and Accommodations

1. If I have a question about the student, who is my primary contact person? How do I reach that person?

2. Does the student have an assistant or interpreter? If there is an assistant, what are his or her major responsibilities? Can that person also help other students in the class?

3. What other services (for example, speech/language services) will the student access? How often? Who will be in touch about arranging these services? Will they be delivered in the classroom or in another location?

4. Do I need to adapt the physical environment for this student? How?

5. Do I need to adapt my expectations for this student because of physical or health needs? How? Are there restrictions on this student's participation in any class activities?

6. How can I adapt my teaching approach to accommodate the student's needs?

◤ Students with Moderate to Severe Developmental Disabilities

Students with moderate to severe developmental disabilities are significantly limited in their cognitive abilities and adaptive skills and have ongoing needs for intensive supports during their school years and into adult life. Most provinces use scores on intelligence tests and adaptive behaviour scales to determine the

Connections: Information on assessing students' cognitive abilities and adaptive behaviours is described in Chapter 8.

presence of this disability, but many in the field are beginning to argue that a more appropriate strategy would be to define the disability on the basis of student needs for services (Beirne-Smith, Patton, & Ittenbach, 1994). For example, Jeffreys of Windsor Community Living Support Services and Gall of the University of Lethbridge argue for "evolving service from 'just in case' to 'just in time'" (1996, p. 22). The Ontario Ministry of Education and Training's (1995a) proposed definition for "developmental disability" is "varying degrees of general intellectual ability such that significant curriculum modification and support services for academic learning are required. Some students will also require support to develop social skills and independent living skills" (p. 11).

Generally, students with moderate or severe developmental disabilities have several noticeable characteristics (Alper & Ryndak, 1992). First, their rate of learning is exceptionally slow. Because these students are limited in the amount of information they can learn, it is crucial to emphasize skills that will help them live independently as adults. Such skills include those related to living and working in the community and to choosing appropriate recreational activities (York, Vandercook, & Stave, 1990). Second, students with moderate and severe developmental disabilities have difficulty maintaining their skills without ongoing practice. This means teachers should stress skills they will use both in and outside of school. Third, students in this group have difficulty generalizing skills learned in one setting or situation to another setting or situation. Thus, they must learn as many skills as possible in context. For example, rather than asking students to practise buttoning and unbuttoning out of context, encourage them to apply this skill in the morning and afternoon as they enter and leave school wearing coats or sweaters. An additional challenge facing students with moderate to severe cognitive disabilities is combining small skills into a larger one. For example, a student may be taught each step involved in making a sandwich, but unless the steps are taught in an integrated way, the student will probably have difficulty carrying them out in a logical sequence.

Helen is a young woman with **Down syndrome,** a condition that often includes a moderate developmental disability. She attended elementary school with her peers even though she did not always learn the same things they were learning. Her teachers expected her to behave appropriately, and her peers helped her when she became confused by classroom directions. In junior high school, she participated with peers in co-taught science and social studies and in elective classes such as foods and computers, and she received some of her reading and math instruction in a resource room. In high school, she took several classes, including choir, vocal music, history, home economics, career exploration, and family living. She also participated in a cooperative education work experience program so she would be ready to get a job after high school. At age 21, Helen graduated from high school. She now works in a local medical office. Her job includes duplicating medical records, doing simple filing tasks, running errands, and preparing to send mail. Helen's success as an adult is largely the result of learning many skills fostered in inclusive schools.

Two principles usually guide instruction for students with moderate or severe developmental disabilities (Ford, Davern, & Schnorr, 1990). The first is the principle of a **functional curriculum,** wherein the goals for students are based on real-life skills they need to succeed. For example, such a student might benefit

✓ **Your Learning:** What are the general characteristics of students with moderate or severe developmental disabilities?

Cultural Awareness: In rural areas, parents of children with severe or multiple disabilities face the problem of isolation. They are likely to be the only parents in the area with a child with complex needs, and they may not have a network to provide support and information. Advances in telecommunications can help alleviate this dilemma.

more from learning to wait in line than learning to write a story, since waiting in line is a behaviour that most adults practise regularly. Some of the most important job skills that Helen learned during her school career were punctuality, following multiple-step directions, and keeping her voice appropriately low.

The second principle is that education should be **community-based;** that is, it should relate what is learned in school to what occurs in the community. For example, in a unit on the economy, a community-based activity might include going to a bank. A lesson on the local community might include learning about the public library, and exploring job possibilities in local restaurants, hotels, businesses, and other establishments. Part of Helen's community-based instruction included learning how to ride the bus from her home to her job.

The skills and confidence gained in community-based education may be critical to the later inclusion of adults with developmental disabilities in community life and to their autonomy and mental health. In an interview study of 23 adults with disabilities, half of whom had developmental disabilities, Lord (1991) of Kitchener, Ontario found that personal empowerment or taking charge of their own lives always occurred in the context of the community. Participants who demonstrated personal empowerment "were involved in community organizations, self-help groups and other aspects of community life" (1991, p. 75). In her work fostering independent living and empowerment, Carpenter of Toronto also asserts the importance of community and of education: "access to information and knowledge of how best to use it is the key to empowerment" (1988, p. 4).

Instructional Adaptations for Students with Moderate to Severe Developmental Disabilities

Most successful inclusive programs use many strategies and many variations of them, as you can see in the Case in Practice. In fact, many of the adaptations and general school conditions needed by students with moderate and severe disabilities are the same ones that make learning more successful for all students, as the following list illustrates.

Clarify expectations and use instructional approaches that match those expectations.   As a teacher, you should know what a student is expected to learn, regardless of whether that student has a disability. For example, in a social studies class, the goal for a student with a moderate developmental disability might be to understand that mountains are high and valleys are low, while the goal for other students might be to understand detailed topographical maps. A fundamental ingredient for adaptation is to make learning standards appropriate for the student as well as a natural part of the instructional environment. You should work with a special educator or consultant to arrange learning activities suitable for reaching those standards using age-appropriate materials (Giangreco, Dennis, Cloninger, Edelman, & Schattman, 1993; Stainback & Stainback, 1988). One detailed system designed by the Canadian researchers Forest and Lusthaus (1990) accomplishes this planning by examining the overall goals for the student and clarifying expectations that should exist all day (for example, approaching adults and peers without hugging them) as well as those for specific subject areas (for example, choosing between two items during math).

Do It! With a classmate, generate ideas for making an elementary or secondary curriculum area more functional and community-based. Share your ideas with others in class.

Connections: Additional instructional adaptations for students with moderate or severe disabilities are suggested in Chapters 9 to 11.

✓ **Your Learning:** How does meeting the needs of students with moderate or severe disabilities in your class help you meet the needs of your other students?

Use heterogeneous classroom groups.   Most professionals who write about adapting general education classrooms to include students with moderate and severe disabilities stress the importance of strategies such as peer tutoring, cooperative learning, and friend support systems in classrooms with a heterogeneous group of learners, including a few students with disabilities (Wisniewski & Alper, 1994). By structuring your teaching so that students work with each other, you foster a sense of classroom community and help students learn to value and respect their classmates with disabilities as individuals (Beveridge, 1997; York, Vandercook, MacDonald, Heise-Neff, & Caughey, 1992).

Identify optimal times for specialized instruction.   Students with moderate or severe disabilities sometimes need to learn skills that are unlikely to arise as part of the traditional school curriculum. For example, a grade five student who needs to learn to tie her shoes is unlikely to have many opportunities to do so when she is with her peers. However, if a peer works with her as classmates are entering the room during the morning or for a few minutes between lunch and the beginning of afternoon activities, critical instruction can occur without the need for teaching shoe-tying out of context in an isolated setting.

Enlist natural support systems.   Peers, older students, parent volunteers, student teachers, interns, and other individuals at school can all assist a student with a moderate or severe disability (York & Vandercook, 1990). Peers can often answer simple questions or respond to basic requests without adult intervention. In some cases, they understand their classmate with a disability better than adults do. Older students can serve as peer tutors or special buddies, both for instruction and for the development of appropriate social skills.

Connections: In Chapter 2, you learned about strategies for communicating with parents of students with disabilities. Such strategies can foster a positive educational experience for students with moderate or severe disabilities.

Create a collaborative effort with families.   When you teach a student with a moderate or severe disability, you should communicate regularly with the student's parents. Families know their children better than school professionals do, and parents can provide valuable information about teaching them (Thousand & Villa, 1990). They might also have questions about how to reinforce skills learned at school at home. Occasionally, you will encounter a family that does not want to be actively involved in the education of their child. In these cases, you must accept their decision without judging it.

Take advantage of assistive technology.   Consider, for example, the many low-tech and high-tech means for enhancing communication. Many students who cannot use language to communicate use various forms of **augmentative communication;** that is, alternative communication forms that enable students to convey their message. Augmentative communication can be either simple or complex, as shown in the Technology Notes.

Multiple Disabilities

The needs of students with multiple disabilities can be extraordinary. Most students with multiple disabilities have a cognitive delay and a physical or sensory impairment. Jesse, the kindergarten student you met at the beginning of this

Case in Practice

Teaching a Student with a Moderate Developmental Disability

GABRIEL is a student in grade one with a moderate developmental disability. He is a member of Ms. Biernat's class for about three-quarters of the school day. During the late morning, he receives intensive instruction from a resource teacher or speech therapist. Gabriel is functioning at about a three-year-old level. He knows his name, colour words, and some functional words such as *exit* and *boys*. Gabriel's speech is indistinct. For the word *big*, he says "bi-i-"; for the word *orange*, he says, "o-onge." However, Gabriel is also learning sign language and knows many words in sign. Gabriel thoroughly enjoys being in grade one with other students and enthusiastically participates in activities with them. He has a tendency, however, to shout instead of using words or signs as a means of interacting, and when he becomes excited, as sometimes happens climbing the monkey bars at recess, he has accidental bowel movements.

Ms. Biernat says the following about Gabriel: "He's a real charmer. When I first met him, he looked so scared and little. I realized that even though I was worried about Gabriel being in my class, he was nearly terrified about joining a large class group. I've learned that there are some things about Gabriel that I have to attend to. For example, he doesn't like changes in anything. On days that we have a school program in the auditorium, I have to tell him several times what is going to happen and remind other students to help him as we go to and from the program. I still need to stay close in case he panics. At least, he gives me clear cues. If he sits down on the floor and yells "No!" I know I've pushed him past the limits of his ability to change.

"In class, one problem I've had to deal with is his tendency to yell. When he wants to tell someone something, he tends to get louder and louder. The students and I know that saying 'Sign it, Gabe' is the right way to respond. We also start asking him questions he can answer with one word or a sign. That helps.

"Gabe can be as mischievous as any other student. The other day in math he was supposed to be finding all the fives on the page while the other students were computing answers to the addition problems. Instead, Gabe began systematically dropping his crayons in the space between the desks. When I stopped him, he grinned. He had definitely done it just to get attention.

"I've learned a lot from Gabe and I know the other students have, too. There are definitely days when I can't think of the right adaptations for him, but the resource teacher or paraprofessional always has an idea. It helps when the speech therapist comes to class, too. She has been very helpful in showing me how to encourage Gabe to use both signs and speech and to do it without making a big deal. Gabe knows his name and address, he matches colour words and a few functional words, and he can count to five and match objects to numbers. He is interested in everything that we do in social studies and science. With support from the special educators, Gabe is having a successful grade one experience, and I'm learning a lot about meeting student needs."

Reflections

What are the strengths and needs that Gabriel brings to his grade one classroom? If you were Gabriel's teacher, what questions would you ask about his educational program? What other situations might cause Gabriel to panic in the way that can occur during school programs without careful advance planning and intervention? How is Ms. Biernat ensuring that Gabriel is a full member of grade one? How is Ms. Biernat drawing on special education professionals as resources to support Gabriel's instructional program in grade one?

chapter, has a cognitive disability and a physical disability. The needs of these students and the adaptations that will help them succeed can be similar to those for students with moderate and severe developmental disabilities, differences being a matter of degree and complexity. For example, in one school integrating students with multiple disabilities into general education classes, the primary challenges teachers faced included the following:

- Providing a functional curriculum within the context of the regular education classroom
- Providing community-based instruction for all students
- Scheduling staff coverage
- Promoting social integration between students with multiple disabilities and other students (Hamre-Nietupski, McDonald, & Nietupski, 1992)

Because many students with multiple disabilities have limited speech and do not easily convey their preferences and needs, communicating with them can be a challenge. One strategy for communication includes the use of augmentative communication systems—the same systems that students with moderate or severe developmental disabilities sometimes use.

✔ **Your Learning:** What questions would you add to the lists on page 109 if you were going to teach a student with multiple disabilities?

As a teacher, you can expect that some but probably not all students with multiple disabilities will participate in regular education activities in your school. They are likely to receive considerable support from a special education teacher or a paraprofessional who thus becomes available for co-teaching and other class-wide integration activities. These professionals and other members of the multidisciplinary team can assist you in setting expectations for students, planning appropriate educational experiences, monitoring their performance, and problem solving when concerns arise. In an elementary school, a student with multiple disabilities might attend your class for part of the day and also receive some services in a resource room, especially if a specific service needs to be delivered privately to preserve student dignity (for example, an exercise that must be practised as part of physical therapy). In a secondary school, a student with multiple disabilities might attend some core classes with peers and spend part of the school day learning to function in the broader community and to perform job-specific skills.

Deaf-Blindness

FYI: Marjorie Wood (1903–1988) was the founder of Canada's first Braille magazine for the deaf-blind, called *Dots and Taps*. Born in Vancouver, she became deaf and blind at the age of seven due to an illness. She raised three children, was a consultant to the Canadian National Institute for the Blind from 1957 to 1971, and was awarded the Order of Canada in 1976. Her autobiography is called *Trudging Up Life's Three-Sensed Highway*.

Students with a dual-sensory impairment have extraordinary needs related to staying in touch with the environment, making sense of events that most teachers and students take for granted, and learning without access to vision and hearing (Rikhye, Gothelf, & Appell, 1989). These students sometimes have average or above-average intelligence (as did Marjorie Wood and Helen Keller), but they often have cognitive or other disabilities. Although a student with **deaf-blindness** might attend the school where you teach, he or she is unlikely to be a member of your class for academic instruction without extensive supports. What is more likely is that you might include this student, along with a special education teacher or personal assistant, on some field trips, at assemblies, in selected class activities, or for particular school programs. The specialists working with the student can prepare both you and your students, letting you know how to approach

vidual students, only used for administrative purposes. In the Northwest Territories, programs are to build on student strengths. Increasingly, we are attempting to guarantee exceptional students the advantages of identification (appropriate services) without the disadvantages (labels).

Placement

In the past, placement referred to the settings for a pupil's educational program. With inclusion, the regular classroom in the neighbourhood school has become the first choice unless this has proven unsuccessful in the individual case. Writers have argued that what is important is that students are accepted and participate as full members of regular classrooms. We now describe programs in terms of the needs they meet rather than their locations. Meeting needs and full acceptance have begun to replace the previous emphasis on placement.

Participation of Parents

Parents are viewed as partners in the education of exceptional students. Nova Scotia describes parents as knowledgeable about the exceptionalities of their children and their primary advocates. Decisions are to be reached by mutual agreement among team members, including parents. One of Saskatchewan's Guiding Principles is that parent/guardian involvement is critical to planning appropriate educational programs, and Quebec requires parental participation. You will learn the expectations for parental participation in your province and find ways to involve parents as partners.

Service Delivery

Service delivery refers to the provision of appropriate educational and disability-related services. To describe an individual planning process, most provinces use the term "Individual Education Plan" (IEP) (Prince Edward Island, Manitoba, the Yukon, Ontario, British Columbia, the Northwest Territories, and Quebec). Three provinces (Nova Scotia, Alberta, and Newfoundland) use the expression, "Individual Program Plan" (IPP). New Brunswick refers to a "Special Education Plan" and Saskatchewan to a "Personal Program Plan." Each consists of a plan to adapt materials, instruction, assessment, and, perhaps, the curriculum. You may feel apprehensive when you first develop an IEP. However, an IEP is not necessarily long and most can be documented in one page.

What Is Inclusive Education and Why Is It Controversial?

There are many signs of the growing movement to ensure access and full participation in all aspects of Canadian society for persons with disabilities. On one hand, the development of inclusive schools reflects a movement that is evident

Do It! Review your local newspaper for articles on inclusion. What viewpoints are expressed? Does your local school district have a written set of guidelines on inclusion? How could you find out?

Do It! Participate in a class debate that presents alternative views on inclusion. What are your own beliefs about your responsibility to teach students who may not be able to meet traditional classroom expectations?

in all parts of Canadian society. On the other hand, schools play a unique role in educating individuals with disabilities so they can take roles as educated adults, and in educating people without disabilities to accept and foster inclusion. A recent publication by the federal Office for Disability Issues suggests, "Attitudes can be the most difficult barrier persons with disabilities must face in gaining full integration, acceptance and participation in society" (1997, p. 1).

Many have argued that inclusion is a value judgment. Fullwood (1990), an Australian educator, makes a persuasive case that inclusion is about people with disabilities having the same chances and choices in life as other people to participate in activities and become members of communities. She focuses on both physical and social relationships, where physical refers to people being in the same places, participating in the same activities, and social refers to people interacting and being interdependent. Canadian writers have argued, "A major goal of inclusive education is to integrate all children and ensure that they have fair and equal access to normal school experiences. This type of educational system regards all children as equally accepted members of heterogeneous classrooms" (Andrews & Lupart, 1993, p. 9). The emphasis on acceptance is also evident in American writing on inclusive education. Stainback and Stainback (1992) wrote that the goal in inclusive schools is that

> all students, including those who have been labeled severely and profoundly mentally and physically disabled, chronically disruptive, typical, gifted, or at risk, are accepted as equal members, recognized for what they have to offer to the school community, and provided an appropriate educational program and any necessary supports (p. xi).

Inclusive education is a relatively new term, replacing terms such as mainstreaming from the 1970s and integration from the 1980s. The two earlier terms emphasized returning students from segregated and marginal settings to classrooms in the mainstream. The emphasis in inclusive society is not on the placement, but on participation. The intent is not that people are returned to inclusive settings, but that they are always included; as preschoolers, they attend daycare and preschool with the other children in their community; they play in the neighbourhood, and join community activities; at all ages they are preparing for full adult participation in employment and all other aspects of a democratic society. In Canada, the context for discussions about inclusion is society.

FYI: In *pullout* or *withdrawal programs*, students leave the regular classroom to receive specialized services. Resource teachers often offer pullout programs, but so do speech therapists, occupational and physical therapists, counsellors, and even remedial teachers.

The practice of inclusive education has thus far proved an elusive goal in schools. This may be because our social values precede our knowledge about how best to accomplish these goals. Some wonder if we have found inclusion so challenging because we haven't put adequate human and financial resources into our efforts so far. Others suggest inclusive education may be harder to realize in large, departmentalized secondary schools than in neighbourhood elementary schools. Controversies abound about inclusive schooling. Two American critiques of inclusive education are the book called *The Illusion of Full Inclusion* (Kauffman & Hallahan, 1995) and the article, "Inclusive Schools Movement and the Radicalization of Special Education Reform" (Fuchs & Fuchs, 1994). Both argue against what they call "full inclusion." They acknowledge that the inclusive classroom may meet the needs of students with severe disabilities for social development. However, they argue that full inclusion does not provide instruction that is intense enough to meet the needs of students with high-incidence mild disabilities,

Case in Practice

Problem Solving in Inclusive Schools: The Classroom Teacher's Role

At Highland Elementary School, staff members are meeting to discuss David, a grade three student with autism. Ms. Dowley is David's teacher; Ms. Jackson is the special educator who provides needed support. Ms. Janes, the school psychologist, is also present.

MS. DOWLEY: David is really a puzzle and a challenge. He is doing so much better at being in class than he was at the beginning of the year, but he can still disrupt the entire class when he tantrums. One of the parents called yesterday to complain about David taking time away from her daughter and the rest of the class. I'm starting to feel the same way. I hope we can come up with some ideas to improve the whole situation.

MS. JACKSON: What kinds of things seem to trigger the tantrums?

MS. DOWLEY: That's part of the problem. I'm still pretty new at teaching and I have my hands full with the whole class. I don't even have time to think carefully about what's happening with David. I just deal with him when a problem occurs.

MS. JANES: The tantrums seem like a serious problem, but before we start addressing them, are there other things we should be discussing, too?

MS. DOWLEY: No. Right now, it's the tantrums—and I want to be clear that I really can see all the other gains David has made. I *want* this to work for David. I know inclusion is right for him if we can just deal with this problem.

MS. JANES: It seems like we need more information. One question I have is this. What happens with you and the other students when David has a tantrum?

MS. DOWLEY: Well, I try to ignore him, but that usually makes it worse. A few of the other students laugh, and that's not helping, either.

MS. JACKSON: Maybe we should focus for a minute or two on when David doesn't tantrum. What are the times of the day or the activities that David does without having behaviour problems?

MS. DOWLEY: Let's see . . . He's usually fine and makes a good contribution when we're talking about science concepts. He loves science. If math is activity-based, he's fine there, too.

MS. JANES: Our meeting time is nearly up. I'd be happy to make time in my schedule to observe David, and perhaps Ms. Jackson could, too. I know you need answers right away, but I hope we can get a clearer sense of the pattern to David's behaviour so we can find the right strategy for addressing it. If we can get in to observe this week, could we meet next Tuesday to try to generate some strategies?

MS. DOWLEY: Sure. That would be great. Let's just work out the details on observing.

Reflections

Why was this meeting a positive example of teachers addressing a student problem in an inclusive school? What did they do that has set them up for success? If you were trying to understand David better, what other questions would you ask about him? What do you think will happen at the next meeting? On the basis of this case, how would you describe the role of classroom teachers in addressing the challenges of inclusion?

such as learning disabilities. Recent research suggests that approaches such as collaborative learning are effective strategies for inclusion (e.g., Putnam, 1993), and there are many accounts of exceptional learners achieving acceptance and learning successfully in inclusive classrooms (e.g., Harris, 1994; Hutchinson, in press).

An Analysis of the Inclusion Debate

✓ **Your Learning:** What impact have provincial policies had on exceptional education? How has the teaching of students with disabilities changed over the years?

As you read professionals' views on inclusion, you might notice that several related themes run through them. These themes include inclusion as a philosophical issue, as a social value issue, as an economic issue, and as an instructional issue. We believe that services for exceptional students will continue to change rapidly and that past programs have been valuable steps in the evolution of effective education, but they are quickly becoming obsolete because of issues in the inclusion debate. Given appropriate supports, most exceptional students can receive much or all of their education in the regular classroom. The Case in Practice illustrates how classroom teachers, special educators, and other school staff members can make inclusion successful by working together. However, a few students, because of the nature of their individual needs, require occasional or ongoing separate programming. And what is most clear is that we must continue to commit financial and other resources to ensure that exceptional students receive quality education.

Who are Exceptional Students?

Connections: More complete descriptions of the characteristics and needs of students with disabilities and other exceptionalities are found in Chapters 4, 5, and 6.

At this point you may be wondering who are these exceptional students that we have discussed throughout this chapter. Here we will introduce you to some specific types or categories of exceptionality. As we have seen, with the ascendance of inclusion, many provinces and territories are downplaying the identification of the particular type of exceptionality, avoiding labelling, and focusing on the individual needs of students. While reading the following generic descriptions, it is important to remember that we are discussing children and adolescents, but they *are* children and adolescents with characteristics that require us to adapt our teaching and other aspects of our classroom interactions with them. They *are not* their exceptionalities, but sometimes using the accepted expressions to describe their characteristics and learning will make it easier for us to communicate. For example, when we read that Nicki, described in the opening of the chapter, has an emotional disability, we know that the ways we can expect to adjust our teaching will most likely have to do with her self-control, which sets different expectations for us than if we were teaching Amber, who is blind and needs adaptations that replace all printed material with Braille and auditory or hearing formats. It is also important to remember that the specific definitions vary across jurisdictions, and when you begin teaching you will be introduced to the definitions used in your province or territory.

Categories of Exceptionalities

Students who are gifted or developmentally advanced.   Students who demonstrate ability far above average in one or several areas including specific academic subjects, overall intellectual ability, leadership, creativity, athletics, or the visual or performing arts are considered gifted. Erin is included in this group; she seems to learn anything new without effort, and she is also eager to learn about almost everything. Evan is also gifted; still in elementary school, he has par-

Some general modifications will also help a student with a visual impairment in your classroom. Meet with the itinerant vision specialist or other resource persons to discuss the student's needs and the extent of assistance required. Based on that information, some or many of these accommodations might be appropriate: Assign a buddy to assist the student at the beginning of the school year, and discontinue the buddy later in the school year to avoid creating unneeded dependence. Some students with visual impairments need additional time to complete assignments or the task needs to be shortened or otherwise modified. Be alert for a student's need for a change-of-pace activity. A student who is fidgeting or refusing to work might be fatigued, which is a common problem for students who must make extraordinary efforts to learn using vision. Allowing the student to take a break or substitute an alternative activity both helps the student and prevents discipline problems. Also keep in mind how to plan alternative learning opportunities for students. A vision specialist will help you develop such alternative learning opportunities. Many provinces have resource guides in specific areas of exceptionality. For example, the Ontario Ministry of Education (1987) published *Vision: Resource Guide*.

Assistive Technology for Students with Visual Impairments

Students with visual impairments use a wide variety of assistive technology to facilitate their learning. If they have some residual vision, they can use devices to help them acquire information visually. Some use simple devices such as magnifying lenses or bright light in order to read or do other schoolwork. Others might hold their books close to their eyes or at an unusual angle in order to see the print. Students with more severe visual impairments access information using computers that can magnify words and pictures many times, computers that convert speech to print or that change type words to Braille symbols, and specially tape-recorded textbooks. New computer devices are being developed and the technology is changing quickly.

FYI: Some students with vision impairments use a Perkins Braillewriter, a specialized mechanical device that works similarly to a typewriter but types in Braille.

Do It! Contact the Disabilities Office of your university to arrange to observe the devices that are available for use by students with visual impairment.

Accommodations for Students with Hearing Impairments

Students with hearing losses have the same range of cognitive ability as other students. However, if intelligence is assessed using a test based on language, they might have depressed scores. Academically, many students struggle because their hearing loss affects their ability to understand language, which affects their learning. Martina, the student with a hearing impairment introduced at the beginning of the chapter, finds this problem especially frustrating. Students might have difficulty learning vocabulary and as a result understanding the materials they read and the lessons you present. For example, students with hearing impairments often miss subtle meanings of words, which can affect both their learning and their social interactions. One simple example can illustrate the complexity of learning language. Think of all the meanings of the word *can*. As a noun, it refers to a metal container, or is slang for bathroom and prison; as a verb, it refers to being physically able, preserving vegetables, or being fired from one's job.

Connections: Self-advocacy skills for all students, including those with hearing impairments, are presented in Chapter 10.

Socially and emotionally, students with hearing impairments are often immature. This lack of maturity occurs for two reasons. First, these students cannot listen to others and model what they say and do. Second, they can become confused in interactions that involve many people and multiple conversations. Because these types of situations are often uncomfortable for them, they sometimes avoid them and fail to develop the social skills needed in group interactions. For example, Jim is a grade seven student with a moderate hearing impairment in Mr. George's science class. When students work in lab groups, Jim tends to "tune out" because he cannot follow what everyone is saying. Sometimes he tries to participate in the activity, but he often does so by making an exaggerated face or drawing a cartoon even when the other students are working intently. They become annoyed with his antics and Jim withdraws from the group and becomes passive. Mr. George ensures that he monitors the group's work, and reminds his students that unless every group member understands a science experiment, the group is not finished. Jim also receives help on his social interactions in a support group led by a social worker.

Accommodations for students with hearing impairments emphasize helping them use whatever residual hearing they may have and accessing language to promote formal and informal learning.

FYI: Even the best speech readers get only about 25 percent of a spoken communication. Most individuals receive only 5 to 10 percent of spoken communication using this strategy.

Because many students with hearing impairments get some information through **speech reading,** or watching others' lips, mouth, and expressions, teachers should always face the class when presenting information and stand where no glare or shadow would make it difficult for a student to see. They should also stand in one location instead of moving around the room. The student should sit close to them. These adjustments facilitate speech reading but are also necessary if an interpreter is present. Teachers should avoid exaggerating

▶ *This student with a hearing impairment and teacher are using American Sign Language. In what other ways might they communicate? What technologies might they use to receive instruction? What would be the advantage of using an FM amplification system?*

Technology Notes

Learning Tools for Students with Visual Impairments

STUDENTS with visual impairments can benefit from various learning tools. The following list describes some of the available technology that your students who have visual impairments might use.

- **Large-print books.** Books printed in extra-large type.
- **Braille books.** Books using Braille, a language system of raised dots that students read with their fingers.

- **Tape-recorded texts.** Sound-cued tape recordings that permit students to find their way through heard text.
- **Opticon.** Device that magnifies print.
- **Braillewriter.** Specialized machine or computer keyboard with Braille characters.
- **Slate and stylus.** System for manually writing in Braille by puncturing paper.
- **Kurzweil reading machine.** Computer that scans print and reads it aloud.

▶ *A student with a visual impairment uses specialized books and equipment.*

sounds or words; doing this makes comprehension more difficult for the student, not easier. Because some students with hearing impairments do not use speech reading, and even those who do will get only part of the message that way, teachers should use as many visual aids as possible. Important directions can be written on the chalkboard, either with words or, for younger students, pictures. Major points in a lecture for older students can be written on an overhead projector or on the chalkboard. With an overhead projector, the teacher can face students while writing, thus enabling students with hearing impairments to speech read. If teachers talk and write on a chalkboard at the same time, students with hearing impairments can become confused because they cannot see the teacher's lips or facial expressions.

If a student with a hearing impairment speaks to you and you do not understand what has been said, ask the student to repeat the information. If you still do not understand or the student becomes frustrated, switching to paper and pencil is sometimes appropriate. When a student appears confused following directions or answering a question you have asked, the difficulty might be vocabulary. Try using a simpler word as a substitute or offering a word you think the student might be trying to convey. Above all, be patient when communicating with students who have hearing impairments.

As with students with visual impairments, safety also needs to be kept in mind. Assigning a buddy to assist the student during a fire drill is a simple strat-

✓ **Your Learning:** What are some adaptations that teachers can make to help students with hearing impairments succeed in their classrooms?

Case in Practice

Including Students with Hearing Impairments

MS. SKINNER is a grade five teacher at Lunar Elementary School. This year in her class of 31 students she has two students with hearing impairments. The girls, who are twins, have had profound hearing loss since birth. Since they use sign language as their primary means of communication, they are accompanied by Ms. Mohammed, their interpreter.

Ms. Skinner discussed what it is like to teach in this class: "When I first heard I was going to get Jenna and Janice this year, I was worried. I knew they'd been in grade four and done well, but there's so much more curriculum at this level. I didn't know how I was going to teach everything and also do all the work necessary for Jenna and Janice. As it turned out, it hasn't been much of an adjustment at all. Ms. Mohammed interprets for the girls, and she adds further explanations if they need it. The hardest part for me was learning to stand in one place when I talk—for a teacher like me, who is constantly moving around the room, that has been very difficult. Ms. Mohammed has taught all of us some basic signs—that puts us all in touch. Jenna and Janice have some serious academic problems mostly related to vocabulary, but the other kids just think of them as classmates. I've learned a lot this year. I'm a lot more confident that I really can teach any student who comes through my door!"

Reflections

Why might teachers be worried about having students such as Jenna and Janice in their classrooms? What is the best way to overcome this worry? What might be particularly challenging for you if you had students such as Jenna and Janice in your classroom? How would you help them compensate for their difficulty in vocabulary? What do you imagine is the impact of having an interpreter in a classroom most of the time? What might the interpreter need from you in order to feel comfortable? What type of assistance might you ask from the twins' parents to help them master the subjects you will be teaching?

egy for addressing this issue. For other specific adaptations regarding safety, a hearing specialist will assist you.

If a student with a hearing impairment uses sign language, you might consider enrolling in a sign class yourself and inviting a deaf education teacher to your class to teach some signs to the entire group. Students generally enjoy this experience, and both you and they will be better able to communicate with the student who cannot hear. In the Case in Practice, you can learn a little more about what it is like to teach a student with a hearing impairment.

Adaptive Devices for Students with Hearing Impairments

Students with some residual hearing are likely to use amplification devices such as hearing aids. If you have a student who wears a hearing aid, you should be alert for signs of inattention that might signal the hearing aid is not turned on or the battery needs to be replaced. Other students might use an FM system consisting of a microphone worn by the teacher and a receiver worn by the student. When the teacher talks, the sound is converted into electrical energy carried on a specific radio frequency through the air. The receiver converts the electrical energy back to sound, amplifies it, and sends it to the student's ear.

Both hearing aids and FM systems amplify sounds, but they do not discriminate important sounds such as the teacher's voice from other sounds. Thus, a student wearing hearing aids can be distracted by the amplified noise of someone typing on the computer keyboard, or chairs scraping on the floor. A student using an FM device will also receive the sounds from a teacher's fingering the microphone. Any of these extraneous noises can interfere with the student's understanding of spoken information and can be distracting to learning. Amplification clearly assists some students with hearing impairments, but it also has limits.

Students who have a severe or profound hearing impairment often use sign language. Sometimes they use **American Sign Language (ASL),** a separate language not based on standard English grammar and structures. Learning ASL is somewhat like learning Spanish, French, or another language. Other students will use **Signed Exact English (SEE);** that is, spoken English converted to a set of signs. Students will sometimes use **finger spelling,** in which every letter of a word is spelled out. For example, finger spelling is needed for names or technical terms for which no signs exist.

Students who use sign language are often accompanied by an interpreter who translates your words and those of classmates into sign language. The interpreter needs to sit facing the student and near you so that the student can both watch you and follow the interpreter. Some older students also use a note-taker (who could be a classmate) since they cannot both watch an interpreter and a teacher and take notes. Even if a student uses an interpreter, however, you should speak directly to the student when asking questions, giving directions, or otherwise conversing. Do not speak to the interpreter instead of the student. The interpreter will ensure that the student understands what you said. Also keep in mind that interpreters need breaks; you might be asked to make small changes in your instructional pattern to ensure that the interpreter can take a break without negatively affecting student learning.

FYI: Some people who are deaf believe that deafness is its own culture, and ASL is its language. They discourage students from using oral language and encourage them to communicate through sign language.

Do It! Ask an experienced sign language interpreter to discuss this professional occupation with you. Be sure to ask how teachers can help make interpreters' jobs easier.

◤ **What Adaptations Can You Make for Students with Physical or Health Disabilities?**

Some students have physical disorders, chronic or acute medical problems, or health impairments that interfere with their learning. Three categories of disabilities can be loosely grouped in this area: orthopedic impairments, other health impairments, and traumatic brain injury. **Orthopedic impairments** are diseases or disorders related to the bones, joints, or muscles. **Other health impairments** include medical or health conditions such as AIDS, seizure disorders, asthma, and fetal alcohol syndrome. **Traumatic brain injury** is any insult to the brain caused by an external force and includes injuries sustained in auto accidents and during play. Because students in these groups have disabilities because of physical or health problems resulting from a wide variety of causes, they have many different levels of cognitive ability and academic achievement and can have needs that range from mild to severe.

Orthopedic Impairments

The largest group of students with orthopedic impairments in public schools are those who have **cerebral palsy** (CP) (Sirvis, 1988). Cerebral palsy occurs because of an injury to the brain before or during birth and results in poor motor coordination and abnormal motor patterns. These problems can occur in just the arms or legs, in both the arms and legs, or in a combination of limbs. For some students, CP also affects other muscle groups, such as those controlling the head and neck. Thus, some students with cerebral palsy walk on their toes with their knees close together. They might also hold their arms with their elbows bent and their hands near shoulder height. Other students with CP need braces or a walker to move about. Yet others use wheelchairs. For some students, head supports keep their heads from lolling side to side. Cognitively and academically, students with CP can be gifted, average, or below average, or they might have a cognitive disability or a learning disability. Norman Kunc (pronounced Koontz) has CP and is an advocate for people with disabilities. In his book, *Ready Willing and Disabled* (1984), he provides an account of his experiences when he was integrated into a regular classroom for the first time—in a junior high school in southern Ontario. He provides examples of strategies that teachers can use for students like him who can keyboard but who lack the muscle control to complete assignments with a pen or pencil. Although computers make some tasks easier than when Kunc was in school, recording solutions to math questions and science problems with a computer remains a challenge. I think Kunc's most valuable contribution is to speak from the heart to teachers who long to understand the perspective of the students for whom they are making accommodations.

Another orthopedic impairment is **muscular dystrophy,** a disease that weakens muscles. Students have increasing difficulty walking and otherwise moving actively about. Gradually, they lose their ability to stand and they require a wheelchair. They also fatigue more and more easily. Students with muscular dystrophy usually die during their late teens (Sirvis, 1988). Frank was a student with muscular dystrophy. When he began elementary school, he seemed no different from any other student. However, he returned to school after one summer vacation with a wheelchair that he used when he was tired. By the end of that year, he used the wheelchair all the time. By late grade ten, Frank was too weak to attend school and received instruction from an itinerant teacher at his home. He died in late September of his third year of high school.

A third orthopedic impairment is **spinal cord injury.** As the term implies, these injuries exist when the spinal cord is severely damaged or severed, usually resulting in partial or extensive paralysis (Hardman et al., 1993). Spinal cord injuries are most often the result of automobile or other vehicle accidents. The characteristics and needs of students with this type of injury are often similar to those of students with cerebral palsy. Judy suffered a spinal cord injury in a car accident. She was hospitalized for nearly six months, and when she returned to school she could not walk and had the use of only one arm. She is as bright and articulate as ever and still gets into trouble when she challenges teachers' authority. What has changed is how she moves from place to place. Rick Hansen is a well-known Canadian with spinal cord injury. Your students will have heard of his "Man in Motion Tour."

Cerebral palsy, muscular dystrophy, and spinal cord injuries are just a sample of the range of orthopedic impairments students can have. You are likely to teach students who have physical disabilities caused by amputations or birth defects that resulted in the absence of all or part of a limb. Likewise, you might have a student with **spina bifida,** a birth defect in which an abnormal opening in the spinal column results in some degree of paralysis. Whatever the orthopedic impairment a student has, your responsibility is to learn about the student's needs and work with special education professionals to ensure that those needs are met through various adaptations.

The adaptations you make for students with orthopedic impairments will depend on the nature and severity of the disability and on the students' physical status. These accommodations are outlined in the Professional Edge.

A second area of adaptation to consider for students with orthopedic impairments involves their personal needs (Hardman et al., 1993). Many students become fatigued and might have difficulty attending to learning activities late in the school day. A few take naps or otherwise rest. Other students need to stop during the school day to take medication. Some students need assistance with personal care such as using the bathroom and eating. Students who use wheelchairs might need to reposition themselves because of circulation problems. This repositioning can be done readily for young children, who can be moved to sit or lie on the classroom floor during stories or other activities. Paraprofessionals or teaching assistants typically assume personal-care responsibilities and those related to moving students. If you have questions about these areas, a special educator can assist, or in some cases the student's parent can explain what is needed.

Academically and socially, it is not possible to generalize about student needs. Some students with orthopedic impairments enjoy school and excel in traditional academic areas. Others experience problems in learning. Some are charming and gregarious students who are class leaders; others have a low self-concept and are likely to have problems interacting with peers. If you think about a student such as Judy, the student with a spinal cord injury introduced earlier,

Do It! Rent a wheelchair and try completing many of your daily tasks. What did you learn from this experience?

✔ **Your Learning:** What accommodations will a student with orthopedic impairments be likely to need? Who is responsible for ensuring that these accommodations are made?

▼▼▼▼▼▼▼▼▼▼▼▼▼▼▼▼▼▼▼▼▼▼▼▼▼▼

Professional Edge

Classroom Accommodations for Students with Physical Disabilities

BASIC changes in the environment can help students with physical disabilities move around and learn more effectively at school. If you teach students with physical disabilities, you and your school might need to make these accommodations:

1. **Handrails for students who use crutches or braces.** Handrails can make it possible for a student to move around the classroom and nearby hallways more easily.

2. **Desks or worktables adapted for student needs.** Some students in wheelchairs will have a built-in work space in the form of a lap desk. Others, though, will need to have tables or desks high enough to allow them to position themselves so they can work comfortably.

3. **Wide aisles and walkways.** Students with mobility needs, whether braces or a wheelchair, often need extra space in order to move around. Instead of arranging student desks in traditional rows, put groups of desks together to form worktables, saving space for aisles. Pay particular attention to space around supply shelves or students will not be able to access needed materials.

4. **Chalkboards and bulletin boards.** If you expect students to write at the chalkboard, an accommodation might be needed for a student in a wheelchair. You might lower the boards or provide a slate for the student. If you create activities that are displayed on bulletin boards, students in wheelchairs need to be able to access these as other students do.

5. **Safety issues.** Plans should be in place for emergency drills. In addition, if students with poor fine motor control participate in high school lab classes or shop activities, adapted equipment can be requested or changes in procedures made to eliminate safety concerns. For example, a student might need a beaker with a handle for a surer grip, or a lab partner might be reminded to handle the chemicals. In technological education, adaptations might include teaching specific safety procedures or adapting assignments so that they require less or simplified use of equipment. Special educators or resource teachers usually provide assistance when these types of modifications are needed.

you can imagine that her reaction to her accident and her need to use a wheelchair is influenced by many factors, including her family support system, her self-concept, and her peers' reactions. The suggestions included throughout this text for working with students to help them learn and succeed socially are as applicable to this group of students as to any other.

Other Health Impairments

Students with health impairments often are not immediately apparent to a casual observer. For example, one common group of health impairments is seizure disorders, or **epilepsy,** a physical condition in which the brain experiences sudden but brief changes in functioning. The result is often a lapse of attention or consciousness and uncontrolled motor movements. No specific cause is ever determined for most cases of epilepsy.

Epilepsy can result in different types of seizures. **Generalized tonic-clonic seizures** involve the entire body. A student experiencing a generalized tonic-clonic seizure falls to the ground unconscious; the body stiffens and then begins jerking. Breathing may become shallow, and the student might lose bladder or bowel control. After one or two minutes, the movements stop and the student regains consciousness. Steps you should take if a student has a generalized tonic-clonic seizure are summarized in the Professional Edge.

Other seizures do not involve the entire body. **Absence seizures** occur when students appear to temporarily "blank out" for just a few seconds. If they are walking or running, they might stumble because of their momentary lapse of awareness. If you observe a student with these symptoms, alert the school nurse or another professional who can further assess the student. It is not uncommon for students to attend school for several years before someone realizes that their inability to pay attention is actually the result of a seizure disorder. Epilepsy Ontario has developed *A Resource Kit about Epilepsy* to help teachers inform students (for kindergarten to grade eight) about seizure disorders.

FYI: It is usually indicated on a student's file when a student has a seizure disorder.

FYI: Previously, generalized tonic-clonic seizures were referred to as *grand mal* seizures. Absence (pronounced "ob-sonce") seizures were referred to as *petit mal* seizures.

Professional Edge
What to Do if a Student Has a Seizure

As a teacher in an inclusive school and as a responsible citizen, you should know how to respond if someone has a seizure. Here are the recommended steps from Epilepsy Ontario:

1. Keep calm and reassure the other students. Explain what a seizure is and ask the other children not to cluster around.

2. Clear the area around the student of anything sharp.

3. Ease the student to the floor and loosen any tight neckwear.

4. Protect the student's head and body from injury by putting something soft such as a jacket or blanket under them.

5. *Do* kneel on the floor beside the student. *Do not* hold the student down.

6. *Do* turn the student gently onto his or her side. With the head to the side, the air passage should be open.

7. *Do not* insert anything between the teeth.

8. Stay beside the student until the seizure ends. Ask someone to contact the parents. Be friendly and reassuring as consciousness returns. Allow the child to nap if he or she wishes.

9. Note the length and characteristics of the seizure. Follow your school's procedures; usually after a tonic-clonic seizure, the child should be checked by a physician.

10. If the seizure lasts more than 10 minutes or the student has a second tonic-clonic seizure within a few minutes, call an ambulance.

Source: From *Epilepsy: A Teacher's Guide,* 1992, Toronto, Epilepsy Ontario.

tion and recognizing their social and emotional needs and responding to them (Lynch, Lewis, & Murphy, 1993b). In one study of parents' and educators' perceptions of problems faced by children with chronic illness, parents reported that their children's most frequent problems were feeling different, undergoing constant medical procedures, pain, and facing death. Educators listed absences, falling behind in school, the lack of interaction with peers, school's inability to meet the student's needs, and social adjustment as the most serious problems (Lynch et al., 1993a).

Specific strategies for working with students with health impairments include these:

1. Find out students' most difficult problems and help them work these through. Strategies include having students write or draw about their concerns or referring a student to the school counsellor or social worker as you see a need.
2. Provide materials for the students about others who have a similar disease or disorder. Books, videotapes, movies, and informational materials can help students with health impairments understand how others have successfully coped with their illnesses, and they can be useful for explaining the needs of these students to peers without disabilities.
3. Consider including death education in your curriculum if you have a student with a life-threatening condition such as cancer (Peckham, 1993). A special educator, counsellor, or social worker can probably prepare a unit and help you present it.
4. Work closely with families. Parents can often be the most valuable source of information concerning their child's status and needs. They can also alert you to upcoming changes in medications and emotional problems occurring at home, and they can help their children work on missed school assignments. (Lynch et al., 1993b)

In terms of academic and curricular adaptations, you should respond to students with health impairments as you would to other students with disabilities. Using the INCLUDE strategy, you can identify their needs. If modifications in the environment, curriculum, or instruction are needed, you can carry them out using the suggestions made throughout the remainder of this text.

Traumatic Brain Injury

Traumatic brain injury (TBI) occurs when a student experiences an insult to the head from an external physical force that results in an injury to the brain, often including a temporary loss of consciousness. TBI has many causes, including child abuse. The most common causes of TBI, however, are falls and accidents involving bicycles, motor vehicles, and sports (Allison, 1992). Whether TBI is the result of a severe injury or a mild one, it can have a pervasive and significant impact on the student's educational performance (Hurt, 1991).

One of the most perplexing aspects of teaching students with TBI is that they can appear just as they did prior to their injuries and yet have significant learning and social problems. They can also seem to be "back to normal" one day only to seem lethargic and incapable of learning the next day. Because of the extreme

✔ **Your Learning:** What adaptations are students with health impairments likely to need?

FYI: Working with students with TBI has become an important topic because of many recent medical advances. Many students who used to die from their injuries now survive and return to school.

variability in needs of students with TBI, the information presented in this section should be considered illustrative; if you teach a student with TBI, seeking input from a specialist is essential.

Cognitively, students with TBI might have the same abilities they had before, or they might experience a loss of capacity. Students might experience difficulty initiating and organizing their learning tasks, remembering what they have learned, and reasoning or problem solving. They might also have difficulty processing verbal information and producing spoken and written language.

Students with TBI also have physical needs. Some students have limited use of their arms and legs, others have problems in fine motor movements such as those needed to turn the pages of a book. Yet others have limited stamina and may attend school for only part of the day.

Socially and emotionally, students with TBI experience many difficulties. They may have experienced changes in their personalities, so that they are not who they used to be (Lezak & O'Brien, 1988). For example, they often remember what they were able to do prior to their injuries and sometimes become depressed as they recognize their current limitations (Prigatano, 1992). They often need a high degree of structure and do not respond well to change. Some students lose their ability to interpret and respond appropriately to social cues. As a result, they might laugh at inappropriate times, or speak loudly when everyone else has realized a whisper is needed. Some of the most common characteristics and related behaviours of students with TBI, along with potential responses teachers can make, are included in Table 4.2.

Often, parents or siblings have witnessed the student in a totally unresponsive state, and they have psychologically prepared for the possibility of death. They might be tremendously relieved that the student survived, but at the same time they are traumatized. Families can experience a range of emotions, including shock, denial, sorrow, and anger (Martin, 1987). Eventually, many adapt. You must be sensitive to the family's stress and their changing capacity to follow up on schoolwork at home or to otherwise support your efforts.

If you teach a student with TBI, you may attend at least one planning meeting to discuss the details of the student's abilities and needs and to prepare you for helping the student in the classroom. Because students with TBI need structure and routine, you should follow the same pattern in classroom activities, and keep supplies and materials in the same place in the classroom. If a break in routine is necessary, you can prepare the student by alerting him or her, assigning a buddy, and staying in close proximity. Since students might know information one day but forget it the next, and sometimes learn easily whereas at other times struggle, the need for flexibility is ongoing. Students are also likely to become frustrated with their inability to learn the way they did in the past, and so your patience in reteaching, providing additional examples, and using strategies to help them focus attention can be essential. Socially, emotionally, and behaviourally, students with TBI rely on you to set clear expectations but to be supportive and responsive to their changing needs. The uniqueness of students with TBI is that their needs are difficult to predict, change either slowly or rapidly, and vary in intensity.

Connections: Students with TBI can be helped with strategies designed to help them function independently. Examples of such strategies are included in Chapter 10.

✓ **Your Learning:** What characteristics of students with TBI create challenges for teachers working with them?

Connections: Information on communicating with families was emphasized in Chapter 3. Review the strategies that promote positive interactions with families.

Connections: Further information on analyzing instructional environments is found in Chapter 7.

TABLE 4.2   Classroom Behaviours of Students with Traumatic Brain Injury

Characteristics	Behaviour	Solutions
Overestimates abilities	Student brags to friends that he or she is still the fastest runner or will win the spelling bee.	Do not challenge the student. Reassure him or her that individuals change after a head injury.
Lowered social inhibition and judgment	Student tries to touch and hug everyone.	Redirect student's attention to an appropriate behaviour. Model correct or alternative behaviour for student.
Faulty reasoning	Student confronts peers and teachers with unfair accusations.	Do not feel obligated to respond immediately. Reassure student and return later to resolve the problem.
Depression	Student appears uninterested and passive, even in activities once considered highly enjoyable. The emotional stress of the injury may be prolonged and can be overwhelming.	Involve the student directly in the activity. Assign a specific role to hook the student's interest. Individual counselling or support-group participation can be beneficial.
Fatigue	Student may be fatigued as a result of both the injury and the medication. Sleep disorders are common.	Review medical information about physical limitations. Change tasks often and give frequent breaks. Consider a shortened school day.
Impulsivity	Student may be unable to wait his or her turn at a drinking fountain or in the cafeteria. He or she may talk out during a test or speak out of turn.	Restate the classroom rules or limits. Reassure the student that there is plenty of time for the activity.
Rigidity	Student may be unable to adapt to changes in schedule or routine.	Alert the student in advance to anticipated changes in each day's accustomed routine.
Flat affect	Student seems to have no voice inflections. Face seems expressionless; eyes seem vacant; he or she does not laugh or smile appropriately.	Remember that this is characteristic of a person with a head injury and not a demonstration of low motivation. Use stimulating learning activities that are relevant to the student's interests and goals.
Low motivation	What appears as low motivation may be confusion and inability to plan how to do the task.	Ask the student to verbalize the first step toward completing the task. Ask for succeeding steps if necessary.
Agitation and irritability	Varying degrees of agitation and irritability may manifest. Student may become annoyed over picky things or become aggressive.	Try to redirect the student's attention away from the source of agitation, or move her to another area or room where it is quiet and she can regain control.

Source: From "Traumatic Brain Injury: An Overview of School Re-entry" by B. F. Tucker and S. E. Colson, 1992, *Intervention in School and Clinic, 27,* pp. 198–206. Copyright © 1992 by PRO-ED, Inc. Reprinted by permission.

What Adaptations Can You Make for Students with Autism?

Autism has been considered part of various emotional disabilities, including schizophrenia, and has been addressed as a form of cognitive disabilities or developmental disabilities. Currently, however, autism is considered a unique disorder that affects boys more than girls in a ratio of approximately four:one. Autism frequently occurs with other disorders. In particular, it is estimated that 70 percent of individuals with autism also have cognitive disabilities; but that number could be an overestimate because of the communication difficulties that accompany the disability and the resulting problems in obtaining accurate estimates of ability (Freeman, 1994).

Although autism can exist in many forms from mild to severe and cannot be treated as a single disorder, it does have specific characteristics. First, students with autism have seriously impaired social relationships. Many students with autism resist human contact and social interactions from a very early age, and have difficulty learning the subtleties of social interactions (Ratey, Grandin, & Miller, 1992). They often do not make eye contact with others, and can seem disinterested in developing social relationships. For example, young children often ask teachers and classmates to watch them do something ("Look at me!"). A young child with autism would not seek out such opportunities for social interactions. Albert, a 13-year-old with autism, maintained that others view him as extremely ugly, but he did not understand why he does not have friends. When an interviewer asked him what he talked about with others, the two topics he mentioned were wind and smells in the environment (Cesaroni & Garber, 1991). He did not take on the perspective of others, and he did not understand that others' interests are also part of social interaction.

Students with autism also experience problems in both verbal and non-verbal communication. They often have significantly delayed language development, and, if they have language skills, they struggle to maintain a conversation with another person. In writing about her experiences of being autistic, Temple Grandin provides a clear example of her communication problems (Grandin, 1984). She explains that once when her mother wanted her to wear a hat while riding in the car, she didn't have the words to refuse. Instead, she screamed and threw the hat out the window, causing her mother to hit another car. Unlike Temple Grandin, many students with autism cannot write or otherwise clearly communicate about their experiences. They often use inappropriate behaviours instead of words to convey many needs. Some students with autism have **echolalic speech.** They repeat what others have said instead of producing original communication.

Another characteristic of students with autism is a very limited range of interest, such as a student who is fascinated with radios to the exclusion of nearly everything else. Such a narrow range of interest often has a negative impact on social relationships with peers and adults since the student does not discern that others are not as interested in the preferred topic.

Students with autism have a low threshold for and difficulty in dealing with stress (Grandin, 1984). A change in a class schedule could be difficult for a student with autism, as could be the introduction of a new route from the classroom

FYI: Autism is a disorder distinct from mental retardation and emotional disabilities. It is characterized by impaired social relationships, communication problems, a narrow range of interests, and extreme responses to stress.

FYI: In *echolalic speech*, a student repeats words others have said, whether in person, on television or radio, or in other media.

✓ **Your Learning:** What is an example of a stereotypic behaviour?

FYI: Some professionals contend that Asperger's syndrome is distinct from autism, but many consider it a specific subtype of this disability.

to a bus. Particular noises or odours can also be stressful. Many students with autism respond to stress with **stereotypic behaviours.** They complete the same action or motion over and over again. For example, they may rock rapidly in their chairs, spin an object repeatedly, or twirl themselves or their arms. In other situations, students might develop a ritual to complete a task. In your classroom, you should be aware of potentially stressful situations for a student with autism. You can either allow time for the student to prepare for the situation, talk about the situation well in advance, assign a peer partner to assist the student, or enlist the help of a special educator or paraprofessional. If a student's response to stress is demonstrated with aggressive or extremely disruptive behaviour, the student might need to spend part of the school day in a more structured, less stressful environment such as a special education classroom.

Recently, professional attention has turned to students with milder forms of autism, including **Asperger's syndrome.** These students sometimes seem like "perfect students" (Coppola, 1987). They usually develop speech at a normal age, but they sometimes have problems knowing whether to use a first-person, second-person, or third-person pronoun. They have limited facial expression, seem inept at interpreting others' non-verbal communication, are awkward in social situations, and have trouble forming friendships (Carruthers & Foreman, 1989). They are highly intelligent, with interest in one or two topics (Gillberg, 1989).

Supporting Appropriate Behaviour

Students with autism often have behaviours that are unusual and can be disturbing to teachers and students who do not understand this disorder. However, many of the behaviours can be corrected with highly structured behaviour management programs, and some can be ignored. Many students with autism can receive some or all of their education in a regular education classroom, provided that needed supports are in place for them (Pratt & Moreno, 1994).

Connections: Many more strategies for responding to student behaviour are presented in Chapter 13.

Generally, the adaptations you make for students with autism involve creating a structured and predictable environment and encouraging appropriate social interactions (Connor, 1990). Establish clear procedures and routines for classroom tasks and follow them consistently. In addition to having structure, students with autism may need opportunities during the day to work alone and be alone (Christof & Kane, 1991). This time serves as a break from the stresses of the classroom and the social and communication demands of that setting.

✓ **Your Learning:** How can you determine the function of a student's behaviour?

To help students with social interactions and communication, you can observe student behaviour to understand its purpose from the student's perspective (Christof & Kane, 1991). For example, if a student has been working in a small group but suddenly leaves the group and runs to the room next door, it could be a signal that the student has reached the limits of his or her tolerance for social interactions. It might be appropriate to work with the other teacher to provide a safe and isolated location where the student can take a break from the classroom social demands. With these understandings, you can communicate to a special educator or paraprofessional the behaviours of concern and possible explanations for them, thus setting up a positive approach for problem solving. Regular education teachers can accommodate students with autism by teaching them to wait and other social skills. Ideas for addressing these areas are included in the Professional Edge on page 135.

▼▼▼▼▼▼▼▼▼▼▼▼▼▼▼▼▼▼▼▼▼▼▼

Professional Edge
Teaching Social Skills to Students with Autism

STUDENTS with autism have a great need to develop appropriate social skills that will serve them well in school and throughout their lives.

These are some useful skills and ideas for addressing them.

Behaviour	Examples	Strategies for Teaching
Waiting	Waiting in line Waiting for someone else to answer Waiting for a program to start	Establish clear rules, such as "Stand up when the teacher calls your name" Teach the student to occupy wait time doing a favourite activity. Try to keep wait time as short as possible at first; reward the student.
Taking turns being first	Being first in line Being first to answer	Create a chart to show who is to be first in line each day. Set rules about taking turns.
Transitioning before completing something	Stopping before a workbook page is completed Leaving the computer in the middle of a game	Try to avoid this problem by allowing enough time for the student to finish. Give the student warnings when time is about to run out. For example, alert the student with visual cues five minutes, two minutes, and one minute before the end.
Changing topics	Asking endless questions about what is going to happen Talking endlessly about favourite topics	Set a time limit on the amount of time a student can discuss a topic. Use a visual timer. Create a rule about the number of times you will respond to the same questions.
Finishing	Finishing lunch Finishing an assignment Finishing a game or activity	Define "finished" in concrete terms. For example, finishing a paper might be defined as putting an answer in every space. Finishing games or activities might be cued by all the cards being drawn, etc.
Being flexible	Teacher absence Art class cancelled because of an assembly Field trip delayed because of rain	Use pictures to show the expected routine, and cross out the part of the routine that is changing. Explain verbally.
Monitoring behaviour when excited	Learning to stop clapping or laughing when others have done so	Teach a student to watch others and stop clapping or laughing as soon as they do.

Source: From *Some Social Behaviours that Students with Autism Need Help to Learn and Apply in Everyday Situations* by N. Dalrymple, 1990, Bloomington, IN: Indiana Resource Center for Autism, Institute for the Study of Developmental Disabilities. Used by permission of the author.

Communicating with Students with Autism

✓ **Your Learning:** What alternative communication approaches have you learned about in this chapter that students with autism might use? What augmentative communication devices might they use?

Communication with students with autism is accomplished through a wide variety of strategies (Brown, 1994). A few students with autism can communicate adequately with speech, especially if they do not feel pressured. Others learn to communicate through sign language and for some, the motor activity of signing seems to help them successfully convey their needs and preferences. For yet other students, communication boards are a useful tool: By simply touching pictures, students can communicate with others even when they cannot speak the appropriate words. Other communication devices that help students with limited speech, including those with autism, were described earlier in this chapter.

Some students now use a widely publicized and controversial technique called **facilitated communication** (Graley, 1994). Facilitated communication involves a person trained in the technique sitting next to the student with autism and providing touch support to the wrist, elbow, or shoulder as the student types responses or other information on a typewriter, computer, adapted keyboard, or communication board. The purpose of the touch support is not to guide the student's hand, but instead to provide steadiness and support for it. Some professionals and parents have found this technique helpful in enabling students with autism to communicate, often for the first time in their lives (Beirne-Smith et al., 1994). Others question whether the written work produced represents the student's thinking or that of the facilitator. The best communication strategies for a student with autism are generally determined by a multidisciplinary team.

Autism Network International

www.students.uiuc.edu/~bordner/ani.html

Deaf Canada Web

www.deafworldweb.org/int/ca

Down Syndrome Research Foundation and Resource Centre

fas.sfu.ca/kin/ds

◤ Summary

Students with low-incidence disabilities comprise only about 10 to 15 percent of all students with disabilities. Together, these students have tremendously diverse abilities, challenges, and needs. Many of them can succeed in your classroom if you take into account that you will teach only one or two students with these disabilities at any given time and that they are students first and have disabilities second. Many of the teaching strategies you have already learned will be effective in teaching them, and other professionals and parents will be available to assist you in creating successful learning experiences for them.

One group of students with low-incidence disabilities is composed of those with moderate or severe cognitive disabilities, multiple disabilities, and deaf-blindness. These students learn very slowly, have difficulty maintaining and generalizing their learning, and struggle to combine skills into larger skills. They need a functional and community-based education that can be accomplished in general education settings with appropriate supports and a commitment to effective teaching and learning practices such as multiple levels of instruction occurring in one classroom, heterogeneous student grouping, the use of natural support systems, and the development of partnerships with families.

Students with sensory impairments are those with visual and hearing impairments. These students' disabilities can range from mild to severe, and the impact on their education can be slight or significant. They often have needs related to academic learning, social and emotional skills, and skills for living in their environments. They also use adaptive equipment or materials to help them learn.

Some students have orthopedic impairments or other health impairments, including fetal alcohol syndrome and traumatic brain injury. Their disabilities can range from mild to severe, and their special supports and services are determined by their needs. Students in these groups often have medical needs that directly or indirectly affect their learning. Their cognitive levels can include an entire range. Most students in this group have social and emotional needs because of their illnesses, and accommodations in these areas are likely to be necessary.

Autism is another low-incidence disability. Students with autism have impairments in their social relationships, communication, range of interests, and ability to respond to stressful events. They need highly structured learning environments with clear procedures and routines. Recently, more attention is being paid to students with mild forms of autism, including Asperger's syndrome.

Applications in Teaching Practice

Planning Adaptations for Students with Low-Incidence Exceptionalities

Mr. LaPointe teaches English to grade nine students. This year he has several students with learning disabilities and emotional disabilities in his class, but his primary concern is Viral, a young man who is quadriplegic. Mr. LaPointe has been told that Viral has average intelligence and is capable of learning. He is meeting with Ms. Bickel from the special education department to answer his questions about Viral.

MR. LAPOINTE: I need more information about Viral. Can he really do the work? How will he take tests? What is his assistant supposed to be doing? Am I accountable if Viral has a medical problem during class?

MS. BICKEL: It sounds like you haven't gotten the information I thought you had. Let me try to help clarify. Viral is quite a good student. He usually gets A's and B's in his core academic classes, and he is eager to learn. Because he can't use his arms, he "talks" using his communication board. I'll be working with you to be sure the board includes all the key words you want it to contain. All Viral has to do is point his head toward the answer he wants and the laser pointer activates the board, which "says" the answer out loud. Probably one adaptation Viral will need is extra time to answer; he really wants to participate but might need a moment to get the laser beam focused on the answer he wants to give.

MR. LAPOINTE: I'll have to see how that works. What does his assistant do?

MS. BICKEL: Mr. Owen is responsible for Viral's personal care and for making sure he gets from class to class. He also takes notes for Viral, and records answers Viral gives on his communication board. He can help you out in class if there's a chance, but Viral needs his attention much of the time.

MR. LAPOINTE: Oh, I wasn't trying to get more help. I just need a picture of what this will be like. I need an extra place for Mr. Owen in class, don't I?

MS. BICKEL: Yes, he'll need to sit right next to Viral.

The teachers continued talking for another 45 minutes. The next week, Ms. Bickel asked Mr. LaPointe how it was going with Viral. Mr. LaPointe commented that he was surprised how smoothly and easily things were going. Viral "spoke" in class on the first day, and the other students asked a few questions about the equipment, but that was all. He asked if Ms. Bickel could help him deal with two other students who already seemed to have behaviour problems.

Questions

1. What type of disability does Viral have? Why is he included in Mr. LaPointe's English class?
2. What adaptations should Mr. LaPointe make in his classroom and his instruction to accommodate Viral's special needs?
3. If you were meeting with Ms. Bickel, what additional questions would you ask? About Viral? About needed accommodations? About Mr. Owen?
4. What assistance would you need from Ms. Bickel in order to feel comfortable teaching Viral?

Chapter 5

Students with High-Incidence Exceptionalities

After you read this chapter, you will be able to

1. Define high-incidence exceptionalities.
2. Describe adaptations you can make in a regular classroom for students who are gifted.
3. Describe adaptations you can make in a regular classroom for students with communication disorders.
4. Describe adaptations you can make for students with mild cognitive, learning and emotional disabilities.
5. Describe adaptations that students with attention-deficit/hyperactivity disorder (ADHD) might need.

MALCOLM *is in grade four and has difficulty communicating in class. Whether he is having a conversation or trying to answer a question, Malcolm can't seem to find the right words to express himself. The other day, his teacher asked him about the different kinds of dinosaurs he had seen on television. Malcolm responded, "Well, uh, there was this one big uh, I mean it really was a big one. It had a funny uh thing on its back and it uh looked like it uh was like funny." This problem he has with finding the right word makes it hard for Malcolm to make friends. The other day, Malcolm started to ask a classmate to come to his house after school, but the classmate walked away before Malcolm could get the words out to invite him. What kind of a language problem does Malcolm have? How will this problem affect his academic and social adjustment in school? How can Malcolm's teachers help him with this problem?*

SETH *is a grade eight student at King Elementary School. Most people who know Seth outside of school would never guess that he has a learning disability. He converses easily with children and adults, has a great sense of humour, and is renowned among his peers for his "street smarts." Things don't go as well for Seth in school; basic academic skills are particularly problematic. He reads slowly, struggling with each word, and as a result, he often cannot tell you what he has read. Seth's written language is also a problem. His handwriting is illegible, his spelling is inconsistent, and his written essays lack organization. In math, Seth still doesn't know his math facts, and when faced with answering word problems, he simply gives up. What exceptionality does Seth have? What factors do you think may have contributed to Seth's academic problems? What kinds of adaptations should Seth's teacher make for him? What other kinds of support do Seth and his teacher need?*

RICK *is approaching his fifteenth birthday and is having major trouble both in and out of school. Rick's behaviour in school has never been easy to manage. In the primary grades, he was disruptive in class but responded well to rewards given him at home by his parents for good behaviour in school. When Rick was in grade five, his parents divorced. At this time his behaviour problems in school began to worsen. Rick began to talk abusively to peers in class and to refuse loudly to do any work. He began to bully other students, particularly those least likely to be able to defend themselves. In grades seven and eight, Rick attended an alternative school. Although his school behaviour improved somewhat, he became involved in gang activities when he was in grade eight. This year, Rick is in grade nine in high school and is attending all regular education classes in addition to seeing a special education teacher once a day in the resource room. His school and class attendance has been spotty, and he occasionally engages in disruptive behaviour in his classes. What is Rick's exceptionality? How do you think his regular education teacher can accommodate his behaviour? What kinds of support do Rick and his teacher need?*

LYDIA *is a grade four student who is gifted and talented. She has been reading since she was age three, and she frequently borrows her sister's high school literature anthology as a source of reading material. She knew most of the math concepts introduced in grade four before the school year began, and she also has a strong interest in learning French, playing flute and piano, and volunteering to read to residents of a local nursing home. Lydia's idea of a perfect afternoon is to have a quiet place to hide, a couple of wonderful books, and no one to bother her. Lydia's teacher, Mr. Judd, enjoys having her in class because she is so enthusiastic about learning, but he admits that Lydia's abilities are a little intimidating. He has also noticed that Lydia doesn't seem to have much in common with other students in class. She is a class leader but does not appear to have any close friends as other students do. Is Lydia a typical student who is gifted or developmentally advanced? How can Mr. Judd help Lydia reach her full potential? What social problems do students such as Lydia sometimes encounter?*

STUDENTS such as Malcolm, Seth, Rick, and Lydia have high-incidence exceptionalities. These students' exceptionalities affect their language, learning, and behaviour. You probably will teach students with high-incidence exceptionalities in your classroom. All of these students can benefit from being in a regular education setting, but they may require support from general and special education professionals. For example, Lydia's teacher is concerned that he cannot make time to provide the advanced instruction that would benefit her. Malcolm's teacher gives him the questions she will ask him ahead of time so he can rehearse his answers with his parents the night before. Seth is learning word processing skills to help him overcome his problems with spelling and handwriting. He is also using texts on tape in his science and social studies classes, which are sometimes co-taught. Rick and his teachers have developed an individualized behaviour contract in which Rick is allowed extra access to the auto mechanics shop for attending class and complying with teachers' requests.

In this chapter, you will learn about the characteristics and needs of students with high-incidence disabilities and about classroom accommodations that enable these students to learn. We have seen that, with the ascendance of inclusion, many of the provinces and territories are downplaying the identification of the particular type of exceptionality, avoiding labelling, and focusing on the individual needs of students. When reading the generic descriptions of high-incidence exceptionalities in this chapter, it is important to remember that we are discussing children and adolescents. They are, however, children and adolescents with characteristics that require us to adapt our teaching and other aspects of our classroom interactions with them. They are not their exceptionalities, but using the accepted expressions to describe their characteristics and learning makes it easier for us to communicate. The labels are increasingly used to facilitate administrative and funding procedures, while individual needs and strengths drive the design of individual education plans and teaching.

What Are High-Incidence Exceptionalities?

Students with **high-incidence exceptionalities** are gifted, or have speech or language disabilities, learning disabilities, serious emotional disturbances, mild cognitive disabilities, or attention-deficit/hyperactivity disorder. The definitional terms for high-incidence exceptionalities and the characteristics are summarized in Table 5.1. Students with high-incidence exceptionalities share a number of important characteristics. They are often hard to distinguish from their peers who are not exceptional, particularly in non-school settings. In addition, students with high-incidence exceptionalities (other than gifted) often exhibit a combination of behaviour, social, and academic problems. Gifted students benefit from challenge and opportunities to work with developmentally advanced peers. Other students with high-incidence exceptionalities benefit from systematic, highly structured instructional interventions such as those discussed in this chapter and throughout the remainder of this book.

How Can You Accommodate Students Who Are Gifted and or Developmentally Advanced?

In addition to students who are unable to meet typical curricular expectations, you will also have in your classroom students who have extraordinary abilities and skills. The term used to described these students is usually **gifted.** Increasingly in Canada, educators are using the term **developmentally advanced** following the lead of researchers Keating (1990) and Matthews (in press) of University of Toronto. "A student is considered gifted when she/he possesses demonstrated or potential abilities that give evidence of exceptionally high capability with respect to intellect, creativity, or the skills associated with specific disciplines" (British Columbia, 1995, section E, p. 17). The accomplishments of students who are developmentally advanced have recently been described as domain-specific or discipline-specific developmental expertise. Matthews (in press) argued that we

Connections: The use of performance-based assessments, often helpful in identifying students who are gifted and talented, is discussed in more depth in Chapter 11.

criticizing the other students because they do not do their share of the work, know enough about the topic, write fast enough, or make the project look good enough. Willis tends to express his frustration through cynicism and cruel jokes. This attitude does not endear him to classmates.

If gifted students find school boring and have difficulty forming friendships, they can also have poor attitudes toward learning and school activities in general. These students are at risk for dropping out of school (Davis & Rimm, 1994).

Behaviour patterns.   Students who are gifted and talented display the entire range of behaviours that other students do. They can be model students who participate and seldom cause problems, often serving as class leaders (Winebrenner, 1992). However, students who are gifted sometimes show an intense interest in a topic and refusal to change when requested by a teacher (Smith & Luckasson, 1995).

Interventions for Students Who Are Gifted and Talented

Do It! Talk to an experienced teacher in your community. How does he or she use the vocabulary in this section?

Although a few school districts operate separate classes and programs for students who are gifted and talented, you will likely be responsible for meeting some or all of the needs of these students in your classroom (Sapon-Shevin, 1994). Four of the strategies most often used to challenge gifted and talented students are enrichment, acceleration, sophistication, and novelty (Gallagher & Gallagher, 1994). These approaches should help you meet the recommendations that gifted students make about school. The recommendations of one group of Canadian kids are listed in Figure 5.1.

Enrichment is an instructional approach that provides students with information, materials, and assignments that enable them to elaborate on concepts presented as part of the regular curriculum (Gallagher & Gallagher, 1994). This option requires you to find related information, prepare it for the students who need it, and create relevant activities for them. One teacher provided enrichment to her students in math (Winebrenner, 1992). She gave a pretest for each unit to the students who are gifted and talented, and if they had already mastered all the concepts, they were given a choice of alternative activities and assignments. If any concepts had not yet been mastered, the students were required to participate in the lesson on the days those concepts were taught. Students who were excused from lessons were expected to take a unit test with the rest of the class. The expectations for student work, options for enrichment, lessons to attend, and testing requirements were all summarized on a student learning contract. For enrichment to be effective, students must have opportunities to complete alternative assignments designed to encourage advanced thinking and product development, they must do such assignments in lieu of other work instead of as additional work, and must have many learning resources available to them both in and out of the classroom (Maker, 1993).

FYI: Two variations on the instructional approaches presented here include *accelerated integrated learning* and *curriculum compacting*, in which students study the same themes and topics as the rest of the class but in greater detail or depth and with enhanced opportunities for application.

Acceleration is providing students with curriculum that takes them from their current level of learning and moves them forward (Gallagher & Gallagher, 1994). For example, Stephen is a student who is gifted in math. In grades seven and eight, he worked in an individualized and independent program to advance

FIGURE 5.1
Recommendations of Gifted Kids

Thirty-three academically gifted students at Vancouver's University Hill Secondary School were asked: "If we as teachers could provide the very best learning situation for you, what would you have us do?" Responses included:

- Let me go ahead and work at higher levels.

- Let us work with older kids. We can fit in.

- It's not an age difference but an attitude difference that's important here. Older kids are more accepting.

- Give us independent programs. Let us work ahead on our own.

- Know that everyone has talent—and need. Provide challenge (in our talent area).

- Have totally hands-on lessons. If we're studying elections, have a mock election.

- Use more videos, films, and telecommunications.

- Use humour.

- Provide independent study opportunities—let us study something we are interested in.

Source: From British Columbia Ministry of Education, *Gifted Education: A Resource Guide for Teachers,* p. 14. Copyright © 1996 by British Columbia Ministry of Education. Reprinted by permission.

his skills. In high school, he completed the available curriculum during his grade nine year and then began taking math courses at a local university. Stephen's program is based on acceleration. Acceleration can occur in one area, as occurred with Stephen, or can be total. For a few students, acceleration includes entering kindergarten early, and skipping grades.

Sophistication is a strategy in which teachers help students to see the principles or systems that underlie the content being learned by the rest of the class (Gallagher & Gallagher, 1994). For example, in an elementary school classroom, as students are reading stories and answering questions about vocabulary or the main idea, a student who is gifted might analyze how character, plot, and setting are intertwined in the story. In a music class, a student who is talented might be assigned to add harmony to a basic melody that other students are learning.

Novelty is an approach in which teachers provide opportunities for students to explore traditional curricular content in alternative and unusual ways (Gallagher & Gallagher, 1994). For example, students might develop interviews with historical figures to gain their perspectives on world events of the past instead of simply reading about them. Working with a mentor, using problem based learning, and creating learning materials that other students can use are examples of novelty approaches for teaching students who are gifted and talented (Matthews, in press; Winebrenner, 1992).

FYI: Studies show that the most effective teachers of gifted students have high intellectual, cultural, and literary interests; are high achieving and hold high standards of excellence; are flexible and democratic in dealing with students; use innovative, experimental, facilitative, problem-solving approaches; respect students' creativity; and do not view critical thinking, non-conformity, and criticism of authority as discipline problems.

TABLE 5.2 Sample Content Modification for Gifted Students

	Subject			
Modification	*Math*	*Science*	*Language Arts*	*Social Studies*
Acceleration	Algebra in grade five	Early chemistry and physics	Learning grammatical structure early	Early introduction to world history
Enrichment	Changing bases in number systems	Experimentation and data collecting	Short story and poetry writing	Reading biographies for historical insight
Sophistication	Mastering the laws of arithmetic	Learning the laws of physics	Mastering the structural properties of plays, sonnets, and so on	Learning and applying the principles of economics
Novelty	Probability and statistics	Science and its impact on society	Rewriting Shakespeare's tragedies with happy endings	Creating future societies and telling how they are governed

Source: From James J. Gallagher and Shelagh A. Gallagher, *Teaching the Gifted Child* (4th ed.), p. 100. Copyright © 1994 by Allyn and Bacon. Reprinted by permission.

Further examples of these four approaches to intervening with students who are gifted and talented are summarized in Table 5.2. The Case in Practice on page 149 illustrates a teacher using some of these strategies.

What Adaptations Can You Make for Students with Communication Disorders?

✓ **Your Learning:** Can you identify and define the categories of high-incidence exceptionalities?

Malcolm is a member of a large group of students who have **speech** or **language impairments.** One common speech problem is **speech articulation,** or the inability to pronounce sounds correctly at and after the developmentally appropriate age. For example, Clara is in grade two but cannot pronounce the *s* sound—a sound that most students master by age five. Other speech difficulties involve voice (e.g., too loud or too soft) and fluency (e.g., stuttering).

Understanding Speech and Language Problems

FYI: In remembering the distinction between receptive and expressive communication disorders, think of the root words *to receive* and *to express.*

Students who have language problems have difficulty with the two key parts of language: receptive language and expressive language. **Receptive language** involves understanding what people mean when they speak to you. **Expressive language** concerns speaking in such a way that others understand you. Some common receptive and expressive language problems are listed in Figure 5.2.

Students with speech and language problems may also have difficulty using language in social situations. For example, they may be unable to vary their lan-

Case in Practice

Meeting the Needs of a Gifted Student

IT is Wednesday morning and Ms. Ollendorf is preparing for the school day. She is thinking about what to do with Mary Jo, a student in her class who is clearly gifted in several areas. Yesterday afternoon in a conference with Mary Jo's mother, Ms. Ollendorf explained that she was concerned that Mary Jo was not doing as well in science as she had the potential to do. Mary Jo's mother offered this explanation:

> In the past month, Mary Jo has said probably 20 times that science is boring. She thinks the book is too simple and doesn't explain "interesting" things. She says she could finish her reports on the experiments before doing them because they are not complex enough to challenge her. She also said that she doesn't do the extra-credit work that you give students as an option because she can get perfect scores on everything anyway. Why would she want to do extra work?

In thinking about Mary Jo, Ms. Ollendorf must admit that the child has made a few good points. Mary Jo is truly far beyond the science text in her understanding of most of the concepts addressed, and she does not seem pleased, as the other students do, when the day's activities include a science experiment. What concerns Ms. Ollendorf most, though, is the possibility of Mary Jo becoming uninterested in science when she so clearly has the potential to pursue a science-related career if she so chooses.

A week later, Ms. Ollendorf introduces a different sort of science to Mary Jo. She has gathered advanced supplemental science textbooks and has contacted several friends who work in local businesses to be mentors for Mary Jo. She has also spoken with a friend who is a science education professor about how to challenge Mary Jo. She offers Mary Jo these options:

1. She will take unit tests prior to instruction.
2. If she scores at least 80 percent on a unit test, she can work four days per week in the alternative science materials. If she does not achieve 80 percent, she will participate in the lessons on the parts of the unit that she has not mastered.
3. For each unit of instruction completed in this manner, Mary Jo will select and create a product that will demonstrate the science concepts she has explored. For example, during the unit on matter, she may choose to explore the gas laws and create and present an experiment demonstrating her knowledge.
4. Mary Jo will visit with a mentor once each month. Mentors might include a high school student, a local businessperson, or another teacher.

Reflections

What did Ms. Ollendorf do to make science a more challenging subject for Mary Jo? Which of the four approaches described for providing appropriate instruction to gifted students did Ms. Ollendorf use? What other strategies could Ms. Ollendorf implement to expand Mary Jo's science instruction further?

guage to match the person they are talking with or the context in which it is occurring, take turns during a conversation, recognize when a listener is not understanding, and take action to clarify (Bos & Vaughn, 1994). Regular classroom teachers can intervene in the classroom to help such students socially.

Early language development forms the underpinning for much of the academic learning that comes when students go to school. It is not surprising, then,

FIGURE 5.2

Language Problems

Expressive Language Problems

1. Use of incorrect grammar or syntax ("They walk down together the hill").
2. Lack of specificity ("It's over there by the place over there").
3. Frequent hesitations ("You know, uhm, I would, uhm, like a, er, Coke").
4. Jumping from topic to topic ("What are feathers? Well, I like to go hunting with my uncle."). Or repeating same information.
5. Limited use of vocabulary.
6. Trouble finding the right word to communicate meaning (word finding).
7. Poor social use of language (inability to change communication style to fit specific situations and to repair communication breakdowns).
8. Difficulty discussing abstract, temporal, or spatial concepts.

Receptive Language Problems

1. Does not respond to questions appropriately.
2. Cannot abstract or comprehend abstractions as idioms ("mind sharp as a tack"; "eyes dancing in the dark"), figurative language or humour.
3. Cannot retain information presented verbally.
4. Difficulty following oral directions or sequence of ideas.
5. Misses parts of material presented verbally, particularly less concrete words such as articles (the book; a book) and auxiliary verbs and tense markers (He was going; She is going).
6. May confuse the sounds of letters that are similar (b, d; m, n) or reverse the order of sounds and syllables in words (was, saw).
7. Difficulty comprehending concepts showing quantity, function, comparative size, and temporal and spatial relationships.
8. Difficulty comprehending compound and complex sentences.

Sources: Adapting Instruction in General Education for Students with Communication Disorders by D. Barad, 1985, unpublished manuscript, DeKalb, IL: Northern Illinois University; and Strategies for Teaching Students with Learning and Behaviour Problems (2nd ed.) by C. S. Bos and S. Vaughn, 1994. Copyright © 1994 by Allyn and Bacon. Adapted with permission.

Cultural Awareness: It is incorrect to view students as having communication disorders when they use ethnic or regional dialects, speak a form of non-standard English learned at home, or are native speakers of languages other than English and have limited English proficiency.

that students with speech and language disorders are likely also to have difficulty with academics. Problems with speech sounds can result in students having difficulties acquiring phonemic awareness needed for reading and spelling skills. Receptive language problems can make reading for comprehension very difficult and can result in trouble understanding mathematical terms such as *minus* and *regroup* and confusion sorting out words with multiple meanings, such as *carry* and *times* (Mercer, 1991). Language disabilities can seriously impede the content-area learning stressed in upper elementary grades and high school. In these settings, much information is provided orally using lecture formats, the vocabulary and concepts covered are much more abstract, and students are expected to learn with less support from the teacher. Another part of learning independently is solving problems. Students with language disorders may have difficulty verbalizing the steps to solve a problem.

Because communication is social, students with speech and language disabilities, such as **stuttering,** often experience social problems. Students whose language is unclear are often avoided by their peers and sometimes ridiculed. The experience of peer rejection can be devastating, leading to lack of confidence, poor self-image, social withdrawal, and emotional problems later in life (Cowen, Pederson, Babijian, Izzo, & Trost, 1973).

Accommodations for Students with Communication Disorders

As discussed in Chapter 1, the INCLUDE strategy suggests that before you make adaptations, you carefully consider potential student problems in view of your instructional demands. For students with speech and language problems, note especially any areas in which students are required to understand oral language (for example, listening to a lecture or a set of verbal directions) or to communicate orally (for example, responding to teacher questions or interacting with classmates when working in cooperative groups). Here are some specific suggestions for working with students with speech and language disorders.

Create an atmosphere of acceptance.   You need to help students believe they can communicate without worrying about making mistakes. First, when students make an error, model the correct form instead of correcting their mistake directly:

> TEACHER: Kareem, what did Jules do with the frog?
> KAREEM: Put pocket.
> TEACHER: Oh. He put it in his pocket?
> KAREEM: Yes.

Second, try to allow students who stutter or have other fluency problems more time to speak, and do not interrupt them or supply words that are difficult for them to pronounce. Offer praise or other reinforcement for successful efforts and for attempts to communicate.

Finally, minimize peer pressure. One effective way to do this is to model and reinforce tolerance of individual differences in your classroom.

Encourage listening and teach listening skills.   First, listen carefully yourself and praise listening among your students. For example, when Ms. Hernandez listens to a student speak, she leans forward and nods. Many of her students copy these listening actions. Second, engage your students' attention before you begin speaking by increasing your proximity to the listeners, giving direct instruction (such as, "Listen to what I'm going to say"), and reducing competing stimuli (have only one activity going on at once). You can also use verbal, pictorial, or written advance organizers to cue students when to listen (Lenz, Alley, & Schumaker, 1987; Robinson & Smith, 1981). Third, make oral material easier to understand and remember by simplifying vocabulary and syntax, using high-frequency words,

FYI: The most common kind of speech problem involving fluency is stuttering. *Stuttering* is a speech impairment in which an individual involuntarily repeats a sound or word, resulting in a loss of speech fluency.

Connections: Strategies for teaching students to respect individual differences are discussed in Chapter 13.

divorced several months later. Why was Thomas behind in reading? Was it heredity? Was it the new reading program? Was it his parents' marital problems? All of these factors may have contributed to Thomas's problem.

Recently British Columbia provided teachers with a resource guide, *Teaching Students with Learning and Behavioural Differences* (1996). This section takes the same perspective and focuses on the overlap among the means of teaching to accommodate student differences arising from learning disabilities, behavioural disabilities, and mild cognitive disabilities. This is because, whatever behaviours they exhibit and whatever the possible causes of these behaviours, the students benefit from the same kinds of instructional practices (Algozzine, Ysseldyke, & Campbell, 1994). These practices are introduced in this chapter and described in considerable depth throughout the rest of this book. For example, Raeanna has a mild cognitive disability. She has difficulty reading her classmates' social cues. As a result, she does not recognize when she is acting too aggressively with her classmates and often is rejected by many of them. Del is a student with learning disabilities. He also has trouble reading the social cues of his peers. Although Raeanna and Del may learn new social skills at different rates, both can benefit from social-skills training that provides considerable guided practice and feedback on how to read social cues.

Although students with learning disabilities, mild cognitive disabilities, and serious emotional disturbance share many similarities, they also have differences (Hallahan & Kauffman, 1991). The behaviour problems of students with emotional or behavioural difficulties are more severe, and students with mild cognitive disabilities have lower levels of measured intelligence. Students with learning disabilities may have more pronounced learning strengths and weaknesses than students with mild cognitive disabilities, who are likely to show lower performance in all areas. Still, the point to remember is that categorical labels are not particularly useful in describing specific students or developing instructional programs for them (Hardman et al., 1993). You need to analyze each student's needs and then make the necessary adaptations. This individualization is at the heart of the INCLUDE strategy introduced in Chapter 1.

Students with learning and behaviour disabilities have many learning needs. They frequently have difficulty acquiring basic skills in the areas of reading, math, and written language. They may also lack skills necessary for efficient learning, such as attending to task, memory, independent learning skills, language skills, reasoning, conceptualization and generalization, motor, and school survival skills.

✓ **Your Learning:** What does it mean to have a learning disability?

FYI: Students with learning and behaviour disabilities may also have language problems and benefit from the language interventions used with students with communication disorders.

Reading Skills

Students with learning and behaviour disabilities have two major types of reading problems: **decoding** and **comprehension.** Decoding problems involve the skills of identifying words accurately and fluently. They are most readily observed in students' oral reading, when they mispronounce words, substitute one word for another, or omit words (Lerner, 1993). Wong (1996) asserted that the distinctive characteristic of children with learning disabilities is their problems in phonological processing underlying their reading difficulties. Phonological processing refers to skills in using "information about the sound structure of our language in processing written and oral language" (Wagner, 1988, p. 623). Chapter 9 describes adapting the teaching of beginning reading to meet the needs of children with learning disabilities. Many of these reading decoding problems are shown in this oral reading sample of a student with a learning disability.

Here is what the student said:

> Then Ford had uh other i . . . a better idea. Take the worrrk to the men. He deee . . . A long rope was hooked onto the car . . . wheels . . . There's no rope on there. The rope pulled the car . . . auto . . . the white wheels along . . . pulled the car all along the way. Men stood still. Putting on car parts. Everybody man . . . put on, on, a few parts. Down the assembly line went the car. The assembly line saved . . . time. Cars costed still less to buh . . . bull . . . d . . . build. Ford cuts their prices on the Model T again. (Hallahan, Kauffman, & Lloyd, 1985, p. 203)

Here is the actual passage the student was to read:

> Then Ford had another idea. Take the work to the men, he decided. A long rope was hooked on to a car axle and wheels. The rope pulled the axle and wheels along. All along the way, men stood still putting on car parts. Down the assembly line went the car. The assembly line saved more time. Cars cost still less to build. Ford cut the price on the Model T again. (Hallahan et al., 1985, p. 203)

Students who have serious difficulties decoding written words are sometimes referred to as having dyslexia. The Professional Edge on page 156 discusses the meaning of this term and suggests instructional approaches.

Students with learning and behaviour disabilities have problems comprehending stories in the elementary grades and content-area textbooks and advanced literature in the upper grades. Although these difficulties result in part from poor decoding skills, they may also occur because these students lack strategies for identifying the key elements of stories and content-area texts. For example, Todd's teacher asked him questions about a book he had just read as part of his classroom literature program. Todd was unable to tell her where the story took place (setting) or the lesson of the story (moral) because the answers to these questions were not directly stated in the story and Todd lacked the necessary inference strategies to identify them. Patsy was unable to answer a study question comparing the causes of World War I and II because she could not locate key words, such as *differences* and *similarities*. In addition, students may not be able to adjust their reading rate to allow for skimming a section of text for key information or reading more slowly and intensively to answer specific questions.

It appears that the best instructional programs in reading for children with learning problems vary depending on the focus of the instruction. The best ways to develop word recognition in beginning reading involve explicit teaching of phonological processing. The best programs for developing comprehension for older students involve constructivist approaches and teaching of strategies. K. Stanovich of University of Toronto has reviewed the research on teaching reading in a series of papers (e.g., 1994; Stanovich & Stanovich, 1995).

Connections: Specific strategies for teaching reading comprehension skills and other basic academic skills are given in Chapters 7 to 11. Phonological processing is addressed in Chapter 9.

Professional Edge

Understanding Dyslexia

THE term *dyslexia* is used a lot these days. You hear that a friend's child has dyslexia, or you see a "dyslexic" on television, or you read that Albert Einstein and Thomas Edison had dyslexia. The word *dyslexia*, which means developmental word blindness, has a medical sound to it, so you may automatically assume that it is medically based. Yet we really do not know what dyslexia is. Some people believe dyslexia is a brain disorder, that people with dyslexia have a different brain structure that leads to difficulties in processing oral and visual linguistic information and that this faulty brain structure is genetically based (Flowers, 1993). Others believe it is a severe reading disorder that cannot be distinguished from other reading disorders caused by a lack of appropriate teaching or cultural disadvantage (Shaywitz, Escobar, Shaywitz, Fletcher, & Makuch, 1992). Although research using more sophisticated technology (see Flowers, 1993, for a review) provides some support for a genetic, neurological basis for reading problems, the evidence is still largely circumstantial. In any case, knowing the cause of severe reading problems is one thing; knowing how to help students who have these problems is another altogether. Perhaps the best way to describe dyslexia is to say that it is a term used to describe any serious reading difficulty.

Although the cause of dyslexia is unknown, its characteristics are well known. Simply put, students with dyslexia have serious problems learning to read despite normal intelligence, normal opportunities to learn to read, and an adequate home environment. Students with dyslexia have trouble learning the components of words and sentences (Mercer, 1991). For example, they have difficulty discriminating and writing letters (*b, d; p, b*), numbers (39, 93; 15, 51), and words (*was, saw*) that look and/or sound alike. As a result, the oral reading of students with dyslexia is marked by slow, word-by-word reading.

Students with dyslexia also have trouble with the basic elements of written language, such as spelling and sentence and paragraph construction. Finally, students with dyslexia may have difficulty understanding representational systems, such as telling time, directions, and seasons (Bryan & Bryan, 1986). Dyslexia is commonly considered a type of learning disability.

It is important to identify students with dyslexia or other severe reading disabilities early, before they fall far behind their peers in phonetic awareness and word-recognition reading skills. Students who appear to be learning letter names, sounds, and sight words at a significantly slower rate than their classmates are at risk for developing later reading problems. Research shows that these students benefit from a beginning reading program that includes the following elements to facilitate phonological processing:

1. **Direct instruction in language analysis.** For example, students need to be taught skills in sound segmentation or in orally breaking down words into their component sounds.
2. **A highly structured phonics program.** This program should teach the alphabetic code directly and systematically using a simple to complex sequence of skills, teaching regularity before irregularity, and discouraging guessing.
3. **Writing and reading instruction in combination.** Students need to be writing the words they are reading.
4. **Intensive instruction.** Reading instruction for at-risk students should include large amounts of practice in materials that contain words they are able to decode.
5. **Teaching for automaticity.** Students must be given enough practice so that they can read both accurately and fluently (Felton, 1993).

Written Language Skills

The **written language difficulties** of students with learning and behaviour disabilities include handwriting, spelling, and written expression. Handwriting problems can be caused by a lack of fine motor coordination, failure to attend to task, the inability to perceive and/or remember visual images accurately (Smith, 1994), and inadequate handwriting instruction in the classroom (Graham & Miller, 1980). Students may have problems in the areas of formation (whether the letter is recognizable), size, alignment, slant, line quality (heaviness or lightness of lines), straightness, and spacing (too little or too much between letters, words, and lines). As shown in Figure 5.3, students with learning and behaviour disabilities have difficulty writing both manuscript and cursive letters.

FYI: Teachers often mistake natural stages of child and adolescent development for signs of the presence of learning disabilities or emotional problems. Reversing letters or confusing *b* and *d*, for example, is common among children who are learning to write.

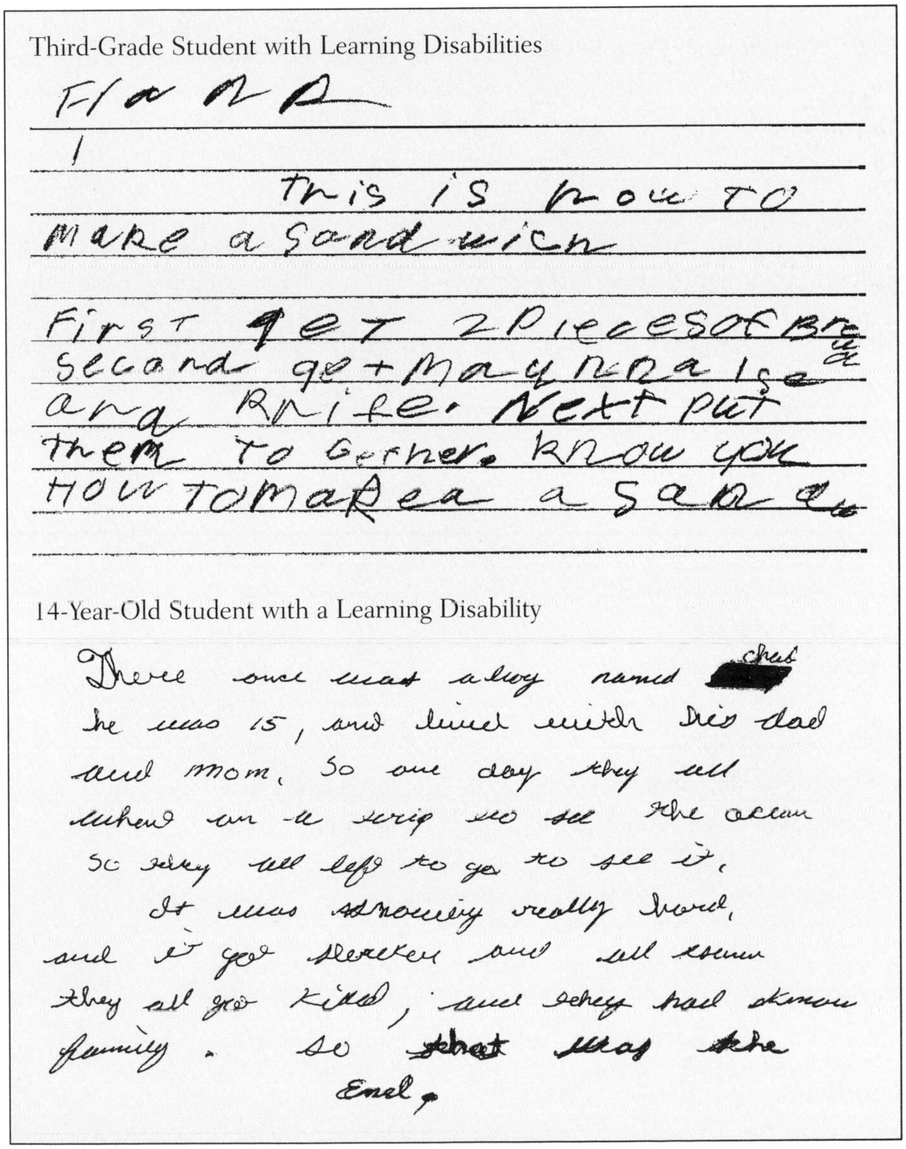

FIGURE 5.3

Handwriting Problems

Students with learning and behaviour disabilities also have trouble with spelling. The English language consists largely of three types of words: those that can be spelled phonetically; those that can be spelled by following certain linguistic rules; and those that are irregular. For example, words such as *cats, construction,* and *retell* can be spelled correctly by applying phonics generalizations related to consonants, consonant blends (*str*), vowels, root words (*tell*), prefixes (*re*), and suffixes (*ion, s*). Words such as *babies* can be spelled by applying the linguistic rule of changing *y* to *i* and adding *es*. Words such as *said, where,* and *through* are irregular and can be spelled only by remembering what they look like. Students with learning and behaviour disabilities may have trouble with all three types of words. Some common types of spelling errors that students with learning and behaviour disabilities make are shown in Table 5.3.

Students with learning and behaviour disabilities have two major types of written expression problems: product problems and process problems (Isaacson, 1987). Their written products are often verb-object sentences, characterized by few words, incomplete sentences, overuse of simple subject-verb constructions, repetitious use of high-frequency words, a disregard for audience, poor organization and structure, and many mechanical errors such as misspellings, incorrect use of punctuation and capital letters, and faulty subject-verb agreements and choice of pronouns (Isaacson, 1987).

These students also have trouble with the overall process of written communication. Their approach to writing shows little systematic planning, great diffi-

TABLE 5.3

Common Spelling Errors of Students with Learning and Behaviour Disabilities

Error	Example
Addition of unneeded letters	dressses
Omissions of needed letters	hom for home
Reflections of a child's mispronunciations	*pin* for *pen*
Reflections of dialectical speech patterns	*Cuber* for *Cuba*
Reversals of whole words	*eno* for *one*
Reversals of vowels	*braed* for *bread*
Reversals of consonant order	*lback* for *black*
Reversals of consonant or vowel directionality	*brithday* for *birthday*
Reversals of syllables	*telho* for *hotel*
Phonetic spelling of non-phonetic words or parts thereof	*cavt* for *caught*
Wrong association of a sound with a given set of letters	*u* has been learned as *ou* in *you*
Neographisms, such as letters put in that bear no discernible relationship with the word dictated	*fest* for *fought*
Varying degrees and combinations of all these or other possible patterns	

Source: "But He Spelled It Right This Morning" by R. Edgington, 1968, in J. I. Arena (Ed.), *Building Spelling Skills in Dyslexic Children* (pp. 23–24), San Rafael, CA: Academic Therapy Publications.

culty putting ideas on paper because of a preoccupation with mechanics, failure to stop to monitor writing, and little useful revising (Isaacson, 1987). Look back at the writing sample of the 14-year-old in Figure 5.3. What types of product problems do you see in this sample? What process problems do you think might have led to these problems?

Math Skills

Math can also be problematic for students with learning and behaviour disabilities. Their problems tend to occur in eight key areas (Smith, 1994; Strang & Rourke, 1985).

1. **Spatial organization.** Students may be unable to align numbers in columns, may reverse numbers (write a 9 backwards; read 52 as 25), or may subtract the top number from the bottom number in a subtraction problem such as

   $$\begin{array}{r} 75 \\ -39 \\ \hline 44 \end{array}$$

2. **Alertness to visual detail.** Students misread mathematical signs or may forget to use dollar signs and decimals when necessary.
3. **Procedural errors.** Students may miss a step in solving a problem. For example, they may forget to add the carried number in an addition problem or subtract from the regrouped number in a subtraction problem.
4. **Failure to shift mind set from one problem type to another.** Students solve problems of one type but when required to solve another type of problem, inappropriately solve them in the way they did the first type.
5. **Difficulty forming numbers correctly.** Students' numbers are too large or poorly formed, which makes solving computational problems awkward, particularly when the students are unable to read their own numbers.
6. **Difficulty with memory.** Students are frequently unable to recall basic math facts.
7. **Problems with mathematical judgment and reasoning.** Students are unaware when their responses are unreasonable. They may also have trouble solving word problems in arithmetic and algebra.
8. **Problems with mathematical language.** Students may have difficulty with the meanings of key mathematical terms such as *regroup* or *rational number* (Cawley, Fitzmaurice, Shaw, Kahn, & Bates, 1979). They may also have trouble participating in oral drills or verbalizing the steps in solving word or computational problems (Cawley, Miller, & School, 1987).

FYI: Adaptations of materials and formats in math instruction include keeping models on the board, providing graph paper to align problems, and using visual cues, such as colour-coded or boldfaced signs and arrows, as reminders of direction, and line boxes to set off problems and answers.

Connections: Specific strategies for teaching math problem-solving skills are discussed in Chapters 7, 9, and 10.

Learning Skills

Students with learning and behaviour disabilities have difficulty performing skills that could help them learn more readily. One such skill is **attention.** Students may have difficulty coming to attention or understanding task requirements (Hallahan et al., 1985). Students may also have problems focusing on the important aspects of tasks. When Arman tries to solve word problems in math, he is unable to tell the difference between information that is needed and not needed

Connections: Specific strategies for helping students remember information are described in Chapter 11.

Connections: Strategies for focusing attention and helping students to process information are given in greater detail in Chapters 7, 9, and 10.

Connections: Teaching strategies for independence is the subject of Chapter 10.

✓ **Your Learning:** What learning needs might students with learning disabilities share? How might you modify instruction in the basic academic skills for these students?

to solve the problem. Finally, students with learning and behaviour disabilities may have trouble sticking to a task once they have started it.

Memory problems may also make learning difficult for students. Some problems occur when information is first learned. For example, Carla cannot remember information when it is presented just once. Students may also fail to retain what they learn. Finally, students sometimes learn something but do not remember to use the information to solve problems or learn other information. For example, a student who learned a note-taking strategy in a resource room failed to use the strategy in her content-area classes.

Students with learning and behaviour disabilities may have trouble organizing and interpreting oral and visual information despite adequate hearing and visual skills. For example, Rodney frequently loses has trouble reading and copying from the chalkboard and is confused by worksheets containing a great deal of visual information. LaTonya, however, has trouble with auditory tasks. She has difficulty following oral directions, differentiating between fine differences in sounds (*e/i; bean/been*), taking notes during lectures, and remembering what she has heard.

Students may also lack the **reasoning** skills necessary for success in school. Important reasoning skills include reading comprehension, generalization (the ability to recognize similarities across objects, events, or vocabulary), adequate background and vocabulary knowledge, induction (figuring out a rule or principle based on a series of situations), and sequencing (detecting relationships among stimuli) (Salvia & Ysseldyke, 1995).

Some students with learning and behaviour disabilities may have motor coordination and fine motor impairments. For example, Denise is a grade one student who has some fine motor and coordination problems, especially when using scissors. Cal is in grade three. His handwriting is often illegible and messy. Cal is also uncoordinated at sports, which has reduced his opportunities for social interaction on the playground since he is never chosen to play on a team.

Independent learning can also be a challenge for students with learning and behaviour disabilities. They have been referred to as **passive learners,** meaning that they do not believe in their own abilities; have limited knowledge of problem-solving strategies; and even when they know a strategy, cannot tell when it is supposed to be used (Hallahan, 1985; Lerner, 1993). Being a passive learner is particularly problematic in the upper grades, where more student independence is expected. When Darrell studies for tests, he reads quickly through his text and notes but does not use any strategies for remembering information, such as asking himself questions, saying the information to himself, or grouping the information he needs to learn into meaningful pieces.

Students with learning and behaviour disabilities may also have problems in the area of **academic survival skills** such as attending school regularly, being organized, completing tasks in and out of school, being independent, taking an interest in school, and displaying positive interpersonal skills with peers and adults (Brown, Kerr, Zigmond, & Haus, 1984). Nicole is always late for class and never completes her homework. Her teachers think she does not care about school at all.

As you can see, students with learning and behaviour disabilities have problems in a number of academic and learning areas.

What Are the Social and Emotional Needs of Students with Learning and Behaviour Disabilities?

Student social needs are crucial to consider because students who have social adjustment problems in school are at risk for developing academic problems (Epstein, Kinder, & Bursuck, 1989) as well as serious adjustment problems when they leave school (Cowen et al., 1973). Students with learning and behaviour disabilities have needs in several social areas, including classroom conduct, interpersonal skills, and personal and psychological adjustment.

Classroom Conduct

Students with learning and behaviour disabilities may engage in a number of aggressive or disruptive behaviours in class, including hitting, fighting, teasing, hyperactivity, yelling, refusing to comply with requests, crying, destructiveness, vandalism, and extortion (Hallahan & Kauffman, 1991). Although many of these behaviours may be exhibited by all children at one time or another, the classroom conduct of students with behaviour disorders is viewed by teachers as abnormal, and their behaviour has a negative impact on the other students in class (Cullinan, Epstein, & Lloyd, 1983). For example, Kenneth is an adolescent with learning and behaviour problems. His father died last year, and his mother has been working two jobs just to make ends meet. Kenneth has been getting into fights in school. He has also been talking back to his teachers frequently and refusing to comply with their demands. Kenneth's behaviour has become so bad that other students and their parents are complaining about it to the teacher.

Connections: Helping students to improve their classroom conduct and interpersonal skills are the subjects of Chapters 12 and 13.

Connections: The use of strategies for responding to student behaviour, including punishment, is the topic of Chapter 12.

Interpersonal Skills

Students with learning and behaviour disabilities are likely to have difficulty in social relations with their peers. Evidence for these problems comes from over 20 years of research showing that these students have fewer friends, are more likely to be rejected or neglected by their peers (Bryan & Bryan, 1986), and are frequently rated as socially troubled by their teachers and parents (Smith, 1994). Many of these problems can be traced to the failure of students to engage in socially appropriate behaviours or social skills in areas such as making friends, carrying on conversations, and dealing with conflict.

Students may have trouble reading **social cues** and may misinterpret the feelings of others (Bryan & Bryan, 1986). For example, a story was told recently about five boys sitting on the floor of the principal's office, waiting to be disciplined. Four of the boys were discussing their failing or near-failing grades and the trouble they would be in when the fifth boy, a student with a learning disability, chimed in to say that his grandparents were coming to visit the next week. Other students may know what to do—but not do it. For example, some students with learning and behaviour disabilities are **impulsive;** they act before they think. Other students may choose not to act on their knowledge because their

Cultural Awareness: Social skills are learned in cultural contexts. Teach your students about the variance in social behaviour within all cultures and emphasize the concept that families and individuals experience their cultures in personal ways.

Connections: Peer relations of exceptional students are included in Chapter 13.

▶ *Students with emotional and behavioural problems might be aggressive, withdrawn, anxious, or depressed, or might exhibit a range of other disruptive or self-destructive patterns of behaviour. What adaptations can you make to help these students in your classroom?*

Technology Notes

Using Computers to Foster Social Development

TEACHERS often think of using computers as a solitary activity in which students rarely interact with either their classmates or their teacher. Computer usage does not have to be this way. Computer activities can be combined with cooperative learning to help students learn important social skills and work habits as well as to enhance their self-esteem (Male, 1994). For example, five students in Mr. May's grade three class worked together on a brainstorming activity in writing. Mr. May gave them the topic of gasoline, and the students tried to see how many ideas they could think of for a story about gasoline. When they were finished, each student chose an idea for his or her story. Luke, a student with a mild cognitive disability, and another student, Levon, liked the same topic so they wrote a story together.

Here is a list of practical ideas for using computers to promote social development in your classroom (Timms, 1991, cited in Male, 1994). You will need to assign and train your groups with care, using the specific guidelines covered in detail in Chapter 13.

1. Combine text and graphics to make book reports.
2. Make book jackets for a story or book.
3. Make a poster to "sell" a book.
4. Make a travel brochure to advertise a story setting for a vacation.
5. Publish a classroom newsletter.
6. Use a word processing program with graphics to write to pen pals.
7. Send interesting questions/information to other schools.
8. Use a crossword puzzle program to study vocabulary words.
9. Make banners or illustrations to decorate class bulletin boards.

attempts at socially appropriate behaviour may have gone unrecognized and they would rather have negative recognition than no recognition at all. The Technology Notes presents strategies to help you foster positive interpersonal skills in your classroom by using computers.

FYI: *Social cues* are verbal or non-verbal signals that people give that communicate a social message.

Personal and Psychological Adjustment

Students with little success at academics and/or social relationships may also have personal and psychological problems (Kerschner, 1990; Torgeson, 1991). One common personal problem is **self-image.** Students with learning and behaviour disabilities often have a poor self-concept; they have little confidence in their own abilities (Licht, Kistner, Ozkaragoz, Shapiro, & Clausen, 1985). Poor self-image, in turn, can lead to **learned helplessness.** Students with learned helplessness see little relationship between their efforts and school or social success. When these students succeed, they attribute their success to luck; when they fail, they blame their failure on a lack of ability. When confronted with difficult situations, students who have learned helplessness are likely to say or think, "What's the use? I never do anything right anyway."

✓ **Your Learning:** What social-emotional needs might students with learning and behaviour disabilities share? Why is it important to address students' social and emotional needs?

▶ *Students operating a television studio*

10. Print invitations to parents or school staff to classroom events.
11. Write poems and include graphics.
12. Create a class book (one page per student).
13. Create flyers to illustrate ways to recycle goods.
14. Allow student experts to tutor fellow classmates or schoolmates on computer or software use.
15. Use a graphing program to graph science project results.

FIGURE 5.4
Diagnostic
Criteria for Major
Depression

A dysphoric mood (unhappy; depressed affect), a loss of interest or pleasure in all or almost all usual activities. At least four of the following symptoms also must have been present consistently *for at least two weeks*.

a. change in appetite or weight
b. sleep disturbance
c. psychomotor agitation or retardation
d. loss of energy
e. feelings of worthlessness
f. complaints of difficulty to concentrate
g. thoughts of death or suicide

Source: Diagnostic and Statistical Manual of Mental Disorders (4th ed.), 1994, Washington, DC: American Psychiatric Association. Used by permission.

Students with learning and behaviour problems may also have severe **anxiety** or **depression**. Heath, a researcher at McGill University, has studied depression, particularly in students with learning disabilities (1992, 1996). Depressed or anxious students may refuse to speak up when in class, may be pessimistic or uninterested in key aspects of their lives, may be visibly nervous when given an assignment, may become ill when it is time to go to school, or may show a lack of self-confidence when performing common school and social tasks. If you have a student in your class who exhibits the signs of depression shown in Figure 5.4, get help for him or her by contacting your school counsellor, psychologist, or social worker.

What Adaptations Can You Make for Students with Learning and Behaviour Disabilities?

As you have just read, students with learning and behaviour disabilities experience a range of learning and social-emotional needs. Although these needs may make learning and socializing difficult for them, these students can succeed in your classroom if given support. Some initial ideas about how you can accommodate students with learning and behaviour disabilities in your classroom are discussed here. You will find much more in-depth treatment of such accommodations in Chapters 7 to 13.

Do It! Interview classroom teachers about their experiences with students who have learning and behaviour disabilities. What approaches work best for teaching these students in inclusive settings?

Addressing Academic Needs

As we have already discussed, you can find out whether students with learning and behaviour disabilities need adaptations by using the INCLUDE strategy to analyze their learning needs and the particular demands of your classroom. You can try three types of adaptations: bypassing the student's need by allowing the student to use compensatory learning strategies; making an adaptation in classroom organization, grouping, materials, and methods; and providing the student with direct instruction on basic or independent learning skills. Several examples of how the INCLUDE strategy can be applied are provided in Table 5.4.

Addressing Social and Emotional Needs

One of the most important reasons given to explain the trend toward inclusive education is the social benefits for students with and without disabilities (Mikkelsen, 1992; Schaps & Solomon, 1990). Unfortunately, experience shows that many students with learning and behaviour problems will not acquire important social skills just from their physical presence in general education classes. Although much of the emphasis in your education as a teacher concerns academics, your responsibilities as a teacher also include helping all students develop socially, regardless of whether they have exceptionalities. As with academics, the support that students need will depend largely on the specific social problem each student has.

Students who have significant conduct problems benefit from a classroom with a clear, consistent behaviour-management system. In classrooms that are effectively managed, the rules are communicated clearly and the consequences for following or not following those rules are clearly stated and consistently applied. Conduct problems can also be minimized if students are engaged in academic tasks that are meaningful and can be completed successfully. Still, conduct problems may be so significant that they require a more intensive, individualized approach. For example, Rick, whom you met at the beginning of this chapter, talked out repeatedly and loudly refused to carry out any requests his teachers made of him. His school attendance was also spotty. Rick's general education teachers met with Rick's special education teacher to develop a

Connections: Review all the steps of the INCLUDE strategy (see Chapter 1). What are they? How can you use them for students with high-incidence disabilities?

Connections: You will learn more about behaviour management, including how to write a behaviour management plan, in Chapter 12.

▶ *In what ways might students who are at risk have difficulty learning? How can teachers address each of these areas of difficulty?*

TABLE 5.4 **Making Adaptations for Students with Learning and Behaviour Disabilities Using Steps in the INCLUDE Strategy**

Identify Class-room Demands	*Note Student Strengths and Needs*	*Check for Potential Successes Look for Potential Problems*	*Decide on Adaptations*
Small-group work with peers	*Strengths* Good handwriting *Needs* Oral expressive language—problem with word finding	*Success* Student acts as secretary for cooperative group. *Problem* Student has difficulty expressing self in peer learning groups.	Assign as secretary of group. Place into compatible small group. Develop social-skills instruction for all students.
Expect students to attend class and be on time	*Strengths* Good drawing skills *Needs* Poor time management	*Success* Student uses artistic talent in class. *Problem* Student is late for class and frequently does not attend at all.	Use individualized student contract for attendance and punctuality—if goals met, give student artistic responsibility in class.
Textbook difficult to read	*Strengths* Good oral communication skills *Needs* Poor reading accuracy Lacks systematic strategy for reading text	*Success* Student participates well in class. Good candidate for class dramatizations. *Problem* Student is unable to read text for information.	Provide taped textbooks. Highlight student text.
Lecture on women's suffrage movement to whole class	*Strengths* Very motivated and interested in class *Needs* Lack of background knowledge	*Success* Student earns points for class attendance and effort. *Problem* Student lacks background knowledge to understand important information in lecture.	Give student video to view before lecture. Build points for attendance and working hard into grading system.
Whole class instruction on telling time to the quarter hour	*Strengths* Good colouring skills *Needs* Cannot identify numbers 7–12 Cannot count by fives	*Success* Student is able to colour clock faces used in instruction. *Problem* Student is unable to acquire telling time skills.	Provide extra instruction on number identification and counting by fives.
Math test involving solving word problems using addition	*Strengths* Good reasoning skills *Needs* Problems mastering math facts, sums of 10–18	*Success* Student is good at solving problems. *Problem* Student misses problems due to math fact errors.	Allow use of calculator.

behaviour contract. According to the contract, each teacher was responsible for keeping tracking of Rick's attendance, talk-outs, and refusals to comply in class. The contract specified that when Rick talked out or refused to comply once, he would be given a warning. If he engaged in these behaviours again, he would be required to serve five minutes of detention for each violation. The contract also specified that for each class Rick attended without incident, he would receive points that his parents would allow him to trade for coupons to buy gasoline for his car.

Adaptations will depend on the types of interpersonal problems your students have. You can use **social-skills training** for students who do not know how to interact with peers and adults (Goldstein, Sprafkin, Gershaw, & Klein, 1980). For example, Tammy is very withdrawn and has few friends. One day her teacher took her aside and suggested that she ask one of the other girls in class home some day after school. Tammy told her that she would never do that because she would not know what to say. Tammy's teacher decided to spend several social studies classes working with the class on that skill and other skills such as carrying on a conversation and using the correct words and demeanour when asking another student whether he or she would like to play a game. The teacher believed that many of the students besides Tammy would benefit from these lessons. First, Tammy's teacher posted the steps involved in performing these skills on a chart in front of the classroom. Then, she and several students in the class demonstrated the social skills for the class. She then broke the class into small groups, and each group role-played the various skills and were given feedback by their classmates and peers. To ensure that Tammy felt comfortable, the teacher put her in a group of students who had a positive attitude and liked Tammy.

For students who know what to do in social situations but lack the self-control to behave appropriately, **self-control training** can be used. In self-control training, students are taught to redirect their actions by talking to themselves. For example, Dominic does not handle conflict well. When his friends tease him, he is quick to lose his temper and lash out verbally at them. His outbursts only encourage the students, and they continue teasing and taunting him. Dominic's teacher taught him a self-control strategy to help him ignore his friends' teasing. Whenever he was teased, Dominic first counted to five to himself to get beyond his initial anger. He then told himself that what they were saying wasn't true and that the best way to get them to stop was to ignore them and walk away. When he walked away, Dominic told himself he did a good job and later reported his efforts to his teacher.

One way to create opportunities for social interaction is to allow students to work in small groups with a shared learning goal. For example, Thomas is a new student with a mild cognitive disability who is included in Mr. Jeffreys's sixth-grade class. Mr. Jeffreys decided to use peer learning groups in science because he thought it would be a good way for Thomas to get to know his classmates and make some friends.

Students who exhibit learned helplessness can benefit from **attribution retraining** (Ellis, Lenz, & Sabornie, 1987). The premise behind attribution retraining is that if you can convince students that their failures are due to lack of effort or lack of strategy rather than ability, they will be more persistent and

Connections: Ways of teaching students self-control are addressed in Chapters 10 and 12.

Connections: Teaching the strategies for independent learning and self-advocacy covered in Chapter 10 helps students who have a poor self-image.

improve their performance in the face of difficulty (Schunk, 1989). Some ideas for how to carry out attribution retraining are shown in Figure 5.5.

You can enhance student self-image by using the following strategies suggested by Mercer (1991):

1. **Set reasonable goals.** When setting goals for students, ensure that they are not too easy or too hard.

2. **Provide specific feedback contingent upon student behaviour.** Feedback should be largely positive, but it should also be contingent upon student completion of tasks. Otherwise, students are likely to perceive your feedback as patronizing. Providing corrective feedback communicates to students that you think they can succeed if they persevere and that you care about them.

3. **Give the student responsibility.** Assigning a responsibility demonstrates to students that you trust them and believe they can act maturely.

4. **Teach students to reinforce themselves.** Students with poor self-images say negative things about themselves. You can help students by reminding them of their strengths, encouraging them to make more positive statements about themselves, and then reinforcing them for making these statements.

5. **Give students a chance to show their strengths.** Part of the INCLUDE strategy is to identify student strengths and then help students achieve success by finding or creating classroom situations in which they can employ

---

FIGURE 5.5

Teaching Positive Attributions

Students attribute their successes and failures to various causes. Negative attributions result when students cite causes that reflect negatively on themselves and are beyond their control. To help students use positive attributions when they talk about their performance in your classroom, try this strategy:

1. Identify the negative attributions you most often hear a student making. Examples include "I got it right. I must have been lucky," "I never do this kind of assignment right," "I'm not smart enough to do this," and "I can't learn this—it's too hard."

2. Create a positive alternative to the negative attribution. Here are some examples based on the attributions given above:

"I must have been lucky."	"And I worked hard to learn the material."
"I never do this . . . right."	"But this time I'll figure out what I need help on and ask for it."
"It's too hard."	"But I know I can learn it."

3. When you hear a student use a negative attribution, take a moment to introduce your alternative, and discuss with the student how to use it. Model the use of a positive attribution.

4. Create opportunities for the student to use the positive attributions and praise their use.

5. Monitor for students' spontaneous use of positive attributions. Call these to the students' attention and praise them.

their strengths. For example, Cara cannot read very well but has an excellent speaking voice. After her group wrote a report on Rick Hansen's "Man in Motion" worldwide tour, Cara was asked to present the report to the whole class.

How Can You Accommodate Students with Attention-Deficit/Hyperactivity Disorder (ADHD)?

Students with attention problems have long been a concern of teachers, especially at the elementary school level. In recent years, this concern seems to have escalated. Whereas this exceptionality was rarely mentioned in earlier Canadian special education policy manuals, Ontario is poised to adopt a separate category of exceptionality called Attention-Deficit Hyperactivity Disorder and British Columbia indicates in its new manual that "for the purposes of this document the term 'learning disability' ... may include students with Attention Deficit/Hyperactivity Disorder (AD/HD)" (1995, section E, p. 11). The definition proposed for use in Ontario says ADHD is "characterized by age-inappropriate degrees of inattention and impulsivity, with or without hyperactivity" (1995a, p. 9).

FYI: Research suggests that many students with ADHD also have a learning disability. Although the connection between ADHD and emotional disabilities is not clear, students with ADHD may have serious behaviour problems, including oppositional behaviours, conduct problems, disruptive behaviours, or depression.

Attention-deficit/hyperactivity disorder (ADHD) is a condition defined in the *Diagnostic and Statistical Manual of Mental Disorders* (DSM-IV) (American Psychiatric Association, 1994). ADHD is characterized by chronic and serious inattentiveness, hyperactivity, and/or impulsivity. You might also hear the term **attention-deficit disorder (ADD)** used to label the condition. ADD is an earlier term for describing attention problems, and some professionals use the terms ADHD and ADD interchangeably.

Estimates of the prevalence of ADHD range from one percent to nearly 20 percent of the student population (Reid, Maag, & Vasa, 1994), but experts seem to agree that it affects no more than three to five percent of students (Barkley, 1990). Although the causes of the disorder are not clear, many professionals suspect it has a neurological basis (Hynd, Voeller, Hern, & Marshall, 1991). Usually, a diagnosis of ADHD is the result of individualized testing for cognitive ability and achievement, a medical screening, and behaviour ratings completed by family members and school professionals (McBurnett, Lahey, & Pfiffner, 1993).

FYI: Parents and teachers often misuse the term *hyperactive* to refer to any students whose high activity levels and easy distractibility make them difficult to control.

Characteristics and Needs of Students with ADHD

The characteristics and needs of students with ADHD can vary considerably. For example, some students with ADHD have primarily an **attention disorder.** They have difficulty sustaining attention to schoolwork or play activities, they often lose things, and they appear forgetful. Other students with ADHD have a **hyperactive-impulsive disorder.** They tend to fidget constantly, need to move around a room even when other students can stay seated, and frequently interrupt others. A third group of students with ADHD have a **combination disorder,** with both the inattentive and hyperactive-impulsive characteristics.

FYI: C.H.A.D.D. (Children and Adults with Attention Deficit Disorders) is a parent organization that provides support for families with children with ADHD. Check to see if there is a C.H.A.D.D. chapter in your area.

✔ **Your Learning:** What characteristics of ADHD does Matt display?

FYI: Behaviour rating scales are frequently used in determining if a student has ADHD. Commonly used rating scales include the *Achenbach Behaviour Checklist for Parents*, the *Connors Rating Scale*, and the *Behaviour Problems Checklist*.

Although all students might occasionally demonstrate some symptoms of ADHD, students diagnosed with this disorder display many of them prior to age seven. Further, their symptoms are chronic and extraordinary. For example, Joyce, the mother of eight-year-old Matt, who has been diagnosed with ADHD, described one memorable morning in the following way: Matt was four years old and had spilled an entire box of breakfast cereal on the kitchen floor and then had a screaming tantrum when Joyce asked him to help her pick it up. He then knocked over a vase of flowers and announced sincerely that he didn't do it. Joyce believed he meant what he said even though she saw him do it. Part of the reason Matt was home that day was because his preschool had asked Joyce not to bring him back. He was too disruptive in class and the parents of other students had complained that he often hit or bit their children. The final straw that morning came when Matt ran upstairs and slammed the bathroom door, locking himself in. He broke the lock mechanism. After an hour of trying to dismantle the lock to open the door, while Matt emptied drawers and cabinets, Joyce declared defeat and called the fire department. The fire fighters rescued Matt by entering the bathroom through a window and bringing him down the ladder. Matt appears incapable of controlling his actions, and he seems not to learn from past experiences.

Cognitively, students with ADHD can function at any level, although the disorder is usually diagnosed for students who do not have cognitive disabilities. Students who are below average in ability and achievement, students who are average learners, and students who are gifted and talented can all have ADHD. Some students with the disorder experience very serious learning problems. Problems can occur in reading, especially with long passages in which comprehension demands are high; spelling, which requires careful attention to detail; listening, especially when the information presented is highly detailed; and math, which often requires faster computational skills than students with ADHD can handle (Zentall, 1993). All of these learning problems can be related to students' inability to focus on schoolwork for extended periods of time and their difficulty in attending selectively only to important aspects of information.

Socially and emotionally, students with ADHD are at risk for a variety of problems (Reeve, 1990). For example, they are more likely to be depressed or to have extremely low confidence or self-esteem. They are often unpopular with peers and have difficulty making friends.

The frequency of behaviour problems of students with ADHD varies. Students whose disorder is inattention might not act out in class, but they can be disruptive. Students with hyperactive-impulsive disorder often come to teachers' attention immediately because of their constant motion and refusal to work.

Interventions for Students with ADHD

To assist students with ADHD academically, you can emphasize key features of their learning and eliminate unnecessary information (Zentall, 1993). For example, keep oral instructions brief. List directions by number using very clear language (for example, "First, put your name on the paper; second, write one sentence for each spelling word; third, put your paper in your spelling folder"). When reading for comprehension, students with ADHD tend to perform better on short passages than on long ones. In math, students should be given extra time to complete computational work or few examples to complete since their attentional problems interfere with their efficiency in this type of task.

Most recommendations for helping students with ADHD academically are similar to those used for students with learning and emotional disabilities, and for other students who need highly structured and especially clear instruction. In the following chapters, you will find many instructional approaches that will meet the needs of students with ADHD.

Behaviour interventions. For responding to behaviour, professionals generally recommend interventions that emphasize structure and rewards, with limited use of reprimands (Abramowitz & O'Leary, 1991). As outlined in the INCLUDE strategy, you should first consider environmental demands and address these as a means of preventing behaviour problems. For example, students with ADHD exhibit less acting-out behaviour when they sit near the front of the room, and they often benefit from working in an area with few visual distractions (for example, away from bulletin board displays). In addition, students often respond well to a systematic use of rewards. You might tell Tamatha, a student with ADHD, that she will earn a sticker for each five math problems she completes. The stickers can later be redeemed for time working on the computer. With older students, contracts for appropriate behaviour can be used.

If a student needs to be corrected, provide a clear and direct but calm reprimand. Say quietly: "Tamatha, do not call out answers. Raise your hand." This message is clear.

Both to address behaviour issues and to teach social skills, some professionals recommend that students with ADHD learn strategies for monitoring their own behaviour through self-talk. Whether these types of strategies are actually effective, however, has been questioned, especially for younger students (Abikoff, 1991). One area in which self-talk strategies are generally recommended is anger control. Students with ADHD often need to learn to control their anger because they experience much frustration that can lead to angry outbursts. If you teach a student who needs to learn anger management, a special education teacher, counsellor, or social worker would probably design a program to meet this need; your responsibility would be to provide follow-through in your classroom. This topic is addressed in Chapter 13.

Use of medication. The most common intervention for students with ADHD is the prescription of psychostimulant medications. Stimulant medications, including drugs such as **Ritalin,** have been demonstrated to be effective in approximately 80 percent of cases in decreasing students' activity level and increasing their compliance (Swanson et al., 1992). These medications do not cure children's choices of inappropriate strategies or the ways they respond; they only reduce the need to engage in stimulation-seeking activity. With medication, the child is more amenable to educational and social intervention (Zentall, 1983).

Despite the apparent effectiveness of stimulant medications in treating ADHD, their use remains somewhat controversial. For example, Swanson et al. (1992) note that most students take stimulant medications for less than three years, and many take them for an even shorter period. This makes medication a short-term treatment, and educators need to work with students and their families

FYI: Because interest in ADHD is so high, parents may ask if you think their child has this disorder. It is essential for you to remember *not* to offer a diagnostic opinion. Refer parents to their family doctor or pediatrician for this information.

Connections: Behaviour and cognitive strategies that are effective for students with ADHD are described in Chapters 10 and 12.

FYI: The three medications most frequently administered to students with ADHD are Ritalin (methylphenidate), Dexedrine (dextroamphetamine), and Cylert (pemoline).

to develop other interventions. Another issue concerns the proper dosage. Some researchers contend that dosages high enough to cause an improvement in behaviour can negatively affect students' academic learning and performance (Swanson et al., 1992). A third area of concern pertains to side effects. For example, approximately 30 percent of students have a **rebound effect** from their medication (DuPaul et al., 1991). As the medication wears off, the student displays behaviours that may be worse than those that existed before the medication was administered. Some students can also experience a loss of appetite accompanied by suppressed weight and height gain (Reeve, 1990). However, once the medication is discontinued, students catch up in height and weight.

Ultimately, a student's physician decides whether to prescribe medication; however, you are likely to be asked to provide educational input into this decision. These are some guidelines to consider when you are thinking about whether medication is likely to have a positive effect:

1. The student's attention is extremely limited, and his or her behaviour is extremely disruptive.
2. Other interventions, in both academic and behaviour domains, have been systematically attempted and have failed.
3. The student does not display symptoms of emotional problems such as anxiety.
4. The parents are supportive of trying medication.
5. The student can be adequately supervised so that medication is taken consistently.
6. The student understands the purpose of the medication and does not have a strong negative opinion about taking it (DuPaul et al., 1991).

Connections: Some families of students with ADHD seek family therapy to help them cope with the stress of having a family member with ADHD.

Before closing this discussion of ADHD, it is important to mention that this disorder still spurs heated discussions. Although most educators and physicians acknowledge the presence of ADHD (for example, Adams, 1994; Adesman & Wender, 1991; Epstein, Shaywitz, Shaywitz, & Woolston, 1991), others question whether ADHD is a distinct condition (for example, Reid et al., 1994). Questions about the existence of ADHD usually centre on the widely different prevalence rates reported, the difficulty in distinguishing ADHD from disabilities such as learning and emotional disabilities, and the absence of a consistent or unique approach for intervening for students with ADHD. Further, some professionals fear that medication has become too easy an intervention for students with attention problems. They comment that giving a pill can be perceived as more efficient than teaching students behavioural or cognitive strategies to monitor their own actions (Swanson et al., 1992), and that even though best practice demands that medication be accompanied by other interventions, too often this does not occur.

Summary

Students with high-incidence disabilities are students who are gifted, or who have speech and language disabilities, learning disabilities, serious emotional disturbances, mild cognitive disabilities, or ADHD. Students with high-incidence disabilities comprise about 80 percent or more of all exceptional students who have disabilities. They are often hard to distinguish from their peers; exhibit a combination of behaviour, social, and academic problems; and all but those who are gifted are likely to benefit from systematic, highly structured interventions.

Students who are gifted include those with generally high intellectual ability as well as those developmentally advanced in specific disciplines. Interventions often used to help them achieve school success include enrichment, acceleration, sophistication, and novelty.

Students with speech and language disorders have a number of learning and social and emotional needs. Their language problems can affect their performance in all academic areas, including reading, math, written expression, and content-area instruction. Socially, they can be withdrawn, rejected by their peers, and have considerable difficulty using language in social situations. The academic and social performance of students with speech and language problems can be enhanced through a number of adaptations, including creating an atmosphere of acceptance, actively encouraging listening skills, stressing words that are important to meaning, presenting many examples of vocabulary and concepts being taught and presenting them several times, using modelling to teach students to expand their language, and teaching within a context that is meaningful for students.

Students with learning and behaviour disabilities are frequently identified as having learning disabilities, emotional disabilities, or mild cognitive disabilities. Students with learning and behaviour disabilities have many learning needs. They have difficulty acquiring basic skills in the areas of reading, math, and written language. They may also lack skills necessary for efficient learning, such as attending to task, memory, independent learning skills, language skills, reasoning, conceptualization and generalization, motor, and school survival skills. You can make adaptations for these students in academic areas using the INCLUDE strategy.

Students with learning and behaviour disabilities have social and emotional difficulties in classroom conduct, interpersonal skills, and personal and psychological adjustment. Their classroom conduct may be characterized by disruptive behaviours in class, including hitting, fighting, teasing, refusing to comply with requests, crying, destructiveness, and vandalism. Students with learning and behaviour disabilities are also likely to have interpersonal problems. They are at risk for being rejected or neglected by classmates, and they may have a number of social skills deficits. The personal/psychological adjustment of students with learning and behaviour disabilities may also be problematic. They sometimes have a poor self-image, are not proactive in academic and social situations, and may experience bouts of depression or anxiety. Adaptations for students with learning and behaviour disabilities in social areas include individualized behaviour management, social-skills training, self-control training, and attribution retraining. Students with attention-deficit/hyperactivity disorder have similar characteristics and needs but demonstrate chronic inattention and/or hyperactivity-impulsivity.

Attention Deficit Disorder Library

qlink.queensu.ca/~3dw18/add.htm

The Centre for Communicative and Cognitive Disabilities

www.uwo.ca/cccd/

Learning Disabilities Association of Canada

edu-ss10.educ.queensu.ca/~lda/

Applications in Teaching Practice

Using the INCLUDE Strategy with Students with High-Incidence Exceptionalities

For each of the four vignettes at the beginning of this chapter,

1. Identify student communication, learning, behaviour, social, and emotional needs.
2. Describe at least three problems the student might have learning and interacting with classmates and teachers.
3. Describe a classroom adaptation you could make for each of these problems.

To help you with this application, refer to Table 5.4 and to the section on the INCLUDE strategy in Chapter 1.

Chapter 6

Teaching for Diversity: Including Students Who Are at Risk and Students From Diverse Cultural Backgrounds

After you read this chapter, you will be able to

1. Explain how regular classroom teachers can address the needs of students from diverse cultural backgrounds.

2. Describe how regular classroom teachers can make adaptations for students at risk for school failure, including students who live in poverty and those who are abused or neglected.

KHAM'S *family has always struggled to make ends meet, but their situation is particularly stressful now. Kham's father left the family two months ago, leaving his mother to care for four children under the age of 11. The family was evicted from their apartment, and they have been living in either a shelter or the family car. Kham is characterized by his teachers as an "average" student, but lately his grade four teacher has been expressing concerns. Kham's homework is not completed, he seems distracted during class, and he has been involved in two playground fights in the past week. The music teacher has noticed that Kham, who had previously been an eager student with a genuine talent for music, is becoming uninterested. When she called on him to choose a song for the class, he said he didn't care. He is also starting to make friends with older students, many of whom have a reputation for gang activity. Kham says these boys are his friends, but his teachers have the sinking feeling that they are "losing" Kham to the life of the streets. How common are problems like Kham's? What other characteristics and behaviours might Kham display in school? What should his teachers do to help Kham stay interested in school?*

Erzsi *is in Ms. Hill's kindergarten class in a small town where her aunt and uncle have lived since their arrival in Canada two years ago. Erzsi and her family have been in Canada only a few weeks. She speaks almost no English and is shy, preferring to talk to herself and hug the toys rather than interact with the other children. Ms. Hill is worried. There are no other children in the school who do not speak English, and it will be difficult to provide an effective English Second Language program for Erzsi. Erzsi does not seem to have much idea what is going on around her and Ms. Hill suspects that she has never attended school before. Erzsi's aunt, who speaks some English, enrolled her in the school and offered to meet with Ms. Hill if she had any questions. Ms. Hill, the principal, and the resource teacher have met twice to assess the situation and generate a list of actions to take to begin to meet Erzsi's needs. What information will Ms. Hill need about Erzsi to begin to include her in the kindergarten classroom? What should Ms. Hill and her colleagues put on their list of actions? What should Ms. Hill do first to help Erzsi? What is the responsibility of school personnel for meeting Erzsi's needs?*

THERE is growing diversity in Canadian elementary and secondary schools. Sources of this diversity include steady immigration to Canada, our willingness to receive people who have been or will be persecuted in their own countries, and the growth of homelessness, poverty, and other social conditions that place Canadian youth at risk for failing to learn in school and for dropping out of school.

As well as pronouncing on the high quality of life in Canada, the United Nations recently declared Toronto the most ethnically diverse city in the world. We observed in Chapter 1 that the Charter of Rights and Freedoms is cited as the basis of rights for exceptional children in Canadian schools. The equality rights that apply to education and are contained in section 15.(1) of the Charter refer to every individual and specifically to children of all racial and ethnic origins:

> Every individual is equal before and under the law and has a right to the equal protection and equal benefit of the law without discrimination and, in particular, without discrimination based on race, national or ethnic origin, colour, religion, sex, age, or mental or physical disability.

A recent article in *The Globe and Mail* focused on the number of students—perhaps as high as 40 percent—who come to school with major preoccupations that take precedence over learning:

> Our schools...to an unprecedented degree, are being expected to cope with physically and emotionally unhealthy children, neglected children, children whose parents lack the time and energy to be with them, substance-abusing children, children with minimum social skills (Valpy, 1993, p. D1).

Teachers work hard to include students such as Kham and Erzsi in their classrooms.

Kham's teachers worry about his future and are frustrated that they cannot make his life better and help him reach his potential. They sometimes feel powerless to influence students, such as Kham, who have so many difficulties in their young lives. Erzsi's teacher is concerned that she cannot possibly make time to provide the English as a Second Language (ESL) instruction that would benefit her. And by the time the school arranges these services, valuable learning time will have been lost.

This chapter is about students who have not necessarily been described as exceptional students in the past but who have exceptionalities and often require special attention from regular classroom teachers. In fact, you may find that you have characteristics similar to those of the students described in this chapter or that you have had similar experiences. If that is the case, you bring to your teacher preparation program knowledge that other teachers may not have, and you may have a perspective on student diversity that you can draw on in understanding student needs. The students described in this chapter include those whose native language is not English and whose cultures differ significantly from that of most of their classmates; and those who are at risk because of situations including poverty and child abuse.

FYI: In most provinces in Canada, programs that support students for whom English is a second language are not considered to be special education programs. However, it is common for teachers of ESL to work closely with resource teachers who are responsible for exceptional learners. Keep in mind that there are students for whom English is a second language who are also exceptional students.

Connections: The Charter of Rights and Freedoms was introduced in Chapter 1. It ensures all Canadians the protection of their rights by law.

The rationale for discussing Kham and Erzsi, and other students like them in this text has three parts. First, these students often benefit greatly from the same strategies that are successful for exceptional students. Thus, one purpose is to remind you that the techniques explained throughout this text apply to many of your students, not just those who have individual education plans. Second, it is important to understand that you will teach many students with a tremendous diversity of needs resulting from many different factors—disability being just one potential factor. You are responsible for creating appropriate educational opportunities for all your students. Third, although many special educators are committed to helping you meet the needs of all your students, you may find that you need to work closely with ESL specialists and social workers to meet the needs of the students described in this chapter. Kham and Erzsi represent the increasingly diverse range of students that all teachers now instruct, and they highlight the importance of creating classrooms that respect this diversity and foster student learning, regardless of students' needs.

✓ **Your Learning:** What are the policies in the school board or district where you are teaching that govern the education of ELS students who also have exceptionalities?

This chapter also highlights how complex student needs have become. For example, you probably realize that exceptional students can also have the exceptionalities described here. A student who is gifted might also be a member of a cultural minority. A student with a cognitive disability might also live in poverty. A student with a learning disability might speak a language other than English at home. You probably also recognize that the student groups discussed in this chapter are not necessarily distinct, even though it is convenient to discuss them as if they are. Students who live in poverty can also be from a cultural minority. An abused student can be at risk for drug abuse. Keep in mind as you read this chapter that your responsibility as a teacher for all students, regardless of their exceptionalities or other special needs, is to identify strengths and needs, arrange a supportive instructional environment, provide high-quality instruction, and foster

Do It! With classmates, discuss the types of diversity found in the schools where you plan to teach. How are you preparing to teach students from diverse backgrounds effectively?

Connections: Chapter 3 described the roles of many professionals who collaborate with teachers.

Students who are gifted and talented are often difficult to identify and challenging to teach. What kinds of intelligence will you recognize in your students? Within your inclusive classroom, how will you address the academic and social-emotional needs of students who are gifted and talented?

Do It! Ask a local school administrator to speak to your class about the guidelines and policies that govern equity in schools. Examine documents on topics such as violence-free schools, multicultural, and anti-racist education in your school.

✓ **Your Learning:** Why are culturally and linguistically diverse students given special attention in a textbook about exceptional students?

Cultural Awareness: Some individuals prefer the term *First Nations People* over Aboriginal or Native Peoples. However, if you can, it is probably best to refer to individuals by the name of their people, such as Cree or Mohawk.

student independence. When students have multiple needs, these tasks can be especially challenging; that is when you should seek assistance from professional colleagues, parents, and other resources. We will also describe briefly recent efforts in Canada to provide equitable education for all students through multicultural and anti-racist education.

▶ What Are the Needs of Students From Culturally Diverse Backgrounds?

The racial, cultural, and linguistic diversity of Canadian classrooms has been growing steadily, and all indications are that it will continue to do so. About 200 000 immigrants arrive in Canada annually, and it is estimated that over 80 percent have a native language other than English and of those half have no English language proficiency (Bosetti & Watt, 1995). For example, in Alberta, more than 1000 children each year—some born in Canada and some who are newcomers to Canada—arrive at school unable to speak English. Research in Canadian schools suggests that ESL students take between four and six years to match the achievement levels of first-language English students on achievement tests (Cummins, 1981; Klesmer, 1994).

Evidence suggests that ESL students experience a high failure rate in school. A study of dropout rates among ESL students was conducted in an Alberta high school with a large number of funded ESL students. It concluded that there was an average dropout rate of 74 percent for ESL students who entered high school between 1988 and 1993 (Watt & Roessingh, 1994). The dropout rate for all students is approximately 30 percent (Human Resources and Labour Canada, 1993).

The reasons for these students' failure to complete school are complex and interrelated, but probably involve several factors (Stephen, Varble, & Taitt, 1993). First, students from racial and ethnic minority groups often lack role models since most teachers are from the majority Anglo-European culture. Second, societal expectations and realities for these students are often contradictory. Although they are told that they can meet high educational standards, they may be discriminated against in assessment practices and through too little support for learning English. Instructional practices can negatively affect students. In particular, textbooks with cultural bias can promote stereotypes and omit culturally important information. Teaching practices that do not allow opportunities for student-centred learning also can put students from different cultures at a disadvantage, because students' background and experiences may lead them to learn more effectively from small-group peer interactions. A mix of teaching approaches is needed. Finally, school policies and organization can penalize students. For example, few schools operate mentor programs specifically designed to connect students from diverse cultures with leaders in business, industry, and education. These contacts can be essential for helping students succeed. Current programs that emphasize multicultural education and anti-racist education for both teachers and students are designed to increase sensitivity to cultural and language difference and to counteract systemic racism (e.g., McLeod & Krugly-Smolska, 1997).

Cultural Awareness

Understanding the characteristics of students who are members of racially and culturally diverse groups involves recognizing that the contradictions between some of these students' home and community experiences and the expectations placed on them at school can lead to learning and behaviour problems. It also involves acknowledging that teachers sometimes misunderstand students and their parents, which can lead to miscommunication, distrust, and negative school experiences.

If you live in an area in which many different cultures are represented in a single classroom, the thought of learning about all of them can be intimidating. It is probably not possible, nor necessary, to learn many details about all the cultures of your students (Wallis, 1993). However, you are responsible for learning fundamental characteristics students might have because of their backgrounds. For example, some students might keep their questions to themselves instead of asking you because of concerns about interacting with the teacher, who is perceived as an authority figure. If you understand this reticence, you can make a special effort to initiate interactions with those students. Further, when a student displays behaviour that you find troublesome, you should determine whether a cultural reason prompted the behaviour before responding to it or assuming that it represents misbehaviour. You can learn this information by talking with students, their families, or teachers experienced in working with students from the culture, or by accessing your district's print or video resources on cultural diversity. Of course, you should also keep in mind that not all students from diverse backgrounds will encounter these problems.

The INCLUDE strategy can be a valuable tool for decision making about instruction for students from culturally and linguistically diverse groups. First, you should consider the demands of the classroom setting, and then identify strengths and interests that students bring to the learning environment. Next, you should look for potential problem areas across your entire instructional program and use that information to brainstorm ideas for alleviating the problems and select those with the most potential for success. As you go through this process, it is essential to monitor student progress and make adjustments as needed.

The impact of cultural and linguistic diversity in educational settings can be examined from three perspectives: how cultural factors affect student behaviour; how teaching approaches can be tailored to culturally diverse groups; and how communication with non-native English speakers can be enhanced. We examine each perspective briefly.

Cultural values and student behaviour.   Varying cultural values have an impact on students' behaviours and the way educators interpret these behaviours. For example, for some students, time is a fluid concept not necessarily bound by clocks. A student might come to school "late" by Anglo-European culture standards that measure time precisely, but "on time" according to events happening at the student's home; for example, after prayer service is completed or morning chores are finished. Another example of the differences between Anglo-European standards and some students' cultures concerns school participation. Students sometimes are more likely to participate when they have established a close rela-

Cultural Awareness: Cultural awareness includes understanding that Canada has been a culturally diverse society for hundreds of years and that families and individuals have maintained their ethnic traditions to varying degrees within our multicultural society. Teachers should not assume cultural traits on the basis of cultural and ethnic identity alone.

Connections: The importance of cultural awareness is discussed in other contexts in Chapters 12 and 13.

tionship with their teachers and peers (Wallis, 1993). Contrast this fact with the common high school structure in which one teacher sees as many as 180 students each day and often uses an instructional format that minimizes interactions. In such settings, students can be at a great disadvantage. Similarly, recent research suggests that some students learn better in cooperative situations (Wallis, 1993). If these small-group learning experiences are not offered in the classroom, some students are being denied access to a potentially powerful learning opportunity. Table 6.1 summarizes traditional values from three different cultures. What impact might these values have on students' learning characteristics and instructional needs? How might teachers overgeneralize and apply these descriptions as stereotypes?

Informed instructional decision making.   Decisions about teaching approaches occur by matching the needs of culturally diverse students in your classroom (Banks, 1993). For example, students from many cultural backgrounds respond well to cooperative rather than competitive learning environments (Adams & Hamm, 1991). Such approaches should become integral to your teaching. Likewise, since some students, including some First Nations students, dislike responding individually and aloud in a large-group situation, you may need to create opportunities for individual contacts, quiet participation, and group response.

Cross-cultural communication.   For students who do not speak English as their native language, school can be a frustrating experience. The following are examples of common problems. Students who do not use English proficiently can easily be discriminated against when they are assessed. As noted earlier, in the past, students were identified as needing special education just because their English skills were limited (Hardman et al., 1993); particular care must be taken to ensure that non-native speakers are not mistakenly labelled. Another example

Connections: Issues related to ensuring that assessment is fair for students of all cultural backgrounds are discussed in Chapters 8 and 11 on assessment.

Connections: Many of the strategies described in Chapter 10 that help students to be independent learners are relevant for assisting students with diverse cultural backgrounds to reach the same goals of independent learning.

▶ *Cultural diversity offers rich opportunities for learning but is also a source of misunderstanding that can lead to school failure. What steps will you take to ensure that you are responding appropriately to all your students as individual members of diverse cultural groups? How will you promote student acceptance of cultural differences in your classroom?*

Polynesian/ Native American	Asian	Western
1. Individual valued as part of family	1. Individual valued as part of family	1. Individual valued apart from family
2. Self-control, humility	2. Self-control, humility	2. Self-expression, pride
3. Reciprocate within family system	3. Submit to family rule	3. Negotiate within family
4. Spiritual harmony	4. Spiritual balance	4. Spiritual duality
5. Reverence/respect for life	5. Partnership with nature	5. Mastery over nature
6. Cooperation, mutual help	6. Cooperation, mutual help	6. Competition, self-reliance
7. Loyalty, obedience, shared responsibility	7. Obedience, duty, honour	7. Self-pride, honour, duty
8. Do what is necessary, play more	8. Work hard, play less	8. Work hard, then play

Source: Reprinted with the permission of Prentice-Hall, Inc. from *Exceptional Children in Focus* (5th ed.) by James R. Patton, James S. Payne, James M. Kauffman, Gwenth B. Brown, and Ruth Ann Payne. Copyright © 1991 by Macmillan College Publishing Company.

TABLE 6.1

Examples of Differences in Traditional Values

concerns the perceptions of teachers and classmates. Students with limited English skills are sometimes considered deficient (Flores, Cousin, & Diaz, 1991); teachers might have difficulty understanding students and might assume they have limited ability, and peers may exclude students from social activities because of language differences. These language-related issues sometimes lead to a third problem, namely, a belief that in order for students to learn when English is not their primary language, they must be segregated from other students. Suggestions for helping students with English as a second language are included in the Professional Edge on pages 184–185.

For culturally and linguistically diverse students, home-school communication is critical. You might have difficulty in even basic communication, though, because of language differences and the lack of availability of an interpreter. Another problem you may face concerns cultural values and parent responses to school personnel (Shea & Bauer, 1991). For example, in traditional Asian families, pride and shame are often emphasized, and indirectness is valued. Imagine a parent conference in which an insensitive teacher describes in detail the academic and learning problems an Asian child is having and directly asks the parents whether they can assist in carrying out a home-school behaviour change program. If they follow traditional Asian values, the parents might be humiliated by the public accounting of their child's failures and embarrassed at the teacher's direct and unnecessary request for their assistance.

Do It! Modify a lesson that you have taught to make it inclusive of students from diverse cultural backgrounds. What kinds of changes did you make? What reminders would help you to consider these issues of inclusion and equity whenever you are planning your teaching?

Connections: The role of cultural awareness in teacher-parent communication and in professional collaboration is introduced in Chapters 2 and 3.

✓ **Your Learning:** What types of communication problems can occur between school professionals and parents of students from racially and ethnically diverse groups?

A third example of the importance of communication relates to the parents' perceptions of school and how they should interact with school personnel contrasted to school staff expectations for parent involvement. For example, the parents of some students might find school foreign and intimidating, and they might believe that their role is to listen passively to what school personnel say. For students from diverse cultural backgrounds who have disabilities, it is particularly important to ensure that adequate information is communicated to parents about the student's instructional program and the procedures used in special education

Professional Edge
Helping ESL Students

As our society continues to become more diverse, you will likely have ESL students in your class. These students can participate actively in and benefit from verbal instruction in your classroom. In fact, active participation will maximize the language benefits they will accrue from your instruction. The following suggestions will help you include ESL students in verbal instruction in your classroom (Simich-Dudgeon, McCreedy, & Schleppegrell, 1988–1989).

1. ESL students may not know the right words to use when they are answering teachers' questions. Before teaching each lesson, identify new and important vocabulary. You can help students understand the meanings of words by using them in relevant contexts. Here is an example of how a teacher effectively defines a word:

    TEACHER: The first question says, "Name the properties used to describe the powders." We didn't call them properties, but what words did we use to describe the powders? Eric?

    STUDENT: Colour, shape, smell . . . [The teacher writes these words on the board.]

    TEACHER: These things are the properties of the powders . . .

    Here is an example of how to guide a student in using the right words:

    STUDENT: . . . because the soap makes the water heavy?

    TEACHER: Is *heavy* a good word to use for that? When something flattens that way, what kind of power do we say it has?

    STUDENT: Adhesive force?

    TEACHER: Good.

2. Sometimes students know the answer but express it in a way that is hard for the teacher to understand. When you realize that a student is having difficulty expressing a correct answer cohesively, let him or her know that the answer is basically correct. Then, rephrase the response and redirect the question to another student:

    TEACHER: What is the most important thing to remember?

    STUDENT: Put the zero... you times...

    TEACHER: [To the whole class] That's correct—who can say it in another way?

3. Make explicit your expectations for a good verbal response. Here are some features of a good verbal response you may want to stress:

    a. Using appropriate words (relevant vocabulary)
    b. Including details and description; being specific
    c. Giving a complete, well-organized answer
    d. Giving an on-topic, thoughtful answer, not just guessing; showing you know what you are talking about
    e. Giving the correct answer

(Sontag & Schacht, 1994). You will share this responsibility with special education professionals.

Multicultural Education

Creating a classroom in which students' cultures are acknowledged and valued is a fundamental characteristic of **multicultural education;** that is, curriculum and instruction that reflects the diversity of our society. Multicultural education

List these features on the chalkboard. As students answer, tell them good qualities about their answers as well as areas they can improve.

4. If you cannot understand a student's English, try these two techniques:

   a. Repeat what the student says, with question intonation, to check your comprehension of the answer.

   STUDENT: Forty-seven.

   TEACHER: Forty-seven? Right...

   b. Tell the student you do not understand. ("Sorry, I don't understand; please say it again.")

To be most effective, these techniques should be explained to all students in the class so that everyone expects them and feels comfortable using them.

5. Rephrase your questions and the answers that other children give so that ESL children have more than one opportunity to understand what is said. For example, when you see a child is having trouble understanding, change questions that require full content answers into questions that give students a simpler choice:

   TEACHER: What happened when you added the drops to the powder?... [no answer]... Did the powder change colour when you added the drops?

6. When students' grammar is incorrect, focus on the content of what the child says and respond to the meaning, while modelling the correct form. One strategy is to repeat what the student said, supplying the correct grammatical form:

   STUDENT: Did the kids went outside already?

   TEACHER: Did the kids go outside already? Yes, they did.

   STUDENT: Some them red.

   TEACHER: Yes, some of them are red.

Writing the correct version of students' responses on the board is a good way to model good grammar without embarrassing the student with an overt correction:

   TEACHER: Okay, what did this prove? Juan?

   STUDENT: If it purple, it's with starch.

   TEACHER: [Writes on board] What did this prove?

"If it turned purple, it had starch in it. If it didn't turn purple, there was no starch in it."

7. For students who do not actively participate in class discussions, check whether different cultural conventions for classroom participation might be the cause. Some cultures do not value children who volunteer answers or speak out. Remember also that ESL children can understand before they can speak. Their seemingly passive behaviour may mask their active role in attending to and learning from the interaction.

Ask students who have recently immigrated to Canada to share with you and their classmates how schools are organized in their native countries, how their teachers teach, how teachers signal their expectations, and what behaviours are expected from students. Parents of these students might be invited to talk to the class and share their experiences.

Do It! Look at the book collection in your school library, the posters on the walls, and the images that define for the students whose school this is. Do these indicators reflect the range of students in the school? Do they reflect the range of Canadians who comprise our society?

Connections: Chapter 7 contains a list of 10 ways to check children's and adolescents' books for racist and sexist attitudes and stereotypes.

begins with examining how you decorate your classroom and how you select learning materials (Allingham, 1992; Lee, 1994). Do your bulletin board displays include students from ethnic and cultural minority groups? When you portray historical events, are members of several cultural groups included? Does your classroom contain stories or literature about successful individuals from various cultures? Is respect for diversity infused throughout your curriculum? Two points are especially noteworthy regarding multicultural education. First, professionals agree that multicultural education should not be an event that occurs for one week out of each school year. It is better addressed through ongoing inclusion of multicultural information in students' education activities. Second, multicultural education is not a topic that is confined to social studies, as some educators believe. It should pervade all subject areas, being reflected in the stories or literature addressed in language arts or English, in assignments given in science and math classes, and in the community contacts that students make in vocational classes.

Lee (1994), a leader in multicultural and anti-racist education, suggests that teachers can do many things to take this perspective seriously, even in kindergarten. She suggests that if all the toys and games in the kindergarten classroom reflect the dominant culture and race and language, then it is a monocultural

Professional Edge

Assessing Your Effectiveness as a Teacher in a Culturally Diverse Classroom

As a teacher, it is your responsibility to respond positively to the cultural and linguistic diversity in your classroom. These questions can help you focus on making your teaching culturally sensitive:

- Do I have an understanding of the cultures that are represented in my classroom?
- Am I aware of culture-based learning styles?
- Are my expectations as high for students of colour as for white students?
- Do I make conscious efforts to engage all students in learning activities?
- Do I make conscious efforts to give equivalent attention and encouragement to all students?
- Do I participate in staff development programs that help teachers better understand student diversity?

- Do the staff development programs for my school and district address multicultural education issues?
- Am I open to identifying racial and cultural biases in myself, my students, and my curriculum materials?
- Do I use methodology that fosters integration (for example, cooperative learning)?
- Do my instruction and methodology conflict with the cultural beliefs of any students in my classroom?
- Do I use a variety of tasks, measures, and materials in assessing student competencies to avoid inadvertent bias in assessment?

Source: Adapted from *How to Respond to Your Culturally Diverse Student Population* by Sarah LaBrec Wyman, 1993, Alexandria, VA: Association for Supervision and Curriculum Development. Copyright © 1993 by ASCD. Used with permission.

rather than a multicultural classroom. You can invite the grandparents of your students to tell their stories and, later in the year, use these stories of their lives in your curriculum. Even on a limited budget, teachers can incorporate multicultural education by using existing materials and asking students about what is missing and whose interest is being served when things are written in the way they are. By drawing attention to inadequacies and biases in monocultural materials and learning to question assumptions, teachers and students together can fashion more multicultural and inclusive classrooms. Matt, a white preservice teacher candidate, bought hundreds of used children's books at garage sales the summer before he entered the faculty of education. Then he went off to his first teaching practice in an Ottawa school. For the first time, he found himself to be a member of a racial and cultural minority. His associate teacher and the children quickly drew to his attention that only white children were pictured in the books that Matt had purchased so inexpensively. These children were accustomed to being critical of books and curriculum materials that did not include their perspectives or pictures of children who looked like them. The students were teaching Matt to teach in a multicultural classroom.

If you develop curiosity about your students' cultures and languages, you will be more sensitive to their learning needs and responsive to them. To guide you in looking at the curriculum and instruction you will use, the Professional Edge provides a list of questions for successful teaching in a diverse classroom. Many resources are available from teachers' federations and associations such as the Canadian Association of Second Language Teachers (e.g., *Multicultural Education: A Place to Start* by McLeod & Krugly-Smolska, 1997) to support teachers in multicultural education.

Do It! Find out whether your province offers and recognizes courses that qualify you to teach English as a second language or teach you to better include ESL students.

Do It! Examine and compare curricula that are called multicultural with curricula that are called anti-racist. What are the essential differences? Which terminology is used in your province or are both used?

Anti-Racist Education

Many Canadian educators have encouraged teachers to move beyond multicultural education to anti-racist education (e.g., Allingham, 1992; Die, 1994). The Ontario Ministry of Education and Training (1993) describes anti-racist education as providing "teachers and students with the knowledge and skills to examine racism critically in order to understand how it originates and to identify and challenge it" (p. 42). The purpose is to prepare all students with the knowledge, skills, attitudes and behaviours to live and work effectively in an increasingly diverse world. If successful, anti-racist education would encourage all students to appreciate diversity and reject discrimination. This approach assumes that existing policies and practices in schools are racist in their impact, if not their intent. Equitable teaching would equalize representation *in the centre* of curriculum of all our students, their values, their history, and their art. Anti-racist education remains controversial in spite of the publication of guidelines such as *Anti-racism and Ethnocultural Equity in School Boards* (Ontario Ministry of Education and Training, 1993). Allingham, a white secondary teacher in Ontario, has written what she calls "a privileged perspective" in which she helps other white teachers to question their assumptions about what makes a good education in a culturally diverse society (1992). She suggests that teachers share books and materials in reading groups to locate teaching materials. "Read, read, read and then talk about reading. Think about who is in and who is not in those materials, and what is said and not said about everybody" (1992, p. 22). Figure 6.1 provides 10 guidelines for selecting materials for secondary courses such as English and history. Although it may be more difficult to maintain this perspective in secondary subjects such as mathematics, science, and technology, this may be because we think of these subjects as acultural. You can provide examples of mathematics, technology, and

FIGURE 6.1

Guidelines for Selecting Materials for Anti-Racist Education

1. Use material from within the cultural or racial experience rather than from an external observer or commentator's point of view. Don't perpetuate the practice of white validation of everyone's experience.

2. Balance the selection: for example, the curriculum should neither exclude all white writers, nor focus exclusively on South Asian writers.

3. Ensure that the materials provide a realistic, authentic, non-patronizing and non-exotic account of their subjects.

4. Canadian material should include the history, culture, and experience of immigration and settlement of visible minority communities. This will include the experience of racism in Canada.

5. Ensure that you are familiar enough with the material to be reasonably certain that it does not confirm existing biases against or stereotypes about racial/ethnic groups. Always acquire material that provides a balance to negative portrayals. The interpreter (often the teacher) must be capable of providing a context that will counteract negative portrayals.

6. First Nations people do not view themselves as part of the "multicultural" community. Identify their work as that of First Nations people, and avoid using the voice of the outsider.

7. The theme or central focus of the material does not necessarily have to do overtly with racism or issues of equity—the work that is done with it can be anti-racist. Choose the material, as always, for age-appropriateness and interest.

8. Ensure that racist, sexist, or classist views are identified as such eventually, even though they may be expressed by a person of colour or the "insider" of the culture.

9. The value of the written material you select is reinforced or diminished by the environment in which it is studied. Ensure that posters, illustrations, symbols, assignments and the seating plan reinforce the value you place on anti-racist work.

10. DO NOT provide this material as an add-on, or as supplementary to the core curriculum. It must be legitimized by its position at the center of the curriculum, along with the conventionally used work.

Source: "Anti-Racist Education and the Curriculum: A Privileged Perspective" by Nora Dewar Allingham, 1992, in Canadian Teachers' Federation (Eds.), *Racism and Education: Different Perspectives and Experiences.* Copyright © 1992 by Canadian Teachers' Federation. Used by permission of Canadian Teachers' Federation.

science as they are practised in other cultures, and highlight the contributions of these cultures to what we think of as western mathematics and so on. These and other suggestions appear in McLeod and Krugly-Smolska (1997).

How Can You Meet the Needs of Students Who Are At Risk?

In addition to all the other special needs you will find among your students, you are likely to encounter one that is found in virtually every public school classroom in Canada. That special need is being at risk for school failure. Students who are at risk are students who have been exposed to some condition that negatively affects their learning. Students at risk include children who are homeless, live in poverty, are abused or neglected.

Some also include additional groups of students on the list. For example, you could include students who are bullies and victims, those who have recently experienced the death of someone close to them, students who are school-phobic, students at risk for suicide, students who are physically unattractive, and students who are socially underdeveloped. Others add slow learners (Watson & Rangel, 1989); children who are parents, and those who drop out of school (Lombardi, Odell, & Novotny, 1990). It is difficult to understand the range of problems that students face and the tremendous impact that these problems have on their lives. One school district committee, formed to identify the district's at-risk learners and to create options for helping them succeed, became overwhelmed at the enormity of their task. One teacher finally suggested that at-risk students were all students who were not achieving in the way teachers believed they could. Another conceptualization of at-risk learners is included in the Professional Edge on page 190.

You might be wondering why students who are at risk are discussed in a text about students with disabilities. The reasons include these: first, with a well-designed education, many students who are at risk for school failure succeed in school. The strategies for accommodating the needs of exceptional students are usually effective for students at risk. Second, it is well known that effective early school experiences for students who are at risk can establish a pattern of success in school learning (Bowman, 1994). Without such experiences, students at risk are more likely to be identified as having learning or emotional disabilities. Third, many students with disabilities also are students at risk. Increasing your understanding of risk factors and approaches for working with students at risk benefits all your students at risk for school failure.

Characteristics and Needs of Students At Risk

Cognitively, socially and emotionally, behaviourally, and physically, students considered at risk are as diverse as students in the general school population. What distinguishes them from other students is the high likelihood that they will drop out of school prior to earning a high school diploma and that they will experience life failure. Some also share other characteristics and needs, including a tendency

Do It! Examine the local newspapers in your community and the larger papers such as *The Globe and Mail* to maintain current knowledge about factors that may place children and adolescents at risk, such as changing social policies that affect the family economically and socially.

FYI: Homeless children must make many educational and personal adjustments as a result of four conditions in their lives: constant moving, frequent change of schools, overcrowded living quarters, and lack of access to basic resources such as clothing and transportation.

▼▼▼▼▼▼▼▼▼▼▼▼▼▼▼▼▼▼▼▼▼▼▼▼

Professional Edge
Identifying Students at Risk

MANY authors have addressed the topic of students at risk for school failure and failure in life. In an effort to better understand issues related to at-risk students, the professional education organization, Phi Delta Kappa, completed a study of the topic in the United States. As part of their work, they conducted a literature search and identified 45 factors associated with being at risk, and educators ranked these factors according to their importance.

1. Attempted suicide during the past year
2. Used drugs or engaged in substance abuse
3. Has been a drug "pusher" during the past year
4. Has a negative sense of self-esteem
5. Was involved in a pregnancy during the past year
6. Was expelled from school during the past year
7. Consumes alcohol regularly
8. Was arrested for illegal activity
9. Parents have negative attitudes toward education
10. Has several brothers or sisters who dropped out
11. Was sexually or physically abused last year
12. Failed two courses last school year
13. Was suspended from school twice last year
14. Was absent more than 20 days last year
15. Parent drinks excessively and is an alcoholic
16. Was retained (held back) in grade
17. One parent attempted suicide last year
18. Scored below 20th percentile on a standardized test
19. Other family members used drugs during the past year
20. Attended three or more schools during the past five years
21. Average grades were below C last school year
22. Was arrested for driving while intoxicated
23. Has an IQ score below 90
24. Parents divorced or separated last year
25. Father is an unskilled labourer who is unemployed
26. Father or mother died during the past year
27. Diagnosed as being in special education
28. English is not the language used most often in the home
29. Mother is an unskilled labourer who is unemployed
30. Lives in an inner-city, urban area
31. Mother is only parent living in the home
32. Is a year older than other students in the same grade
33. Mother did not graduate from high school
34. Father lost his job during the past year
35. Was dropped from an athletic team during the past year
36. Experienced a serious illness or accident
37. Does not participate in extracurricular activities
38. Parent had a major change in health status
39. Had a close friend who died during the past year
40. Had a brother or sister who died during the past year
41. Father did not graduate from high school
42. Changed schools during the year
43. Changed place of residence during the past year
44. Has three or more brothers and sisters
45. Is the youngest child in the family

Source: From "Special Education and Students at Risk: Findings from a National Study" by T. P. Lombardi, K. S. Odell, and D. E. Novotny, 1990, *Remedial and Special Education, 12* (1), pp. 56–62. Copyright © 1990 by PRO-ED, Inc. Reprinted by permission.

to be non-compliant, problems in monitoring their learning and behaviour, language delays, difficulties with social relationships, and problems understanding the consequences of their behaviours (Stevens & Price, 1992). To illustrate further the needs of these students, three representative groups of at-risk students will be briefly discussed: children living in poverty, including those who are homeless; children who have been abused or neglected; and children who live in homes in which substance abuse occurs. Keep in mind that although this discussion treats each group as distinct for the sake of clarity, any single student could be in all three groups.

Students who live in poverty. Students who live in poverty often come to school tired and preoccupied from the stresses they experience in their lives away from school (Kirst, 1991). They might not have nutritious meals, a safe and warm place to play and sleep, or needed supplies to complete homework. They are sometimes worried about their family's circumstances, and older students might be expected to work evenings and weekends to help support the family or to miss school in order to babysit younger siblings. Students living in poverty are also more likely than advantaged students to experience parental neglect, witness violence, and change schools and residences frequently (Cuban, 1989).

Like Kham, whom you met at the beginning of this chapter, some poor families are homeless. Further, many more families are in temporary living arrangements with relatives or friends. Homelessness results in many educational problems. Students sometimes leave their neighborhood school when they move to a shelter or stay with family or friends. This can leave gaps in their learning. Other students are placed in foster care when the family is homeless, and this arrangement affects their social and emotional adjustment. In addition to learning problems, students who live in poverty or who are homeless sometimes (although not always) display acting-out, restless, or aggressive behaviour; depression; regressive behaviours; and anxiety (Linehan, 1992).

Students who are abused or neglected. A second group of students at risk are those who are abused and neglected each year. Recent data show that, in 1996, 3500 cases of physical or sexual maltreatment were investigated by the Metropolitan Toronto Police (Gadd, 1997). There are no national statistics for child abuse in Canada. Each province and territory compiles its own figures according to its own definitions. Although the precise meaning of the term varies, **child abuse** generally refers to situations in which a parent or other caregiver inflicts or allows others to inflict injury on a child, or permits a substantial risk of injury to exist (Bear, Schenk, & Buckner, 1992/1993; Tower, 1989). **Child neglect** is used to describe situations in which a parent or other caregiver fails to provide the necessary supports for a child's well-being, whether these are basic food and shelter, education, medical care, or other items (Bear et al., 1992/1993; Tower, 1989).

Some students who have been abused or neglected will have visible signs such as bruises, burns, or other untreated physical problems. They might also complain of hunger. Germinario, Cerrvalli, and Ogden (1992) also note the following student behaviours that might signal to school professionals the presence of abuse or neglect:

FYI: Because poverty affects life chances in so many ways, students often face multiple risk factors simultaneously. Some children experience both poverty and abuse, for example. Family dysfunction, crime, youth violence, teen pregnancy, and sexually transmitted diseases also place students at risk.

FYI: In addition to the general terms *abuse* and *neglect*, the following terms are frequently used to describe maltreatment of children: physical abuse, sexual abuse, emotional abuse, physical neglect, educational neglect, and emotional neglect.

- Is fearful of contacting parents
- Reports injury by parents
- Displays aggression
- Appears withdrawn
- Asks for or steals food
- Arrives early to or departs late from school
- Reports no supervision at home
- Is fatigued, falls asleep
- Is reluctant to change for gym or participate
- Exhibits regressive, infantile behaviour
- Runs away or displays other delinquent behaviour
- Lags developmentally
- Shows precocious or bizarre sexual behaviour

You should be aware that you have a legal and ethical obligation to report any suspected child abuse among your students (Layman, 1990). If you suspect that one of your students is being abused, you should follow your school district's or board's procedures for reporting it. If you are unsure about those procedures, you should notify your principal or school social worker.

FYI: Children at risk, including those with disabilities, are more likely than other children to be abused. High-risk groups include premature infants, children with cognitive disabilities, children with emotional and behavioural disorders, and children with physical disabilities.

Connections: Fetal alcohol syndrome is discussed in Chapter 4. Children with severe inattention, hyperactivity, and impulsivity are discussed in Chapter 5.

Students who live with substance abuse.   A third group of students at risk for school failure are those involved in substance abuse. Some students' parents have abused drugs and alcohol. The impact on students begins before they are born and often affects them throughout their lives. Babies born to mothers who drink heavily during pregnancy may have a medical condition called **fetal alcohol syndrome (FAS),** or **fetal alcohol effects (FAE).** Babies with FAS or FAE are smaller than expected, may have facial and other slight physical abnormalities, and often experience learning and behaviour problems when they go to school. The prevalence estimate for these disorders is 1 in 500 to 600 children born for FAS and 1 in 300 to 350 children born for FAE (Burgess & Streissguth, 1992). Students with FAS or FAE tend to use poor judgment, leaving a situation when things do not go as planned or failing to predict the consequences of their behaviour (Burgess & Streissguth, 1992). Babies born to mothers who have been abusing cocaine or other drugs are often low in weight. They also are likely to become overstimulated, which leads to a range of irritable behaviours (Griffith, 1992). When these children reach school age, they are likely to experience a wide variety of learning and behaviour problems. They may be inattentive, hyperactive, and impulsive.

Many children grow up in homes in which alcohol or drugs are abused. They are at risk because of a number of factors. For example, they are at risk for being neglected or abused. In homes in which drugs are abused, these students may be passive recipients of drugs that can be inhaled or may accidentally ingest other drugs (Griffith, 1992). Students who live in homes in which alcohol or drugs are abused display at least several of the following characteristics at school:

- Poor or erratic attendance
- Frequent physical complaints and visits to the nurse
- Morning tardiness, especially on Mondays
- Inappropriate fear about the possibility of parents being contacted

- Equating any drinking with being drunk or being alcoholic
- Perfectionistic and/or compulsive behaviour
- Difficulty concentrating, hyperactivity
- Sudden emotional outbursts, crying, temper tantrums
- Regression (for example, thumb sucking)
- Friendlessness, isolation, withdrawn behaviour
- Passivity but becoming active or focused during drug/alcohol awareness lessons
- Lingering after drug/alcohol awareness lessons to ask unrelated questions
- Signs of abuse or neglect (Germinario et al., 1992, p. 106)

A third group of students affected by substance abuse includes students who themselves abuse drugs or alcohol. It is estimated that 18 percent of students have used illicit drugs by the time they are 17 years old, and half of the young adults aged 18 to 25 have done so (Drugs & Drug Abuse Education, 1994). Approximately 90 percent of high school students report by grade 12 having used alcohol sometime in their lives, and 60 percent report having used it in the past 30 days (Morgan, 1993). Students with emotional disabilities are at particularly high risk for alcohol and drug abuse. Students who are substance abusers often have poor diets, sleep disturbances, feel a great deal of stress, and are at risk for depression and suicide. In school, they typically recall only information taught while they are sober, interact poorly with peers and teachers, and display excessive risk-taking behaviour.

As you can see, students who live in poverty, who are abused or neglected, or who live with substance abuse, as well as other at-risk students, collectively have many characteristics and needs that affect their learning. Although some of them are resilient and will not suffer long-term consequences because of their stressful lives, most will not thrive without the support of an understanding school system and knowledgeable and committed teachers.

Interventions for Students At Risk

As a classroom teacher, you will be faced with the sometimes frustrating situation of not being able to eliminate the stresses that often prevent students from learning to their potential. However, you can offer them a safe environment with clear expectations and instructional support that might become an important place in their lives.

Generally, recommendations for intervening to teach students at risk include four areas, none of which is completely unique to these students: set high but realistic expectations; establish peers as teaching partners; seek assistance from other professionals; and work closely with parents or other caregivers. Each recommendation is discussed briefly here.

Set high but realistic expectations. When teaching students who are at risk, it is tempting to make assumptions about how much they are capable of learning. For example, you might think that since the student does not have books at home and the parent is either unable or unwilling to read with the student, the student will not be a successful learner. The result of such thinking is often inappropriately low expectations—which students might "live down" to (Knapp, Turnbull, & Shields, 1990). Low expectations can also lead to your overusing teaching strategies that emphasize drilling students on lower-level academic skills. Although drill activities have a place in educating at-risk students, they must also be balanced with other approaches. For example, students must learn thinking processes along with basic skills, and they need to learn to construct their own knowledge along with receiving it from you (Knapp & Shields, 1990).

One other strategy for setting high expectations should be mentioned. Many professionals now believe that the still-common practice of **streaming** or **tracking**—that is, grouping students for instruction by perceived ability (O'Neil, 1992)—can discriminate against students at risk. Streaming leads to a sense of failure among some students, and it tends to lead to lowered expectations for at-risk students. Grouping students heterogeneously generally does not place

Connections: The topic of grouping students for instruction is addressed in more detail in Chapter 7.

Technology Notes

Using Multimedia for Students at Risk

VIDEODISC technology provides the potential for helping students at risk to focus attention, learn in an environment rich in stimulation, and prepare for the future. It is the most common use of multimedia in classrooms (Lewis, 1993). A videodisc looks like a large compact disc; it goes into a videodisc player that is connected to a television or monitor. The videodisc stores text, graphic, and video information as well as audio. Typically, teachers and students do not view a videodisc from beginning to end; the amount of information stored on one is simply too immense to be used on a linear basis. Rather, they access specific segments pertinent to what they are studying.

Johnson (1992) proposes the use of videodisc technology in these four teaching formats to benefit students at risk:

1. **Format 1: Knowledge acquisition through picture naming.** One great need for students at risk is to learn vocabulary. Many words can be better communicated through pictures or videos (for example, the development of cer-

tain types of clouds during a thunderstorm). Videodisc permits the presentation of hundreds of still pictures as well as video clips to illustrate vocabulary concepts.

2. **Format 2: Picture naming plus an emphasis on function.** In addition to labelling pictures, increasing vocabulary includes understanding the functions of the objects shown in the pictures. One example concerns logarithms: Students may know what they are but have no idea how they are used. Videodisc technology can clarify applications of concepts.

3. **Format 3: Knowledge acquisition in the context of decision making.** Another skill area that students at risk must develop is problem solving. Videodisc programs are being developed that assist in this process in an interesting and challenging way. For example, one videodisc program engages students in saving animals from extinction. Another requires students to balance economic and environmental concerns in a factory simulation.

high-achieving students at a disadvantage, but it may help raise the achievement of at-risk learners (Wheelock, 1992). Although teachers appropriately group students by their need for instruction in specific skills as part of their overall instructional plan, and some secondary schools offer advanced classes that lead to a limited amount of tracking, you should be aware of the potential negative effects of streaming. As a teacher, you can ensure that you do not overuse this type of grouping in your classroom, and you can work with your colleagues to create a school in which students of many different abilities learn together.

One word of caution about setting standards is necessary. Some students who are at risk have such high stresses outside school that they might not have much support from their parents and other family members for school assignments and work. Two examples from teachers help to illustrate this point. One talked about a student who was not returning homework. The teacher was penalizing the student by giving her lower grades and making her complete the work

Interactive multimedia programs

4. **Format 4: Integrating the innovative format into the broader teaching context.** Although videodisc technology is a powerfully motivating teaching and learning tool, information and concepts learned using it must be applied in day-to-day activities in the classroom. Thus, the problem-solving skills that students learn in the environmental dilemma explored on videodisc need to be applied to the issue of garbage in the parking lot or on the playground. Without such specific connections to daily life, the impact of this approach to learning is greatly diminished.

during recess. She later found out that the family was penniless and had a single lightbulb in their tiny apartment. When the bulb burned out, there was no light after sunset, and homework was not the priority. Another teacher described a high school student who always slept in class. Detention did not help, nor did attempts to contact parents. The teacher later learned that this student left school each day, cooked dinner for her younger siblings, and then worked at a fast-food restaurant until midnight. Thus, high expectations are important, but they need to be tempered with understanding the circumstances in the student's life outside school.

Effective instruction for students at risk includes the same strategies you would use for other students, with particular attention to the physical and social/emotional challenges these students often face. Students at risk need a structured learning environment, systematic instruction in basic skill areas, and strategies for learning independence. One instructional approach that holds promise is the use of technology, including videodiscs. This approach is described in the Technology Notes.

Connections: Peer teaching and other forms of peer-mediated instruction are discussed in Chapters 7 and 13.

Establish peers as teaching partners.   Peers learning from one another is a strategy recommended earlier for students from diverse cultural and linguistic backgrounds; it is also useful for at-risk students. For example, in the Success for All Program (Slavin et al., 1994), an intensive early reading program designed to help at-risk learners acquire foundational learning that will help them throughout their school careers, a key ingredient is a cooperative learning approach. Students work with each other in structured groups to learn vocabulary, writing, comprehension, and other reading skills. This program appears to have great potential for helping students achieve school success.

Another example of a peer partner program comes from the Touchstones Project (Comber, Zeiderman, & Maistrellis, 1989). This junior high school program emphasizes restructuring classes to reduce overreliance on teacher-directed, lecture-based instruction. Programs that emphasize learning from peers have been developed to support at-risk adolescents in learning about themselves and about career development. "The BreakAway Company" (Campbell, Serff, & Williams, 1994) uses simulations and self-talk to teach at-risk adolescents about solving personal and interpersonal problems in a reflective way without being impulsive. In simulations of a workplace group, adolescents wear company shirts and produce advertisements for the company. Serff (1996) found that even two years after participating in The BreakAway Company, at-risk youth remembered and used the problem-solving strategies. Another program that uses role-playing and peer partners to enhance self-awareness and career development is *Pathways* (Hutchinson & Freeman, 1994). Adolescents think aloud with partners, and take the roles of employers choosing employees, at one point, while learning to complete application forms and take the roles of disagreeing workmates while learning to solve problems on the job. Adolescents reported increased discussions with adults (parents and guidance counsellors) about employment preparation and about staying in school (Hutchinson, Freeman, & Quick, 1996). Both The BreakAway Company and Pathways, developed at Queen's University in partnership with the Canadian Career Development Foundation, include anger management strategies to help at-risk youth take responsibility for their own actions under stress. These programs emphasize class discussions and active student participation during lessons; the outcome is better learning and enhanced social interactions for students. Students also gain independence as they learn to self-direct their learning and learn from one another instead of relying on the teacher (Landfried, 1989).

Collaborate with other professionals.   A third strategy for teaching at-risk students involves increasing your problem-solving capability by adding the skills and resources of your colleagues. In a survey of teachers' and principals' preferences for providing support to students at risk, these individuals were mentioned as potential resources: special education teachers, other special education professionals, psychologists, social workers, reading teachers, and paraprofessionals (Lombardi et al., 1990). Other programs for at-risk students enlist the assistance of volunteers, counsellors, and administrators.

The purpose of problem solving with your colleagues about at-risk students is that you can check your own perspectives against their, gain access to their expertise, and coordinate your efforts. For example, if you are teaching Shaneal, a student whom you suspect has been abused, you can first ask the counsellor or social worker if there is any past documentation of abuse, and you can request that one of these professionals speak with the student. If you are teaching Jack, a student who is missing quite a few school days and increasingly refuses to complete assignments, you might want to problem solve with colleagues about the causes of Jack's behaviour and how to address them.

Support family and community involvement.   As with all students, it is essential that you maintain positive contact with parents or other caregivers of your at-risk students. However, the level of participation you can expect will vary considerably. Some parents will be anxious to ensure that their children have all the advantages a positive education can give them, and they will do all they can to assist you in teaching. Other parents are not functioning well themselves (Germinario et al., 1992), and they probably cannot be expected to participate actively in their children's education. Stevens and Price (1992) recommend several strategies for improving the involvement of families and communities in their children's education. For example, sometimes it might be more appropriate for a student to bring to school something important from home and to base an assignment on that, rather than being assigned more traditional homework. It can also be helpful to assist parents in connecting with community resources such as health clinics and social service agencies. One school district, struggling because of the rapidly increasing number of at-risk students, worked with local church leaders to connect families with resources and improve the communication between school personnel and families.

When you think about the diversity of students you will teach, it is easy to become overwhelmed by the challenge of meeting all your students' instructional needs. Keep in mind that classrooms structured to celebrate diversity rather than treat it as a deficiency or an exception are classrooms with many options for learning and a blend of structure and flexibility. In the Professional Edge, you will find recommendations for making classrooms and schools inclusive for all students.

FYI: Effective prevention and intervention programs exist for all grade levels. Programs for students at risk are most effective when family and community support are present.

Professional Edge

Best Practices for Including All Students

THESE are considered best practices for creating schools that include all students, whether they have low-incidence or high-incidence exceptionalities:

1. **School climate and structure** includes a mission statement that reflects the school's commitment to inclusive education and an instructional support system for all students and staff.
2. **Collaborative planning** creates opportunities for teachers and others to meet during the school day to develop support systems for students and staff.
3. **Social responsibility** is fostered by creating opportunities for students to demonstrate self-reliance through peer tutoring, participation in school decision making, and so on.
4. **Curriculum planning** ensures that the school curriculum includes age-appropriate content and process-oriented goals and objectives that set high standards of excellence for all students.

5. **Delivery of instructional support services** occurs as part of ongoing school and community activities.
6. **Individualized instruction** takes place for all students using a wide range of materials and methods, with instruction delivered by peers and others as well as by teachers.
7. **Transition planning** so that students move smoothly from one educational setting to another and from school to post-school activities is deliberately and carefully addressed.
8. **Family-school collaboration** is valued and fostered.
9. **Planning for continued best-practice improvement** is addressed by arranging to develop a revised plan every three to five years.

Source: Adapted from "Strategies for Educating Learners with Severe Disabilities within Their Local Home Schools and Communities" by J. S. Thousand and R. A. Villa, 1990, *Focus on Exceptional Children, 23*(3), pp. 1–24.

Canadian Association of Second Language Teachers

www2.tvo.org/education/caslt/entry/homepage.htm

FAS/FAE Information Service

www.ccsa.ca/fasgen.htm

Hooked-On-School

www.schoolnet.ca/english/vp/Hooked/index.html

Summary

You will be teaching students from culturally and linguistically diverse backgrounds. These students and their families sometimes have values that differ from those of schools. Teachers need to learn about students' cultures, teach in a manner that is responsive to the cultures, and acknowledge and value diverse cultures in the classroom in order to teach students from diverse cultural backgrounds effectively.

Students at risk for school failure because of environmental influences such as poverty, child abuse, and drug addiction also have special needs. Because students at risk often live in unpredictable and stressful environments, strategies for teaching them include setting appropriate expectations, understanding the often fluctuating range of their needs, and stressing structure and accomplishment in their classroom instruction.

Applications in Teaching Practice

Developing Strategies to Reach All Your Students

Marta Collings is a grade two teacher in a suburban school district. Although it is only the fourth week of school, she is concerned. She is confident of her teaching skills and has a strong commitment to teaching all the students assigned to her, but she is worried that she won't be able to meet the diverse needs represented in her class this year. She is well aware that student needs in school are becoming increasingly diverse, and her current class group clearly demonstrates that fact. For example, Thuan, who just emigrated to Canada from Vietnam, speaks very little English and seems overwhelmed by nearly everything at school. Ms. Collings can't recall ever seeing Thuan smile. Then there is Sonny. Sonny is supposed to be taking medication for ADHD, but since his family has moved into a shelter, Ms. Collings has noticed that it doesn't seem to be having any effect on him. She wonders whether he is taking the medication. Ms. Collings has been unable to contact his mother during the past two weeks. At the after-school meeting where Ms. Collings, the school psychologist, the counsellor, and the principal discussed the matter, it was noted that Sonny's mother is expected to come to the school for the parents' day in the kindergarten next week, with Sonny's little sister. The counselor is supposed to follow up on this issue and let Ms. Collings know what is happening. Meanwhile, while everyone is sympathetic, Sonny is in her classroom and, as Ms. Collings puts it, "bouncing off the walls." Jenny is a concern as well. She and her twin sister, Jenna, who is in the other grade two class, are struggling academically despite lots of individual attention and supportive parents. Neither girl is reading at grade level; last year's teacher had questioned whether they were ready for grade two, but the school discourages retention except in extraordinary circumstances. Ms. Collings knows that the twins' father has been unemployed for nearly a year and that the family is barely getting by on donations from friends and their church. She wonders how much of the twins' learning problems are related to their home situation. She also teaches Kimberly, who is so far ahead of other students that Ms. Collings wishes she had a complete set of grade six materials to use as resources for her. Two other students—Lisa and Paul—are from families that have very little; they come to school without supplies and seem reluctant to interact with the other children. In thinking about her class, Ms. Collings realizes that at least half the students in her class have exceptionalities of one sort or another. She wants to reach them all. She is unsure whether she can accomplish her goal.

Questions

1. How typical is the type of class group Ms. Collings has? What other types of diverse needs might you expect to have represented in a class you are responsible for teaching?
2. What general strategies might Ms. Collings use in her class that would benefit many students with exceptionalities and harm none?

Chapter 7

Analyzing
Instructional
Environments

After you read this chapter, you will be able to

1. Identify and describe the key elements of an instructional environment.

2. Describe the major components of classroom organization and explain how they can be adapted for exceptional students.

3. Explain various ways that students can be grouped for instruction in an inclusive classroom.

4. Explain how the use of effective classroom materials and instructional methods can benefit students with special needs.

MR. MARFO *teaches history at a large urban high school. When he introduces new content to his students, he teaches to the whole class at once. First, he reviews material that has already been covered, pointing out how that material relates to the new content being presented. Next, he provides any additional background information that he feels will help his students understand the new material better. Before Mr. Marfo actually presents the new material, he hands out a partially completed outline of the major points he will make. This outline helps his students identify the most important information. Every 10 minutes or so, he stops his lecture and allows his students to discuss and modify their outlines and ask questions. When Mr. Marfo completes his lecture, he asks his students to answer a series of questions on the lecture in cooperative learning groups of four. Manuel is a student with a learning disability who is included in Mr. Marfo's class. Manuel has a history of difficulty staying on task during lectures and figuring out what information to write down. He also has trouble remembering information from one day to the next. How well do you think Manuel will perform in Mr. Marfo's class? What changes in the classroom environment might help Manuel to succeed?*

JOSH *has cerebral palsy. His scores on intelligence tests are in the normal range. However, he has lots of trouble with muscle movements; he has little use of his lower body and legs and also has problems with his fine muscle coordination. As a result, Josh uses a wheelchair, has trouble with his speech (he speaks haltingly and is difficult to understand), and struggles to write his letters and numbers correctly. Josh is included in Ms. Kowalski's grade two class. What aspects of the classroom environment do you think Ms. Kowalski will need to adapt for Josh? How do you think she could use technology to facilitate Josh's inclusion?*

FYI: The information in this chapter relates to Steps 1 and 2 of the INCLUDE model presented in Chapter 1.

FYI: This chapter aims to help you answer two questions: How can I teach my whole class so that students' individual difficulties are minimized? and, What adaptations of the instructional environment might I need to make to meet individual students' exceptionalities?

✓ **Your Learning:** Instructional environment includes classroom organization; student grouping for instruction; and the methods, materials, and procedures used to organize instruction and evaluate student performance.

DISABILITIES and other exceptionalities arise when there is an interaction between the characteristics of individual students and the various features of the students' home and school environments. Effective teachers analyze their classroom environment in relation to students' academic and social needs and make accommodations to ensure student success in the classroom. For example, Manuel has difficulty staying on task and retaining new information. However, features of Mr. Marfo's class make it easier for Manuel to function. The partially completed lecture outlines help Manuel focus his attention on specific information as he tries to listen and stay on task; the pauses help him catch any lecture information he might have missed. The review sessions should help Manuel retain information by giving him a mechanism for rehearsing newly learned information. Josh has some serious motor problems, but he may be able to function quite independently if Ms. Kowalski makes her classroom accessible to a wheelchair and works with special educators to use assistive technology to meet Josh's needs in handwriting and oral communication.

In this chapter, the relationship between your classroom environment and the diverse needs of learners will be examined. An important assumption is that the more effective your classroom structure is, the greater the diversity you will be able to accommodate and the fewer individualized adaptations you will need to make. The key aspects of classroom environments are shown in Figure 7.1. These features include classroom organization, classroom grouping, instructional materials, and instructional methods.

◤ How Is an Inclusive Classroom Organized?

Your classroom organization involves physical organization, routines for classroom business, classroom climate, behaviour management systems, and time management. You may need to make reasonable accommodations for exceptional students in all of these areas.

Physical Organization

Although the direct effects of physical organization on student academic performance are open to interpretation (Doyle, 1986), how a classroom is physically organized can affect student learning and behaviour in a number of areas. For example, carefully arranged classrooms can decrease noise and disruption, improve the level and quality of student interactions, and increase the percentage of time that students spend on academic tasks (Paine, Radicchi, Rosellini, Deutchman, & Darch, 1983). Classroom organization influences learning conditions for all students and the accessibility of instructional presentations and materials for students with sensory and physical disabilities. Physical organization includes the appearance of the classroom and the use of space, including wall areas, lighting, floor space, and storage.

Wall areas can be used for decorating, posting rules, displaying student work, and reinforcing class content, sometimes through the use of bulletin boards. For

FIGURE 7.1 Overview of Classroom Environments

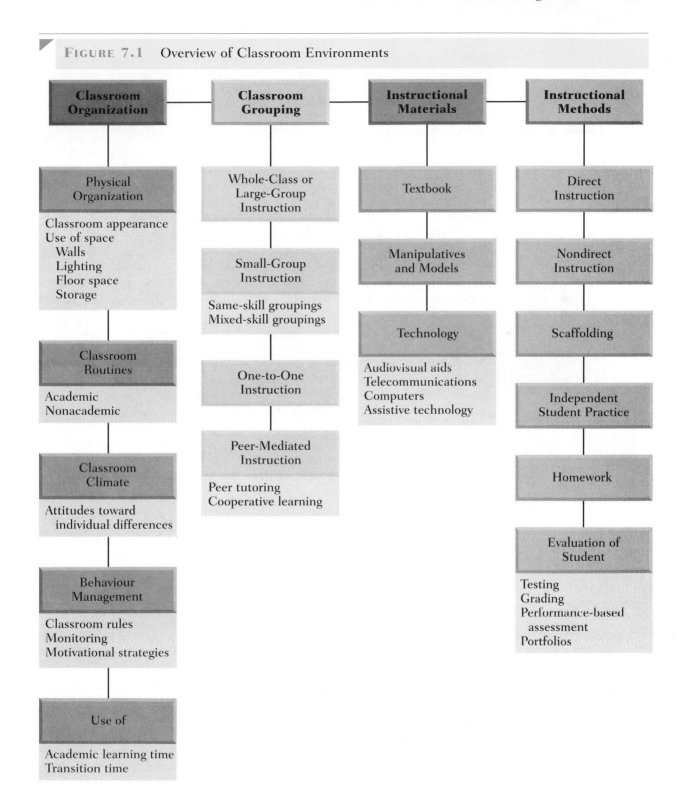

example, one teacher taught a note-taking strategy and posted the steps on a bulletin board to help her students remember them. In using wall space, keep in mind two possible problems. First, wall displays may divert students with attention problems from concentrating on your instruction. Place these students where they are least likely to be distracted by displays. Second, students may not notice that important information appears on a display, and you may need to direct their attention to it. For example, Ms. Tremblay posted a display showing graphic representations of the basic fractions. She reminded her students to look at these fractions while they were doing their independent math work.

Lighting, either from windows or ceiling lights, can also be problematic for exceptional students. Students with hearing impairments might need adequate light to speech read; they also are likely to have problems with glare in areas where the light source comes from behind the speaker. Students with visual impairments also have difficulty working in areas that are not glare-free and well lit. Occasionally, students with learning disabilities or severe emotional disturbances may be sensitive to and respond negatively to certain types of light. In most cases, problems with lighting can be remedied easily by seating students away from glare caused by sunshine.

The way in which floor space is organized and the kinds and placement of furniture used also need to be considered. For example, floors that do not have a non-slip surface can make wheelchair travel difficult. Furniture that is placed in lanes that provide access to the chalkboard or materials such as computers can make mobility difficult for students in wheelchairs or students with visual impairments. Tables, pencil sharpeners, and chalkboards that are too high may prevent access for students who use wheelchairs. Desks that are too low can interfere with students who have prostheses (artificial limbs). Special equipment in science labs, computer centres, and vocational areas can also present access problems for exceptional students. For example, the lathe in the woodworking shop might be positioned too high for a person in a wheelchair to operate; the space between work areas in the science lab might not be wide enough for a wheelchair to get through. Finally, the arrangement of your class should be predictable. This means that you should not make major changes without first considering their impact on exceptional students and then informing these students so they have time to adapt. For example, Mr. Tate decided to move one of the bookshelves in his classroom. He noticed, however, that the new location blocked the passageway from the door to the desk of a student in his class who was blind. Mr. Tate informed the student of the move in advance and together they worked out an alternative route to the student's desk.

The arrangement of student desks, whether in rows, circles, or small groups, can have considerable impact on exceptional students. For example, traditional row configurations, which provide students with an immediate, unobstructed view of the teacher, have been shown to help students with attention disorders focus better when the teacher is instructing the whole group at one time. On the other hand, the placement of desks into clusters of four works better when you are using mixed-ability, cooperative learning groups to help integrate a student who is socially withdrawn. Another important consideration about floor space concerns student monitoring: Teachers should be able to see all parts of the classroom at all times, whether they are teaching large or small groups, or are working at their desks. Designing such visual access means that all specially designated areas in the classroom, such as learning/interest centres, computer stations, small-group instructional areas, or study carrels, need to be positioned so they can be monitored.

An additional area of physical organization is storage. For example, students with visual disabilities may need to store equipment such as tape recorders, large-print books, Braille books, and magnifying devices. For students with severe disabilities, space might be needed to store book holders, paper holders, page turners, braces, crutches, and communication boards.

Routines for Classroom Business

Establishing clear routines in both academic and non-academic areas is important for two reasons. First, routines that are carefully structured (that is, clear to students and used consistently) reduce non-academic time and increase learning time. Second, you can prevent many discipline problems by having predictability in your classroom routines.

Most students, especially exceptional students, find stability in knowing that classroom activities will be similar each day. In the absence of this stability, misbehaviour often follows. You can find many examples of breaks in school routines. On the day of a field trip, elementary school students are more likely to hit or push, to delay beginning assignments, and to do poor work. In junior and senior high schools, teachers often dread shortened schedules for assemblies and other school programs because of increased student behaviour problems.

You can create daily classroom routines that help students learn. For example, you might expect grade four students to enter your classroom each morning, to begin their morning work, and to read quietly if they finish before instruction begins. Having routines for sharing time, setting up science experiments, preparing to go to physical education, moving to the computer lab, and so on will help students meet your expectations. Routines are especially helpful to students who need a strong sense of structure in classroom life. In secondary schools, routines might include having specific lab procedures, starting each class with a five-minute review, or scheduling a particular activity on the same day every week. For example, in a geometry class, students who complete their assignments might choose to begin the day's homework, complete a Math Challenger worksheet from the activity file, or work on research papers or other long-term projects.

You can also create routines for student accountability that help students to be clear about your expectations. Dworet of Brock University and his colleagues (e.g., Dworet, Davis, & Martin, 1996) have described how students need to know your expectations for quantity and quality of academic work, along with timelines and procedures to follow when they encounter difficulties. In a descriptive study carried out with a teacher in an urban school, Hutchinson (in press) demonstrated that teaching exceptional adolescents to be accountable for completing collaborative problem solving contributed to a high level of learning in mathematics. Applying the negotiated consequences, for failing to make group submissions, changed the activity patterns in the classroom within a week. In subsequent weeks, the teacher and class modelled accountability routines for other subjects on their successful routines in mathematics.

Classroom Climate

A number of authors have noted that classroom climate contributes significantly to the number and seriousness of classroom behaviour problems (Bennett & Smilanich, 1994; Jones & Jones, 1990; Morse, 1987). The **classroom climate** concerns the overall atmosphere in the classroom—whether it is friendly or unfriendly, pleasant or unpleasant, and so on. Climate is influenced by the attitudes of the teacher and students toward individual differences: Is the classroom characterized by a cooperative or competitive atmosphere? Is the classroom a safe place for all students to take risks? Are skills for interacting positively with children and adults actively supported in the classroom?

Connections: Specific strategies for teaching students to respect individual differences are described in Chapter 13.

Teachers who communicate respect and trust to their students are more successful in creating positive classroom environments in which fewer behaviour problems occur (Deluke & Knoblock, 1987). For example, Mr. Elliott reprimanded a student who talked out of turn by saying, "I know you have a question about your work, and I'm glad you care enough to ask for help; but I need to have you raise your hand because I can only help people one at a time." Mr. Elliott showed respect for the student and built the student's trust by not putting her down. Yet, Mr. Elliott stuck to his rule about not speaking before being called on and explained why it was important.

FYI: Checking for student strengths is an important step in the INCLUDE model.

You build the overall quality of your communication with your students in numerous small ways. For example, finding the time each week to speak privately with students lets them know that you care about them as individuals. Asking older students sincere questions about their friends, out-of-school activities, or part-time jobs also conveys your interest in them. Taking the time to write positive comments on papers lets students know that you appreciate their strengths and do not focus only on their needs. When you encourage each student to achieve his or her own potential, without continually comparing students, you are communicating the idea that each class member has a valuable contribution to make. Teachers who fail to take these small steps toward positive communication with students, or who publicly embarrass a student or punish a group for the behaviour of a few, soon may create a negative classroom climate that thwarts appropriate and effective learning.

Behaviour Management

FYI: Classrooms in which instruction is relevant, interesting, and active are classrooms with fewer behaviour problems. Strategies to design instruction effectively to maximize student learning are covered in Chapters 9 and 10.

Behaviour management is a critical precursor to learning. When clear expectations for student behaviours and systematic procedures for helping students meet those expectations are lacking, even the best lessons or adaptations lose their effectiveness. Three major components of **behaviour management systems** are essential: rules, monitoring, and the use of consequences or other motivational techniques.

Classroom rules.   What rules do you intend to establish in your classroom? Rules help create a sense of order and expectations for a classroom, and they form a significant first step in setting up a learning environment based on preventive classroom management. Teachers who are effective classroom managers have well-defined rules for their classrooms (for example, Bullara, 1993; Smith & Mirsa, 1992).

Effective classroom rules share three key characteristics: they are brief and specific; positively worded; and clearly understood by students (Doyle, 1990).

First, rules should be few in number but as specific as possible. For example, a list of 10 or 12 rules that urge students to be fair, kind, and respectful are not as useful as three or five rules such as "Speak one at a time," "Keep your hands to yourself," and "Be prepared to start class when the bell rings by having all your learning materials ready."

Second, rules should be worded in a positive way (Bullara, 1993). Consider the difference between a rule that states "Don't call out answers" and one that says "Raise your hand to speak." If students assist in making classroom rules, you can encourage positive wording by rephrasing rules that students suggest if they are inappropriately worded. Keep in mind that students who participate in rule making might be more motivated to obey rules.

Third, rules should be explained carefully to your students. Post rules during the first weeks of school, explain and discuss them, and model them for students. Violations of the rules should be pointed out and corrected immediately. For example, after you and your students have established and reviewed classroom rules, explain their use, congratulate students for following them, and ask students whom you reprimand to explain why their behaviour violated the rules. Younger students could draw pictures about their classroom rules and procedures. Older students could write about the need for rules. This early attention to setting your classroom expectations will pay off throughout the school year. By rehearsing and focusing student attention on them, the rules will become part of students' understanding of their classroom. If you do not take this time to teach the rules, too often they become merely a bulletin board display, ignored by teachers and students alike.

Monitoring. In addition to having clear expectations, you also need to monitor student classroom behaviours frequently. For example, scan the room to check that students are following the rules. If student behaviour is not carefully monitored, students choose not to follow the rules consistently. For example, Charmaine is a student with behaviour problems who is included in Ms. Patrick's grade five class. Ms. Patrick has a rule that students must complete all of their independent work before they can go to the computer station to play a problem-solving game. Ms. Patrick did not have time to monitor Charmaine's behaviour. One day, she saw Charmaine at the computer station and asked her if she had completed her assignments. Not only had Charmaine not completed her assignments on that day, but she also hadn't done any work for the past three days. Thereafter, Ms. Patrick was careful to monitor the work completion behaviour of all her students.

Motivational strategies. In an effective behaviour management system, consequences and other motivational strategies such as goal setting and self-monitoring are used to maintain appropriate classroom behaviour. It is easier for you and students to set goals and monitor progress within an individual lesson when you provide a written agenda. When Duquette (1996) conducted research in secondary schools in eastern Ontario, she found that one feature of classrooms with effective management and motivational strategies was a written agenda. The agenda can be written on the board or on chart paper. You can direct individuals' attention to a particular element of the agenda or ask individuals to add sub-goals whose accomplishment will serve as a motivator for them.

FYI: Research suggests that the most effective classroom rules are ones that students develop themselves and express with teacher guidance.

Cultural Awareness: If your classroom includes students who are not native English speakers, you need to ensure that these students understand the rules.

Connections: Arranging your classroom to ensure an unobstructed view was discussed earlier in this chapter.

Connections: Strategies for effective classroom management, goal setting, and self-monitoring programs are presented in more detail in Chapters 10 and 12.

Behaviour consequences involve the type of rewards and punishment you use as well as the ways in which you present the rewards and punishments to students. For example, if rewards are to be effective, they need to be things students like; rewards also need to be delivered *soon after* and *only if* the student behaves appropriately. Consider the case of Tim, a boy who constantly talks out of turn in class. One day, Tim raised his hand before he spoke. His teacher, Mr. Ali, immediately praised Tim for raising his hand, which motivated Tim to raise his hand three more times that day. Mr. Ali used rewards effectively because he selected one that Tim liked (teacher recognition) and delivered it right after Tim raised his hand. You can also use other methods of motivating students, such as goal setting and self-monitoring. These methods involve students directly in their own interventions and can help students become more independent. For example, Tim's teacher asked him to set a goal for himself regarding the number of his talkouts and also asked Tim to keep track of his own talkouts and record them on a chart.

Use of Time

The amount of time that students are meaningfully and successfully engaged in academic activities in school is referred to as **academic learning time** (Arends, 1991). Research has shown that the greater the academic learning time in a classroom, the more students learn (Fisher et al., 1980). Time usage is particularly important for exceptional students, who may need more time to learn than their peers. If you use the strategies described in this chapter and throughout this book to organize your classroom, group your students, and adapt your materials and methods, you can greatly increase the academic learning time for all your students.

Just as important as the amount of time spent in academic activities is the management of transition time. **Transition time** is the time it takes to change from one activity to another. Transition time can occur when students remain at their seats and change from one subject to another, move from their seats to an activity in another part of the classroom, move from somewhere else in the classroom back to their seats, leave the classroom to go outside or to another part of the school building, or come back into the classroom from outside or another part of the building (Paine et al., 1983, p. 84).

Research studies show that teachers sometimes waste instructional time by not managing transitions carefully (Ornstein, 1990). Arlin (1979) found that better-managed classrooms had fewer transitions. On the other hand, Smith (1985) of Queen's University found that, for a teacher who created smooth transitions, a large number of transitions was not a problem. Smith's videotaped data showed that the teacher with smooth transitions verbally and non-verbally marked clearly the beginnings and endings of transitions, remained task-oriented through the transitions, and addressed any inappropriate behaviours as soon as they occurred. You may also find it helpful, especially for exceptional children who dislike disruption, to prepare for the transition in advance, "You have five more minutes to work on your towers (or shared problem solving) and then it will be time to tidy up the blocks (or to finish the rest for homework tonight)."

How you organize classroom materials can also affect the management of your transitions. For example, you need to have all your materials ready for each subject and activity. In addition, your materials should be organized so that they

Professional Edge

Using "Sponges" to Increase Academic Learning Time

You almost always have times during the day when you have a minute or two before a scheduled academic activity or before the class goes to lunch, an assembly, or recess. You can fill that extra time with productive activities by using "sponges." Sponges are activities that fit into brief periods of time and that give students practice or review on skills and content you have already covered in class. The following lists of sponges will help you "soak up" that extra classroom time.

Beginning Sponges (Lower Grades)

1. Be ready to tell one playground rule.
2. Be ready to tell me the names of the children in our class that begin with *J* or *M*, and so on.
3. Be ready to tell a good health habit.
4. Say numbers, days of the week, months— and have children tell what comes next.
5. What number comes between these two numbers: 31–33, 45–47, and so forth.
6. What number comes before/after 46, 52, 13, and so on?
7. Write a word on the board. Ask children to list words that rhyme with it.
8. Think of animals that live on a farm, in the jungle, in water, and so forth.
9. List things you can touch, things you can smell, and so on.

Dismissal Sponges

1. "I Spy"—Who can find something in the room that starts with *M*, *P*, and so on?
2. Who can find something in the room that has the sound of short *a*, long *a*, and so forth?
3. Number rows or tables. The teacher signals the number of the table with fingers, and children leave accordingly.
4. Count in order or by 2s, 5s, and so on.
5. What day is it? What month is it? What is the date? What year is it? How many months

in a year? How many days in a week? and so on.
6. Reward activity: "We have had a good day! Who helped it be a good day for all of us? Betty, you brought flowers to brighten our room. You may leave. John, you remembered to rinse your hands, good for you. You may leave. Ellen showed us that she could be quiet coming into the room today. You may leave, Ellen. Bob remembered his library book all by himself." Some students can be grouped together for good deeds to speed things up. The teacher can finish with, "You're all learning to be very thoughtful. I'm very proud of all of you and you should be very proud of yourselves."
7. To review the four basic shapes, each child names an object in the room either in the shape of a triangle, circle, square, or rectangle.

Upper Grade Sponges

1. List the continents.
2. Name as many gems or precious stones as you can.
3. Write an abbreviation; a Roman numeral; a trademark; a proper name (biological); a proper name (geographical).
4. How many countries and their capitals can you name?
5. List five parts of the body *above the neck* that have three letters.
6. List one manufactured item for each letter of the alphabet.
7. List as many nouns in the room as you can.
8. How many parts of a car can you list?
9. List as many personal pronouns as you can.
10. Name as many politicians as you can.

Source: From *Effective Teaching for Higher Achievement* by D. Sparks and G. M. Sparks, 1984, Alexandria, VA: Association for Supervision and Curriculum Development. Copyright © 1984 by ASCD. Used with permission.

✓ **Your Learning:** What are the key elements of classroom organization? How is classroom organization related to student behaviour in the classroom?

are easily accessible. No matter how well organized your transitions, you still may need to adapt them for some exceptional students. Students with physical disabilities may need more time to take out or put away their books. Students with physical and visual disabilities may have mobility problems that cause them to take more time with transitional activities such as getting into instructional groups or moving from room to room. Another way to increase the academic learning time of your students is described in the Professional Edge on page 211.

How Can You Group All Your Students for Instruction in Inclusive Classrooms?

Exceptional students benefit from a variety of classroom grouping arrangements, including large- or small-group instruction, mixed- and same-ability groupings, and teacher-centred or peer-mediated group instruction. It is important to remember that the particular arrangement you choose depends on your instructional objectives as well as your students' particular needs.

Whole-Class or Large-Group Instruction

FYI: An advantage of co-teaching (see Chapter 3) is that it gives teachers more grouping options and students more time with the teacher.

Exceptional students benefit from both whole-class and small-group instruction. One advantage of whole-group instruction is that students spend the entire time with the teacher. In small-group instruction, on the other hand, students spend part of the time with the teacher but also spend time working independently while the teacher works with the other small groups. Research shows that the more time students spend with the teacher, the more they learn (Rosenshine & Stevens, 1986). This increase in learning may be because students are more likely to go off task when they are working on their own, particularly if they have learning or behaviour problems. Whatever grouping arrangements you use, ensure that students spend as much time as possible working with you. Another advantage of whole-group instruction is that it does not single out exceptional students as being different from their peers. However, you may need to adapt whole-group instruction for exceptional students. For example, students in a grade four class were reading *Charlotte's Web* as a large-group instructional activity. One student in the class read more slowly than the rest of the class. To help her keep up, the teacher made a list of hard words for each chapter, which a peer tutor taught the student before she read. The teacher also gave the student more time to answer comprehension questions about the story in class because it took her longer to look up some of the answers. In another example, a high school science teacher identified technical words he was going to use in a lab ahead of time and worked on them with a small group of students with vocabulary problems before school.

Small-Group Instruction

You may encounter situations in which small-group instruction is more appropriate for exceptional students. You can use either same-skill groupings or mixed-skill groupings in setting up your small groups.

Same-skill groupings are helpful when some but not all students are having trouble mastering a particular skill and need more instruction and practice. For example, a teacher was showing her students how to divide fractions that have a common denominator. She gave her class a mini-quiz to see who had learned how to do the problems. She found that all but five students had mastered the skill. The next day, the teacher worked with these five students while the rest of the class did an application activity. It is important to recognize that small-group instruction is not only for special education or remedial students; most students benefit from extra help in a small group at one time or another. In fact, many times your exceptional students will not need extra instruction.

Small, same-skill groups are also used in basic skill areas when students are performing well below most of the class. For example, Lori is in Ms. Patel's grade four class and is reading at the grade two level. Lori is learning decoding and vocabulary skills in a small group with other students who are at her level. Because the group is small and homogeneous, Ms. Patel is able to proceed in small steps, present many examples, and allow students to master skills before they move on. Lori is making progress and feels good about herself because she is becoming a better reader. But keep in mind that small, same-skill groups should be used only when attempts to adapt instruction in the large group have been unsuccessful. Same-skill groups tend to become permanent and take on a life of their own, and students are more likely to become stigmatized when they are entrenched in low groups. Although some students do require instruction that is more individualized and intensive than can be provided in the large group, the ultimate goal of any small group should be its eventual dissolution. Also, on many days, students can benefit from instruction with the rest of the class. For example, Lori's group participates in large-group reading when the teacher is reading a story and working on listening comprehension. Another potential problem in using same-skill groupings is the danger that students who are in a low-achieving group in one area will be placed in low groups in other areas even though their

Connections: Strategies for grouping students for instruction are discussed in more detail in Chapter 8.

Cultural Awareness: Research suggests that students can sometimes benefit from working in same-sex groups. The achievement scores of girls grouped together for math and science instruction are generally higher than for girls grouped with boys.

Do It! Observe student groupings in action. Based on your observations, what factors contribute to effective grouping procedures, group characteristics, and group dynamics?

▶ *This is a teacher-centred grouping arrangement for small-group instruction. What are some advantages and disadvantages of this strategy for exceptional students? What other ways of grouping students should be part of a teacher's instructional repertoire?*

skill levels do not justify it. For example, just because Lori is in the lowest group in reading does not automatically mean she needs to be in low groups in other areas such as math.

Small, same-skill groups are also used to enable gifted students to work with peers of similar ability in specific curriculum areas when they are performing well above the rest of the class. For example, Rob and two of his peers are reading about the solar system and preparing a report to present to the class while Ms. Patel is teaching comprehension and decoding skills to the other students. These three children do not need advanced instruction in mathematics; thus, they work in mixed-skill and whole-class groupings for math. Keating (1991) and Matthews (in press) of the University of Toronto have described many ways in which same-skill groupings can be used at some point in the day to stimulate students who are gifted and challenge them to keep learning.

The major advantage of **mixed-skill groupings** is that they provide exceptional students with a range of positive models of both academic and social behaviour. In mixed-skill groupings, students often help each other, so such groups can also be a vehicle for providing direct instruction to individual students, something for which classroom teachers do not often have time. In addition, mixed-skill groups, like large groups, tend not to single out exceptional students.

One-to-One Instruction

FYI: Co-teaching gives students more opportunities for one-to-one instruction in class.

Providing **one-to-one instruction** for exceptional students can be very effective under some circumstances. In this grouping arrangement, students work with either a teacher or computer in well-sequenced materials that are geared to their specific level and proceed through the materials at their own pace. For example, Waldo is having trouble with addition and subtraction facts. For 15 minutes each day, he works at the classroom computer station on an individualized drill-and-practice program. Right now he is working on his addition facts through 10. When he masters these, the computer will automatically place him into more difficult problems. Although one-to-one instruction may be appropriate in some circumstances, it is not necessarily the grouping arrangement of choice. First, it is inefficient; when it is carried out by the classroom teacher, the extensive use of one-to-one instruction will result in less instructional time for everyone. Second, the logistics of one-to-one instruction sometimes require that students complete much independent work while the teacher moves from student to student. This can lead to high levels of off-task behaviour—a problem many exceptional students experience (Hardman, Drew, Egan, & Wolf, 1993; Mercer, 1991). Third, the lack of peer models in one-to-one instruction makes it more difficult to motivate students—a problem particularly relevant at the high school level (Ellis & Sabornie, 1990). Sometimes, its exclusive use can exclude students from critical social interactions and reduce the feeling of belonging and community in the classroom. Finally, if a student requires one-to-one instruction for extended periods of time, further analysis of his or her needs and instructional setting is needed.

Peer-Mediated Instruction

All of the instructional groups described so far are **teacher centred.** In teacher-centred groups, the classroom teacher is primarily responsible for instruction. In

peer-mediated instruction, students are primarily responsible for instruction. The most common examples of peer-mediated instruction are peer tutoring and cooperative learning.

Peer tutoring.   Another form of small-group instruction is peer tutoring. **Peer tutoring** is a system of instruction in which pairs of students help one another and learn by teaching (Jenkins & Jenkins, 1988). The tutor role is most often held by a peer in the same class or school. Tutees are the students who receive the instruction from peer tutors. When peer tutoring is used with exceptional students, the goal is often to accommodate their individual differences, provide them with additional instructional time, and ensure that the additional instructional time is spent in highly focused, academically relevant activities (Jenkins & Jenkins, 1988).

Peer tutoring has many potential benefits in inclusive classrooms. First and most important, it has been advocated as a means for improving the achievement of the students who receive tutoring, and research tends to support that tutees' achievement increases after tutoring. For example, in a study in which grade six students taught math concepts to younger students with moderate cognitive disabilities, the younger students' knowledge of beginning mathematics improved (Vacc & Cannon, 1991). Similar results have been found when the tutees are students who have high-incidence disabilities or are at risk for school failure and when the subject matter is either reading or mathematics (Beirne-Smith, 1991; Fantuzzo, King, & Heller, 1992; Mathes & Fuchs, 1994; Scruggs, Mastropieri, & Richter, 1985). For example, students at risk for school failure have been found to increase the amount of time they spend on school tasks and their achievement in a peer tutoring program (Greenwood, 1991).

Peer tutoring has a positive impact on the students who tutor as well as on the recipients of this instruction, particularly when older tutors with marginal skills work with younger students. Students who serve as tutors learn their academic content better, and they have more positive attitudes toward school and learning (Cohen, Kulik, & Kulik, 1982). Not surprisingly, these results are most pronounced when the tutor has not already mastered the academic content used in tutoring (Jenkins & Jenkins, 1981).

Recent studies of peer tutoring have examined how it affects students' interactions between students with disabilities and their non-disabled tutors (Haring, Breen, Pitts-Conway, Lee, & Gaylord-Ross, 1987). It also helps students who are disliked by classmates to become more socially accepted (Garcia-Vasquez & Ehly, 1992).

One final component in the rationale for peer tutoring concerns its efficiency and cost effectiveness. In tutoring programs, more students are able to participate actively in meaningful academic activities longer than can typically be arranged in a traditional classroom. This alone makes it a worthwhile instructional approach. In addition, when peer tutoring programs are structured properly, the instruction is far more cost effective than hiring professionals. This does not mean that children can replace teachers in schools, but it does mean that peer tutoring is an inexpensive way to magnify the instruction that one teacher is able to deliver.

Cooperative learning.   An instructional system in which students work in small mixed-ability groups with a shared learning goal is **cooperative learning.** Students in cooperative groups have two responsibilities: to learn the information

Connections: Guidelines for developing peer-mediated instructional programs—peer tutoring and cooperative learning—are provided in Chapter 13.

FYI: Give all your students, not just those who are high achieving, a chance to be tutors. Lower-achieving students can benefit socially and academically from tutoring younger students.

for which the cooperative group is responsible and to ensure that all the other members of the cooperative group also learn the information (Johnson & Johnson, 1989).

Cooperative learning generally has four fundamental and essential characteristics (Johnson & Johnson, 1992). First, the students in the groups have positive interdependence. They either reach their goal together, or no one is able to achieve it. For example, in Mr. Reilly's classroom, the students earn points if all the members in their cooperative group get at least 70 percent on their weekly spelling test. Group members work very hard to help all members learn spelling words. Second, cooperative learning requires face-to-face interactions. In Mr. Reilly's class, students have opportunities to work directly with their group members to achieve their learning goals. Third, members of cooperative groups have individual accountability. On the weekly spelling tests, students who have difficulty learning their words are not excused from taking the test, nor are high achievers permitted to answer for all group members. Each member is required to make a contribution. Finally, cooperative learning stresses student interpersonal skills. A primary reason for using cooperative learning is to foster peer relationships. One way it promotes healthy peer relationships is by stressing the importance of teaching students needed interpersonal skills, such as how to ask questions, how to praise classmates, and how to help another student learn.

These four characteristics of cooperative learning distinguish it from other approaches to learning common in schools. For example, much school learning is competitive; that is, based on winners and losers. Spelling matches or other instructional games in which only one student wins are competitive. A second type of traditional learning approach is individualistic. In individualistic learning, student achievement is not dependent on how others achieve. For example, a teacher sets up a system in which all students who complete 90 percent of their homework are listed on the class "good work habits" honour roll. If all the students in the class meet the standard of 90 percent, all can be listed. All students can be winners; one student's winning does not affect other students' chances of success.

All three approaches—cooperative, competitive, and individualistic—have a place in schools. Cooperative learning, however, is relatively new and thus still needs to be carefully nurtured. In addition, the social and interactive components of cooperative learning are not possible in either of the other two approaches, and so this approach needs to be added deliberately to the school curriculum.

The value of cooperative learning lies in its potential for creating positive peer interactions while also serving as an effective instructional approach. Thus, many researchers have studied whether students in cooperative learning groups learn as much as students in traditional competitive or individualistic approaches. As with social benefits, the results have generally been positive. For example, in a study comparing various types of cooperative learning programs, Sharan (1980) found that all the programs had a significant positive effect on student achievement. These results were echoed in a review by Slavin (1994). More recently, cooperative learning has been found to be an effective instructional approach for student achievement in reading, math, science, and thinking skills (Ellis, 1989–1990; Lazarowitz & Karsenty, 1990; Lew, Mesch, Johnson, & Johnson, 1986; Ross, 1988). For a description of how to implement cooperative learning in an inclusive classroom, see Hutchinson (1996).

Cultural Awareness:
Research shows that students with limited English proficiency and minority students benefit both academically and socially from cooperative learning arrangements.

✓ **Your Learning:** What are the different student grouping options used in inclusive classrooms?

How Can You Evaluate Instructional Materials for Inclusive Classrooms?

The nature of the **instructional materials** you use is another very important consideration in accommodating exceptional students in your classroom. Classroom instructional materials include textbooks, manipulatives and models, and technology.

Textbooks

Basal textbooks (often called **basals**) are books used for instruction in any subject area that contain all the key components of the curriculum being taught for that subject. The careful evaluation of basals is vital because the selection of well-designed textbooks can save you much time and energy since better books require fewer adaptations for exceptional students. For example, a math basal that contains enough practice activities will not need to be adapted for students who require lots of practice to master a skill. Similarly, a history textbook that highlights critical vocabulary and includes clear context cues to help students figure the words out on their own may make it unnecessary for teachers to prepare extensive vocabulary study guides. Texts that contain challenge questions and activities that promote application of new learning to authentic problems may meet the needs of students who are gifted or advanced in particular academic domains.

Fortunately, over the past 20 years, guidelines for distinguishing well-designed texts have been developed (Armbruster & Anderson, 1988; Kameenui & Simmons, 1991). A set of questions to help you evaluate basals and other basic-skills materials is included in the Professional Edge on pages 218–219.

Many teachers are choosing to develop or collect their own materials rather than depending on pre-published basal series. For example, some teachers have their students read trade books instead of traditional reading books; others have their students engage in the actual writing process rather than or in addition to answering questions in a book. Still others involve their students in real-life math problem solving rather than basal math books. Even if you choose not to use basals, however, the guidelines for teaching basic skills discussed here apply.

If you use **content-area textbooks,** which are books used for instruction in content areas such as science or social studies, they also need to be evaluated. In secondary schools, students are expected to access curriculum content, often by reading their textbooks (Armbruster & Anderson, 1988; Deshler, Putnam, & Bulgren, 1985). Because students are required to read and understand their texts, often without previous instruction, the texts should be written at a level at which students can easily understand them. Ciborowski (1995) describes ways teachers can help students to understand texts that are written at a high level when the text cannot be replaced. Armbruster and Anderson (1988) refer to readable textbooks as "considerate." "Considerate" textbooks are easier for students to use independently and require fewer teacher adaptations. The guidelines here refer to features involving organization and quality of writing:

FYI: Workbooks are commonly used to practise skills taught in basal materials. The material on practice activities in this chapter and in Chapter 9 applies to workbooks as well.

▼▼▼▼▼▼▼▼▼▼▼▼▼▼▼▼▼▼▼▼▼

Professional Edge

Guidelines for Evaluating Basals or Other Basic-Skills Curricula

BEFORE evaluating any material, read the evaluative questions here and mark with an asterisk the ones that are critical for the type of material you are examining. Answer each question with a yes or no. Examine all your responses in a single area, paying special attention to the questions you designated as critical. Rate each area inadequate (1), adequate (2), or excellent (3). If the area is inadequate, designate if the features could be easily modified (M).

Rating Scale:	Inadequate	Adequate	Excellent	Easily modified
	1	2	3	M

1 2 3 M   *Effectiveness of Material*

Yes No   Is information that indicates successful field testing or class testing of the material provided?

Yes No   Has the material been successfully field tested with students similar to the target population?

Yes No   Are testimonials and publisher claims clearly differentiated from research findings?

1 2 3 M   *Prerequisite Skills*

Yes No   Are the prerequisite student skills and abilities needed to work with ease in the material specified?

Yes No   Are the prerequisite student skills and abilities compatible with the objectives of the material?

Yes No   Are the prerequisite student skills and abilities compatible with the target population?

1 2 3 M   *Content*

Yes No   Does the selection of subject matter, facts, and skills adequately represent the content area?

Yes No   Is the content consistent with the stated objectives?

Yes No   Is the information presented in the material accurate?

Yes No   Is the information presented in the material current?

Yes No   Are various points of view, including treatment of cultural diversity, individuals with disabilities, ideologies, social values, gender roles, and socio-economic status, represented objectively?

Yes No   Are the content and the topic of the material relevant to the needs of students with disabilities?

1 2 3 M   *Sequence of Instruction*

Yes No   Are the scope and sequence of the material clearly specified?

Yes No   Are facts, concepts, and skills ordered logically?

Yes No   Does the sequence of instruction proceed from simple to complex?

Yes No   Does the sequence proceed in small, easily attainable steps?

Rating Scale:	Inadequate	Adequate	Excellent	Easily modified
	1	2	3	M

1   2   3   M   *Behavioural Objectives*

Yes   No   Are objectives or outcomes for the material clearly stated?

Yes   No   Are the objectives or outcomes consistent with the goals for the target population?

Yes   No   Are the objectives or outcomes stated in behavioural terms, including the desired behaviour, the conditions for measurement of the behaviour, and the desired standard of performance?

1   2   3   M   *Initial Assessment and Placement*

Yes   No   Does the material provide a method to determine initial student placement in the curriculum?

Yes   No   Does the initial assessment for placement contain enough items to place the learner accurately?

1   2   3   M   *Ongoing Assessment and Evaluation*

Yes   No   Does the material provide evaluation procedures for measuring progress and mastery of objectives?

Yes   No   Are there enough evaluative items to measure learner progress accurately?

Yes   No   Are procedures and/or materials for ongoing record keeping provided?

1   2   3   M   *Instructional Input (Teaching procedures)*

Yes   No   Are instructional procedures for each lesson either clearly specified or self-evident?

Yes   No   Does the instruction provide for active student involvement and responses?

Yes   No   Are the lessons adaptable to small-group and individualized instruction?

Yes   No   Are a variety of cueing and prompting techniques used to gain correct student responses?

Yes   No   When using verbal instruction, does the instruction proceed clearly and logically?

Yes   No   Does the material use teacher modelling and demonstration when appropriate to the skills being taught?

Yes   No   Does the material specify correction and feedback procedures for use during instruction?

1   2   3   M   *Practice and Review*

Yes   No   Does the material contain appropriate practice activities that contribute to mastery of the skills and concepts?

Yes   No   Do practice activities relate directly to the desired outcome behaviours?

Yes   No   Does the material provide enough practice for students with learning problems?

Yes   No   Are skills systematically and cumulatively reviewed throughout the curriculum?

Source: From *Instructional Materials for the Mildly Handicapped: Selection, Utilization, and Modification* by A. Archer, 1977, Eugene, OR: Northwest Learning Resources System, University of Oregon. Used by permission of the author.

FYI: Taped textbooks can be helpful for students with reading problems. Deshler and Graham (1980) suggest that you tape only key sections of texts and that you highlight the main points in the text to help students focus on the most critical information.

Do It! Examine textbook materials for the subject area and grade level you plan to teach. What do the evaluation criteria presented in this chapter tell you about the adaptability of these materials for students in inclusive classrooms?

✔ **Your Learning:** On what key factors can you evaluate basals and other basic-skills materials? What criteria can you use to evaluate content-area textbooks?

1. **Check the organization of the headings and subheadings.** Make an outline of the headings and subheadings in a few chapters. Is the structure consistent with your knowledge of the organization of the subject matter?

2. **Check the consistency of organization in discussions of similar topics.** For example, in a science chapter on vertebrates, information about the different groups of vertebrates should be similarly organized; that is, if the section on amphibians discusses structure, body covering, subgroups, and reproduction, the section on reptiles should discuss the same topics, in the same order.

3. **Look for clear signalling of the structure.** A well-signalled text includes information headings and subheadings. The most helpful headings are those that are the most specific about the content in the upcoming section. For example, "Chemical Weathering" is a more helpful content clue than "Another Kind of Weathering." A well-signalled text also includes format clues to organization. Page layouts, marginal notations, graphic aids, and the use of boldface or italics can all serve to highlight or reinforce the structure.

4. **Look for explicit or obvious connectives, or conjunctions.** The absence of connectives can be particularly troublesome when the connective is a causal one (for example, *because, since, therefore*), which is frequently the case in content-area textbooks. Therefore, look especially for causal connectives. For example, "Because the guard cells relax, the openings close" is a better explanation than "The guard cells relax. The openings close."

5. **Check for clear references.** One reference problem to watch for is confusing pronoun references when more than one noun could be used. For example, "Both the stem of the plant and the leaf produce chloroform, but in different ways. For one, the sun hits it, and then. . . ." Here, the pronouns *one* and *it* could be referring either to *the stem* or *the leaf.*

6. **Look for transition statements.** These transitions help the reader move easily from idea to idea. Given that a text will be covering many topics, make sure that the topic shifts are smooth.

7. **Make sure the chronological sequences are easy to follow.** In a discussion of a sequence of events, the order of presentation in the text should generally proceed from first to last.

8. **Make sure graphic aids are clearly related to the text.** Graphic aids should be important for understanding the material rather than simply providing decoration, clearly referenced in the text so the reader knows when to look at them, and should be easy to read and clearly labelled.

▶ Children's and Adolescents' Books

Books written expressly for children and adolescents to read independently can help students to elaborate on the understanding they develop from textbooks. However, close examination shows that many of these books expose children to racist and sexist attitudes and show stereotypes of people with disabilities that are also destructive. These attitudes can be portrayed in texts, media, and models as well. The following 10 ways to analyze children's books are based on publications by the Council on Interracial Books for Children (1994) and the Federation of Women Teachers Associations of Ontario (1996):

1. **Check the illustrations.** Look for stereotypes. Are there oversimplified generalizations about a particular group? Look for tokenism. Look at who is doing what. Are females and persons with disabilities inactive observers?

2. **Check the story line.** Does it use "white" standards of behaviour for a person of colour to "get ahead"? Is poverty accepted as inevitable and associated with Aboriginals or people with disabilities? Could the same story be told if the sex roles were reversed?

3. **Check the lifestyle.** For example, are camels shown as transportation in middle eastern countries, a dated portrayal? Or do illustrations and text go beyond oversimplifications to offer insights into another way of life?

4. **Weigh the relationships between people.** Who takes power, shows leadership, functions in supporting roles? How are family relationships depicted? In black families, is the mother always dominant?

5. **Note the heros.** Is the hero serving sexist or racist interests, perhaps acting patronizing or telling offensive jokes? Are minority heroes admired for their struggles for justice or for serving those already in power?

6. **Consider the effects on a child's self-image.** Does the story build and reinforce the positive self-image of a student by being inclusive and empowering? Does it contain positive role models for Aboriginal children?

7. **Check the background of the author or illustrator.** Do life experiences provide specific knowledge to recommend them to be creators of the book?

8. **Check the perspective of the author.** Is the view Eurocentric? Or is it balanced, for example, showing respect for perspectives of Aboriginal people?

9. **Check the language.** Are words loaded? Do they have offensive overtones (e.g., lazy)? Are words sexist or do they use male nouns or pronouns for both genders (e.g., forefathers)?

10. **Check copyright date.** Books on minority themes began to appear in the 1960s, mainly written by white authors. Only recently is the world of children's books beginning to reflect the multicultural society that Canada has become or the concerns of feminists. In this period of change, the copyright date is only one clue and no guarantee of a book's sensitivity.

You can write to authors and publishers to express your concerns about children's books, and start a "news-watch" or a "bias-in-books" project with your students. Children and adolescents can be shown how to detect racism and sexism in a book. Enid Lee, an anti-racist educator in Toronto, said in an interview, "We can take some of the existing curriculum and ask kids questions about what is missing, and whose interest is being served when things are written in the way they are" (Miner, 1994, p. 20-21). You can also inform your school librarian about balanced, accurate, sensitive books and resources for your school library.

Manipulatives and Models

Manipulatives, models, and audiovisual tools can help students make connections between the abstractions often presented in school and the real-life products and situations that these abstractions represent. **Manipulatives** are concrete objects or representational items, such as blocks and counters (for example, base-10 blocks for math), used as part of instruction. **Models** are also tangible objects;

FYI: Research suggests that some students learn best through manipulation of the environment and direct experience in authentic learning situations.

they provide a physical representation of an abstraction (for example, a scale model of the solar system). Strategies to help students make these connections have great potential benefit for exceptional students, who may lack the background knowledge and reasoning skills to understand abstractions. Still, manipulatives, models, and audiovisual tools should be used carefully. When using these valuable tools, consider these guidelines (Marzola, 1987; Ross & Kurtz, 1993):

1. **Select materials that suit the concept and the developmental stage of the student.** When you are first introducing a concept, materials should be easy to comprehend. Generally, the order in which you introduce materials should follow the same order as students' understanding: from the concrete to the pictorial to the abstract. For example, in a biology lesson on the heart, many students will benefit from viewing a three-dimensional model of a human heart, whereas other students will be able to understand how a heart works just by seeing a picture of one.

2. **Use a variety of materials.** Exceptional students may have trouble transferring their understanding of a concept from one form to another. For example, Wally's teacher always demonstrated place value using base-10 blocks. When Wally was given a place-value problem using coffee stirrers, he was unable to do it. Wally's teacher could have prevented this problem in the first place by demonstrating place value using a range of manipulative materials such as base-10 blocks, coffee stirrers, paper clips, and so on.

3. **Use verbal explanations whenever possible to accompany object manipulation.** Models, manipulative demonstrations, and audiovisual aids should be preceded and accompanied by verbal explanations of the concept or skill being demonstrated. Verbal explanations are important because students may be unable to identify the important features of the model on their own. For example, Ms. Balou put a model of a two-digit by two-digit multiplication problem on the board. She explained all the steps in computing the problem to her students and wrote each step on the chalkboard as it was completed.

4. **Encourage active interaction.** It is not enough just to have the teacher demonstrate with manipulatives or models and students observe. Allow your students to interact actively with models and manipulatives. This hands-on experience will help them construct their own meaning from the materials.

5. **Elicit student explanations of their manipulations or use of models.** Encourage your students to verbalize what they are doing as they work with models and manipulatives. This is useful for assessing whether they really understand the concept or skill. For example, Mr. Abraham had his students explain out loud how they would subtract 43 from 52 using base-10 blocks. Although explanations can help you evaluate how your students process information, exceptional students may not be able to articulate concepts right away because of language problems or a lack of reasoning skills. These students may require more frequent demonstrations of how to articulate what they are doing.

6. **Move your students beyond the concrete level when they are ready.** Exceptional students may have trouble moving from one learning stage to another. One effective way to help students make the transition from the concrete to the abstract is to pair concrete tasks with paper-and-pencil tasks.

For example, Ms. Wong asked her students to label a picture of a human heart after they had observed and discussed a physical model. Mr. Parks asked his grade two students to solve subtraction problems using manipulatives and then record their answers on a traditional worksheet.

Technology

Teachers today have available to them a broad array of technology to enhance the presentation of material to their students. These technologies range from traditional audiovisual aids, such as audiotape, videotape, and overhead projectors, to more advanced technologies of microcomputers, videodiscs, and telecommunications and electronic networks.

A number of guidelines for using all types of technology in your classroom have been suggested (Schuller, 1982). First, you should have clearly defined objectives for why you are using the technology. You should also know the content of the film, software, or other materials you are using. Being familiar with the content will make it easier to decide which technologies will work for you and how you can best utilize them. You should also guide learners on what to look for. This guidance is especially relevant for exceptional students, who often have trouble focusing on the essential information. Finally, evaluate the results to see whether the technology has helped students meet your instructional objectives.

One common use of computers in inclusive classrooms is to provide instruction to students through drill-and-practice programs, tutorials, and simulations. In general, drill-and-practice programs are used most often with exceptional students. Drill-and-practice programs have been shown to be effective for exceptional students largely because they allow students to learn in small steps, provide systematic feedback, and allow for lots of practice to mastery. Still, not all drill-and-practice programs are created equal (Okolo, 1993). Some guidelines for

Cultural Awareness:
Research suggests that teachers can reduce classroom gender bias by providing boys and girls equal access to all hands-on instructional materials, including computer time.

▶ *Computer technology, telecommunications networks, and assistive technology for students with disabilities promise to revolutionize education in Canadian schools. In what ways might technology serve as a "great equalizer" in inclusive classrooms?*

Do It! Interview teachers to find out how they use assistive technology with their exceptional students.

what to look for and what to avoid in these programs are given in the Professional Edge on pages 224–225.

Computers can also provide initial, sequenced instruction for students, using **tutorials,** as well as instruction in problem solving, decision making, and risk taking, using **computing applications** and **simulations.** Each of these forms of computer-assisted instruction has potential advantages and disadvantages (Bos & Vaughn, 1994). For example, tutorials can present instruction to mastery in small, sequential steps, an instructional approach shown to be effective with exceptional students. Tutorials can also provide one-to-one instruction at varying levels of difficulty, something teachers usually do not have time to do. On the other hand, you need to check to ensure that students have the necessary prerequisite skills to benefit from the tutorials. In addition, tutorials may not provide sufficient review for students, and students may not be motivated enough to work through them independently (Bos & Vaughn, 1994). During the past decade there has been a shift to using computer applications such as databases and spreadsheets for teaching problem solving and critical thinking. Hollingsworth (1996), an

Professional Edge

Features of Effective Drill-and-Practice Software

THE introduction of technology in the classroom has given teachers a new array of tools to use in presenting material to students. Exceptional students can especially benefit from using drill-and-practice software, which allows them to learn at their own pace. Keep in mind the following guidelines when choosing an effective drill-and-practice program for your students who have special needs.

What to Look for	What to Avoid	Rationale
Programs that provide high rates of responding relevant to the skill being learned	Programs that take too much time to load and run or that contain too many activities unrelated to the skill being learned	The more time students spend on task, the more they learn.
Programs in which animation and graphics support the skill or concept being practised	Programs with animation or graphics that are unrelated to the program's instructional objective	Although animation and graphics may facilitate student interest in an activity, they may also distract students, and reduce practice time.
Programs in which reinforcement is clearly related to task completion or mastery	Programs in which the events that occur when students are incorrect (for example, an explosion are more reinforcing than the events that occur when the student is correct (for example, a smiling face)	Some programs may inadvertently encourage students to practise the incorrect response in order to view the event that they find more interesting.

Alberta educator, describes how students can interact with the data, generating and checking hypotheses, and quickly formulating new ideas as a result of creating new information from existing information; for example, secondary students can compute energy deficiency for countries based upon the amount of energy consumed and the amount of energy produced. Gifted adolescents may be able to accelerate in the social studies curriculum without leaving the classroom. Similarly, spreadsheets enable students to develop or use problem-solving templates. Exceptional adolescents who are not efficient at calculations can use templates to focus on learning concepts such as rate and change over time in business studies, physics, or algebra without being held back by their lack of skills in calculation (Hollingsworth, 1996). Simulations are of great potential benefit in teaching students to be active learners by confronting real-life situations. However, simulations may be difficult to integrate with academic curriculum, may require much teacher assistance, and can be time-consuming (Bos & Vaughn, 1994).

Computer technology is an important part of an inclusive classroom. Researchers in Saskatchewan have developed and implemented software, called

What to Look for	*What to Avoid*	*Rationale*
Programs in which feedback helps students locate and correct their mistakes	Programs in which students are merely told if they are right or wrong or instructed to "try again"	Without feedback that informs them of the correct answer, students may become frustrated and make random guesses.
Programs that store information about student performance or progress that can be accessed later by the teacher	Programs without record-keeping features	Teachers often find it difficult to monitor students as they work at the computer. Access to records of student performance enables the teacher to determine whether a program is benefitting a student and whether the student needs additional assistance.
Programs with options for controlling features such as speed of problem presentation, type of feedback, problem difficulty, and number of practice trials	Programs that must be used in the same way with every student	Options are cost-effective; they enable the same program to be used with a broad range of students, and enable more appropriately individualized instruction.

Source: From "Computers and Individuals with Mild Disabilities" by C. M. Okolo, 1993, in *Computers and Exceptional Individuals*, edited by J. Lindsey. Austin, TX: PRO-ED. Copyright © 1993 by PRO-ED, Inc. Adapted with permission.

Technology Notes

Teaching Writing Skills Through Telecommunications

TELECOMMUNICATIONS systems are ideal for fostering the writing skills of all your students, including exceptional students. Telecommunication systems allow students to communicate from one computer to another over telephone lines using a modem. Students can write and receive messages using electronic bulletin boards or mail boxes. For example, they can write letters to get acquainted; write formal reports on different topics; write poetry to share thoughts, feelings, and

▶ *How is technology enhancing the instruction and learning in this classroom?*

CoPlanner Worksheet, that supports the cooperative work of a team planning for students in inclusive settings (Haines, Sanche, & Robertson, 1993). A great variety of **assistive technology** is available to enable students with both low- and high-incidence disabilities to communicate or have access to information by allowing them to bypass their disability. Students with physical disabilities such as Josh, whom you met at the beginning of the chapter, can operate computers with a single key or switch rather than through a regular keyboard. Students with physical disabilities can use voice command systems to enter information into a computer verbally. Students who are deaf can communicate with hearing students or other deaf students using computer-assisted telecommunication devices such as those described in Chapter 4. Computer-generated large print, Braille translations, and synthesized speech can assist students with visual disabilities in communicating. Students with communication problems can benefit from augmentative communication devices, which are computers equipped with speech

images of the world; do electronic journalism; and have dialogues on social issues. They can share questions, answers, research, and creative writing with students all over the world. Male (1994) suggests a number of important benefits in using telecommunication systems to build your students' writing skills:

1. **Risk-free self-expression.** In most cases, students do not know the students they are communicating with. Therefore, they feel comfortable expressing themselves freely.

2. **Focus on content rather than personality and physical attributes.** In telecommunications, people communicate invisibly. They can interact free of barriers that often isolate them, such as wheelchairs, appearance, and race.

3. **Cross-cultural respect and curiosity.** Using telecommunications, students can communicate readily across provincial and national boundaries. Such access can motivate students to find out more about other cultures and promote respect for these cultures. In one Ontario school, students co-produced a newsletter with a school in the Northwest Territories.

4. **Self-worth.** Students feel important when they receive electronic mail and have their work acknowledged by people from around the world.

5. **Elimination of time pressure from communication.** Students receive messages and can work on them off-line, which gives them an opportunity to receive input and feedback from peers or teachers and to revise.

Here are some activities that you might want to try with your students to get them started using a telecommunications system:

1. Students brainstorm a list of important aspects of their school and community.
2. Students write the beginning of a story, and students at a sister school complete the story.
3. Students research and/or write legends from their region.
4. Students create a monthly newsletter about events in their school, community, state, or country.
5. Students describe favourite meals and include instructions for preparing them, allowing the receiving students to experience something new and different to eat from a different region or culture. (Male, 1994, p. 130)

For a list of telecommunication projects you might want to access, see Male (1994, p. 128).

Source: From *Technology for Inclusion: Meeting the Special Needs of All Students* by M. Male, 1994. Copyright © 1994 by Allyn and Bacon. Adapted with permission.

---

synthesizers that can type text and produce speech heard by everyone. These devices can also be programmed with words and phrases for particular situations. Students with learning disabilities can compensate for poor handwriting, spelling, and grammatical skills using word processing equipment. Uses of telecommunications technology for teaching writing skills are presented in the Technology Notes on pages 226–227.

How Can You Analyze Instructional Methods in Relation to Student Needs?

Teachers use a number of instructional methods in class, including direct instruction, non-direct methods of instruction, scaffolding, independent student practice, and evaluation of student performance. Each method should be analyzed in relation to student needs and then used and/or adapted as needed.

Elements of Direct Instruction

Several decades of teaching effectiveness research have shown that many students learn skills and subject matter more readily when it is presented very explicitly, often referred to as **direct instruction** (Aber, Bachman, Campbell, & O'Malley, 1994; Christenson, Ysseldyke, & Thurlow, 1989; Rosenshine & Stevens, 1986). Direct instruction consists of six key elements:

Connections: Presenting new content also involves using strategies for activating students' prior knowledge. These strategies are explored further in Chapter 9.

1. **Review and check the previous day's work (and reteach if necessary).** This aspect of direct instruction may include having established routines for checking homework and reviewing relevant past learning and prerequisite skills. All these procedures are important because exceptional students might not retain past learning and/or know how to apply it to new material. For example, on Thursday, Ms. Guzik taught her students how to round to the nearest whole number. On Friday, she gave her class a story problem to solve that required rounding. Before the students solved the problem, she pointed to a chart in the front of the room that showed a model of how to round numbers and suggested that they refer to this chart when they reached the end of solving the problem.

2. **Present new content or skills.** When content or skills are presented, teachers begin the lesson with a short statement of the objectives and a brief overview of what they are going to present and why. Material is presented in small steps, using careful demonstrations that incorporate illustrations and concrete examples to highlight key points. Included within the demonstrations are periodic questions to check for understanding.

3. **Provide guided student practice (and check for understanding).** At first, student practice takes place under the direct guidance of the teacher, who frequently questions *all* students on material directly related to the new content or skill. You can involve all students in questioning by using unison oral responses or by having students answer questions by holding up answer cards, raising their hands if they think an answer is correct, or holding up a number to show which answer they think is right. For example, when asking a yes or no question, tell your students to hold up a one if they think the answer is yes and a two if they think the answer is no. This approach can also be used with spelling. Ask your students to spell words onto an index card and then hold up their answers. Unison responses not only give students more practice, but they also allow you to monitor student learning more readily. Prompts and additional explanations or demonstrations are provided during guided practice where appropriate. Effective guided practice continues until students meet the lesson objective. For example, Mr. Hayes was teaching his students how to add *es* to words that end in *y*. After modelling two examples at the board, he did several more examples *with* the students, guiding them as they applied the rule to change the *y* to *i* before they added *es*. Next, Mr. Hayes asked them to do a word on their own. Students put their answers on an index card and held the card in the air when directed by the teacher. Mr. Hayes noticed that five students did not apply the rule correctly.

He called these students up to his desk for additional instruction and had the rest of the students add *es* to a list of words on a worksheet independently.

4. **Provide feedback and correction (and reteach if necessary).** When students answer quickly and confidently, the teacher asks another question or provides a short acknowledgment of correctness (for example, "That's right"). Hesitant but correct responses might be followed by process feedback (for example, "Yes, Yolanda, that's right because . . ."). When students respond incorrectly, the teacher uses corrections to draw out an improved student response. Corrections can include sustaining feedback (that is, simplifying the question, giving clues), explaining steps, giving process feedback ("The reason we need to regroup in this subtraction problem is because the top number is smaller than the bottom number"), or reteaching last steps. Corrections continue until students have met the lesson objective, with praise used in moderation. Specific praise ("I'm impressed at how you drew a picture of that story problem!") is more effective than general praise ("Good boy, Leon").

5. **Provide independent student practice.** Students practise independently on tasks directly related to the skills taught until they achieve a high correct rate. Practice activities are actively supervised and students are held accountable for their work.

6. **Review frequently.** Systematic review of previously learned material is provided, including the incorporation of review into homework and tests. Material missed in homework or tests is retaught (Rosenshine & Stevens, 1986).

✓ **Your Learning:** What are the steps in an effective direct-instruction lesson?

Rosenshine and Stevens (1986) are careful to note that for older students or for those who have more subject-matter knowledge or skills, these six steps can be modified, such as by presenting more material at one time or spending less time on guided practice. For example, when a grade two teacher presented a unit on nutrition, she spent a whole week defining and showing examples of complex carbohydrates, fats, sugar, and protein. In a grade eight health class, this material was covered in one day, largely because students already had much background information on this topic. Although each direct-instruction step is not required for every lesson, they are particularly helpful to students with learning and behaviour problems, who benefit greatly from a high level of classroom structure (Algozzine, Ysseldyke, & Campbell, 1994; Christenson et al., 1989; Hutchinson, in press).

The Case in Practice presents an example of a direct-instruction lesson.

Non-direct Methods of Instruction

Non-direct instruction is used by classroom teachers when the goal of instruction is higher-level thinking skills and problem solving. The most common non-direct method is called **inquiry,** or **discovery, learning** (Hoover & Hollingsworth, 1982; Jarolimek & Foster, 1993; Putnam & Wesson, 1990). Unlike direct instruction, which is very teacher-centred, in the inquiry approach, the teacher's role is "that of a guide-stimulator, a facilitator who challenges learners by helping them identify questions and problems and who guides their inquiry" (Jarolimek & Foster, 1993, pp. 142–143). The learners, then, are placed "in a role that requires considerable initiative in finding things out for themselves.

Case in Practice

A Direct-Instruction Lesson

THIS direct-instruction lesson is designed to teach two-digit subtraction problems that involve renaming. Notice that the teacher first reviews the pre-skills of knowing when to rename. Then she guides students through several problems.

TEACHER: Yesterday we learned a rule about renaming with subtraction problems. What is that rule?

STUDENTS: When we take away more than we start with, we must rename.

TEACHER: Great! Now tell me whether we need to rename in doing this problem. [Teacher writes

$$\begin{array}{r} 42 \\ -37 \\ \hline \end{array}$$

on the board.]

STUDENTS: Yes, we need to rename.

TEACHER: Why is that?

STUDENTS: Because we're taking away more than we start with. We start with 2 and take away 7. Seven is more, so we have to rename.

TEACHER: Okay. Today we're going to learn how to rename in subtraction. [Teacher writes

$$\begin{array}{r} 53 \\ -26 \\ \hline \end{array}$$

on the board.] Read this problem.

STUDENTS: 53 take away 26.

TEACHER: The 1s column tells us to start with 3 and take away 6. What does the 1s column tell us to do?

STUDENTS: Start with 3 and take away 6.

TEACHER: Do we have to rename?

STUDENTS: Yes.

TEACHER: Right! We start with 3 and have to take away more than 3. Here's how we rename: First we borrow a 10 from the five 10s. What do we do first?

STUDENTS: Borrow a 10 from the five 10s.

TEACHER: How many 10s will be left?

STUDENTS: Four 10s.

TEACHER: So I cross out the 5 and write 4 to show that the four 10s are left. [Teacher crosses out 5 and writes 4.]

TEACHER: We borrowed a 10. What do we do next?

STUDENTS: Put the 10 with the three 1s.

TEACHER: Right. Put 10 with the three 1s. [Teacher writes 1 in front of 3.] Now we have 13 in the 1s column. Figure out what 13 minus 6 is. [Pause] What's 13 minus 6?

STUDENTS: Seven.

TEACHER: We write 7 in the 1s column. [Teacher writes 7 under the 1s column.]

TEACHER: The 10s column says four 10s minus two 10s. How many is four 10s minus two 10s?

STUDENTS: Two 10s.

TEACHER: What is 53 minus 26?

STUDENTS: 27.

[Teacher repeats with two more problems.]

Reflections

What direct-instruction steps did the teacher use here? Think about the characteristics of exceptional students discussed in Chapter 5. Why do you think direct instruction is effective for these students? Can you think of some situations in which you would not want to use direct instruction?

They must be actively engaged in their own learning" (Jarolimek & Foster, 1993, p. 143). The teacher guides the students through five steps: (1) defining a problem, (2) proposing hypotheses, (3) collecting data, (4) evaluating evidence, and (5) making a conclusion. Authentic inquiry tasks engage students and help them

With the appropriate support, non-direct instruction can be effective for exceptional students. What steps should this teacher take to ensure effective instruction using scaffolding?

to see the relevance and utility of their learning. Hull (1989) described the intense engagement and learning of at-risk adolescents who wrote letters and carried out anthropological fieldwork. Such authentic tasks were once thought appropriate only for students who were gifted.

Scaffolding

Non-direct methods of instruction have great potential for use with students with disabilities, many of whom are characterized as being passive learners who lack skills in these areas. Still, in order to succeed in a discovery format, exceptional students need support from the teacher. An approach that has been used successfully to support students as they develop problem-solving skills is called **scaffolding.** Scaffolds are "forms of support provided by the teacher (or another student) to help students bridge the gap between their current abilities and the intended goal" (Rosenshine & Meister, 1992, p. 26).

Before using scaffolding, you need to determine whether students have the necessary background ability to learn a cognitive strategy (Rosenshine & Meister, 1992). For example, a strategy for helping a student read a physics textbook would not be useful if the student lacked a basic knowledge of mathematics and physical properties. Similarly, teaching a strategy for solving math word problems would not be successful for a student who did not have basic math computation skills unless the student knew how to use a calculator while solving word problems. Using scaffolding to teach higher-order cognitive strategies consists of the following six steps:

1. **Present the new cognitive strategy.** In this step, the teacher introduces the steps in the strategy concretely, using a list of strategy steps. The teacher

Connections: Ways to use scaffolding to teach students study skills are described in the discussion of learning strategies in Chapter 10.

then models the strategy, including all *thinking* and *doing* steps. For example, Mr. Zikakis is teaching his social studies class how geographic features and natural resources affect the growth and location of cities. First, he introduces the problem-solving strategy to his students: (1) define the problem, (2) propose hypotheses to explain the problem, (3) collect data to evaluate your hypotheses, (4) evaluate the evidence, and (5) make a conclusion. These steps are posted on the chalkboard for easy reference. Mr. Zikakis then models the strategy steps by showing students a map of the province of Ontario and saying the following:

> The problem here is finding out why Toronto came to be located where it is and not anywhere else in Ontario. Some possible factors that might affect where big cities are located might include the presence of water (rivers and lakes), mountains, valleys or other land forms, climate, access to other cities, and whether mineral or oil deposits are located nearby. Next, I'm going to collect some data or information to see which of these factors had an influence on the development of Toronto. Toronto is located on a large lake—Lake Ontario. This makes it easier for people and goods to travel in and out. It is also centrally located; it is in the middle of the country; people from other cities can get to it easily. There are also no mountains around it so this also makes it easy to get to. There are no major mineral deposits nearby, so that doesn't seem to be important here. The climate is cold, so I don't think people came to Toronto for the weather. The evidence leads me to conclude that Toronto is where it is because of Lake Ontario and because it is easy to get to from a lot of places.

2. **Regulate difficulty during guided practice.** Students begin practising the new strategy using simplified materials so they can concentrate on learning the strategy. At first, the strategy is introduced one step at a time. Students are guided carefully through the steps, with the teacher anticipating particularly difficult steps and completing these difficult parts of the task as necessary. For example, before tackling more difficult examples, such as the geography example above, Mr. Zikakis first asks his students to use the problem-solving steps to solve simpler problems on topics familiar to them. For example, he asks them to solve problems such as why the cookies someone made were dry, why a hypothetical student was late for school every day, or why the school lunches tasted awful. He also helped students brainstorm ideas for how to collect data, a step that can be difficult. Mr. Zikakis did this by compiling an initial list of data collection procedures for each problem. For the problem of why the cookies were dry, Mr. Zikakis gave his students a list of possible data collection procedures such as identifying the ingredients, finding out how long the cookies were baked, and determining how old the cookies were.

3. **Provide varying contexts for student practice.** Students practise the strategy on actual classroom tasks under the teacher's direction. The teacher starts out leading the practise, but the students eventually carry out the practice sessions in small cooperative groups. In Mr. Zikakis' class, students practised the problem-solving strategy using examples from their social studies textbooks.

4. **Provide feedback.** The teacher provides corrective feedback to students using evaluative checklists based on models of expert problem solving carefully explained to the students. Students are encouraged to evaluate their performance using these checklists. For example, each time Mr. Zikakis' students used the problem-solving strategy, they evaluated their performance by asking themselves questions such as, Did we clearly state the problem? Did we state a complete list of hypotheses? How thorough were our data collection procedures? Did the information collected allow us to evaluate all the hypotheses? Did we interpret the results accurately? Were our conclusions consistent with our results?

5. **Increase student responsibility.** Next, the teacher begins to require students to practise putting all the steps together on their own. Student independence is encouraged by removing elements of the scaffold. For example, prompts and models are diminished, the complexity and difficulty of the materials are increased, and peer support is decreased. The teacher checks for student mastery before going to the last step, independent practice.

6. **Provide independent practice.** Finally, the teacher provides the students with extensive practice and helps them apply what they have learned to new situations. For example, Mr. Zikakis showed his students how problem solving could be used in their other subjects, such as science (Rosenshine & Meister, 1992).

✓ **Your Learning:** How can scaffolding be used to make non-direct instruction more effective for exceptional students?

Independent Student Practice

The major purpose of practice is to help students refine or strengthen their skills in various areas. Consider these guidelines for using practice activities effectively in your classroom:

1. **Students should practise only skills or content they have already learned.** This guideline is particularly important if students are to be able to perform practice activities independently. Tasks that are too difficult can lead to high levels of off-task behaviour.

2. **Practice is more effective if students have a desire to learn what they are practising.** Whenever possible, point out to students situations in which they can use the skill in other phases of learning.

3. **Practice should be individualized.** Exercises should be organized so that each student can work independently.

4. **Practice should be specific and systematic.** Practice should be directly related to skills and objectives you are working on in class. This guideline is particularly important for exceptional students, who need more practice in order to master academic skills.

5. **Students should have much practice on a few skills rather than a little practice on many skills.** Focusing on one or two skills at a time is less confusing and gives students more practice on each skill.

6. **Practice should be organized so that students achieve high levels of success.** Correct answers are reinforcing to students and encourage them to do more. Most students need at least 90 percent accuracy when doing practice activities, though higher-achieving students can tolerate a 70 percent

rate as long as the teacher is present to give them needed assistance (Good & Brophy, 1988).

7. **Practice should be organized so that students and the teacher have immediate feedback.** You need to know how students do so you can decide whether to move to the next skill. Students need to know how they are doing so they can make meaningful corrections of their work (Ornstein, 1990).

Connections: Use the INCLUDE strategy to adapt practice activities for your exceptional students.

For your exceptional students, consider these additional questions. First, what are the response demands of the activity? Do students have to answer orally or in writing? How extensive a response is required? Do the students have enough time to finish the activity? Response demands are important because students who are unable to meet them will be unable to do the practice activity independently. For example, Mr. Edwards is having his class practise weekly vocabulary words orally in class by giving their definitions. Ross stutters and is unable to give his answer out loud. Mr. Edwards allows him to submit a written list of definitions. Ms. Osborne is asking her students to answer short-answer questions in their history books. Clarice has a physical disability and is unable to write her answers independently. She uses an adapted classroom computer to prepare her answers. Mr. Nusbaum asked his students to write a paragraph summarizing the reasons for the stock market crash of 1929. Maurice cannot write a coherent paragraph but can answer orally into a tape recorder. Amanda writes very slowly, so Mr. Nusbaum gave her more time to complete the activity.

Homework

Perhaps the most common form of practice used by teachers is **homework.** Research shows that homework can have a positive effect on student achievement if it is assigned properly (Cooper, 1989; Cooper & Nye, 1994). Here are some guidelines for the effective use of homework:

1. Homework should have different purposes at different grades. For younger students, it should foster positive attitudes toward schoolwork and build good work habits. For older students, it should reinforce knowledge acquisition in specific topics.

2. The frequency and duration of mandatory assignments should vary by grade:
   - *Grades 1 to 3*—One to three assignments a week, each lasting no more than 15 minutes.
   - *Grades 4 to 6*—Two to four assignments a week, each lasting 15 to 45 minutes.
   - *Grades 7 to 9*—Three to five assignments a week, each lasting 45 to 75 minutes.
   - *Grades 10 to 12*—Four to five assignments a week, each lasting 75 to 120 minutes.

3. Homework should include mandatory assignments. Failure to turn in these assignments should result in clear consequences. However, homework should not be used as a punishment.

4. Homework should also include voluntary assignments meant to meet the needs of individual students or groups of students.

5. All homework assignments should not be formally evaluated; however, feedback should be provided. Homework assignments can be used to locate problems in student progress and to individualize instruction.

6. Topics should appear in assignments before and after they are covered in class, not just on the day they are discussed.

7. Homework should not be used to teach complex skills. It should generally focus on simple skills and material or on the integration of skills that students already have.

8. Parents should rarely be asked to play a formal instructional role in homework. Instead, they should be asked to create a home environment that fosters independent student work.

9. Reasons students do not do, turn in, or complete homework must be explored. Is it a poor home situation? Pressures of a part-time job? Competing after-school or out-of-school activities? Poor study skills? Inappropriate assignments? (Ornstein, 1990, p. 450).

Homework is often a challenge for exceptional students. For example, most teachers expect homework to be completed independently, and students must have the sensory, academic, and organizational skills to do so. A student with a severe reading disability might be unable to read a chapter in a history book and answer the questions without some form of adaptation such as a peer reader or taped text. Similarly, a student with fine motor difficulties might be unable to answer the written questions unless allowed to do so orally or with an adapted word processor. In addition, you may need to provide this same student more time or to assign fewer problems. Therefore, it is important that you carefully examine your own homework requirements and adapt them to ensure full participation by all your students.

Connections: Strategies for adapting seatwork, independent practice activities, and homework for exceptional students are presented in Chapter 8.

Evaluation of Student Performance

The major purpose of student evaluation is to determine the extent to which students have mastered academic skills or instructional content. The results of student evaluations are often communicated through grades or marks, which are determined in a number of ways, including tests and assignments. Because student evaluation is so important, you need to consider how classroom tests and assignments may interact with student learning needs. Most critical is that the method of evaluation measures skill or content mastery, not the student's disability. For example, Carson, a student who has an attention deficit, should be given tests in small segments to ensure that the test measures his knowledge, not his attention span. Similarly, Riesa, a student with a severe learning disability in writing, needs to be given an essay test in history orally if the test is to be a valid measure of her history knowledge, not her writing disability. Carefully consider the types of evaluation measures you plan to use and each student's learning characteristics to ensure that your tests will measure the right thing.

Adaptations in Testing and Grading

You may need to make adaptations for exceptional students in each of the key testing demand areas of preparation, administration, and feedback. For prepara-

Connections: Chapter 11 explores strategies for adapting classroom tests and report-card grades for exceptional students. It also covers potentially valuable additions to testing and grading, such as performance-based assessments and portfolios.

tion, if the content stressed is factual material such as names and dates, students with memory problems may need more practice in class or at home. If test and assignment due dates are announced orally, students with hearing impairments, or listening or organizational problems, may require written instructions as well. With regard to administration, students with severe reading problems may need to take a written test orally; students with visual disabilities may need their tests written in Braille and are usually given more time to complete them. For feedback, students with problems in written language may require modified grading criteria that emphasize the quality of the writing content rather than mechanics. Of course, for some students, traditional paper-and-pencil classroom testing might not be appropriate at all. For example, Sybil has severe developmental disabilities and is included in Ms. Barnaby's grade three class. While the classroom is being tested on geometry, Sybil is asked by her teacher to identify orally, with the help of a language board, the shape and meaning of road signs, a skill included on her IEP.

The type of report-card grade used as well as the system used to arrive at that grade might need to be adapted for some students. For example, Hal was discouraged about always getting a C in English no matter how hard he tried. His teacher decided to supplement his grade with an A for effort to encourage Hal to keep trying. Mr. Henning encouraged his students to come to class on time by giving them credit for punctuality.

Summary

Various aspects of classroom environments can affect the learning of all students, including exceptional students. Fewer individualized accommodations for exceptional students will be required in classrooms that are well structured and organized. However, even in the best situations, some adaptations will be needed. To determine what adaptations are necessary, carefully examine the demands of your classroom environment and identify ones that may be problematic for students.

Demands covering four major areas should be analyzed: classroom organization, classroom grouping, instructional materials, and instructional methods. Classroom organization includes physical organization, classroom routines, classroom climate, behaviour management, and the use of time. Key aspects of classroom grouping involve the use of whole-class and small instructional groups, same-skill and mixed-skill groups, one-to-one instruction, and peer-mediated and teacher-centred groupings.

Features of basic-skills materials to consider are their effectiveness, prerequisite skills, content, sequence of instruction, behavioural objectives, initial assessment and placement procedures, ongoing evaluation and assessment procedures, instructional input, and practice. For content-area textbooks, check the quality of organization and the writing. For children's and adolescents' books, check for racist, sexist, and stereotypical representations.

Manipulatives and models can help students make connections between abstractions and real-life products and situations. You can also use a variety of technology in your classroom to enhance your presentation and student learning, including videotape, audiotape, overhead projectors, chalkboards, videodiscs,

Access First
www.inforamp.net/~access/
afl.htm

Access Technology Services
www.dorton.demon.co.uk/
ATS/atshome.htm

WebABLE!
www.yuri.org/webable/

telecommunications, and microcomputers. Computers serve three main purposes in teaching students: to provide instruction to students; as learning tools to help students access, process, and file data; and as assessment tools to assist teachers.

Two common instructional models used in the schools are direct and non-direct instruction. Direct instruction is effective in teaching basic skills. Non-direct methods of instruction are used when the goal of instruction is higher-level thinking skills and problem solving. Sometimes, exceptional students require support when participating in non-direct teaching. One way of helping these students is scaffolding. Scaffolds are forms of support provided by the teacher (or another student) to help students acquire cognitive strategies.

Guidelines for using student practice and homework effectively should be followed. In addition, the oral, written, and academic response demands of practice and homework tasks and the nature and difficulty of the directions need to be analyzed. Student evaluation procedures include testing and grading. For tests, analyze demands related to preparing for tests, taking tests, and receiving feedback on test performance. Adaptations may need to be made in each of these areas. For report-card grades, the type(s) of grades used as well as the system by which a grade is determined will need to be considered.

Applications in Teaching Practice

Planning Adaptations in the Instructional Environment

1. Verna is a student with a learning disability who is included in Ms. Chang's grade four class. Ms. Chang uses whole-group instruction in math. This method is sometimes hard for Verna, who is behind her peers in math; Verna is slow to answer her math facts, has trouble keeping her numbers straight in columns, and sometimes forgets a step or two when she is computing a problem that requires two or more steps. How can Ms. Chang help Verna succeed in the large group?

2. In Chapter 4, you read about students with low-incidence exceptionalities. For each of the students described at the beginning of that chapter, describe how each element of classroom organization may need to be adapted.

3. Design a lesson to teach students to round numbers to the nearest 10 using direct instruction.

4. How could Mr. Howard teach the following textbook reading strategy to his grade nine history students using scaffolding?

   R Review headings and subheadings.
   E Examine boldface words.
   A Ask, "What do I expect to learn?"
   D Do it: Read!
   S Summarize in your own words (Bartlett, Marchio, & Reynolds, 1994)

5. Find a drill-and-practice computer program and evaluate it using the criteria discussed in this chapter.

Chapter 8

Assessing
Student Needs

Learner Objectives

After you read this chapter, you will be able to

1. Explain how regular classroom teachers contribute significantly to the assessment process.
2. Describe the uses of standardized achievement and psychological tests in making educational decisions for exceptional students.
3. Define curriculum-based assessment and explain how it can help regular classroom teachers.
4. Construct and use probes of basic academic skills, content-area prerequisite skills, and independent learning skills.
5. Use curriculum-based assessments to make decisions about exceptional students.

MS. LYONS *is concerned that Rob, a student in her grade two class, is not keeping up with the rest of the class in math. Mr. Blair, the resource teacher, suggests that Ms. Lyons do some informal assessment herself before considering referring Rob for an assessment and an IEP. What kind of assessments can Ms. Lyons use to clarify Rob's problems in math? How might these assessments help Ms. Lyons make adaptations for Rob in math? Under what circumstances should she refer Rob for an IEP?*

MR. BLOUNT *teaches a high school history class. He has learned that three exceptional students will be included in his class next fall. Mr. Blount was told that these students have some reading problems and that they may have trouble reading the textbook. Mr. Blount decided to make up a test to give at the beginning of the year to see how well the students were able to use the textbook. Using a section of a chapter from the text, Mr. Blount wrote questions to test how well students could identify the meaning of key vocabulary words, use parts of the book (for example, table of contents, glossary, index), read maps, and read for information (for example, note main ideas, draw conclusions). When Mr. Blount gave the test in the fall, he found that the three exceptional students had trouble reading the text, but that many other students also had difficulty. What decision might Mr. Blount make on the basis of the assessment?*

ROBERTO *is a student with moderate to severe disabilities who is included in Ms. Benis's grade six social studies class. As a result of Roberto's cerebral palsy, he has significant cognitive, language, and motor deficits. Roberto can read his name as well as some high-frequency sight words. He uses a wheelchair, and he has trouble with fine motor movements such as cutting and handwriting. Roberto speaks with the aid of a communication board. Ms. Benis is doing a unit on recycling with her class. The students are working in small, mixed-skill groups, with each group constructing a graphic of the recycling process for either paper products, plastic, or metal. What assessment process can Ms. Benis carry out to help her develop a plan for including Roberto in this unit?*

As more and more exceptional students are served in regular education classrooms, teachers will need to make many important decisions that can greatly affect these students' success. For example, in the vignettes above, Ms. Lyons was trying to determine whether Rob needed intensive math instruction from a resource teacher or whether his needs could be met through adaptations in her regular math program. Mr. Blount wanted to find out whether his students with disabilities could read the textbook for his history class to help him decide whether he would need to adapt the book. Ms. Benis wants to include Roberto, who has moderate to severe disabilities, in her social studies class. To answer their questions, these teachers needed accurate, relevant information. Thus, they developed informal measures to help them make a number of instructional decisions as well as participate in special education decision making. This chapter explores assessment strategies that help regular classroom teachers contribute to the process of decision making for exceptional students. This decision making involves, for example, determining if a student needs special education services, when a student is ready to learn in inclusive settings, and what classroom accommodations to try, continue, or change.

◤ How Do Your Student Assessments Contribute to Special Education Decisions?

Connections: Review the discussion in Chapter 2 of the roles of regular classroom teachers in decision making by the school-based team.

Connections: The assessment types of procedures described in this chapter are used in Steps 2, 3, and 4 of the INCLUDE model presented in Chapter 1.

In a recent book, Wilson (1996) of Queen's University described the array of roles the classroom teacher plays in assessment. This array includes mentor, guide, accountant, reporter, and program director. Assessment in the regular classroom must satisfy many goals: feedback to all students, diagnostic information for the teacher, summary for record keeping, evidence for reports, and guidance for curriculum revision. In addition, as a classroom teacher, you make an important contribution to the process of identifying and meeting the needs of exceptional students. A major part of that contribution involves assessing student needs. **Assessment** has been defined as the process of gathering information to monitor progress and make educational decisions if necessary (Overton, 1992). The two most common ways of collecting information are through standardized, commercially produced tests and informal, teacher-made tests. Much of the information in this chapter is about ways in which these measures can be used to make decisions about exceptional students during the school-based team process described in Chapter 2.

Assessment in Initial Interventions

One of the first decisions a teacher must make is whether a student's performance is different enough from that of his or her peers to merit further, more in-depth assessments. For example, to clarify Rob's problems in math, Ms. Lyons, whom you met at the beginning of this chapter, examined the most recent group achievement-test scores for her class in math and found that Rob's total math score was one to two years below grade level. Ms. Lyons then gave Rob and his classmates some mini-tests on various math computation skills she had taught them to see whether Rob was behind his peers on these skills. Using this information, Ms. Lyons found that a number of students were performing similarly to Rob. She therefore consulted with the resource teacher and decided not to refer Rob for a more comprehensive evaluation until she tried some adaptations in the classroom first, with Rob and several other students.

FYI: The curriculum-based assessment probes described later in this chapter can help measure the effects of pre-referral interventions.

When the Initial School-Based Interventions are Unsuccessful

As described in Chapter 2, if initial interventions are unsuccessful, a school-based team may refer a student for in-depth assessment. This assessment seeks to answer the question: What is the nature and extent of the student's exceptionality? For example, Ms. Clark referred Paula for a case-study evaluation because she suspected that Paula had a learning disability. The school psychologist administered an individual intelligence test and found that Paula's performance was in the above-normal range. The school psychologist also gave Paula a test of cognitive functioning, including a test of memory, attention, and organization, and an individual achievement test. She found that Paula was slow in processing visual information (letters, numbers, shapes) and that her achievement in reading was significantly lower than that of other students her age. Her achievement in math was at grade level. Ms. Clark evaluated Paula's classroom reading performance by having her and five "average" students read orally and answer questions from a grade-level trade book that was part of the classroom literature program. Paula read slower and with less accuracy than her peers, and she was able to answer only 40 percent of the comprehension questions. Because Paula showed problems processing visual information quickly enough, and because her potential as measured by the intelligence test and her achievement as measured by both a standardized achievement test and informal classroom reading tests differed significantly, Paula was identified as having a learning disability.

✓ **Your Learning:** What questions are involved in identifying an exceptional student?

Placement of the Exceptional Student

The major **program-placement** decision involves where a student's intervention and services will take place (for example, in a regular classroom, resource room, or full-time special education classroom). The IEP team must make this decision with great care. In the past, the tendency was to pull students out of regular classrooms without carefully considering whether they could be supported within the regular education program. In this book, the emphasis is on doing all that you can

✓ **Your Learning:** What questions are involved in making a program placement decision?

FYI: Program-placement decisions for students with moderate to severe learning disabilities should be based on the curricular goals outlined in their IEPs.

within the regular education classroom first. Still, students have different needs, and some may require instruction in an area at a level of intensity that cannot be delivered in the general education classroom. That is why it is important to make placement decisions based on measures that accurately reflect student performance in class. For example, Carlos has been shown to be eligible for receiving services for learning disabilities in math. His IEP team is trying to decide whether his learning needs can be met by adapting the math methods and materials in the regular classroom or whether he should be provided more intensive instruction in a resource room setting. Carlos's classroom teacher gave Carlos and his classmates a series of informal math tests. She found that Carlos was significantly behind his peers on some but not all of the tests; his math problem solving was deficient compared to that of his classmates, but his math computational skills were fine. The IEP team decided to keep Carlos in his regular education class and support his instruction in problem solving by providing him extra teacher-guided practice whenever a new problem-solving skill was introduced. The team also decided that they would carefully monitor Carlos's problem-solving skills; if those skills showed little improvement, they would consider other options at his next review.

Curriculum Placement

✓ **Your Learning:** What questions are involved in placing students into the classroom curriculum?

Curriculum-placement decisions involve where to begin instruction for students. For an elementary school teacher, such a decision may mean choosing a reading or math book. For example, Ms. Fontaine asks her students to read orally and answer questions to find the appropriate trade books in which to place them (that is, the level of difficulty at which the books are neither too easy nor too hard in her literature-based reading program). At the secondary level, curriculum-placement decisions are likely to involve which class in a sequence of classes a

▼ *Students' needs can be identified, addressed, and monitored through assessments based on observation and instructional evaluation. What role do regular education classroom teachers play in assessing students' needs?*

student should take. For example, Mr. Nowicki, Scott's math teacher, is trying to decide whether to place Scott in his Algebra 1 class. Mr. Nowicki identifies basic math skills that he feels all students entering algebra should have. He constructs a test based on those skills and gives it to Scott as well as other incoming grade nine students.

Instructional Evaluation

Decisions in **instructional evaluation** involve whether to continue or change instructional procedures that have been initiated with students. For example, Ms. Bridgewater is starting a peer tutoring program to help Cecily, a student with severe developmental disabilities, read her name and the names of her family members. Each week, Ms. Bridgewater tests Cecily to determine how many of the names she has learned. Mr. Shulha decides to accompany each of his history lectures with a graphic organizer of the material. He gives weekly quizzes to determine whether his students' performance is improving.

Do It! When teaching an instructional unit, give a probe of material taught. Examine the results. You might be surprised at what you discover.

Program Evaluation

Program-evaluation decisions involve whether intervention and services for the student should be terminated, continued as is, or modified. A key consideration is whether students are meeting their IEP goals. For example, Amanda is receiving social work services twice per week. Her IEP goal is to decrease the number of times she has a verbal confrontation with Mr. Aboud, her teacher. Mr. Aboud is keeping track of the number of times daily that Amanda refuses to comply with his requests to determine whether sessions with the social worker are improving Amanda's behaviour.

✓ **Your Learning:** What questions are involved in evaluating the program of an exceptional student?

▶ What Information Sources Are Used in Programming for Exceptional Students?

A number of information sources are used in programming for exceptional students. The use of multiple assessment sources is consistent with the principle of non-discriminatory testing, which says that no single measure should be used to make important educational decisions for individual students. The measures described in this section include standardized achievement tests, reports of psychological tests, the environmental inventory process, and curriculum-based assessments.

Standardized Achievement Tests

A common source of information for making educational decisions is the **standardized achievement test.** These tests are designed to measure academic progress, or what students have learned in the curriculum. Standardized achievement tests are norm-referenced. In a norm-referenced test, the performance of one student is compared to the average performance of other students in Canada

✓ **Your Learning:** What are two ways of telling how a student compares on a task to other students his or her age from different parts of the country?

who are the same age or grade level. Student performance is often summarized using grade equivalents and/or percentile ranks. Grade equivalents simply indicate the grade level, in years and months, for which a given score was the average, or middle, score in the norm group. For example, a score of 25 with the grade equivalent of 4.6 means that in the norm group, 25 was the average score of students in the sixth month of grade four. Percentile ranks represent the percentage of students who scored at or below a given student's score. A percentile score of 75 percent, then, means that the student scored higher than 75 percent of all students in his or her age group who took the test. Keep in mind that grade-level equivalencies and percentiles look at student performance only from the standpoint of how different they are from average, *not* according to how well they performed a skill from the standpoint of mastery. For example, a grade equivalent score of 3.2 in reading comprehension means that the student achieved the same score as the average of all students in grade three, second month, who were in the normative sample; it does not say anything about how well the student is able to answer the various kinds of comprehension questions that may be in the grade three reading curriculum.

Group-administered tests.   There are two major types of standardized achievement tests: group-administered and individually administered diagnostic tests. As the name implies, group-administered standardized achievement tests are completed by large groups of students at one time; this usually means that the regular education teacher gives the test to the entire class. *Principles for Fair Student Assessment Practices for Education in Canada* was published in 1993 by a Joint Advisory Committee. Group tests assess skills across many areas of the curriculum, none in much depth. They are intended to be used solely as screening measures. These tests are used less in Canadian schools than in the past, and are not used for making decisions about individuals:

1. Administration in a group environment does not allow students to ask the teacher questions about directions or to clarify test questions (Overton, 1992). For example, Alicia has a learning disability in reading and has problems comprehending written directions.
2. Many group tests are timed, which may limit the responses of students with disabilities. For example, Carmen has a problem with eye-hand coordination and makes errors in transferring her answers to a computer-scored answer sheet.
3. National or even local norms might not match actual distribution of classroom achievement (Deno, 1985; Marston, 1989; Salvia & Ysseldyke, 1995). For example, Darryl is in grade four and scored at the grade two level on a standardized achievement test in reading, a score that was at least six months below the rest of his classmates. However, the results of an informal reading probe based on his classroom literature-based program revealed that four other students in class were reading at a level roughly equivalent to Darryl's. The teacher decided to form an instructional group composed of these students to help them with their literature books and did not refer Darryl for further assessment.
4. The results of standardized tests provide little useful data to guide instruction (Bursuck & Lessen, 1987; Deno, 1985; Marston, 1989; Salvia & Ysseldyke,

✓ **Your Learning:** What are the drawbacks in using group-administered standardized achievement tests to make educational decisions for students?

1995). For example, Ellen's math achievement scores showed that she was one year below grade level in math computation. However, the test contained too few items to find out the particular kind of errors she was making.

5. Standardized achievement tests might be culturally biased, and they can lead to the overrepresentation of minority groups in exceptional education services (Garcia & Pearson, 1994; Oakland, 1981). For example, Bill comes from a single-parent home in a high-rise apartment building in the city. When he read a story on a standardized achievement test about an affluent two-parent family in the suburbs, he had difficulty predicting the outcome.

6. The content of a standardized achievement test might not match what is taught in a particular classroom (Deno, 1985; Deno & Fuchs, 1987; Marston, 1989). For example, one teacher stressed problem solving in his science class, whereas the standardized achievement test given in his district stressed the memorization of facts. Therefore, he had to give his own tests to see if students were learning the material.

7. Because it is not possible to administer standardized tests frequently, their utility as a tool for evaluating day-to-day instruction is limited (Bursuck & Lessen, 1987; Deno, 1985). For example, Clark was not allowed into Algebra 1 because of his poor performance on a standardized achievement test in math. After one month, Clark's teacher felt he was ready for Algebra 1. Because the achievement test could not be given again until May, the algebra and basic math teachers developed their own test of skills prerequisite for Algebra 1 and gave it to Clark.

Group-administered standardized achievement tests can be useful in some circumstances. One such situation involves making administrative and policy

▶ *What are some advantages of individually administered diagnostic tests? What are other sources of assessment information used in educational decision making for exceptional students?*

Do It! Ask an administrator at your local school district or school board whether students with disabilities take the district's standardized achievement tests and whether they are allowed accommodations (for example, an oral test for students with learning disabilities). Also ask whether the scores for students with disabilities are counted in the district's overall test results.

decisions on a school-district or school-board level. For example, a school board found that their students were below the national average on the problem-solving portion of a math achievement test and decided to spend more time on math problem solving at all levels in the district. Educators mistrust standardized tests for other reasons. They often feel that when standardized tests are administered they gradually influence the curriculum and what teachers teach. Teachers are right to express this concern. In a study conducted in Ontario and British Columbia, Wilson (1990) found that classroom assessment was influenced by provincial evaluations and was carried out more to confirm student marks than to guide and change teaching for individuals or the class. The validity of group-administered achievement tests for making decisions about individual students at the classroom level is limited. These tests should be used with great caution and only in conjunction with informal, classroom-based measures.

Individually administered tests.   A special education teacher, resource teacher, or the school psychologist usually gives **individually administered diagnostic tests** as part of a student's case-study evaluation. Although these tests may screen student performance in several curricular areas, they tend to be more diagnostic in nature. For example, an individually administered diagnostic reading test may include subtests in the areas of letter identification, word recognition, oral reading, comprehension, and phonetic skills; a diagnostic test in math might include math computation, fractions, geometry, word problems, measurement, and time. Because individually administered diagnostic tests provide information on a range of specific skills, they can be useful as an information source in making educational decisions. For example, Tamara scored two years below grade level on the comprehension subtest of an individually administered diagnostic test in reading. Yet in an oral reading sample taken from her grade four reader, she read both fluently and accurately. On the basis of these two findings, her teacher placed her in a literature-based reading program that stressed skills in reading comprehension.

Although individually administered diagnostic tests may be more helpful than group-administered achievement tests, they are still subject to many of the same problems. Again, you should always verify findings from these tests using more informal measures based on what you teach.

Psychological Tests

Psychological tests are used as part of the process of evaluating some exceptional students, particularly to determine if a student is gifted or has cognitive or learning disabilities. Reports of the results of these tests are often written by school psychologists and consist of a summary of the findings and the implications for instruction. **Psychological tests** can include intelligence tests and tests related to learning disabilities (Overton, 1992; Salvia & Ysseldyke, 1995).

✓ **Your Learning:** What do psychological tests measure?

The overall purpose of psychological tests is to measure abilities that affect how efficiently students learn in an instructional situation. These abilities are inferred based on student responses to items that the test author believes represent that particular ability. For example, abilities commonly assessed by psychological tests include generalization (the ability to recognize similarities across objects, events, or vocabulary), general or background information, vocabulary, induction (the ability to figure out a rule or principle based on a series of situations), abstract reasoning, and memory (Salvia & Ysseldyke, 1995). Student scores are then compared to a norm group of other same-aged students, with an average score being equal to 100.

Psychological tests can be helpful if they clarify why students may not be learning in class and lead to effective changes in instruction. For example, the results of Lina's test showed that she had difficulty with visual memory. Her teacher, Ms. Fasbacher, felt that this was related to her poor performance in spelling. As a result, Ms. Fasbacher provided Lina with extra practice on her weekly spelling lists. Interpreting the results of psychological reports will seem less daunting if you follow the general guidelines suggested here. First, do not be scared off by the technical terms and/or jargon. You have the right to expect that reports be translated into instructionally relevant language. Second, the results of psychological tests are most valid when corroborated by classroom experience. Further, in the event of discrepancies between psychological reports and your experience, do not automatically discount your experience. Keep in mind that your impressions are the result of many more hours of observation than are psychological evaluations, which are based on fewer samples of student behaviour that take place outside the classroom. Third, be sure to ask about or check the technical adequacy of the psychological tests included in your report. You will be surprised to find that many of these tests may not be acceptable. Fourth, psychological tests may discriminate against students from culturally different or disadvantaged backgrounds in the following ways:

FYI: Psychological tests may not be reliable or valid and may not have appropriate norms. Check the test manual or ask your school psychologist about the technical adequacy of tests used in your school.

1. **Inappropriate content.** Students from minority cultures may lack exposure to certain items on the instrument.
2. **Inappropriate standardization samples.** Cultural and ethnic minorities may not have been represented in the normative sample at the time the instrument was developed.
3. **Misunderstood examiner or language.** Anglo, English-speaking examiners may be unable to establish rapport with students from minority groups and students from different linguistic backgrounds.
4. **Inequitable social consequences.** As a result of discriminatory assessment practices, students from minority groups may be relegated to lower educational streams or placements, with the ultimate result that they obtain lower-paying jobs.
5. **Ineffective measurement of constructs.** Test developers design instruments assumed to measure academic or cognitive ability for all students. When used with students from minority groups, however, the instruments may measure only the degree to which the students have absorbed middle-class culture.
6. **Different predictive validity.** Instruments designed to predict the educational or academic outcomes or potential for students of the majority culture may not do so for students from minority groups (Reynolds, 1982).

Cultural Awareness: Psychological tests can be biased against students from diverse backgrounds. Use them only in conjunction with other formal and informal measures.

Finally, the primary purpose of psychological tests is to establish possible explanations for particular learning, behavioural, or social and emotional problems. Keep in mind that such causes should be springboards for helping students overcome these problems, not excuses for a student's lack of achievement.

Do It! Examine sample copies of some of the standardized tests described in this chapter. What questions would you ask to ensure your correct interpretation and appropriate use of information from these sources?

Connections: Characteristics of students with moderate to severe developmental disabilities are described in Chapter 4.

The Professional Edge below contains lists of standardized tests commonly used in special education decision making. These include standardized group and individual achievement tests and psychological tests used to assess intelligence or cognitive functioning.

Environmental Inventory Process

Traditional formal and informal testing practices may be inappropriate for students with moderate to severe developmental disabilities. These students often lack the critical language and motor skills necessary to respond to such tests. In addition, the abstract nature of the test items has little relation to the functional living skills that are so important to assess for these students. The **environmental inventory** is an alternative assessment process for students with moderate to severe disabilities. Sometimes this is referred to as community-referenced assessment. The purpose of this type of assessment is to determine what adaptations or supports are needed to increase the participation of these students in classroom as well as community environments (Freagon, Kincaid, & Kaiser, 1990; Vandercook, York, & Forest, 1989). The environmental inventory process involves asking yourself three questions:

Professional Edge
Standardized Tests Commonly Used in Special Education Decision Making

YOU have many standardized tests to choose from to help you in making decisions about exceptional children and adolescents. When selecting an instrument, make sure it is appropriate for the student being tested. If you have questions about the suitability of a particular test, consult your school psychologist or special education teacher. The following lists provide the names of commonly used standardized tests for decision making about exceptional learners.

Standardized Achievement and Diagnostic Tests

Canadian Test of Basic Skills
Canadian Achievement Tests
Woodcock-Johnson—Revised Tests of Achievement
Peabody Individual Achievement Test—Revised

Kaufman Test of Educational Achievement: Comprehension Form
KeyMath Diagnostic Arithmetic Test—Revised
Woodcock Reading Mastery Tests—Revised
Test of Written Language—2
Test of Written Spelling—2
Test of Reading Comprehension—Revised
Gray Oral Reading Test—Revised
Wide Range Achievement Test—3

Intelligence Tests and Tests of Cognitive Functioning

Wechsler Intelligence Scale for Children—III
Woodcock-Johnson—Revised: Tests of Cognitive Abilities
Stanford-Binet IV
Kaufman Assessment Battery for Children

1. What does a person who does not have a disability do in this environment?
2. What does a person who has a disability do in this environment? What is the discrepancy?
3. What types of supports and/or adaptations can be put in place in order to increase the participation level or independence of the person who has a disability?

An example of how this process is used in a classroom environment is shown in Figure 8.1. This example involves Roberto, the student with moderate to severe developmental disabilities whom you met at the beginning of the chapter, who is included in Ms. Benis's grade six social studies class. The class is working in small groups on depicting the steps in the recycling process for paper, metal, and plastic. Roberto lacks the motor and cognitive skills necessary to participate like everyone else. Ms. Benis has decided to assign Roberto to the group that his friend Seth is in. She also decides to use different materials for Roberto. Ms. Benis will ask a paraprofessional to help Roberto find pictures of sample recycled products; Seth will help Roberto paste these pictures onto the group's diagram. Mr. Howard, Roberto's resource teacher, will help Roberto identify recycled products in grocery stores and restaurants. Roberto's parents will help him sort the recycling at home.

✔ **Your Learning:** Why are standardized achievement tests and psychological tests not useful for students with moderate to severe cognitive disabilities?

Curriculum-Based Assessments

Because of the limited utility of standard achievement tests and psychological reports for day-to-day instructional decisions, you need other tools to be a partner in the evaluation process. **Curriculum-based assessment (CBA)** is a promising option, and in many instances can be an alternative to standardized tests. CBA has been defined as a method of measuring the level of achievement of students in terms of what they are taught in the classroom (for example, Blankenship & Lilly, 1981; Bursuck & Lessen, 1987; Tucker, 1985). CBA has a number of attractive features. First, in CBA, you select the skills that are assessed based on what you teach in class, thus ensuring a match between what is taught and what is tested. CBA compares students within a class or school to show learning differences, not national norms (Marston, Tindal, & Deno, 1984), thus ensuring that a student referred for special education services is significantly different from his or her peers (Bursuck & Lessen, 1987). For example, in the vignettes at the beginning of this chapter, Ms. Lyons gave Rob some curriculum-based assessments in math to identify what specific kinds of problems he was having. She then implemented a peer tutoring program and used these same tests to measure its effectiveness. Mr. Blount used an informal reading assessment based on his American history textbook to see how well his students were able to read this text. The Case in Practice illustrates a scenario in which both standardized and curriculum-based assessments are used to help make decisions about an exceptional learner.

Before we describe the specifics of how to use curriculum-based assessments, we must point out that curriculum-based assessments are not without drawbacks. First, test items that accurately measure student performance may be hard to construct. Second, because curriculum-based assessments test what is taught, they may fail to measure other important information or skills that may not be taught directly. Third, because curriculum-based assessments relate to

Connections: This chapter involves assessment for identifying and addressing students' special needs. Chapter 11 is devoted to adapting assessment for evaluating student performance and improving instruction.

Connections: Strategies for assessing student problem-solving skills using performance-based assessments are explained in Chapter 11.

FIGURE 8.1

Environmental
Inventory Process

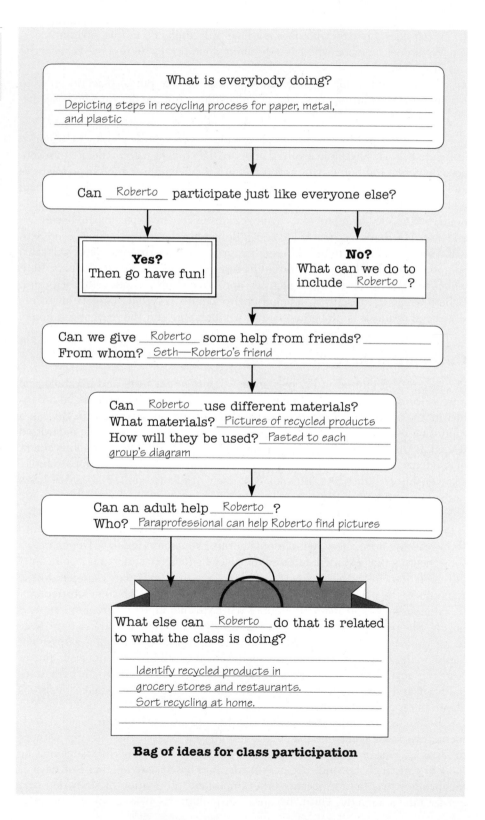

What is everybody doing?

Depicting steps in recycling process for paper, metal,
and plastic

Can __Roberto__ participate just like everyone else?

Yes?
Then go have fun!

No?
What can we do to
include __Roberto__ ?

Can we give __Roberto__ some help from friends? _____
From whom? __Seth—Roberto's friend__

Can __Roberto__ use different materials?
What materials? __Pictures of recycled products__
How will they be used? __Pasted to each__
group's diagram

Can an adult help __Roberto__ ?
Who? __Paraprofessional can help Roberto find pictures__

What else can __Roberto__ do that is related
to what the class is doing?

Identify recycled products in
grocery stores and restaurants.
Sort recycling at home.

Bag of ideas for class participation

Case in Practice

Assessments in Special Education Decision Making

DARNELL is nine years old. He was referred for testing for a learning disability by his grade four teacher, Ms. Davis. Ms. Davis was particularly concerned about Darnell's lack of progress in written language (for example, paragraph writing and spelling). Following an evaluation, an IEP meeting was held. Present at the meeting were the school psychologist, Mr. Earl; the learning disabilities teacher, Mr. Bryant; Darnell's grade four teacher, Ms. Davis; and Darnell's mother, Mrs. Lewis. The following information was presented after introductions were made.

MR. EARL: We're all here today to take a careful look at some of the problems Darnell has been having with his writing to see if he may have a learning disability and be eligible for some extra help. I'll start by sharing the results of the intelligence testing I did with Darnell. Then, Mr. Bryant will discuss the results of a standardized achievement test in writing that he gave Darnell. Ms. Davis will share the results of some informal testing she has been doing in her class. Finally, Mrs. Lewis will tell us about Darnell's use of language at home.

I gave Darnell the Wechsler Intelligence Test for Children–III, a commonly used intelligence test for children. His overall score was 105, well within the average range. I think it's also important to point out that Darnell's verbal IQ of 103 was also in the normal range; he may be having trouble with his written language, but his oral language seems okay. Darnell seems to have the ability to be successful in writing.

MR. BRYANT: I gave Darnell the Woodcock-Johnson—Revised Tests of Achievement. His scores in all areas of written expression were well below what we might predict based on the IQ scores presented by Mr. Earl. His overall grade equivalence score in written expression is grade two, month three. Darnell scored particularly low in writing mechanics such as spelling, proofing, capitalization, punctuation, and flu-

ency. His score in this area was grade one, month eight.

MS. DAVIS: At the end of last month, I was teaching my class to write "how to" papers, such as "how to make a peanut-butter-and-jelly sandwich." After about a week, I noticed that Darnell was having problems with this kind of writing. I wasn't surprised, since he was also having problems with other kinds of writing. I decided to do some extra things to help Darnell. First, I gave him a visual grid to help him organize his paper. For example, there was a specially marked spot for the introduction and conclusion, as well as for the steps for whatever was being described. I also went over to Darnell's desk as he was writing to give him some extra help. I did this for another week but saw no improvement. I think Darnell lacks more basic skills, such as how to write a complete sentence.

Let me show you what I mean. Yesterday, I asked all of my students to do a written language probe in class. I asked them to write a paragraph about how they wash their hair. I gave the students five minutes to write their paragraphs. This is what Darnell wrote:

> *waat you haid and pot sopo in haid*

First, I wanted to see whether Darnell wrote as much as the rest of the class. As you can see, Darnell wrote eight words, which is less than two words per minute. The average for the rest of the class was 30 words, or about six words per minute. I also judged Darnell's paragraph for quality; his paragraph lacked such features as a title, topic sentence, closing sentence, and the use of signal words, like "*First* you do this, and *next* you do that." The papers of all the other students in class except one had these features.

MRS. LEWIS: This sounds a lot like Darnell is at home. He has never had trouble following oral directions, but his handwriting and spelling have always been a problem. Getting him to write a letter to his grandmother is like pulling teeth.

Reflections

What different kinds of assessment were used here? What other measures might have been used?

What instructional changes did Ms. Davis try before referring Darnell? Can you think of some other interventions that she could have tried? Do you think Darnell should be identified as having exceptional learning disabilities on the basis of this information? Why or why not?

student performance at the individual classroom level, their use for evaluating student performance on a provincial or even boardwide basis is limited. In the past decade, some urban school boards have developed "benchmarks" that fall between norm-referenced and classroom-based assessments (e.g., Toronto Board of Education, n.d.) to overcome the drawbacks of both. Finally, curriculum-based assessments are most appropriate for assessing academic skills taught in school. As such, they are not as effective when assessing problem-solving skills in real-world contexts.

What Kinds of Curriculum-Based Assessments Can You Create for Your Students?

Two major kinds of curriculum-based assessments are commonly used: probes of basic academic skills (for example, reading, math, and writing) and content-area strategy assessments (for example, probes of prerequisite skills, textbook reading, and note-taking). Although probes of basic academic skills relate more directly to elementary school teachers and content-area strategy assessments to junior high and high school teachers, each of these measures is relevant for both groups. For example, high school students need to perform basic skills fluently if they are to have ready access to curriculum content; elementary school students need early training in learning strategies to facilitate the difficult transition to high school instruction.

Probes of Basic Academic Skills

Probes are quick and easy measures of student performance in the basic skill areas of reading, math, and written expression. They consist of samples of academic behaviours and are designed to assess skill accuracy and, when they are timed, to assess skill fluency.

Probes can sample a range of skills in a particular area, such as a mixed probe of grade five math computation problems in addition, subtraction, multiplication, and division; or they can sample one skill area, such as letter identification or writing lowercase manuscript letters.

Probes are classified according to how students take in task information (seeing, hearing) and how they respond (writing, speaking). They include four major types: see-say, see-write, hear-write, and think-write (Bursuck & Lessen, 1987). For example, when reading orally from a textbook, students *see* the text and *say* the words. Hence, oral reading is referred to as a see-say probe. Similarly, in a spelling probe, students *hear* the teacher dictate words and *write* the words as they are dictated. This is a hear-write probe.

As you develop curriculum-based assessments, keep in mind the following suggestions:

1. Identify academic skills that are essential in your particular room or grade. In the elementary grades, include skills in handwriting, spelling, written expression, reading (for example, letter identification, letter sounds, oral reading accuracy, comprehension), and math (for example, number identification, computation, problem solving, time, and money). By repeating probes of basic academic skills with students, you are carrying out self-referenced assessment in which students are compared to themselves. This means that what you are seeking is evidence that student performance is improving compared to the same student's performance at an earlier time.

2. Select skills representing a sample of skills that are taught, not necessarily every skill. Performance on these skills then acts as a checkpoint for identifying students in trouble or measuring student progress. For example, in assessing reading performance, asking students to read a passage aloud from their reading or literature books and answer comprehension questions may not represent all reading skills you have taught (for example, words in isolation), but it does include a representative sample of many of these skills.

Probes of reading skills.   The critical reading skills in the elementary years include letter identification, letter sounds, word recognition, and comprehension. Student ability to identify letter names and sounds can be assessed using a see-say probe. Word recognition and comprehension can be assessed using a see-say oral passage reading probe.

Although the easiest method for assessing comprehension is to use the questions that accompany most classroom reading series, if you are using a literature-based reading program, you may need to design your own questions, which can be a difficult task. Carnine, Silbert, and Kameenui (1990) have suggested one practical model for designing comprehension questions based on story grammar. A **story grammar** is simply the description of the typical elements found frequently in stories. These include theme, setting, character, initiating events, attempts at resolution, resolution, and reactions. These elements of story grammar can be used to create comprehension questions that may be more appropriate than traditional main-idea and detail questions, because story grammar describes the organization of most stories that elementary school students are likely to read. The Case in Practice on pages 254–255 shows how a teacher uses a story grammar with one of her grade two students.

You can also have students retell stories after they read them. Students then must organize the information that they think is important. You can then evaluate the completeness of their recall without questions that offer clues to what you think is important. Such a situation has two requirements in order for effective evaluation to occur: a standard set of criteria to evaluate the completeness of the retelling, and the opportunity to evaluate each student's retelling individually.

✓ **Your Learning:** What are the four major types of probes? Give an example of each.

Connections: Probes of academic skills will help you evaluate the instructional progress of students with special needs—an application of the *E* step of the INCLUDE strategy.

Probes of written expression. Written expression can be assessed using a think-write probe. In this probe, the teacher reads the students a story starter. The students then have one minute to plan a story and three minutes to write it. This probe is scored according to the number of "intelligible" words the student can write per minute. Intelligible words are those that make sense in the story. This way of scoring is useful for screening students for serious writing difficulty. If you are interested in more diagnostic information, such as grammar usage, spelling, handwriting, punctuation, vocabulary, or ideas, you can score this probe

---

Case in Practice

Using Story Grammars

Ms. PADILLA's grade two students have just read the story *Chakapesh Snares the Sun*, a legend retold by Linda Guebert (McInnes, 1987). The story is about an Algonquin boy who is setting snares in the bush. The boy, Chakapesh, sets a snare on the sun's trail even though his sister warned him not to. The sky is dark when Chakapesh discovers he has snared the sun. He asks a mouse to chew the ropes of the snare to set the sun free. This works and the sun lights the sky once again.

Ms. Padilla is assessing Chantille's comprehension of the story using the story grammar retelling format.

Ms. PADILLA: Chantille, you have just read *Chakapesh Snares the Sun*. Would you tell me in your own words what the story is about?

CHANTILLE: The story is about a boy named Chakapesh who sets snares and one day he sets a snare on the sun's trail and he traps it.

Ms. PADILLA: Chantille, where does this story take place?

CHANTILLE: In the bush where he was setting the snares.

Ms. PADILLA: Chantille, what was the problem when the sun was caught in the snare?

CHANTILLE: Chakapesh caught the sun in the snare, so it didn't give light to the sky anymore.

Ms. PADILLA: You said that the sun was trapped. What did Chakapesh do to solve that problem?

CHANTILLE: Well, he got the sun free.

Ms. PADILLA: How did you feel at the end of the story?

CHANTILLE: I felt happy.

Ms. PADILLA: Why did you feel happy?

CHANTILLE: Well, 'cause the sun was free.

Ms. PADILLA: Chantille, what lesson do you think this story teaches us?

CHANTILLE: That the sun is important because it gives us light.

A score sheet that Ms. Padilla completed for Chantille is shown in Figure 8.2. A plus (+) means that Chantille responded accurately to that element without any prompting or questioning; a checkmark (✓) means that Chantille mentioned the element after she was questioned or prompted; a minus (−) means that she failed to refer to the element even after questioning or prompts.

Look at Chantille's scores. As you can see, she had a good idea of who the main characters were and received a plus for this component ("Characters"). Chantille identified the problem of the sun being trapped, and the problem of the sky going dark with prompts; thus, a + and a [catch checkmark] were scored for "Goal/Problem." It was unclear from Chantille's response exactly how the characters tried to solve their problem, so she received a − for "Attempts." Chantille did say the problem was

differently or give another probe designed to measure these areas specifically (see Deno & Fuchs, 1987; Evans, Evans, & Mercer, 1986; and Howell & Morehead, 1993, for sample informal assessments in these areas).

Probes of math skills.   Teachers in the primary grades need to measure student identification of numbers, coins, and geometric figures. This assessment can be done as a see-say probe using numbers and symbols. Math computation and math problem solving can be assessed using see-write probes such as the one in Figure 8.4 on page 256.

Do It! Create a sample learning probe for each area of curriculum-based assessment described in this section. Base each probe on the subject area and grade level you plan to teach.

solved when the sun was set free; she received a + for this element of "Resolution." However, she did not say how this resolved the problem of the darkened sky so she received a −. Chantille's reaction to the story was appropriate, so a + was scored. For "Setting," Chantille received a [catch checkmark]; she identified the setting after Ms. Padilla prompted her. Finally, Chantille received a − for "Theme." This response was lacking, even after prompting.

Notice that Ms. Padilla's prompts included explicit references to the various story grammar components. For example, she asked, "You said that the sun was trapped. What did Chakapesh do to solve that problem?" as opposed to a more general question, such as, "What happened to the sun?" This use of specific language makes the story grammar components more clear, a necessary structure for younger, more naive learners.

Reflections

How could story retelling be incorporated into a classroom literature-based program? How do you think these results will be helpful to Ms. Padilla?

▶ **FIGURE 8.2**   Story Retelling Checklist

Student Name	Story Grammars Evaluated											
	Theme		Setting		Characters		Goal/ Problem		Attempts		Resolution	Reactions
Chantille	−		✓		+		+	✓	−		⊢	—	+

+ Responded correctly without prompting
✓ Responded correctly after prompting
− Did not identify relevant story grammar component

FIGURE 8.3   See-say: Oral Passage Reading

Time	1 minute
Materials	*Student*—Stimulus passage *Examiner*—Duplicate copy of stimulus passage, pencil, timer
Directions to Student	"When I say 'Please begin,' read this story out loud to me. Start here [examiner points] and read as quickly and carefully as you can. Try to say each word. Ready? Please begin."
Scoring	Place a slash (/) on your copy of the materials where the student started reading. As the student reads, place a mark (X) on your copy over any errors (mispronunciations, words skipped, and words given). (If student hesitates for 2–3 seconds, give him or her the word and mark it as an error.) If student inserts words, self-corrects, sounds out, or repeats, do not count as errors. When the student has read for 1 minute, place a (/) on your copy to indicate how far the student read in 1 minute. (It is usually good practice to let students finish the paragraph or page they are reading rather than stopping them immediately when 1 minute is over.) Count the total number of words read during the 1 minute (the total number of words between the two slashes). Tally the total number of errors (words mispronounced, words skipped, and words given) made during the 1-minute sample. Subtract the total number of errors from the total words covered to get number correct (total words – errors = correct words).
Note	Probe administered individually.

Billy decided to go down by the river and	(9)
demonstrate his fishing ability. He always could deceive	(17)
the fish with his special secret lure. He had his best	(28)
luck in his own place, a wooded shady spot downstream	(38)
that no one knew about. Today he was going to try	(49)
to catch a catfish all the boys called Old Gray. Old Gray	(61)
was a legend in this town, because even though many boys	(72)
had hooked him, he always managed to get away.	(81)
This time Billy knew that if he sat long enough, he could	(93)
catch his dream fish!	(97)

1. Where did Billy like to fish?
2. Who was Old Gray?
3. How was Billy planning to catch Old Gray?
4. Why do you think Billy was so interested in catching Old Gray?

Source: From *Curriculum-Based Assessment and Instructional Design* by E. Lessen, M. Sommers, and W. D. Bursuck, 1987, DeKalb, IL: DeKalb County Special Education Association. Used with permission.

> **FIGURE 8.4** See-Write: Math Computation
>
> | | |
> |---|---|
> | ***Time*** | 1 minute |
> | ***Materials*** | *Student*—Response sheet, two pencils
Examiner—Timer |
> | ***Directions to Student*** | "When I say 'Please begin,' write the answers to these math problems as quickly and carefully as you can. Go across the page [examiner demonstrates]. If you have trouble with a problem, try it, write something, and then move on. Do not erase. Ready? Please begin." After one minute, say "Please stop. Put your pencils down. Thank you." |
> | ***Scoring*** | Count the number of correct digits (not answers) written. For example, here is a student's work for the problem 43 + 49: |
>
> $$\begin{array}{r} 1 \\ 43 \\ + 49 \\ \hline 92 \end{array}$$
>
> Score this as three correct digits: The answer has two correct digits (92) and the number carried represents one correct digit. Digits correct is often used because it is more sensitive to changes in student performance (see Tindal & Marston, 1990, for a more complete explanation).
>
> *Source:* From *Curriculum-Based Assessment and Instructional Design* by E. Lessen, M. Sommers, and W. Bursuck, 1987, DeKalb, IL: DeKalb County Special Education Association. Used with permission.

Content-Area Assessments

Content-area teachers may need to take a somewhat different approach to student assessment. Content-area classrooms are characterized by increased curricular demands with fewer opportunities for individualization; students are expected to learn more material and to take responsibility for learning much of it on their own. Students who enter a class significantly behind their classmates either in background knowledge or independent learning skills are likely to struggle. Thus, it is important to identify these students early so that they can be better prepared when they enter a content class. For example, at the beginning of this chapter, Mr. Blount assessed his history students' ability to read the class textbook independently since students in his class were expected to read much of the material on their own.

Do It! Give an academic skill probe in an elementary school class. summarize the results and share them with the teacher.

Probes of prerequisite skills. Unfortunately, the decision whether to place a particular student in a given high school class can be problematic, partly because of the difficulty of identifying which skills are prerequisite. For example, the English department at a high school developed a test of prerequisite skills for grade nine English. Clarise, a student with a learning disability, was given this test at the end of grade eight to find out whether this class was appropriate for her to take. For skill-oriented classes such as math and English, prerequisite skills

Connections: Using probes of prerequisite stills is a good way to identify classroom demands as part of the INCLUDE strategy.

would be those taught in elementary school or previously taught courses, such as computation skills for algebra and sentence writing for English. For classes that stress content rather than basic skills (for example, science), having the necessary background information to understand the material currently being presented is also vital.

Unfortunately, the process of determining whether students have necessary prerequisite skills can be problematic. A key problem involves identifying these skills. Teachers' choices of prerequisite skills often include skills that a student can bypass and still have access to course content, such as reading in a history class (which can be bypassed by using an oral text) or written expression in a science class (which can be bypassed by using oral tests and reports). When testing for prerequisite skills, you must be careful that you do not inadvertently exclude exceptional students, many of whom are capable of passing content classes despite their problems in certain basic-skills areas.

This and other problems suggest the need for a fair way of making placement decisions for exceptional students at the high school level. A potentially useful method is for teachers to develop probes to evaluate student performance on critical prerequisite skills. The probe-development process, which is similar to the process of developing curriculum-based assessments described earlier in the chapter, consists of the following steps:

1. Identify critical content learning or skills for your class.
2. Identify entry-level content or skills needed. Be certain these are not skills for which a bypass strategy would be possible.
3. Develop a probe to measure the identified skills.
4. Administer the probe to current classes to ensure that students passing the class are able to pass the probe test.
5. Set a minimum score necessary for student course entry based on the results of the preceding step. You may want to use an acceptable range rather than a single score, particularly during the initial stages of this process.
6. As with all educational decisions, no one score should be the sole basis for a decision. Other factors, such as student motivation and level of supportive assistance, will need to be considered.

Measures of independent learning skills.   When students enter secondary school, they find an environment often not as supportive as the smaller elementary and junior high school environments they left. The student body is often larger and more diverse. Daily routines change and curriculum is more difficult (Schumaker & Deshler, 1988). Secondary schools also demand a much higher level of student independence through the application of a range of **independent learning skills.** These skills, often referred to as learning strategies or study skills, include note-taking, textbook reading, test-taking, written expression, and time management. Student ability to perform these various skills independently can make the difference between passing or failing a class. For example, at the beginning of the chapter, Mr. Blount decided to assess textbook reading skills since these were important for success in his class. A sample instrument to measure textbook reading skills, which was originally developed by Voix (1968) and later adapted by Lessen, Sommers, and Bursuck (1988), is shown in Figure 8.5. Notice in Figure 8.6 on page 263 that the reading tasks for this measure are

FYI: Your tests of prerequisite skills should include only skills that are critical for performing in your class, not skills that the student could bypass.

Do It! Ask a high school teacher what the prerequisite skills are for his or her class. Develop a probe to measure these skills.

✔ **Your Learning:** What is the process for developing probes of prerequisite skills?

▶ *What curriculum goals might a physical education teacher observing this class be assessing?*

taken directly from the students' history and science textbooks. Doing so ensures that the results are relevant for the particular classroom situation. Note also that

FIGURE 8.5

Evaluating Content-Area Textbook Reading Skills

Suggestions for specific types of questions are included here. The information in parentheses explains or offers additional information about a particular item.

Using Parts of the Book

1. On what page would you find the chapter called _____? (Tests ability to use table of contents.)

2. Of what value to you are the questions listed at the end of each chapter? (Tests understanding of a specific study aid.)

3. How are the chapters arranged or grouped? (Tests knowledge of text organization.)

4. What part of the book would you use to find the page reference for the topic _____? (Tests knowledge of index.)

5. On what page would you find the answer to each of the following questions? (Tests ability to use index.)

Using Source Materials (examples)

1. What library aid will tell you the library number of a book so that you would be able to find the book on the shelves? (Tests knowledge of functions of card catalogue and computerized cataloguing systems.)

2. What is a biography? (Tests knowledge of a type of reference book.)

3. Explain the difference between science-fiction and science-factual materials. (Tests knowledge of important types of science materials.)

Comprehension

The following questions would be based on a three- or four-page selection from the textbook.

Vocabulary

1. Turn to page _____. How does the author define the word _____? (Tests ability to use context clues and the aids the author uses to convey the meaning of the word.)

2. Define _____.

3. What is a _____?

4. *Vocabulary in context*: From the paragraph on page 584 beginning "In Poland, the Soviet Union . . . ," write an appropriate and brief definition of each of the following words: ____, ____, and ____.

Noting Main Ideas

These questions would ask for main points of information, such as main ideas of longer, important paragraphs of the chapter introduction or summary or of an experiment. (*Examples:* What are atoms composed of? What reason was given for the conservation of human resources? What is the result of the photosynthetic process?)

Noting Details

These questions would ask for specific bits of information, such as an aspect of a process, the application of a law, the principal steps in an experiment, a life cycle, or incidents in the life of a scientist. (*Examples:* Describe the photosynthetic process. What are the different stages in the cycle of precipitation and evaporation? List the major incidents in the life of Mme. Marie Curie.)

Drawing Conclusions

Ask questions about the significance or value of a finding, the implication of a description of some species or natural phenomenon, causes and effect, or a comparison of two or more types of organisms. The questions should call for answers that are not stated in the text. (*Examples:* Illustrate the term *balance of life.* What conclusion can you draw from the importance of the photosynthetic process? What is the principle difference between mitosis and meiosis?)

Applying Theoretical Information

These questions would ask for examples of practical uses of scientific law and principles. (*Examples:* Explain the relationship of photosynthesis to the conservation of plant life. Explain the idea that air confined in a small area exerts pressure in all directions, in relation to the action of air in a football.)

Following Directions

These questions would ask learners to show the sequence of steps or ideas for solving a problem or performing an experiment or the sequence of a chain of events. (*Examples:* What is the second step of the experiment? What should you do after you have placed the flask over the burner?)

Understanding Formulas and Symbols

These questions test student understanding of how symbols and formulas are used with scientific data. (*Example:* What does the "H" refer to in the symbol H_2O?)

Maps and Graphs

Use questions that require knowledge of map and graph symbols and how to use them. (*Examples:* Use the graph on page 602 to answer these questions: By 1925, how many millions of people inhabited Earth? How many times will the world population have increased from 1900 to 2000? Use the map on page 174 to answer these questions: Who ruled Gascony in the 1300s? Who governed the major portion of Flanders after 1550?)

Study Reading

Directions: Read pages 584–586. Take notes. Then close your book and keep it closed. However, you may use the notes you made to help you answer the following questions. (Have questions on a separate sheet for distribution after notes have been made.) *Note:* Ask detail, main idea, and inference questions.

Source: Adapted from Evaluating Reading and Study Skills in the Secondary Classroom: A Guide for Content Teachers by R. G. Voix, 1968, Newark, DE: International Reading Association.

Student 1	Student 2
Percentage of Accuracy	Percentage of Accuracy
96	70

FIGURE 8.6
Percentage of Accuracy in Passage Reading for Two Students

this textbook reading assessment can be given to the entire classroom at once; this will be helpful since many students may have trouble reading their textbooks, not just exceptional students.

As with the basic and prerequisite skills mentioned earlier, probes can be developed to assess independent learning. A key consideration is that the tasks used for assessment should parallel the tasks that students face in your classroom: If you are evaluating textbook reading, the reading task should come from the textbook you are using in class; if you are measuring a student's ability to take lecture notes, the task should involve elements similar to a typical lecture delivered in your class.

Once the task has been selected, decide what kind of measure to use. Three possible choices are direct-observation checklists, analysis of student products, and student self-evaluation. With **direct-observation checklists**, a list of observable steps necessary to perform a given strategy is developed. Next, the teacher asks a student to perform a classroom task that requires him or her to use the strategy and records on the checklist the behaviours that the student did or did not perform.

Although direct observation of student behaviour can provide much useful information, it is time-consuming, particularly when you are a secondary school teacher who teaches many students each day. For most students, you can use either analysis of student products or student self-evaluations. Nonetheless, if you should have the luxury of a free moment with an individual student, such as before or after school or during a study period, the time spent directly observing a student perform a task is very worthwhile.

Analysis of **student products** involves examining student notebooks, tests, papers, and other assignments or written activities to find evidence of effective or ineffective strategy performance. In most cases, you can evaluate your whole classroom at once, and you do not have to score the products while you are teaching.

In **student self-evaluations,** students perform a task such as taking a test, are given a checklist of strategy steps, and are then asked to tell which of these steps they did or did not use (Bursuck & Jayanthi, 1993). Student self-reports are useful for several reasons. They can provide information about strategy behaviours that cannot be directly observed. Student evaluations also stimulate student self-monitoring, a behaviour critical for independent learning. Self-report measures can also include interview questions that further clarify strategy usage. For example, one teacher asked, "What was the first thing you did when you received your test?" As with all measures, student self-evaluations will need to be corroborated by information from other sources (for example, direct-observation checklists and student products), particularly for exceptional students, many of whom have difficulty evaluating their own behaviour.

Do It! Develop and give a textbook reading probe such as the one shown in Figure 8.6 in a high school class. Share the results with the teacher.

Connections: Sample direct-observation checklists can be found in Chapter 11.

Connections: Chapter 10 focuses on strategies for helping students become independent, self-advocating learners.

Cultural Awareness: Student-centred assessment strategies such as self-evaluation are an important part of empowering students through multicultural education.

Technology Notes

Computerized Curriculum-Based Measurement

RESEARCHERS have developed software that makes scoring and interpreting curriculum-based measures in math much easier (Fuchs, Fuchs, Mamlett, Philips, & Bentz, 1994). Students take a weekly probe test that measures required math operations for that grade. After students enter their data into a computer program, it scores their tests, summarizes the results, and makes graphic displays of each student's rate and accuracy on tests over time, and of each student's mastery skills profile. Teachers may also receive a comparable display for the class of rate and accuracy on tests over time and of skills mastered and skills that need to be retaught.

The Technology Notes above describes a way in which you can use software to help you assess your students.

◢ How Are Learning Probes Used to Make Teaching Decisions About Exceptional Learners?

Academic probes can help teachers make many evaluation decisions about exceptional students.

Skill Mastery and Curriculum Placement

Connections: Issues involving same-skill and mixed-skill groupings are discussed in more depth in Chapter 7.

As we have already discussed, inclusive education involves the use of various instructional grouping arrangements: same-skill groups, mixed-skill groups, and individualized instruction. Exceptional students benefit from all three of these arrangements. You can use curriculum-based assessment probes to form all of these grouping types by rank-ordering and then visually inspecting your students' probe scores. For example, Mr. Glass wanted to form mixed-skill cooperative groups in math. He used probe scores on a problem-solving task form by choosing one lower performer, two middle performers, and one higher performer for each group. Ms. Robins, on the other hand, found that three of her students were having difficulty with capitalization but the rest of the class was not. She formed a small group to review capitalization rules.

✓ **Your Learning:** How can curriculum-based assessment probes be used to place students in reading books?

Curriculum-based probes can also be used to place students appropriately within classroom instructional materials. Because students who are consistently working in materials that are too easy or hard for them are more likely to be off task in class and are at risk for eventually becoming discipline problems, placing students at the right spot in the curriculum is essential. The Professional Edge on page 263 describes a method often used to place students in a reading curriculum.

Professional Edge

Using Curriculum-Based Assessment for Reading Placement

F INDING books on topics your students are interested in is important in motivating them to read. But just as important is ensuring that students are able to read their books accurately and fluently. The following method has been used for years to place students in reading material that is at their reading level. As you will see, this method can be used for both basal and literature-based reading programs.

1. For basal readers, select three 300-word passages—one from the beginning, one from the middle, and one from the end—of each level book in a given series. For grades one and two, select briefer passages of between 100 and 200 words. For literature-based programs, first group books into levels of difficulty using one of the many available readability formulas. Beginning books can also be arranged according to predictability. Then proceed as noted for basals.
2. Select passages that contain few proper names, are related to topics familiar to most students, and are primarily flowing narratives rather than dialogue or poetry.
3. For each passage, construct a teacher score sheet similar to the one shown in Figure 8.3.
4. Give the probes starting at a level at which you feel the student will be reasonably successful. (See Figure 8.2 for oral reading probe directions.)
5. Average the students' correct and error rates for the three passages and then compare them to the following placement figures. If the average scores fall at the instructional level or greater, continue to go up a level. *Stop at the highest level at which the student scores at the instructional level.* (The rate guidelines specified below were derived from Carnine et al., 1990; Deno & Mirkin, 1977; Starlin, 1982.) If the student's average scores are below the instructional level, sample student reading behaviour at lower levels. Thus,

if any of a student's scores are at the frustration level, drop down a level or two and sample from three 300-word passages at that level. *Remember, these placement figures are to be used as general guidelines, not perfect predictors of future student performance.* Therefore, we strongly suggest that you continue to monitor student performance and make placement changes as necessary.

Grades 1–3

Frustration Level
29 words/minute or less and/or 8 or more errors/minute.

Instructional Level
30–49 words/minute and/or 3–7 errors/minute

Mastery Level
Grade 1 = 50–60
     2 = 50–110
     3 = 50–135 and/or 2 or fewer errors/minute

Grades 4–6

Frustration Level
49 words/minute or less and/or 8 or more errors/minute

Instructional Level
50–99 words/minute and/or 3–7 errors/minute

Mastery Level
100–150 words/minute or better and 2 or fewer errors/minute

Above Grade Six

Frustration Level
0–69 words read correctly per minute and/or 8 or more errors/minute

Instructional Level
70–149 words read correctly per minute and/or 3–7 errors/minute

Mastery Level
150–250 words read correctly per minute and 2 or fewer errors/minute

Monitoring Student Progress and Instructional Evaluation

✓ **Your Learning:** How can probes be used to monitor student progress?

Although education has come a long way in terms of researching what constitutes effective teaching, it is still difficult to predict whether a given technique will work for a given student in a particular situation. It is thus important that we carefully monitor the results of our teaching. This monitoring is particularly relevant for exceptional students who, by definition, are less likely to respond favourably to commonly used instructional methods.

Curriculum-based assessment probes, because they are time-efficient, easy to give, and match what is taught in the classroom, are ideal for monitoring student progress in class. For example, Mr. Harris was interested in whether Maria, a student with learning disabilities, was retaining any of the words included on weekly spelling lists. She had scored 90 and above on her weekly tests, but Mr. Harris was still unsure whether she was remembering the words from one week to the next. He developed a spelling probe using words from previous spelling lists. He gave the probe to his entire class and found that Maria and 10 other students were retaining only 20 percent of the words. As a result, he started a peer-tutoring program to help students review their words. Mr. Harris also set up group competitions and had awards for groups scoring the highest on the review probes. With these two activities implemented, Maria's and the other students' retention improved significantly.

✓ **Your Learning:** Reread the three scenarios at the beginning of this chapter. Using what you have learned in this chapter, answer the questions at the end of each scenario, and then review the chapter content to improve your answers.

A final example is worthy of mention. Mr. Rigaud recently switched his reading program from a basal series to a literature-based program. He wanted to ensure that several of the lower-performing students in his class were adding new words to their sight vocabularies. He randomly selected three 300-word passages from a literature book that all of these students had recently completed. He found that two of the students read the passages at mastery levels, but one student was reading at the frustration level. Mr. Rigaud decided to drop the student to an easier level of book and provide some high-frequency word drill with the student using a peer tutor. Again, teaching approaches, no matter how promising, may not work for all students. By monitoring his students' progress using CBA probes, Mr. Rigaud was able to make a helpful adaptation in a student's instructional program.

▰ Summary

The assessments that regular classroom teachers make can contribute to educational decisions about exceptional students. Curriculum-placement decisions concern where to begin instruction for students. Decisions in instructional evaluation involve whether to continue or change instructional procedures that have been initiated with students. The purpose of program-evaluation decisions is to determine whether a student's education program, interventions, and services should be terminated, continued as is, or modified.

Classroom teachers can approach a number of information sources to help them program for exceptional students. Group-administered standardized achievement tests can be used to compare students in difficulty to their peers,

The Bell Curve

www.cycad.com/cgi-bin/
Upstream/Issues/
bell-curve/index.html

Identification and Testing of Gifted Children

www.jayi.com/jayi/aagc/
ident.htm

but they have serious drawbacks for making other types of decisions. Individually administered diagnostic tests provide more specific information but are susceptible to many of the same problems as group-administered tests. Psychological tests, such as tests of intelligence and tests related to learning disabilities, measure abilities that affect how efficiently students learn in an instructional situation. These tests can clarify why students may not be learning in class, but they are most helpful when corroborated by classroom experience. Be aware that psychological tests may discriminate against students from culturally different or disadvantaged environments. The purpose of an environmental inventory is to identify what adaptations or supports students with moderate to severe disabilities need to increase their participation in the classroom and the community. Curriculum-based assessments measure student achievement in terms of what they are taught in the classroom. As such, they are helpful in making a range of decisions about exceptional students, particularly decisions involving day-to-day instruction.

There are two major kinds of curriculum-based assessments: probes of basic academic skills and content-area strategy assessments. Probes of basic academic skills consist of samples of academic behaviours and are designed to assess skill accuracy and, sometimes, skill fluency. Probes can be developed for all basic skill areas, including reading, written expression, and math. Content-area assessments include probes of prerequisite skills and measures of independent learning skills. Probes of prerequisite skills help teachers make decisions about whether to place students in particular high school classes. Measures of independent learning skills, often referred to as learning strategies or study skills, include note-taking, textbook reading, test-taking, written expression, and time management. Three ways to measure skills in these areas include direct-observation checklists, analysis of student products, and student self-evaluations.

Curriculum-based assessment probes can be used to help make special education decisions. A peer comparison method can help screen students who are in academic difficulty. Probes can also be used to help teachers diagnose specific skill deficits by determining whether academic problems involve accuracy, fluency, or both. In addition, academic assessment probes can be used to help form instructional groups, as well as to place students into the appropriate reading materials. Finally, curriculum-based probes can help teachers monitor the progress of students in class by measuring student performance over time.

Moving from Testing to Assessment

www.schoolnet.ca/sne/
snenews/volume1/issue9/
section5.html#b

Applications in Teaching Practice

Collecting and Using Assessment Information

1. It is November 1, and you are concerned about two students in your literature-based reading program. The students' parents have commented that they have not seen improvement in their children's reading at home. You have also noticed that both of these students seem to choose trade books that are too hard for them. In addition, you have concerns about what progress they have made in their word identification

and comprehension skills. You wonder if you should make some changes in their reading program.

a. What areas of reading would you want to assess here? Why?

b. How would you assess each area using the curriculum-based assessment procedures described in this chapter? What probes would you give? What would your probes look like? How would you score them?

c. What additional assessment information (for example, standardized tests, psychological tests, portfolios) would you collect?

d. How would you use the information you obtained in (b) and (c)? Under what circumstances would you decide to adapt the current program? Use an alternative program? Advocate for intensive instruction from a resource teacher?

e. What would you do to evaluate the changes suggested in (d)? What measures would you give? How often? What kinds of decisions would you be making?

2. Sara is a student with a learning disability in your class who has been receiving indirect support in the area of (choose one: reading, math, written expression). You are interested in knowing how she is doing in relation to the rest of the class.

a. Select a subject area in which Sara has been receiving indirect support.

b. Select a particular skill in that subject-matter area that you have been working on in your class (for example, in reading—sight-word reading, passage reading, comprehension, letter or letter-sound identification; in math—any math computation skill, word problems, money, geometry; in written expression—writing mechanics, writing productivity, quality of ideas).

c. Describe a curriculum-based assessment strategy you would use to judge how well Sara is doing on that skill as compared to her classmates. Respond to the following questions in your description:

(1) What probe would you use to measure this skill?

(2) How would you administer and score the probe?

(3) How would you use this information to evaluate Sara's progress?

(4) What additional information might you collect?

3. The high school resource room teacher has suggested that Howard, who has a learning disability, be included in your second semester _____ (choose whatever area you will eventually be teaching) class. He has asked you to help collect some information to assist him in deciding what support service (if any) Howard should receive.

a. If you are a math teacher, describe a strategy for determining whether Howard has the prerequisite skills for your class. Your strategy should respond to the following questions:

(1) What kind of prerequisite skill probe would you give?

(2) How would you administer and score it?

(3) Describe how you would use the information to determine needed support services.

b. If you are teaching a class for which the ability to read the textbook is an important skill:

(1) Select a sample textbook from your content area.

(2)   Develop a probe of content-area reading skills using the model shown in Figure 8.5.

(3)   How did you select the skills to be included on your measures? How would you use the information collected to determine the nature and extent of classroom support needed?

Chapter 9

Instructional
Adaptations

▰ *Learner Objectives*

After you read this chapter, you will be able to

1. Adapt lessons when students do not have the preskills necessary to learn new skills.

2. Select and sequence instructional examples to help students acquire basic skills.

3. Adapt instruction by providing the direct instruction, practice, and review needed to help students acquire basic skills.

4. Describe adaptations you can make in providing background knowledge, organizing content, and teaching terms and concepts to help students acquire academic content.

5. Implement strategies for improving the clarity of your written and verbal communication with students.

6. Adapt independent practice activities for students.

Ms. Diaz *was teaching her grade four class how to write percents for fractions using this example from her math book:*

Write a percent for $\frac{7}{8}$.

$\frac{7}{8}$ means $7 \div 8$.

$$8\overline{)7.00} = 0.87\frac{4}{8} = 0.87\frac{1}{2} = 87\frac{1}{2}\%$$

$$\begin{array}{r} 0.87\frac{4}{8} \\ 8\overline{)7.00} \\ \underline{64} \\ 60 \\ \underline{56} \\ 4 \end{array}$$

Divide until the answer is
in hundredths. Give the
remainder as a fraction.

$\frac{7}{8} = 87\frac{1}{2}\%$, or 87.5%

Ms. Diaz showed her students how to do this problem by writing the sample on the board and then pointing out that the fraction $\frac{7}{8}$ means 7 divided by 8 and that they have to divide until the answer is in hundredths and to give the remainder as a fraction. Following this instruction, Ms. Diaz assigned the students 15 similar problems to do independently. Abdul is a student with a learning disability in this class. Abdul has difficulty learning new skills unless he is given many opportunities for instruction and practice. Abdul answered none of the 15 problems correctly. He missed converting the fractions to percents because he forgot that $7 \div 8$ means 7 divided by 8; Abdul divided 8 by 7 instead. How could this lesson have been taught to Abdul to prevent this misunderstanding?

CECILY is a student with a hearing impairment who is in Ms. Boyd's history class. Cecily is failing history because the tests are based mainly on the textbook and she has trouble identifying main ideas in the text and understanding important vocabulary words. Cecily can read most of the words in the text but she reads very slowly, word by word. Last week, she was assigned a chapter to read for homework; it took her almost two hours to read 15 pages, and when she was done, she couldn't remember what she had read. The key words are highlighted, but Cecily can't figure them out from the context and doesn't know how to use the glossary. How can Ms. Boyd help Cecily read and remember key ideas in her textbook? What can she do to help Cecily understand new vocabulary words?

As you have already learned, the curriculum methods and materials that teachers use have a strong influence on how readily students learn in the classroom. In fact, the better the materials and teaching, the fewer the adaptations required for exceptional students. However, for various reasons, you may not have control over the materials used in your school. Further, despite your best teaching efforts, some students will still need **instructional adaptations** if they are to master important skills and content. For example, in the vignettes above, merely showing Abdul how one problem is done is not enough. He needs guidance through a number of examples before he is ready to do problems independently. You could help Cecily identify important information in her textbook by giving her a study guide that has questions pertaining to the most important content in each chapter. You could also ask Cecily to identify words she does not know and ask a classmate to help her with the meanings before she reads.

The purpose of this chapter is to provide you with strategies for adapting curriculum materials, teacher instruction, and student practice activities that are reasonable to carry out and that increase the likelihood of success for exceptional students. Remember, reasonable accommodations are those adaptations that can help a student without taking so much time and effort that they interfere with the teacher's responsibilities to other students. Further, these accommodations may be helpful for other students in class without formally identified exceptionalities.

FYI: This chapter presents guidelines for Steps 5 and 6 of the INCLUDE model presented in Chapter 1:

Step 5. Use information from Steps 1–4 to brainstorm instructional adaptations.

Step 6. Decide which adaptations to use.

► How Can You Adapt Basic-Skills Instruction for Exceptional Students?

Basic-skills instruction primarily means instruction in the tool skills of reading, writing, and math. However, you may also apply effective principles for adapting basic-skills instruction to content areas such as science. Four aspects of basic-skills instruction that may need to be adapted for exceptional students are preskills, selection and sequencing of examples, rate of introduction of new skills, and direct instruction, practice, and review.

Teaching Preskills

Darrell is included in Ms. Rayburn's grade two class. In language arts, he is experiencing a problem common to many exceptional students. On Tuesday, Darrell was at his desk reading a book on his favourite topic: magic. However, when Ms. Rayburn asked Darrell specific questions about the book, he was unable to answer them. It turned out that Darrell was unable to decode most of the words in the book and was just pretending to read.

Preskills are basic skills necessary for performing more complex skills. Before teaching a skill, you should assess students on the relevant preskills and, if necessary, teach these skills. Darrell was unable to comprehend the magic book because he lacked the phonological word-identification skills needed to read the words. He may need instruction in processing and word-attack skills; he may also need to be encouraged to read trade books at his reading level. Since commercially produced materials do not generally list preskills, you need to ask yourself continually what preskills are required and be on the lookout for students who lack them. This may mean informally assessing such skills. For example, before Mrs. Tong taught her kindergarten students to tell time, she checked to see whether they could identify the numbers 1 to 12 and count by fives to 60. Before teaching students to look up words in a dictionary, Mr. Thurman checked to see whether his students could say the alphabet, could alphabetize words to the third letter, and knew whether to turn to the front, middle, or end of the dictionary when looking up a certain word.

If you are teaching a skill and find that most of your students lack the necessary preskills, teach these preskills directly before teaching the actual skill. If only one or two students lack preskills, you can provide these students with extra practice and instruction through a peer or parent volunteer, or with the help of a special service provider. For example, Ms. Cooper is preparing a lesson on how to find the area of a rectangle. Before beginning the lesson, she gave her students a multiplication probe and found that almost half the class was still having problems with their multiplication facts. Ms. Cooper set up a peer tutoring program in which students who knew their facts were paired with students who did not; they practised facts for 10 minutes each day for a week. Ms. Cooper still introduced finding areas as scheduled, but she allowed students to use calculators until they had mastered their facts in the peer tutoring sessions.

Selecting and Sequencing Examples

The way you select and sequence instructional examples can affect how easily your students learn. For example, Alex completed practice activities in Mr. Huang's grade three class. Mr. Huang has been teaching two-digit subtraction with regrouping. On Monday through Thursday, Alex was given five of these problems and got them all right. On Friday, he was asked to do a mixture of problems, some requiring regrouping and some not. Alex got only three of the problems correct because he was unable to discriminate between subtraction problems that required regrouping and those that did not. He was unable to differentiate these two types of problems in part because his daily practice pages had included only one problem type.

You can help students make key discriminations between current and previous problem types by at first using examples that require only the application of that particular skill (Carnine, Silbert, & Kameenui, 1990). When students can perform these problems without error, add examples of skills previously taught to

Cultural Awareness: Children learn many basic preskills both directly and vicariously before they reach school age. Children's cultural backgrounds and life conditions greatly affect what they know and can do.

FYI: Assessing student preskills does not always have to be done using paper-and-pencil tasks. Simply questioning your students orally takes less time and can give you relevant information immediately.

help students discriminate between the different problem types. Doing this also provides students with needed review. An easy adaptation for Alex would have been to add several problems that did not require regrouping to each daily practice session.

Ms. Owens ran into another example-related problem when teaching her students word problems in math. In her examples, if a word problem included the word *more,* getting the correct answer always involved subtracting, such as in the following problem:

> Alicia had 22 pennies. Juanita had 13. How many more pennies does Alicia have than Juanita?

However, on her test, Ms. Owens included the following problem:

> Mark read three books in March. He read four more books in April. How many books did Mark read?

Several exceptional students in Ms. Owens's class subtracted three from four because they thought the presence of the word *more* signalled to subtract. Ms. Owens needed to include problems of this latter type in her teaching to prevent such misconceptions.

The following example shows a different example-selection problem. Tawana's class was covering several high-frequency sight words that appeared in trade books they used in their literature-based reading program. On Wednesday, Tawana learned the word *man,* but on Tuesday, after the word *men* was presented, she was unable to read *man* correctly. Tawana's word-identification problem illustrates an example-selection problem that concerns sequencing. The visual and auditory similarities of *man* and *men* will make learning these words difficult for many at-risk students and students with learning disabilities, who may have trouble differentiating words that may look and/or sound the same. One way to prevent this problem is to separate the introduction of *man* and *men* with other, dissimilar high-frequency words, such as *dog, house,* and *cat.*

This same sequencing idea can be applied to teaching the alphabet. For example, when deciding on the order in which to teach the letters, consider separating letters that look and sound the same, such as *b* and *d*, *m* and *n*, and *p* and *b*. The careful sequencing of instruction can also be applied to teaching higher-level content. For example, when Mr. Roosevelt, a high school chemistry teacher, taught the chemical elements, he separated those symbols that looked and/or sounded similar, such as bromine (Br) and rubidium (Rb), and silicon (Si) and strontium (Sr).

Deciding the Rate of Introduction of New Skills

Students sometimes have difficulty learning skills when they are introduced at too fast a rate. For example, Mr. Henry is teaching his grade six students how to proofread rough drafts of their writing for errors in using capital letters and punctuation marks. He reviews the rules for using capital letters, periods, commas, question marks, and exclamation points. Next, he asks students to take out their most recent writing sample from their portfolios to look for capitalization and punctuation errors. Carmen found that he had left out capital letters at the beginning of two sentences, but he did not find any of the punctuation errors he had made. He missed them because Mr. Henry taught his students to proofread their papers for capital letters and punctuation marks simultaneously. A better pace would have been first to work on proofreading for capitalization errors and then to add one punctuation mark at a time (first periods, then commas, followed by question marks and then exclamation points).

In another example of the **rate of introduction** of new skills, Ms. Smolska is working on reading comprehension with her students. She introduces three new comprehension strategies at once: detecting the sequence, determining cause and effect, and making predictions. Carlos is a student who has a mild cognitive disability; he learns best when he is taught one strategy at a time. Ms. Smolska adapted Carlos's instruction by forming a group with three other students who, like Carlos, will benefit from learning these comprehension strategies one by one. She also deleted cause-and-effect and prediction questions from these students' written comprehension exercises until they had been taught these strategies directly in their small group. When Mr. Wallace, the resource teacher, came to co-teach, he worked with these students on detecting the story sequence.

These examples demonstrate an important principle about introducing new skills to students with special needs: New skills should be introduced in small steps and at a rate slow enough to ensure mastery prior to the introduction of more new skills. Further, you may want to prioritize skills and even delete some, as Ms. Smolska did. Many commercially produced materials introduce skills at a rate that is too fast for exceptional students. As just illustrated, a common adaptation is to slow down the rate of skill introduction and provide more practice. Other students in the class, including those with no formally identified special needs, often benefit from such adaptations as well. If a student happens to be the only one having a problem, you can seek additional support from the resource teacher, paraprofessionals, peers, and/or parent volunteers. Slowing down the rate of skills introduced is an adaptation in the way curriculum is presented, but it is not the same as reducing the amount of curriculum to be learned. For some students, though, you may need to decrease the amount of curriculum. For example, Ms. Evers reduced Robin's curriculum by shortening her spelling lists from 15 to five words and selecting only words that Robin used frequently in her writing.

Providing Direct Instruction and Opportunities for Practice and Review

Exceptional students may require more direct instruction and review if they are to acquire basic academic skills. Consider this example: Lashonda is included in Ms. Howard's spelling class. On Monday, Ms. Howard gave students a pretest on the 15 new words for the week. On Tuesday, the students were required to use each word in a sentence. On Wednesday, the teacher scrambled up the letters in all the words and asked the students to put them in the correct order. On Thursday, students answered 15 fill-in-the-blank questions, each of which required one of the new spelling words. On Friday, Lashonda failed her spelling test even though she had successfully completed all the spelling activities for that week. She did poorly on her spelling test because the daily spelling activities did not provide her with enough direct instruction and practice on the spelling words.

Connections: The steps in a direct-instruction lesson are described in Chapter 7.

Connections: Direct instruction could help Abdul, whom you met at the beginning of the chapter. His teacher could teach the skill directly by listing the steps in solving these problems on the board; asking students to say all the steps; solving several sample problems for the students by following the listed steps; leading the students through solving similar problems using the steps until they can do them independently; and assigning problems for the students to do independently, reminding them to follow the steps listed on the board.

Although activities such as using spelling words in sentences are valuable in the right context, they do not provide practice on the more primary objective of this particular lesson, which is spelling all 15 words correctly from dictation. One way to help Lashonda would be to have a peer tutor give her a daily dictation test on all 15 words, ask Lashonda to write each missed word three times, and then retest her on all 15 words again.

These examples demonstrate another problem that exceptional students have when learning basic skills: **retention.** Melissa had mastered her addition facts to 10 as measured by a probe test in October, but when she was given the same test in January, she got only half of the facts correct. Thomas could state the major causes of the First World War in October, but he could not remember them when asked to compare them to the causes of World War II in January. A common adaptation you can use for these students is to schedule more skill review for them. This review should be more frequent following your initial presentation of the skill, and then can become less frequent as the skill is established. For example, instead of waiting until January to review addition facts, Melissa's teacher could provide review first weekly, then every other week, and then every month. Thomas's teacher could periodically review key concepts and information that he will need to apply later, either as homework, an instructional game or contest, or an activity in a co-taught class.

Earlier in the chapter we met Darrell who was pretending to read about magic. Darrell kept guessing at the words in his book. He didn't know the sounds associated with the letters and even when Ms. Rayburn told him the sounds of the letters, Darrell couldn't combine them. Growing evidence supports the notion that for the young child, the most critical factor in forming the building blocks of early reading is phonological awareness (Vandervelden & Seigel, 1997). Typically this awareness develops during grade one, allowing the child to discover how letter-sound relationships are used to decode the printed word. A number of Canadian researchers have demonstrated the strong relationship between progress in early literacy and phonological awareness or phonological process-

Do It! Use the probes described in Chapter 8 to find out if your students retain information you have taught them.

▶ *Some students need additional direct instruction and guided practice when they are learning new skills. What prerequisite concepts and skills might you teach for this assignment on essay writing?*

ing—Stanovich of University of Toronto (1986), Seigel of University of British Columbia (1993), and Kirby of Queen's University (1996). Although it would have been better if Darrell had begun to receive systematic instruction in letter-phoneme matching and other aspects of phonological awareness earlier, Darrell learned quickly after the resource teacher began direct instruction of phonological processing with a small group during grade two language arts classes. Examples of two activities used to teach phonological processing are shown in Table 9.1.

This discussion of Darrell raises an important issue: classroom teachers may need to know approaches such as direct instruction of phonological awareness to meet the needs of individual students. While most children learn to read in a literature-based language arts program, Darrell cannot. If he is not taught phonological processing, Darrell is likely to end up identified as having a learning disability or a reading disability, because deficits in phonological processing characterize most non-readers and poor readers.

Some of your exceptional students may need more direct instruction and practice. Mr. Thomas is teaching his grade six students the format for writing a letter to a friend, including where to put the date and inside address and how to write a salutation and closing using correct punctuation. First, he reviewed the various circumstances in which people write letters to friends. Next, he showed a sample letter using the overhead projector and wrote a letter with the class. Finally, he asked the students to write a letter for homework. Brenda handed in her letter the next day; although her ideas were good, she had the inside address

Connections: Recall the ways of adapting non-direct instruction described in Chapter 7.

FYI: Research shows that many students with learning disabilities need direct instruction in letter sounds in order to learn to identify words systematically.

◣ **TABLE 9.1**   Teaching Phonological Processing: Examples of Letter-Phoneme Match and Initial Consonant Deletion and Substitution

---

Introductory Activity for Initial-Consonant Letter-Phoneme Match

1. Teacher introduces the preparatory language activity (a poem with many letters starting with *p* and many rhyming words), and the target consonant *p*.

2. Children identify the spatial position of the target consonant (first letter) and mark this with a plastic letter *p* on the target consonant:

The teacher models and practices the letter-sound connection for the model consonant in a word written on a card: "This word reads *proud*. Put your finger on the first letter."

Then the teacher says "*proud* starts with *p*. Find *p* here" while keeping a finger on the first letter of the word, and pointing to three plastic letters placed above the card.

3. After two words have been introduced, the teacher asks, "Which one reads *proud*? Which one reads *kite*?"

4. The teacher asks for context-cued selection: "I feel _____ when I help my teacher" (for the word *proud*).

Later Activity: Initial consonant deletion and substitution:

1. The teacher says: "Say *pride*. Say it again without the *r*." (deletion of *r*)

"Say *frog*. Say it again without the *r*." (deletion of *r*)

2. The teacher says: "Say *train*. Say it again, only say *b* instead of *t*." (substitution of *b* for *t*)

✓ Your Learning: How can basic-skills instruction be adapted for exceptional students through attention to preskills, example selection and sequencing, rate of introduction of new skills, and direct instruction with opportunities for review?

in the wrong place, left out commas in the salutation, and forgot to include a closing. Brenda needed more instruction and guided practice on how to format a letter than Mr. Thomas had provided. He had shown the students one letter and had written one letter with them before assigning them to write a letter on their own for homework. Mr. Thomas could have continued to write letters with the class until even the lower performers seemed comfortable performing the task. He could also have asked the students to write a letter independently in class so that he could monitor their performance and provide corrective feedback if necessary.

Clearly, you may need to adapt instruction to enable exceptional students to acquire basic skills. These adaptations include teaching preskills, selecting and sequencing examples, adjusting the rate of introduction of new skills, and providing additional direct instruction, practice, and review. Students may also need adaptations in the presentation of subject-matter content, the primary teaching focus as students move into the upper grades.

◤ How Can You Adapt the Instruction of Subject-Area Content for Exceptional Students?

The instruction of academic content includes areas such as history and science. This instruction mainly involves the use of textbooks and lecture-discussion formats but can also include other activities, such as videos, films, computer-assisted instruction, and cooperative learning. Although content-area instruction is generally associated with instruction in secondary schools, the information presented here is also relevant for elementary teachers. In this section, you will learn how you can adapt your teaching and materials to help exceptional students learn subject-area content. Strategies for making adaptations are stressed for the areas of activating background knowledge, organizing information, and teaching terms and concepts.

Activating Background Knowledge

The amount of background knowledge that students have can greatly influence whether they can read subject matter with understanding. The knowledge that students bring to a content-area lesson is often as important for understanding as the quality of the textbook or instructional presentation (Langer, 1984). For students to understand content material, they need to relate it to information they already know. Unfortunately, teachers often fail to consider background information. Students with disabilities and students who are at risk may have two problems with background knowledge: They may simply lack the necessary knowledge, or they may know the information but be unable to recall it and relate it to the new information being presented.

Using the PReP strategy.   A teaching strategy for determining how much knowledge students already have about a topic so that you can decide how much background information to present in class before a reading assignment is called the **PReP** (*PreReading Plan*) **strategy** (Langer, 1984). The Professional Edge describes how to use the PReP strategy.

Professional Edge

How to Use PReP

YOU can use the PReP (PreReading Plan) strategy to help you determine what background information your students have about a particular concept or topic and what gaps, if any, exist in their knowledge of it. The following example shows how one teacher used the PReP procedure to find out what the students in his science class already knew about photosynthesis.

Step 1: Preview the text or lesson and choose two to three important concepts.

Before a grade eight science class reads about photosynthesis in their texts, the teacher conducts a PReP activity to help students recall and organize their knowledge of this concept and to determine which students are ready to read the material. The following dialogue focuses on the concept of photosynthesis. Other key words selected are *cycle* and *oxygen*.

Step 2: Conduct a brainstorming activity with students that includes the following three phases.

Phase 1: Initial association of concept

TEACHER: We're going to be reading in our texts about a process called photosynthesis. I'd like you to tell me anything that comes to mind when you hear the word *photosynthesis*. I'll write what you say on the board. Anyone?

During this phase, it becomes apparent that none of the students has much knowledge of the concept. The following responses are typical:

STUDENT 1: Sun shining on a plant.

STUDENT 2: Photograph.

STUDENT 3: Pictures.

Phase 2: Reflections on initial associations

TEACHER: Now I'd like each of you to think about what you said and to try to tell us what made you think of that response.

STUDENT 2: Photosynthesis sounds like a *photograph*. The first part of it anyway.

STUDENT 3: Yeah, I thought at first you said *photograph* and that made me think of pictures.

STUDENT 1: I remembered reading in a book about photosynthesis. There was this picture that showed rays coming out of the sun and going down to a plant. I just remembered the picture when I heard that word.

During this activity, the teacher helps the group see that they do know something about the concept. A discussion grows out of the meaning of the morpheme (word part) *photo* and how *photo* could be related to the sun and plants. This helps all of the students refine their responses in the third phase and helps some of them raise the level of their responses.

Phase 3: Reformulation of knowledge

TEACHER: Now that we've been thinking about this for a while, do any of you want to change or add to your previous responses, before we read about photosynthesis?

STUDENT 1: It is when the sun shines on plants and that helps the plants give oxygen.

STUDENT 2: Light like in photographs.

STUDENT 3: Like taking pictures.

Step 3: Evaluate student responses to determine the depth of their prior knowledge of the topic.

The teacher concludes that although Student 1 could successfully read the text, the others need help building the concept from what they know before reading about it. Students 2 and 3 receive help to ensure that they understand the morpheme photo and the role of light in the process of photography. They then can extend this knowledge to the role of light in the process of photosynthesis. Of course, concept teaching takes place, but it always begins with the knowledge students display.

Source: Adapted from "Examining Background Knowledge and Text Comprehension" by J. Langer, 1984, *Reading Research Quarterly, 19*, pp. 468–481. Used by permission of International Reading Association.

Preparing anticipation guides.   Anticipation guides can help you activate student knowledge about a particular topic and construct bridges to new information by encouraging students to make predictions (Moore, Readance, & Rickelman, 1989; Vacca & Vacca, 1986). **Anticipation guides** consist of a series of statements, some of which may *not* be true, related to the material that the student is about to read (Burns, Roe, & Ross, 1992). Before teaching, students read these statements that either challenge or support ideas they may already have about the subject. This process catches their interest and gives them a reason for listening and reading. Providing questions or statements prior to reading also aids comprehension for all students, including those with exceptionalities.

Anticipation guides completed by students with advanced development in the curriculum area may alert you that these gifted students are already knowledgeable about many of the topics you intend to teach. Then you can prepare to compact the curriculum and provide more challenging teaching for these students. When Ms. Czarny found that Frankie and Hema knew most of what she intended to teach in the grade two unit on transportation, she enlisted the resource teacher to help the two students learn about commuting and its impact on suburban families. Hema had asked a question about commuting while completing the anticipation guide. The two gifted students interviewed commuters and their families, examined recent information that showed family members spend less time together than they did 15 years ago, and prepared a report about commuting in the life of people living in suburban Montreal—the location of their community.

You can make anticipation guides for your students by following the steps suggested in the Professional Edge. A sample anticipation guide for a secondary science class is shown in Figure 9.1.

Providing planning think sheets.   Activating background information and building bridges to current knowledge is also of concern to teachers when asking students to write. Some researchers recommend a **planning think sheet** to help writers focus on background information as well as the audience and purpose of a paper (Englert, Raphael, Anderson, Anthony, Fear, & Gregg, 1988). For audience, students are asked to consider who will read the paper. For purpose, students clarify why they are writing the paper (for example, to tell a story, to convey information, or to persuade someone). Finally, students activate background knowledge and organize that knowledge by asking themselves questions such as, "What do I know about the topic? How can I group/label my facts?" (Englert et al., 1988, pp. 107–108). A planning think sheet for a paper assignment might contain write-in lines on which students answer the following questions:

- What is my topic?
- Why do I want to write on this topic?
- What are two things I already know that will make it easy to write this paper?
- Who will read my paper?
- Why will the reader be interested in this topic? (Raphael, Kirschner, & Englert, 1986)

Do It! Design an anticipation guide and a planning think sheet for a particular activity or assignment in a subject area you plan to teach.

Connections: Other strategies that help students write independently are described in Chapter 10.

FIGURE 9.1

Sample
Anticipation
Guide

Anticipation Guide for Chapter 16: The Nervous System

Section 1: The Control System

Directions: Read the statements below. If you think the statement is true, write T on the line next to the sentence and in the column labelled "Before." If you think the statement is false, write F in the space. Check to make sure that you are marking in the "Before" column. Read Section 1 to see if you were right. After you have finished reading, go back and read the sentences again. This time, write your responses in the column labelled "After." How do your answers compare? What new things have you learned about the nervous system from reading this section?

After	Before	
_____	_____	1. A person cannot function without the nervous system.
_____	_____	2. Our nervous system helps us study and learn about new things.
_____	_____	3. There are gaps between the nerve cells in our body.
_____	_____	4. Nerve cells do different jobs in the body.
_____	_____	5. The central nervous system is only one part of our nervous system.
_____	_____	6. Our brain does not control our reflexes.
_____	_____	7. A person cannot hold his or her breath until he or she dies.
_____	_____	8. Some people can swim without thinking about it.

Source: From *Anticipation Guide for the Nervous System* by M. Bursuck, 1993, unpublished manuscript, Northern Illinois University, DeKalb. Used by permission.

Organizing Content

When students read textbooks or listen to their teachers present content information, their understanding of important ideas and their interrelationships is enhanced when advance organizers are used (Lenz, Alley, & Schumaker, 1987). **Advance organizers** include information that makes content more understandable by putting it within a more general framework. They are particularly effective for exceptional students, who may have limited background knowledge and reading and listening comprehension skills. Examples of advance organizers include the following:

- Identifying major topics and activities
- Presenting an outline of content
- Providing background information
- Stating concepts and ideas to be learned in the lesson
- Motivating students to learn by showing the relevance of the activity
- Stating the objectives or outcomes of the lesson (Lenz, 1983)

FYI: Advance organizers help activate prior learning, keep students on task, and provide reference points for remembering tasks that need to be completed.

▼▼▼▼▼▼▼▼▼▼▼▼▼▼▼▼▼▼▼▼▼▼▼▼▼▼▼

Professional Edge

How to Make Anticipation Guides

You can use anticipation guides to prompt your students to think about a particular concept or topic and to help them use what they know to make predictions about the new material. The following steps describe how you can prepare these helpful tools for your students.

Procedure

1. **Step 1.** Identify the major concepts and details in the reading. (What information or ideas should be the focus of the students' attention?)

2. **Step 2.** Consider student experiences or beliefs that the reading will challenge or support. (What do students already know or believe about the selection they will be reading?)

3. **Step 3.** Create three to five statements that may challenge or modify your students' pre-reading understanding of the material. Include some statements that will elicit agreement between the students and the information in the text.

4. **Step 4.** Present the guide on the board, on an overhead projector, or on paper. Leave space on the left for individual or small-group responses. As each statement is discussed, students must justify their opinions. You may wish to have students first fill out the guide individually and then defend their responses to others in small groups or within a class discussion.

5. **Step 5.** After reading, return to the anticipation guide to determine whether students changed their minds about any of the statements. Ask students to locate sections in the reading that support their decisions.

6. **Step 6.** Another option for responding is to include a column for predictions of the author's beliefs. This can be completed after students have read the selection and can lead into your discussion of the reading.

Source: Adapted from *Content Area Reading* (2nd ed.) by R. T. Vacca and J. L. Vacca, 1986, Boston: Little, Brown.

Connections: Teaching techniques to foster active listening are described in Chapter 5.

Advance organizers often take the form of organizational signals. These signals include introductory statements that act as advance organizers (for example, "The purpose of today's lesson is to identify the nine planets and to be able to list them in order of size."); cue words, such as "first," "second," or "third," and "it is important that you know"; or textual cues, such as boldface print words. Organizational signals are important for exceptional students, many of whom have difficulty telling the difference between important and unimportant information.

Two commonly used options for assisting students in organizing content material are study guides and graphic organizers.

Constructing study guides.　The general term **study guide** refers to outlines, abstracts, or questions that emphasize important information in texts (Lovitt & Horton, 1987). Study guides are very helpful in improving comprehension for exceptional students in content-area classrooms (Lovitt, Rudsit, Jenkins, Pious, & Benedetti, 1985). For example, at the beginning of this chapter, Cecily was

1. A mollusc is a _____ bodied animal with a _____.
2. A bivalve is a mollusc whose _____ has _____ _____ joined by a _____.
3. An example of a bivalve mollusc is _____.
4. A univalve is a mollusc that has a _____ _____ shell.
5. An example of a univalve mollusc is a _____.
6. _____ are animals without backbones.

FIGURE 9.2

Sample Study Guide for Molluscs

having trouble identifying key ideas in her history text, a common problem for students at all educational levels. She might benefit from study guides that cue students to important information by asking them questions about it. Procedures for constructing study guides are shown in the Professional Edge. A sample study guide for a section of an elementary science text on molluscs is shown in Figure 9.2 above.

Horton (1987) has suggested the following additional modifications you might want to try:

1. Allow five to eight centimetres of margin in which students can take notes. Draw a vertical line to indicate the margin clearly. For example, in the study guide in Figure 9.2, the answer to question 1 is, "A mollusc is a *soft*-bodied animal with a *mantle*." You may want to define *mantle* for your students and ask them to write the definition in the margin. Some exceptional students will find new words easier to understand if you first write the definition on the study guide on the overhead and then have them copy it.
2. Print page numbers alongside the sentences in the study guide to show where to find the missing word in the textbook.
3. Print the missing words on the bottom of the page to serve as cues.
4. Leave out several words for the more advanced students and fewer for exceptional students. For example, question 2 on the mollusc study guide could be simplified as "A bivalve is a mollusc whose shell has _____ parts joined by a hinge."
5. Arrange for peer teaching situations; pair students and ask them to take turns being the teacher and the student.
6. Use the study guide for homework assignments. Assign students a passage in the text and give them accompanying study guides (either with or without the pages marked for easy reference). Ask them to complete the guides and study the material for homework.
7. Ask students to keep and organize their study guides from a number of passages and to study them as they review for unit or end-of-semester tests.
8. Place reading passages, study guides, and tests on a microcomputer.
9. Whenever possible, write the study guide at a reading level that fits most of your students. Students with reading and writing problems may need to have the study guide read to them or to respond to the questions orally.

Do It! Design a study guide for a chapter in a textbook that you plan to teach.

10. Include only key information on the guide. When necessary, reduce the content load by having students answer fewer items. For example, Ms. Hall required that Al, a student with a mild cognitive disability in her grade four class, answer only four of 10 questions on a study guide. When the students were tested on the content covered in the guide, Al was held responsible for answering only questions related to the four items he had answered.

Of course, study guides are not a substitute for direct instruction. The amount of direct instruction necessary will vary with the difficulty of the material. In general, students need more help completing study guides for texts that

---

Professional Edge
How to Develop Study Guides

STUDY guides will help improve the comprehension of all your students, especially those exceptional students who are included in content-area classrooms. The following steps show you how to develop a study guide from a content-area textbook. A sample study guide appears after the development process is described.

1. Go through the entire book and mark the chapters you will cover throughout the term and those you will not.

2. Indicate the sequence in which you will assign the chapters; that is, note the one that comes first, second, and so forth.

3. Read the material in the first chapter carefully. Mark the important vocabulary, facts, and concepts that you expect students to learn. Cross out any material you do not intend to cover.

4. Divide the chapter into logical sections of 1000- to 1500-word passages. (The length will depend, of course, on how detailed the material is and how much of it you deem important.)

5. Write brief sentences that explain the main ideas or emphasize the vocabulary, facts, or concepts from the passage. Write 15 sentences per passage.

6. Place those sentences in order so that the material in one leads to the next, and so forth.

7. To create questions, either leave out a few words in each sentence or change each sentence into a question. For example, one important statement identified in a chapter on natural disasters was as follows:

A 2 percent sales tax was passed to pay for relief efforts after the massive of 1997.

This statement could be turned into a question by leaving out several words:

_____ was passed to pay for relief efforts after the massive floods of 1997.

You could also change the statement into a question:

How did the people pay for the relief efforts after the massive floods of 1997?

8. Make a transparency of sentences and/or questions using large type.

9. Prepare sheets for the students, using regular type.

10. Prepare an answer sheet for the teacher.

11. Develop a multiple choice test to cover the material in the study guide. The test should have 10–15 items, with four possible choices for each question.

Source: From Study Guides: A Paper on Curriculum Modification by S. V. Horton, 1987, University of Washington.

assume high levels of student background knowledge and in which key information needs to be inferred as opposed to being explicitly presented. Guidelines for using study guides are presented in the Professional Edge.

Creating graphic organizers. Another way teachers can help students organize content is to use graphic organizers. This strategy gives students a visual format to organize their thoughts while looking for main ideas. Archer and Gleason (1990) suggest the following guidelines for constructing graphic organizers:

1. Determine the critical content (for example, vocabulary, concepts, ideas, generalizations, events, details, facts) that you wish to teach your students. Helping students focus on the most critical information is important for several reasons. First, exceptional students may have trouble identifying the most important information in an oral lesson or textbook chapter. Second, it

FYI: Teachers successfully use graphic organizers at all phases of instruction, from advance organizers to review. Graphic organizers, which are sometimes called concept maps or semantic webs, help make your lessons multisensory and are helpful for exceptional students.

Professional Edge
How to Use Study Guides

ONCE you have prepared study guides, you will need to teach your students how to use them. As with any adaptation, you will want to explain study guides clearly and specifically, ensuring that both your students with and without disabilities understand them. The following suggestions offer a systematic way to present these useful tools for understanding content.

1. Require your students to read the material before they use the study guides.

2. Pass out study guide sheets to students *after* they have read the material.

3. Place the transparency on the overhead projector. Expose only the first sentence or question.

4. Encourage students who can read and answer the question to raise their hands.

5. Call on a student to read and answer the question.

6. Distribute requests for answers to all students. From time to time, call on students who do not raise their hands.

7. Ask students to fill in the answers on their sheets, as they are identified.

8. Repeat the same process with the remaining questions. Cover those items on the transparency that have not yet been answered.

9. Ask related questions from time to time. The study guide sentences should serve as an outline for discussion.

10. Amplify on the sentences. Occasionally, give additional examples and illustrations.

11. Allow the students a few minutes to study their finished study guides after they have been completed and discussed.

12. Administer a test on the material.

13. Score the tests as soon as possible and inform students about their performance.

14. Show students the class average and discuss items that a number of students missed.

15. Show students how to keep a progress chart of their scores from the various tests.

Source: From Study Guides: A Paper on Curriculum Modification by S. V. Horton, 1987, University of Washington.

is easier for students to remember several main ideas than many isolated details. Third, trying to put too much information on a graphic organizer can make it so visually complex that students may have trouble interpreting it.

2. Organize the concepts in a visual representation that reflects the structure of the content, such as stories, hierarchies (top-down and bottom-up), feature analysis, diagrams, compare-contrast, and timelines. Since the purpose of a graphic organizer is to clarify interrelationships among ideas and information, you should keep the visual display as simple as possible. Figure 9.3 shows a completed compare-contrast graphic organizer.

3. Design a completed **concept map.** Completing the map before you teach with it ensures that the information is clear and accurate and can be presented to your students in a timely manner. Figure 9.4 shows a filled-in concept map.

4. Create a partially completed concept map (to be completed by students during instruction). Asking students to fill out the map as you present your lesson is an excellent way to keep them on task. Also, many students with exceptionalities benefit from a multisensory approach; seeing the information on the graphic, hearing it from the teacher, and writing it on the map helps them better retain the information presented.

5. Create a blank concept map for students to use as a postreading or review exercise. This structure for review will be easy for students to use.

FIGURE 9.3

Compare-Contrast Graphic Organizer

Logging in Algonquin Park in 1897 and 1997

Attribute	1897	1997
Size of trees logged	More than 1 metre in diameter	Less than one metre in diameter
Life of loggers	Lived in shanties that housed 50 loggers	Live at home with families and commute to logging
	Ate salt pork, bread, baked beans	Eat fresh foods
Transportation of logs	Hauled by horses to water Hauled by train to saw mill	Hauled by "skidders" to logging road
	Floated down Ottawa River to Quebec City, went by boat to England	Hauled by truck to saw mill or paper mill
Relationship between logging and other uses of the park	Logging seen as preferable to settlement of park by farmers, because area contains headwaters of five river systems	Constant discussion of conflict between logging and recreation, and between logging and environmental health of the park

Information drawn from *A Pictorial History of Algonquin Park* by R. Tozer and D. Strickland, 1986, Ontario Ministry of Natural Resources and the Friends of Algonquin Park.

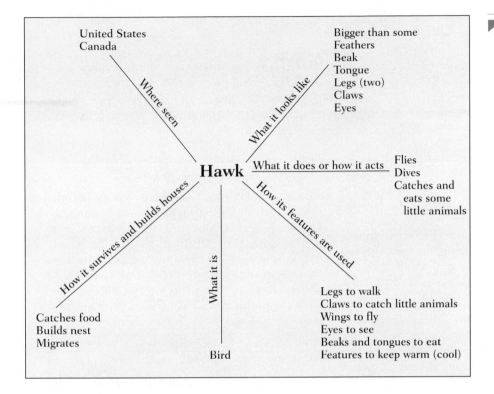

FIGURE 9.4

Sample Concept Map for a Science Selection on Hawks

Once you have constructed graphic organizers, you can use them as follows:

1. Distribute partially completed concept maps to your students.
2. Place a transparency of the completed map on an overhead projector. Place a piece of paper under the transparency so that you will expose only those portions you wish students to attend to. This limiting of the amount of information you present at one time helps students with attention problems, who have trouble focusing on more than one piece of information at a time.
3. Introduce the information on the concept map, proceeding in a logical order; stress the relationships between the vocabulary, concepts, events, details, facts, and so on.
4. At natural junctures, review concepts you have introduced. You can do this by placing the blank map on the overhead and asking students questions about the content. This review is essential for exceptional students, who have difficulty learning large amounts of information at one time.
5. At the end of the lesson, review the critical content again using the blank concept map. You can also have students complete the blank maps for homework. These maps will help your students organize their studying and also help you find out what they have learned. (Carnine et al., 1990)

The Case in Practice on pages 286–287 illustrates how one teacher uses a graphic organizer called a story map to help her students better comprehend a particular story.

Case in Practice

Teaching with Story Maps

STORY maps are graphic organizers that provide students with a visual guide to understanding and retelling stories. They have been shown to help exceptional students read with better comprehension (Bos & Vaughn, 1994). In the account that follows, Ms. Barrows, a grade two teacher, is using the story map in Figure 9.5 to teach her students the Algonquin legend, *Chakapesh Snares the Sun* retold by Linda Guebert in *Networks: Weave a Dream* (McInnes, 1987). She has demonstrated using the maps for a week now, so her students are familiar with the format. Today, she is providing guided practice for her students on how to use the maps.

MS. BARROWS: Boys and girls, today we're going to read a story entitled *Chakapesh Snares the Sun*. Chakapesh is a boy who belongs to the Algonquins. What do you think the story is going to be about?

JULIANE: Maybe it's going to be about a boy who has special powers.

LEE: Maybe he wants to keep the sun all for himself.

MS. BARROWS: Well, before we read and find out, who can tell me what a story map is?

DARWAIN: It's a map that guides us through a story—kind of like a regular map tells us where we're going when we're driving a car.

MS. BARROWS: That's right, Darwain. Now let's read the first page and find out who the main characters in this story are and where the story takes place. When you find out, we'll fill them in on our story maps. [She distributes a blank story map to each student.]

HARLEY: I know, the story is about Chakapesh and his sister, a mouse, and the sun. I think Chakapesh is the main character.

MS. BARROWS: That's right, Harley. Let's all fill in the main characters on our maps.

MS. BARROWS: Where do you think the story takes place?

LOVELL: I think it takes place in a forest.

MS. BARROWS: Why do you think so, Lovell?

LOVELL: Because it says at the beginning of the story that he lived in a camp in the bush. That's a woods or forest.

MS. BARROWS: Good thinking, Lovell. Stories often start by telling us about the setting. You know where to look. And a bush is a forest, you're right. Let's all fill in the setting on our maps. [They do.] Remember, we said last week that all stories have a problem that needs to be solved. Read the next three pages and find out what the problem is here. [The students read the passage.] Okay. What's the problem?

HARLEY: Well, Chakapesh doesn't listen to his sister and snares the sun.

MS. BARROWS: Right. That's one problem. Write it on your maps. Now, does anyone see another problem?

ELISEO: I know. The sky went dark.

MS. BARROWS: Eliseo, what's wrong with a dark sky?

ELISEO: Well, I think it was because it was day, and the sun should be shining.

MS. BARROWS: That's right, Eliseo. Let's all put this problem on our maps. [They do.] Okay, let's read the next page and find out what Chakapesh attempted to do about the sun that was caught in a snare.

LOVELL: Chakapesh tried to get close to the sun to untie the ropes.

MS. BARROWS: Do you think this will solve the problem?

LESA: I don't think so. The sun is too hot for him.

MS. BARROWS: Well let's all finish the story and find out. [They finish reading the story.] So, did the sun shine again?

JULIANE: Yes. Chakapesh asked a mouse to chew through the ropes.

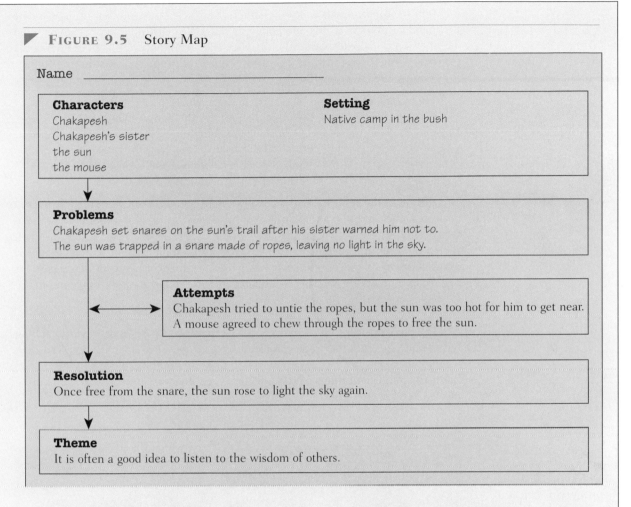

▰ **FIGURE 9.5   Story Map**

Name _____

Characters
Chakapesh
Chakapesh's sister
the sun
the mouse

Setting
Native camp in the bush

Problems
Chakapesh set snares on the sun's trail after his sister warned him not to.
The sun was trapped in a snare made of ropes, leaving no light in the sky.

Attempts
Chakapesh tried to untie the ropes, but the sun was too hot for him to get near.
A mouse agreed to chew through the ropes to free the sun.

Resolution
Once free from the snare, the sun rose to light the sky again.

Theme
It is often a good idea to listen to the wisdom of others.

MS. BARROWS: That's right. Let's fill in how Chakapesh solved the problem on our story maps. [They do.] Was the world returned to normal?

JULIANE: Yes. There was light in the sky from the sun.

MS. BARROWS: That's right. How do you think Chakapesh felt at the end?

LOVELL: I think he felt happy.

MS. BARROWS: Why do you think that, Lovell?

LOVELL: Well, because he was able to walk home in the light.

MS. BARROWS: Good thinking, Lovell. I'd like the rest of you to put how *you* think Chakapesh felt, and why, on your maps. Remember, we said

a part of stories is a lesson that they teach us. What lesson do you think this story teaches?

HARLEY: Well, it is good to mind your parents and your sister.

MS. BARROWS: Good thinking, Harley. Let's all put down the lesson of this story on our maps.

Reflections

How did Ms. Barrows use the story map to help her students comprehend the story? Which students do you think would benefit most from this approach? What should Ms. Barrows do to get her students ready for completing story maps on their own? How could you incorporate the use of story maps into a literature-based classroom reading program?

Teaching Terms and Concepts

Content-area instruction is often characterized by a large number of new and/or technical vocabulary words and concepts. Exceptional students or students who are at risk are likely to have difficulty with the vocabulary and concept demands of many content-area texts and presentations. For example, consider the following passage from a general science text:

> Thousands of years ago, Scandinavia was covered by a thick ice sheet. The mass of the ice forced the crust deeper into the denser mantle. Then the ice melted. The mantle has been slowly pushing the land upward since. This motion will continue until a state of balance between the crust and mantle is reached again. This state of balance is called *isostasy* (ie-soss-tuh-see) (Ramsey, Gabriel, McGuirk, Phillips, & Watenpaugh, 1983).

Although the term *isostasy* is the one highlighted, other technical terms and concepts, such as crust and mantle, may also pose a problem for students. These words may be particularly difficult because students are likely to be familiar with their non-scientific meanings, which differ from their technical meanings (for example, *mass* as in church; *crust* as in bread). You will need to check student understanding and teach the vocabulary directly if necessary, using one of the strategies covered in the next section.

Modelling examples, synonyms, and definitions.   Another way of teaching terms and concepts has been proposed by Carnine et al. (1990). They suggest three related ways of teaching new vocabulary to students: modelling examples, synonyms, and definitions. Although there is some variation across these three methods, all of them use the following steps:

▶ *This teacher is modelling positive and negative examples to clarify the meaning of a new concept. How can using both examples and non-examples help make the meaning of new terms and concepts clear?*

1. Choose a range of both positive and negative examples to teach your new word. Example selection is most important. A range of positive examples is used to ensure that students can apply the word to various contexts or forms. For example, if you are teaching your students to identify a *rectangle*, you want them to identify a rectangle whether it is big, small, empty, or shaded. Therefore, when showing students examples of rectangles, show them big rectangles, small rectangles, empty rectangles, and shaded rectangles. If you are teaching your students what a *vehicle* is, you want them to recognize a vehicle whether it is a car, boat, or bicycle. Whereas positive examples help students learn the range of a word, non-examples help them discriminate the new word from other words that may be similar. For example, in teaching *rectangle*, use figures such as triangles, circles, and trapezoids as non-examples. In teaching *vehicle*, use chair, house, or even an exercise bike as non-examples. Generally, you should use at least six examples to teach a new word and include at least two non-examples.

2. If you are teaching your word using a synonym, the student must already know the synonym. For example, when teaching the word *gigantic* using the synonym *huge*, make sure the students know what *huge* means. If you are teaching your word using a definition, the definition should be stated simply and clearly and should contain only words for which students know the meaning. Here is a definition of *vehicle* for third grade:

   Vehicle: A method of transportation that takes a person from one location to another.

   This definition uses a number of words that students in grade three might not know. Here is a simpler definition that younger students might understand:

   Vehicle: An object that takes you from place to place.

3. Tell students the meaning of the words either through modelling positive and negative examples or by presenting positive and negative examples using a synonym or a definition. For example, if you are teaching *rectangle* by modelling positive and negative examples, you would say the following as you pointed to your examples:

   This is a rectangle . . . This is a rectangle . . . This is not a rectangle . . . This is a rectangle.

   If you were teaching the word *gigantic* using the synonym *huge*, you might say this:

   Today we're going to learn the meaning of the word gigantic. What's the word? Gigantic means huge. [point to elephant] An elephant is a gigantic animal. It is huge. [point to a picture of a redwood tree] This is a redwood tree. It is gigantic. It is huge. [point to a smallish dog] This is a dog. The dog is not gigantic. The dog is not huge.

4. Ask students a series of yes or no questions to see whether they can discriminate examples from non-examples. For example, "Is this a rectangle?" If students have been taught a word using a definition or synonym, follow your question with, "How do you know?" Their reasons for answering "yes" or "no"

will tell you if the students are correctly using the definition or just guessing. For example, to test whether students know what a vehicle is, you might say

> What is this? (a car) Is a car a vehicle? (yes) Why do you say that? (because it is an object that takes you from place to place). What is this? (a chair). Is a chair a vehicle? (no). Why do you say that? (because it doesn't take you from place to place).

5. The purpose of this step is to find out whether students can discriminate the new word from words they have learned previously. This step is carried out through a series of open-ended questions. For example, in teaching *rectangle*, the teacher points to a rectangle along with other figures already taught and asks, "What is this?"

Teaching vocabulary by modelling examples or using synonyms and definitions can benefit all of your students. Use modelling examples when students do not understand words that could explain the meaning of the new word (for example, teaching students what a herringbone design is). Use teaching synonyms when students already know a word with a meaning similar to the new word; for example, the word *bow* could be taught by using the synonym *front*. Use definitions when a longer explanation is needed to define a word and students already understand the words that make up the explanation.

Cultural Awareness: Teaching vocabulary by modelling examples or using synonyms and definitions is especially helpful for students with limited English proficiency.

Making concept diagrams.   Constructing **concept diagrams** is a method that combines the definition, examples, and non-examples approach just described with graphic organizers (Bulgren, Schumaker, & Deshler, 1988). First, the teacher selects key words from a story or lecture. Next, he or she constructs a diagram that features the word's definition; characteristics that are always present, sometimes present, and never present; and examples and non-examples. Finally, the concept diagram is presented to students as follows:

Connections: Ways to teach students to remember vocabulary words using mnemonics are described in Chapter 10.

1. Present the word and its definition.
2. Discuss the always, sometimes, and never characteristics.

FIGURE 9.6
Concept Diagram

Concept Name:	Non-violent resistance	
Definition:	Protesting in a peaceful way	

Always	*Sometimes*	*Never*
Peaceful	Done in a group Done individually	Violent

	Examples	*Non-examples*
	Picketing Boycott Sit-in Hunger strike	Shouting match Physical attack Riot

3. Discuss one of the examples and one of the non-examples in relation to the characteristics.
4. Check other examples and non-examples to see if they match the characteristics (Carnine et al., 1990).

A sample concept diagram for the concept of non-violent resistance is shown in Figure 9.6.

How Can You Improve Clarity in Written and Oral Communication?

In effective instruction, if ideas are clearly tied together, they are easier for students to understand. The need for instructional clarity applies to written communication, which in many school situations involves the use of textbooks, and oral communication, which includes teacher instructional behaviours such as giving directions, asking questions, and delivering lectures. When a textbook is not written clearly or a lecture is not presented clearly, students have to make critical connections between ideas on their own—a skill that many at-risk students may not have. Exceptional students may not be able to recognize when they do not understand the material, or they may be unaware of strategies to try when instruction is difficult to understand. For example, when reading a text, they may not know how to use key words and headings or to look at the end-of-chapter questions to get main ideas. During oral presentations, students may not feel comfortable asking questions to clarify the information presented because they often are unsure what to ask and are afraid of looking stupid. Finally, exceptional students may lack the background knowledge necessary to construct meaning on their own. The implication here is that if you communicate clearly and use materials that do so as well, your exceptional students needs will be more successful.

✓ **Your Learning:** What are the major areas for making adaptations in subject-areas instruction?

Connections: Recall the discussion of evaluating and adapting textbooks and materials in Chapter 7.

Clarity in Written Communication

If you select structurally and organizationally coherent textbooks, then you should have to make few adaptations to the text; however, you may want to rewrite the sections containing the most important information. Problems with textbook organization and clarity can occur in explanations, especially when a sequence of events is being described. The ease with which students can understand the sequence depends on a number of factors, including the number of steps, the format used (list or paragraph form), and the presence of distracting information or material that is not related to the sequence.

Here is a passage about how baby alligators are hatched that exceptional students may struggle to understand:

Adult female alligators make large cone-shaped nests from mud and compost. The female lays from 15 to 100 eggs with leathery shells in the nest and then covers it. The heat from both the sun and the decaying compost keeps the eggs warm. The eggs hatch in about nine weeks. Unlike other reptiles that hatch from eggs, baby alligators make sounds while they are still in the shell. The mother then bites off the nest so the baby alligators can get out. When first hatched, baby alligators are about 15 to 25 cm long (Berger, Berkheimer, Lewis, & Neuberger, 1979, p. 55, cited in Armbruster, 1984).

As you can see, the passage states a sequence of events leading up to the hatching of a baby alligator. It is written in paragraph format rather than a list, which makes it harder to decipher. Although the events are written in the correct order, the presence of a distractor, the sentence "Unlike other reptiles that hatch from eggs, baby alligators make sounds while they are still in the shell," breaks up the sequence and makes it harder for students to comprehend. A relatively easy adaptation would be to highlight the sentences in the sequence, or ask the students to put numbers next to each key sentence in the sequence. Of course, if a number of students in your class are having trouble with distracting information, you could provide direct instruction on how to identify and/or ignore distracting or irrelevant information.

Another aspect of written language that can make comprehension more difficult is the use of pronoun referents. A general rule is that the closer the pronoun is to its referent, the easier it is to translate. Many readers may have trouble determining who *he, she,* and *they* refer to in passages they read. Although the placement of most pronouns is not always problematic, understanding pronouns can be especially difficult for exceptional students. However, students can be taught to make sense of pronouns (Carnine et al., 1990). Before students read, identify unclear pronouns. Ask students to underline the pronouns and then show them how to find their referent by asking questions such as these:

Passage

Curtis and Dorva skipped school. They were grounded for a week. He was sorry. She got mad.

Student Questioning

TEACHER: Curtis and Dorva skipped school. Who skipped school?
STUDENTS: Curtis and Dorva.
TEACHER: They were grounded for a week. Was Curtis grounded?
STUDENTS: Yes.
TEACHER: Was Dorva grounded?
STUDENTS: Yes.
TEACHER: He was sorry. Was Curtis sorry?
STUDENTS: Yes.
TEACHER: Was Dorva sorry?
STUDENTS: No.
TEACHER: She got mad. Did Dorva get mad?
STUDENTS: Yes.

Clarity in Oral Communication

Just as the quality of textbook writing affects student learning, so, too, does the quality of teachers' oral language. Three particularly important areas of oral language include giving directions, asking questions, and presenting subject matter (such as in a lecture).

Giving oral directions. Giving oral directions is the most common way that teachers tell their students what they want them to do. When directions are not clear, valuable instructional time is wasted having to clarify them repeatedly. Consider this set of directions given by a junior high school teacher at the beginning of a social studies lesson:

Unclear Instruction
All right, everyone, let's settle down and get quiet. I want you all to get ready for social studies. Shh. . . . Let's get ready. Alice and Tim, I want you to put those worksheets away. We need our books and notebooks (Evertson et al., 1983, p. 143).

How clear is the teacher about what she wants her students to do? Now read this alternative set of directions:

Clearer Instruction
All right, everyone, I want all of you in your seats facing me for social studies. Now, I want you to get out three things: your social studies book, your spiral notebook, and a pencil. Put everything else away so that you just have those three things—the social studies book, the spiral notebook, and the pencil—out on your desk. [As students get out their materials, the teacher writes "Social Studies, page 55, chapter 7 on Italy" on the chalkboard. She waits until students have their supplies ready and are listening before she begins talking.] (Evertson et al., 1983, p. 143).

In the first example, the teacher does not get the students' attention before giving them directions. This is a major problem. She is also unclear about what she wants her students to do. For example, words such as "settle down" and "get ready" are not defined for the students. In the second example, the teacher first gets her students' attention, and then very specifically states all the things they need to do. Lavoie (1989) has suggested a number of guidelines for giving directions that are helpful for exceptional students:

1. State commands specifically, using concrete terms. In the Clearer Instruction example, the teacher was specific about what the students needed to do to get ready for social studies. They had to get out three things: their book, notebook, and pencil. The first teacher told them only to "get ready."
2. Give "bite-size" directions; avoid a long series of directions. The second teacher first had her students sit down and face her; then she had them take out their materials; finally, she had them turn to the chapter they were going to read that day.
3. Whenever possible, accompany explanations with a demonstration. For example, Mr. Gaswami asked his students to take out their science books, turn to the beginning of the chapter, identify five key words, and define them using the glossary. Mr. Gaswami showed his students what he wanted them to do by opening his book to the chapter, pointing out that the key words were the ones that were italicized, and then demonstrating how to find and paraphrase the meanings using the glossary in the back of the book by doing several examples. He also wrote these directions on the board to help students remember all the steps.

FYI: Another use of cueing is to let a student know that he or she can expect to be called on to respond orally only when you present a particular cue that only the student will know. This way the student can attend to a lesson with less anxiety about speaking in class.

4. Use cueing words such as "Look up here" and "Listen, please" before giving directions. Gestures such as a raised hand are also effective in getting students' attention.

Asking questions.   Asking students questions is a vital part of instructional clarity. The way you question your students is important for several reasons. Questioning is a quick way of assessing what your students have learned. In addition, questioning through the use of follow-up probes can help you analyze your students' errors. For example, Ms. Dilworth's grade three class was given the following math problem:

> Three-fourths of the crayons in Bob's box of a dozen crayons are broken. How many unbroken crayons are there?

Ms. Dilworth asked Kareem what the answer was, and Kareem answered that four unbroken crayons are left. Ms. Dilworth asked Kareem to explain how he got that answer. Kareem said, "Because three-fourths means three groups of four and since there is only one group left that group has four in it." By asking a question, Ms. Dilworth found out that Kareem did not know the concept of three-fourths. Questions can also be used to redirect students to the correct answer when they make mistakes. For example, Ms. Dilworth might have asked Kareem a number of follow-up questions:

> How many crayons did you start with? How many is a dozen? What fraction of the crayons were broken? What does three-fourths mean? What would one-fourth of twelve be?

Connections: Exceptional students benefit from being taught to think because efficient thinking may not come naturally to them and/or they may not have been exposed to good models of thinking. Strategies for teaching students thinking skills are described in Chapter 10.

Last, and perhaps most important, it is through effective questioning that your students can learn thinking skills. Well-constructed questions provide students with a model for effective thinking; in time, students learn to ask themselves these same questions as they solve problems. A reading comprehension strategy that uses questions to teach students how to think while they are reading is shown in Figure 9.7. First, the teacher asks the students the questions in Figure 9.7 as they read stories. Over time, students are taught to ask themselves these questions as they read independently.

Although asking questions can be a very potent teaching strategy, to achieve maximum benefit, questioning needs to be carried out correctly. Kindsvatter, Wilen, and Ishler (1988) have suggested the following guidelines for using questioning in your classroom:

1. Phrase questions clearly to ensure that students know how to respond. For example, a vague question, such as "What about the Great Depression?" forces students to guess rather than carefully to consider a direct response to the question. A better wording would be, "What were the two primary causes of the Great Depression?"

Connections: Strategies for questioning students with limited English proficiency are described in Chapter 6.

2. Provide a balance between higher- and lower-level questions. The important point to remember is that both kinds of questions are important. Lower-level, or convergent, questions help you find out whether students have the basic understanding necessary for higher-level thought. Further, critical and creative thinking can be developed by using convergent and evaluative questions. Although the current emphasis on incorporating more higher-level

> ▌**FIGURE 9.7**   **Questions Students Can Ask as They Read**
>
> ### To Get the General Idea To Summarize
> - What is the story about?
>   What is the problem?
>   What is the solution?
> - What makes me think so?
>
> ### To Predict-Verify-Decide
> - What's going to happen next?
>   Is my prediction still good?
>   Do I need to change my prediction?
> - What makes me think so?
>
> ### To Visualize-Verify-Decide
> - What does this (person, place, thing) look like?
>   Is the picture in my mind still good?
>   Do I need to change my picture?
> - What makes me think so?
>
> ### To Summarize
> - What's happened so far?
> - What makes me think so?
>
> ### To Think Aloud
> - What am I thinking?
> - Why?
>
> ### To Solve Problems or Help When I Don't Understand
> - Shall I
>   Guess?
>   Ignore and read on?
>   Reread or look back?
> - Why?
>
> *Source:* From "SAIL: A Way to Success and Independence for Low-Achieving Readers" by J. L. Bergman, 1992, *Reading Teacher,* 49(8), pp. 598–602. Used by permission of International Reading Association, T. Schuder, and J. Bergman.

skills into the curriculum is positive, it is important to realize that lower-level knowledge is still important, particularly for exceptional students. Exceptional students may not readily acquire lower-level knowledge. Failing to help them acquire these understandings can prevent them from ever developing higher-level understandings. Also, lower-level questions can give students an opportunity to succeed in class. Finally, research suggests that lower-level questions may be most appropriate in teaching basic skills to students who are at risk (Emmer, Evertson, Sanford, Clements, & Worsham, 1983; Rosenshine, 1979).

3. Adapt questions to the language and skill level of the class, including individual students in the class. Your questions should accommodate a range of needs, from lower-performing students to gifted students. For example, a question for a lower-performing student might be, "From what you have just read, how does the demand for a product affect its supply?" For students with more skills, the question might become, "Going beyond the article a little, how does price affect supply and demand and at what point is market equilibrium reached?"

4. Vary the "wait time" you give your students to answer questions. **Wait time** is the amount of time you give students to respond to questions in class.

5. Involve all of your students in classroom questioning by calling on nonvolunteers as well as volunteers. Calling on all of your students also allows

FYI: Wait time gives students a chance to think and respond orally to teachers' questions. The duration of wait times should reflect the types of questions: one or two seconds for low-level questions and three to five seconds for higher-level questions.

Cultural Awareness: For students with limited English proficiency, pause three to five seconds for lower- and upper-level questions.

you to monitor student learning efficiently. In addition, calling on non-volunteers (who frequently are exceptional students) demonstrates that you hold them accountable for listening and leads to higher levels of on-task behaviour. However, as mentioned before, you should match questions with student ability to maximize the likelihood of student success. Finally, for lower-level questions, consider using **unison responding,** or having all students respond at once, together. Unison responding allows more student opportunities for practice and recitation and can lead to higher levels of correct responses and on-task behaviour (Carnine, 1981) as well as providing shy students with opportunities to participate as a group.

Presenting content orally. Communicating clearly to your students when you are presenting subject-matter content orally, such as in a lecture, is also important. This section of a lecture was delivered during a geography lesson about Italy:

> Italy is in southern Europe, down by France and the Mediterranean Sea. It's a peninsula in the Mediterranean. There are a lot of beautiful islands in the Mediterranean off of Italy and Greece as well. Sardinia and Sicily are islands that are part of Italy. Corsica, Capri, and some other islands like Crete and Cyprus are in the same part of the world, but they don't belong to, although they may be close to, Italy. You could turn to the map of Europe that's in your text to see where Italy is (Evertson et al., 1983, pp. 143–144).

The language used by this teacher lacks clarity. For example, he presents information about a number of islands but is unclear how these islands relate to the main topic, which appears to be the location of Italy. The teacher is also vague when he says, "[the islands] don't belong to, although they may be close to, Italy." In addition, the teacher uses the word *peninsula* but does not define it. Finally, this explanation needs the visual display of a map to bring clarity to it, but the teacher refers to a map at the end almost as an afterthought and makes use of the map voluntary. The only students who will know where Italy is after this lecture will be those who already knew in the first place. Many exceptional students could be left behind. Additional guidelines for presenting instruction clearly are shown in Table 9.2.

Do It! Rewrite this section of a lecture following the guidelines for presenting instruction in Table 9.2.

✓ **Your Learning:** List general and specific strategies for improving the clarity of your written and oral communication.

▶ What Adaptations Can You Make to Help Students Succeed in Independent Practice?

As discussed in Chapter 7, the main purpose of practice activities is to provide students with opportunities for refining their skills while also allowing you to monitor their performance. To achieve these purposes, students should be able to complete practice activities such as seatwork and homework independently.

Even under ideal circumstances and with the best intentions, it is difficult to design practice activities that meet the needs of all the students in your class. Problems arise because of individual characteristics, and adaptations must be made. For example, students with severe reading problems may have difficulty reading directions that may be quite clear to everyone else. Students with attention

TABLE 9.2   Instructional Clarity

Poor Clarity	*Being Clear*
Not telling students what they are expected to learn or the purposes of the activity.	Stating lesson goals; listing major objectives on the board.
Using verbal mazes; that is, starting a sentence and stopping to start again, pausing and repeating words to buy time, and halting in midsentence.	Using complete sentences in a straightforward way; focusing on the expression of one thought, point, direction, and so on at a time.
Presenting information or directions out of sequence; starting and stopping in the middle of a lesson.	Presenting information in the appropriate sequence; emphasizing important points; working from an outline with complex content and providing it to the students visually (for example, on a transparency or the board) as well as orally.
Moving from a major topic or skill to another without signalling the change.	Beginning and ending activities clearly; preparing students for transitions by giving them warnings; telling students what to expect and why the activity has changed.
Inserting extraneous information into the lesson; interrupting the lesson's flow with irrelevant comments or questions.	Sticking to the topic; ensuring that the main concept is understood before adding complexity.
Presenting concepts without ample concrete examples; teaching skills without sufficient demonstration and practice time.	Having many, varied examples; planning adequate demonstrations and practice time.
Introducing complexity before the students are ready for it.	Teaching basic skills to an overlearned (highly developed) level before presenting refinements.
Using phrasing and vocabulary that is overly complex for the age or grade level.	Using words the students understand; repeating and restating major points and key ideas; checking frequently to see that students are with you.
Overusing negative adjectives and adverbs, such as "not all rocks," "not many countries," or "not very happy."	Being specific and direct: "the igneous rocks," "one-fourth of the countries," or "upset" or "annoyed."
Using ambiguous phrases and pronouns with vague or unidentifiable referents: "these," "them," "things," "etc.," "maybe," "more or less," "this thing," "all of this," "and so forth," "you know."	Referring to the concrete object whenever possible; using the noun along with the pronoun: "these bacteria," "this sum," "those problems," "all of the spelling words on page 20."
Being vague and approximate about *amount*— "a bunch," "a few," "a couple," "some"; *likelihood*— "may," "might," "chances are," "could be," "probably," "sometimes"; *nature*—"aspects," "sorts," "kinds."	Being as precise as possible. Specific information is more interesting and easier to remember than vague facts.

Source: From *Organizing and Managing the Elementary School Classroom* by C. M. Evertson et al., 1983, Austin: Research and Development Center for Teacher Education, University of Texas.

problems may have trouble with questions that have multiple steps. Students with physical disabilities may be unable to perform the writing requirements of their assignments. In the case of students with severe cognitive disabilities, practice activities may need to be revamped totally so that they are consistent with the students' skill levels and goals and objectives on their IEPs.

Adapting Seatwork Assignments

Connections: Recall the information on evaluating workbook pages in Chapter 7.

One problem with seatwork is that the practice activities may not contain enough items. This limitation is important since students with disabilities often require more practice to master skills or content. For example, Ms. Jennings has just taught her students to solve two-step story problems in math that require adding first and then subtracting. She first demonstrated three problems in front of the class and then guided her students through three more. Ms. Jennings then asked her students to complete independently five problems in the math book. She found that only half the students answered all of the problems correctly and that the rest of the class needed more practice. Many math books have extra problems for students who need more practice, but some do not. You may need either to make up your own items or to find similar items from other commercially produced books.

Another common problem with seatwork is that the directions are too difficult. Complicated or confusing directions can prevent students from completing their seatwork successfully. For example, some directions are excessively wordy: "Use the words letters stand for and the sense of the other words to find out what the new word in heavy black print is" (Center for the Study of Reading, 1988, p. 14). This is just a convoluted way of saying, "Read." Other directions have too many steps: "Read the first sentence, and fill in the missing word. Read the second sentence. Find the word from the first sentence that makes sense in the second sentence and print it where it belongs. Then, do what the last sentence says. Repeat for all the other sentences" (Center for the Study of Reading, 1988, p. 14).

Affleck, Lowenbraun, and Archer (1980) have suggested a number of adaptations you can make for exceptional students when they encounter directions that are too difficult:

1. Verbally present the tasks. This adaptation can be done with the whole class, particularly when many students are having problems with the directions. You can accommodate the needs of individual students by pairing a worksheet with an auditory tape that explains the directions.
2. Add practice examples that you can do with the whole class or a small group of students who are having particular difficulty.
3. Write alternative sets of directions. You can project these onto a screen using an overhead projector or distribute individual copies to students.
4. Highlight the important words in the directions.
5. Ask students to help each other when the directions are difficult.

FYI: Before starting independent practice, complete sample items for the students. Talk through each step, modelling your thought process and decision making. Use questioning to check that students understand directions. What other strategies will you use for adapting seatwork and homework?

Students may also have trouble when single pages of seatwork contain a number of different tasks. This combination of tasks can cause problems for exceptional students, who often have difficulty making the transition from one task to another. Consider the example shown in Figure 9.8. This worksheet has

Name _____

The Sound of Short *i*

A. Say each word. Circle the words that have the vowel sound you hear in "hit."

lick	milk	cane	time
might	away	drink	gone
rabbit	house	sing	girl
this	come	five	fish

B. Make new words by changing the first letter or letters.

pick _____ _____ _____

wing _____ _____ _____

slip _____ _____ _____

C. Finish each sentence by underlining a word that you circled above.

1. The boys and girls will _____ a song in school.
2. My father and I went to the river and caught a big _____.
3. _____ is not the book I want to read.
4. The fluffy little _____ ran across the road.
5. My mother gave me a glass of _____.

FIGURE 9.8
Seatwork Activity

three different tasks that are repeated twice. Students need to make a number of transitions within one worksheet to complete the activity successfully. If you were to adapt this worksheet, you could cut the page into segments and have students do them one at a time. You could also visually cue the change of task on the page (for example, draw a line between tasks).

Finally, seatwork should provide opportunities for students to practise functional skills. When seatwork tasks are non-functional, much valuable practice time is wasted. Before you give a seatwork assignment to your students, ask yourself what the objective is and whether this task meets the objective. If you have a hard time answering either question, consider not using the worksheet.

Providing Feedback on Independent Practice Activities

You can also adapt student practice by the feedback you provide on students' performance. It makes good sense to correct and return students' work as soon as possible. Timely feedback allows you to find out immediately where your students are making mistakes so you can reteach material if necessary. Providing feedback as quickly as possible is particularly important for exceptional students, who are less likely to learn material the first time it is presented. Returning papers soon after they are handed in also helps students know what they are doing correctly or incorrectly, and it gives them the opportunity to make corrections when the material is still fresh in their minds. In addition, regular feedback makes students feel more accountable for what they put on their papers.

Although providing timely feedback to students is a good practice, as a professional teacher and as an individual with a personal life as well, your time during and after school may be limited. Therefore, in grading your students' papers, efficiency is imperative. Here are some suggestions designed to help save you time:

1. **Correct papers as you circulate.** You can correct some papers as you circulate throughout the room during the seatwork period. First, carry a pen with different colour ink than those used by students when they correct their own papers. Begin circulating and correcting the papers of exceptional students first. This will ensure that those who are most likely to need your help receive it. Each time you stop at a student's desk, correct at least two items. Correct answers can be marked with a C, star, happy face, or whatever you prefer. Mark errors with a dot. When you find an error, try to determine whether the student simply made a careless mistake or did not know how to do the item correctly. If the student does not know how to do the item, show him or her how to do it, assign several similar problems, and say that you will be back to check the work in several minutes (Paine, Radicchi, Rosellini, Deutchman, and Darch, 1983, pp. 122–123).

2. **Use spot checking.** Reading three of the 10 comprehension answers assigned will give you a fairly good idea of whether students understand the material (Lavoie, 1989).

3. **Use shared checking.** Allow the first two students finished with an assignment to go to a corner and compare their answers. When they reach agreement on the answers, they design a "key." They can then check the other students' answers. If students exchange papers, ask the corrector to sign the paper at the bottom. This strategy helps to ensure that students correct fairly and accurately (Lavoie, 1989).

4. **Use easy checking.** Design assignments in a way that makes them easy to correct. For example, put problems or questions in neat, orderly rows. When checking assignments from consumable workbooks, cut off the corners of the pages you have checked or corrected. This helps you (and the student) find the next page quickly (Lavoie, 1989).

5. **Use self-checking.** Dictate or show answers using an overhead projector while students correct their own papers. Require that pencil assignments be corrected in pen and vice versa. Making corrections in a different shade or colour enables you to monitor the number of mistakes students make before completion of their final corrected copy. Asking students to colour over each answer with a yellow crayon before the correction activity serves the same purpose, since their original answers are impossible to erase. After collecting papers, spot check them for accuracy and provide consequences accordingly (Lavoie, 1989).

Adapting Homework Assignments

Some schools may feel pressure to assign more homework because of societal pressures to boost student achievement. Unfortunately, as with in-class independent practice activities, exceptional students may have difficulty completing traditional homework assignments. The problems of exceptional students involve

Do It! Select a commercially prepared student workbook page in the subject area and grade level you plan to teach. Critique the worksheet in light of the guidelines for adapting seatwork. How might you adapt this worksheet for an exceptional student?

primarily two factors: students' lack of time management and academic skills to complete these assignments independently, and the failure to establish a clear line of communication between home and school. Patton (1994) recently reviewed the research literature on effective homework practices for exceptional students and developed these strategies for adapting homework, which apply especially to students in secondary schools:

1. **Involve parents from the outset.** Establish an effective home–school communication system and inform parents of the role they should play in the homework process. Regular classroom teachers are often confused about who is responsible for communicating with the parents of exceptional students—the regular classroom teacher or the resource teacher (Jayanthi, Nelson, Sawyer, Bursuck, & Epstein, 1995). Usually, whoever assigns the homework should communicate with the parents, and this is typically the classroom teacher.

2. **Assign homework from the beginning of the school year.** This strategy gets students accustomed to the routine of having homework.

3. **Schedule time and establish a routine for assigning, collecting, and evaluating homework.** You need to ensure that you allow enough time to explain assignments to exceptional students. A quick explanation immediately before or after the bell is often not enough and results in homework either not done or done incorrectly. According to Patton (1994), a thorough explanation of a homework assignment should include the following components: state the purpose; give directions for completing the assignment; provide an estimate of how long the assignment should take; note in writing when the assignment is due; clarify the format to be used; identify the materials needed to complete the assignment successfully; indicate how the assignment should be evaluated; and always give both oral and written instructions.

▶ *All students can benefit from homework and other independent practice activities. What are some strategies you can use to adapt homework and other assignments for exceptional students?*

4. **Coordinate with other teachers.** Students may have several different teachers. Students could conceivably be assigned homework in most or all of their classes on a given night, which could lead to a difficult situation for them. You should coordinate your planning with your fellow teachers, if only for the students in your classes who you feel are at risk for not completing homework.

5. **Verify the clarity of your assignments.** Do this by asking students to tell you what they are supposed to do, responding either as a group or individually.

6. **Whenever possible, allow students to start their assignments in class.** This strategy allows you to see if any problems arise, *before* students take their assignments home.

7. **Use assignment books and/or folders.** Many exceptional students lack critical organizational and memory skills. Having places to write down due dates and keep their papers can be helpful. Assignment books can provide a valuable communication link with parents. Teachers can initial the book after class, indicating the assignment has been properly recorded. Parents can initial the book as well, confirming that they have seen the assignment.

8. **Implement classroom-based incentive programs.** Students who are rewarded for completing their homework accurately will be more likely to do their homework regularly. Incentives may be particularly important for exceptional students, for whom homework is often a struggle with no obvious benefit.

9. **Ask parents to sign and date homework**. This adaptation is particularly powerful. Research shows that students whose parents are required to sign off on their homework spend more time doing their homework.

10. **Evaluate assignments**. As with independent practice in class, homework that is collected, evaluated, and graded is more meaningful to students. Many of the correcting strategies recommended for in-class activities can also be applied to homework.

11. **Establish relevance**. Show students how a particular assignment relates to their lives in and out of school.

12. **Give homework on skills students can already perform**. Homework is a good way to help students build skill fluency, maintain their skills, or apply their skills to new settings or situations. Homework should not, however, require skills that the students have not yet acquired.

Even in the best homework systems, exceptional students will still need adaptations. For example, students with reading problems may need extra assistance with homework directions. Students with physical disabilities may need assignments shortened, or they may need to respond orally rather than in writing. Remember to use the INCLUDE strategy introduced in Chapter 1 in developing adaptations that fit your assignments and the individual characteristics of your exceptional students. A recent survey of regular classroom teachers (Polloway, Epstein, Bursuck, Jayanthi, & Cumblad, 1994) showed that teachers favoured these homework adaptations: adjust length of assignment; provide extra teacher help; provide a peer tutor for assistance; set up student study groups; provide auxilliary learning aids, such as computers and calculators; check more frequently

Connections: For more ideas on building student independence in completing assignments, see Chapter 10.

Connections: Recall the discussion of homework in Chapter 7. Enlisting family support for students' independent practice is vital. Chapters 2 and 3 contain guidelines for communicating with family members.

with students about assignments, such as when they are due and what is required; and allow alternative response formats, such as oral or written.

Of course, successful homework also depends on individual student skills. Not only do students need to be proficient in basic academic skills, but they also need to be able to learn independently. For example, they need to recognize their homework problems and seek help when necessary. They also need to manage their time effectively. Strategies for teaching these and other independent learning skills will be covered in more depth in Chapter 10.

FYI: Sometimes, homework is not a viable option, as in the case of students who work so hard during the day that they need a break or students whose life circumstances make homework irrelevant.

Adapting Materials for Students with Moderate to Severe Disabilities

Students with moderate to severe disabilities often cannot perform some or all of the steps in tasks performed every day by students without disabilities. In the past, this inability to perform tasks in the same way as other students was interpreted to mean that students with moderate to severe disabilities could not benefit from these activities. Today, the emphasis is on making adaptations and providing support for these students so that they can increase their participation level or level of independence in performing classroom activities (Freagon, Kincaid, & Kaiser, 1990). You can use this five-step self-questioning process to ensure that students with moderate to severe disabilities are maximally included in your class:

1. **Can the student perform the same task, using the same materials?** Answering yes to this question means that goals and objectives from the student's IEP can be addressed within the general education curriculum. For example, Meg is in a grade five class involved in a unit on nutrition. During math, they will be measuring ingredients for making fat-free blueberry muffins. In this case, Meg participates in the measurement activity under the same expectations for performance as her peers. No adaptations are required.

2. **Can the student perform the same task but with an easier step?** At this level, the student participates in the regular classroom curriculum at a more basic level compared to his or her peers. This means that the activity is the same but the objectives are different. For example, in the nutrition example, Meg only measures out ingredients that do not involve fractions (for example, 1 cup, 1 teaspoon). Or, Meg identifies the words *cup* and *teaspoon* in the recipe.

✔ **Your Learning:** What adaptations can you make in your practice activities to help all students succeed?

3. **Can the student perform the same task but with different materials?** At this point in the process, the objectives continue to be the same but the materials are changed to ensure that the student is an equal partner in the lesson. For example, Meg uses an adapted recipe that uses visual symbols to depict the ingredients and measurements. Meg also uses measuring spoons and cups that have enlarged handles that enable her to use them.

4. **Does the student need to perform a different task having the same theme as the classroom lesson?** In this option, the student participates in activities drawn from the regular education curriculum that are thematically linked to what his or her peers are doing. The focus for the student with

Connections: Other information on including students with moderate to severe disabilities is included in Chapter 4 and 8.

moderate to severe disabilities is on core IEP goals that are embedded in general education classroom activities. For example, Meg practises filling measuring cups and spoons; Meg tells another student in the class what her favourite breakfast foods are.

5. **Does the student require a different theme and a different task?** This option focuses on functional tasks that have a direct bearing on the day-to-day life of the student. The student's IEP goals and objectives are not dependent on the regular education curriculum and are addressed independent of classroom routines and activities. For example, Meg leaves the classroom to work on toileting, dressing, and handwashing; she leaves school to learn cleaning skills at a local fast-food restaurant; and she hands back papers to other students, with the teacher or a peer reading her the names on each paper (Lowell York, Doyle, & Kronberg, 1995).

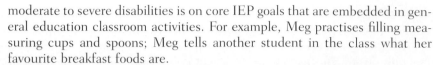

Summary

Teachers who communicate clearly through the curriculum materials they use or the information they present orally in class will meet the needs of a broad range of their students without having to make adaptations. Nonetheless, despite your best efforts, you will still need to make some adaptations for students who are at risk or have other exceptionalities.

In teaching basic skills, you may need to make adaptations in the areas of preskills, selecting and sequencing examples, rate of introduction of new skills, and the amount of direct instruction, practice, and review. Preskills are basic skills necessary for performing more complex skills. Before teaching a skill, you should assess the relevant preskills, and, if necessary, teach them. The range of examples you present should correspond directly with the types of problems you want students to solve, both in and out of class. Examples can also be sequenced to make learning easier for students. Students sometimes have difficulty learning skills when they are introduced too quickly. Introduce skills in small steps and at a slow enough rate to ensure mastery before you present more new skills. Finally, in learning basic skills, students at risk or with exceptionalities may need more direct instruction, practice, and review.

In teaching subject-matter content to exceptional students, adaptations may need to be made in the areas of activating background knowledge, organizing content, and teaching terms and concepts. Students who have disabilities may lack background knowledge necessary for learning a content area, or they may know the information but be unable to recall it and relate it to the new information being presented. The PReP strategy, anticipation guides, and planning think sheets can help activate students' background knowledge. When content is well organized, students' understanding of important ideas and their interrelationships is enhanced. Student understanding also increases when study guides and graphic organizers are used. Students may also need help comprehending the large number of new and/or technical vocabulary words and concepts in content-area instruction. Strategies for teaching vocabulary that are effective for exceptional students include modelling examples, synonyms and definitions, and concept diagrams.

Educational Solutions

www.excalnet.com/gchron

The KEEN (Key Enrichment of Exceptional Needs) Foundation

www.keen.org

Laureate Learning Systems

www.llsys.com

Your oral and written communication with students must be clear. Clear written communication requires fewer inferences by the reader, which helps exceptional students, who may lack the background knowledge and reasoning skills to make such inferences. Effective written communication also explains sequences of events logically and uses obvious pronoun referents. Clear oral communication involves the effective use of directions, questions, and lectures.

You may also need to make adaptations in student independent-practice activities. Seatwork can be adapted by increasing the number of practice items, clarifying the directions, and reducing the number of different activities on a page. Providing feedback on independent practice activities can be facilitated by correcting papers as you circulate and using spot checking, shared checking, easy checking, and self-checking. Effective homework adaptations for exceptional students include adjusting assignment length; providing extra teacher help; providing a peer tutor; setting up student study groups; providing auxilliary learning aids, such as calculators and computers; and allowing alternative response formats, such as oral or written responses.

Students with moderate to severe disabilities often cannot perform some or all of the steps in tasks. You can use a five-step questioning process to adapt your classroom activities for these students.

Applications in Teaching Practice

Developing a Repertoire of Instructional Adaptations

1. You want to teach a group of at-risk students to spell the following contractions: *can't, aren't, couldn't, shouldn't, wouldn't, don't, won't,* and *isn't.* In designing your instruction, how would you respond to the following questions related to teaching basic skills:
    a. How will you evaluate whether your students have learned the contractions?
    b. What preskills should you be concerned with, how will you assess them, and what will you do with students who do not know them?
    c. How would you sequence your instruction? Why did you choose this particular sequence?
    d. How will you provide direct instruction, practice, and review for your students?
    e. At what rate will you introduce the contractions?
2. Design a study guide for a section of Chapter 2 of this text. Explain how you would use the guide with at-risk or other students with exceptionalities.
3. Develop a graphic organizer for a major concept or section of information in Chapter 1 of this text. Explain how you would teach the concept to students who are at risk or who have exceptionalities.
4. Design a concept diagram for the concept of "reasonable accommodation."

Chapter 10

Strategies for Independent Learning

▼ Learner Objectives

After you read this chapter, you will be able to

1. State ways that teachers can encourage student self-awareness and self-advocacy.
2. Describe ways that learning strategies can be developed and taught.
3. List and describe successful learning strategies in the areas of reading comprehension, note-taking, written expression, math problem solving, and time management.
4. Describe ways that students can learn to use learning strategies independently.

GERALD *is a student with learning disabilities in Mr. McCrae's grade nine English class. Gerald has had problems in the area of written expression throughout his school years. It is not that he does not have good ideas. When Gerald talks about what he is going to write, it sounds great. However, when he tries to get his ideas on paper, writing becomes a very frustrating experience for him. First, Gerald's papers lack organization. They rarely have a good introduction and conclusion, and the body is usually out of sequence. Gerald also makes a lot of mechanical errors; his papers are full of misspellings, and he frequently leaves out punctuation marks and capital letters. When asked by Mr. McCrae why he does not proofread his papers, Gerald responded that he does. What can Mr. McCrae do to help Gerald learn to organize his papers better? What can be done to help Gerald proofread his papers better for mechanical errors?*

TRACI *is a student in Ms. Wiens' grade three class. Although Traci was referred for an assessment and IEP meeting last year, the committee recommended more classroom adaptations for Traci, rather than special services. Traci has difficulty solving story problems in math because she does not have a systematic way of working on them. When Traci starts a problem, she looks for the numbers right away rather than reading the problem carefully first. For example, one day she saw the numbers 23 and 46 in a problem and automatically added them to get an answer of 69. The problem called for subtraction, but Traci did not know that because she had not read the problem. What can Ms. Wiens do to help Traci solve math word problems more successfully? How can Ms. Wiens help Traci become a more independent problem solver?*

RONALD *is a student with a moderate developmental disability who has problems with organization. He is often late for school because, according to his parents, he rarely plans ahead and is always getting his materials ready for school at the last minute. Ronald is usually late for class as well. He says that he cannot keep track of what he needs to bring to each class so he is constantly going back to his locker, which makes him late. His locker is a complete mess. Afternoons, Ronald has a part-time job bagging groceries as part of a cooperative education program. His supervisor has expressed concern that Ronald has been late for work several times, frequently forgets his uniform, and several times has missed his bus and has had to be driven home by one of the clerks. What can Ronald's teachers do to help him become better organized?*

ALL of these students share a common problem: They are unable to meet independently the academic and organizational demands of school. Being able to work independently is a skill that becomes increasingly important as students move through the grades. Gerald needs to be able to organize his papers better, not just in English, but in all areas—teachers often judge quality on the basis of organization, neatness, or the number of spelling or punctuation errors. Traci needs to solve problems more systematically, not just in math, but in her other classes and out of school as well. Ronald will need a strategy for managing his time; being punctual and having the necessary supplies or materials are essential in school as well as in the world of work. The fact is, as students move through the grades and on to careers or post-secondary education, more and more independence is expected by teachers and necessary for student success.

Connections: How does this chapter relate to the INCLUDE model presented in Chapter 1?

The key areas in which students need to perform independently include the following five areas: gaining information, storing and retrieving information, expressing information, self-advocating, and managing time. Gaining information involves skills in listening to directions during lessons and on the job, or in reading and interpreting textbooks, source books, or other media. Storing information consists of strategies for taking notes and preparing for tests or other evaluations. Students also need to retrieve information when needed. For example, they need to remember how to carry out a job task such as cleaning and clearing a table or safety procedures to follow during science lab. Expressing information includes the school tasks of taking tests and writing papers. It also involves tasks such as carrying out an employment interview and negotiating interpersonal problems in the workplace. Self-awareness and self-advocacy skills help students set realistic school or life goals and develop and carry out a plan to meet those goals. Finally, students must have the time-management skills to organize their time and effort toward meeting their goals. Although all of these skills become more important as students progress through school, independence should be stressed at all levels of instruction. Unfortunately, many students, including those who are at risk or have other exceptionalities, lack basic independent learning skills. Traditionally, when students needed learning-strategy instruction, they were referred to special education classes, remedial reading or math programs, or special study-skills courses. In inclusive classrooms, learning strategies can be taught to exceptional students in several ways. Most often, learning strategies can be taught in class so that all students can benefit. For example, when Mr. Cooper discovered that many of his students in history were having trouble taking notes, he presented a note-taking strategy to his whole class. Ms. Au and the other members of the mathematics department at Forest View Secondary School taught problem solving on the job to all the grade nine students, in a unit on mathematics problem solving. They capitalized on the common processes used to solve all kinds of problems, and taught all students so everyone would benefit, rather than teaching only the exceptional students. Similarly, Ms. Carpenter taught her biology class a strategy for taking multiple-choice tests because her students were scoring low as a group on these kinds of questions. Occasionally, because of extraordinary student needs, strategy instruction might take place outside the classroom. For example, some exceptional students may need to have a strategy broken down into small steps, view multiple demonstrations of a strategy, and practise the strategy many times before they learn it. If the collaborative support of other education professionals is lacking, this level of instruction may be difficult to deliver within the time and curricular constraints of the regular education classroom. Ronald, the student you met at the beginning of this chapter, has such extraordinary needs. Ronald needed a strategy designed specifically for his organizational problems; a plan for getting to his afternoon job on time would not be relevant for the rest of his classmates. In cases such as these— where a resource teacher teaches strategies to individual students—your job will be to encourage and monitor student usage of the strategy in your class and to provide students with feedback on their performance. However, in most cases, you can teach many of these skills in your class while still covering the required academic content. In fact, teaching learning strategies to students will allow you to cover more material because your students will be able to learn on their own. You should do all you can to encourage and teach independent learning strategies to your students. This chapter will focus on three major ways you can build student independence in learning: (1) encouraging student self-awareness and self-advocacy skills; (2) developing and teaching learning strategies directly in class; and (3) teaching students to use strategies on their own. Keep in mind that the strategies discussed apply most directly to students with high-incidence exceptionalities such as learning and behavior disabilities or to students who are at risk.

Connections: Strategies for independence that are relevant for students with moderate to severe cognitive or developmental disabilities are discussed in Chapters 4 and 9.

How Can You Encourage Student Self-Awareness and Self-Advocacy?

As students move through elementary, junior, and senior high school and on to post-secondary education or the world of work, the level of independence expected by those around them increases. Teachers expect students to come to class on time, master content through reading and lectures, keep track of assignments, organize study and homework time, set realistic career goals, and participate in curricular and extracurricular activities to meet these career goals. Students are also expected to recognize when they have a problem and to know where to go for help. Clearly, students need to look out for themselves—to become self-advocates.

In effective student **self-advocacy,** students must be aware of their strengths and weaknesses, the potential impact of these strengths and weaknesses on their

FYI: Self-advocacy also includes social interaction skills, the subject of Chapter 13.

performance, the support they need to succeed, and the skills required to communicate their needs positively and assertively.

Adjusting to these changing expectations can be difficult for all students, but especially for exceptional students. Many exceptional students are unaware of their strengths and weaknesses (Aune, 1991; Bursuck & Jayanthi, 1993). Figure 10.1 contains an activity designed to encourage self-awareness and help adolescents recognize their personal strengths. It is important that teachers think out loud when modelling such activities and that students each have a partner to record their thinking aloud. They also lack self-advocacy skills (Durlak, Rose, & Bursuck, 1994). They will need to learn these skills while still in school.

Generally speaking, resource teachers and special educators have much of the responsibility for teaching self-advocacy directly. However, you are in a good position to teach all students about the opportunities and expectations of the adult world related to self-awareness and self-advocacy. For example, Cecil is a student with a vision impairment who is included in Mr. Jordan's algebra class. Even though Cecil sits in the front row, he is still unable to see the problems on

Cultural Awareness: Self-advocacy relates to social and cultural factors that affect a student's self-concept and self-esteem. Strategies for independence can help students at risk or with special needs overcome learned helplessness and develop a stronger sense of self-efficacy.

FIGURE 10.1

Self-Awareness of Personal Strengths

Name: _____

Partner: _____

Have your partner record your answers to the questions below and list your three greatest strengths.

	Yes	Sometimes	No
1. Do I value other people's opinions?	___	___	___
2. Do I make good decisions?	___	___	___
3. Do I like talking to people?	___	___	___
4. Do I like fixing things?	___	___	___
5. Do I organize my time well?	___	___	___
6. Am I a responsible person?	___	___	___
7. Do I like to write about my ideas?	___	___	___
8. Do I think for myself?	___	___	___
9. Am I a team player?	___	___	___
10. Do I work hard?	___	___	___
11. Do I try to look my best?	___	___	___
12. Do I finish what I start?	___	___	___

My three greatest strengths:

1. _____
2. _____
3. _____

Source: From *Pathways: Knowing About Yourself, Knowing About Careers* by N.L. Hutchinson and J.G. Freeman, 1994. Copyright © 1994 by Nelson Canada. Reprinted by permission.

Student's Name _____

Date _____

Rater _____

Instructions

This evaluation asks you to examine the student's skills in the area of self-advocacy (assertiveness and interpersonal skills). Please read each statement and indicate how you think this student compares to other students his or her age in these specific areas.

5 = Very high		2 = Below average
4 = Above average		1 = Very low
3 = Average		N/O = Not observed

1. _____ Recognizes he or she needs help.

2. _____ Knows when and how to request help.

3. _____ Participates verbally in class (appropriately).

4. _____ Makes eye contact with person to whom speaking.

5. _____ Is aware of kinds of accommodations available for testing and other needs and understands which are appropriate for his or her characteristics (for example, oral exams, extended time for tests, books on tape).

6. _____ Asks for appropriate help from peers.

7. _____ Actively participates in setting, establishing, and discussing IEP goals.

8. _____ Speaks in appropriate voice tone for situation.

9. _____ Cooperates when asked.

10. _____ Persists when necessary.

11. _____ Asks questions if does not understand.

12. _____ Works independently.

13. _____ Indicates confidence in academic abilities.

14. _____ Initiates work, participation, and questions.

15. _____ Volunteers answers in class.

16. _____ Indicates confidence in social abilities.

Other Comments/Concerns

_____

_____

_____

_____

Source: From *Preparing High School Students with Learning Disabilities for the Transition to Postsecondary Education: Training for Self-Determination* by C. M. Durlak, 1992, unpublished doctoral dissertation, Northern Illinois University, DeKalb. Used by permission.

Do It! Adapt the self-advocacy checklist in Figure 10.2 to make it a self-rating form for students to complete. Use language that reflects the grade level you plan to teach. How could you use such a form to plan instruction in self-advocacy skills?

✓ **Your Learning:** Why might guiding students in establishing or choosing their own learning goals be an effective approach for introducing self-advocacy skills?

the board because Mr. Jordan forms his numbers too small. However, Cecil does not feel comfortable asking Mr. Jordan to write larger. Cecil practised asking Mr. Jordan for help with his resource teacher. Cecil then asked Mr. Jordan directly, who responded that it would be no problem to write bigger. Mr. Jordan also gave Cecil some additional suggestions on how to describe his disability and ask his teachers for accommodations. A checklist of self-awareness and self-advocacy skills is shown in Figure 10.2. Suggested practices that you can follow to help your students increase their level of self-awareness and self-advocacy are presented in the Professional Edge below.

How Can You Teach Independent Learning Strategies Effectively in Class?

Another way you can help your students become more independent is to teach them strategies for learning how to learn. These methods are collectively referred to as learning strategies. Wong (1996), a researcher at Simon Fraser University, describes **learning strategies** as techniques or principles that enable a student

---

Professional Edge
Supporting Self-Advocacy Skills

LEARNING to be a self-advocate can be a challenge for students, and especially for exceptional students. You can help all your students learn to be more self-aware and to look out for themselves by fostering the skills and strategies they will need to become more sure of themselves. Following the suggestions described here will help you create a safe environment in which students can practise self-advocacy skills.

1. Support a schoolwide self-advocacy system. Some common classroom situations that require students to self-advocate or assert themselves are asking for clarification of lecture material; telling a teacher that they have a disability or other learning problem; making an appointment with the teacher to discuss needs or accommodations, such as extended time on tests; asking the teacher if they may tape-record class lectures; and obtaining teacher approval for having another student

take notes or for them to copy another student's notes.

2. Establish a classroom climate in which students are comfortable enough to assert themselves. To foster such an atmosphere, you should provide students with constructive feedback on their self-advocacy skills. For example, part of being a good self-advocate is being able to assert oneself firmly but positively. Tom, a student with a physical disability, told his science teacher, Mr. Collins, that he was legally required to let him use a tape recorder in class. Mr. Collins explained to Tom that he could have been more positive, and, as a result, more effective in his request if he had explained carefully his disability and asked for permission to use the tape recorder rather than demanding it.

3. Many exceptional students have low self-esteem, often because much of the attention

to learn to solve problems and complete tasks independently. Learning strategies, which are similar to study skills, not only emphasize the steps needed to perform a strategy (for example, steps to follow in reading a textbook), but they also stress why and when to use that strategy as well as how to monitor its usage. For example, when Ms. Blankenship taught her students a strategy for reading their textbook, she pointed out that the strategy would save them time yet improve their test scores. She also taught them how to judge how well they are using the strategy by completing a simple checklist as they read.

An important component of teaching learning strategies effectively is to present well-designed strategies. As you recall from the discussions of effective materials in Chapters 7 and 9, the better your materials are designed, the greater the chance that they will work for exceptional students, without requiring you to make major adaptations. Some effective guidelines for designing learning strategies are presented in the Professional Edge on page 314.

For students to perform learning strategies independently, they must first learn to perform them accurately and fluently. The following teaching steps have been shown to be effective for teaching learning strategies (e.g., Hutchinson, 1993; Schumaker, Deshler, & Denton, 1984; Wong, 1996). These steps include many of the effective teaching practices described in Chapters 7 and 9.

FYI: This discussion of learning strategies relates to the concept of metacognitive skills—learning how to learn—including, for example, the test-taking skills presented in Chapter 11.

FYI: Collaboration with a school counsellor or resource teacher can help you design effective self-advocacy skills for your exceptional students.

Do It! Develop a list of ways in which you might incorporate content about self-advocacy in your classroom.

they receive focuses on their weaknesses rather than their strengths. You can help students acquire a more balanced perception of themselves by giving them opportunities to use their strengths. For example, John, who has a good memory (but poor reading skills), is asked to remind the teacher when announcements need to be made. The teacher praises him for having a good memory.

4. Continually demonstrate in class that all of us are better at some things than others. Students are more accepting of their own problems when they realize that they are not the only ones who experience difficulty. For example, Melissa is a straight-A grade five student but is not good in sports. Alexis is just the opposite. She has a severe reading disability but is the best athlete in the class. Their teacher set up a peer-tutoring program whereby Melissa taught Alexis to recognize common reading words and Alexis helped Melissa learn to throw a softball during recess. Students also benefit from seeing that even teachers are not proficient at everything, and that the trick is to identify ways to adjust to your weaknesses. Ms. Edwards explains

that certain spelling demons still give her trouble and that she keeps a card in her purse with the correct spelling of these words that she can refer to as needed.

5. Help your students take charge of their lives by teaching them to set goals for themselves. An important first step is helping students understand their strengths and weaknesses. Understanding their strengths and weaknesses helps to ensure that their goals will be realistic. Next, show your students examples of both short- and long-term goals. Short-term goals could involve passing the next algebra test, doing all your math homework for the week, or ensuring that you have written down all your assignments. Long-term goals could include graduating from high school with a C average or better, becoming a computer programmer, or joining the Coast Guard.

When they are setting their goals, have students keep in mind these questions: Does my goal state what I want to achieve? Do I believe I can reach my goal? Can I really achieve my goal? How will I know when I have achieved my goal?

Professional Edge

Developing Your Own Learning Strategies

You can use the guidelines here either to create your own learning strategies or to evaluate ones that are commercially produced. By following these suggestions, you will not always need to depend on commercial publishers for your learning materials. Rather, you can develop learning strategies to fit the students in your class.

1. Identify skill areas that are problematic for most of your students, such as taking multiple-choice tests or lecture notes.
2. For each skill area, specify student outcomes, such as scoring 90 percent or better on multiple choice tests or writing down key main ideas and details from a lecture.
3. List a set of specific steps students need to follow to reach the identified outcomes. You may want to think about what you do when you take multiple-choice tests or lecture notes and pattern your suggestions on your own best study habits. You may also want to ask other students who have good test-taking and note-taking skills what they do. Shown here is a sample reading comprehension strategy called RAP:

R Read a paragraph.
A Ask yourself what were the main idea and two details.
P Put main idea and details in your own words. (Ellis & Lenz, 1987)

4. Your strategy should contain no more than seven steps. Having more steps will make the strategy difficult to remember.
5. Your steps should be brief; each should begin with a verb that directly relates to the strategy.
6. To help students remember the steps, you may find it helpful to encase the strategy in a mnemonic device (for example, the acronym RAP for the reading strategy above).
7. The strategy should cue students to perform thinking (remember), doing (read), and self-evaluative (survey or check your work) behaviours.

Source: Adapted from "Generalization and Adaptation of Learning Strategies to Natural Environments: Part 2. Research into Practice" by E. Ellis, K. Lenz, and E. Sabornie, 1987, *Remedial and Special Education,* 8(2), 6–23.

Assessing Current Strategy Usage

Connections: The assessment strategies described in Chapter 8 apply to this discussion. Also recall the information in Chapter 9 on teaching preskills and providing direct instruction.

Students are often receptive to instruction when they can clearly see problems they are having and how the strategy you are teaching will help them overcome these problems. Therefore, learning-strategy instruction begins with an assessment of how well your students can currently perform a skill. As you learned in Chapter 8, specific learning strategies can be assessed using direct-observation checklists, analyses of student products, and student self-evaluations.

You also need to assess whether your students have the preskills necessary to perform the strategy. For example, students who can read all the words on a test and understand the class content will benefit most from a test-taking strategy. On the other hand, students who cannot identify most of the words in their texts would not be logical candidates for learning a textbook-reading strategy. As you have learned, exceptional students often lack critical preskills. Before you decide to teach a particular strategy, you should identify its preskills and assess them separately. If most students lack the preskills, they can be taught as part of your everyday instruction. If only a few have problems with preskills, these students need to receive additional instruction in class, with a peer or adult tutor, through co-taught lessons, or in a learning assistance centre or special education setting.

Clarifying Expectations

Learning strategies have the potential of empowering your students because they enable students to learn and succeed in and out of school on their own, without undue help from others. When you introduce learning strategies to students, you need to point out their potential benefits clearly and specifically. Carefully explained expected outcomes can be motivating, particularly as students get older and teacher encouragement alone may not be enough to keep them interested. The first step in getting and keeping students motivated to learn is to give a strong rationale for why learning the strategy is important. This rationale should be directly linked to current student performance as well as to the demands of your class. For example, when introducing a new note-taking strategy, Mr. Waska pointed out that the class was able to identify on average only half of the main ideas presented on a note-taking pretest. He also told his class that half of the material on his tests would come from information presented during his lectures. Finally, Mr. Waska explained that taking good notes can help students out of school as well; in many job situations, employers give directions that need to be written down.

The next step in clarifying expectations is to explain specifically what students will be able to accomplish when they have learned the skill. For example, Ms. Thompson told her class that after learning a textbook-reading strategy, they would be able to do their homework faster. Also, give students an idea of how long it will take them to learn the strategy. For example, you could make a chart showing the instructional activities to be covered each day and the approximate number of days it will take to learn the strategy. The advantage of presenting the information on a chart is that steps can be publicly crossed out or checked off as completed. The act of checking off completed activities can be very motivating for students. It is also a way of demonstrating self-monitoring, an effective independent learning skill that we will discuss later in this chapter.

Demonstrating and Modeling Strategy Use

In demonstrating strategies, keep in mind three important points. First, remember that the process one goes through in performing a task or solving a problem should be carefully explained. For example, demonstrate both thinking and doing behaviours. Talking aloud to yourself while performing the skill is particularly important for many exceptional students, who often do not develop spontaneously organized thinking patterns. Second, present both examples and non-examples of appropriate strategy usage, carefully explaining why they are examples or non-examples. This explanation can help students distinguish between doing a strategy the right way and doing it incorrectly—a distinction that can be difficult for exceptional students to make without direct instruction. For example, Mr. Waska demonstrated effective and ineffective note-taking strategies using the overhead projector. As a student listened to a short lecture, he took notes systematically, writing down key ideas and details. Next, using the same lecture, he demonstrated ineffective note-

Connections: Applying the INCLUDE strategy is an effective way to identify strategies that students need to succeed in your class.

Do It! Talk to an experienced teacher in your community. How does he or she use the vocabulary in this section?

▶ *Demonstrating the use of a learning strategy involves explaining both the thinking and doing parts of a process, showing examples and non-examples of effective strategy usage, and checking learners' understanding. How do these steps help exceptional students acquire learning strategies?*

Case in Practice

Teaching Script for Demonstrating KWL Plus Strategy

AN important component of teaching a learning strategy effectively is to demonstrate and model its appropriate use. The following script shows how one teacher combines demonstration and modelling to present a textbook-reading strategy to her grade eight class.

TEACHER: Let's review the textbook-reading strategy we talked about yesterday. Please take out the cue cards you made in class yesterday.

The teacher will ask students to read each step individually and will ask them what each step involves. Questions such as, "What are the steps? What might you do with the information you think of when brainstorming? What do you do after you read the passage?" might be used.

TEACHER: Now that we've reviewed each step, we need to learn how to use the whole strategy effectively. Before we move on, though, let's read aloud all of the steps together as a group. When I point to the letter, say the letter, and when I point to the meaning, you read its meaning.

The students read the steps aloud: "*K* means 'what you already know,' *W* means 'what you

want to know,' and *L* is 'what you learned.'"

TEACHER: Good. Now I'm going to demonstrate how to use the strategy with a story I found about crayons. I'll put the passage on the overhead, as well as give each of you a copy so you can follow along at your desk. I'll work through each step of the strategy orally and write the information obtained at each step on the board. Use your cue cards to help you see what step of the strategy I'm on.

The teacher then goes through the story, demonstrating correct usage of the steps and asking for feedback after. The teacher also goes back over each step asking the students to verify if all of the steps to the strategy were followed and to explain how they were followed.

TEACHER: What do we do now that we have a passage assigned to read? First, I brainstorm, which means I try to think of anything I already know about the topic and write it down.

The teacher writes on the board or overhead known qualities of crayons, such as "made of wax," "come in many colours," "can be sharpened," "several different brands."

taking by trying to write down every word. Finally, after you demonstrate, ask frequent questions to test student understanding. Frequent questioning can help you monitor student understanding and determine whether more demonstration is needed. Keep in mind that for many students, including those with disabilities, one demonstration may not be enough. See the Case in Practice below for a sample script for demonstrating the **KWL** (**K** = what you already know; **W** = what you want to know; **L** = what you learned) **Plus** textbook-reading strategy.

FYI: Modelling as an instructional strategy based on social learning is explained further in Chapter 13.

Encouraging Students to Memorize Strategy Steps

The purpose of having students memorize the steps in the strategy is to make it easier for them to recall the strategy when they need to use it. To help students learn the steps, you can post them prominently in your classroom at first so that you and your students can refer to them throughout the class or day. Students may also need to be drilled on saying the strategy steps. To practise, students could pair off and quiz each other; or you could ask students the strategy steps before and after class. For example, each day during the last several minutes of class, Ms. Henry quizzed four of her social studies students on the steps of the KWL reading strategy.

Connections: Strategies for memorizing information are also described in Chapter 11.

TEACHER: I then take this information I already know and put it into categories, such as "what crayons are made of" and "crayon colours." Next, I write down any questions I would like to have answered during my reading, such as "Who invented crayons? When were they invented? How are crayons made? Where are they made?" At this point, I'm ready to read, so I read the passage on crayons. Now I must write down what I learned from the passage. I must include any information that answers the questions I wrote down before I read and any additional information. For example, I learned that coloured crayons were first made in the United States in 1903 by Edwin Binney and E. Harold Smith. I also learned that the Crayola Company owns the company that made the original magic markers and Crayola magic markers are currently made at a factory in Lindsay, Ontario. Last, I must organize this information into a map so I can see the different main points and any supporting points.

At this point, the teacher draws a map on the chalkboard or overhead.

TEACHER: Let's talk about the steps I used and what I did before and after I read the passage.

A class discussion follows.

TEACHER: Now I'm going to read the passage again, and I want you to evaluate my textbook reading skills based on the KWL Plus strategy we've learned.

The teacher then proceeds to demonstrate the strategy incorrectly.

TEACHER: The passage is about crayons. Well, how much can there really be to know about crayons besides there are hundreds of colours and they always seem to break in the middle? Crayons are for little kids, and I'm in grade eight so I don't need to know that much about them. I'll just skim the passage and go ahead and answer the question. Okay, how well did I use the strategy steps?

The class discusses the teacher's inappropriate use of the strategy.

TEACHER: We've looked at the correct use of the strategy and we've seen how mistakes can be made. Are there any questions about what we did today? Tomorrow we will begin to memorize the strategy steps so that you won't have to rely on your cue cards.

Source: From *A Script for How to Teach the KWL Strategy* by S. Butson, K. Shea, K. Pankratz, and M. Lamb, 1992, unpublished manuscript. DeKalb: Northern Illinois University. Used with permission.

Even though memorizing a strategy can help students recall it, you may not want to spend too much time on this step, particularly for some of your exceptional students, who may have memory problems. For these students, you might include the steps to all the strategies they are learning in a special section of their assignment notebooks. For strategies used most often, cue cards listing strategy steps can be made to tape to the inside cover of textbooks or notebooks. You can also post a chart in your classroom that contains the strategy steps.

Providing Guided and Independent Practice

Connections: Providing support for students when they first learn a skill is discussed in Chapter 7 as part of scaffolding.

Connections: Students who are gifted can benefit from learning strategies, but, as discussed in Chapter 6, may not need as much practice learning them. An advantage of co-teaching (Chapter 3) is that one of you can give students more strategy practice while the other works on another activity with students who do not need more practice.

Connections: Additional strategies for changing students' attributions were discussed in Chapter 5.

As we have already stated, students must learn how to perform strategies accurately and fluently before they can attempt them independently. Such proficiency requires considerable practice. Five ways of providing practice on learning strategies are suggested:

1. Ask students to practise on **controlled materials** when they are first learning a strategy; these materials are at their reading level, without complex concepts, and are of high interest; for example, when teaching a strategy for taking essay tests, have students practise on familiar materials such as sports or rock music.
2. Provide guided practice in which you ask questions to cue students to the steps in the strategy (like "What will you do first? What will you do next?") and gradually stop asking questions.
3. Give specific feedback that encourages self-assessment; ask students how they think they did and say "Good job showing the relationships in the word problem" rather than just "Good job."
4. Give praise only when students have produced praiseworthy work, otherwise they may attribute your praise to you feeling sorry for them.
5. Encourage students to reinforce themselves and take responsibility for their successes and failures (e.g., get them to attribute their success to their own strategies and effort; these are factors under their control).

Administering Posttests

FYI: Knowing which strategies to teach your students is an important outcome of using the INCLUDE strategy.

When it appears from your practice sessions that most students have acquired the strategy, give them the pretest again to test their mastery. If according to your posttest, students have not acquired the strategy, problem solve to identify where the breakdown occurred and then provide additional instruction and/or practice. If more than 20 percent of the students need extra practice or instruction, they can receive additional help in a large or small group. If less than 20 percent of the students require more assistance, those needing more individualized practice can be provided with peer tutors or support staff.

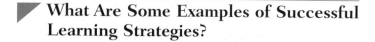

What Are Some Examples of Successful Learning Strategies?

There is a growing research base of learning strategies that work for exceptional students or students who are at risk. These strategies cover many areas, including reading comprehension, written expression, math problem solving, and time and resource management. An array of strategies that incorporate many of these effective practices are summarized in the following sections.

Reading-Comprehension Strategies

Reading-comprehension strategies are intended to help students meet the independent reading demands of content-area classes successfully, particularly in the middle and upper grades. Although reading primarily involves textbooks, students must also be able to read and understand a variety of source books.

PARS is a simplified textbook-reading strategy for expository prose that is good for younger students or students without much experience using textbook-reading strategies (Cheek & Cheek, 1983). The four steps of PARS follow:

1. **Preview the material.** In this step, students scan the chapter to identify main ideas by surveying the introductory statement, headings, graphic aids, and chapter summary.
2. **Ask questions** that relate to the main ideas discovered when surveying the chapter.
3. **Read the chapter** in order to answer the questions developed.
4. **Summarize** the main ideas in the chapter.

CAPS is a self-questioning strategy that can be used to help students find answers to questions about what is important in a story (Leinhardt & Zigmond, 1988). Here are the steps:

C   Who are the *characters*?
A   What is the *aim* of the story?
P   What *problem* happens?
S   How is the problem *solved*?

Another reading-comprehension strategy is **POSSE** (Englert & Mariage, 1991). This strategy includes many reading practices that have been shown to aid reading comprehension, such as graphic organizers, text structures, stimulation of student background knowledge, and self-monitoring. The steps in this strategy are as follows:

P   Predict ideas.
O   Organize the ideas.
S   Search for the structure.
S   Summarize the main ideas.
E   Evaluate your understanding.

When students are *predicting*, they can be given a sentence starter such as, "I predict that. . . ." For this step, students are taught to use signals from a variety of sources, including the title, headings in bold, pictures, key words, and so on. Brainstorming is very important in this step. For example, look at the completed POSSE strategy sheet in Figure 10.3 for a section of text on the Bermuda Triangle. Before they read, students studied pictures, headings, and boldfaced vocabulary words in the text. On the basis of this information, as well as their background knowledge, they predicted that the story would be about ideas such

Connections: Strategies for developing and using graphic organizers were described in more depth in Chapter 9.

Case in Practice
Reciprocal Teaching

THE students in this small group have just read a section of text that focuses on Loch Ness. They are now applying the search, summarize, and evaluate steps of POSSE.

TEACHER: What is the main topic the text is talking about?

PEG: The Loch Ness monster.

TEACHER: What was this section about? What was the main idea?

PEG: Oh, the lake. I have two questions: "What is a lake?" and "What lives in it?"

TEACHER: Do you mean this particular lake or any lake?

PEG: This lake. Joe?

JOE: It's foggy, it's deep, and it's long and narrow.

PEG: Don?

DON: The land beside the lake, you don't know if it is real soft and you could fall through it.

TEACHER: So it could be soft and swampy.

ANN: I think the Loch Ness monster lives there.

TEACHER: Is Ann answering your question, Peg?

PEG: No.

TEACHER: What was your question?

PEG: I had two: "What is a lake?" and "What lives in the lake?"

JOE: But they never answered that. I have a question about the main idea. Aren't we supposed to do a question about the main idea?

TEACHER: Just about what we read.

JOE: Yes, but she asked us, "What lives in the lake?" but it doesn't really mention that in the book.

TEACHER: That's true. The major idea has to do with Loch Ness and what it looks like. A minor idea that we really inferred rather than directly read in the article was that the Loch Ness monster lives in the lake.

PEG: Are there any clarifications?

STUDENTS: [No response.]

TEACHER: I have a clarification. You had trouble reading some of these words and I wondered if you knew what some of them mean? What does ancestors mean?

[The teacher continues discussing vocabulary.]

Source: From "Making Students Partners in the Comprehension Process: Organizing the Reading 'POSSE'" by C. S. Englert and T. V. Mariage, 1991, *Learning Disability Quarterly, 14,* 133–134.

Note-Taking Strategies

Because lecturing is a common way for teachers to present information to students, particularly in upper elementary and secondary school, students need strategies for recording key information in lectures so they can study it later.

The **five *R*'s of note-taking** (Pauk, 1989) is a helpful strategy for note-taking. The steps are listed here:

Record main ideas and important details.
Reduce to concise phrases.
Recite key information using your concise phrases as cues.
Reflect on your notes by adding your own ideas.
Review all the key information in your notes.

An important preskill for this strategy is identifying main ideas and details. Students may need direct instruction on this skill. This strategy can be enhanced

◤ *These students are engaged in a structured dialogue about the newspaper they are reading, a peer-modelled comprehension strategy called reciprocal teaching. What four strategies must students be taught before they can practise reciprocal teaching?*

by combining it with a column note-taking format. Students can have a 10-centimetre column for *recording*, a five-centimetre column for *reducing*, and a two-centimetre column for *reflecting*.

A note-taking strategy is called **PASSING.** This strategy includes the following steps:

Prepare for class.
Attend to the teacher.
State the topic.
State the source.
Identify key words and ideas.
Note their meaning.
Give the meaning in your own words.

Students can record information using the PASSING strategy on a note-taking sheet such as the one shown in Figure 10.4, which Inez kept. For example, Inez's science teacher lectured on koala bears. For the *P* step, Inez read the section on koala bears in her science book. For the *A* step, she attended to the lecture by keeping her eyes on the teacher and her notes and by trying to think about what her teacher was saying. For the two *S* steps, Inez stated the topic of the lecture (koala bears) as well as the source (science class). She then identified key words (the *I* step) *marsupials, herbaceous,* and *nervous.* In the *N* step, she noted their meaning. After the lecture, Inez gave the meanings of key words and ideas in her own words (the *G* step).

To learn this or other note-taking strategies, students need the preskill of being able to distinguish between main ideas and details. For example, Inez chose key words that represented main ideas. Some students attempt to write down everything and need to be taught directly how to differentiate main ideas and details. For example, Mr. Abeles discovered that many students in his history class were unable to identify main ideas from his lectures. First, he gave his stu-

FIGURE 10.4
PASSING Note-
Taking Form

Name _____Inez_____

Class _____Science_____

Date _____3/13/97_____

Topic _____Koala bears_____   Source _____Lecture_____

Identify key words	Note their meaning	Give the meaning in your own words
Marsupials	Like kangaroos— have pouch to carry young	Koala bears are marsupials. Marsupials are animals that carry their young in a pouch like kangaroos do.
Herbaceous	Live on eucalyptus leaves Never drink water— suck water from leaves	Marsupials are herbaceous animals. They eat eucalyptus leaves almost entirely.

dents rules to follow: main ideas are what a whole section or passage is about; details are what just one part of a section or passage is about. For several weeks, he stopped after presenting a section of material and put three pieces of information on the board—one main idea and two details. He asked the students which was the main idea and why. When his students were doing well at these tasks, Mr. Abeles asked them to write their own main ideas after a section of lecture; these were then shared with the class and corrective feedback was provided as necessary. A group of researchers at Simon Fraser University (Winne, Graham, & Prock, 1993) provided convincing evidence that most poor readers' problems with inferencing from text stem from their inability to identify the main ideas or most important ideas when reading. When they can't distinguish the important from the unimportant in the passage, they overemphasize their background or prior knowledge. This supports Wong's (1996, pp. 163-166) emphasis on teaching students to find the main idea sentence in a paragraph. Students must also be able to summarize material in their own words. One effective strategy for writing summaries involves the following steps: (1) skim the passage (or listen to a section of lecture); (2) list the key points; (3) combine related points into single statements; (4) cross out the least important points; (5) reread the list; (6) combine and cross out to condense points; (7) number the remaining points in logical order; and (8) write points into a paragraph in numbered order (Sheinker & Sheinker, 1989, p. 135). Finally, students should learn strategies for studying their notes, such as covering up one column and trying to say what is in the column, and then uncovering the column and comparing their responses to the actual information. Although some students can master this study strategy with only a verbal explanation, others may need more support in the form of a demonstration and guided practice.

Writing Strategies

Another area that requires student independence is writing and proofreading papers. One strategy that helps students organize themselves to carry out all the steps in the writing process is called **POWER** (Englert et al., 1988). The process involves the use of self-questioning, graphic organizers, and peer editing using the following steps:

Planning
Organizing
Writing
Editing
Revising

The POWER strategy teaches students four different organizational structures for writing papers: stories, compare/contrast, explanations, and problem/solution (Englert et al., 1988). When writing stories, students use key story elements—Who? When? Where? What happened? How did it end?—to organize their papers. A compare/contrast structure includes information about what is being compared (for example, logging in Algonquin Park in 1897 and 1997), on what characteristic they are being compared (where the loggers live), and on how they are alike and/or different (in 1897, they lived in shanties in the woods; in 1997, they live with their families and commute to the logging site). Explanations involve telling how to do something, such as explaining the steps in changing a tire. Finally, in a problem/solution structure, a problem is identified (for example, it was arduous to travel from East to West in the 1800s in Canada), the cause of the problem is explained (there were no roads, there were mountains and rough terrain for stagecoaches), and the solution is stated (the Canadian Pacific Railway was built).

For the *planning* stage, students focus on the audience for the paper, the purpose, and the background knowledge that will be necessary to write the paper. In the *organizing* step, students decide which organizational pattern fits their paper (for example, story, compare/contrast) and then complete a pattern guide to help them organize their ideas. A **pattern guide** is a graphic designed to help students organize their papers. A sample pattern guide for a compare/contrast paper is shown in Figure 10.5. Notice that the words that are not in boxes—"both same," "in contrast to," "similarly," and "however"—are key words that are used frequently when making comparisons. These words help students make the transition to writing sentences. For example, in Figure 10.5, two kinds of pizza are being compared/contrasted. The student might write, "The crusts of deep dish and regular pizza are *both the same* in that they both are made of white flour. This is *in contrast to* their thickness; deep-dish pizza crust is much thicker."

In the *writing* stage, the teacher demonstrates and thinks aloud to show students how to take the information gathered in the planning and organizing steps and produce a first draft. For example, you can compose an essay comparing two kinds of pizza using the overhead projector, thinking out loud as you write. You can involve students by asking questions such as, "What would a good topic sentence be?" "Is this a good example?" "How do you think I should end this?" "Why?" You could also have students write the paper along with you.

Connections: The organizational structures for writing papers are similar to the text structures in content-area textbooks discussed in Chapter 7 and the story grammars described in Chapter 8.

Compare/Contrast

What is being compared/contrasted?
Deep dish pizza and regular pizza

On what?
Crust

both same | Alike? White flour | Different? Deep dish is thicker | in contrast to

On what?

similarly | Alike? | Different? | however

Source: From "A Case for Writing Intervention: Strategies for Writing Informational Text" by C. S. Englert, T. E. Raphael, L. M. Anderson, H. M. Anthony, K. L. Fear, and S. L. Gregg, 1988, *Learning Disability Quarterly,* 3(2), p. 108. Used by permission of Council for Learning Disabilities.

The *editing* step teaches students to critique their own writing and identify areas in which they need clarification or assistance, an important self-evaluation skill. Editing is a two-step process involving student self-evaluation and peer editing. For self-evaluation, students reread and evaluate their draft, marking with a star sections of the paper they like best and putting question marks in the margins by parts they think may be unclear. Finally, students think of two questions to ask their peer editors. For example, Jorge asked his peer editor whether he had used capital letters and punctuation correctly. He was also concerned about whether his paper was long enough and asked for suggestions on how to add information.

For **peer editing,** several steps are followed. First, writers read their papers to a peer editor while the editor listens. The peer editors then summarize the paper. Next, the editor evaluates the paper, giving an analysis of salient features of the writing that might guide a revision or lead to improvement. For example, the peer editor might suggest that the writer add key words to or reorganize the paper for clarity. These suggestions are shared with the writer. Then the peer editor and the writer brainstorm ways to improve the paper.

A research-based strategy called TAG can also help students with the peer-editing process (Carlson & Henning, 1993; MacArthur & Stoddard, 1990). The **TAG** strategy involves three simple steps:

T   Tell what you like.
A   Ask questions.
G   Give suggestions.

As discussed previously, students need to be provided with models and guided practice on these steps prior to doing them independently. They should be taught to always start off positively, telling what they like about the paper before criticizing.

In the *revise* step, students decide on changes to be made using their self-evaluation sheets and peer feedback. Englert et al. (1988) suggest that the teacher model how to insert or change the order of information, while providing a rationale for any changes. All modifications are made directly on the first draft. Last, the teacher and student have a conference, and changes in writing mechanics are suggested. Following this conference, a final draft is composed on a clean sheet of paper.

When students have to proof their papers independently, they might use a strategy called COPS (Alley, 1988). In the **COPS** strategy, students question themselves as follows:

C   Have I *capitalized* the first word and proper nouns?
O   How is the *overall* appearance of my paper? Have I made any handwriting, margin, or messy errors?
P   Have I used end *punctuation*, commas, and semicolons carefully?
S   Do words look like they are *spelled* right; can I sound them out or use the dictionary?

✓ **Your Learning:** In what ways might the COPS strategy be helpful to Gerald, whom you met at the beginning of this chapter?

Although COPS has been shown to be effective, students need pre-skills to perform this strategy adequately. Prior to teaching COPS, consider the following questions: Can the students recognize misspelled words? Do the students know rules for using capital letters and punctuation? Can they apply these rules? Can the students use a dictionary? If the answer to any of these questions is no, teach these skills directly before teaching students the COPS strategy.

Do It! Develop a pattern guide for student writing in a subject area you plan to teach. Use the compare/contrast grid in Figure 10.5 or create a new pattern for problem/solution, explanations, or stories.

Several additional strategies can be used to help students with the various aspects of written expression. **SLOW CaPS** (Levy & Rosenberg, 1990, p. 27) is a strategy for writing four kinds of paragraphs: list or describe, show sequence, compare and contrast, and demonstrate cause/effect. Here are the steps:

Show the type of paragraph in the first sentence.
List the details you want to write about.
Order the details.
Write details in complete sentences and CAP off the paragraph with a *C* (concluding), *P* (passing/transition), or *S* (summary) sentence.

(Notice that the *a* in CaPS is not used and so is lowercased.)

A composition strategy called **DEFENDS** (Ellis & Lenz, 1987) is designed to help students write a paper defending a position.

Decide on an exact position.
Examine the reasons for the positions.
Form a list of points that explain each reason.
Expose the position in the first sentence.
Note each reason and supporting points.
Drive home the position in the last sentence.
Search for errors and correct.

The five-step study strategy here will help students learn unknown spelling words (Graham & Freeman, 1986). Students are required to:

1. Say the word.
2. Write and say the word.
3. Check the word.
4. Trace and say the word.

Technology Notes **Word Processing for Exceptional Students**

THE capabilities of word processing equipment hold great promise in helping exceptional students become more independent writers. Although promising, however, word processing is by no means a panacea. In deciding whether to introduce word processing to exceptional students, you will want to keep in mind what it can and cannot do.

Pros

1. Allows students to focus on the meaning of their communication by freeing them from the mechanical aspects of writing.
2. Eliminates the physical act of recopying a paper and reduces the feeling that revisions are punishment. Revisions are more palatable because rewriting every word is not necessary.
3. Makes correcting errors easier, making writing less of a risk; students are willing to experiment more with word choice and sentence structure.
4. Fosters collaborative writing because of the text accessibility on the computer monitor.
5. Helps to identify many errors by using spelling and grammar checkers.
6. Helps students produce neat, easy-to-read papers, in multiple copies if needed, with the aid of a printer. This attractive finished product gives students a sense of pride in their work and enhances their self-image.
7. Frees teachers of repetitive instructional tasks, such as handwriting and appropriate

formatting, so they can spend more time on content programming.

Cons

1. Encourages students to rely on programs for checking and proofreading. As a result, students do not practise editing skills or develop the habit of checking. This overreliance on the computer's proofreading capabilities is a problem because some word processors do not recognize all errors (for example, the incorrect use of homonyms such as *their* and *there*).
2. Requires typing skills, which may be a problem for some students with visual motor or fine motor problems.
3. Use command structures with a high readability level or complex language, making independent usage more difficult (see the guidelines for selecting software programs that follow).
4. Does not necessarily by itself lead to gains in the ability to write; word processing is no substitute for effective writing instruction.
5. Requires spelling skills since spell-check programs require students to select the "correct" word from a series of options.
6. Has proofreading functions that on average pick up only 25 percent of grammatical errors.
7. Requires knowledge of grammatical rules; even if the program flags probable errors, students may not understand the program's suggestions.

5. Write the word from memory and check your spelling.
6. Repeat the first five steps if you misspell the word in step 5.

Word processing software can also help exceptional students become independent writers. The Technology Notes gives some of the pros and cons of the available word processing programs and some guidelines for selecting the correct word processing program for exceptional students.

▶ *Students using computers for written expression.*

Guidelines for Selecting Word Processing Software

Here are guidelines for selecting word processing software that is easy for exceptional students to use.

1. The overall structure of the program should be logical.
2. Programs should have a simple procedure for cursor movement, insertion, and deletion rather than the most sophisticated. For example, "control-S" means "save."
3. Picture displays (icons) are helpful for some students to describe the mode or command. For example, a picture of a typewriter means "print."
4. Plain English menu choices are helpful. For example, "move text" is easier to conceptualize than "block insertion."
5. Menu choices should not provide too many or irrelevant choices.

6. Saving and loading features should include prompts for verification. Highlighting is one type of prompt.
7. A "what you see is what you get" format may help eliminate confusion about the way text is formatted on the screen versus the way it is printed.
8. Vocabulary, language, and reading level should be suitable for the students.
9. The documentation accompanying the program should be as complete, clear, and devoid of jargon as possible.
10. The program should have the capability to handle greater writing demands than the students will make initially. Do not, however, invest in software that has more capabilities than the students will need.

Source: From "LD Students and Word Processors: Questions and Answers" by C. Keefe and A. Candler, 1989, *Learning Disabilities Focus, 4*(2), 78–83. Reprinted by permission of Lawrence Erlbaum Associates, Inc.

Strategies for Problem Solving in Math

Connections: The NCTM standards also stress the use of manipulatives, covered in Chapter 7, and performance-based tests, examined in Chapter 11.

Increasingly, teachers are focusing on problem solving as a major component of the math curriculum. This concentration is consistent with the math standards developed by the National Council of Teachers of Mathematics (1990), which also stress the importance of teaching problem solving. However, research indicates that if exceptional students are to become good problem solvers, they must be taught *how to* problem solve directly. A common (but by no means the only) way to introduce problem solving to students in a classroom context is through story or word problems. Techniques for teaching word problems that are effective for exceptional students are presented in the Professional Edge.

As the ideas in the Professional Edge suggest, problem solving can be taught as a process involving self-instruction whereby learners talk themselves through tasks. **RIDGES** is a self-instructional strategy designed to teach exceptional students to solve math word problems independently (Snyder, 1988).

Do It! Using the guidelines in the Professional Edge, develop a story problem for curriculum content you plan to teach. Then write a teaching script for showing your students how to solve the problem.

Read the problem carefully.
I know.

What I know from reading the problem is that Roberto started with 45 cents and spent 35 cents.

Draw a picture.

Let's see, Roberto starts with 45 cents.
He spent 35 cents for a chocolate bar.

Goal statement.

My goal is to find out how much money Roberto has left.
Equation development.

If he started with 45 cents and spent 35 cents, to find out how much he has left I take away, or subtract. The equation would be

45 cents − 35 cents = ?

Solve the equation.

$$
\begin{array}{r}
45 \text{ cents} \\
-35 \text{ cents} \\
\hline
10 \text{ cents}
\end{array}
$$

Roberto has 10 cents left.

Connections: What strategies other than self-instruction might be taught to help Traci (who was introduced at the beginning of this chapter) learn to solve problems like this one?

FYI: More information on how to use self-instruction is included later in this chapter and in Chapter 12.

The **LAMPS** strategy (Reetz & Rasmussen, 1988) can be used as an aid to remember the steps in regrouping or carrying in addition. Here are the steps:

Line up the numbers according to their decimal points.
Add the right column of numbers and ask . . .
"**M**ore than 9?" If so, continue to the next step.
Put the 1s below the column.
Send the 10s to the top of the next column.

▼▼▼▼▼▼▼▼▼▼▼▼▼▼▼▼▼▼▼▼▼▼▼▼▼▼▼▼▼▼

Professional Edge
Teaching Word Problems

SOLVING story problems is a challenge for many students and can be especially difficult for exceptional students. Use the following techniques to ensure that your exceptional students learn to master math word problems.

1. Be certain the students can perform the arithmetic computation before introducing the computation in story problems. This could be on a calculator.
2. Develop a range of story problems that contain the type of problem you want the student to learn to solve.
3. Instruct with one type of problem until mastery is attained.
4. Teach the students to read through the word problem and visualize the situation. Ask them to read the story aloud and tell what it is about.
5. Ask the students to reread the story—this time to get the facts.
6. Identify the key question. In the beginning stages of problem solving, students should write the key question so they can refer to it when the computation is complete.
7. Identify extraneous information.
8. Reread the story problem and attempt to state the situation in a mathematical sentence. The teacher plays an important role in this step by asking the students questions and guiding them in formulating the arithmetic problem.
9. Tell the students to write the arithmetic problem and compute the answer. (Some problems can be computed by the students in their heads without completing this step.)
10. Tell the students to reread the key question and be sure they have completed the problem correctly.
11. Ask the students if their answer is likely, based on their estimate.

Source: From *Strategies for Teaching Students with Learning and Behaviour Problems* (2nd ed.) by C. S. Bos and S. Vaughn, 1994, pp. 334–335. Copyright © 1994 by Allyn and Bacon. Reprinted by permission.

The **FOIL** strategy (Crawford, 1980) helps prevent algebra students from missing one of the four products needed to calculate multiplication of a binomial by another binomial. Four steps are followed:

F   Multiply *F*irst terms
O   Multiply *O*utermost terms
I   Multiply *I*nnermost terms
L   Multiply *L*ast terms

For example, apply the FOIL strategy to this problem:

$(x + 4) (x + 3)$
$A \quad B \quad C \quad D$

In the *F* step, the student multiplies the first two factors in each binomial, $(x) (x) = x^2$, or using the letters, *AC*. Next, in the *O* step, the student multiplies the first factor in the first binomial and the second factor in the second binomial, $x \times 3 = 3x$, or *AD*. Then in the *I* step, the student multiplies the second factor of the first binomial and the first factor of the second binomial, $4 \times x = 4x$, or BC. Finally, in the L step, the second factors of both binomials are multiplied: $4 \times 3 = 12$, or BD. This strategy applies *only* to the special case of multiplying two binomials.

Algebra word problems are difficult for many exceptional adolescents, although they are one of the major elements in most grade nine and ten mathematics programs. Hutchinson (1986, 1993) developed a self-questioning strategy similar to the RIDGES strategy (Snyder, 1988) shown earlier in this chapter. The questions that students asked themselves to guide their representation (or understanding) of a problem were:

1. Have I read and understood each sentence? Are there any words whose meaning I have to ask?
2. Have I got the whole picture, a representation, for this problem? (drawing)
3. Have I written down my representation on the worksheet? (goal; unknowns; knowns; type of problem; equation)
4. What problem features should I focus on in a new problem so I know whether I can use the representation I have been taught?

The questions students asked themselves to guide their solving of the equation they had already written were:

1. Have I written an equation?
2. Have I expanded the terms?
3. Have I written out the steps of my solution on the worksheet? (collected like terms; isolated unknowns; solved for unknowns; checked my answer with the goal; highlighted my answer)

FIGURE 10.6

Structured Worksheet for Algebra Problem Solving

Goal: _____

What I don't know: _____

What I know: _____

I can write/say this problem in my own words or draw a picture:

Kind of problem: _____

Equation:

_____

Solving the equation:

Solution:

[compare to goal]

Check:

Source: From *Instruction of Representation and Solution in Algebraic Problem Solving with Learning Disabled Adolescents.* by N.L. Hutchinson, 1986, unpublished doctoral thesis, Simon Fraser University, Burnaby, BC.

4. What problem features should I focus on in a new problem so I know whether I can use the solution I have been taught?

The worksheet that is referred to in these self-questions appears in Figure 10.6.

Strategies for Managing Time and Resources

In the early 1980s, an informal survey about the kinds of problems that lead to a student being referred for special education (Lessen & Bursuck, 1983) found the problem mentioned most often was a lack of organization. This is a common characteristic of students with disabilities (C. Smith, 1994; S. Smith, 1980). Ronald, one of the students introduced at the beginning of the chapter, has trouble organizing.

Organizing study materials involves having the appropriate school supplies, ensuring that these supplies are brought to class when they are needed, and having an organized notebook to ensure easy access to information. First, you can ensure that your students obtain the appropriate school supplies by requiring that they communicate with their parents about what materials they need. Second, you can encourage students to write the information down rather than trying to remember it. Presenting the information on the board or overhead will ensure that their lists are accurate. You may also want to duplicate the list and distribute it to your students. Finally, encourage your students to ask themselves these or similar questions, which can help them remember school supplies as well as assignments throughout the school year:

- What is due tomorrow in school?
- What do I need to do to get it done tonight?

Connections: Review Chapter 7 on the impact of classroom environments on learning. How might you modify your classroom to help students develop the independent learning skills described in this chapter?

Strategies for managing time and organizing materials help provide the structured routines that many students need to succeed in school. What are the three steps in teaching students how to use weekly assignment calendars?

- What materials or other things do I need to get the job done?
- Who can I ask for help in doing this?

Cultural Awareness:
Teachers with a multicultural perspective take into account that students from different cultural backgrounds might have different routines as well as different resources for addressing, structuring, and completing projects. For example, some will have books to consult at home and access to the Internet, while others will lack these resources at home and will only have access to them in the school.

These questions can be posted on the board at first to help students remember them and to prompt their use. You can help motivate students to bring needed materials by providing positive recognition for those who do bring their supplies to school. For example, Mr. Fayed gave school pencils to students who had all their supplies in school. Ms. Habner put the names of her students on a "responsible students" list from which she chose people for classroom jobs. You may need to make adaptations for exceptional students. For example, students with physical disabilities may need a classmate or parent to bring their supplies into school. Students who live in poverty might be unable to afford supplies other than materials the school or teacher provides.

Besides having to organize their materials, students also need to organize their time, particularly as they get older and the demands made on their time increase. More schools are now teaching their students to use schedule books to help them arrange their time (Jenson, Sheridan, Olympia, & Andrews, 1994; Patton, 1994). You can teach your students to use a weekly schedule book in the following ways:

1. **Teach students to differentiate between short- and long-term assignments.** Short-term assignments are those that can be completed in one or two days and that take one or two steps to get done, such as reading a chapter in history and answering the questions at the end of the chapter. Long-term assignments take more than two days to complete and take more than two steps to get done. Writing a five-page report on a current event is an example of a long-term assignment. The difference between short- and long-term assignments can be taught readily to the whole class at once by giving them the definitions and teaching them to apply these definitions to a series of examples.

2. **Teach students to task analyze long-term tasks** by breaking them into component tasks, estimating the amount of time it will take to perform each subtask, and then scheduling time to complete the subtasks in their schedule books. Start by modelling the task-analysis process. You can do this by distributing an already completed task analysis and timeline for your first several long-term assignments. Then, ask students to begin to develop their own task analyses, first under your guidance, and eventually, independently. The steps for performing a **task analysis** are explained in the Professional Edge on pages 336–337.

Do It! Perform a task analysis for an assignment in a course you are currently taking. How will your experience help you teach students this strategy?

3. **Show students how to record information in their schedule books** by entering fixed activities or activities you do every week; entering occasional activities, or activities that will differ from week to week; entering the due dates for assignments; prioritizing assignments; scheduling time to work on assignments; and monitoring assignment completion, including rescheduling or adding time to work on assignments.

Cultural Awareness:
Family and home supports can play an important role in student management of time and resources, but

Many schools have had success with schoolwide programs with a single system of keeping track of assignments in a schedule book used in every class. The consistency and repetition that are naturally a part of such a system seem to benefit students, including those with exceptionalities, many of whom are more successful when teachers stick to a daily routine. Exceptional students may need additional adaptations, however, such as having the classroom teacher check and/or initial their schedule book before they leave class. This step is particularly important when students are first learning to use a schedule book.

How Can Students Learn to Use Strategies Independently?

Some students may have trouble using a learning strategy independently, even after they have learned how to do it. Their problem could be that they may not know when to use a strategy, or if they are using it, how to keep track of how well they are doing and change their behaviour if necessary.

Four strategies that can help students perform tasks more independently are self-instruction, self-monitoring, self-questioning, and self-reinforcement. Like all learning strategies, these "self" strategies may need to be carefully taught using the teaching practices described in this chapter.

Self-Instruction

In **self-instruction,** learners are taught to use language to guide their performance. In essence, students are taught to talk themselves through a task. The idea is, if they can talk themselves through a task, they will not need help from anyone else. The first step needed to teach students self-instruction techniques is to explain that self-instruction involves giving yourself instructions on how to do a task. For example, self-instruction can be used to help get seatwork done or remember to use a strategy for a multiple choice test. Demonstrate how to write down the steps needed to perform that task. After you have demonstrated how to apply self-instruction, ask the students to practise in a role-play situation and give them feedback. The students can practise in pairs and give each other feedback, with you monitoring and also giving feedback. Students can keep a chart or index card listing the task steps, which they should be encouraged to glance at periodically while performing the task.

Self-Monitoring

In **self-monitoring**, students watch and check themselves to ensure that they have performed targeted behaviours. Self-monitoring is a critical aspect of independent learning, since being independent often requires students to check their performance to see if it is effective and make a change when a particular strategy is not working. Self-monitoring can also be a strong motivator for students by providing them concrete evidence of their progress. In teaching self-monitoring to your students, first explain to them that self-monitoring is a way that they can check their own behaviour to ensure that they are doing the right thing. Ask the students to identify a behaviour or a learning strategy that they need to do in class.

The next step is to select a practical and expedient way for students to measure the behaviour. One possibility is to keep track of behaviours as they occur

teachers cannot assume that these supports exist or are understood. Communicating information about independent learning skills and explaining expectations can lead to effective family involvement.

Connections: The "self" strategies covered in this chapter apply to academic learning. These same strategies are sometimes referred to as *cognitive behaviour management*, which is discussed in Chapter 12.

FYI: Self-monitoring is discussed again in Chapter 12 as a strategy in student behaviour management.

Professional Edge
Teaching Students Task Analysis

An important part of time management is knowing how to task analyze assignments. Students who can judge the difficulty of their assignments and break them into manageable steps are better able to budget time for completing their work. Unfortunately, task analysis is a skill that is problematic for students, including those with exceptionalities. Strategies for teaching students to analyze their assignments are described here.

Write the Assignment

Write a two-page paper comparing the baseball strike of 1994 to the baseball strike of 1981.

Before you begin a task analysis of your assignment, review the following steps:

Step 1: Decide exactly what you must do.
Step 2: Decide how many steps are needed to complete the task.
Step 3: Decide how much time each step will take.
Step 4: Set up a schedule.
Step 5: Get started.
Step 6: Finish the task.

Now you are ready to begin a task analysis of your assignment. Check off steps as they are completed in the boxes (p).

Step 1: Decide exactly what you must do

❑ Notice the key words in the directions. Look at the exact wording. List key words for this project.

1. _Two-page paper_
2. _Compare 1994 baseball strike to 1981 strike_

❑ Tell yourself aloud what you must do.

❑ Go over the directions again.

Step 2: Decide how many steps are needed to complete the task

❑ List all the steps needed to do the task.

❑ Number the steps in the order of their importance.

Steps	Order
Find source information for both strikes in library	1
Write first draft	4
Edit	5
Write final draft	6
Make outline of paper	3
Read sources and take notes	2

Step 3: Decide how much time each step will take

❑ Rewrite your steps in the order in which you numbered them.

❑ Now, consider the amount of time you would need to complete each step.

❑ Record the amount of time in the appropriate space.

Steps (List in sequence beginning with priorities)	Order
Find source information for both strikes in library	1 hour
Read sources and take notes	21-2 hours
Make outline of paper	1 hour
Write first draft	3 hours
Edit	1-2 hour
Write final draft	1-2 hour

Step 4: Set up a schedule

❑ Count the number of days you have to do the task. How many days?

❑ Look at a calendar.

❑ Plan a time for every step. Look back to where you estimated how much time each step would take.

❑ Make changes in your time plan. Some things will take less time. Some things will take more time.

Step 5: Get started

❑ Stay on schedule. Check your calendar each day to see if you are proceeding on schedule.

❑ Make changes if needed. You can make changes in the time plan. You can make changes in the materials.

❑ Stop and look at your progress after each step is finished. Are you still on schedule?

❑ Get help if you find a problem you cannot solve. Whom did you ask for help?

Step 6: Finish the task

❑ Complete your project on time.

❑ Evaluate the finished product. How do you think you did?

❑ Give yourself a reward. What is your reward?

Source: From Blueprint for Study Strategies by Montgomery County Public Schools, 1985, Rockville, MD: Board of Education of Montgomery County.

using a checklist. The checklist shown in Figure 10.7 was developed to help students monitor their use of a self-questioning program in handwriting.

Teach students to use the measurement system through demonstration, practice, and feedback, and continue to encourage and reinforce the use of self-monitoring in your class. Self-monitoring can be applied to any learning strategy.

Self-Questioning

Self-questioning is a form of self-instruction in which students guide their performance by asking themselves questions. The idea behind self-questioning is that if students can guide their own behaviour by asking themselves questions, then they will not always need a teacher or other adult present in order to perform. In teaching your students self-questioning, ask the students first to identify a set of behaviours, duties, or tasks that are required in class. For example, the students could identify steps needed to proof a writing paper, such as checking the correct use of capital letters, punctuation, spelling, and appearance. Ask the students to write these tasks in question form, for example, "Have I capitalized all words correctly? Have I used the right punctuation marks in the right places? Have I spelled all the words correctly? Is my paper neat?"

FIGURE 10.7   Self-Monitoring Checklist for Handwriting

	Monday	Tuesday	Wednesday	Thursday	Friday
Preparing to Write					
How is my posture; am I sitting up straight?	+				
Is the paper aligned correctly? Is it straight?	+				
Am I holding my pen correctly?	+				
Checking Mechanics					
Are the words written on the line?	+				
Are the capitals touching or nearly touching the top line?	0				
Are the lowercase letters filling one-half the space of the line?	0				
Checking Spacing					
Is there enough space between words but not too much?	+				

+ = Done
0 = Not done

As in self-monitoring, the next step is to select a practical and expedient way for students to measure the behaviour, such as recording behaviours as they occur using a checklist. Students might practise self-questioning in pairs for feedback. Other practical measures include keeping task questions on index cards and putting them in a convenient place. For example, students might put the proofing questions on an index card and tape it to the inside cover of their notebooks.

Self-Reinforcement

As the term implies, **self-reinforcement** occurs when students reward themselves for behaving appropriately or achieving success in learning tasks. Teaching self-reinforcement is an effective way of helping students replace negative attributions with more positive ones. Students need to be coached to use self-reinforcement by praising or rewarding themselves explicitly for doing something right or being successful academically. The first step is to ask students to set a particular goal for themselves, such as getting all their homework in on time. Allow students to decide when and how they can reinforce themselves. For example, younger students might give themselves a star or sticker each time they beat their highest score on a math facts timed test. Older students might give themselves a point for each day they completed their homework. If they have four points by the end of the week, they could go out to lunch with a friend. Self-praise is also a good way of rewarding progress toward personal goals.

Practise setting goals, acknowledging when a goal has been attained, and using different kinds of self-reinforcement. You will want to model for students how self-reinforcement works by demonstrating how you set goals for yourself, know when you have reached a goal, and reinforce yourself for reaching the goal. For some students, being an independent learner does not come naturally. These students need to be taught directly independent learning and self-advocacy skills. They also need to be taught how to apply those skills in school and real-world settings with minimal support.

FYI: Reinforcement and related behavioural principles are explored further in Chapter 12.

✓ **Your Learning:** How can students learn to initiate the use of strategies on their own?

 Summary

General education teachers can help all their students, including exceptional students, become independent learners. One way teachers can build student independence is to encourage student self-awareness and self-advocacy.

Another way to help your students become more independent is to design and teach effective learning strategies in class. Effective learning strategies can be developed by identifying skills that are problematic for most of your students, specifying relevant student outcomes, and listing a set of specific steps students need to follow to reach the identified outcomes, these steps should be brief (no more than seven) and are often encased in a mnemonic device. They should also cue students to perform thinking, doing, and self-evaluative behaviours. Methods of teaching learning strategies to students include assessing current strategy usage, clarifying expectations, demonstrating and modelling strategy use, encouraging students to memorize strategy steps, providing guided and independent practice, and administering posttests.

Assistive Media Inc.
comnet.org/local/orgs/
assistmedia/index.html

Dyslexia, Learning Disabilities, and Literary Resource Site
www.greenwood.org

The Room 13 Project

www.schoolnet.ca/sne/
room13/initia/inet/paper.html

Many strategies that can help students become independent learners are available. Reading-comprehension strategies include PARS, CAPS, and POSSE. The reciprocal teaching technique provides teacher and peer models of effective thinking behaviours and then allows students to practise these behaviours with their peers. Some note-taking strategies are the five *R*'s of note-taking (record, reduce, recite, reflect, and review), and PASSING (prepare, attend to the teacher, state the topic and the source, identify key words and ideas, note their meaning, and give the meaning in their own words). POWER (planning, organizing, writing, editing, and revising) is a writing strategy that helps students organize themselves to carry out all the steps in the writing process through the use of self-questioning, graphic organizers, and peer editing.

Other strategies for written expression include TAG, COPS, SLOWCaPS, and DEFENDS. Strategies for problem solving in math include RIDGES, LAMPS, and FOIL. Students also need to learn strategies for managing their time and resources.

Four strategies that can help students learn to use strategies independently are self-instruction, self-monitoring, self-questioning, and self-reinforcement. In self-instruction, students are taught to use language to guide their performance. In self-monitoring, students watch and check themselves to make sure that they have performed targeted behaviours. Self-questioning is a form of instruction in which students guide their performance by asking themselves questions. Self-reinforcement occurs when students reward themselves for behaving appropriately or making progress in learning.

Applications in Teaching Practice

Designing Strategies for Independence

1. Latasha is a student who has a moderate hearing loss. Although her hearing aid helps, she still has to depend a lot on speech reading to communicate. She also speaks slowly and has trouble saying high-frequency sounds such as *sh* and *t*. Latasha has a poor self-image and is reluctant to interact with her peers and teachers. Design a self-advocacy program for Latasha. What skills would you teach her? How would you get her to use these skills in your class and in other school and out-of-school situations?

2. Cal is a student with organizational problems; he is chronically late for class and rarely finishes his homework.
   a. Design an organizational strategy using the guidelines for developing strategies covered in this chapter.
   b. Describe how you would teach the organizational strategy described using the guidelines for effectively teaching a learning strategy covered in this chapter.
   c. Describe how you would teach Cal to use the strategy independently using self-instruction, self-monitoring, self-questioning, and self-reinforcement.

3. Do the following analyses for any learning strategy in this chapter.
    a. Evaluate the strategy's design using the guidelines in the Professional Edge on page 314.
    b. Describe how you would teach the strategy using the six steps described in this chapter.
    c. State how you would help students apply the strategy independently using the four "self" strategies discussed in this chapter.

Chapter 11

Adapting Assessment
for Exceptional
Students

Learner Objectives

After you read this chapter, you will be able to

1. Identify and describe adaptations that can be made prior to testing and when administering tests to exceptional students.

2. Explain ways to construct clear tests.

3. State alternative ways to grade tests for exceptional students.

4. Describe ways to teach students to study for and take tests.

5. Describe ways to adapt report card grades.

6. Explain how performance-based and portfolio assessments can be used with exceptional students.

Mr. Stevens *is a secondary school science teacher. One of his students, Stan, has a learning disability that causes him to have trouble reading his textbooks. Stan also has difficulty figuring out multiple-choice test questions, the kind that Mr. Stevens uses on his exams and quizzes. Stan says that he knows the material but just needs more time to take the tests because he reads slowly. During the past term, Mr. Stevens gave four multiple-choice tests, each worth 20 percent of the final grade. Scores on homework assignments counted for the remaining 20 percent. Stan earned a grade of B on his homework, but he had two D's, one C, and one F on the tests. Mr. Stevens assigned him a grade of D for the term. Mr. Stevens felt this was a fair grade since most of Stan's peers scored much higher on the tests. Mr. Stevens is also committed to keeping his reputation as a teacher with high standards. When Stan received his grade for the term, he asked his parents why he should work so hard when he couldn't seem to get good grades anyway. Stan's parents felt that he had improved last term but that his grade did not show it. They were afraid that Stan would stop trying and eventually drop out of school. What are the issues here? What could Mr. Stevens do to help Stan?*

Jennifer *is in Ms. Robinson's grade three class. She has a hearing impairment and has some trouble in reading but is doing well in Ms. Robinson's literature-based reading program. Ms. Robinson is pleased with her progress and has given her an A in reading on the first two report cards. Recently, Jennifer's parents became very upset when they learned that Jennifer was only reading at the grade one level according to district standardized tests. They wondered how she could have done so poorly on the standardized tests when she has been bringing home A's on her report card. What would you tell Jennifer's parents if she were in your class? How could you change your grading procedures to prevent communication problems like this from occurring?*

LUCILLE *is a student with mild to moderate developmental or cognitive disabilities who is in Ms. Henry's grade four class. On the basis of her current performance in math, which is at the grade one level, Lucille's IEP team set math goals for her in the areas of basic addition and subtraction. The rest of the class is working on more difficult material based on the grade four math curriculum. Lucille's IEP objective for the second marking period was to compute in writing 20 two-digit by two-digit addition problems with regrouping with 80 percent accuracy within 20 minutes. She received direct instruction on these problems from Mr. Brook, her resource teacher, who was co-teaching with Ms. Henry. As a result, she met her goal for the marking period. How should Ms. Henry grade Lucille? School and provincial policies require letter grades.*

ONE of a teacher's major responsibilities is to assess the educational progress of students. The information collected during assessment activities can indicate if teaching has been effective and can allow teachers to alter instruction as needed. Classroom evaluations are also helpful in giving students (and their parents) an idea of how well they are performing in school, and they can be used by principals and school boards to evaluate the effectiveness of their schools (Wilson, 1996).

Even though assessment activities are very important, the ways in which students are assessed most frequently—testing and grading—can be problematic for exceptional students, their teachers, and parents. For example, Stan and his science teacher have a problem because Stan's test scores reflect his learning disability more than his knowledge of science. Jennifer's teacher has a problem in communicating the meaning of Jennifer's grades to parents. She graded Jennifer based on her progress and her effort in class. Jennifer's parents, however, thought she was being graded in comparison to her peers and therefore expected their daughter to be performing at or above grade level, not below. Lucille's teacher must give Lucille a grade even though she has different curricular goals than the other students in the class. As you work with students who are included in your classroom, you will experience these and other challenges in assessing the learning of students with disabilities and other exceptional students. In this chapter, you will learn a number of ways to solve these problems.

How Can Classroom Tests Be Adapted for Exceptional Students?

Connections: How do the topics in this chapter fit into the INCLUDE framework presented in Chapter 1?

Connections: The assessment of academic skills is stressed in this chapter. For information on assessing students' social skills, see Chapter 12.

Although testing has always been a major part of education, the recent emphasis on school reform, and parents' concerns about raising educational standards, may make educators rely even more on tests in the future. With the current focus on inclusion, any increase in emphasis on test performance will bring concerns about the performance of students with disabilities on tests. As shown in the vignette about Stan at the beginning of this chapter, testing can be a very trying experience for many of these students and their families.

Most important in testing exceptional students is ensuring that test results reflect their knowledge and skills, not their disabilities. Fortunately, classroom tests can be adapted in ways that can help you test exceptional students fairly and with a reasonable amount of accuracy. As shown in Table 11.1, adaptations can be made in three contexts: before the test; during test administration; and after the test, in grading procedures. Many of these adaptations will also benefit students who are not exceptional.

Adaptations Before the Test

You can do a number of things before the test to help students with disabilities. First, you can prepare a study guide that tells students what to study for the test. A study guide can help students who waste valuable time studying everything indiscriminately instead of concentrating on the most important information. Study guides can also assist students with memory problems by focusing their efforts on only the most critical material. Second, you can give a practice test. This test can clarify your test expectations and also benefits the class by familiarizing students with the test format. Practice tests are also helpful to students who have trouble following directions or for those who are anxious about taking tests and often fail to cope immediately with an unfamiliar test format. Finally, many students with disabilities also benefit from tutoring before tests. This help can be offered before or after school by peer tutors or paraprofessionals. Tutors can provide guidelines for what to study or help directly with particularly difficult content.

Teaching test-taking skills.   Another option is to teach students **test-taking skills.** Students may need a number of test-taking skills, including ones for studying for tests, for taking objective tests, and for writing essay tests. At first, you might start working with students on test-taking strategies by helping them analyze the kinds of mistakes they usually make on tests. They can then use a test-taking strategy that fits their particular problem. For example, Bill and his teacher looked over his history tests for the last grading period and noticed that most of the questions he missed were taken from class lectures rather than the textbook. Bill begins to check his notes after class with one of his classmates, a kind of "study buddy," to ensure that he does not miss any main ideas. He also decides to spend more time studying his notes before the test. Eric, on the other

FYI: Planning your tests and test adaptations at the beginning of instruction helps you clarify what is essential to teach and achieve a good match between your tests and instruction.

Connections: Strategies for developing and using study guides appear in Chapter 9.

◣ TABLE 11.1   Examples of Testing Adaptations

Before the Test	During the Test	After the Test
Study guides	Alternative forms of response	Change letter or number grades
Practice test	Alternative means of response	Change grading criteria
Teaching test-taking skills	Alternative sites	Use alternatives to number and letter grades
Modified test construction	Direct assistance	
Individual tutoring	Extra time	

Connections: Ways to teach your students to perform study skills independently are described in Chapter 10.

hand, notices that he tends to choose the first response (a.) on multiple-choice tests and that he is not reading the other answer choices carefully. His teacher suggests that he read each choice carefully before responding and put a check next to each answer as a way of ensuring that he has read each choice. At the secondary level, students might use a mistake analysis form such as the one shown in Figure 11.1 to help them focus on these and other types of test-taking problems. The teacher should first show students how to use the form by providing a number of examples in class.

When studying for tests, students often are required to remember a lot of material. This can be difficult for students with learning or cognitive disabilities, who may have memory problems. Students can benefit from strategies that help them remember important content for tests. For example, Greg uses a memo-

FIGURE 11.1

Form for Analyzing Test-Taking Mistakes

Check (✔) any of the following mistakes you made when you took tests for three of your courses. Write DNA (does not apply) for a statement that does not apply to a test. For example, if a test has no true-false or multiple-choice questions, write DNA for mistake 4 and mistake 5.

Test-Taking Mistakes	**English**	**Social Studies**	**Science**
1. Directions not followed.	_____	_____	_____
2. Not all questions answered in allotted time.	_____	_____	_____
3. Answers not checked carefully.	_____	_____	_____
4. True-false or multiple-choice questions left unanswered.	_____	_____	_____
5. Correct true-false or multiple-choice answers changed to incorrect ones.	_____	_____	_____
6. Wrong answer about information in notes and text.	_____	_____	_____
7. Wrong answer about information in notes but *not* in text.	_____	_____	_____
8. Wrong answer for information written on the chalkboard.	_____	_____	_____
9. Wrong answer for information the teacher said to learn.	_____	_____	_____
10. Wrong answer about a topic stated in a textbook heading.	_____	_____	_____
11. Wrong answer for a term printed in special type in the text.	_____	_____	_____
12. Wrong answer about information in a numbered list.	_____	_____	_____

Courses (column group heading above English, Social Studies, Science)

rization technique called **chunking.** After he studies a chapter in his text, he tries to recall five to seven key ideas. These key thoughts help to trigger his recall of more significant details. After reading a chapter about the life of Nellie McClung, for example, he remembers information in chunks—her *works of fiction and non-fiction,* her experiences as a *social activist and suffragist*, and so on. These general ideas help him remember details such as when and where she was born and her role in securing the vote for Canadian women in provincial and federal elections. Mnemonic devices can also help students remember information for tests. **Mnemonics** impose an order on information to be remembered using poems, rhymes, jingles, or images to aid memory. For example, Mr. Charles wants his class to remember the six methods of scientific investigation. He tells the students to think of the word *chrome* (Cermak, 1976). Here are the six steps of the **CHROME** strategy:

C Categorization
H Hypothesis
R Reasoning
O Observation
M Measurement
E Experimentation

Many students do poorly on tests because they do not study for tests systematically. Teach your students to organize their materials so that they avoid wasting time searching for such items as notes for a particular class or the answers to textbook exercises. Making random checks of your students' notebooks is one way to find out how well organized they are. For example, Ms. Barber stresses note-taking in her grade five social studies class. Every Friday afternoon, she checks the notebooks of five students in her class. She gives students bonus

Connections: What types of graphic organizers (see Chapter 9) might be used in helping students prepare for tests?

▶ *Students can help each other prepare for tests effectively using directly taught study strategies. What strategies might these students be using to prepare for an upcoming test?*

Connections: What roles do self-questioning and self-monitoring (see Chapter 10) play in the test-taking strategies presented in this chapter?

points if they have notes for each day and if their notes are legible and include key information. Also, teach your students strategies for how to process material when they are studying. For example, Ms. Cybulski shows her grade three students a verbal **rehearsal strategy** for learning their spelling words. She demonstrates how she says the word, spells it out loud three times, covers the word, writes the word, and then compares her spelling to the correct spelling. Mr. Huang shows his class how they can summarize text and class material on the topic of "The Group of Seven" using a concept map such as the one shown in Figure 11.2. Another effective rehearsal strategy is for students to ask themselves questions about the most important information to be learned.

Teaching test-taking strategies.   Many students, including exceptional students, do not test well because they lack strategies for taking the actual tests. For example, Sal rarely finishes tests in science because he spends too much time on questions that he finds difficult. Laura has trouble with true-false questions because she does not pay attention to key words such as *always, never, usually,*

▶ **FIGURE 11.2**   Concept Map: Studying for Tests

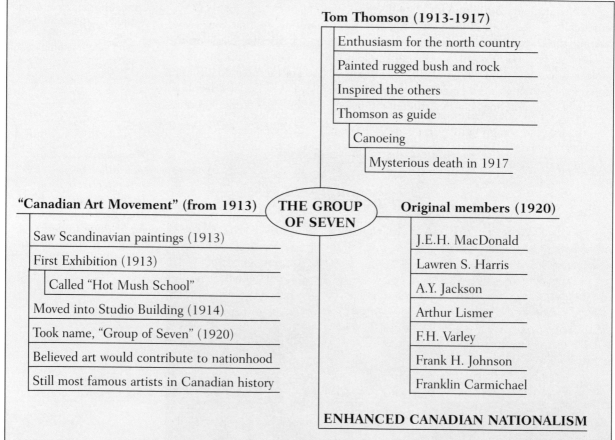

and *sometimes*. Lewis's answers to essay questions contain much irrelevant information and do not focus on what the questions are asking. The Professional Edge on pages 350–351 offers suggestions for teaching students strategies for taking objective tests.

Students also need strategies for taking essay tests. Performing well on essay tests requires that students know the content; can follow directions, including identifying and understanding key words; and can organize their ideas. All these areas can be problematic for students with disabilities. The following suggestions from Langan (1982) might prove helpful to students taking essay tests:

Connections: You can design your own test-taking strategies using the guidelines presented in Chapter 10.

1. Read over the entire exam before you begin. If you have memorized information related to specific questions, jot it down before you write your answer.
2. Look for key instructional words in the questions to help you determine how to structure your answer and determine what information to include. For example, you would include different information and use a different structure if you were asked to *list* the reasons for the rebellion led by Louis Riel versus *discuss* them. Key words often used in essay tests are listed and defined in Table 11.2 on page 352.
3. Organize your answers. A general rule in answering essay questions is that you should spend at least one-fourth of your time planning what you will write.
4. Leave time to proofread your answers for clarity, legibility, spelling, and grammar.
5. When writing an answer, leave margins and do not write on the back of the paper. If your writing is large, write on every other line. Leaving some extra space makes the exam easier for the teacher to mark.
6. If you do not have time to write an answer, write your outline for the answer. Often, teachers will give you a substantial amount of credit if they can see that you knew the information and simply did not have time to write the answer.

Do It! Rewrite or adapt the strategies for taking essay tests as an illustrated handout for younger students who are expected to write one or two complete paragraphs in response to a question. Which key words would you teach younger students to help them answer appropriately?

Adaptations in Test Construction

All students benefit from tests that are written clearly and assess pertinent knowledge or skills. Thus, everything that you have learned about writing good tests in your teacher education program applies here. Still, test items can be well written but constructed in a way that results in problems for exceptional students. For example, Carmen has difficulty reading tests that are visually cluttered. She might benefit from triple spacing between test items and extra space between lines. Juan scores poorly on tests because he is unable to read many of the words used in the items; the items contain complex sentences with many words that are above his reading level and that his teacher did not use while teaching.

In essay-test construction, several adaptations might benefit students with problems in reading and written expression. For students with reading problems, highlight key words such as *analyze*, *compare/contrast*, *describe*, and *list*. You can also give students a form to complete to help them organize their responses. For example, this question was used on a science test:

Connections: What adaptations might you make for Stan, whom you met at the beginning of this chapter, before he takes tests? What adaptations in test construction might you also use?

```
▼▼▼▼▼▼▼▼▼▼▼▼▼▼▼▼▼▼▼▼▼▼▼▼▼▼▼▼▼
```

Professional Edge

Teaching Strategies for Taking Objective Tests

MANY students flounder when taking tests because they do not approach tests in any organized way. You can help your students approach their objective tests more systematically by teaching them the strategies described here. The following six rules for responding to multiple-choice and true-false items are based on a comprehensive review of the research literature.

1. **Respond to the test maker's intention.** Answers to test questions should take into account the way material is treated in class. For example, Rob had this item on his social studies test:

   > During the settlement of Saskatchewan, buffalo played a major role.
   >
   > True
   > False

   Although Rob had learned at the Royal Museum of Natural History that the buffalo were even more significant to the lives of the First Nations people who had lived in Saskatchewan before the settlers, his teacher had not brought up this point in class. Therefore, Rob responded by circling "True."

2. **Anticipate the answer.** Before students attempt to answer the question, they should fully understand its meaning. Therefore, they should try to determine the answer before they read the possible answers. For example, Armand was answering the following multiple-choice item:

   > What does an astronomer study?
   >
   > a. plants
   > b. music
   > c. history
   > d. stars

   After he read the question, Armand thought about the word *astronomy* and what his teacher had talked about in class, such as the fact that astronomers use telescopes and that they look at stars and planets. He then read all the possible choices and circled "d. stars" as the correct answer.

3. **Consider all alternatives.** Many exceptional students, such as students with learning disabilities, tend to answer too quickly, choosing the first available choice. Students should be encouraged to read all the choices before responding. Students can monitor their

---

Compare and contrast plant and animal cells by describing three ways they are alike and three ways they are different.

Do It! Construct a test for a lesson you might teach containing objective items and essay or short-answer questions. Then create a modified version of this test for your exceptional students.

The following **response format** might aid students in writing an answer:

Ways that plant and animal cells are alike

1. _____

2. _____

3. _____

Ways that plant and animal cells are different

1. _____

behaviour by putting a checkmark next to each choice after they have read it.

4. **Use logical reasoning strategies to eliminate unlikely answers.** Even if students do not know the answer to a question, they can improve their chances of getting it right by using what knowledge they do have to eliminate unlikely choices. For example, Dolores read the following item:

> In which province would you expect to find the oldest buildings?
>
> a. Quebec
>
> b. Manitoba
>
> c. Saskatchewan
>
> d. Ontario

Dolores did not know the answer to the question at first, but she did know that Manitoba and Saskatchewan joined Confederation later than Ontario and Quebec. Thus, she eliminated the two western provinces. Because the European settlers crossed the Atlantic, she reasoned that they would have reached Quebec and put up buildings sooner than they reached Ontario. So she chose Quebec by a process of elimination. Quebec was the correct answer.

5. **Use time wisely.** As already mentioned, a frequent test-taking problem is failing to budget time. Some students spend so much time on some items that they have little time left for others. While taking tests, students should check the time periodically to ensure that they have enough time left to answer the remaining questions. You can assist students by writing the time remaining on the chalkboard several times during the testing period. Students can also be taught to estimate the amount of time they should spend on each question. For example, if students are taking a 100-item test in a 50-minute period, they plan to spend no more than 30 seconds per question. After 25 minutes, they can then check to see that they have completed at least 50 items. Finally, teach students to spend more time on items on which they have at least partial knowledge and less time on questions for which they have no knowledge.

6. **Guess if all else fails.** Most tests do not have a penalty for guessing. On standardized tests especially, tell your students that if they do not answer a question, they have no chance of getting it right, but if they guess they have a 50 percent chance of getting true-false questions right and a 25 percent chance of getting most multiple-choice questions right.

Source: From "Are Learning Disabled Students 'Test-Wise'? A Review of Recent Research" by T. Scruggs and M. Mastropieri, 1988, *Learning Disabilities Focus*, 3(2), 87–97.

2. _____

3. _____

Other practical ways of constructing both objective and essay tests that will allow you to measure student knowledge more accurately are shown in the Professional Edge on pages 354–355. Note that if changes in test construction are intended for the whole class, they can be incorporated into the original master before photocopying. When changes are intended only for one or two students, you can make them as students take the test. For example, Ms. Minter's co-teacher, Ms. James, crossed out two of the four choices on Barry's multiple-choice items and changed a matching question from having 12 items to three groups of four items each. For another student, she underlined key words in each question and changed several completion questions into true-false items.

FYI: Another consideration in constructing tests is to arrange test items in chronological order to match the sequence of instruction.

TABLE 11.2

Key Words in
Essay Questions

Key Word	Definition
Compare	Show similarities between things.
Contrast	Show differences between things.
Criticize	Give the positive and negative points of a subject as well as evidence for these positions.
Define	Give the formal meaning of a term.
Describe	Tell in detail about something.
Diagram	Give a drawing and label it.
Discuss	Give details and, if relevant, the positive and negative points of a subject as well as evidence for these positions.
Enumerate	List points and number them 1, 2, 3. . . .
Evaluate	Give the positive and negative points of a subject as well as your judgment about which outweighs the other and why.
Illustrate	Explain by giving examples.
Interpret	Explain the meaning of something.
Justify	Give reasons for something.
List	Give a series of points and number them 1, 2, 3. . . .

Outline	Give the main points and important secondary points. Put main points at the margin and indent secondary points under the main points. Relationships may also be described with logical symbols, as follows:
	
	1. _____
	   a. _____
	   b. _____
	2. _____

Prove	Show to be true by giving facts or reasons.
Relate	Show connections among things.
State	Give the main points.
Summarize	Give a condensed account of the main points.
Trace	Describe the development or history of a subject.

Source: From *Reading and Study Skills* (2nd ed.) by J. Langan, 1982, p. 193, New York: McGraw-Hill.

Adaptations Involving Test Administration

The ways that tests are given to exceptional students can also affect the accuracy of the results. Students who, like Stan, have reading-comprehension problems might do better on tests if given more time to finish them or if permitted to take them orally. Students with written expression problems might benefit from a dictionary or a handheld spell checker, or by dictating their answers. Seating students with attention problems near you when they take a test might help them stay on task longer. The test administration adaptations shown in the Professional Edge on pages 356–357 are grouped according to students' areas of difficulty.

As the Professional Edge shows, students might also benefit from the use of an alternative **test site** such as a resource room. For example, testing in the resource room might help students with attention problems (by allowing them to take their tests in a setting with fewer distractions) and students with written language problems (by permitting them to answer test questions orally). Changing the test site also protects students who are taking the test in a different way from being embarrassed. However, before sending a student out of class to take a test, you should first try other options. For example, Ms. Edwards lets her students choose whether to have a test read to them. She allows those who do not want the test read aloud to work independently while she reads the test to the rest of the students. She also gives the students to whom she reads the test more help with directions and the meaning of key vocabulary or difficult questions. Mr. Collins and Ms. Klein are co-teaching. Mr. Collins supervises the students taking the test silently while Ms. Klein reads the test to a group of students. If you do find it necessary to send a student out to take a test, be sure to coordinate your plans in advance with the resource teacher to avoid scheduling problems.

> **Connections:** Issues of fairness and other topics concerning student relations are discussed in more detail in Chapter 13.

Alternative Test-Marking Procedures

You may also need to adapt the ways you mark student tests. For example, Matt has a learning disability. Because of his disability, he has trouble remembering large amounts of information for tests. This memory problem has affected Matt's test scores, which so far include two F's and one D. Matt's teacher, in collaboration with the resource teacher and Matt's parents, identifies the most important information in the chapter and asks Matt to study that for the test. When Matt takes the test, he answers only the 15 questions that his teacher asterisked, which test the key information he was told to study. The rest of the class answers 30 questions, the 15 that Matt answers plus 15 more covering other material contained in the chapter. Out of his 15 questions, Matt gets 13 correct. In deciding how to grade Matt, the teacher considers three grading options: changing student grades, changing the grading criteria, and using alternatives to traditional letters and numbers.

> **Connections:** The IEP team (see Chapter 2) provides guidelines for making test adaptations.

You can change student grades with written comments or symbols, or by giving multiple grades. These options can help clarify what a grade means. In Matt's case, his teacher could give him a B on the test, but with an asterisk meaning that the test was on a different amount of content than that of the rest of the class. Giving multiple grades can be helpful on tests that require written responses. For example, on an English test, Jacinto is required to write an essay on the character of Morag in the novel *The Diviners*. When his teacher marks his essay, she assigns him one grade based on the quality of his analysis of Morag and another grade for writing mechanics.

A second option is to change the **grading criteria,** or the standard upon which the grade is based. For example, Matt's teacher could give him a grade of

▼▼▼▼▼▼▼▼▼▼▼▼▼▼▼▼▼▼▼▼▼▼▼▼▼▼▼

Professional Edge

Modifications in Test Construction for Students with Disabilities

ALL your students will do better on clearly written tests that ask questions that pertain specifically to the material covered in class and in the textbook. But your exceptional students especially require well-phrased and visually accessible tests if they are to succeed at test taking. The following modifications, although beneficial to all your students, can be crucial for exceptional students.

1. Tests should be typewritten and photocopied.

2. Make tests visually uncluttered by leaving sufficient space between items (triple space) and between lines of items (1.5 spaces). Do not crowd pages with items; keep wide margins.

3. Use symmetrical spacing. For multiple-choice tests, align possible responses vertically rather than horizontally, and type the question and possible responses on the same page. Permit students to circle the letter of the correct answer rather than write it in front of the item.

4. Provide additional spacing between different types of test questions. Provide separate

directions and a sample item for each type of test question.

5. For completion, short-answer, and essay questions, leave sufficient space to write the answer. Students do not do as well when they must carry over their answers to the back of the page or onto the next page.

6. Leave space for students to answer on the test rather than using machine scoring or answer sheets. Some students have difficulty transferring answers from one page to another.

7. For students who have difficulty with multiple-choice questions, reduce the number of possible answers. Students might choose the correct answer from three, for example, rather than from four or five possible responses.

8. For students who read slowly and for students who have organizational problems, avoid the following constructions in matching items: long matching lists—keep lists to five or six items and group by concepts; lengthy items; and having students draw lines to the correct

B by basing his grade on a different standard: 15 questions rather than 30. You may also want to base a student's "percentage correct" on items tried instead of on the total number of questions. This alteration may help students who do accurate work but work slowly. Giving partial credit is another possible option. For example, when Ms. Jordan marks student answers to math story problems, she gives students points for underlining key words in the question and setting up the equation correctly. These extra points can motivate students who are improving but do not increase their test scores significantly. Students can also be allowed to retake tests. They can then be marked by using their score on the retake or averaging their original score with their retake score.

answer, which can be confusing for students with visual-motor problems (Wood, Miederhoff, & Ulschmid, 1989). Lists with 10 to 15 entries in the first column can be simplified by pre-selecting three to four choices from the second column for each item in the first column. Record the selected choices beside the item in the first column and ask the student to select the correct answer from the smaller pool. Consider this example:

Match the definition on the left with the word on the right by writing the letter for the word in the blank next to the definition.

1. in a sudden way __	a. brightness
2. not able __	b. visitor
3. to make bright __	c. suddenly
4. one who visits __	d. happiness
5. in a happy way __	e. rearrange
6. to tell again __	f. brighten
7. to arrange beforehand __	g. retell
8. state of being happy __	h. prearrange
9. to arrange again __	i. unable
10. state of being bright __	j. happily

These questions will be less confusing for exceptional students if you modify them using the guidelines just described:

1. in a sudden way __	a. brightness
	b. visitor
	c. suddenly
	d. retell
2. to make bright __	a. happily
	b. unable
	c. brighten

9. Change fill-in-the-blank items to a multiple-choice format, providing three or four choices for the blank. Students select the correct answer only from the choices given. This modification changes the task from one of recall (memory) to one of recognition.

10. For essay questions, review the questions, key words, and tasks with students individually and help students develop answer outlines. Permit dictated or taped responses when appropriate.

11. Consider colour coding, underlining, enlarging, or highlighting key words and mathematical symbols.

Source: Adapted from: *Accommodations for Secondary Learning Disabled/Mainstreamed Students on Teacher-Made Tests* by J. N. Williams, 1986, Wheaton, MD: Wheaton High School.

A third grading option you may want to try is using alternatives to letter and number grades, such as pass-fail grades and checklists of skill competencies. For example, Matt could be given a grade of P (Pass), because he has mastered 7 of 10 key concepts in the chapter, or rated on a **competency checklist** showing which key concepts in the chapter he had learned.

What do regular classroom teachers think of the testing adaptations described in this chapter? In a recent study, a sample of over 300 regular classroom teachers in the United States were asked if they found certain adaptations helpful and easy to use. The results of this survey are shown in Table 11.3.

✓ **Your Learning:** What are some specific adaptations you can make in test preparation, construction, administration, and grading that will help exceptional students do better on tests in your class?

Professional Edge

Adaptations in Administering Classroom Tests

EVEN a well-constructed test will fail to measure the knowledge of exceptional students accurately if it is inappropriately administered. The adaptations you will make in administering tests to your exceptional students will depend on the students' area of difficulty. Use the following chart to help you decide which modifications to try with exceptional students included in your class.

| | *Area of Difficulty* | | | | |
Adaptation	Reading	Writing	Listening	Speaking	Organizing; Paying Attention
Oral explanations of directions	X				X
Repetition of directions; student repetition of directions	X		X		X
Oral, taped, or dictated test; oral clarification of written answers by student	X	X			X
Written versus oral test; written versus oral directions			X	X	
Extra time	X	X		X	
Time checks during test					X
Segmented test with separate directions for each section	X		X		X
Peer or other assistance:					
to read directions	X				
to check comprehension	X				
to check spelling		X			

◢ How Can Report Card Grades Be Adapted for Exceptional Students?

Report card grading is perhaps the most prevalent and controversial evaluation option used in schools. The practice of grading by letters and percentages began in the early twentieth century (Cohen, 1983), a time of great faith in the ability of educational measures to assess students' current levels of learning accurately and also predict future levels of learning. High grades were viewed as a sign of accomplishment, intended to spur students on to greater achievements. Those who received low grades were encouraged to join the workforce.

Adaptation	Area of Difficulty				
	Reading	Writing	Listening	Speaking	Organizing; Paying Attention
Technological aids:					
placemarks or markers	X				X
word processor		X			
tape recorder	X	X		X	
Visual aids and cues; verbal and visual prompts for word retrieval			X	X	
Use of outlines, diagrams, charts, tables, and webs to organize or answer	X	X			X
Permitted use of non-cursive writing		X			
Use of previously prepared notes or rehearsed answers				X	
Alternative sites:					
to minimize noise/distraction			X		X
for alternative testing	X	X			
Seating proximity to teacher			X		
Teacher paraphrase or summary of student answers in complete thoughts				X	
Checklist for materials needed and preparation					X
Allowing answering directly on test rather than answer sheet		X			

Source: Adapted from Accommodations for Secondary Learning Disabled/Mainstreamed Students on Teacher-Made Tests by J. N. Williams, 1986. Unpublished manuscript. Wheaton, MD: Wheaton High School.

Times certainly have changed. Laws have been passed guaranteeing appropriate education for all students, not just those who can succeed with minimal intervention. Further, our ability to compete in the emerging global economy will depend on better educational outcomes for *all* our citizens, not just a privileged few. These changes have led to new demands that go beyond the relatively simple matter of identifying "good" and "poor" students. For example, how can evaluations be modified to assure that they do not discriminate against students with disabilities? How can they be used to motivate students to stay in school, communicate educational competence and progress to parents and students, and guide our teaching as we move to meet the needs of an increasingly diverse student body? Although answers to these questions are beginning to emerge, in large

▸ TABLE 11.3

Testing Adaptations Regular Classroom Teachers Find Helpful and Easy to Use

Adaptation	Description
Test preparation	Give extra help preparing for tests.
	Teach students test-taking skills.
	Give practice questions or the actual test as a study guide.
Test construction	Provide extra space on test for answering.
	Test on a lesser amount of content.
	Simplify wording of test questions.
	Change the type of test item used.
	Highlight key words in questions.
	Use typewritten photocopied tests.
	Use tests with enlarged print.
Test administration	Read test questions to students.
	Give frequent quizzes rather than exams only.
	Give open-book or open-notes tests.
	Give extended time to finish tests.
	Allow use of technological learning aids during test.
	Give individual help with directions during test.
	Allow students to answer fewer questions.
	Give feedback to individual students during test.

Source: From Testing Adaptations: A National Survey of the Testing Practices of General Education Teachers by M. Jayanthi, M. Epstein, M. Polloway, & W. D. Bursuck, in press.

Cultural Awareness: What do grades mean in Canada? How are grades used and to what ends? How do values about grades in the Canadian culture affect exceptional students?

part we continue to use a grading system that was intended to fulfil a purpose much more narrow in scope.

The use of traditional letter and number grades has caused problems for teachers, who must communicate with many audiences, including parents, students, administrators, and legislators. These audiences are often looking for information that is not readily communicated using a single number or letter (Carpenter, Grantham, & Hardister, 1983). For example, students may be interested in how much progress they have made, whereas their parents want to know how their children compare to their classmates as well as to children nationwide. Schools, on the other hand, may need to provide university admissions offices with indicators of student potential to do university work. Teachers also are increasingly left with conflicting concerns about grading, including upholding the school's standards, maintaining integrity with other teachers, being honest with students, justifying grades with other students, motivating students for better future performance, communicating accurately to the students' next teacher, and avoiding the reputation of being an "easy" teacher (Rojewski, Pollard, & Meers, 1990, 1992; Vasa, 1981).

Cultural Awareness: In what ways might grading systems be unfair? Which student groups would be affected the most? What provisions do school districts make for evaluating students who are culturally different or whose first language is not English?

Do It! Develop grading criteria for the test you constructed in the previous section. How might you modify your grading criteria for the exceptional students in your class?

Increased inclusion in schools has put even more burdens on grading systems. As shown in the vignettes at the beginning of the chapter, grading can present serious challenges for exceptional students and their teachers. For example, Stan was not a good test taker, yet 80 percent of his report card grade in science was based on his test performance. He was concerned that his grade did not accurately reflect his effort or progress in class.

In spite of their many limitations, grades are likely to be used by teachers and schools for many years to come for the reasons discussed above. Teachers need to recognize the limitations of certain types of grades, however, and adapt grading systems to ensure they are fair to all students. As summarized in Table 11.4, grades can be adapted by changing grading criteria, making changes to letter and number grades, and using alternatives to number and letter grades.

▶ TABLE 11.4   Examples of Grading Adaptations

Change Grading Criteria	Change to Letter and Number Grades	Use Alternatives to Letter and Number Grades
Vary grading weights.	Add written comments.	Use pass-fail grades.
Change to letter and number grades.	Add student activity logs.	Use competency checklists.
Modify curricular expectations.	Add information from portfolios and/or performance-based assessments.	
Grade on the basis of improvement.		
Use contracts and modified course syllabi.		

Changes in Grading Criteria

One way to adapt report card grades is to change the criteria on which they are based. Teachers often consider a number of factors when assigning student marks, including in-class work or seatwork, homework, ability, attendance, class participation, effort, attitude, reports or papers, extracurricular work, preparedness, organization, notebooks, and progress (Bursuck et al., 1994; Wilson, 1996). One common adaptation is to vary the grading weights of criteria in terms of how much each one counts toward the final grade. In the case of Stan, for example, his teacher counted tests as 80 percent of the grade and homework as 20 percent. Mr. Stevens could help Stan by reducing the amount tests count from 80 percent to 60 percent and giving Stan more credit for other things he does well, such as being prepared, attempting all class activities, and participating in class. Grading students in areas such as effort should be based on the same objective standards that you use to measure the learning of academic content. In Stan's case, Mr. Stevens could define effort as the percentage of school days on which Stan has his materials for class, completes his homework, and asks at least one question in class.

Another way to adapt grading criteria is to base student performance on **modified curricular expectations.** Expectations such as these are reflected in IEP goals and objectives, behavioural contracts, or course syllabi. For example, in the vignette at the beginning of this chapter, Lucille's IEP stated that she had a modified curriculum in math. While the rest of the class was working on decimals, she was working on two-digit by two-digit addition problems with regrouping. Because her IEP objective was to score 80 percent or better when given 20 of these problems, her grade four teacher and resource teacher agreed to give her an A if she met her objective, a B if she scored between 70 and 80 percent, a C if she scored between 60 and 70 percent, and so forth. To ensure that Lucille's parents had an accurate overview of her standing in relation to her peers, Lucille's teacher included a written comment on Lucille's report card indicating that her grade was based on different curricular expectations.

Grading criteria can also be adapted through the use of **grading contracts** or **modified course syllabi.** Both of these adaptations help ensure that grading modifications are clearly defined, based on objective criteria, and explained to the student and his or her parents. A grading contract is an agreement between the classroom teacher and the student about the quality, quantity, and timelines required to obtain a specific grade (Hess, 1987). An example of a grading contract follows:

- If (student) comes to class regularly, turns in all the required work that is completed with _____ percent accuracy, and does one extra credit assignment/project, he or she will receive an A.
- If (student) comes to class regularly and turns in all the required work with _____ percent accuracy, he or she will receive a B.
- If (student) comes to class regularly and turns in all the required work, he or she will receive a C.
- If (student) comes to class regularly and turns in 80 percent of the required work, he or she will receive a D.
- If (student) does not come to class regularly and turns in less than 80 percent of the required work, he or she will receive an F. (Hess, 1987)

FYI: Changing grading criteria for an exceptional student often requires collaborating with the IEP team to make decisions about the student's IEP goals.

In a modified course syllabus, you and the in-school team or IEP team state the specific course requirements, expectations, grading criteria, and any other changes required because of the student's disability. Figure 11.3 shows an example of an adapted syllabus for an Introduction to Foods course in broad-based technologies (Hess, 1987).

Teachers can also base grades on the amount of improvement students make. **Improvement grades** can be incorporated into a traditional grading system by assigning extra points for improvement or by moving students up a grade on the scale if they improve, particularly if they are on the border between grades. A high C, for example, could be changed to a B if the student's test average or total points for the marking period were much higher than those of the previous marking period. Consider the case of Aretha, whose average on spelling tests for the last marking period is 77 percent, an improvement of over 40 percentage points over the preceding marking period. Although her true grade for spelling is a C, her teacher raises her grade to a B– because she has improved so much. Another student, Roberto, read five trade books this marking period as compared to one book the period before. Although most students in the class have read more books at more difficult levels, Roberto still receives a grade of O (outstanding) in reading because he read so many more books than before. His teacher will note on his report card that the books Roberto read were one to two years below grade level.

Connections: How might the strategy of grading on the basis of improvement help Stan and his parents, whom you met at the beginning of the chapter?

Changes to Letter and Number Grades

Number and letter grades can be clarified by supplementing them with other ways of evaluating and reporting student progress, such as written or verbal comments, logs of student activities, and portfolios. Written or verbal comments can be used to clarify areas such as student ability levels as compared to peers and the extent of student effort. For example, Roberto's teacher gave him an Outstanding in reading but commented on his report card that the books he read were below grade level. Such comments about student ability levels can prevent misunderstandings. In the case of Jennifer in the chapter opening vignette, Jennifer's mother thought her daughter's high grade in reading meant that she was reading at grade level. An explanation on Jennifer's report card would have put her grade in context. But keep in mind a word of caution as you make report card comments denoting student ability levels. Students sometimes compare report cards with their classmates and might be embarrassed by comments that indicate they are working below grade level. To prevent this situation, you might use an alternative procedure, such as talking to the parents or sending them a separate note of clarification. In addition, report-card comments typically should not state that the student is receiving special services; this could be a violation of student confidentiality. Finally, when a number or letter grade is given on a report card, the basis for arriving at that grade is often not clear. For example, does the grade represent student performance compared with his or her classmates, or is it based on the student's progress toward meeting objectives on his or her IEP? Failure to clarify the bases for grades can lead to communication problems with parents, as shown in the Case in Practice.

Cultural Awareness: Cultural expectations and standards strongly influence the way families interpret and react to their children's grades. Teachers cannot take for granted that all parents will respond appropriately to their children's grades. Communication is the key.

FIGURE 11.3

Adapted Course Requirements for Introduction to Foods Course in Broad-Based Technologies

1. Types of work to be completed by students:
   a. Read test and pamphlets
      - Recipes with abbreviations and equivalents
      - Tables
      - Menus
   b. Demonstrate ability to:
      - Measure ingredients
      - Use and care for large and small appliances
      - Follow kitchen safety rules
      - Practise good nutrition and weight control
      - Recognize four basic food groups
      - Write menus
      - Prepare meals
   c. Successfully complete written, oral, and performance competency tests

2. The quantity of work to be completed by student:
   a. Read Chapters 1–10, 12, and 16 of the text
   b. Participate in two group projects
   c. Prepare a meal for four people individually
   d. Take weekly quizzes, 10 unit tests, and one final examination

3. The grade for the course will be determined as follows:

Weekly quizzes—10 points each	= 180 points
Unit tests—25 points each	= 250 points
Group project—50 points	= 100 points
Meal preparation	= 300 points
	830 points

   747–830 points = A   498–580 points = D
   664–746 points = B   0–497 points = F
   581–663 points = C

4. The quality of work will be determined by the instructor based on objective test data and direct observation of the students.

5. Timelines for completion of work are:
   a. Complete assigned readings weekly.
   b. Complete group projects within two weeks after assignment.
   c. Complete individual meal preparation prior to end of semester.

This course was reviewed on _____

Signatures

Student _____

Special Education Teacher _____

Parent _____

Home Economics Teacher _____

Guidance Counsellor _____

Principal _____

Source: From Grading-Credit-Diploma: Accommodation Practices for Students with Mild Disabilities by R. Hess, 1987, Des Moines: Iowa State Department of Education.

Because report card grades are primarily summaries of student performance, they provide little information about student performance over a period of time. You can use **daily activity logs** of student activities and achievement to provide ongoing information for students and their parents. One system uses self-sticking notes to record daily observations of students (Einhorn, Hagen, Johnson, Wujek, & Hoffman, 1991). The notes include the date, student's name, classroom activity,

Do It! Grace, a student with developmental disabilities, is doing poorly despite your efforts to adapt evaluations for her, and she is discouraged. You know Grace is doing the best she can. Now it's report card time. What are you going to do?

Case in Practice
Explaining Grades

OMAR is a student in Ms. Wittrup's grade four class. When Ms. Murji, Omar's mother, received Omar's most recent report card, she had some questions and made an appointment to see Ms. Wittrup and Ms. Talbot, Omar's special education teacher.

MS. WITTRUP: Ms. Murji and Omar, I'm so glad you came in today. Ms. Murji, I understand you have some questions about Omar's report card.

MS. MURJI: Thank you for taking the time to see me. Yes, I do have some questions about Omar's report card. First of all, I noticed that Omar got a B in reading. This is an area where he's getting help in special education. Does this mean he doesn't need any more help?

MS. TALBOT: Omar's IEP objective for the first grading period was to read fluently and comprehend literature books that are at the grade two reading level. His word-identification skills in that material are good, but he is still having some trouble with comprehension. Sometimes he has trouble summarizing what he has just read; other times he has a hard time answering questions that I ask him. That is why he received a B rather than an A. I think Omar has a good chance of meeting this objective by the end of this marking period. Still, he is pretty far behind his grade four classmates, so I think he needs to keep getting help from me.

MS. MURJI: I think I understand better what his reading grade means, but I don't understand how Omar got only a C in math. He has always done better in math than in reading. Has he been fooling around in class and not paying attention?

MS. WITTRUP: No, Omar has been working hard in math. Omar doesn't have any special needs in math so he is in the regular program. As you can see from looking at my grade book, Omar scored an average of 75 percent on his math tests. His average for homework and in-class work was 80 percent. His overall average for the marking period was 78 percent, which is a C.

MS. MURJI: Is there something I can do to help Omar with his math so that maybe he can get a B next time?

MS. WITTRUP: One thing that hurts Omar on his tests is that he is still making careless mistakes on his math facts, particularly the multiplication facts. If you could help him with these at home, I think Omar might be able to pull his grade up to a B.

MS. TALBOT: We're very proud of Omar for getting an A in social studies. Remember we had all agreed that because Omar had reading problems we would let him use a taped text and take his tests orally. Well, Ms. Wittrup told me that Omar had an average of 95 percent on the two tests, which is an A. Good for Omar!

Reflections

Ms. Murji had a difficult time understanding what Omar's grades meant. What could Omar's teachers have done to prevent this confusion from occurring? Omar received a grade of A in social studies because he was allowed to use a taped textbook and to take the tests orally. How would you explain this adaptation to a concerned student who took the test without any of these supports and received only a C?

FIGURE 11.4

Notation System
for Ongoing
Evaluation

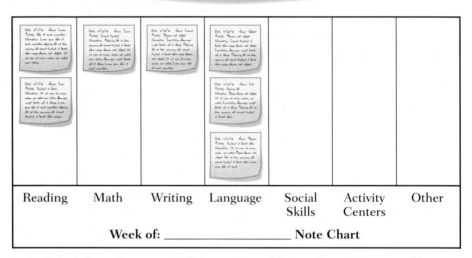

Date: 4/1/97   Name: Annie Hoffman
Activity: Reading story to peer
Observation: While reading a new story to a
peer, Annie spontaneously used the initial letter
sound /r/ to sound out the word "rabbit."

Reading	Math	Writing	Language	Social Skills	Activity Centers	Other

Week of: _____ Note Chart

Source: From *Authentic Assessment: A Collaborative Approach* by R. Einhorn, C. Hagen, J. Johnson, C. Wujek, and L. Hoffman, 1991, p. 16, SMA Communication Development Project.

Do It! Interview experienced teachers about their values and practices in establishing student grades. Reflect and write on your own beliefs and values about evaluating student learning.

and a brief description of the observation. Figure 11.4 shows an example of a self-stick note from an observation of a classroom reading period and a chart on which notes can be collected and summarized periodically for evaluations. Information taken from the self-stick notes can be summarized periodically. These summaries can then be shared with parents as often as necessary to clarify student grades. For example, Leroy receives a D in math for the marking period. His parents call Leroy's teacher to set up a conference to discuss the grade and identify how Leroy can improve. Leroy's teacher shares a notes summary indicating that Leroy did not follow along while she was demonstrating solutions to math problems on the chalkboard. Leroy's teacher and parents set up a contract for Leroy that encourages him to pay attention to such demonstrations.

Alternatives to Letter and Number Grades

The most common alternatives to letter or number grades are pass/fail, credit/no credit grades, and checklists of competencies and skills. In **pass/fail** or **credit/no credit systems,** a list of minimum understandings or skills for a class is determined by the regular classroom teacher in consultation with the resource teacher. These minimums may or may not relate specifically to a student's IEP. A grade of Pass or Credit is assigned if the identified understandings and skills are successfully mastered. No letter grades are given.

The major advantage of this alternative is that it relieves the teacher of the responsibility of grading students based on peer comparisons. Grades based on peer comparisons can be discouraging for students who try hard but do not have the ability to compete on an equal basis. Another advantage of pass/fail and credit/no credit systems is that the student knows what is expected and works toward a goal. A disadvantage of pass/fail grades is that their "all or nothing" nature puts a lot of pressure on the teacher, particularly in situations where minimum standards are not well defined. It is important, therefore, to be as specific as possible in setting your minimum standards. Here is an example of pass/fail requirements developed for a history course that has the necessary specificity:

1. Be in attendance and on time for 90 percent of all class periods each semester.
2. Complete 75 percent of the daily work with at least 60 percent accuracy.
3. Complete a class project (with peer assistance if necessary), earning at least 60 percent of the available points.
4. Participate in class discussions at least once per week and attend all small-group project meetings held in class.
5. Score 60 percent or better on all weekly and semester tests. (Hess, 1987)

In using **competency checklists,** the regular classroom teacher lists the goals and objectives of a given course and then checks off the objectives as the student achieves or masters them (Hess, 1987). A key advantage of checklists is that they give more detailed information about student performance than grades, which makes them potentially more valuable to students, parents, and future employers. Checklists have several disadvantages, however. They may be time-consuming for teachers to keep up to date, the tasks and objectives may not be understood by teachers, and they tend to focus on student weaknesses unless care is taken to state objectives in positive terms.

Cultural Awareness: Effective evaluation involves collaboration among students, parents, professionals, and administrators, and it seeks to empower students in the learning process by making them the centre of all evaluation activities (Dean, Salend, & Taylor, 1994, p. 41).

✔ **Your Learning:** What are the three options for adapting report-card grades for exceptional students? What are some specific strategies for each option? What are the advantages and disadvantages of each strategy?

How Can Performance-Based Assessment Benefit Exceptional Students?

Ms. Johnson has just completed a unit on persuasive writing and ask her students to write letters to the editor of a local newspaper, trying to persuade readers to support the building of a new county facility for elderly people. Mr. Radic has been teaching drawing to scale as part of a map-reading unit and asks his students to make a map of the neighbourhood that could be used by visitors from Japan.

All of these teachers are checking their students' progress by using a method of evaluation called performance-based assessment. **Performance-based assessment** measures what students "can do with knowledge, rather than with the isolated specific bits of knowledge the student possesses" (Poteet, Choate, & Stewart, 1993, p. 5). Performance-based assessments measure learning processes

Do It! Review the test you constructed and modified earlier in this chapter. Does it include items you could test using authentic tasks? How might you use performance-based assessment instead?

rather than focusing only on learning products. They frequently involve using **authentic learning tasks,** or tasks that are presented within real-world contexts and lead to real-world outcomes. Mr. Radic could have asked his students to compute the number of kilometres between several cities using a kilometrage key, a more traditional map-reading assignment. Instead, he asks them to create their own maps, within a real context, because he wants to see how well they can apply what they have learned to an actual problem. Not only does he evaluate their maps, but he also evaluates parts of the learning process, such as how well his students select and implement learning strategies and collaborate with their classmates during problem solving.

Using performance-based assessments can be very helpful for students with disabilities or other exceptionalities who may be included in your classroom. Performance-based assessments can offer students options for demonstrating their knowledge that do not rely exclusively on reading and writing, areas that often impede the successful testing performance of students with disabilities. For example, Calvin, a student with reading problems in Mr. Radic's class, completed the map activity successfully but would have had trouble with a traditional paper-and-pencil test of the same material. Performance-based tests are also not subject to the same time constraints as traditional tests. Time flexibility can benefit students who may need more time, such as students with reading fluency problems, or students who need to work for shorter time periods, such as students with ADHD. Again, using the example of Mr. Radic's map-drawing activity, students had some time limits (they had to finish in one week) but did not have to do the entire project in one sitting. Students with disabilities may also have particular difficulty making the connection between school tasks and tasks in the real world. Performance-based assessments can help them understand this connection, particularly if the assessment is followed up with instruction directly geared to skill applications. For example, Ms. Johnson, whose students were required to write letters to the editor, discovered that many of her students were unable to support their arguments directly with specific examples. She therefore spent some class time demonstrating to students how they could support their arguments and guiding them through several practice activities.

Developing and Evaluating Tasks for Performance-Based Assessment

FYI: In *Pathways*, a career development program for inclusive classrooms, performance-based assessments include employment interviews, job applications, and self-assessments of match to job descriptions.

Performance-based assessments, such as standardized tests and curriculum-based assessments, must be carefully designed and scored so that they can provide information that is helpful for instruction and that is viewed with credibility by parents, students, and administrators. A summary of a number of considerations in designing, administering, and scoring performance-based assessments (Wiggins, 1992) follows:

1. **Choose learning outcomes that are not covered by your current classroom and standardized testing program.** Traditional standardized and classroom tests are likely to assess student knowledge but to underassess the application of that knowledge. Therefore, choose **learning outcomes** for your performance-based tests that stress how well students apply, analyze,

or synthesize information. In choosing your learning outcomes, try to think of the knowledge you teach as a tool for helping your students perform an important real-world function. For example, reading comprehension can be viewed as a tool for reading an auto mechanics manual. Learning the steps in the scientific method can be viewed as a tool for designing science experiments to test your own hypothesis. Identifying and using coins can be seen as a tool for making change at a supermarket checkout.

2. **Design tasks within contexts that are meaningful for students.** The tasks you choose should provoke student thought and interest. Wiggins (1992) suggests that a well-designed task will engage students so much that they will forget they are being evaluated. Tasks can be made more engaging by embedding them within a meaningful, motivating context. In addition, well-designed tasks are worth doing for the learning they engender (Hutchinson, 1994, 1996).

3. **Clarify task expectations by giving students scoring standards and models of excellent performance during teaching.** Although developing a specific solution to a performance-based task is always the student's responsibility, the goal of the task, as well as the standards on which it is based, should be clearly presented by the teacher. For example, in Mr. Barnes's class, the students were responsible for creating an experiment to see which station played the most music by female artists. However, the students were already familiar with characteristics of effective research design, because Mr. Barnes discussed these in class and showed the students model research projects completed by previous students.

4. **Make testing conditions as authentic as possible.** Standardized and traditional classroom tests require many constraints, such as time limits and limited access to references. In real life we have deadlines, but these deadlines rarely involve brief artificial periods of time, such as having to perform within 45-minute periods. Instead, timelines for performance-based tests should be based on performance of similar tasks in the real world. For example, individuals training to be auto mechanics will need to perform tasks based on time limits established by professional mechanics. Access to resources during performance-based tests is also generally not prohibited; in fact, it is encouraged. Imagine denying a lawyer access to case law books while he or she is constructing a defence for an upcoming case! Of course, students must be skilful enough to be able to absorb and apply these resource materials in a timely fashion.

5. **Identify standards based on what is most important for doing an effective job.** You must take great care in selecting the standards for judging performance-based assessments; a scoring system based on qualities that are widely agreed upon can assure that the results of your performance-based assessments will be useful. Identify key areas of performance by consulting the research literature, colleagues, students, administrators, and parents. These areas can involve both the products of performance-based tests and the processes that students perform in constructing these products. For example, effective performance in math problem solving might include understanding the problem, solving the problem, and answering the problem (Hutchinson, 1993; Szetela & Nicol, 1992).

FYI: Authentic learning tasks motivate students to perform their best. Student motivation is a critical ingredient for an accurate evaluation.

Connections: In Chapter 10, there were descriptions of strategies for solving math word problems that emphasize process and product.

Connections: Review Chapters 8 and 9 for information on testing and teaching pre-skills.

of money, some of which involve grocery-store products. This adaptation helps Cleo make the connection between money and the supermarket.

Exceptional students also lack important pre-skills that are necessary for problem solving. You need either to teach them these pre-skills or to allow them to bypass the pre-skills altogether in order to carry out your performance-based tasks. For example, Sam has a learning disability in math; he does not know his math facts and as a result cannot get Ms. Riley's product comparisons correct. Ms. Riley allows him to perform the task with a calculator. She also requires that he spend five minutes per day using a computer-based math fact program until he learns his basic facts. Anna has visual disabilities; she asks another student to read her the prices of the brands and she writes them down.

For students with more severe disabilities, you may need to modify or scale down performance-based tasks by using the curriculum adaptation process described in Chapter 9. For example, Derek has severe developmental disabilities and lacks basic math skills other than simple number identification. Ms. Riley asks Derek to participate in the same task as the other students but asks him to perform an easier step. She has Derek choose groups of products that students are to compare. This task is more consistent with Derek's IEP goal of being able to classify "like" objects, such as three kinds of pop or two types of bread.

Finally, exceptional students may have trouble meeting the problem-solving demands of performance-based tests. For example, Peter has attention deficits and approaches problems impulsively; he rushes to find an answer and fails to consider all the options. For Peter, performance-based tests are important because they give him the opportunity to learn critical problem-solving skills. Nonetheless, for stu-

Connections: Scaffolding (see Chapter 7) and learning strategies instruction (see Chapter 10) are good ways to support students as they learn to carry out performance-based tasks.

▶ *As an alternative to pencil-and-paper tests, performance-based assessments allow students to demonstrate their knowledge and skills through application in real-world contexts. What are some ways to adapt performance-based assessments for exceptional students?*

dents such as Peter to succeed, performance-based tasks need to be modified and problem-solving skills need to be taught directly. For example, Mr. Kelsey's class is applying work they have done in computing areas and perimeters to the task of planning a garden. Before asking students to design their own gardens, Mr. Kelsey carefully demonstrates how he would design his. This demonstration is very helpful for students in the class, such as Peter, who are not natural problem solvers and need a model to guide them. Mr. Kelsey also scales down Peter's assignment, asking him to design only one section of a smaller garden.

As you can see, the use of performance-based tests with exceptional students can be helpful, but it can also be problematic. For this reason, use performance-based tests in conjunction with other classroom-based and standardized tests.

How Can Portfolio Assessment Benefit Exceptional Students?

Another promising type of evaluation currently in use is **portfolio assessment.** A portfolio is "a purposeful collection of student work that exhibits the student's efforts, progress, and achievement in one or more areas. The collection must include student participation in selecting contents, the criteria for selection, the criteria for judging merit, and evidence of student self-reflection" (Paulson, Paulson, & Meyer, 1991, p. 60).

A portfolio collection typically contains the observable evidence or products of performance assessment, evidence that may or may not reflect authentic tasks (Poteet et al., 1993). Portfolios include many different sources of information, including anecdotal records, interviews, work samples, and scored samples such as curriculum-based assessment probes. As an example, sources of information for language arts that can be placed into a portfolio are shown in Table 11.5.

Cultural Awareness: Student-centred evaluation, a key component of portfolio assessment, is an important part of effective multicultural education. Student-centred evaluation strategies include self-evaluation questionnaires, interviews, student entries in journals and learning logs, and think-alouds (Dean et al., 1994, p. 41).

Emphasizing Progress

Portfolios can be very helpful for teachers working with students with disabilities. Portfolios can assist teachers in evaluating student progress and guiding instruction. For example, Ms. Pohl is interested in finding out whether the extra math practice sheets she is sending home with Robert are improving his scores on weekly math computation tests. She consults Robert's portfolio and finds that his performance has improved significantly over the past two months. Ms. Pohl tells Robert's parents of his progress. They agree to continue the extra practice for at least another month.

Portfolios also emphasize student products rather than tests and test scores. This emphasis benefits exceptional students, many of whom are poor test takers. It may also highlight student strengths better than traditional tests, which tend to have a narrow academic focus. For example, Leshonn's teacher uses portfolios to evaluate her social studies students. Leshonn has problems in reading and writing but has good artistic ability and excellent oral language skills. During the last marking period, his class studied the growth of suburban areas after World War II. Leshonn designed a scale model of one of the first planned communities.

FYI: Student activities should always demonstrate achievement or mastery of instructional objectives. Teachers should avoid choosing activities that are too fragmented, narrow, or shallow.

3. The portfolio is separate and different from the student's cumulative folder. Scores and other cumulative folder information that are held in central depositories should be included in a portfolio only if they take on new meaning within the context of the other exhibits found there.

4. The portfolio must convey explicitly or implicitly the student's activities; for example, the rationale (purpose for forming the portfolio), intents (its goals), contents (the actual displays), standards (what is good and not-so-good performance), and judgments (what the contents reveal).

5. The portfolio may serve a different purpose during the year from the purpose it serves at the end of the year. Some material may be kept because it is instructional, such as partially finished work on problem areas. At the end of the year, however, the portfolio may contain only material that the student is willing to make public.

6. A portfolio may have multiple purposes, but these must not conflict. A student's personal goals and interests are reflected in his or her selection of materials, but information included may also reflect the interests of teachers, parents, or the district. One almost universal purpose of student portfolios is to show progress on the goals represented in the instructional program.

7. The portfolio should contain information that illustrates growth. There are many ways to demonstrate growth. The most obvious is by including a series of examples of actual school performance or other real-world performance-based activities that show how the student's skills have improved. Changes observed on interest inventories, on records of outside activities such as reading, or on attitude measures are other ways to illustrate a student's growth.

8. Finally, many of the skills and techniques that are involved in producing effective portfolios do not just happen by themselves. By way of support, students need models of portfolios as well as examples of how others develop and reflect upon portfolios. (Paulson et al., 1991, pp. 61–62)

Do It! Develop a list of possible portfolio contents for a unit you plan to teach. How might you modify your list for exceptional students?

You may have to make adaptations when using portfolios with exceptional students, particularly in selecting and evaluating portfolio pieces. For example, Jerome was asked to select an example of his "best" work in written expression for his portfolio. However, he was uncertain what "best" work meant: Was it a paper that he tried his hardest on? Was it a paper that was the hardest to write? Or was it one that he or his teacher liked best? Because he did not know, Jerome simply selected one paper at random. Similarly, when LaShonda was asked to evaluate her efforts to solve a word problem in math, all she could come up with was whether she had the correct answer. You need to teach students such as Jerome and LaShonda how to select and evaluate portfolio pieces through the use of models, demonstrations, and guided practice.

Connections: Portfolios and performance-based tests can also be helpful in making the assessment decisions described in Chapter 8. However, portfolios should supplement, not supplant, standardized achievement, psychological, and curriculum-based measures.

Finally, although portfolios are a valuable assessment tool, they are also a relatively new tool; clear guidelines for selecting and scoring portfolio contents are still emerging (Salvia & Ysseldyke, 1995). Therefore, if you are using portfolios to evaluate the progress of exceptional students, such as whether they are meeting their IEP objectives, use them as a supplement, to other assessment procedures such as testing, grading, and curriculum-based assessments.

Summary

As a teacher, you have a number of tools at your disposal for assessing your students' progress, including tests, performance-based assessments, and portfolios. Although each of these assessment methods can also help you measure the progress of exceptional students included in your class, they may need to be adapted to ensure that the evaluation information demonstrates the students' skill levels or content knowledge, not their disabilities or other special needs.

Testing adaptations can be made before testing, during testing, and after testing, when tests are graded. Adaptations before the test include study guides, practice tests, tutoring, teaching test-taking skills and strategies, and modifying test construction. During the test, you can allow alternative forms of response, alternative means of response, alternative testing sites, extra time, and direct assistance. Adaptations after the test involve grading tests and include changing letter or number grades, using alternatives to letter and number grades, and changing the criteria upon which grades are based.

Adaptations in report card grades involve changing the grading criteria, making changes to letter and number grades, and using alternatives to letter and number grades. Ways of changing grading criteria include varying grading weights, modifying curricular expectations, using grading contracts and modified course syllabi, and grading on the basis of improvement. Letter and number grades can be changed by supplementing them with other ways of evaluating and reporting student progress, such as written comments, daily activity logs, and recording daily observations. Alternatives to letter and number grades include pass/fail grades, credit/no credit systems, and competency checklists.

Performance-based assessments measure learning processes rather than focusing exclusively on learning products and they frequently involve authentic, or real-world, tasks. They can be helpful in evaluating the performance of exceptional students because they do not rely exclusively on formats that create problems for students with disabilities. These assessments are not subject to the same time constraints as traditional tests, which often pose a problem for exceptional students, and they also help students see the connection between school work and real-world tasks. Performance-based assessments can be developed, administered, and scored according to several guidelines, such as choosing learning outcomes not covered by your current testing programs, designing tasks within meaningful contexts, clarifying task expectations by providing scoring standards and models of excellence, making testing conditions authentic, and designing a scoring system based on what is most important for effective performance. Performance-based tests may need to be adapted for exceptional students by scaling down the task, allowing students to bypass pre-skills, and teaching problem solving directly using performance-based tasks.

Portfolio assessment can also benefit exceptional students. Portfolios are collections of student work that exhibit student efforts and achievements. Portfolios typically contain the observable evidence or products of performance assessment, such as anecdotal records, interviews, work samples, and scored samples. Necessary features of portfolios include student participation in collecting the

Academic Therapy Publications

www.atpub.com

Achievement Tests

www.psychtest.com/ ESLtest.htm

Test Specifications

www.schoolnet.ca/sne/ snenews/volume2/issue4/ section4.html#b

contents, criteria for judging merit, and evidence of student self-reflection. Portfolios can benefit exceptional students because they de-emphasize traditional tests and teach students critical self-evaluation skills. However, exceptional students may need to be taught how to select and evaluate their portfolio pieces.

Applications in Teaching Practice

Adapting Evaluations for Exceptional Students

 Eugene, Abdul, Tara, and Jamie are students in your classes. Eugene has been identified as having a specific learning disability. He has good study skills, but his problems in reading and written expression place him at a disadvantage when he takes tests. Failure on tests has increased his test anxiety; he often misses items he knows because when he is anxious during a test he tends to get careless. What tests will you be giving in this class? What adaptations might you need to make for Eugene before testing? in constructing the test? in administering the test? and in grading the test?

Abdul is a motivated student who gives 100 percent to everything he does. He has some reading and written language problems that make it hard for him to perform well on classroom tests. You have been weighting your grades in your class as follows:

Requirement	*Percentage of Grade*
Three quizzes (objective)	45
One exam (essay)	30
Homework	10
One project	15

A 90–100
B 80–89
C 70–79
D 60–69
F Below 60

Abdul attended all of the classes and participated in class discussions approximately once per class. He completed all his homework assignments on time, with an accuracy of 90 percent. Abdul's average on the three quizzes was 61 percent, and his score on the essay exam was 60 percent. On the project, Abdul scored 95 percent. You made no testing adaptations for Abdul this term. His overall percentage for the term was 69 percent, or D. How do you think Abdul will feel about getting a D for the term? What grading adaptations might you try for Abdul?

Tara has a learning disability and receives intensive reading instruction in the resource room. Her short-term objectives for this term are that she will read a grade one literature book at a rate of 20 words correct per minute with four or fewer errors per minute and will be able to tell who the main character of the story is, what the main problem in the story is, and how the problem is solved. It is now the end of the term. Should you give Tara a grade in reading? Why or why not? Assuming that Tara met her short-term objectives in reading, what do you think her grade for the marking period should be? Should her grade be adapted in any way?

Jamie is a student with mild cognitive or developmental disabilities. You are about to start a unit on adding and subtracting fractions. The IEP objective for Jamie is to identify the fractions 1-4, 1-3, and 1-2. Describe a performance-based test that you could use to measure Jamie's knowledge of these fractions. How would you score this test? How could you use portfolio assessment to measure Jamie's progress on this unit?

Chapter 12

Responding to
Student Behaviour

After you read this chapter, you will be able to

1. Outline strategies for promoting positive behaviour with groups of students, including exceptional students.
2. Explain simple techniques for responding to individual student misbehaviour.
3. Outline systematic approaches for increasing students' positive behaviours and decreasing their negative behaviours.
4. Identify how to help students manage their own behaviour.
5. Describe a problem-solving approach for deciding how to respond to individual student behaviour.

JOSEPH, *a grade nine student with a learning disability, comes late to his applied algebra class at least twice each week. He seldom participates in class discussions, and he does not ask questions. Unless Mrs. Akers asks him not to, Joseph sits with his head down on his desk. When discussing Joseph with the resource teacher, Mrs. Akers describes his demeanour as sullen. Mrs. Akers has been teaching high school math for many years, and she believes that students have the responsibility to be interested in the subject, to attend class, and to participate. She knows that Joseph is heading toward a failing grade for this term, even though she thinks he could do the work with a little more effort. What is Joseph's responsibility for his learning? What is Mrs. Akers's responsibility for making instruction appealing to students like Joseph? What strategies could help Joseph meet Mrs. Akers's class expectations for him?*

DARRYL *has a moderate cognitive disability. Every time he enters the classroom he says loudly, "I'm ba-ack," even if he has only been gone for a moment. Although he is in sixth grade, he frequently sucks his thumb and rocks in his chair. When he needs help, he calls out, "Teacher, Teacher," regardless of what is happening in the classroom at that moment. If assistance is not immediate, he continues to call out—with increasing volume. Darryl's teacher, Mr. Lowell, is losing patience with these "babyish" behaviours. He believes that Darryl is learning many social skills through the small-group work the class does, and he knows Darryl's teaching assistant is ensuring that he is learning basic pre-reading skills. Mr. Lowell is most concerned about the impact of Darryl's behaviours on the class. Despite class discussions about how best to respond to Darryl's outbursts, several students continue to snicker when Darryl calls out, which often leads to other behaviour problems. How could Mr. Lowell address both Darryl's inappropriate classroom behaviours and the class response to them?*

MARYSHA *is extremely shy. Although her hearing impairment is moderate and she is an excellent speech reader, she rarely volunteers information in class. If she has a question about an assignment, she sits quietly until Mr. Davis notices her and asks what she needs. She usually stands alone on the playground, and in groups she agrees with anything class-mates wish to do. Her acquiescence sometimes causes problems, as it did when she and two other students decided to sneak back to their classroom during recess without adult supervi-sion. The incident was a minor one, but Mr. Davis is concerned about Marysha's gullibility; he worries that in the future she might be easily enticed by others to try alcohol or drugs or to join a gang. Why might Marysha be so reluctant to participate in interactions with her teachers and peers? What skills could Marysha learn to help her make decisions about her activities with her peers?*

ALL teachers spend a portion of their time and energy monitoring student behaviour and addressing inappropriate behaviour. Whether you teach five-year-olds in a kindergarten class or 17-year-olds in secondary English, the classroom climate you create and how you respond to student behaviour will significantly affect students' learning. In recent reports, Canadian teachers in Newfoundland (Covert, Williams, & Kennedy, 1991), Manitoba (Manitoba Teachers' Society, 1990), Saskatchewan (Sanche, Schwier, & Haines, 1990), and in other provinces across the country (Martin & Sugarman, 1993) have expressed concerns related to student behaviour in schools. Preservice teachers from British Columbia reported classroom management as an area in which they felt least prepared early in their teacher education and in which they had learned most during teacher education (Housego, 1990). Further, the Canadian public has a high degree of interest in discipline in classrooms, as shown in a recent *Maclean's*/Decima poll of 1500 Canadians (*Maclean's*, 1991, p. 38).

To begin this discussion about classroom discipline, we present some basic understandings that will provide a context in which you should consider manag-ing student behaviour. First, it is essential to recognize that the word **discipline** has as its root the word *disciple*, or the follower of a teacher. Even though in cur-rent use discipline is often associated with obedience, discipline is really mostly about learning. It is a means to ensure that students have maximum opportunity to learn from their teachers. Discipline is never an end in and of itself. As you learn about approaches for increasing classroom discipline in this chapter, you will be finding ways to enhance your students' learning.

Second, some professionals view discipline and classroom management as negative, implying that these subjects are about teacher control and power. That view fails to take into account the very real dilemma that teachers face in attempting to keep a class full of students interested in learning in a way that is safe and respectful of all students. If you are effective in classroom management, you will be providing conditions that enable your students to succeed (Martin & Sugarman, 1993). Rather than managing student behaviour for your convenience or to command compliance, you will be guiding students in ways that contribute to their own best interests.

Third, teacher beliefs about discipline are strongly culturally based, and some evidence suggests that teachers are far more likely to refer students for dis-cipline problems when they are from a culture other than the teacher's (Bullara,

1993). All teachers have an obligation to monitor their behaviour to ensure that their responses are not based on racial bias or cultural ignorance. Further, they have a responsibility to recognize when their expectations are inconsistent with a student's culture. For example, a teacher recently described a dilemma his school faced in working with students from Somalia. The students were spitting, a clear violation of school rules. However, school professionals soon learned that the students were not misbehaving. Part of their religious custom called for complete fasting, including not swallowing their own saliva. Spitting, acceptable in their homeland, was perceived as misbehaviour in a Canadian school.

Teachers who actively, carefully, and creatively apply approaches for classroom management and who monitor the success of their strategies, adapting them as needed, can have a positive influence on student learning (Bennet & Smilanich, 1994; Deluke & Knoblock, 1987; Duquette, 1996). Many issues are beyond a teacher's control—you do not have the power to increase the financial support available to schools, nor can you remove the public pressures that surround many curriculum and school reform initiatives. However, you can affect and are ultimately accountable for the learning of your students. Using effective classroom management strategies will increase their learning by creating a positive classroom environment. Further, teachers who use effective management strategies will have far less need to change inappropriate student behaviour.

In the sections that follow, you will learn procedures for group behaviour management, strategies for responding to individual student behaviours, and a problem-solving approach for changing student behaviour. Together, these techniques will provide you with a foundation for effective classroom management.

◤ How Can You Prevent Discipline Problems?

Strategies for responding to disruptive student behaviour and promoting positive academic and social behaviour are discussed later in this chapter. The best topic with which to begin a discussion of discipline issues is prevention behaviour (Doyle, 1990; Stainback, Stainback, & Froyen, 1987). In many cases, you will make the difference between having a classroom in which the stress level is high and "keeping control" is a constant struggle or having a classroom in which student learning is supported by the environment and behaviour problems are rare. You can make this difference by creating an instructional environment that is conducive to learning and using effective communication to foster a positive classroom climate.

Instructional Environments Conducive to Learning

In Chapter 7, you learned that many factors contribute to creating an instructional environment that fosters student learning. Many of these same factors also promote appropriate classroom behaviour. For example, you found out that teachers need to set clear expectations in their classroom through rules that students understand and follow (Dworet, Davis, & Martin, 1996). You need only a few rules, but they should be specific, worded positively, posted and discussed with

Do It! Refer to Chapters 7, 9, and 10. Make a list of six key principles of effective instruction that also help reduce classroom behaviour problems.

students early in the school year, and rehearsed while students learn them. Rules should also be monitored and changed as needed. Figure 12.1 contains sample rules for students at the elementary level.

Another key factor related to the instructional environment and discipline is establishing clear classroom routines. These routines include those for beginning the school day or class period, those for transitioning from one activity to another, those for moving about in the classroom, and those for ending the school day or class period. Students who have routines are less likely to misbehave because they can meet classroom expectations for behaviour.

Effective Classroom Communication

Cultural Awareness:
Students who have limited English proficiency can be inadvertently overlooked in teacher-student communication because of their language difficulties and possible reluctance to interact. Misunderstandings are also more likely (Bosetti & Watt, 1995). You are responsible for fostering positive communication with this group of students.

Teachers who treat their students with respect and trust are more successful in creating positive classroom environments in which fewer behaviour problems occur (Bennett & Smilanich, 1994; Deluke & Knoblock, 1987). Communication between teacher and students is integral to fostering this trust and respect. However, teacher-student communication is a complex matter, and problems often arise. Sometimes, teachers provide students with too much information or information that is unclear. Students become confused when information is not relevant to the instruction being delivered. And sometimes, teachers give one message with words but convey another message with their tone of voice or non-verbal behaviours. The following communication factors affect classroom management (Bauer & Sapona, 1991):

1. The complexity and level of abstraction of the message
2. Students' background knowledge and experience to understand the content of the message

FIGURE 12.1

Examples of Classroom Rules and Routines

Classroom Rules

   Be respectful of yourself and others.
   Respect other people's property.
   Listen quietly while others are speaking.
   Obey all school rules.

Classroom Routines

   When you finish your work:
     1. Place it in the red basket.
     2. Choose a word game or book.
     3. Quietly play the game or read.

3. Students' understanding of classroom interactions and routines
4. Teacher and student awareness of non-verbal communication
5. Cognitive organization that teachers provide before launching into specific content
6. The expectation that teachers and students listen to one another

Teacher-pupil interactions that affect learning and behaviour include both formal interactions that are part of instruction and informal interactions in the classroom (Hutchinson, 1996). One way to gain a sense of students' perceptions of your communication in class is to ask them.

The overall quality of your communication with your students is built in numerous small ways. For example, finding time each week to speak privately with students lets them know that you care about them as individuals. Asking older students sincere questions about their friends, out-of-school activities, or part-time jobs also conveys that you care. Taking the time to write positive comments on papers shows students that you appreciate their strengths and are not focusing only on their needs. When you encourage each student to achieve his or her own potential without continually comparing students to one another, you are communicating the idea that each class member has a valuable contribution to make. Teachers who fail to take these small steps toward positive communication with students, or who publicly embarrass a student or punish a group for the behaviour of a few, soon create a negative instructional environment that thwarts appropriate behaviour and effective learning.

Cultural Awareness: Another type of diversity to monitor in your interactions with students is gender. You need to ensure that you interact with boys and girls equitably and that you respond to their behaviour needs without bias.

Effective Teaching Methods

One other critical strategy for preventing behaviour problems is to provide instruction that is relevant, interesting, and active. Recall from Chapters 9 and 10, for example, how learning is enhanced through the use of clear and systematic instructional approaches and learning strategies that actively engage students in their learning. We remind you of this information because effective instruction plays a critical role in classroom behaviour management. Students who are given boring or outdated materials, who are asked to complete dozens of worksheets with little instructional value, and who have few opportunities to create their own learning through projects or activities are likely to resort to misbehaviour.

Not all behaviour problems can be prevented. Some will occur despite your best efforts to prevent them. Before you decide that the student is the one who must change to resolve the behaviour problem, remember to examine how your expectations, communication, teaching behaviour, and other factors you control might be part of the problem.

How Can You Promote Positive Group Behaviour?

In effective classrooms, teachers and students respect each other and students are busily engaged in learning. Students attend to their work, they interact with each other politely and without verbal or physical fighting, and they ignore the occasional misbehaviour of classmates instead of encouraging it. In many class-rooms, you can promote positive behaviours such as these by using behaviour management strategies that are designed specifically for the whole class. For example, all students might participate in earning privileges or rewards, as individuals or as members of cooperative learning groups. The following sections describe effective whole-group strategies such as the Good Behaviour Game, other peer-mediated approaches to behaviour management, and token economies.

The Good Behaviour Game

The **Good Behaviour Game** has long been regarded as a powerful strategy for reducing disruptive behaviours especially in elementary classrooms (Barrish, Saunders, & Wolf, 1969). Even though it was first described three decades ago, it still has value for today's classrooms. These are the procedures used in the game:

1. Explain to students that they will be divided into two teams, one seated on each side of the classroom. These teams will compete with each other to have the fewest number of negative behaviours during a class period or school day. The game can also be played so that students compete to have the greatest number of positive behaviours, and more than two teams can be used.

2. Describe the target behaviours for students. These behaviours should be specific. For example, out-of-seat behaviour might be included, along with talking out during large-group instruction or making disruptive noises (for example, loud burps, audible sighs). Examples of positive behaviours might include promptly putting away materials when requested and remembering to place completed work in the teacher's "IN" basket. Examples and non-examples of the behaviours should be given to ensure that all students under-

▶ *What group strategies can be used for managing student behaviour? What student behaviours might have preceded this teacher's use of card-game privileges as a reward?*

stand expectations. Select only two or three misbehaviours that are particularly relevant to your classroom. If you select too many behaviours, the game is less likely to be effective because students will have difficulty remembering the targeted behaviours and you will have difficulty monitoring them. Similarly, select only a limited number of positive behaviours that you are encouraging students to display.

3. Set a time period each day in which the game will be played. You might schedule it during language arts instruction or during the first half of the class period in a secondary setting.

4. Let students know that each time you notice one of the targeted behaviours being displayed, you will tell the person who has misbehaved and also tally a point against that person's team. In the positive version, appropriate behaviours noted are tallied.

5. At the end of each day, tally the points and announce which team won (least number of points or most number of points, depending on the variation of the game used).

6. You might also wish to set an "all win" condition. For example, if both teams have fewer than 5 points or, positively, more than 10 points, a tie might be declared.

7. The winning team (or both teams) receives a reward. The reward should be based on a list of student preferences, keeping in mind feasibility. As explained later in this chapter, the amount of the reward and the type of reward should be based on student needs.

To maintain student interest in the Good Behaviour Game, you could vary the rewards earned, or change the instructional activity or time of day during which the game is played. You might also find that it is most effective to save this approach for periods of the school year that are stressful for students, such as the late November through late December holiday time with its many classroom interruptions, or the three weeks prior to spring break or the close of the school year. This type of game approach could be very effective for Darryl, the student with a moderate cognitive disability you met at the beginning of the chapter. Darryl's teacher could identify ignoring Darryl's occasional talking out as a positive behaviour for the class. By doing this, the class would be learning that it is not helpful to encourage Darryl's talking out and Darryl would not be inadvertently rewarded for this inappropriate classroom behaviour. Of course, this program would need to be accompanied by additional instruction for Darryl in how to interact appropriately.

One problem that can occur with the Good Behaviour Game is when one student deliberately misbehaves, causing his or her team to lose repeatedly. If this happens, it might be preferable to create an individual behaviour management plan of the sort described later in this chapter. Part of the plan could include allowing the student to earn the privilege of playing the game with the rest of the class.

✓ **Your Learning:** At what other times of the school year might the Good Behaviour Game be useful? Why might it lose its effectiveness if used for prolonged periods?

Other Peer-Mediated Approaches

How you group students for instruction can also serve as a group behaviour management technique. For example, if you ask students to work with a learning buddy or peer tutor, you can probably reduce the amount of misbehaviour because students will be more actively engaged in their learning and will have the added responsibility of serving as a "teacher." Similarly, if you ask students to work in small instructional groups so that either all of them can earn a reward for completing their work or no one can earn a reward, students have a natural incentive for focusing on their learning activities and are less likely to misbehave. For a shy student such as Marysha, introduced at the beginning of this chapter, peer-mediated instructional approaches can foster appropriate social interactions because they create a small-group, structured instructional environment. Peer-mediated instruction is also highly recommended as a strategy for promoting positive behaviour for students from racially and culturally diverse backgrounds by Piper (1993) who has conducted research in Alberta and Nova Scotia.

Connections: Chapter 13 provides more detailed information on peers teaching each other.

Token Economy

FYI: A token economy is a group or individual behaviour management technique in which students earn individual privileges and other rewards for displaying desired classroom behaviours.

Another group behaviour management procedure that might be effective in your classroom is a **token economy** (Kazdin, 1977). This procedure may be cumbersome for whole class implementation, but could work well for a small group within a class or an individual student like Darryl, described at the beginning of this chapter, to reduce his interruptions. This strategy creates a system in which students earn "money" that they exchange for rewards. As in any economy, certain tasks have more or less value than others, and rewards have more or less cost. One form of token economy has students receive imaginary money that they record in cheque books. When they purchase a privilege, the cost is subtracted from the balance.

Use the following steps to create a classroom token economy:

1. **Identify the behaviours for which students will earn credit.** A number of behaviours can be specified and posted in the classroom such as bringing learning supplies to class or completing work. Students can be involved in deciding what behaviours to include.
2. **Decide on the classroom "currency."** You could use points, punches on a card, play money, or any other system.
3. **Assign a value to each target behaviour.** Values may vary or be the same for all target behaviours.
4. **Decide on the privileges or rewards students will earn.** It is important to include on the reward list at least one item that costs the minimum amount of currency a student might earn (for example, one point) so that all students will have the opportunity to participate in the economy.
5. **Assign purchase "prices" to the privileges and rewards.** One teacher had access to hundreds of sets of plastic beads; the beads became quite the rage in the classroom, but they were not very costly. However, lunch alone with the teacher was a high-priced privilege.
6. **Explain the economy to students.** As you have probably discerned, you can make an economy as simple or complex as you have the creativity to develop and implement and your students have the ability to understand.
7. **Establish a systematic way for students to exchange their currency for privileges or rewards.** By having a consistent time and a system for the exchange, perhaps once weekly, you avoid a constant stream of student

✓ **Your Learning:** What versions of a token economy would be most effective for elementary school students? For high school students?

requests for privileges or rewards and the aggravation of the constant monitoring this would require.

How you establish your token economy will depend partly on the age of your students. For younger students, you may need to use tangible currency (for example, tokens, beads, play money). Older students are more capable of using points or other symbolic currencies. Likewise, younger students will need more opportunities to exchange their currency, whereas older students are more able to save their currency to earn more expensive privileges or rewards over a longer period of time. Rewards might include stickers or a pencil for young children, and a discount movie pass or a book for older students.

To work effectively, a token economy should be carefully planned with flexibility for adjustment as the need arises. For example, you might need to change the reward list or the amount of currency required to obtain particular rewards.

Do It! With a classmate, create a token economy for a class of students at the level you plan to teach. What will you use for tokens? What will the rewards be? How many tokens will it take to obtain each reward? How will rewards be distributed?

▶ What Are Some Simple and Effective Responses to Individual Behaviour?

For some students, including exceptional students, the steps you take to create a positive and productive learning environment will not be sufficient to eliminate behaviour problems; nor will group behaviour management strategies always work. For some individuals, more specialized approaches are needed, and you will find it helpful to follow the steps of the INCLUDE model outlined in Chapter 1. However, before you decide to use specialized approaches in responding to a student's behaviour, you can try a number of simpler strategies first. Teachers have long relied on this "principle of least intervention" in addressing student behaviour needs. In this section, the strategies described include minimum interventions, such as "catch 'em being good," and techniques for managing students' surface behaviours.

Minimum Interventions

Teachers sometimes contribute unintentionally but significantly to student misbehaviour. They do this by inadvertently bringing out negative student behaviours and by responding directly to minor student misbehaviours, actions that sometimes cause the student to misbehave more. For example, when asked directly to begin work, a student might refuse. However, when given choices among which assignment to do first, the student might comply. Similarly, when reprimanded for using foul language in the classroom, some students will use the reprimand as a signal to continue the language to get further attention. Ignoring occasional inappropriate language might lessen the problem.

On questionnaires, 300 adolescents in Ontario identified the problems they thought occurred most frequently in the classroom and the corrective or disciplinary actions they saw their teachers use most often. They also identified the responses that they thought teachers should make to individual behaviours (Coathup, 1988). The inappropriate behaviours they identified as happening most frequently were students not paying attention to the teacher, talking out of turn, being unprepared for class, and showing little or no interest in schoolwork. They reported that teachers frequently used the same strategies to respond to all these problems—public correction of the student or detention. They preferred simple strategies that did not draw attention to the student such as private correction, looking at the student, and holding a conference. The exception was that they did support publicly correcting a student for speaking out of turn. By listening to your students, you might be able to arrive at cooperative, negotiated responses to individual behaviour.

When working with exceptional students, it is essential to stay alert to how you might be contributing to a student's behaviours, either through your own responses to the behaviour or through your classroom structure and lesson format. Here are four examples of very simple strategies teachers use to address minor student misbehaviour.

Cultural Awareness: For students from diverse backgrounds, especially those with limited English proficiency, a private "catch" on good behaviour can be more effective than a public one because you can better gauge the student's understanding of your message.

Catch 'em being good. A versatile and long-recognized strategy for reducing inappropriate student behaviour and increasing appropriate behaviour is called **"catch 'em being good."** When a student is behaving according to expectations, you acknowledge and reward the behaviour. For example, if grade three student Jeff enters the room and immediately begins his work, you might say to him, "I like the way you went right to your desk, Jeff. That's exactly what you're supposed to do!" This comment has the effect of rewarding Jeff's behaviour. At the same time, it clearly lets other students know that going directly to one's seat is a behaviour they should do, too. In a grade seven class, a teacher might privately say to a student who is chronically late, "I noticed you were at your seat with materials ready when the bell rang. Nice going." Although the privacy of the comment eliminates its potential positive impact on other students, it is likely to prevent student embarrassment.

✓ **Your Learning:** What is a low-demand request? For which students is this technique most likely to be effective?

Make low-demand requests first. Sprague and Horner (1990) described a successful strategy for helping students with significant cognitive disabilities who have difficulty transitioning between activities such as coming in from recess or moving from one activity to another within the classroom. With this approach, make several low-demand and unrelated requests of the student prior to expecting the targeted request. For example, if it is time for Thuy to put away his crayons to join a group reading a story, first get Thuy's attention by saying something like, "Thuy, give me five." Follow this with asking Thuy to tell you his address (or another appropriate piece of personal information that he is learning). Next ask him to shake hands. Finally, request that Thuy leave his colouring and join the reading group. Each request is followed by verbal praise (for example, "Right," or "Good job").

✓ **Your Learning:** What does it mean to respond to a student's apparent intent? How does this approach differ from traditional responses to student behaviour?

Respond to apparent intent. Another strategy for designing minimum interventions is based on the apparent **intent** of the behaviour (Foster-Johnson & Dunlap, 1993). For example, a student begins pinching others every morning at around 11:00. Hypothesizing that the student is hungry, the teacher provides a snack for the student. Many other examples of this approach to using behaviour intent to identify and change factors surrounding the student can be generated. For example, a student who becomes belligerent when an assignment is given may be signalling that he does not want to do the work or that the work is too difficult. Breaking the task into smaller parts or giving an assignment that begins with easier questions may decrease or eliminate the behaviour. Likewise, a student who makes outrageously untrue statements in class (for example, "My sister is going to marry Prince William"; "my job [at a restaurant] pays $50 an hour") may have the intention of getting adult attention. Chatting with the student for a moment before school or class, or creating individual time with an adult at school, may eliminate the need for further intervention. In all these cases, the teacher, acting as a sort of behaviour detective, found that a simple modification effectively changed the behaviour.

Use grouping strategies. In many schools, students with disruptive behaviours tend to seek out others who misbehave as seatmates or groupmates. One group of researchers documented that a very simple strategy may significantly reduce misbehaviour in such situations (Stainback, Stainback, Etscheidt, & Doud, 1986). They arranged for a highly disruptive student to be partnered in science class with students who were not disruptive. When this was done, the student's disruptive behaviours declined dramatically. When the student sat with disruptive peers, disruptive behaviours were far more frequent. The authors argue convincingly that grouping strategies are easily managed and should be part of any plan for addressing disruptive behaviour. This strategy also has potential for a student such as Marysha, one of the students described at the beginning of the chapter. Because she is extremely quiet, a teacher might decide to place her with a group of students who model positive social skills and who are unlikely to take advantage of her tendency to go along with whatever the group decides. Teachers should be careful to avoid creating dependencies by overusing this kind of strategy. Marysha must be able to function independently, too.

Connections: Grouping strategies were introduced in Chapter 7. Their use to promote student social interactions is described in Chapter 13.

Managing Students' Surface Behaviours

Another relatively simple strategy for responding to student behaviours is the concept of managing their **surface behaviours.** Long and Newman (1971) propose that many times a teacher's initial response to student behaviour can determine whether a problem situation will develop. If a teacher treats a minor misbehaviour as a major infraction, the result might be a strong negative student response followed by a stronger teacher response until a serious behaviour problem comes to exist. For example, if a student mutters something negative about an assignment under her breath and the teacher responds by stating in a stern voice, "What did you say?" the incident will escalate. The student might reply, "Nothing"; the teacher repeats the request, and the student eventually says something that gets her in trouble. Such interactions can be avoided if teachers are prepared to shift the focus of the interaction. Suggestions for heading off such problems include purposefully ignoring minor incidents and using humour to defuse tense classroom situations. Examples of initial response techniques are outlined in the Professional Edge.

These initial response techniques are most suited to minor misbehaviours and are unlikely to resolve serious discipline issues. Also, responding to students' surface behaviours can have the effect of increasing those behaviours. For

FYI: Surface behaviours are student reactions to classroom situations or events that might signal the beginning of a more serious discipline problem.

Professional Edge

Strategies for Managing Students' Surface Behaviours

KNOWING how to manage students' surface behaviours effectively can often head off a potentially tense classroom situation. The following strategies, most suited for responding to minor misbehaviours, can help you deal with problem behaviours as soon as they occur.

1. **Planned ignoring.** If a student's behaviour is not likely to harm others or to spread to others, you might decide to ignore it, especially if the behaviour signals another problem. For example, a student who repeatedly sighs loudly could be signalling a loss of interest; instead of responding to the sighing, recognize that student's need to change activities soon.

2. **Signal interference.** Communicate with students about surface behaviours by using nonverbal signals such as eye contact or gestures (for example, finger to lips to request silence).

3. **Proximity control.** Sometimes, simply moving closer to a misbehaving student resolves the problem.

4. **Interest boosting.** If a student appears to be losing interest in a task or activity, refocus attention by asking a specific question about the student's progress or by otherwise paying specific attention to the student's work.

5. **Tension reduction through humour.** For some minor misbehaviour, your best response might be humour. For example, a student frustrated with an assignment tossed a textbook into the garbage can. Instead of scolding or lecturing, the teacher exclaimed, "Two points!" and then went to the student to assist with the assignment.

6. **Hurdle help.** For some students, beginning an assignment can be overwhelming. As a result, they refuse to start working or they misbehave to avoid the work. You can help them begin by assisting with the first example, asking questions to facilitate their thinking, or prompting them to follow steps, avoiding a behaviour issue.

7. **Support from routine.** Creating more structure in the classroom can avert discipline problems. For example, asking Rhonda to begin each day by hanging up her coat, going to her seat, and colouring the picture you have placed on her desk might help her avoid being disruptive. Each day when secondary students enter the classroom, ask them to tackle a two-minute mystery or crossword related to the current instructional unit or a mathematics challenge that they find on their desk.

8. **Removing seductive objects.** When students bring radios, toys, or other distracting items to school, including dangerous objects, teachers should usually hold them for "safe-keeping." Other objects in the classroom environment can also become a focus for misbehaviour and should be hidden. For example, if you have costumes at school for the class play, keep them in a closet; if you set up an intriguing science experiment, cover the materials until time to use them.

Source: Adapted from "Managing Surface Behaviour of Children in School" by N. J. Long and R. G. Newman, 1971, in N. J. Long, W. C. Morse, and R. G. Newman (Eds.), *Conflict in the Classroom: The Education of Children with Problems* (2nd ed.), pp. 442–452. Belmont, CA: Wadsworth.

example, if you use humor with a student and the student responds by talking back, then your humour may be increasing rather than defusing the inappropriate behaviour. If this happens, switch to another approach or try a more systematic response to the behaviour, such as the ones described in the next section.

How Can You Respond to Individual Student Behaviour When Simple Approaches Are Not Enough?

In many instances, students' behaviour problems may need a more long-term and systematic intervention; that is, you may need to increase the desirable behaviour a student displays or decrease the undesirable behaviour, and a single conversation with the student or your sporadic attention to the problem is not enough to address it. Although the principles for responding to student behaviour are the same whether you are using simple or more systematic interventions, the latter responses are usually carried out across time in a consistent manner as part of a behaviour intervention plan resulting from problem solving. The former, simple interventions, are used informally and occasionally.

Increasing Desirable Behaviours

All students, even the most challenging, have some appropriate behaviours you would like to increase. The primary strategy for increasing appropriate behaviour is called **reinforcement**. Reinforcement is any response or consequence that increases a behaviour (Alberto & Troutman, 1994). It is important for you to realize that reinforcement can increase negative as well as positive behaviours. For example, when a teacher puts a sticker on a student chart because the student completed his assignment without calling out for unneeded help, the student is more likely in the future to continue to work independently. However, when a teacher says to a student who is wandering around the classroom, "Sit down!" the student is also more likely in the future to wander again. In both instances, reinforcement was applied. In the first case, it rewarded a desirable behaviour; in the second, it rewarded an undesirable behaviour.

Positive and negative reinforcement.   Any time you respond to a behaviour with a consequence that makes it more likely for the behaviour to occur again, you are using **positive reinforcement** (Gardner et al., 1994). When you reward a student for appropriate behaviour and that behaviour increases, it is an example of positive reinforcement. Specifically, if you tell a student that after she completes five math problems she may use the classroom computer and she completes all of the problems, you are reinforcing math problem completion through the computer rewards.

Negative reinforcement operates somewhat differently. Suppose you set up a system with your grade nine English students that they must have their homework signed each night by their parents until they have brought it back to school on time at least 9 out of 10 times. Because students see having homework signed by parents as an undesirable consequence, they will increase their promptness in turning in homework to avoid the consequence. Any increase in behaviour to avoid a response is called **negative reinforcement** (Gardner et al., 1994). Although negative reinforcement can be effective, positive reinforcement should usually be tried first since it is preferable to have students working toward a positive outcome rather than under the threat or perception of a negative consequence.

Do It! Ask experienced teachers about their views on using rewards with students. What do they believe? Do the teachers' beliefs about using rewards differ?

✓ **Your Learning:** What is reinforcement? How do positive and negative reinforcement differ?

Some educators, parents, and researchers question the wisdom of rewarding students for doing something that they are already doing for its own sake. For example, in one study in a series that showed the potential drawbacks of rewards, Lepper, Greene, and Nesbitt (1973) observed young children who spent much of their free time in preschool drawing. They told one group of children they would receive a certificate for drawing, so that group expected a reward. Another group did not know in advance, but received a certificate for drawing, and a third group received no reward for drawing. After the children had received their rewards, the researchers observed that only those in the group who expected rewards spent less time drawing. Members of the other two groups continued to draw at the high rates seen before the intervention. The researchers were not concerned about the rates of drawing *per se*, but about the notion that drawing was no longer engaged in for its own sake by the group that expected rewards. They warned that there could be hidden costs to rewards; play seemed to have been turned into work for preschoolers. For students who struggle to learn, it may be necessary to provide external rewards; the questions really arise when rewards are provided unnecessarily.

Types of reinforcers.   For positive reinforcers to be used for exceptional students, keep these considerations in mind. First, recognize that many different types of reinforcers can be used:

1. **Social reinforcers** are various types of positive interactions that a teacher, parent, or peer can give students for appropriate behaviour and that increase the behaviour. These reinforcers might include a positive phone call home to parents, a pat on the back, verbal praise, or selection as Citizen of the Month. Social reinforcers, especially clear and specific verbal praise, should always be tried before other positive reinforcers since they are the most natural type of reward in a school environment. If you find it necessary to employ other types of rewards, they should be used only in conjunction with social reinforcers since your long-term goal should always be to have students respond to rewards that occur naturally in their classroom environment.

2. **Activity reinforcers** involve activities such as playing games, helping a teacher in another class, and participating in other coveted individual or group pastimes. Generally, activities that directly relate to a student's educational goals (for example, practising math skills on the computer) are preferable to those that are solely recreational (for example, playing a non-educational computer game).

3. **Tangible reinforcers** are prizes or other objects that students can earn as symbols of achievement and that students want to obtain. A student who is earning baseball cards or stickers for completing assignments is receiving a tangible reinforcer. Tangible rewards can often be naturally integrated into classroom activities. For example, a student can earn the rocket pieces and household chemicals needed to create a highly interesting science experiment not offered to other students. However, ensure that the amount of the tangible reinforcer is appropriate for the amount of positive behaviour required. Students earning the science materials just mentioned are expected to display appropriate behaviours over an extended period, not just for an afternoon. Conversely, if the tangible reinforcer is a sticker, perhaps an

▶ *What individual strategies can you use in responding to individual behaviour? How can teacher feedback strengthen positive behaviour? How will you find out what types of rewards your students will respond to?*

afternoon of appropriate behaviour is the right amount for the reward being given.

4. **Primary reinforcers** are food or other items related to human needs that a student finds rewarding. They are much more basic than secondary reinforcers, which include social reinforcers, activity reinforcers, and tangible reinforcers. Primary reinforcers used in schools are often edible and might include a piece of candy, a soft drink, or a piece of fruit. Although you might occasionally employ primary reinforcers as a special treat, generally they should be used only if a student is incapable of understanding more natural rewards, or if other types of rewards are not effective. This is important for two reasons. First, food reinforcers and their impact on student health is a concern. Second, food reinforcers are not a natural part of the school learning process. If you plan to use primary reinforcers such as food, check with a school administrator to find out about local policies governing their use. Also check with parents, both for permission and about a student's possible food allergies. You should also keep in mind nutritional effects.

Effective use of positive reinforcers.   In addition to understanding that there are different types of positive reinforcers, you need to know some principles for effectively using them (McIntyre, 1992). These include the following:

1. Make sure that the positive reinforcers are clear and specific and that students understand the relationship between their behaviour and rewards. The rewards that students earn need to be specific and not otherwise available; for example, the amount of computer time for the specific behaviour displayed should be clarified if computer time is a reward. Clarity and specificity are especially important when you use verbal praise. Say, "Good job! You asked three other students for help before you asked me" because this praise explicitly states what behaviour is being rewarded.

2. Vary how much and how often you reward students. If a student has very little positive behaviour, you may reward it heavily at first just to increase it. As the student learns to use the appropriate behaviour more readily, you should decrease the amount of reward and the intensity of it. For example, if you were first rewarding a student with free-choice computer time for each two assignments completed, you might gradually change the reward so that the student must complete four assignments—and get at least 90 percent on each—in order to use the computer to practise math skills.

3. Make sure the student desires the rewards selected. If you propose to make a positive phone call home when a student participates in group work but the student does not care what his or her parent thinks, your reward is unlikely to work. A sample list of rewards favoured by some students is included in Figure 12.2. You can determine your students' preferences by asking them what types of rewards they like or by asking them to rank their preferences from a list of rewards you provide.

Related to the concept of reward desirability is that of **satiation**. Simply stated, a student who receives the same reward over a period of time may no longer find it rewarding (Schloss & Smith, 1994). If five minutes of free time is given repeatedly, after a while the student may come to expect the free time and

✓ **Your Learning:** What are the four different types of reinforcers? What is an example of each? How should you decide which type of reinforcer to use?

FYI: Adults need variety in the types of intensity of their rewards, too. Think of examples from your life that demonstrate this concept—for example, getting yourself to speak in front of other people by rewarding yourself with a CD for doing your class presentation, but recognizing that eventually you need to speak in front of others without such rewards.

> ▶ **FIGURE 12.2**   Sample Rewards Suggested by Students

- Working with a friend in the hall
- Collecting the lunch money
- Taking attendance
- Taking the attendance cards to the office
- Photocopying and collating papers
- Early dismissal
- Writing something and photocopying it
- Sitting at the teacher's desk to work
- Viewing videotapes on Friday afternoon
- Extra shop or physical education time
- Special picnic lunches or food treats
- More assemblies
- Working on games or puzzles
- Typing on a typewriter
- Extra library time
- Helping the class line up at the door
- Reading a magazine
- Listening to a tape with headphones
- Working on the computer
- Feeding the class animals
- Sitting next to a friend

- Running errands for the teacher
- Taking notes to other teachers
- Taking good work to the principal or counsellor
- Free time for special projects
- Extra recess
- Sticker on a behavioural report card
- Lunchtime basketball games, with the teacher serving as referee
- Popcorn during educational films
- Special parties
- Field trips
- Special art projects
- Listening to the radio
- Decorating the bulletin board
- Being a group leader
- Leading the class to the library
- Lunch with the teacher
- Note home to parents
- Watering the plants
- No-homework pass for one night
- Going to another classroom as a cross-age tutor

Source: From *Effective Discipline* (2nd ed.) by D. D. Smith and D. M. Rivera, 1993, p. 77, Austin, TX: Pro-Ed. Copyright © 1993 by PRO-ED, Inc. Reprinted by permission.

✓ **Your Learning:** How could you apply these principles for using reinforcers effectively in designing a Good Behaviour Game as described earlier in this chapter?

not work to receive it. When this happens, it is important to change the reward. You can often avoid the problem of satiation by using a **reinforcement menu;** that is, a list of rewards from which students may choose. The menu, consisting of a few items, can be posted in the classroom, or students can keep individual lists.

Decreasing Undesirable Behaviours

Most teachers find that exceptional students have some inappropriate classroom behaviours that need to be decreased. These might include aggressive behaviours such as calling classmates' names or poking, pinching, or hitting others; verbal outbursts such as calling out answers, swearing, or making nonsense statements during large-group instruction; or other behaviours such as fleeing the classroom when feeling stressed, copying others' work, or refusing to work. Just as there are strategies to increase desirable behaviours, there are specific strategies you can use to decrease undesirable behaviours.

Decreasing behaviour is generally accomplished through one of these four sets of strategies: (1) differentially reinforcing behaviours that are incompatible with the undesirable behaviour; (2) extinction, or ignoring the behaviour until the student stops it; (3) removing something desirable from the student; and (4) presenting a negative or aversive consequence (Alberto & Troutman, 1994). The latter two sets of strategies, removing something desirable and presenting a negative or aversive consequence, are considered **punishment.** Punishment occurs when a consequence applied has the effect of decreasing a behaviour. Each of the four sets of strategies is explained in the following sections.

Differential reinforcement of incompatible behaviours.   Reinforcers can be used to decrease inappropriate behaviour by increasing related appropriate behaviour. Perhaps in your classroom you have a student such as Patrick. Patrick has a severe learning disability. He tends to be very dependent on you for affirmation that he is doing his work correctly; he seems to be constantly at your elbow asking, "Is this right?" To change this behaviour, you might want to try praising Patrick when you notice him working independently at his desk. This technique is called differential reinforcement of incompatible behaviours. You are reinforcing a positive behaviour—working at his desk—that is incompatible with the negative behaviour—being at your desk asking for affirmation (Schloss & Smith, 1994). Your goal in this case is to get Patrick to come to your desk less by systematically rewarding him for appropriate behaviours that prevent him from being at your desk. Other examples of how to use this strategy are included in the Professional Edge on page 396.

Extinction.   Another approach to decreasing negative behaviour is **extinction**. To extinguish a behaviour, you stop reinforcing it; eventually the behaviour will decrease. This strategy is often appropriate when a student has a minor but annoying undesirable behaviour, such as tapping a pencil or rocking a chair, and when you have been reinforcing the behaviour by calling attention to it or otherwise responding to it (Alberto & Troutman, 1994). However, extinction is appropriate only when the behaviour is minor and does not threaten student well-being. Also, before an ignored behaviour decreases, it is likely to increase; that is, at first the student might tap the pencil more loudly or rock more rapidly before stopping. If you respond to the behaviour at this higher level (by telling the student to stop the noise or to keep still), you inadvertently reward the student for the exaggerated behaviour through your response. If you think you cannot ignore a behaviour while it increases, extinction is not the strategy to use.

Removing reinforcers.   In some instances, you will decrease inappropriate behaviour by taking away from the student something desired, a strategy called **removal punishment**. One example of removal punishment is **response cost,** which involves taking away a privilege, points, or some other reward (Schloss & Smith, 1994). An informal use of response cost occurs when teachers take away recess or an assembly because of misbehaviour. More systematically, a student may lose a certain amount of free time each time he or she swears in class.

> ✔ **Your Learning:** What is extinction? What are the risks of using extinction to decrease students' undesirable behaviour?

▼▼▼▼▼▼▼▼▼▼▼▼▼▼▼▼▼▼▼▼▼▼▼▼▼▼

Professional Edge

Rewarding Positive Behaviour to Reduce Negative Behaviour

THE following examples show how you can help students be more successful in your classroom by responding to positive behaviours that are incompatible with negative behaviours and rewarding the positive behaviours when you see them occurring.

Undesired Behaviour	Positive Alternative Student Behaviour That the Teacher Rewards
Talking back	Responding to positive responses such as "Yes, sir" or "Okay" or "I understand"; or to acceptable questions such as "May I ask you a question about that?" or "May I tell you my side?"
Cursing	Using acceptable exclamations such as "Darn" or "Shucks."
Being off task	Pursuing any on-task behaviour: looking at book, writing, looking at the teacher, and so on
Being out of seat	Sitting in seat (bottom on chair, with body in upright position)
Noncompliance	Following directions within seconds (time limit will depend on student's age); following directions by the second time a direction is given
Talking out	Raising hand and waiting to be called on
Turning in messy papers	Making no marks other than answers; no more than a few erasures (depending on student needs and abilities); no more than three folds or creases
Hitting, pinching, kicking, pushing/shoving	Using verbal expression of anger; pounding fist into hand; sitting or standing next to other students without touching them
Tardiness	Being in seat when bell rings (or by the desired time)
Self-injurious or self-stimulatory behaviours	Sitting with hands on desk or in lap; hands not touching any part of body; head up and not touching anything (for example, desk, shoulder)
Inappropriate use of materials	Holding/using materials appropriately (for example, writing only on appropriate paper)

Source: From "Accentuate the Positive . . . Eliminate the Negative!" by J. Webber and B. Scheuermann, 1991, *Teaching Exceptional Children, 24*(1), pp. 13–19. Used by permission of Council for Exceptional Children.

If you are considering using response cost, keep in mind that it is effective only if the student currently has reinforcers that you can remove. For example, denying a student access to a special school program will decrease negative behaviour only if the student wants to attend the program. Also, response cost sometimes fails because the negative behaviour is being reinforced so strongly that the response cost is not effective. In the example just described, if the student receives a lot of peer attention from acting out in class, the response cost of not attending the school program might be too weak to counteract the strong appeal of peer attention. Finally, because response cost teaches a student only what not to do, it is essential that you simultaneously teach the student desired behaviours.

Another widely used removal punishment strategy is **time-out**. Time-out involves removing a student from opportunities for reward (Jones & Jones, 1990). Many elementary school teachers use a simple form of time-out when they require students misbehaving on the playground to spend a few minutes in a "penalty box." The reward from which students are removed is playtime with classmates. Time-out can be used in a number of ways, depending on the age of the student, the nature of the inappropriate behaviours, and the student's response to isolation. For example, it may be sufficient in a kindergarten or first-grade classroom to have a time-out chair in a quiet corner of the classroom. When Heather pushes another child, she is told to sit in time-out where she can observe other students in the reading circle and yet cannot interact with them. If this is not effective, placing a carrel on the student's desk or using a screen (possibly made from a large box) around a chair might be the next step. For older students and those with more challenging behaviours, time-out may need to be in a location totally removed from the student's class. For example, when Louis swears at his teacher, he is sent to the time-out room, a small, undecorated room with just a desk and chair that adjoins the counsellor's office. However, for Cherri, time-out means going to Mrs. Eich's room across the hall, where she doesn't know the students.

If you use time-out, keep in mind the following considerations:

1. The length of the time-out should vary depending on the student's age, the type of challenging behaviour, and the amount of time it takes for the time-out to achieve the result of decreasing an undesirable behaviour. Younger students and those with limited cognitive ability often require shorter time-out periods than older students with learning and behaviour problems.
2. When using time-out, students should be given a warning, should know why they are given a time-out, and should not have access to attractive activities during time-out. The warning provides students an opportunity to correct the behaviour; the explanation ensures that students understand the reason for time-out; and the absence of attractions guarantees that time-out does not become a reward for the student. The last point is especially important. In one school, a student with autism was being "timed out" from his inclusive classroom for running around the room. He was being sent to a special education classroom where he was using coloured chalk on the chalkboard to entertain himself for long periods of time. Not surprisingly, his running behaviour began increasing!
3. Giving a student attention as part of a time-out process sabotages its effectiveness. Sometimes, teachers who are using time-out accompany a student to the time-out area, explaining the student's behaviour on the way, arguing with the student about the time-out procedure, or otherwise providing the student with a great deal of attention. This attention may reinforce the student's behaviour and, in effect, negate the effect of using time-out. The

Do It! Ask a school professional to talk to your class about how to use time-out. When does it work best? When is it ineffective? Does your local school district have policies about the use of time-out?

student may increase the behaviour because of the few minutes of undivided teacher attention that results from it.

4. If a student refuses to go to a time-out location, you may need to ask for assistance in enforcing your decision. However, you should also keep in mind that if time-out becomes a power struggle between you and a student, it might not be the appropriate strategy to use.

5. Be aware that for some students, isolation is in itself rewarding. For time-out to be effective, the environment from which the student is removed must be rewarding. Some students are happy to be left completely alone for as long as possible. For students who prefer isolation, time-out is clearly not an appropriate strategy for reducing misbehaviour.

6. Attend to the safety needs of students in time-out settings. It is highly unethical to send an upset student to an unsupervised time-out location. If time-out is employed, it must include adult supervision, a safe location for the student, and monitoring for student comfort and safety. Your school district probably has written policies about the use of time-out. If not, it is especially important to work closely with a special educator, counsellor, or administrator to ensure that you use it appropriately.

Cultural Awareness:
Punishments vary from culture to culture. Your students may come from families that use punishments such as shame, ostracizing, or severe physical punishment. Your knowledge of how students are punished at home should help you understand how they respond to punishment in school.

Presenting negative consequences.   The final set of strategies for decreasing undesirable student behaviour is the least preferable because it involves presenting negative consequences to students (Gardner et al., 1994). It is referred to as **presentation punishment**. For example, when a teacher verbally reprimands a student, the reprimand is a negative consequence intended to decrease student misbehaviour. It is a mild punishment, one of the most common used in schools (Alberto & Troutman, 1994; Coathup, 1988).

Natural consequences refers to asking a student to suffer the logical and naturally occurring effects of his or her behaviour. If Perry knocks Lisa's pot of paint to the floor, Perry must clean up the mess, and restore the floor to its prior condition. You can emphasize that the floor belongs to the community, not to the child, because everyone in the room walks over it. The child then knows that if someone else wrongs the property of the community, he can count on you to enforce the natural consequences in favour of him and the rest of the community. This requires vigilance on your part or the students may perceive you as unfair.

Another type of presentation punishment is **overcorrection**, in which a student is directed to restore a situation to its original condition or a better condition than existed before the misbehaviour. This strategy is useful when a student has damaged classroom property or otherwise created a mess. For example, a student who scribbles on a chalkboard might be assigned to erase and wash all the boards in the room. A student who writes on a desktop might be required to stay after school to clean all the desktops in the class. A student who throws garbage on the floor might be given the task of sweeping the classroom and adjoining hallway. This strategy can make clear the undesirable consequences of negative behaviours, but it is not without problems. First, the student must be willing to complete the overcorrection activity; it might be extremely difficult to compel this behaviour. If a student refuses to complete the task, a confrontation might occur. In addition, the overcorrection requires close teacher supervision. A student should not be left alone to complete the assigned task, which translates into a significant time commitment from the teacher.

In Canada, **physical punishment** is "a thing of the past." For example, in their recent discussion about the crisis of authority in schools, Clifton and Roberts (1993) of the University of Manitoba do not refer to physical punishment. Whatever the criterion—legal, ethical, or effectiveness—punishment is viewed as less desirable than increasing positive behaviours through reward. Morris (1985) summarized the following potential negative effects of physical punishment and other types of presentation punishment:

1. The punishment often suppresses a student's undesirable behaviour but does not change it. Once a student realizes or observes that physical punishment will no longer follow a behaviour, that behaviour is likely to recur. Thus, a student who is physically punished for stealing is likely to steal again if he or she is relatively sure that no one will discover the theft.

2. Although the punishment might reduce or eliminate a particular behaviour, other undesirable behaviours might be substituted. For example, a student strongly scolded for talking out might at the first opportunity deface a bulletin board as a way of "getting even."

3. The punishment often produces strong emotional responses in the student, such as anxiety and fear. These responses can interfere with the student's new learning in the classroom or in social situations. In one unfortunate cafeteria incident, a student with a learning disability was threatened with punishment when she threw food, a clear and serious violation of school rules. The student was so frightened that she left school and walked home along a busy highway, causing much consternation on the part of teachers and administrators who could not find her.

4. The student who is punished might respond with aggression and hostility toward the person who administers the punishment. This side effect would also influence the relationship between that person and the student. In a classroom in which the teacher uses punishment, the student might withdraw or lash out at the teacher in anticipation of the punishment about to be delivered.

5. When punishment is used, students might begin to avoid participating in a wide range of activities. Thus, when an art teacher repeatedly punishes a student for using materials carelessly, the student might become reluctant to use the materials at all, and this reluctance might extend to instruments in a music class or to equipment in a physical education class. The student might misbehave to avoid having to go to art, music, or gym.

6. The punishment sometimes has an opposite effect on behaviour, increasing instead of decreasing it. This is especially true when the student craves adult attention. For example, if you verbally correct a student for using foul language, the student may enjoy your attention and increase the use of foul language in order to obtain your attention. In this case, the intended punisher clearly has not served its purpose.

7. Through the teacher's modelling, students might learn that they, too, can control people by using punishment. For example, a student might imitate a teacher's scolding when tutoring a younger student.

In general, then, the message for you as a teacher responding to student behaviours in class is this: Increasing positive behaviours through the use of reinforcers, especially when these desirable behaviours can substitute for student undesirable behaviours, is the preferred approach to behaviour management. If you find it necessary to decrease undesirable behaviours, the preferred strategies are reinforcing the positive incompatible behaviours and extinction. The use of removal or presentation punishment should be a last resort, only as part of an ongoing behaviour intervention plan, and should involve a team decision. If you do use punishment, keep in mind all the potential problems with it and monitor its use closely.

◢ How Can You Help Students Manage Their Own Behaviour?

The strategies just outlined for increasing positive and decreasing negative student behaviour rely on the teacher providing rewards or consequences to the student. Another set of strategies, far less teacher-directed, involves having students take an active role in managing their own behaviour (Coleman, Wheeler, & Webber, 1993). These strategies are preferred because they promote student independence by giving students skills they can use in many school settings and outside of school as well.

Cognitive Behaviour Management Strategies

Donald Meichenbaum of Waterloo University conducted the first research on **cognitive behaviour management (CBM)** strategies. Meichenbaum and Goodman's (1971) study with impulsive children generated much excitement and subsequent research (Ryan, Weed, & Short, 1986).

Connections: CBM strategies are presented in an instructional context in Chapter 10.

In cognitive behaviour management (CBM), students are taught to monitor their own behaviour, to make judgments about its appropriateness, and to change it as needed (for example, see Meichenbaum, 1977). Many elements of CBM have already been introduced in Chapter 10 as a means of increasing student independence in academic learning and organization. Here they are applied to helping students manage their own classroom conduct and social behaviour in various situations. For example, Joseph, the student with a learning disability introduced at the beginning of this chapter, might be able to use CBM to manage his own classroom behaviour.

Two types of CBM are commonly used to teach students how to manage their own behaviour (Hughes, Ruhl, & Peterson, 1988). These are self-monitoring and self-reinforcement.

Self-monitoring.   Students learn to monitor and record their own behaviour in **self-monitoring.** For example, a student might keep a daily record of the number of assignments completed or the number of times he or she waited until the teacher was between groups to ask a question. Students with more advanced skills could even wear headphones to listen to an audiotape with prerecorded sig-

FIGURE 12.3
Countoons: Sample Self-Recording Forms

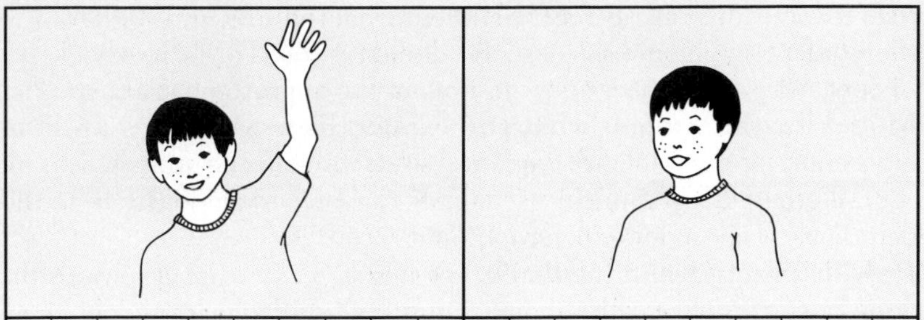

1	2	3	4	5	6	7	8	9	10	1	2	3	4	5	6	7	8	9	10
11	12	13	14	15	16	17	18	19	20	11	12	13	14	15	16	17	18	19	20
21	22	23	24	25	26	27	28	29	30	21	22	23	24	25	26	27	28	29	30
31	32	33	34	35	36	37	38	39	40	31	32	33	34	35	36	37	38	39	40
41	42	43	44	45	46	47	48	49	50	41	42	43	44	45	46	47	48	49	50

Count your hand raising | Count your talk outs

Source: From *Comprehensive Classroom Management* by V. Jones and L. Jones, 1990. Copyright © 1990 by Allyn and Bacon. Reprinted by permission.

nals and record whether they were on task at the sound of each tone. Students can also self-record their social behaviours. They could tally the number of times they left their seat without permission or asked permission before leaving the classroom. An example of a student self-recording form is a countoon, illustrated in Figure 12.3.

Self-reinforcement. Another type of CBM, **self-reinforcement,** is often used in conjunction with self-evaluation. In this approach, students self-evaluate and then judge whether they have earned a reward. For example, Erik might award himself three points for a high score, two points for an average score, and no points for a low score. When he accumulates 20 points, he chooses a reward from his personal reinforcement menu. His favourite reward might be working with the kindergarten students during their physical education period. The teacher periodically checks the accuracy of Erik's self-evaluation and self-reinforcement. He earns a bonus point for being accurate in his assessment of himself, even if that assessment is occasionally negative. If Erik must give himself no points for a low score, if his teacher checks his accuracy that day, he will receive a bonus point because he accurately assessed his work.

Teaching CBM Strategies

Generally, teaching CBM strategies to a student with special needs has three main steps:

1. **Discuss the strategy with the student and present a rationale for its use.** If you cannot clarify for the student what the strategy is or how it works, the student might not be a good candidate for CBM. To check student understanding, ask the student to explain the approach back to you.
2. **Model for the student what you expect.** For example, you might use an old sample of the student's work and walk through the strategy you plan to use. Alternatively, you might use a brief role-play to demonstrate to the student how to self-monitor behaviour and record it.
3. **Provide practice and feedback.** For this step, the teacher rewards the student for correctly using the approach until the student is confident enough to use the approach without such support. If you are teaching a student to use CBM, use reinforcers with the student until he or she has mastered the strategy. Even after mastery, it is helpful to reward the student periodically for successfully self-managing behaviour. This step can be enhanced by helping the student develop a personal reinforcement menu so rewards are meaningful. Parents and colleagues can sometimes assist in implementing this step.

Although CBM is not appropriate for every student behaviour problem, it has the advantage of teaching a student to monitor and take responsibility for his or her own behaviour. Because of increased student responsibility, cognitive behaviour management is a far more effective strategy for many students than are more traditional classroom rewards. Students can transfer self-management strategies to other classrooms and teachers and even into adult life.

▶ How Can a Problem-Solving Approach Help You Respond to Student Behaviour?

Connections: In Chapter 3, you learned who participates in shared problem solving and the steps for effective problem solving. Student behaviour could be a topic you address through a shared problem-solving process.

In this chapter, you have learned many approaches for responding to individual student behaviour. However, we have not yet addressed one key issue: How do you know how serious a student behaviour problem is, and which type of approach should you use in responding to it? The answer is to think of responding to student behaviour as a problem-solving process, much like the interpersonal problem-solving process introduced in Chapter 3. By thinking systematically about student behaviour problems, including using information you gather through the INCLUDE strategy, you will make sound decisions about how to intervene and will be better able to determine if the strategy you select is effective.

The steps for problem solving about a student's behaviour include (1) identifying the problem by increasing your understanding of the behaviour; (2) confirming your understanding of the behaviour by observing it and recording your observations; (3) creating a plan for responding to the behaviour by using rewards or consequences; (4) implementing your plan; and (5) monitoring the plan for effectiveness.

Identify the Behaviour Problem

When a student displays behaviours that are especially aggravating or seem directed at purposely causing a classroom disruption, it is tempting to respond by

TABLE 12.1 Possible Student Intents

Intent	Goal	Example of Behaviour
Power/Control	Control an event or a situation	Acts to stay in the situation and keep control: "You can't make me!"
Protection/Escape	Avoid a task or activity; escape a consequence; stop or leave a situation	Has a tantrum at the start of every math lesson; skips social studies class
Attention	Become the centre of attention; focus attention on self	Puts self in the forefront of a situation or distinguishes self from others; for example, burps loudly during class instruction
Acceptance/Affiliation	Become wanted or chosen by others for mutual benefit	Hangs out with troublemakers; joins a clique or gang
Self-expression	Express feelings, needs, or preoccupations; demonstrate knowledge or skill	Produces drawings, for example, of aerial bombings, body parts, occult symbols
Gratification	Feel good; have a pleasurable experience; reward oneself	Acts to get or maintain a self-determined reward, for example, hoards an object; indulges in self-gratifying behaviour at others' expense
Justice/Revenge	Settle a score; get or give restitution, apology, or punishment	Destroys another's work; meets after school to fight; commits an act of vandalism

Source: Adapted from "Behavioural Intent: Instructional Content for Students with Behaviour Disorders" by R. S. Neel and K. K. Cessna, 1993, in Colorado Department of Education Special Education Services Unit, *Instructionally Differentiated Programming: A Needs-Based Approach for Students with Behaviour Disorders.* Used by permission.

trying to stop the behaviour in order to get back to the business of educating the student. First, however, you need to identify the problem, which involves understanding why the student is displaying a particular behaviour. Inappropriate behaviours can be viewed as clues for diagnosing the student's goal or intent, and intent helps you understand the problem the student is displaying (Neel & Cessna, 1993). Students with inappropriate behaviours often have the same goals as students who display appropriate behaviours, but are unskilled in expressing their intent in an acceptable way. If you understand intent, you can better plan interventions. Table 12.1 describes some common student behaviour intents. Put simply, this conceptualization of student behaviours suggests that before responding you should ask, "Why is the student doing this?"

The following example might help to clarify the idea of identifying students' intents. Daniel is in grade six. When the grade six teaching team meets to discuss student problems, Mr. Adams expresses concern that Daniel sometimes swears in class. Ms. Schultz adds that he sometimes picks fights with other students in class. Dr. Hogue agrees that Daniel is having problems and recounts a recent incident in which Daniel was sent to the office. As the teachers talk, they begin to look past Daniel's specific behaviours and focus instead on his intent. They realize that in one class, Daniel was disruptive when a difficult assignment was

Connections: Student intent was introduced earlier in this chapter. Do you remember how intent affects student behaviour?

Do It! For common student intents, generate at least three additional appropriate ways in which the student could accomplish the intent.

being given; in another, the problem was occurring as quizzes were being returned; and in the other, the incident was immediately prior to Daniel's turn to give an oral book report. The teachers agree that Daniel's intent has been to escape situations in which he might fail.

Once you identify the probable intent of a student's behaviour, it becomes important to assist the student in changing the behaviour to a more acceptable form, while still enabling the student to achieve the original intent. In Daniel's case, it would be easy for the teachers to decide on a reward system to get Daniel to swear less in Mr. Adams's class. However, this has more to do with the teachers' intent of having well-mannered students than it does with Daniel's intent to escape a potential failure experience. An alternative approach would be to permit Daniel to receive his quizzes prior to the start of class, or perhaps to participate in the after-school homework club that includes a group that studies for the quiz. Another behaviour to teach Daniel might be for him to ask to give oral reports to one peer or to audiotape them beforehand. The question of intervening to address Daniel's behaviour has shifted from "How can we get Daniel to be less disruptive in the classroom?" to "How can we help Daniel use more appropriate strategies to avoid situations in which he fears he will fail?"

This approach to understanding student behaviour is more complex than looking at the surface behaviour the student displays. However, if you carefully analyze the student's intent, you greatly increase the likelihood that you will be able to assist the student in displaying more appropriate behaviours. In the following sections, specific procedures for measuring student behaviour and intervening to change it are recommended. All the strategies assume that you have completed the critical first step of clearly understanding the intent of the student's words or actions.

Observe and Record Student Behaviour to Better Understand the Problem

One component of understanding student behaviour is creating a systematic way to measure its occurrence. By doing this, teachers are better able to judge if the behaviour follows a particular pattern (for example, it occurs during certain types of activities or at certain times of day). Patterns assist in understanding the behavioural intent and the seriousness of the behaviour in relation to teachers' classroom expectations. At the same time, by accurately measuring the behaviour when it becomes a concern and continuing to do so after a plan for addressing the behaviour is implemented, teachers can see if their efforts to change the behaviour have been successful. Sometimes, you will observe and record student behaviour yourself. However, if you find that it is not feasible to collect observational information about your students, a school psychologist, a resource teacher, or an administrator can probably help you in this task. Likewise, a parent volunteer, teaching assistant, or student teacher can gather information by observing. The key is to create a support system for yourself rather than decide against the strategy.

Anecdotal recording. One useful strategy for measuring student behaviour is to record specific incidents, including what happened immediately before the behaviour (antecedents) and what happened as a result of the behaviour (consequences). This approach is called an **ABC** (antecedents-behaviours-consequences) **analysis.** For example, Ms. Carlisle is observing Carlos. When the class is directed to form cooperative groups (antecedent), Carlos gets up from his seat and heads for the pencil sharpener (behaviour). Ms. Carlisle asks Carlos to join his group (consequence). By keeping an ongoing ABC log of Carlos's behaviours in the classroom, Ms. Carlisle found out that whenever the class is transitioning from one activity to another, Carlos is likely to be off task. A sample ABC analysis is shown in Figure 12.4.

✓ **Your Learning:** What is an ABC analysis?

Event recording.   One easy way to measure a behaviour is to count how many times the behaviour occurs in a given period of time. This approach is most useful when the behaviour is discrete, that is, has a clear starting and stopping point. For example, it might be appropriate to use **event recording** to count the number of times John is late to class during a week or the number of times David blurts out an answer during a 30-minute large-group social studies lesson. On the other hand, event recording probably would not be helpful in measuring Jane's tantrum or Jesse's delay in starting his assignment, because these behaviours have more to do with how long they last than the number of times they occur.

Event recording is relatively easy. You could keep a tally on an index card taped to your desk or planbook or kept as a bookmark in one of your textbooks. Some teachers use a "beads-in-a-pocket" strategy, transferring any small object from one pocket to another when a count is observed. The key to this type of recording is to have an accurate total of the number of times a behaviour occurred.

Permanent product recording.   If your concern about student behaviour relates to academics, it may be simplest to keep samples of work as a means of measuring behaviour, a strategy called **permanent product recording.**

Student Name ___Denton R.___   Date ___2/26___

Location ___Science–Mr. B___   Observer ___Mr. D___

Start Time ___1:02___   Stop Time ___1:15___

Antecedents	Behaviors	Consequences
1:03 Students getting books out and open to begin class.	Denton pulls out his cap and puts it on.	Students around D. start laughing and saying "hey."
1:05 Teacher notices D. and tells him to remove cap.	D. stands, slowly removes cap, and bows.	Students applaud.
1:14 Teacher asks D. question.	D. says, "Man, I don't know."	Student says, "Yeah, you're stupid." Others laugh.

FIGURE 12.4
ABC Analysis

▶ *How might a behaviour chart help you collaborate with others to develop a plan for responding to a student's behaviour? What other methods of recording behaviour might you use to determine if your behaviour management plan is working?*

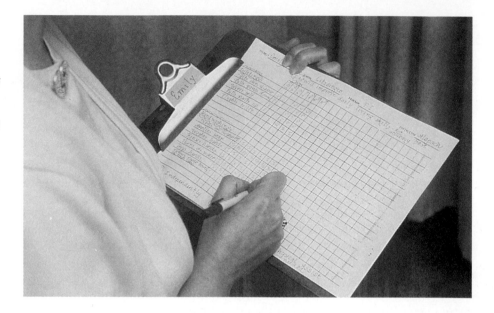

For example, if students in history class regularly have to respond to 10 discussion questions during a single class session, you might keep Sam's completed work to document the percentage of questions he is attempting or the percentage of his responses that are correct.

✓ **Your Learning:** For what behaviours besides tantrums might you want to record the duration of a student's behaviour?

Duration recording.   For some behaviours, your concern is the length of time the behaviour lasts. The strategy of **duration recording** might apply to a young student who cries each morning at the start of the school year, a junior school student who takes an extraordinary amount of time to locate all her learning materials, or a secondary school student who delays beginning assignments. Often, accurately recording duration requires that you have a stopwatch and are able to notice the moment the behaviour begins and the moment it ends. However, duration recording can also measure how long students take to complete assignments by asking them to write on their papers the time when they began and finished their work. A sample duration recording form is included in Figure 12.5.

Interval recording.   Sometimes, you have concerns about a student's behaviour not addressed by any of the systems just described. For example, you might be concerned about how well a student is staying on task during an independent assignment or the extent to which a student plays with others during free-choice time. In these cases, **interval recording** may be the best measuring strategy. To use this approach, you specify a length of time for the observation and then divide the time into smaller intervals. For example, you might observe a 10-minute work or play period divided into 20-second intervals. As you observe the student for each 20-second interval, you indicate whether the behaviour has been present for that entire interval by marking a + or − on the recording form.

Time sampling.   Whereas interval recording requires that you observe a student continuously, **time sampling** uses a similar strategy but involves only peri-

FIGURE 12.5   **Sample Duration Recording**

Student Name		Observer		

Target Behavior ___Refusal to begin assigned work___

Date	Location	Start Time	Stop Time	Comments
10/13/95	Classroom	10:15 a.m.	10:24 a.m.	Writing assignment
10/14/95	Classroom	10:37 a.m.	10:55 a.m.	Peer edits; P.E.-11 a.m.
10/17/95	Music	11:15 a.m.	11:22 a.m.	Group singing; kept head down and ears covered

odic observations of the student. For example, if you wanted to observe whether Patricia played alone or with others during a 30-minute recess, you could divide the time period into 10 three-minute observations. At the end of each three-minute interval, you would glance to see *at that moment* whether Patricia was playing with others or alone and record your observation accordingly. In the completed form in Figure 12.6, you can see that Patricia was on task for approximately 40 percent of the intervals. Time sampling is less demanding than interval recording because you observe only momentarily instead of continuously, but it does include the risk that the behaviours you observe at each sampling are not typical of what has occurred until that moment. This system can also be expedient when your goal is to observe several students at one time; by glancing at three different students and immediately recording the behaviour of each one, you can look at the behaviour patterns of each student during a single observational period.

✓ **Your Learning:** What is the difference between interval and time sampling as strategies for observing and recording student behaviour?

FIGURE 12.6   **Time Sampling**

Student Name	Patricia	Date	11/21/95	
Location	Classroom	Observer	K. Powers	
Behavior	On-task	Start time	1:10	Stop time 1:40

Interval Length: 3 minutes

+ = Behavior occurred at end of interval   − = Behavior did not occur at end of interval

Minute:

1		2		3		4		5		6		7		8		9		10	
+	+	−	−	−	−	+	−	−	+	+	+	+	−	−	−	−	+	−	−

On-task = 40% (eight intervals out of 20)

Technology Notes

Technological Aids for Recording Behaviours

SEVERAL simple forms of technology can assist you in recording student behaviour. Here are a few suggestions.

Anecdotal Recording

The computer is a powerful tool for keeping anecdotal records about a student. If you create a file and record your ABC analyses or other anecdotal information in chronological order, you will have a clear and accurate record that can be shared with others or used as a basis for deciding how to intervene to help a student and whether a particular intervention is successful.

Event Recording

Any of the counters available for golf or other sports can be used to keep track of classroom events. For example, if you want to count how many times Yvonne appropriately calls out an answer during a 20-minute lesson, you could wear a wrist counter and simply "click" it each time Yvonne calls out. At the end of the lesson,

▶ *Teachers evaluating a program for behavioural observation and record keeping.*

you could then transfer your tally to a computer or paper record.

Permanent Products

If part of your problem solving concerns the amount of work a student begins, finishes, or completes accurately, a computer record might be a preferred strategy. For example, if a student begins to write a story on the computer but does not complete it, this record can be saved for future reference. Another alternative is to ask students to use a tape recorder for assignments that can be completed out loud. This specific evidence of the student's work can give a sense of how much of an assignment the student completed.

Duration Recording

If a student's behaviour is audible (for example, a tantrum), you can create an accurate record of duration. When the behaviour begins, you simply start tape-recording and stop when it ceases. You can then later time the behaviour.

Interval and Time Sampling

A tape-recorded signal to remind you to observe for a behaviour, or a watch that will emit a tone at specified intervals, can help you systematically gather information about student behaviour. In addition, you could record the behaviour using a printing calculator. For example, if you plan to indicate with a "+" or "−" whether a student is working appropriately with peers at the end of each five-minute segment, you could simply strike either of those keys on a calculator. After the recording period, you would have a printed record of your observations.

Source: From "Recording Behaviour with Ease" *by M. A. Koorland, L. E. Monda, and C. O. Vail, 1988, Teaching Exceptional Children, 21*(1), 59–61. Used by permission of Council for Exceptional Children.

Other considerations.   Teachers sometimes say that measuring behaviour with the precision implied by these approaches is not realistic. It is certainly true that you will not routinely have the time to use these strategies with many students. However, when you are faced with a student whose behaviour is particularly persistent and puzzling, the time you take to record it systematically will give you a clearer picture of how to address the problem. In addition, if you create several generic behaviour-recording forms that can be adapted to a number of approaches, and if you enlist the assistance of other school professionals, as mentioned earlier, you may find that recording observations is not as burdensome as you might imagine. See the Technology Notes for more ideas for recording observations.

Develop a Plan

The result of observing and recording behaviour is a profile of the student's behaviour. This profile gives you a sense of the seriousness of the behaviour and can help you develop a plan that is either relatively unobtrusive (for minor misbehaviour) or extremely systematic (for chronic, serious behaviour problems). It can also alert you to whether you might also be contributing to the problems and help you decide how to change your own teaching behaviour. For example, you might realize through your observations that the student begins to misbehave only when you have asked students to sit listening to you for extended periods of time. Instead of considering a student-change plan, the first strategy might be to consider a teacher-change plan!

If you decide that you need a systematic response to student behaviour, review the options presented in this chapter to select an approach. Specifically, first consider whether you can prevent the behaviour by changing your classroom arrangement or instructional practices. Next, decide if a group behaviour management technique is indicated so you do not single out one student. If these options do not seem appropriate, you might employ simple strategies directed at a single student that do not require ongoing attention. The final set of approaches are reserved for persistent and serious behaviour problems. This set includes all the options for increasing positive and decreasing negative behaviours. If appropriate, you might also use a cognitive behaviour management strategy. The Case in Practice on page 410 models the development of a behaviour plan.

Connections: What are the options presented earlier in this chapter for responding to student behaviour?

Implement the Plan

Once you have identified how to change the student's behaviour, you are faced with the task of implementing your plan. It is important to have a clear structure for implementation because the key to managing student behaviour effectively is a systematic response.

Contracts.   One straightforward way to use one or combine several of the strategies for increasing or decreasing behaviour is through **behaviour contracts**. A behaviour contract is an agreement between the teacher and student that clearly specifies the expectations for the student, the rewards for meeting expectations, the consequences of not meeting expectations, and the timeframe

▼▼▼▼▼▼▼▼▼

Case in Practice

Analyzing a Behaviour Plan

MISTY is a student who has many charming characteristics, but she can also create major disturbances in her classroom. Misty is categorized as having a mild cognitive or developmental disability, but her teachers agree that her disability also has an emotional component. In her grade two classroom, Misty craves teacher attention and often brings flowers or other small gifts to her teacher. However, when Misty is asked to complete a challenging assignment, she is likely either to have a loud and lengthy tantrum or to cross her arms, put her head down, and say over and over again, "I can't, I can't, I can't."

Mr. Kennedy has worked with the special education teacher and school psychologist to devise a plan to address this negative behaviour. When Mr. Kennedy is about to assign Misty work to do, he alerts her that he is about to give it, and then presents only half the assignments at one time. Misty has learned to say "I know I can, I know I can" before she ever sees the assignment. When Misty looks at the first item, she is to raise her hand for help if she does not know how to complete it. If she does her steps— saying "I know I can," accepting the assignment,

and raising her hand if she is stuck—she earns 10 points toward her favourite activity in school: helping the art teacher clean up at the end of the day. It takes 50 points to reach this goal. Although Mr. Kennedy does not want Misty to work only to get to help the art teacher and has concerns about whether helping the art teacher is instructionally appropriate for Misty, he sees that she is making progress. He will gradually remove the reward system after she is more confident of herself.

Reflections

How is Mr. Kennedy implementing the behaviour plan for Misty? Why do you suppose he and his colleagues decided on this set of procedures? How did they discover what type of reward Misty would work for? What does Mr. Kennedy mean when he says he is worried about the art-helping activity being "instructionally appropriate"? What do you think? How would you deal with this concern? If this plan does not work for Misty, what alternative plan could be tried? How could the reinforcers and the frequency of reinforcement be altered?

for which the agreement is valid. Contracts are best used with students such as Joseph and Marysha, who are old enough to understand their content and whose disabilities either do not affect their cognitive functioning or affect it only marginally. However, simple contracts can be used with almost any student (Downing, 1990). As you review the sample contract in Figure 12.8, notice that it has more detail than some very simple student contracts you may have seen. For exceptional students who have behaviour challenges, simple contracts are often ineffective in changing behaviour. The added components of the contract in Figure 12.7 significantly increase its impact on the student.

The original and still most comprehensive information on how to write student behaviour contracts comes from Homme (1970). He stresses these points:

1.   The reward that goes with the contract should be immediate; that is, as close in time as possible to the performance of the desired behaviour.
2.   Initial contracts should call for and reward small amounts of the desired behaviour. For example, requiring a student to read an entire book in order

For _____Marta_____
(Student name)

I agree to do these things (what, how much, how well, how often, how measured):
In the lunchroom, eat my lunch quietly and without causing a disruption to
children around me for 10 minutes of the 20-minute lunch period. Ms.
Longleiter will tell me if I'm doing ok.

For doing them I will receive (what, how much, how often, when):
I will leave the lunchroom with Ms. Longleiter for an extra 10 minutes of
recess.

Outstanding performance will be if I
Keep my contract 3 days in a row

My bonus for outstanding performance is
15 extra minutes of reading game time with one of my friends (in the
afternoon of the same day, the bonus is earned).

If I don't meet the terms of my contract, this is the consequence:
I will have time-out until recess begins and I will not be allowed to choose
an activity during Friday morning "Choices" time

This contract will be renegotiated on
April 3, 1996

Marta	*Ms. Kornick*
Student signature	**Teacher signature**
March 17, 1996	*March 17, 1996*
Date	Date

FIGURE 12.7
Sample Student Contract

to earn a reward would probably be too frustrating a task for a student with a reading problem. Instead, the student could be rewarded for each chapter (or even each chapter section or page) completed.

3. Reward frequently with small amounts. This approach has been proven a more effective method than fewer, larger rewards.

4. A contract should call for and reward accomplishments rather than obedience; that is, reward the completion of assigned work or appropriate behaviour rather than "teacher pleasing" behaviours such as staying in seat.

5. Reward the performance only after it occurs. This rule seems obvious, but it is often overlooked. Students who are allowed privileges or rewards before or

during work performance are far less likely to complete the performance successfully than those rewarded after it.

6. The contract must be fair. The amount of work required of the student and the payoff for completing the work must be balanced.

7. The terms of the contract should be clear to the student. The contract should be put in writing and discussed with the student. Each component of the contract should be expressed in language the student understands. If the student is not able to understand a contract, this strategy is probably not the best one. The student and teacher should sign the contract.

8. The contract must be honest. The teacher should be willing to carry out the contract as written and to do so immediately. In practice, this means that you should be sure you can deliver on the promises you make.

9. The contract should be positive. It should specify student accomplishments and rewards rather than restrictions and punishments.

10. Contracts should be used systematically. If the contract is enforced only occasionally, the result may be worse (or at least very confusing) for the student than not using one at all.

Other implementation strategies. For young students or students with limited cognitive abilities, contracts might be too complex. In such cases, you can use simpler strategies. For example, you might note in your planbook that you need to check student work at the end of each 15-minute segment. Alternatively, you might set an egg timer at the beginning of the independent work period to remind yourself to reward a student after five minutes of sustained work. If you are using a group strategy, you can announce to the class that the strategy is in effect for the class period or a certain period of time. There is no single right way to implement a behaviour response plan. As long as you have clearly identified the behaviour of concern, have a specific approach for addressing it, and create a systematic strategy for responding to it, your plan will probably succeed.

Monitor the Plan

You began gathering information about the student's behaviour prior to thinking about how to respond to it. You should continue to keep behaviour records as you implement your plan so you can determine if it is working. To do this, use the same recording strategies presented earlier in this chapter. Remember that some students' behaviour will not change rapidly; you should be committed to following your plan for at least two or three weeks before deciding it is ineffective.

As you monitor your plan, any of these situations might occur: First, the inappropriate behaviour may cease completely, or the desired behaviour may be displayed consistently. If this happens, you may decide gradually to withdraw the rewards and consequences you have implemented. For example, if you are using a contract with a student to eliminate his use of profane language in class and no profane language is occurring, you can gradually make it more difficult for the student to earn a reward, and then stop using a contract altogether. This is called **fading out** the reward system.

Second, the plan you are implementing may have value but need modification. Perhaps it takes too much time to implement, or the rewards need adjustment. Such alterations are not unusual; simply modify the plan and continue to monitor its effectiveness. For example, if you created a point system for your grade ten keyboarding class that includes points for being seated when the bell rings, points for turning homework in at the beginning of class, and points for having an assignment notebook and pen in class, you might discover that the system is too difficult to monitor. You might eliminate the points for everything except homework for all but the two students who chronically fail to come to class on time with supplies in hand.

Third, the plan may not be working. As you track the number and duration of tantrums for one of your students, you might learn that time-out seems to be causing more tantrums that last longer. If a situation like this occurs, try to analyze what happened. A resource teacher, psychologist, or counsellor might be able to assist you in this analysis and to suggest an alternative plan. In fact, in instances in which problem solving about a student fails to achieve the results you had hoped for, shared problem solving with colleagues as outlined in Chapter 3 is highly recommended as your next course of action. Special educators often have had extensive preparation in behaviour modification and considerable experience in designing effective behaviour management systems. In some schools, the school counsellor or school psychologist might also be available as a resource. Of course, school administrators might also assist you on behaviour topics, particularly if you have students who are particularly disruptive. A shared problem-solving session involving all or at least some of these individuals can be very helpful for both you and the student.

Finally, it is imperative that you work closely with parents to resolve student behaviour problems if the parents are willing to participate. Parents can sometimes clarify why a student is behaving in a particular way (for example, a death in the family or a divorce; a weekend trip; a cultural response to a school activity). In addition, they can reinforce school messages at home, and they can help provide tangible or activity rewards at home earned by appropriate behaviour during the school day. By creating partnerships with parents, you increase options for responding to student behaviour. However, if parents are unable to work closely with you, it is imperative that you devise a response to student behaviour using school resources.

Do It! Obtain permission to attend a meeting at which professional educators problem solve about a student's behaviour. What procedure do they use? What role does a parent play? What types of strategies are proposed? How will the plan they develop be monitored?

Summary

Responding to student behaviour begins with creating a classroom learning environment that encourages appropriate behaviour and discourages inappropriate behaviour. The next option for responding to behaviour is to promote positive behaviours in your entire class group through techniques such as the Good Behaviour Game, peer-mediated instruction, and perhaps token economies.

A next alternative is to employ simple interventions designed to respond to the behaviour of an individual student. These include low-intrusion strategies such as strategically grouping students and responding to surface behaviours. If needed, the next set of options for responding to student behaviour are systematic individual strategies for increasing positive and decreasing negative behaviours.

Behavior Home Page
www.state.ky.us/agencies/behave/homepage.html

Perceptual Control Theory, Reinforcement Theory, and the Responsible Thinking Process

www.edford.com/rtpvrft.html

Why Children Misbehave

www.allkids.org/Epstein/ Articles/Misbehavior.html

For some students, self-management through cognitive behaviour management is an additional option.

To decide how serious a student behaviour is and which set of alternatives might be needed to address it, you can use a problem-solving approach that includes identifying the problem behaviour, confirming it by observing and recording the behaviour, developing a plan to address the problem, implementing the plan, and monitoring its effectiveness. Professional colleagues and parents can be important allies in making this problem-solving process successful.

Applications in Teaching Practice

Developing Strategies for Responding to Individual Student Behaviour

Ms. Bind teaches grade nine English. One of her students is Russell, a student with learning and behaviour problems. Russell tends to be a class clown. He makes flippant remarks that border on being disrespectful of other students and Ms. Bind. He is often reprimanded for chatting with other students instead of listening, and then he will complain that he doesn't know how to do an assignment that was just explained. The other students generally like Russell, and they sometimes urge him to further classroom antics. Ms. Bind is not alone in her concern about Russell's behaviour. His other teachers report a similar pattern. All are concerned about his slipping grades and worry that in high school it will be difficult for him to get the adult supervision that helped him be more successful in elementary school. Ms. Bind's tally of classroom incidents from the last week suggests that Russell is reprimanded at least three times per class period. The reprimands tend to occur when the class is transitioning from one activity to another, for example, from a large-group lecture to an individual assignment.

Ms. Bind, resource teacher Mr. Chow, and counsellor Ms. Lassaux have been meeting about Russell. Their first step was to think about Russell's intent. They decided that the behaviours he is displaying probably have to do with seeking attention, from both peers and teachers. They spend a considerable time discussing what type of attention is available to Russell through more appropriate sources, and they weigh the pros and cons of various alternatives for responding to Russell's behaviour. They also drift into a conversation about the impact the other students are having on maintaining Russell's behaviour. Ms. Bind is convinced that if Russell's audience were not so attentive, many of his problems might take care of themselves.

Questions

1. What strategies could Ms. Bind and the other teachers use to address the group response to Russell's behaviour? What cautions would you have for them in trying these strategies?
2. What simple strategies could Ms. Bind use to help Russell behave more appropriately in class? For each strategy, identify potential positive outcomes that could occur but also outline potential problems that could arise.

3. What types of reinforcement might work for Russell? How could Ms. Bind ascertain what reinforcers to use if reinforcement is the strategy decided upon? Which types of reinforcers would you avoid in this case?

4. How do you think Russell would respond to strategies designed to decrease his negative behaviour? For example, how might Russell react if he received a detention each time he disrupted class? What type of negative consequence is detention?

5. Is Russell likely to be able to use cognitive behaviour management? Why or why not? If you decided to try a CBM strategy, how would you go about it?

6. What are the next steps Ms. Bind and her colleagues should take? For each problem-solving step, outline what you think might occur.

into groups of five or six. Kathleen's group has five members of varying abilities and skills. Behaviour stemming from Kathleen's emotional disability is usually not evident in this group. Her peers do not respond to her teasing and inappropriate comments. They help her be a constructive group member to help the team get extra points and a possible "free pass" on a future assignment. The two other students in the class who have identified exceptionalities are in two other groups. Mr. Geib distributes materials to the students and gives directions. When everyone is working, he goes from group to group, answering questions and helping students stay focused on their assignment. What is the impact of this type of grouping arrangement in a diverse classroom? Is it more or less effective than traditional instruction? How can Mr. Geib avoid the problem of some students doing all the work for their groups while other students contribute little? What is the social benefit of this classroom grouping arrangement?

MATT is a grade 12 student with learning disabilities and ADHD. When his resource room tutor, Ms. Benoit, asked him to describe his friendships at school, Matt told her, "I get really bored here. It seems that I know lots of people, but I just don't know how to react to these people." He said that he had not been looking forward to returning to school after the winter vacation because he thought the other students didn't like him or found him annoying. Ms. Benoit wrote in her notes that "Matt endures the burden of the academic challenges without the social benefits that most students take for granted." She then set about to use her knowledge about Matt to work with him so that Matt would feel more a part of his school and to foster friendships with peers. How could Ms. Benoit use her knowledge of Matt's perceptions of his relationships with peers to help him? What would you suggest she do in her resource room? How might she work with other teachers to enhance the social acceptance of students like Matt?

Connections: Chapters 4, 5, and 6 address some of the social characteristics of students with disabilities and other special needs.

ONE of the most important reasons given for the trend toward inclusive education for exceptional students is the social benefit (Brown et al., 1989; Mikkelsen, 1992; Schaps & Solomon, 1990). Many educators believe that students with disabilities and other exceptional needs learn appropriate social behaviours and develop friendships only when they have opportunities to interact with their non-disabled peers. At the same time, students without exceptionalities learn that individuals with disabilities are people very much like other people; and they develop sensitivity to people who are not exactly like them and a sense of social responsibility to include exceptional individuals in the classroom community.

How do the social benefits of inclusive education occur? Is it sufficient to integrate exceptional students into a classroom? Does integration alone help other students to become more sensitive and responsive? If not, what does nurture a positive classroom social environment for all students? How are exceptional students perceived by peers? How do exceptional students perceive their relationships with friends and peers? How can these thoughts influence their attitudes toward school? Can this information help teachers promote friendships of exceptional students? What if some students continue to have difficulty in their social interactions with peers, teachers, and other adults in school? What if classmates complain that adaptations for exceptional students are not fair? These are the topics we will explore in this chapter on approaches for building positive social relationships.

As you begin to think about this aspect of inclusive education, you need to keep in mind a few ideas. First, although much of the emphasis on teaching and learning in teacher preparation, including much of the emphasis in this book, concerns academics, your responsibilities as a teacher also include helping all students, whether or not they are exceptional, to learn social skills. Attention to social skills must begin at a very early age and must continue throughout students' school years. Second, you do not need to teach social skills to students apart from your regular class time. As you read this chapter, you will realize that many skills related to developing positive social relationships can be incorporated into your daily instruction, as Mr. Geib was doing in Kathleen's class in the example at the beginning of this chapter. When you think about inclusive education, the issue of social relationships becomes part of your classroom expectations; that is, for some students the social component of their education is the primary classroom goal, whereas for others it is just a part. For example, Lucy's purpose in being in her grade five classroom might have as much to do with learning important life social skills, such as talking to peers and participating in group activities, as it does with learning arithmetic skills. She has further opportunities to refine her social skills working as a teacher's assistant. Kathleen is learning how to be a member of a group without being disruptive. For Matt, however, it appears that social skills and social acceptance are troublesome and are having an impact on how he perceives school and himself in school. This may mean that in his case, however, academic expectations and social expectations are equally important. One of your responsibilities as a teacher in an inclusive classroom is to clarify these expectations with special educators and others who work with exceptional students.

◤ What Is the Teacher's Role in Promoting Positive Social Interactions Among Students With and Without Disabilities?

A beginning point for understanding how to create a classroom in which students interact with each other appropriately is to look at what we know about children's interactions. This knowledge provides a basis for thinking about how you can then group students and supervise their interactions to accomplish the social goals of inclusion.

Students with exceptionalities want to succeed in the classroom. However, they often experience low levels of acceptance by their peers. They are more likely than their peers to lack social development and social acceptance. This seems to be true whether they have, for example, learning disabilities (Gresham, 1993; Levesque, 1997) communication disorders (Lass, 1991), behaviour problems (Sabornie, Kauffman, Ellis, Marshall, & Elksnin, 1988), or hearing loss (Jaussi, 1991). Recent research suggests that it is not exceptionalities per se, but peer norms, that have such influence on students' social status among peers

The Special Friends and Circle of Friends programs are only two of many strategies for promoting friendship and support. Other strategies include pairing students on the basis of shared interests so that they have a natural basis for becoming friends (Fox, 1989) and having students brainstorm ideas for welcoming and making friends with a new class member with a disability (Stainback et al., 1992). In addition, teachers can nurture supportive interactions. For example, a classmate might volunteer to explain cafeteria procedures to the peer and to share lunch with him or her. A secondary student with a similar class schedule might volunteer to help the classmate move from class to class.

Sometimes, you will have to address problems related to student support and friendship. Some students (and some teachers, too) express concern about the fairness of making accommodations for exceptional students, such as changing the consequences for misbehaviour, altering the amount or type of work expected, grading on a different scale, or using rewards to which other students may not have access. The Professional Edge below offers advice about responding to issues of fairness.

Professional Edge
Responding to Issues of Fairness

A PROBLEM that seems to exist in schools is confusion between fairness and equality. As Richard LaVoie, in his videotape *How Difficult Can This Be,* points out, responding to every student in the same way is equal. However, responding to each student based on need is the meaning of fairness. He contends that schools should try to be places of fairness, not equality. Here are some suggestions for addressing fairness:

1. Be clear about your own beliefs and values concerning the appropriateness and justice of making accommodations for exceptional students.

2. Discuss issues related to fairness openly with students. This openness includes alerting them to accommodations that exceptional students in class might receive, discussing their own exceptionalities, and role-playing situations that could occur in class that might not be perceived as "fair" and how to respond to them.

3. Prevent students from basing their perception of themselves and their achievement on other students. It is your responsibility to avoid conversations in which students compare themselves to classmates, either positively or negatively.

4. If a student says something like, "Yeah, but Stanley yelled in the room and *he* didn't get his name on the board. That's not fair!" the best way for you to respond is to say, "Let's just talk about you. What was it that made you yell?" The worst response is to engage in a conversation about Stanley's exceptionalities.

5. If parents attempt to compare their child to another, politely but firmly explain that it is ethically and legally inappropriate for you to discuss other students. Then ask them to clarify their concerns about their child. If they are dissatisfied with your response, enlist the support and assistance of your principal or vice-principal.

Providing Positive Role Models

A third component of promoting positive peer relationships is offering positive role models. There are several ways to do this. First, as a teacher in an inclusive school, you might be the most influential model for students learning how to interact with a peer with a disability. If you are positive in your interactions and treat a student with a disability as a full classroom member, students will respond in a similar way. For example, if you talk to a student with a severe disability as though he or she is a very young child even though you are teaching a grade eight

Connections: Chapter 3 describes findings of some of the research about families of exceptional children.

FYI: A colleague or community member who has a disability might be a great resource as a positive role model for students.

Professional Edge

Tips for Interacting with Siblings of Students with Disabilities

SOMETIMES, having a child with a disability has little effect on the siblings in a family. In other cases, a child with a disability profoundly influences family and sibling dynamics. The effect of having a sibling with a disability is determined by many factors and is not easy to predict. If you have students with siblings who are disabled, keep these points in mind.

1. Siblings' attitudes toward their brother or sister with a disability are often most influenced by their parents' attitudes.

2. Siblings' attitudes might also be affected by the nature and severity of the disability, the difference in their ages, the number of children in the family, the family's ability to provide needed specialized care, and the amount of accurate information the sibling receives about the disability.

3. Girls might feel more sense of responsibility toward their sibling than boys do. This may occur because they are asked more often to help care for their sibling with a disability.

4. Young children sometimes believe they can "catch" a disability. An older sibling might think he or she "caused" a disability by wishing the new baby would not be born. If you have a student with these beliefs, you should alert the parents.

5. If your student does not seem to feel that having a brother or sister with a disability is extraordinary, you should take the cue and not draw attention to that fact.

6. Some siblings of students with disabilities will look for attention at school because they feel, correctly or not, that the brother or sister gets a disproportionate amount of attention in the family. You need to be understanding. If you feel the student's need for attention is interfering with education, you might refer the student to the counselor or social worker.

7. Some students will gladly talk about their sibling's abilities as part of school awareness activities, but others might feel embarrassed by this request. You should check with the student and his or her parents before planning this type of activity.

8. If a student with a disability experiences a problem in school, a brother or sister might be asked to help. For some, this is a burden. They feel they cannot have their own life because of their sibling's needs. If a school problem occurs, it is often more appropriate to contact the student's parents and inform the siblings so they know what is happening.

Connections: Follow the second INCLUDE step, noting student strengths and needs, to help identify students' social-skills abilities.

Do It! Identify and contact local and national support groups for people with disabilities. Ask a representative of each about the availability of speakers and other resource materials. With your peers, arrange to invite these speakers to speak at your university or school.

✓ **Your Learning:** Why should your instructional program include information about individuals with disabilities? What strategies can you use to ensure that your instructional program educates your students about people with disabilities?

class, other students will probably treat the student as a young child. However, if you speak in an age-appropriate voice, so will your students. Interacting with students with disabilities in the same way as you would interact with anyone else provides the modelling that will help shape all student interactions.

Students without disabilities also need to see that students with disabilities and other special needs have many *abilities*. Pointing out contributions made by a student with a disability (Cohen, Lotan, & Catanzarite, 1990), giving students with disabilities standard classroom responsibilities, and recognizing a student's best effort—whether or not it fits within traditional curriculum standards—all these actions lead peers to recognize that the student is a valuable classroom community member (Stainback, Stainback, & Jackson, 1992). Teachers can also promote participation in extracurricular activities by all students and encourage participation in community groups such as Cubs and Guides. Family and community or national support groups also can be resources for providing positive role models. Parents or siblings might discuss a student's abilities as part of school awareness activities. As the Professional Edge on page 423 suggests, however, there are some special considerations relating to siblings of students with disabilities.

How Can Teachers Provide Education about Students with Disabilities?

Besides promoting positive social interactions between students with and without disabilities, teachers play an important role in educating their students about all types of differences among individuals, including disabilities (Andrews, 1996). Even during years in which you have few or no students with disabilities in your class, you can positively affect student understanding and attitude toward individuals with disabilities by building information about them into your curriculum. In this section, these strategies are described: informing students through direct instruction; using video and print media; demonstrating and using adaptive technology; and arranging simulation activities. The Case in Practice suggests why there is a strong need for school-based disability awareness and sensitivity training.

Informing through Direct Instruction

One of the most straightforward strategies for teaching students about individuals with disabilities is to provide them with relevant information. For example, you might invite guest speakers to your class to discuss what it is like to have a disability and how people with disabilities lead successful lives. You can also find an individual to speak to your class through a local disability advocacy group or parent group. A local college or university might also be a valuable resource.

You can also educate students about disabilities by incorporating relevant topics into the curriculum. As you teach, you can mention famous individuals with disabilities who contributed to various fields. For example, when studying American history, you can raise the fact that Franklin D. Roosevelt had polio and

Case in Practice

Intervening to Promote Positive Social Interactions

MRS. HAYNES is in a quandary. This afternoon during her last-period grade eight science class, she discovered that four girls who share a lab station had taped a sign to their lab table that said, "Only really cool and cute people are allowed to sit here." The girls had told a less popular student with a mild cognitive disability and mild cerebral palsy that she couldn't join them for the lab because she wasn't cool and certainly wasn't cute. The girl, Shana, had quietly sat at the end of the lab station for the entire period, fighting back tears. The other girls had been giggling the entire time. With many student questions and an interruption from the office, Mrs. Haynes had not realized what was happening until near the end of the period. She had felt like strangling the four girls, and her heart was broken for Shana. She had decided that Shana needed attention more immediately than the other girls and had spent nearly a half hour after school with her. She would call the girls' parents tonight, as she had told them she would, but she was still extremely disappointed that four of her students could be so cruel. The incident also made her wonder what else went on that she was unaware of. She resolved to spend the evening deciding how to take proactive steps to influence the thinking of these and her other students.

Reflections

Why might girls in grade eight be so insensitive? How might younger students or high school students convey the same message? If you were Mrs. Haynes, what would you have said to Shana after school? Why? How would you talk to the other girls' parents? What consequence would you impose for the girls' cruel prank? How would you go about educating these students about exceptional individuals and the diversity that exists across all people? What activities could be incorporated into this science class? What similar activities could be used in a primary class or high school classroom?

used a wheelchair. In science, you can explain Thomas Edison's hearing loss and Albert Einstein's alleged learning disability, or modern-day Stephen Hawking's disabilities. In the fine arts, examples of individuals with disabilities include singer Stevie Wonder, and composer Ludwig von Beethoven. In sports, Rick Hansen provides a modern-day Canadian example. Students' understanding and respect for individuals with disabilities are better fostered through an ongoing education program rather than occasional "special events" that highlight this topic (Sapon-Shevin, 1992). For example, if your school participates in an ongoing program to increase students' understanding of racial, cultural, religious, and other types of diversity, disability awareness is appropriately included as another type of diversity.

A third source of direct information about disabilities is special awareness programs. An example of a program for use in inclusive classrooms is *Kids on the Block,* a set of puppets and supporting materials and books about disabilities. The puppets "talk" to students about having disabilities and interacting with classmates and others who have them. This program, typically staffed by volunteers, is available in many communities. The goal of volunteers who participate is to promote awareness that people with disabilities are individuals and to make non-

FYI: In addition to a puppet program, *Kids on the Block* has a series of books about many different types of disabilities.

disabled students more comfortable interacting with them. The special educators in your school should know what programs are available in your area and how you can access them.

Using Video and Print Media

Do It! Create a resource list of videos, television programs, and books about people with disabilities.

Individuals with disabilities have gained a greater voice in all aspects of our society, and their visibility has also increased in the media. A trip to your local library or video store or a casual reading of your newspaper can lead you to a wealth of information. You could identify how the information relates to your instructional goals, find ways to incorporate it into your lessons, and arrange discussions so that your students feel free to ask questions and share their insights.

Your school or district might have educational videos about students with disabilities. Many award-winning movies also address disability and are appropriate for older students. These films include *My Left Foot, Rainman, The Miracle Worker, If You Could See What I Hear, The Other Side of the Mountain, Children of a Lesser God* (McGookey, 1992), and *Forrest Gump.* Television shows and made-for-TV movies also address disability topics.

Books written by and for children exist about virtually every type of disability and other special need. For example, Ontario author Jean Little, who is blind, has written a number of award-winning books about exceptional children including *Listen for the Singing* (about a girl with low vision whose brother is blinded), *Take Wing* (whose main character has a younger brother with developmental disabilities), and *Mine for Keeps* (in which the main character has cerebral palsy).

▶ *How do students without disabilities learn about their peers with disabilities? How can teachers promote friendships between students with and without exceptionalities?*

Her autobiography about growing up blind, written for children, is called *Little by Little*. Two British Columbia authors have written about exceptional children. *Finders, Keepers* by Andrea Sparling is about a boy who discovers he has learning disabilities, and *Can't You Be Still* and *Nobody Knows*, about a young girl with cerebral palsy, were written by Sarah Yates. Reading or assigning an appropriate book to your class can be an excellent strategy for introducing a new student and his or her special needs. A reading assignment can also help open a discussion about interacting and treating a classmate respectfully.

Newspapers carry stories about individuals with disabilities, and trends toward inclusive education. Newspapers such as *The Globe and Mail* are a source of this type of information, but your local paper also carries stories you can use.

Do It! For the next four weeks, read the newspaper carefully for stories about people with disabilities. What topics are covered? How could you use these stories in your classroom?

Demonstrating and Using Adaptive Technology

Another means of educating students about individuals with disabilities is by taking advantage of both high-tech and low-tech adaptations. You can teach students about these adaptations or help them learn to interact with classmates who use them. Some of the adaptive materials available include talking computers, calculators, and watches; adaptive communication devices such as communication boards; and adapted tools with easy-grip handles and simplified movement requirements (for example, lever door handles instead of knobs). Examples of adaptations are included in the Technology Notes on pages 428–429.

Arranging Simulation Activities

In addition to teaching students about disabilities directly, through the use of films, books, other media, and demonstrations of adaptive technology, you can help students understand what it is like to have a disability by arranging simulations (Anderson & Milliren, 1983; Hallenbeck & McMaster, 1991). A **simulation** is an activity in which students experience what it might be like to have a disability as they carry out typical school, home, or community activities. An important component is providing opportunities for students to discuss what they learn from simulation experiences and how they could be more sensitive and respectful to their classmates with disabilities. In one school district, all secondary students attended an assembly at which class members who had participated in simulation activities shared their experiences (Hallenbeck & McMaster, 1991). The following sections describe effective simulations for specific types of disabilities. Keep in mind, however, that students also need to understand that simulating a disability is not exactly like having the disability. Classroom discussions based on simulations should address this fact.

Simulations for physical disabilities.   Physical disabilities can be safely simulated in a number of ways using simple materials. For example, to show students what it is like to have limited dexterity, ask them to perform fine motor tasks such as picking up a paper clip, sorting papers, and writing while wearing a bulky glove. Another way of demonstrating limited motor control is to ask students to keep their dominant hand in their pocket and complete schoolwork or eat lunch using only their non-dominant hand.

Technology Notes

Communications Technology for Individuals with Disabilities

TECHNOLOGY is making it easier for people with disabilities to communicate. Computers and other technological aids are powerful tools for fostering social relationships among students with and without disabilities. Here are some of the products available from Apple Computer, Inc. for Apple, Macintosh, or PowerBook computers to assist individuals with special needs:

1. **Touch screen.** With this computer screen, the computer can respond to touch instead of traditional keyboard strokes.

2. **Talking word processor.** When an individual types letters, words, or sentences into the computer, the computer can "say" them back.

3. **Screen image enlarger.** This adaptive device makes print on the screen up to 16 times larger than the standard image.

4. **Talking computer commands.** This software package enables the computer to add "spoken" words to the computer icons, windows, and menus.

5. **TTY modem.** This modem is a full-functioning text telephone (TTY). It can place and receive telephone calls for individuals with hearing impairments. It also doubles as a standard send/receive fax modem.

6. **Customized keyboard—large.** This keyboard is larger than a standard keyboard and has a touch-sensitive surface instead of keys. Users can adjust how light or heavy a touch is needed for a keystroke. They can also use different keyboard overlays for specialized applications.

7. **Customized keyboard—small.** For individuals who have a very limited range of motion, a small keyboard is also available. People who can use only one hand, for example, find this keyboard easier to use than other keyboards.

8. **Ultrasonic head control.** This adaptive headset enables an individual to operate the computer by moving his or her head and blowing on a straw. Its primary use is for people with severe physical disabilities. With this equipment, neither a keyboard nor a mouse is needed to operate the computer.

9. **Computer voice input.** With this adaptive equipment, computer users can speak aloud computer commands and the computer will recognize them and carry them out. In addition, the computer will enter dictated letters and other information into a word processing package.

10. **Portable computer for wheelchair users.** With a battery adapter, a notebook computer can be plugged into a wheelchair's power supply.

11. **Word prediction tool.** Software makes it easier for some individuals to write because it predicts the words they are typing, thus making spelling more accurate and reducing the amount of typing needed.

Students might also experience what it is like to use a wheelchair, which you could borrow from your special services office or rent from a health supply store. In one activity, students are paired for a schoolwide scavenger hunt, with one student in a wheelchair and the other as a companion. Students perform simple tasks that they normally take for granted, such as getting a drink from a drinking

Customized keyboard and head control device

IBM and companies making peripherals for use with IBM computers also have many products that facilitate communication for individuals with disabilities. Here are examples of products that can be used with IBM and IBM-compatible computers:

1. **Unicorn Smart Keyboard.** This keyboard has a large 20 cm × 30 cm touch-sensitive surface and includes special overlays for customizing the keyboard layout. This keyboard is helpful for students with visual impairments and those with limited motor control.

2. **Speech synthesizers.** Speech synthesizers convert information typed or scanned into a computer into speech, complete with appropriate inflection, tone, and pitch. They can also be used with equipment such as the Smart Keyboard. Some of the speech synthesizers available for use with IBM-compatible computers are Type 'n Talk, Braille 'n Speak, Personal Speech System, and Apollo Speech Synthesizer.

3. **VoiceType.** This software is a flexible speech-recognition program that lets the user control many software programs by speaking.

4. **Screen Magnifier.** This software magnifies words and images on the computer monitor from two to 32 times. It can also reverse the colours on the screen.

5. **Kurzweil Personal Reader.** This piece of hardware scans print material and translates it to speech. The scanned material can be listened to immediately or stored for later use.

6. **Portable computing.** IBM and compatible computers are available in a wide variety of notebook styles. With appropriate adaptations, they can often be used to enable students with disabilities to communicate better with their peers and teachers as well as to assist them in completing homework.

fountain, using the bathroom, making a phone call from a public phone, and getting to a second-floor classroom or out to a sidewalk.

Simulations for sensory disabilities.   Swimmer's earplugs can be used to simulate a hearing impairment. Activities that students might try while "hearing impaired" include eating lunch with friends in a noisy cafeteria, watching a television show or video with classmates with the sound unamplified, and talking on the phone. Students could discuss visual clues they used to tell what others were saying and how they felt when they missed important messages. For vision impairments, a blindfold or eye patch can be an effective simulation. Partial sight can be simulated by using waxed paper or crumpled plastic wrap inserted into glasses frames. Activities while "vision impaired" might include eating lunch, completing a written assignment, reading from the board, or locating a book on a shelf. Discussion topics might include the difference between not being able to see at all and not being able to see well, and how others were and were not helpful to the student experiencing impaired vision.

Do It! Think of other ways that you could arrange simulation activities for your students using simple materials. Try to generate ideas for each type of exceptionality.

Simulations for learning and cognitive disabilities.   Students can learn what it is like to have a learning or cognitive disability by experiencing some of the inherent frustrations of these disabilities. For example, asking students to write or trace a pattern by watching their hands in a small mirror is effective. One other strategy is to give students a reading assignment far above their reading level and then ask complex questions about it. Discussion based on these simulations can highlight the frustration of knowing that one is not "dumb" but not being able to complete certain activities successfully; of wanting to give up when tasks are difficult; and of worrying about what others think when one cannot do as well as others.

Simulation activities can be divided among classroom teams, with each team reporting their experiences to the whole class. Older students might extend their experience by preparing simulation activities for younger students, leading them through the activities, and conducting follow-up discussions.

▨ How Can You Develop and Support Peer Tutoring?

Connections: Peer tutoring in relation to student groupings is defined in Chapter 7.

Students also learn about disabilities and other special needs through direct experience and interaction with classmates. Peer tutoring has been discussed as a small-group student grouping arrangement in the classroom and as an instructional approach. It is also a means for facilitating positive social relationships in diverse and inclusive classrooms by helping students develop social skills and providing a context for positive interactions. In some secondary schools, peer tutoring is a daily source of positive social interactions for exceptional adolescents as well as a major source of academic learning (e.g., Levesque, 1997).

Research on peer-tutoring programs has addressed factors such as the age of the tutor and the tutee, the amount of time allocated for tutoring, the content selected for peer tutoring, and the amount of program structure. All these factors influence peer-tutoring outcomes. The Professional Edge on page 431 summarizes advice about all types of peer tutoring based on such research (Rekrut, 1994).

Professional Edge

Tips for Successful Peer Tutoring

PEER-tutoring outcomes are influenced by many factors, including the type of material being learned, the age and sex of the students involved, and the level of achievement and amount of training the tutors and tutees have. Keep in mind the following tips for fostering successful peer tutoring.

1. Many aspects of the school curriculum are amenable to instruction and practice via peer and cross-age tutoring.

2. A student of any age may be either the tutor or tutee; the older student does not necessarily have to be the tutor.

3. Peer and cross-age tutors are often high achievers, but an achiever at any level might serve well as a tutor. More important than

actual ability is the tutor's ability to teach without making value judgments about the tutee.

4. Same-sex partners work best in both cross-age and peer tutoring, especially for older students.

5. Tutors should be trained both in how to interact with their tutees and in how to present content to them and record their learning.

6. Tutoring can influence both cognitive and affective objectives for students.

Source: Adapted from "Peer and Cross-Age Tutoring: The Lessons of Research" by M. D. Rekrut, 1994, *Journal of Reading,* 37(5), pp. 356–362. Used by permission of International Reading Association.

Developing Peer Tutoring Programs

Developing a **peer tutoring program** can be as simple or complex as you want it to be. You can create your own system within your classroom, partner some or all of your students with another group of students, or help coordinate a school-wide tutoring program (Jenkins & Jenkins, 1985). Established and researched programs also exist, such as the *Classwide Peer Tutoring Program* (Greenwood, Delquadri, & Hall, 1989).

In the *Classwide Peer Tutoring Program,* teachers assign all students to tutoring pairs that are changed weekly. Each tutoring pair is also assigned to one of two classroom teams. Pairs work on instructional content that is broken into daily assignments. The tutoring format is highly structured. Tutors have explicit instructions on how to present information, and tutees have many opportunities for practice, with immediate correction if they make errors. When a tutee answers a question correctly, that student earns a point for his or her team. Tutors keep track of points earned. The winning classroom team is announced and posted daily or weekly, depending on the structure of the program. This team earns a special privilege or the applause of all class members.

Steps for setting up a peer tutoring program of your own are listed in Figure 13.2 and described in the following sections.

FYI: Use more than one tutoring arrangement in your classroom to avoid the problem of tutees feeling stigmatized because they are receiving assistance.

Connections: Reciprocal tutoring is very similar to reciprocal teaching, which was introduced in Chapter 10.

their list, they review it until the end of the tutoring session. This example illustrates the need for a clear set of procedures for tutors to follow, whatever format you use. Clear procedures help keep participants in tutoring sessions on task.

Training tutors. Many authors distinguish between effective and less effective peer-tutoring programs on the basis of the preparation tutors receive for their teaching roles. Evidence suggests that intensive tutor training results in better tutoring outcomes (Barron & Foot, 1991). Sample topics for a peer tutor training program are outlined in Figure 13.3.

Supporting Peer-Tutoring Programs

Part of a tutor training program includes follow-up and assessment. For example, in a cross-age tutoring program, it is important to bring tutors together periodically to discuss how they are doing and how they have resolved problems and to thank them for their work. When tutoring extends beyond your own class group, it is a nice touch to provide tutor appreciation certificates or other tokens of appreciation.

Do It! With classmates, develop a manual you could use for training peer tutors at the grade level you expect to teach. What illustrations will you include? How will you organize the critical information? Try out your manual by setting up a small peer tutoring program as part of your field experiences.

FIGURE 13.3

Topics for Training Peer Tutors

1. Sensitivity to others' feelings, needs for acceptance, and fears of rejection.
2. Ways to develop positive relationships with tutees, including using respectful language, giving positive reinforcement, showing personal interest, and offering constructive feedback.
3. Effective communication and interactions skills
   - Giving clear directions
   - Making teaching interesting to the tutee
   - Acting interested—and being interested
   - Explaining things in another way
   - Correcting the tutee without criticism
   - Praising correct responses
   - Admitting mistakes
4. Tutoring procedures and guidelines
   - Having all needed materials prepared
   - Beginning a session without teacher assistance
   - Breaking big steps into smaller ones
   - Showing how to do something if the tutee does not understand
   - Giving the tutee time to think before responding
   - Helping but not doing the work for the tutee
   - Monitoring time to finish on time
   - Reviewing what has been taught
5. Procedures for gathering data on the tutee's learning, such as using a checklist or helping the tutee chart progress.
6. Problem solving about issues that could come up during peer tutoring.
7. The tutoring schedule and the need for commitment.

Several other factors go into the supports needed for a successful peer tutoring program. These factors are discussed below:

1. Keep supervising and monitoring your peer tutoring program once it is established so you can catch small problems before they become large problems and provide support and praise to tutors and tutees.
2. Support from the staff and administration of your school can provide ideas and classrooms with which to partner. Administrators can also help with scheduling, budget, and communication with parents.
3. Volunteers can not only tutor, but they may be able to take over day-to-day management of the details.
4. Communication with parents before a peer-tutoring program starts about the rationale and organization should help to allay fears of tutors losing instructional time. Periodic updates during the program serve to keep parents informed. Be prepared to answer any questions parents may have.

Do It! Volunteer to help set up a peer-tutoring program in a local school. What are the program's objectives? What difficulties did you encounter? What were the most rewarding aspects of the project?

Connections: Chapters 2 and 3 included strategies for parent communication. These strategies could be part of your approach to communicating with parents about peer tutoring.

How Can You Use Cooperative Learning Strategies to Facilitate Social Inclusion?

Another option for promoting peer relations is cooperative learning, introduced in Chapter 7 as an instructional grouping strategy. For nearly three decades, cooperative learning has been proposed as a strategy for promoting positive student interactions in diverse classrooms. It has been used as a strategy for achieving racial and cultural integration (Kemp, 1992), for assisting socially isolated learners (Lew, Mesch, Johnson, & Johnson, 1986), for fostering inclusive education for students with disabilities and other exceptionalities (Gelzheiser & Meyers, 1990; Hutchinson, in press; Stevens & Slavin, 1991), and for accommodating culture-based learning styles.

FYI: Cooperative learning is defined in Chapter 7 as an instructional system in which students work in small groups to achieve shared goals.

Understanding the Rationale for Cooperative Learning

The primary purpose of cooperative learning is to increase students' ability to interact with each other in appropriate ways while they learn. Many studies over the past 20 years have addressed this topic. For example, Solomon and his colleagues (1990) have carefully monitored the social skills development of elementary school students participating in classrooms that stress cooperative learning. They have found that the students spontaneously express more concern for other students and help each other more than do students in comparable classes in which cooperative learning is not emphasized. The students in the cooperative classrooms also are more likely to show affection toward other class members, invite others to join a group activity, and thank or praise each other. Other researchers have demonstrated similar positive effects of cooperative learning on students' social skills and interactions with their peers (Hutchinson, in press; Nastasi & Clements, 1991). Although fewer studies are available on secondary students, the same trend exists. For example, in a study of cooperative learning in a grade ten biology class, students experienced a higher level of self-esteem than did students in a comparison class; they felt their class was treated more fairly; and they displayed more cohesiveness and less competitiveness as a group (Lazarowitz & Karsenty, 1990).

For students with disabilities, the social benefits of cooperative learning appear to accrue in the same way that they do for other students, which in turn helps to promote inclusive education. In one review of nearly 100 studies of cooperative learning (Johnson, Johnson, & Maruyama, 1983), the positive social impact existed for exceptional students, especially when these students receive specific instruction in collaborative skills (Putnam, Rynders, Johnson, & Johnson, 1989). In fact, cooperative learning is often recommended as a fundamental component of inclusive classrooms (Andrews & Lupart, 1993; Hutchinson, in press; Putnam, 1993b; Villa & Thousand, 1992; Wong, 1996). Johnson and Johnson (1989, 1992) summarized the influence of cooperative learning on student social development. On the basis of the 80 studies they have conducted, they concluded that cooperative learning leads to more caring and committed relationships between students with and without disabilities, increased student self-esteem, higher levels of cooperative and social skills, and greater use of critical thinking and higher-order reasoning.

The value of cooperative learning lies in its potential for creating positive peer interactions while at the same time serving as an effective instructional approach. For example, in a study carried out in an inner-city school in Ontario, Hutchinson (in press) worked with a grade eight teacher who was implementing cooperative learning in mathematics problem solving. Twelve of the 25 students in the class had been identified as having learning disabilities or behavioural difficulties. The students were taught to work with a partner and think out loud. In the first session, many of the students would try a problem and then drift into talking with their friends or daydreaming. In that session, Hutchinson described James: "...he was doodling. He refused my offer of help. For the rest of the math class, James sprawled back in his desk and waited for the period to end" (p. 11). In the twelfth session, "James had a really good day today ... When he finished the set of five problems for the day, he made a big show of getting the next set so he could 'get ahead of all you guys'" (p. 11). Around the same time, "Look at that Tom. Jeff helps him, and he turns around and helps Dave. The three of them are working together" (p. 14). Over the six weeks of the cooperative problem solving, the students came to work in pairs and trios, thinking aloud, and helping one another. The class made significant improvement on all six measures of problem solving. And, because it had worked so well, the teacher and students modelled the organization of their science and social studies courses on the cooperative learning methods they had used in mathematics.

✓ **Your Learning:** What are the social benefits of cooperative learning for students with disabilities as well as for other students?

Developing Cooperative Learning Programs

Given the many positive effects of cooperative learning for all students, you will probably want to use it as an instructional approach in your classroom. You might decide to use cooperative groups three times each week for language arts activities, for instance, or once each week for test review. Regardless of how you incorporate cooperative learning into your classroom, you can achieve the best results by following some basic guidelines.

✓ **Your Learning:** Compare the steps for creating a peer-tutoring program with those for establishing a cooperative learning program. How are they alike? How do they differ? What accounts for the similarities and differences?

Form cooperative learning groups.　One of your first considerations in creating a **cooperative learning program** is deciding on the size and composition of the groups. Regardless of the specific cooperative learning approach you choose, the age, abilities, and needs of your students help determine group size. For example, if you teach a primary grade, you will probably use groups of two or three at the beginning of the school year and consider larger groups after students become accustomed to cooperative learning procedures. With older students, maturity and experience with cooperative learning will influence group size. Notice that the range of group size is from two to five or six. Larger groups become difficult for students to participate in and for teachers to manage.

You should assign students to cooperative groups to create heterogeneous groupings; that is, if your class group includes four students with disabilities, you should distribute them among the cooperative groups. Likewise, your students who are high achievers and low achievers should be assigned across groups. The success of cooperative learning is based on students learning to value and respect the contributions each makes. Deciding to place students together in groups according to ability undermines the purpose of this instructional approach (Harvard Graduate School of Education, 1992).

Teachers sometimes ask how long cooperative groups should be kept intact. If you change groups too frequently, students will not have enough opportunity to reach a high level of cooperative functioning. However, if you keep the same groups for too long, students do not have the opportunity to work with other classmates. A general guideline is to keep cooperative groups for at least a two- or three-week unit but to change them at least at the end of each reporting period.

Prepare students for cooperative learning.　A high school English teacher participated in a class on cooperative learning and decided that she and the

> **Connections:** Additional information on student grouping arrangements can be found in Chapter 7.

▶ *How can cooperative groups be used to teach both academic content and skills for working with peers? What skills do students need to work successfully?*

resource teacher could use this strategy in their inclusive class. They carefully planned a series of cooperative activities, assigned students to their groups, and waited for positive results. They quickly learned why teaching students to cooperate is such an important component in developing cooperative learning programs! The high school students bickered with each other and were impatient with students who did not immediately answer questions. Some decided to try to complete their work alone, even though it required input from others. Before students work together, it is essential to teach them cooperative skills.

The skills for cooperative group members have been categorized under the headings forming, functioning, formulating, and fermenting (Johnson, Johnson, Holubec, & Roy, 1984). These skills are summarized in Figure 13.4. Forming skills are skills that students need to move into cooperative groups and carry out basic tasks with politeness and respect. Functioning skills are procedural, including monitoring time limits, asking for help, and clarifying other group members' statements. Formulating skills are more advanced procedural skills and include asking other students to elaborate on their comments so that everyone understands them better, devising strategies for remembering important information, and relating new information to information previously learned. Fermenting skills are skills that students use to participate in their groups as critical thinkers and problem solvers. These skills include integrating members' ideas to form a new idea, questioning others about their ideas to analyze them further, attempting to provide multiple answers, and expressing or testing hypotheses.

Cooperative group members often have assigned **group roles** that help the group function effectively. In some classrooms, group-member assignments include the encourager, the monitor, the leader, and the recorder. The *encourager* has the responsibility of making positive comments to other group members. The *monitor* helps keep the group on task and watches the time. The *leader* gets the group started on its task and facilitates its work. The *recorder* writes down any information the group is responsible for producing. Depending on students' ages and skills, additional responsibilities can be added. In some classrooms, group roles rotate so each student has an opportunity to try all roles. If a student with a disability cannot carry out a role (for example, recorder), a classmate might help out, or that student is not assigned that role.

In general, preparing students for cooperative groups includes identifying the skills they need to learn, planning how you will teach them, teaching the skills and allowing students opportunities to practise them, and gradually increasing your expectations for students' cooperative behaviour. Steps for preparing students for cooperative learning are outlined in the Professional Edge.

Select curricular content. Almost any subject matter you teach can be adapted for cooperative learning. The key to selecting content is to ensure that you have already provided initial instruction to the students so that they are not expected to master new information without your guidance. Further, the content needs to be formatted clearly. It might be a chapter from one of their textbooks, print materials you have photocopied, or a structure for preparing a report on the topic at hand. Students should be able to understand the assignment and how to go about completing it readily.

FYI: Encourager, monitor, leader, and recorder are group-member roles that students might assume during cooperative learning. You can add other roles as needed or eliminate one of these roles for smaller groups.

Forming Skills

- Move into cooperative learning groups without making undue noise and without bothering others.
- Stay with the group during cooperative lessons; don't move around the room.
- Use quiet voices.
- Encourage everyone to participate.
- Use names.
- Look at the speaker.
- Avoid put-downs.
- Keep one's hands and feet to oneself.

Functioning Skills

- Give direction to the group's work by stating or restating the assignment's purpose, setting or calling attention to time limits, and offering ideas on how to complete the assignment.
- Express support and acceptance verbally and non-verbally (for example, praise, eye contact).
- Ask for help or clarification if you do not understand.
- Offer to explain or clarify if you do understand and someone else does not.
- Paraphrase others' contributions.
- Energize the group by being enthusiastic or suggesting new ideas.
- Describe one's feelings as appropriate.

Formulating Skills

- Summarize out loud what has just been read without referring to notes or other materials.
- Seek accuracy by correcting someone else's summary or adding important information to it.
- Seek elaboration by asking others to relate the information to other lessons and other things they know.
- Seek clever ways to remember important ideas.
- Ask others to explain their reasoning process.
- Ask others to plan out loud how they would teach the information to another student.

Fermenting Skills

- Criticize ideas, not people.
- Identify sources of disagreement within the learning group as the disagreement occurs.
- Integrate a number of different ideas into your point of view.
- Ask others to justify their conclusions or answers.
- Extend others' answers or conclusions by adding other information.
- Probe by asking questions that lead to deeper analysis.
- Go past the first answer to generate other plausible answers.
- Test reality by checking time and instructions.

Source: Adapted from *Circles of Learning* by D. W. Johnson, R. T. Johnson, E.J. Holubec, and P. Roy, 1984, Alexandria, VA: Association for Supervision and Curriculum Development. Copyright © 1984 by ASCD. Used with permission.

FIGURE 13.4
Student Cooperative Group Skills

Professional Edge
Steps for Teaching Cooperative Skills

FOR cooperative learning programs to be successful, it is critical that students learn social skills to guide their interactions with classmates. These are some suggestions for effectively teaching cooperative skills to your class.

1. Identify the skills that students need to learn, based on your observations and other assessments of their skills and needs.

2. Clarify for students why they are being asked to learn cooperative skills and explain how they should interact. For example, you might use a playground or hallway altercation as a non-example of cooperative interactions, or stage spontaneous role-plays in which you model positive or negative responses.

3. Identify the skills to students. For example, label one skill "Encouraging."

4. Demonstrate the skill for students. For encouraging, use phrases such as "Keep trying," "That's a good response," and "You really did a good job on that." Use a few examples of poor skills to teach students to discriminate between positive and negative examples.

5. Ask students to practise skills, first with a partner, then with a small group.

6. As students learn several skills, ask them to play an instructional game in their cooperative group, stressing practice on cooperative skills. Ask the groups to identify examples of positive skills used and examples of situations in which skills were not used well.

7. Praise examples of student skills that you observe. If a student consistently fails to use cooperative skills, speak with that student's group and, if necessary, work privately with the student.

Do It! Visit the library and check for additional resources related to cooperative learning. What are some other popular approaches?

Choose cooperative learning programs. The number of approaches to cooperative learning seems to grow each year. For our discussion, two approaches will be outlined: Jigsaw II and Numbered Heads Together. Other cooperative learning programs are presented in Table 13.1.

In a **Jigsaw II** classroom (Aronson, Blaney, Stephen, Sikes, & Snapp, 1978), students are assigned to heterogeneous work groups. Each member of the work group is also assigned to an expert group. Work groups meet and decide which part of the assigned material each member is to become an expert on. For example, in a unit on the Canadian Prairies, experts might be assigned for these topics: geography, economy, culture, and cities. All team members then read the material, with each member focusing on his or her expert topic. After reading, team members join their expert group, composed of all students in the room with a shared expert topic. The expert groups review their portion of the instructional material, then return to teach it to their work-group members. Group members ask each "expert" questions to help clarify the information being presented. After all group members have taught their segment of the information and the groups have had an opportunity to review their learning, a quiz or other evaluation procedure is used, and each group member is graded individually on this assessment.

TABLE 13.1	Cooperative Learning Approaches	

Approach	*Source*	*Description*
Group Investigation	Shlomo Sharan and Rachel Hertz-Lazarowitz	Heterogeneous teams of two to six members plan how to complete an assigned project by identifying tasks to do and resources needed and deciding which group members will have which task responsibilities. Once tasks have been completed, group members develop a shared report that is presented to the class. The class provides feedback to the team.
Jigsaw	Elliott Aronson and colleagues	Each of the four members of the heterogeneous work groups is assigned as an expert on a specific part of the assigned materials. Experts from all class work groups meet and learn material on their specific topic as provided by the teacher. Experts then return to their work groups and teach the materials to work-group members. Work-group members have access only to the materials on which they are the expert. Individual quizzes are then given.
Learning Together	David Johnson and Roger Johnson	Heterogeneous groups of two to six members learn specific skills for interacting with one another. They then work together in various formal and informal group structures to learn material.
Student Teams–Achievement Division (STAD)	Robert Slavin and colleagues	Heterogeneous four-member teams learn materials together and take quizzes separately. Students earn points based on their own improvement over past quiz scores. These points are contributed to a team score.
Team Assisted Individualization (TAI)	Robert Slavin and colleagues	The four members of heterogeneous teams work at their own pace on individualized math materials. Members help each other and check each others' work, even though they might be on different units. Individual tests are taken to pass out of a unit. Teams earn points each week based on the number of units members have successfully completed.
Teams-Games-Tournaments (TGT)	David DeVries and Keith Edwards	Three-member teams help each other learn material. Team members are then assigned to tournament tables for competition with others from class with similar achievement levels. Quizzes are given or an instructional game based on the material learned is played. Members contribute points to their teams based on their performance at their tournament table.

Source: Based on *Cooperative Learning* (2nd ed.) by R. E. Slavin, 1994, Boston: Allyn and Bacon; *Learning Together and Alone* (4th ed.) by D. W. Johnson and R. T. Johnson, 1994, Boston: Allyn and Bacon; and *Cooperative Learning and Strategies for Inclusion* by J. W. Putnam, 1993, Baltimore: Brookes.

✓ **Your Learning:** How are the cooperative learning approaches presented here alike and different? When might each be most appropriate?

Connections: Observe whether students are using learning strategies from Chapter 10 while monitoring cooperative groups.

Connections: Review information in Chapters 9 and 10 to help you recall other strategies that could be incorporated into cooperative learning activities.

In **Numbered Heads Together** (Kagan, 1990), students are assigned to cooperative groups and count off by numbers. The teacher then poses a question to the group and students are asked to put their heads together to ensure that all group members know the answer. After a brief time, the teacher brings the students back and calls out a number. All the students with that number stand and one student responds to the question, or they write the answer on a slate and hold it up for the teacher to see. Students responding correctly score points for their teams.

Monitor program effectiveness. Once students are established in cooperative groups, your role becomes one of monitoring and managing your class. For example, if you notice that a student is having difficulty in a group, you might decide to join that group briefly. If a student seems to be struggling because of the complexity of the lesson content, you can make an on-the-spot adaptation to help the student and the group. If a student is being disruptive, your proximity might be sufficient to settle that student. By observing, you can plan your next lessons and address any issues concerning cooperative skills.

Many of the teaching strategies presented in this text can be incorporated into cooperative learning experiences. For example, a student in a cooperative group could have adapted materials. The group could use a learning strategy to practice problem solving. You can use an entire array of instructional interventions and strategies for independence as part of your cooperative learning activities. Cooperative groups provide a constructive classroom structure—one that provides opportunities for adapting instruction for individual needs, building self-esteem and group spirit, addressing students' own goals, and promoting positive attitudes toward others. You have an almost limitless number of options for using this structure to accomplish your academic and social goals for students. One example of this approach in action is presented in the Case in Practice.

How Can You Help Exceptional Students Improve Their Social Skills and Enhance Their Friendships?

"Each of us dreams about the same things. We dream about having friends, being loved, doing interesting things, and having a sense of importance or that our life is not wasted" (O'Brien et al, 1989, p. 21).

For many students with disabilities and other exceptionalities, your efforts to create a classroom learning environment that fosters positive peer relationships will enable them to be class members who are liked and valued by their peers. For some students, though, you will need to go further. Research has shown that some students with disabilities have persistent problems in their social interactions (Cartledge & Milburn, 1983; MacCuspie, 1996; Schonert-Reichl, 1995; Weiner, Harris, & Shirer, 1990) and that these students benefit from specific instruction to help them learn needed social skills and enhance their friendships (Coleman, Wheeler, & Webber, 1993; Pray, Hall, & Markley, 1992; Weiner, 1994).

▼▼▼▼▼▼▼▼▼▼

Case in Practice
Cooperative Learning in Action

IN Mrs. Robinson's grade three classroom, students are preparing for today's lesson on ecology and the environment. The students move into their work groups and check to see that all group members remember their expert assignments. They also check to see that each group member has paper and pencil as directed by Mrs. Robinson. Once all are settled, the students move to their expert groups. Today's expert groups are reviewing the topics addressed during the past week: (1) information about littering and its impact; (2) recycling programs; (3) products made from recycled materials; and (4) landfills and why they are controversial. Greg's expert group is reviewing littering. Greg has a moderate developmental disability and was deliberately assigned to this group by his teacher since the topic is immediately related to life skills Greg needs to learn. He joins his group with another member of his work group. In this way, Greg can participate in the review but is not totally responsible for all the information addressed. Greg's learning about littering is that it is wrong. He also participated earlier in the week in the class litter pick-up on the school grounds. After 15 minutes, the students return to their work groups. For the next 30 minutes, they take turns leading the review on their part of the environment information. Greg tells his group, "Don't litter. Pick it up." He also shows the "before" and "after" photos of the schoolyard. The group's other littering "expert" eventually takes over, and

Greg listens for awhile, but eventually he leaves the group and gets paper and crayons. He comes back to the group saying, "I make a picture about litter." A group member clears a space at the table for him and he begins to draw, showing his classmates his picture several times. The group asks him what several of the objects drawn are, and they continue their other expert reports. On the next day, the students complete their review test on ecology and the environment. Greg answers simple questions about ecology out loud as they are asked by the student teacher. Mrs. Robinson monitors the larger group taking the written test.

Reflections

What approach to cooperative learning is being used in this classroom? What has Mrs. Robinson done to ensure that the lesson will run smoothly? How can you tell that Mrs. Robinson has taught students cooperative skills? Which skills do you think she might have emphasized? What did Mrs. Robinson do to ensure that Greg would be a valued class member while also taking into account that he could not learn much of the information presented during the unit? In what other way could she have addressed this issue? If you were Mrs. Robinson, what would you be particularly interested in observing as you monitored the students in this class working in their cooperative groups? How else could Greg's learning about the unit have been assessed?

Social skills can be thought of as the behaviours that help students interact successfully with their peers, teachers, and others and that help students win social acceptance. They include engaging in and sustaining conversation; accurately recognizing and responding to emotions expressed by others; identifying and effectively solving social problems, such as disagreements about who can play with a toy or decisions about sneaking out of school with a group of peers; expressing preferences in socially acceptable ways; and initiating kind or helpful acts. Social skills range from very simple to complex. For example, for a young student or a student with a moderate cognitive disability, social skills might include learning how to greet others by saying "Hi" instead of hugging, to take turns during games or large-group activities, and to ask to join a group (Schulze, Rule, & Innocenti, 1989). For adolescents with learning or behaviour problems—students such as Kathleen and Matt, whom you met at the beginning of this chapter—social skills might include expressing emotions appropriately, disagreeing with others (especially adults) in acceptable ways, and avoiding situations in which confrontation is likely to occur (Williams, Walker, Holmes, Todis, & Fabre, 1989). Although special educators and resource teachers may play an active role in teaching social skills to students with especially strong needs, you can also address them in your classroom.

Social-skills training should occur as part of ongoing classroom instruction (Vaughn, McIntosh, & Hogan, 1990; Wiener, 1994) and may occur as a separate "subject." Ways in which you can bring social-skills training to your classroom include behavioural interventions and social skills training.

Friendship is reciprocal; that means that to have a friend, one must be a friend. But being a friend takes practice and opportunities to be with peers to learn how. Reciprocity also means that exceptional children must not only choose others to be their friends, but they must also be chosen by others. And to have a best friend or best friends, exceptional children and adolescents must choose those who choose them. This may sound straightforward, but think of Matt who was described in the introduction to the chapter. As a teacher, what can you do so that other adolescents no longer find Matt annoying and what can you do to help Matt so that he does not behave in ways that are annoying to his peers?

Two Canadian researchers have recently used interviews to learn about the friendships and peer relations of two groups—children with visual impairments and adolescents with learning disabilities—who are included in neighbourhood schools (Levesque, 1997; MacCuspie, 1996). MacCuspie (1996) explored the friendships of five children from grades one to six, one of whom was blind and four of whom had severe visual impairments. She observed them in their classrooms and interviewed peers from each classroom. The children with visual impairments thought friends were children who didn't "make fun of" their eyesight and who helped them. Sighted children described friends as children with the same interests and with whom they "did a lot." Sighted children reported they didn't choose children with visual impairments as friends because they could not play games in the school yard and, in school tasks, they worked too slowly (with large print rather than regular print). Children also disliked the way the exceptional children did not look them in the eye. MacCuspie suggests that in addition to general strategies relevant for all exceptionalities, teachers need to adopt specific strategies that focus on the specific exceptionalities of children who are included. You can help other students understand how much sight each visually impaired child has, which games they can play, and why they cannot maintain eye contact with a sighted peer. Young children seem puzzled by disabilities and although they want to help exceptional peers, they seem reluctant to be their friends if they are very different.

Levesque (1997) conducted observations and extensive interviews with two adolescents with learning disabilities. A young woman, Lynn, described her friends as "what gets me through school" and thought friendships were based on

Do It! Create a lesson plan that you could use to teach social skills in your anticipated classroom. Try your lesson plan on a group of students in your field experiences.

common interests and mutual support and trust. Despite her weak literacy skills, Lynn thrived in high school and enjoyed the social opportunities; she was a cheerleader and a member of a tightly knit group of young women. Matt, who was introduced at the beginning of this chapter, equated school with boredom and wandered the halls at noon hour trying to join groups that stood around and talked. He reported that he did not know "how to relate" and had no friends in his school. He has ADHD and seemed unable to focus on a conversation for long or discuss someone else's interests; Matt's only interest was computer games. He did not have a clear idea of what a friend was, perhaps because he had never really formed reciprocal friendships. Levesque's work implies that secondary teachers may need to help students to form extracurricular groups with others who share their interests (such as computer games) and you may need to draw reluctant students out in small-group or paired conversations in the classroom. Perhaps learning the views of and needs for friendship expressed by students such as Matt and Lynn will help you tailor your interventions to their needs. Friendships are necessary if we are to move "from tolerance to inclusion" as MacCuspie suggests in the title of her book.

Using Behavioural Interventions

Another strategy for teaching social skills to students is to use behavioural interventions such as the ones you learned about in Chapter 12 (Sabornie & Beard, 1990). For example, you can reward your entire class for treating a new class member with respect and friendship. If you have a student whose social problems include teasing class members or talking out of turn, you can reward your class for not responding to the inappropriate behaviours. To use these types of behavioural interventions, you need to identify the behaviours you want to foster clearly and choose an appropriate reward structure, create a simple record-keeping system, explain the intervention to students, and systematically implement your plan. For example, in grade one classroom, a student with a mild cognitive or developmental disability joined the group. Ashi would periodically leave his seat or group and roam from desk to desk, sometimes leaving the classroom. At the beginning of the school year, the teacher explained to the other grade one students that Ashi needed to move more than other students and that this behaviour was acceptable for Ashi but not for the rest of the class. She then asked students not to stop working if Ashi came to their desks and not to make a commotion if he left the room. When she noticed that students were following her directions, she would reward the class with five extra minutes of recess or an extra story in the afternoon. As the school year progressed, she gradually quit this type of reward and transitioned to thanking students for understanding Ashi's needs.

Behavioural interventions can also be used to reinforce appropriate social skills. When teachers see a student with social-skills needs interacting appropriately, they should make a positive comment to the student. In secondary schools, these comments are usually offered in private to avoid embarrassing the student. For example, a student advisor overheard a conversation between a chemistry teacher and a student with an explosive temper. The teacher was chiding the student for failing to turn in assignments on time. The student replied, "Yeah, I know

Connections: Chapter 12 addressed strategies for increasing desirable student behaviour. These strategies also can be applied in teaching social skills.

I haven't been doing too well on the homework." Later, the advisor congratulated the student for acknowledging the teacher's feedback without becoming defensive or making a comment that might have led to detention.

Teachers can also point out to students that using social skills is rewarding in itself. They can point out positive consequences for students who have interacted with peers appropriately. For example, when Pamela played an entire board game with her classmates, taking her turn like everyone else, the teacher commented to her, "Pamela, I see that you had fun playing the game today. You did a nice job taking your turn. Clare and Rebekeh enjoyed playing with you."

Using Social-Skills Training Packages

✓ **Your Learning:** How could you apply what you have learned about social skills and student social relationships to the students introduced in the vignettes at the beginning of this chapter? If you were Lucy, Kathleen, or Mark's teacher, what strategies would you include to foster positive student interactions with each of them?

If you have several students who need social-skills instruction, you might find one of the many prepackaged **social-skills training programs** available to teachers useful. For example, *Think Aloud* (Camp & Bash, 1985) is a social problem-solving package designed for use with elementary school students. Students are taught to ask themselves a series of questions whenever they are faced with a problematic situation. The questions are, What is the problem? What should I do? What is my plan? and, Am I following the plan? Teachers rehearse these steps with students and provide opportunities for students to practice the steps in structured situations. Teachers also remind students to use the steps when they observe students in appropriate situations.

An example of a social-skills package for adolescents is *Skillstreaming the Adolescent* (Goldstein, Sprafkin, Gershaw, & Klein, 1980). This package includes structured procedures for teaching nearly 50 different social skills using modelling, role-playing, and feedback. Teachers can select and use only the skill lessons most pertinent to their class groups. For example, if a high school class is having problems because several students are extremely aggressive, the module on that topic might be helpful. Two modules in *Pathways* (Hutchinson & Freeman, 1994) focus on *Solving Problems on the Job* and *Anger Management* and use similar methods of role-playing. They help students to use social skills in the classroom and prepare them for post-secondary social challenge.

However you decide to help students develop social skills, keep in mind that several other professionals are available in your school who may have advanced training in teaching social skills and who can assist you in this aspect of your curriculum. For example, if your school has a teacher for students with emotional disabilities, he or she might be able to co-teach social-skills lessons with you. Similarly, a school counsellor or social worker could help you build social-skills lessons into your instructional program.

With your understanding of strategies and approaches for building student social relationships, you now have the final ingredient for making your classroom a place where students want to come and want to learn. You know about the foundations of exceptional education and the procedures followed for identifying exceptional students. You have a strategy–INCLUDE–for guiding your decisions about student needs and interventions. You know how important the support and assistance of colleagues and parents is, whether for planning an instructional program for a student, teaching with you in the classroom, or problem solving when concerns arise. You also understand some of the most important characteristics and needs of exceptional students. You have learned many strategies for helping students succeed in your classroom, including creating a positive instructional environment, assessing student needs, making instructional interventions, helping students to be independent, and evaluating their learning. You have learned, too, several approaches for responding to students' discipline and behaviour needs and for fostering positive social relationships among students.

What is most important, however, is the statement that appeared in the first chapter of this text: Students with disabilities and other exceptionalities are people first. If you keep that in mind and use the knowledge you have gained, you will positively touch the lives and learning of all the students who call you teacher.

Summary

In addition to fostering the academic growth of students in inclusive schools, teachers also work to ensure that their students with and without disabilities and other special needs build positive social relationships. Learning to interact positively is especially important since research over the past four decades has demonstrated that students with disabilities are more likely than other students to be disliked or not accepted by their peers and less likely to be liked and accepted.

Teachers can help students develop positive peer relationships in inclusive classrooms by creating ways for students to have face-to-face interactions, nurturing the development of friendship and support among students, and providing positive role models. Another aspect of addressing the social curriculum in general education classrooms is educating students without special needs about individuals who have disabilities or other exceptionalities. Direct presentation of information, the use of print or video media or adaptive technology, and the use of simulation activities are approaches to introducing students to the characteristics and needs of exceptional students.

One specific instructional approach that helps create positive student relationships is peer tutoring. Peer tutoring has a long history and has recently received renewed attention. It benefits both tutors and tutees, including students with disabilities. Teachers can create tutoring programs that are contained within their classrooms or that use several class groups or even an entire school. A second instructional approach recommended for inclusive classrooms is cooperative learning. In cooperative learning, students accrue both social and academic benefits. To set up a cooperative learning program, teachers need to decide on group issues, prepare students to work cooperatively, identify the instructional content to be used in the groups, and select a cooperative learning approach, such as Jigsaw II, Numbered Heads Together, or Cooperative Integrated Reading and Composition.

Sometimes, students with disabilities need additional intensive instruction to learn social skills and enhance their friendships. This instruction can involve social-skills training, including the use of behavioural interventions and social-skills training programs.

Cooperative/Collaborative Learning

www2.emc.maricopa.edu/innovation/CCL/CCL.html

Peer Tutoring

www.quasar.ualberta.ca/ddc/inclusive/obrien.htm

School Psychology Resources Online

www.bcpl.lib.md.us/~sandyste/school_psych.html

Applications in Teaching Practice

Planning for Promoting Positive Peer Relations

 Mr. Barkley is reviewing his class roster and his plans for the upcoming school year. He knows that he will have four students with learning and behaviour disabilities—Jay, Doug, Ray, and Jasmine—in his class. He also will have Theodore, a bright young man with cerebral palsy who uses a wheelchair and has a personal attendant. Theodore cannot write or type; he points to symbols on his communication board. Having talked to other teachers, Mr. Barkley is a little worried about this group because several of the other students in the class also have exceptionalities, including Kusi, with ADHD, and Micki, who is gifted. Right now, his planning list looks like this:

1. Talk to Ms. M. [resource teacher]. What are reasonable expectations for the exceptional students? Does Theodore need any extraordinary assistance? What is he going to be like in class? Do I need to know anything special about having the personal attendant in my classroom? Does she know what to do for Theodore? Can she also work with other students if it doesn't negatively affect Theodore? Should Jay, Doug, Ray, or Jasmine sit near each other or be separated? What should they be able to do in class—everything? Eighty percent? What are the social goals for these students? Could we review the students' IEPs to clarify what I should stress with them? Do these students have best friends at school and are these friends in the same class?
2. Talk to counsellor. Can she teach some basic social-skills lessons with the class during the first six weeks? Twice each week for 20 minutes?
3. Set up cooperative learning groups for first six weeks and get all materials ready. Goal: Two cooperative learning activities per week, with the first two weeks spent on teaching social skills in groups. Group size? Maybe three, given class composition, with a move to four later in the term.
4. Check on availability of after-school tutoring program at elementary school this year. Reward for some of the students? Other peer tutoring options?
5. Request more information on Jasmine—see note about her participation in a social work group on Thursdays during advisory period.

Mr. Barkley's planning list goes on along these lines for two more pages.

Questions

1. Why is Mr. Barkley concerned about the social interactions and friendships of his students? Why is this part of his responsibility as much as teaching his academic subject matter? How does having students with disabilities in his room increase needs in the social-skills area?
2. What could Mr. Barkley do to sensitize his students to Theodore8s needs? What might he do if Jay, Doug, Ray, or Jasmine becomes the object of student complaints about fairness during the course of the school year?
3. What approach to peer tutoring is Mr. Barkley considering? What options might he try to arrange? Who in his class might be the best candidates for each of the peer tutoring approaches?

4. What questions might Mr. Barkley have concerning the social needs of Kusi and Micki?

5. Mr. Barkley notes that he needs to spend the first two weeks of cooperative learning sessions on social skills. What skills might he teach? How can he teach them? What academic content could be included in the lessons in which social skills are being taught?

6. It appears that Mr. Barkley has one student who will receive social-skills instruction in a separate group, and he is requesting that the counsellor help him teach social skills during the first six weeks of school. How could a resource teacher also help Mr. Barkley address the social needs of all his students?

Glossary

ABC analysis. Systematic recording of antecedents, behaviours, and consequences as a strategy for analyzing student behaviour.

absence seizure. Seizure that is brief and often characterized by momentary lapses of attention. Also called a *petit mal seizure*.

academic learning time. The time students are meaningfully and successfully engaged in school.

academic survival skills. Skills needed to succeed in school, including regular and punctual attendance, organization, task completion, independence, motivation, and appropriate social skills.

acceleration. Approach for educating gifted students based on allowing them to move through all or part of the curriculum at their own, accelerated pace.

accuracy. The extent to which a student's academic performance is without errors.

acquired immune deficiency syndrome (AIDS). Disease resulting from HIV, in which the body becomes unable to fight infection.

activity reinforcer. Positive activity that causes a behaviour to increase. An example of an activity reinforcer is a student being rewarded with extra time to work on the computer.

adapted education program. For an exceptional student, a program based on ongoing assessment with specific goals and approaches that meet the student's needs.

ADD. *See* attention deficit disorder.

ADHD. *See* attention-deficit/hyperactivity disorder.

administrator. Professional responsible for managing some aspect of schools; includes principals, assistant principals, department chairpersons, team leaders, special services coordinators, district administrators, and others.

advance organizer. Information, often presented as organizational signals, that makes content more understandable by putting it within a more general framework.

advocate. Individual who works to ensure that parents understand their rights and that school professionals provide an appropriate education for parents' exceptional children.

AIDS. *See* acquired immune deficiency syndrome.

alternative teaching. Co-teaching option in which students are divided into one large and one small group. The large group receives the planned instruction. The small group receives reteaching, preteaching, enrichment, or other special instruction.

American Sign Language (ASL). A sign language not based on the grammar or structures of English, used by some people with hearing impairments.

anecdotal recording. Strategy for recording behaviour in which incidents before and after a behaviour are recorded along with a description of the behaviour.

annual goal. Broad statement describing estimated yearly outcomes for an exceptional student. Annual goals address areas of identified needs.

annual review. Yearly process of convening a team that includes a parent, teacher, an administrator, and others as needed to review and update a student's IEP.

anticipation guide. Series of statements, some of which may not be true, related to material that is about to be presented during instruction, given to students as a way of activating their knowledge by making predictions about the topic.

anti-racist education. Approaches to education that examine racism critically in order to understand how it originates, to identify and challenge it.

anxiety. Condition in which an individual experiences extraordinary worry in some situations or worries excessively about future situations.

articulation. Production of speech sounds.

Asperger's syndrome. Mild form of autism in which an individual develops speech but has chronic difficulty in forming and sustaining social relationships, gross motor problems, and intense interests in a narrow range of topics.

assessment. Process of gathering information to monitor progress and make educational decisions.

assistive technology. Any of a wide variety of technology applications designed to help students with disabilities learn, communicate, and otherwise function more independently by bypassing their disabilities.

asthma. Physical condition in which an individual experiences difficulty breathing, especially during physically or psychologically stressful activities.

at risk. Term used to describe students who have characteristics, live in conditions, or have experiences that make them more likely than others to experience failure in schools.

attention-deficit disorder (ADD). Term sometimes used as a synonym for attention-deficit/hyperactivity disorder.

attention-deficit/hyperactivity disorder (ADHD). Medical condition in which students have significant inability to attend, excessive motor activity, and/or impulsivity.

attention disorder. Type of ADHD characterized by difficulty sustaining attention.

augmentative communication. Alternative systems of communication, often using pictures, symbols, and/or words accessed through computer or other technology, sometimes used by students with disabilities.

authentic learning tasks. Tasks used in performance-based assessment that are based in real-world contexts and lead to real-world outcomes.

autism. Condition in which an individual lacks social responsiveness from a very early age, has a high need for structure and routines, and demonstrates significant language impairments. These characteristics interfere with learning.

basal textbook. A book used for instruction in basic-skills areas that contains all key components of the curriculum to be taught for that subject. Often called a *basal.*

basic-skills instruction. Instruction in the tool skills of reading, writing, and math.

behaviour contract. Agreement between a teacher (or other adult) and student that clearly specifies student performance expectations, rewards for meeting expectations, consequences of not meeting expectations, and the time frame for which the agreement is valid.

behaviour disability. *See* emotional disability.

behaviour management system. Systematic approaches to responding to student behaviour that include rules, strategies for monitoring student behaviour, and the use of rewards, consequences, and other motivational techniques.

blind. Condition in which an individual has little or no residual vision and relies on auditory and other input for learning.

braille. Writing system used by individuals who have vision impairments that uses various combinations of six raised dots punched on paper read with the fingertips.

brainstorming. Strategy for generating solutions to problems in which participants call out ideas, building on one another's responses, deferring all evaluation.

Brown v. Board of Education. Supreme Court decision in 1954 that established that it is unlawful and discriminatory to create separate schools for African-American students. This "separate cannot be equal" concept was later applied to students with disabilities.

Canadian Charter of Rights and Freedoms (1982). Guarantees equity rights of every individual including those with disabilities.

CAPS. Four-step learning strategy for helping a student decide what is important in a story: ask who the characters are; identify the aim of the story; decide what

problem happens; and determine how the problem is solved.

career counsellor. *See* transition specialist.

catch 'em being good. Behaviour management strategy in which a teacher notices appropriate student behaviour and positively comments on it, either privately to the student or publicly to the class.

CBA. *See* curriculum-based assessment.

CBM. *See* cognitive behaviour management.

cerebral palsy. Most common type of orthopedic impairment among public school students, caused by brain injury before or during birth and resulting in poor motor coordination and abnormal motor patterns. Can result in learning disabilities.

child abuse. Situation in which a parent or other caregiver inflicts or allows others to inflict injury on a child, or permits a substantial risk of injury to exist.

child neglect. Situation in which a parent or other caregiver fails to provide the necessary supports for a child's well-being.

CHROME. Mnemonic for remembering the six methods of scientific investigation: categorization, hypothesis, reasoning, observation, measurement, and experimentation.

chunking. Memorization strategy in which students are taught to remember five to seven key ideas at one time.

Circle of Friends. Program designed to help students without disabilities understand how important it is to have friends with disabilities and to encourage them to form friendships with classmates with disabilities.

classroom climate. The overall atmosphere of a classroom, including whether it is friendly and pleasant, based on the expectations of teachers and their interactions with students.

classroom grouping. Various grouping arrangements, such as teaching the whole class at once or in small groups, that modify the classroom environment. Classroom grouping may be teacher centred or peer mediated.

classroom instruction. Strategies through which a teacher presents curriculum content to students.

classroom organization. Strategies through which a teacher establishes and maintains order in a classroom.

classwide peer tutoring program. Peer tutoring program in which all students in a class are assigned to tutoring pairs to instruct each other in a highly structured format.

cognitive behaviour management (CBM). Behaviour management strategy in which students learn to monitor and change their own behaviour.

cognitive disability. Mild developmental disability. *See* developmental disability.

collaboration. A style of interaction professionals choose to use in order to accomplish a goal they share, often stressed in inclusive schools.

communication disorders. Conditions in which student has great difficulties in communicating with others and that interferes with learning.

community-based education. Approach to instruction in which what is learned in school is related to activities that occur in the community.

competency checklist. Evaluation technique in which student learning is checked against a listing of key concepts or ideas being taught.

comprehension. Reading skill involving understanding the meaning of what has been read.

concept diagram. Specific type of graphic organizer used to present vocabulary words that includes definitions and characteristics.

concept map. Graphic organizer showing relationships among concepts of instruction as well as essential characteristics of the concepts.

consultant. Specialist who provides particular expertise to teachers and others when an extraordinary student need arises.

consultation. Specialized problem-solving process in which one professional with particular expertise assists another professional or parent who needs the benefit of that expertise; used as an instructional approach for some students with disabilities.

consulting teacher. Special education teacher who meets with regular education teachers to problem solve and monitor student progress but who typically has little or no direct contact with students.

content-area textbook. A book used for instruction in science, social studies, or other content areas.

controlled materials. Instructional materials at the student's reading level, of high interest and free of complex vocabulary and concepts, often used while teaching students a learning strategy.

cooperative learning. Student-centred instructional approach in which students work in small mixed-ability groups with a shared learning goal.

cooperative learning program. Program in which cooperative learning approaches are integral to instruction.

COPS. Learning strategy for proofreading papers with these steps: Have I capitalized the first word and proper nouns? How is the overall appearance of my paper; have I made any handwriting, margin, or messy errors? Have I used end punctuation, commas, and semicolons carefully? Do words look like they are spelled right; can I sound them out or use a dictionary?

co-teaching. Instructional approach in which two or more teachers or other certified staff share instruction for a single group of students within a single classroom setting.

counsellor. Specialist with expertise in meeting students' social and affective needs.

cross-age tutoring. Peer tutoring approach in which older students tutor younger ones.

cross-categorical approach. Instructional approach in which the cognitive, learning, affective, and social and emotional needs of students, not their disability labels, form the basis for planning and delivering instruction.

curriculum-based assessment (CBA). Method of measuring the level of achievement of students in terms of what they are taught in the classroom.

curriculum placement. Type of assessment decision concerning where to begin instruction for students.

cystic fibrosis. Genetically transmitted disease in which the body produces excessive mucus that eventually damages the lungs and causes heart failure.

daily activity log. Strategy for providing ongoing information for students and their parents about learning by noting daily observations of student work, effort, and outcomes.

deaf. Hearing impairment in which the individual cannot process linguistic information through hearing with or without the use of hearing aids and relies on visual and other input for learning.

deaf-blind. Condition in which an individual has both significant visual and hearing impairments that interfere with learning.

decibel (dB). Unit for measuring the loudness of sounds.

decoding. Reading skill involving accurately identifying words and fluently pronouncing them.

DEFENDS. Learning strategy for compositions defending a position with these steps: Decide on an exact position; examine the reasons for the position; form a list of points to explain each reason; expose the position in the first sentence; note each reason and supporting points; drive home the position in the last sentence; and search for errors and correct.

depression. Condition in which an individual is persistently and seriously unhappy, with a loss of interest or pleasure in all or almost all usual activities. Symptoms of depression include changes in appetite or weight, sleep disturbances, loss of energy, feelings of worthlessness, and thoughts of death or suicide.

developmentally advanced. Condition in which an individual has domain-specific or discipline-specific expertise, e.g., in mathematics or languages. Also referred to as gifted.

developmental disability. Condition in which an individual has significant limitations in cognitive ability and adaptive behaviours that interfere with learning. Also referred to as cognitive disability. In the past was referred to as mental retardation.

diabetes. Disease in which the body does not produce enough insulin to process the carbohydrates eaten.

diagnostic teaching. Sample lessons and other instructional activities carried out with students experiencing extreme academic or behaviour difficulty to decide upon teaching approach.

differential reinforcement of incompatible behaviours. Reinforcing an appropriate behaviour that is incompatible with another undesirable behaviour in order to increase the positive behaviour.

direct instruction. Research-based instructional approach in which the teacher presents subject matter using a review of previously taught information, presentation of new concepts or skills, guided practice, feedback and correction, independent student practice, and frequent review.

disability. Condition characterized by a physical, cognitive, psychological, or social difficulty so severe that it negatively affects student learning.

discipline. Term to describe the set of classroom expectations, including rules for behaviour, that serves as a means for facilitating student learning.

discovery learning. *See* inquiry learning.

Down syndrome. Most prevalent type of biologically caused cognitive disability caused by the failure of one pair of chromosomes to separate at conception.

duration recording. Strategy for recording behaviour in which the length of time a behaviour occurs is recorded.

echolalic speech. Occurs when an individual communicates by repeating what others have said instead of producing original speech.

emotional disability. Condition in which individual has significant difficulty in social and emotional domain.

enrichment. Approach for educating gifted students based on helping them elaborate on or extend concepts being presented to all students.

environmental inventory. Assessment procedure, often used for students with moderate or severe disabilities, designed to find out what adaptations or supports are needed to increase student participation in classroom and community environments.

epilepsy. Physical condition in which the brain experiences sudden but brief changes in its functioning leading to seizures.

ESL programs. Educational programs for students for whom English is a second language.

evaluation. Procedures used to determine whether teaching was effective, to provide feedback to students and their parents about student learning, and to inform school boards and communities about school effectiveness.

event recording. Strategy for recording behaviour in which each occurrence of the behaviour is counted.

example selection. Teacher choice of examples during instruction. Example selection directly affects student understanding of instruction.

example sequence. Order of presentation of examples during instruction. Example sequence directly affects student understanding of instruction.

exceptional learners. Expression used to describe students with disabilities, students who are gifted, and students at risk, all of whom may need adaptations in the classroom in order to learn.

exemplar. A sample student performance designed to specify a level of achievement in authentic learning evaluation. For example, a writing sample of an "average" grade seven student is an exemplar against which other students' writing can be compared.

expressive language. An individual's ability to communicate meaning clearly through speech.

extinction. Strategy for decreasing negative behaviour by no longer reinforcing it; most effective when the undesirable behaviour has been inadvertently reinforced by the teacher.

facilitated communication. Method of assisting individuals with autism and other disabilities to communicate by gently supporting the wrist, arm, or shoulder on a typewriter or computer keyboard. This method is controversial.

fading out. Gradual process for decreasing the use of behavioural strategies to support appropriate student behaviour.

FAE. *See* fetal alcohol effects.

FAS. *See* fetal alcohol syndrome.

fetal alcohol effects (FAE). Form of fetal alcohol syndrome (FAS), often without physical characteristics. Students with FAE often experience a variety of learning and behaviour problems in school.

fetal alcohol syndrome (FAS). Medical condition caused by prenatal maternal abuse of alcohol, often resulting in slight physical abnormalities and learning, cognitive, or emotional disabilities.

finger spelling. Communication system in which each alphabet letter is assigned a specific hand position. Finger spelling is often used to communicate proper names or technical words for which no other sign language signs exist.

five R's of note-taking. Learning strategy for note-taking with these steps: record the main ideas and important details; reduce to concise phrases; recite key information using your concise phrases as cues; reflect on your notes by adding your own ideas; and review all the key information.

fluency. The rate at which a student performs an academic task such as calculating math problems or reading.

FOIL. Four-step learning strategy for multiplying binomials in algebra: multiply the first terms; multiply the outermost terms; multiply the innermost terms; and multiply the last terms.

friendship. A reciprocal relationship in which two individuals must both be a friend to the other; each must choose the other and be chosen by the other.

functional curriculum. Instructional approach in which goals and objectives are based on real-life skills needed for adulthood. Examples of skills addressed in a functional curriculum include shopping and making purchases; reading common signs such as exit, stop, and sale; riding public transportation; and interacting with peers and adults.

generalized tonic-clonic seizure. Seizure involving the entire body. Also called a *grand mal seizure*.

gifted. Demonstrated ability far above average in one or several areas including overall intellectual ability, leadership, specific academic subjects, creativity, athletics, or the visual or performing arts. Also called talented.

Good Behaviour Game. Strategy for reducing disruptive and promoting positive behaviour in the classroom in which students work on teams to earn points for appropriate behaviour toward a reward.

grading contract. Agreement between a teacher and student that specifies the quantity, quality, and timeliness of work required to receive a specific grade.

grading criteria. The standard on which a student's academic performance is evaluated and graded.

grand mal seizure. *See* generalized tonic-clonic seizure.

graphic organizer. Visual format that helps students to organize their understanding of information being presented or read and the relationships between various parts of the information.

group-administered standardized achievement test. Standardized achievement test given to large groups of students at one time, usually administered by general education teachers, useful as a screening measure.

group investigation. Cooperative learning program in which teams of two to six members plan and carry out shared projects and develop a report that is presented to the class. Class members provide feedback to each team.

group roles. Assigned roles for students in cooperative groups that help the group function effectively. Roles commonly assigned include encourager, monitor, leader, and recorder.

handicap. Term, generally no longer preferred, to describe disabilities.

hard of hearing. Hearing impairment in which an individual has some hearing through which to process linguistic information, possibly with the assistance of hearing aids or other assistive devices.

hearing impairment. Condition in which an individual has the inability or limited ability to receive information auditorily such that it interferes with learning.

hemophilia. Genetically transmitted disease in which blood does not properly coagulate.

hertz (Hz). Unit for measuring the pitch or tone of sounds.

heterogeneous grouping. *See* mixed-skill grouping.

high-incidence disability. Any of the most common disabilities, including learning disabilities, speech or language impairments, mild mental retardation, and serious emotional disturbance.

HIV. *See* human immunodeficiency virus.

homework. The most common form of student practice.

homogeneous grouping. *See* same-skill grouping.

human immunodeficiency virus (HIV). Viral disease in which the body loses its ability to fight off infection. Individuals with HIV often become infected with AIDS.

hyperactive-impulsive disorder. Type of ADHD characterized by excessive movement and other motor activity including fidgeting, a need to move around a room even when others are seated, and rapid changes in activities.

IEP. *See* individual education plan.

improvement grade. Giving credit in evaluation of student performance for progress made, based on the student's level of learning prior to instruction.

impulsivity. The extent to which an individual acts before thinking, often a characteristic of students with learning disabilities or ADHD.

INCLUDE. Strategy for accommodating exceptional students in the regular classroom.

inclusion. Term to describe a professional belief that students with disabilities should be integrated into general education classrooms whether or not they can meet traditional curricular standards and should be full members of those classrooms.

inclusion specialist. Resource teacher or special education teacher responsible for providing a wide variety of supports to students with disabilities and regular classroom teachers who teach them. Sometimes called a *support facilitator*.

independent learning skills. Skills students need to manage their own learning, including note-taking, textbook reading, test-taking, written expression, and time management.

Individual Education Plan (IEP). Document prepared by a multidisciplinary team or annual review team that specifies a student's level of functioning and needs, the instructional goals and objectives for the student and how they will be evaluated, the nature and extent of in-school interventions and related services to be received, and the initiation date and duration of the services. Normally each student's IEP is updated annually.

individualized instruction. Instruction designed to meet the specific needs of an exceptional student.

individually administered diagnostic test. Diagnostic achievement test given to one student at a time, often administered by a special education teacher or school psychologist, useful as a diagnostic measure. These tests provide more specific information than group-administered achievement tests do.

in-school team. Team of teachers, specialists, and administrators that problem solves about students experiencing academic or behaviour difficulty and decides whether students should be individually assessed for possible special education services.

instructional adaptation. Any strategy for adapting curriculum materials, teacher instruction, or student practice activities that increases the likelihood of success for exceptional students.

instructional evaluation. Type of assessment decision concerning whether to continue or change instructional procedures that have been initiated with students.

instructional materials. The textbooks, manipulatives, models, and technology used as part of instruction.

inquiry learning. The most common method of non-direct instruction. *See also* non-direct instruction.

intent. The purpose or goal of a student's behaviour, not always clear from the behaviour itself. An example of an intent occurs when a student repeatedly calls out in class to gain the teacher's attention; that is, the intent is teacher attention.

interval recording. Strategy for recording behaviour in which observation occurs for brief segments of time and any occurrence of the behaviour during the segment is noted.

itinerant teacher. Special education teacher who provides services to students with disabilities and teaches in two or more schools.

Jigsaw. Cooperative learning program in which work group team members are assigned to expert groups to master part of the assigned material to which no other group has access. In the work group, each team member has an opportunity to present his or her part of the material. Students are then assessed for mastery individually.

Jigsaw II. Cooperative learning program in which students interact in both work groups and expert groups to learn assigned materials. Students are then assessed separately.

job coach. A special education professional who accompanies students with disabilities to job sites and helps them master the skills needed to perform the job.

KWL Plus. Three-step learning strategy for reading comprehension: what you already know; what you want to know; what you learned.

LAMPS. Learning strategy for remembering the steps in regrouping in addition with these steps: line up the numbers according to their decimal points; add the right column of numbers and ask . . . ; if more than nine continue to the next step; put the 1s below the column; and send the 10s to the top of the next column.

LD. *See* learning disability.

learned helplessness. Characteristic of some students with disabilities in which they see little relationship between their own efforts and school or social success, often resulting in a belief that they cannot do challenging tasks.

learning and behaviour disabilities. Term used to describe collectively learning disabilities, serious emotional disturbance, and mild cognitive disabilities.

learning disability (LD). Condition in which a student has dysfunction in processing information typically found in language-based activities, resulting in interference with learning. Students with a learning disability have average or above-average intelligence but experience significant problems in learning how to read, write, and/or use a computer.

learning outcomes. Specific goals or outcomes students are expected to accomplish as a result of a unit of instruction.

learning strategies. Techniques, principles, or rules that enable a student to learn to solve problems and complete tasks independently.

least restrictive environment (LRE). The setting as similar as possible to that for students without exceptionalities in which a student with an exceptionality can be educated, with appropriate supports provided. For most students, the LRE is a regular education classroom.

legal blindness. Visual impairment in which an individual's best eye, with correction, has vision of 20/200 or less, or the visual field is 20 percent or less.

low demand request. Behaviour management strategy in which the teacher helps a student transition from one activity to another by making a series of simple requests of the student that are unrelated to the targeted task.

low-incidence exceptionality. Any of the less common exceptionalities outlined in P.L. 101-476, including multiple disabilities, hearing impairments, orthopedic impairments, other health impairments, visual impairments, deaf-blindness, autism, and traumatic brain injury.

LRE. *See* least restrictive environment.

mainstreaming. Term for placing students with disabilities in regular education settings when they can meet traditional academic expectations with minimal assistance, or when those expectations are not relevant.

maintenance goal. Type of goal teams set that describes what the team wants to accomplish in terms of its own effectiveness.

manipulatives. Concrete objects or representational items used as part of instruction. Examples of commonly used manipulatives include blocks and counters.

mental retardation. *See* developmental disability.

minimum intervention. Strategy for promoting positive behaviour that is non-intrusive and often spontaneous instead of systematic and long term. Examples of minimum interventions include noticing positive student behaviour and commenting on it and transitioning students from one activity to another by making unrelated but easily accomplished requests first.

mixed-skill grouping. Classroom grouping arrangement in which students are clustered for instruction without focusing on specific skill needs. Also referred to as heterogeneous grouping.

mnemonic. A device or code used to assist memory by imposing an order on the information to be remembered.

mobility specialist. Specialist who helps students with visual impairments learn to be familiar with their environments and able to travel from place to place independently and safely.

model. Concrete representation that can help students make connections between abstractions and real-life physical objects or processes.

modified course syllabi. A document, usually produced by the IEP team, that states the specific course requirements, expectations, grading criteria, and other changes necessary because of a student's disability.

modified curricular expectations. Individualized expectations, different from those of other students, set for exceptional students on the basis of the goals and objectives summarized in the IEP.

multicultural education. Approaches to education that reflect the diversity of society.

multiple disabilities. Condition in which individuals have two or more disabilities although not one can be determined to be predominant.

muscular dystrophy. Disease that weakens muscles, causing orthopedic impairments. This disease is progressive, often resulting in death during the late teenage years.

natural consequences. Type of presentation punishment in which a student suffers the logical outcome of a misbehaviour. An example of natural consequences is a student cleaning the desk as a consequence for writing on that desk.

negative example. Instructional stimulus that does not illustrate the concept being taught, used with examples to ensure that students understand the instruction. Also called non-example.

negative reinforcement. A potential negative consequence to a behaviour that causes the behaviour to increase.

non-direct instruction. Instructional approach often used for teaching higher-order thinking skills, including problem solving, in which the teacher guides learning by challenging students' thinking and helping them address problems.

novelty. Approach for educating gifted students based on allowing students to learn traditional content using alternative or unusual strategies that might include working with an adult mentor, creating materials for other students to use, or using a problem-based learning approach.

Numbered Heads Together. Cooperative learning program in which students number off. The teacher poses a question; the students work together to ensure all members know the answer, and then the teacher calls a number. Students with the number stand, and one is called upon to respond to the question, with correct responses scoring points for the team.

nurse. Specialist who has expertise in understanding and responding to students' medical needs and who sometimes serves as a liaison between medical and school professionals.

occupational therapist. Specialist with expertise in meeting students' needs in the area of fine motor skills, including self-help skills such as feeding and dressing.

one-to-one instruction. Classroom grouping arrangement in which individual students work with either a teacher or computer in materials geared to their level and at their own pace.

orthopedic impairments. Condition in which an individual has a physical condition that seriously impairs the ability to move about or to complete motor activities so that it interferes with learning.

other health impairments. Condition in which an individual has a disease or disorder so significant that it affects his or her ability to learn. An example is AIDS.

overcorrection. Type of presentation punishment in which a student makes restitution for misbehaviour. An example of overcorrection is a student cleaning all the desks in a room as a consequence for writing on one desk.

paraprofessional. Non-certified staff member employed to assist certified staff in carrying out education programs and otherwise helping in the instruction of students with disabilities. Sometimes called teachers' assistant or educational assistant.

PARS. Learning strategy for reading textbooks with these steps: Preview the material, ask questions, read the chapter, and summarize the main ideas.

partially sighted. Condition in which an individual has a significant visual impairment but is able to capitalize on residual sight using magnification devices and other adaptive materials.

pass/fail grading system. Evaluation procedure in which minimum competency levels established by the teacher are identified; students meeting or exceeding these are given a passing evaluation and those not meeting them are given a failing evaluation.

PASSING. Learning strategy for note-taking with these steps: Prepare for class, attend to the teacher, state the topic, state the source, identify key words and ideas, note their meaning, and give the meaning in your own words.

passive learner. Learner who does not believe in his or her own ability, has limited knowledge of problem-solving strategies, and is unable to determine when to use a strategy.

pattern guide. A graphic organizer designed to help students organize their written papers.

peer editing. Component of student writing in which students review, evaluate, and provide feedback to each other about their written work.

peer tutoring. Student-centred instructional approach in which pairs of students help one another and learn by teaching.

peer tutoring program. Program emphasizing the use of peers as teachers.

peer-mediated instruction. Classroom instructional arrangement in which the pattern of interaction is among students, with the teacher serving as a facilitator of learning.

performance-based assessment. Method of evaluation that measures what students can do with knowledge rather than measuring specific bits of knowledge the student possesses.

permanent product recording. Strategy for recording behaviour in which samples of student work and other permanent evidence of student behaviour are collected and evaluated.

personal assistant. Paraprofessional specially trained to monitor and assist a particular student with a disability.

personal role. One of the roles individuals bring to a team, consisting of characteristics, knowledge, skills, and perceptions based on life experiences broader than those in the professional area.

petit mal seizure. *See* absence seizure.

phonological awareness. Recognizing how letter-sound relationships are used to decode the printed word.

phonological processing. Processing the sounds of the language.

physical punishment. Type of presentation punishment, not recommended for use by teachers, that involves a negative physical consequence for misbehaviour.

physiotherapist. Specialist with expertise in meeting students' needs in the area of gross motor skills.

placement. Location in which education will occur for an exceptional student.

P.L. 94-142. Legislation also called the Education for the Handicapped Act (EHA), passed in 1975, which set federal guidelines for special education and related services and the procedures for establishing and monitoring them.

planning think sheet. Set of questions to which students respond as a strategy for assisting them to activate background knowledge in preparation for writing.

portfolio assessment. Method of evaluation in which a purposeful collection of student work is used to assess student effort, progress, and achievement in one or more areas.

positive reinforcement. A consequence to a behaviour that causes it to increase. Also called a reward.

POSSE. Learning strategy for reading comprehension with these steps: Predict ideas, organize the ideas, search for the structure, summarize the main ideas, and evaluate your understanding.

POWER. Learning strategy for writing with these steps: planning, organizing, writing, editing, and revising.

PReP strategy. Strategy for determining how much background information students have about a topic.

prereferral assistance team. *See* in-school team.

present level of functioning. Information about a student's current level of academic achievement, social skills, behaviour, communication skills, and other areas that is included on an IEP.

presentation punishment. Presenting negative consequences as a strategy for decreasing behaviour.

preskill. Basic skill necessary for performing a more complex skill.

primary reinforcer. Food or other items related to human needs that cause a behaviour to increase, used only occasionally in schools. An example of a primary reinforcer is a piece of licorice earned for appropriate behaviour.

probe. Quick and easy measure of student performance (accuracy and fluency) in the basic-skill areas of reading, math, and written expression consisting of timed samples of academic behaviours.

probe of basic academic skills. *See* probe.

probe of prerequisite skills. Specific type of probe designed to assess whether a student has the prerequisite skills needed to succeed in the planned instruction.

professional role. One of the roles individuals bring to a team, including knowledge, skills, and perceptions based on professional training and experience.

program evaluation. Type of assessment decision concerning whether interventions and services for an exceptional student should be terminated, continued as is, or modified.

program placement. Type of assessment decision concerning where a student's interventions and services will take place.

psychological test. Test designed to measure how efficiently students learn in an instructional situation; often used to assess intelligence and to determine whether learning disabilities exist.

psychologist. *See* school psychologist.

psychometrist. Specialist with expertise in assessment who in some provinces completes much of the individual assessment required to determine whether a student is exceptional and needs interventions and services.

pullout model. Instructional approach in which students with disabilities leave the general education classroom once or more each day to receive special education services.

punishment. Any response or consequence that has the effect of decreasing a behaviour.

rate of introduction. The pace at which new skills are introduced during instruction.

rebound effect. Potential side effect of medication in which as medication wears off the individual displays symptoms worse than those that existed before medication was given. Rebound effects are a particular concern for medications prescribed for students with ADHD.

receptive language. An individual's ability to understand what people mean when they speak.

reciprocal teaching. Teaching students to comprehend reading material by providing them with teacher and peer models of thinking behaviour and then allowing them to practice these thinking behaviours with their peers.

reciprocal tutoring. Same-age tutoring approach in which students in the same class are randomly assigned and take turns teaching each other. *See also* reciprocal teaching.

regular class. One placement for exceptional students with peers without exceptionalities. Also referred to as a general education class.

regular classroom teacher. Elementary or secondary teacher whose primary responsibility is teaching one or more class groups.

rehearsal strategy. Test-taking strategy that involves saying information out loud, repeating it, checking it for accuracy, and repeating it as part of studying.

reinforcement. Any response or consequence that causes a behaviour to increase.

reinforcement menu. List of rewards from which students may choose, often most effective if students participate in its development.

related services. Services students with disabilities need to benefit from their educational experience. Examples of related services include transportation, speech therapy, physical therapy, and counselling.

removal punishment. Taking away from a student something that is desired as a strategy for decreasing inappropriate behaviour.

residential facility. Placement for students with disabilities when their needs cannot be met at a school. Students attend school and live at a residential facility.

resource room. Classroom to which students come for less than 50 percent of the school day to receive special education, often for 30 to 60 minutes per day.

resource teacher. Special education teacher who provides direct services to students with disabilities either in a special education or general education classroom and who also meets to problem solve with teachers. Resource teachers most often work with students with high-incidence disabilities.

response cost. Type of removal punishment in which a student loses privileges or other rewards as a consequence of inappropriate behaviour.

response format. The way in which a student is expected to respond to test items. Examples of response formats include writing true or false, circling a correct answer from a list of four, drawing a line to match items, or writing an essay.

retention. Ability to remember information after time has passed.

RIDGES. Learning strategy for problem solving in mathematics with these steps: read the problem carefully, identify what I know, draw a picture, make a goal statement, develop an equation, and solve the equation.

Ritalin. Psychostimulant medication commonly prescribed for individuals with ADHD.

same-age tutoring. Peer tutoring approach in which students in the same class or grade level tutor one another, typically with higher-achieving students assisting lower-achieving students.

same-skill grouping. Classroom grouping arrangement in which all students needing instruction on a particular skill are clustered for that instruction. Also referred to as homogeneous grouping.

satiation. Situation in which a positive reinforcer, used repeatedly, loses its effectiveness.

scaffolding. Instructional approach for teaching higher-order thinking skills in which the teacher supports student learning by reviewing the cognitive strategy to be addressed, regulating difficulty during practice, providing varying contexts for student practice, providing feedback, increasing student responsibility for learning, and creating opportunities for independent student practice.

school psychologist. Specialist with expertise to give individual assessments of students in cognitive, academic, social, emotional, and behavioural domains. This professional also designs strategies to address students' academic and social behaviour problems.

self-advocacy. Extent to which a student can identify supports needed to succeed and communicate that information effectively to others, including teachers and employers.

self-awareness. Extent to which a student has an accurate perception or his or her learning strengths, learning needs, and ability to use strategies to learn independently.

self-control training. A strategy in which students who lack self-control are taught to redirect their actions by talking to themselves.

self-image. Individual's perception of his or her own abilities, appearance, and competence.

self-instruction. Strategy in which students are taught to talk themselves through tasks.

self-monitoring. Strategy in which students are taught to check whether they have performed targeted behaviours.

self-questioning. Strategy in which students are taught to guide their performance by asking themselves relevant questions.

self-reinforcement. Strategy in which students reward themselves for behaving appropriately or achieving success in learning tasks.

sensory impairment. Disability related to vision or hearing.

separate class. Classroom in which students with disabilities spend 50 percent or more of the school day.

serious emotional disturbance. Condition in which an individual has significant difficulty in the social and emotional domain, so much so that it interferes with learning.

shared problem solving. Process used by groups of professionals, sometimes including parents, for identifying problems, generating potential solutions, selecting and implementing solutions, and evaluating the effectiveness of solutions.

short-term objective. Description of a step followed in order to achieve an annual goal.

signed exact English (SEE). A form of sign language in which spoken English is converted word-for-word into signs.

sign language interpreter. Specialist who listens to instruction and other communication and relays it to students with hearing impairments through sign language.

simulation. Activity in which students experience what it might be like to have a disability; in a technology context, simulations are computer programs that teach problem solving, decision making, and risk taking by having students react to real-life and imaginary situations.

SLOW CaPS. Learning strategy for writing four kinds of paragraphs with these steps: show the type of paragraph in the first sentence; list the details you want to write about; order the details; write details in complete sentences; CAP off the paragraph with a concluding, passing, or summary sentence.

slow learner. Student whose educational progress is below average, but not so severe as to be considered a cognitive disability, and is consistent with the student's abilities.

social cues. Verbal or non-verbal signals people give that communicate a social message.

social reinforcer. Positive interpersonal interaction that causes a behaviour to increase. An example of a social reinforcer is a teacher praising a student's appropriate behaviour.

social skills. Behaviours that help students interact successfully with their peers, teachers, and others and that help them win social acceptance.

social-skills training program. Systematic instruction designed to help students acquire social skills.

social worker. Specialist with expertise in meeting students' social needs and fostering working relationships with families.

sophistication. Approach for educating gifted students based on helping students learn complex principles about subject matter being presented to the entire class.

special education. Specially designed instruction provided by the school district or other local education agency that meets the unique needs of students identified as exceptional.

special education teacher. Teacher whose primary responsibility is delivering and managing the delivery of special education services to students with disabilities.

Special Friends. Program designed to promote friendships between students with disabilities and those without disabilities.

special services coordinator. Administrator responsible for interpreting guidelines related to educating students with disabilities and assisting other school district personnel in carrying out those guidelines.

speech articulation. The ability to produce sounds correctly beyond the age where they would normally be expected to develop.

speech or language impairment. Condition in which student has extraordinary difficulties in communicating with others due to causes other than maturation and that interferes with learning.

speech reading. Strategy used by individuals with hearing impairments to gain information by watching a person's lips, mouth, and expression. Only a small proportion of a spoken message can typically be discerned through speech reading.

speech and language therapist. Specialist with expertise in meeting students' communication needs, including articulation and language development.

spina bifida. Birth defect in which there is an abnormal opening in the spinal column, often leading to partial paralysis.

spinal cord injury. Condition in which the spinal cord is damaged or severed because of accident or injury, leading to orthopedic impairments.

standardized achievement test. Norm-referenced test designed to measure academic progress, or what students have retained in the curriculum.

stereotypic behaviour. An action or motion repeated over and over again. Examples of stereotypic behaviours include spinning an object, rocking the body, and twirling.

story grammar. Description of the typical elements of stories, including theme, setting, character, initiating events, attempts at resolution, resolution, and reactions.

story map. Graphic organizer for narrative material.

streaming. Educational practice of grouping students for instruction by their perceived ability level.

student evaluation. Determination of the extent to which students have mastered academic skills or other instructional content, frequently communicated through grades.

student self-evaluation. Assessment approach in which students are asked to perform a task, are given a checklist of strategy steps for the task, and then are asked to tell which of these steps they did or did not use.

study guide. General term for outlines, abstracts, or questions that emphasize important information in texts.

stuttering. Speech impairment in which an individual involuntarily repeats a sound or word, resulting in a loss of speech fluency.

support facilitator. *See* inclusion specialist.

surface behaviour. Initial student behaviours that teachers could interpret as misbehaviour. Responding appropriately to surface behaviours can prevent them from escalating into more serious discipline problems.

TAG. Learning strategy for peer editing with these steps: tell what you like, ask questions, and give suggestions.

TAI. *See* Team Assisted Individualization.

talented. *See* gifted.

tangible reinforcer. Prizes or other objects students want and can earn through appropriate behaviour and that cause that behaviour to increase. An example of a tangible reinforcer is a school pencil earned for appropriate behaviour.

task analysis. Six-step strategy for managing time: Decide exactly what you must do; decide how many steps are needed to complete the task; decide how much time each step will take; set up a schedule; get started; finish the task.

task goal. Type of goal teams set that describes the business the team exists to accomplish.

TBI. *See* traumatic brain injury.

teacher-centred instruction. Classroom instructional arrangement in which the pattern of interaction is between teacher and students, with the teacher as the central figure.

team. Formal work groups that have clear goals, active and committed members, leaders, clear procedures followed in order to accomplish goals, and strategies for monitoring effectiveness.

team role. One of the formal or informal roles individuals bring to a team, consisting of contributions made to help ensure effective team functioning. Examples of formal team roles include team facilitator, recorder, and timekeeper. Examples of informal team roles include compromiser, information seeker, and reality checker.

team teaching. Co-teaching option in which students remain in one large group and teachers share leadership in the instructional activity of the classroom.

test administration. The conditions under which a test is given to students.

test construction. The way in which test items are worded, ordered on the test, and formatted.

test site. The location in which a test is given.

test-taking skills. Learning strategies taught to students to help them succeed in studying for and taking tests.

3R strategy. Three-step learning strategy to help students prepare for lectures: Review notes and materials from the previous class; read materials related to today's class; relate lecture topic to other topics.

Think-Pair-Share. A cooperative learning strategy in which students think alone briefly, then pair with a classmate to discuss the question, and during share a few students report to the class.

time-out. Type of removal punishment in which a student is removed from opportunities for reward. An example of time-out is a "penalty box" for misbehaviour on the playground.

time sampling. Strategy for recording behaviour in which a behaviour is periodically observed and measured during a specified time period.

token economy. Group behaviour management procedure in which students earn a representative or token currency for appropriate behaviour that can later be exchanged for rewards.

tracking. *See* streaming.

transition specialist. Special educator or career counsellor who helps prepare students with disabilities for postschool activities, including employment, vocational training, or higher education.

transition time. The time it takes a group of students to change from one classroom activity to another.

traumatic brain injury (TBI). Condition in which an individual experiences a significant trauma to the head from accident, illness, or injury and that affects learning.

tutorial. Computer program designed to present new material to students in small sequential steps and/or to review concepts.

unison responding. All students responding at once to teacher questions or other instruction.

visual impairment. Condition in which an individual has an inability or limited ability to receive information visually, so much so that it interferes with learning.

wait time. Amount of time a teacher gives a student to respond to a question.

written agenda. A list written on the blackboard, chart paper, or an overhead transparency of the tasks for the class.

written language difficulties. Problems that students with learning and behaviour disabilities have with skills related to handwriting, spelling, and written expression.

References

Abelson, M. A., & Woodman, R. W. (1983). Review of research on team effectiveness: Implications for teams in schools. *School Psychology Review, 12*, 125–136.

Aber, M. E., Bachman, B., Campbell, P., & O'Malley, G. (1994). Improving instruction in elementary schools. *Teaching Exceptional Children, 26*(3), 42–50.

Abikoff, H. (1991). Cognitive training in ADHD children: Less to it than meets the eye. *Journal of Learning Disabilities, 24*, 205–209.

Abramowitz, A. J., & O'Leary, S. G. (1991). Behavioral interventions for the classroom: Implications for students with ADHD. *School Psychology Review, 20*, 220–234.

Adams, D., & Hamm, M. (1991). Diversity gives schools infinite learning possibilities: Learning cooperatively proves successful tool to highlight many cultural values. *School Administrator, 4*(48), 20–22.

Adams, L. (Ed.). (1994). *Attention deficit disorders: A handbook for Colorado educators.* Denver: Colorado Department of Education.

Adams, L., & Cessna, K. (1991). Designing systems to facilitate collaboration: Collective wisdom from Colorado. *Preventing School Failure, 35*(4), 37–42.

Adelman, P. B., & Olufs, D. (1986). *Assisting college students with learning disabilities.* A manual written for the Association on Handicapped Student Service Programs in Postsecondary Education. Columbus, OH.

Adesman, A. R., & Wender, E. H. (1991). Improving the outcome for children with ADHD. *Contemporary Pediatrics, 8*, 122–139.

Affleck, J. Q., Lowenbraun, S., & Archer, A. (1980). Teaching the mildly handicapped in the regular classroom. Columbus, OH: Merrill.

Affleck, J. Q., Madge, S., Adams, A., & Lowenbraun, S. (1988). Integrated classroom versus resource model: Academic viability and effectiveness. *Exceptional Children, 54*, 339–348.

Alberta Education. (1995). *Individualized program plans: Programming for students with special needs.* Edmonton: Author.

Alberta Education. (1995). *Guide to education for students with special needs.* Edmonton: Author.

Alberta Education. (1996). *Policy, regulations and forms manual.* Edmonton: Author.

Alberta Education, Special Education Branch. (1996). *Partners during changing times: An information booklet for parents of children with special needs.* Edmonton: Alberta Education.

Alberto, P. A., & Troutman, A. C. (1994). *Applied behavior analysis for teachers: Influencing student performance* (4th ed.). New York: Merrill/Macmillan.

Algozzine, B., Morsink, C. V., & Algozzine, K. M. (1988). What's happening in self-contained special education classrooms? *Exceptional Children, 55*, 259–265.

Algozzine, B., Ysseldyke, J. E., & Campbell, P. (1994). Strategies and tactics for effective instruction. *Teaching Exceptional Children, 26*(3), 34–36.

Alley, G. R. (1988). Effects of generalization instruction on the written language performance of adolescents with learning disabilities in the mainstream classroom. *Reading, Writing, and Learning Disabilities, 4*, 291–309.

Allingham, N. D. (1992). Anti-racist education and the curriculum: A privileged perspective. In Canadian Teachers' Federation (Ed.), *Racism and education: Different perspectives and experiences* (pp. 15–29). Ottawa: Canadian Teachers' Federation.

Allison, M. (1992). The effects of neurologic injury on the maturing brain. *Headlines, 3*(5), 2–6.

Allport, G. (1954). *The nature of prejudice.* Cambridge, MA: Addison-Wesley.

Alper, S., & Ryndak, D. L. (1992). Educating students with severe handicaps in regular classes. *Elementary School Journal, 92*, 373–387.

American Psychiatric Association. (1994). *Diagnostic and statistical manual of mental disorders* (4th ed.). Washington, DC: Author.

American Speech-Language-Hearing Association. (1982). Definitions: Communicative disorders and variations. *ASHA, 24*, 949–950.

Anderson, K., & Milliren, A. (1983). *Structured experiences for integration of handicapped children.* Rockville, MD: Aspen.

Andrews, J. (Ed.). (1996). *Teaching students with diverse needs: Secondary classrooms.* Toronto: Nelson Canada.

Andrews, J., & Lupart, J. (1993). *The inclusive classroom: Educating exceptional children.* Scarborough: Nelson Canada.

Archer, A., & Gleason, M. (1990). Direct instruction in content area reading. In D. Carnine, J. Silbert, & E. Kameenui. *Direct Instruction Reading* (2nd ed.) (pp. 339–393). Columbus, OH: Merrill.

Arends, R. I. (1991). *Learning to teach*. New York: McGraw-Hill.

Arlin, M. (1979). Teacher transitions can disrupt time flow in classrooms. *American Educational Research Journal, 16*, 42–56.

Armbruster, B. B. (1984). The problem of "inconsiderate text." In G. G. Duffy, L. R. Roehler, & J. Mason (Eds.), *Comprehensive instruction: Perspectives and suggestions* (pp. 202–217). New York: Longman.

Armbruster, B. B., & Anderson, T. H. (1988). On selecting "considerate" content area textbooks. *Remedial and Special Education, 9*(1), 47–52.

Armstrong, T. (1994). *Multiple intelligences in the classroom*. Alexandria, VA: Association for Supervision and Curriculum Development.

Aronson, E., Blaney, N., Stephen, C., Sikes, J., & Snapp, M. (1978). *The jigsaw classroom*. Beverly Hills, CA: Sage.

Aune, E. (1991). A transition model for postsecondary-bound students with learning disabilities. *Learning Disabilities Research and Practice, 6*, 177–187.

Banks, J. A. (1993). Multicultural education: Development, dimensions, and challenges. *Phi Delta Kappan, 75*, 22–28.

Barad, D. (1985). Adapting instruction in general education for students with communication disorders. Unpublished manuscript. DeKalb, IL: Northern Illinois University.

Barkley, R. A. (1990). *Attention deficit hyperactivity disorder: A handbook for diagnosis and treatment*. New York: Guilford Press.

Barrish, H. H., Saunders, M., & Wolf, M. M. (1969). Good Behavior Game: Effects of individual contingencies for group consequences on disruptive behavior in a classroom. *Journal of Applied Behavior Analysis, 2*, 119–124.

Barron, A. M., & Foot, H. (1991). Peer tutoring and tutor training. *Educational Research, 33*, 174–185.

Barth, R. S. (1990). *Improving schools from within*. San Francisco: Jossey-Bass.

Bauer, A. M., & Sapona, R. H. (1991). *Managing classrooms to facilitate learning*. Englewood Cliffs, NJ: Prentice-Hall.

Bauwens, J., & Hourcade, J. J. (1991). Making co-teaching a mainstreaming strategy. *Preventing School Failure, 35*(4), 19–23.

Bauwens, J., & Hourcade, J. J. (1994). *Cooperative teaching: Rebuilding the schoolhouse for all students*. Austin, TX: Pro-Ed.

Bauwens, J., Hourcade, J. J., & Friend, M. (1989). Cooperative teaching: A model for general and special education integration. *Remedial and Special Education, 10*(2), 17–22.

Bay, M., & Bryan, T. (1992). Differentiating children who are at risk for referral from others on critical classroom factors. *Remedial and Special Education, 13*(4), 27–33.

Bear, T., Schenk, S., & Buckner, L. (1992/1993). Supporting victims of child abuse. *Educational Leadership, 50*(4), 42–47.

Beirne-Smith, M. (1991). Peer tutoring in arithmetic for children with learning disabilities. *Exceptional Children, 57*(4), 330–337.

Beirne-Smith, M., Patton, J. R., & Ittenbach, R. (1994). *Mental retardation* (4th ed.). New York: Merrill.

Bennett, B., & Smilanich, P. (1994). *Classroom management: A thinking and caring approach*. Ajax, ON: VISUTronX.

Bergan, J. R., & Tombari, M. L. (1975). The analysis of verbal interactions occurring during consultation. *Journal of School Psychology, 13*, 209–226.

Berger, C. F., Berkheimer, G. D., Lewis, L. E., & Neuberger, H. J. (1979). *Houghton Mifflin Science*. Boston: Houghton Mifflin.

Bergman, J. L. (1992). SAIL: A way to success and independence for low-achieving readers. *Reading Teacher, 45*(8), 598–602.

Beveridge, A. (1997). *Successful inclusion of children with disabilities into regular classes: The practices and beliefs of four elementary teachers*. Unpublished master's thesis, Queen's University, Kingston, Ontario.

Blankenship, C., & Lilly, M. S. (1981). *Mainstreaming students with learning and behavior problems*. New York: Holt, Rinehart & Winston.

Bos, C. S., & Vaughn, S. (1994). *Strategies for teaching students with learning and behavior problems* (2nd ed.). Boston: Allyn and Bacon.

Bosetti, L., & Watt, D. (1995). Structural marginalization in educational policy: The case of English as a second language. *Exceptionality Education Canada, 5*(1), 25–41.

Bowman, B. T. (1994). The challenge of diversity. *Phi Delta Kappan, 76*, 218–224.

Brandenberger, J., & Womack, S. T. (1982). Division of labor in special team teaching situations. *Clearinghouse, 55* (5), 229–230.

Brent, R., & Anderson, P. (1993). Developing children's listening strategies. *Reading Teacher, 47*(2), 122–126.

British Columbia Special Education Branch. (1995). *Special education services: A manual of policies, procedures and guidelines*. Victoria: Author.

British Columbia Special Education Branch. (1995). *Gifted education: A resource guide for teachers*. Victoria: Author.

British Columbia Special Education Branch. (1996). *Teaching students with learning and behavioural differences: A resource guide for teachers*. Victoria: Author.

British Columbia Special Education Branch. (1996). *Individual education planning for students with special needs*. Victoria: Author.

British Columbia Special Education Branch. (1996). *Teaching students with fetal alcohol syndrome/effects: A resource guide for teachers*. Victoria: Author.

Brown v. Board of Education, 347 U.S. 483 (1954).

Brown, G. (1994). Augmentative communication systems: Practical ideas for home and school programs. In F. LaRoy & J. Streng (Eds.), *A new dawn of awakening: Proceedings of the 1994 conference*. Arlington, TX: Future Education.

Brown, G. M., Kerr, M. M., Zigmond, N., & Harris, A. (1984). What's important for student success in high school? Successful and unsuccessful students discuss school survival skills. *High School Journal, 68*, 10–17.

Brown, L., Long, E., Udvari-Solner, M., Davis, L., VanDeventer, P., Ahlgren, C., Johnson, F., Gruenewalk, L., & Jorgensen, J. (1989). The home school: Why students with severe intellectual disabilities must attend the schools of their brothers, sisters, friends, and neighbors. *Journal of the Association for Persons with Severe Handicaps, 14*(1), 1–7.

Bryan, T. H., & Bryan, J. H. (1986). *Understanding learning disabilities* (3rd ed.). Palo Alto, CA: Mayfield.

Bulgren, J. A., Schumaker, J. B., & Deshler, D. (1988). Effectiveness of a concept teaching routine in enhancing the performance of LD students in secondary-level mainstream classes. *Learning Disability Quarterly, 11*, 3–17.

Bullara, D. T. (1993). Classroom management strategies to reduce racially biased treatment of students. *Journal of Educational and Psychological Consultation, 4*(4), 357–368.

Bunch, G., Lupart, J., & Brown, M. (1997). *Resistance and acceptance: Educator attitudes to inclusion of students with disabilities*. North York: York University, Faculty of Education.

Burgess, D. M., & Streissguth, A. P. (1992). Fetal alcohol syndrome and fetal alcohol effects: Principles for educators. *Phi Delta Kappan, 74*, 24–29.

Burke, W. W. (1988). Team building. In W. B. Reddy & K. Jamison (Eds.), *Team building: Blueprints for productivity and satisfaction* (pp. 3–14). Alexandria, VA: NTL Institute for Applied Behavioral Science.

Burns, P. C., Roe, B. D., & Ross, E. P. (1992). *Teaching reading in today's elementary schools*. Boston: Houghton Mifflin.

Bursuck, M. (1993). Anticipation guide for the nervous system. Unpublished manuscript, Northern Illinois University, DeKalb.

Bursuck, W. D., & Jayanthi, M. (1993). Programming for independent study skill usage. In S. Vogel & P. Adelman (Eds.), *Programming for success for college students with learning disabilities* (pp. 177–205). New York: Springer-Verlag.

Bursuck, W. D., & Lessen, E. (1987). A classroom-based model for assessing students with learning disabilities. *Learning Disabilities Focus, 3*(1), 17–29.

Bursuck, W. D., Polloway, E. A., Plante, L., Epstein, M. H., Jayanthi, M., & McConeghy, J. (in press). Report card grading and adaptations: A national survey of classroom practices. *Exceptional Children*.

Butson, S., Shea, K., Pankratz, K., & Lamb, M. (1992). A script for how to teach the KWL strategy. Unpublished manuscript, Northern Illinois University, DeKalb.

Camp, B. W., & Bash, M. A. (1985). *Think aloud*. Champaign, IL: Research Press.

Campbell, D., Serff, P., & Williams, D. (1994). *The BreakAway Company*. Toronto: Trifolium.

Campbell, J. (1992). Laser disk portfolios: Total child assessment. Educational Leadership, 49(8), 69–70.

Canadian Charter of Rights and Freedoms, Part I of the *Constitution Act*, 1982, being Schedule B of the *Canada Act* 1982 (U.K.), 1982, c.11.

Canning, P.M. (June, 1996). *Special matters: The report of the review of special education*. St. John's: Newfoundland Department of Education and Training.

Careless, J. (May, 1994). A checklist for caring. *University Affairs*, May, pp. 6–7.

Carlson, C., & Henning, M. (1993). *The TAG peer editing procedure*. DeKalb: Northern Illinois University.

Carnine, D. W. (1981). High and low implementation of direct instruction teaching techniques. *Education and Treatment of Children, 4*, 42–51.

Carnine, D., Silbert, J., & Kameenui, E. (1990). *Direct instruction reading*. Columbus, OH: Merrill.

Carpenter, D., Grantham, L. B., & Hardister, M. P. (1983). Grading mainstreamed handicapped pupils: What are the issues? *Journal of Special Education, 17*(2), 183–188.

Carpenter, S. (1988). *The Centre for Independent Living in Toronto: An overview*. Toronto: Centre for Independent Living.

Carruthers, A., & Foreman, P. J. (1989). Asperger syndrome: An educational case-study of a preschool boy *Australia and New Zealand Journal of Developmental Disabilities, 15*(1), 57–65.

Cartledge, G., & Milburn, J. F. (1983). Social skills assessment and teaching in the schools. In T. R. Kratochwill (Ed.), *Advances in school psychology* (Vol. 3) (pp. 175–235). Hillsdale, NJ: Erlbaum.

Cawley, J. F., Fitzmaurice, A. M., Shaw, R., Kahn, H., & Bates, A. (1979). LD youth and mathematics: A review of characteristics. *Learning Disability Quarterly, 2*(1), 29–44.

Cawley, J. F., Miller, J., & School, B. (1987). A brief inquiry of arithmetic word problem solving among learning disabled secondary students. *Learning Disabilities Focus, 2*(2), 87–93.

Center for the Study of Reading. (1988). *A guide to selecting basal reading programs: Workbooks*. Cambridge, MA: Bolt, Beranck and Newman.

Cermak, L. S. (1976). *Improving your memory*. New York: Norton.

Cesaroni, L., & Garber, M. (1991). Exploring the experience of autism through firsthand accounts. *Journal of Autism and Developmental Disorders, 21*, 303–313.

Chan-Marples, L. W. (1993). *Immigrant women, disability, and culture*. Unpublished M.Ed. thesis, University of Alberta, Edmonton.

Cheek, E. H., Jr., & Cheek, M. C. (1983). *Reading instruction through content teaching*. Columbus, OH: Merrill.

Christenson, S. L., Ysseldyke, J. E., & Thurlow, M. L. (1989). Critical instructional factors for students with mild handicaps: An integrated review. *Remedial and Special Education, 10*(5), 21–31.

Christof, K. J., & Kane, S. R. (1991). Relationship building for students with autism. *Teaching Exceptional Children, 24*(2), 49–51.

Ciborowski, J. (1995). Using textbooks with students who cannot read them. *Remedial and Special Education, 16*, 90–101.

Cipani, E. C., & Spooner, F. (1994). *Curricular and instructional approaches for persons with severe disabilities*. Boston: Allyn and Bacon.

Clark, B. (1992). *Growing up gifted* (4th ed.). New York: Merrill.

Clifton, R. A., & Roberts, L. W. (1993). *Authority in classrooms*. Scarborough: Prentice Hall Canada.

Coathup, G. (1988). *Discipline problems and corrective actions within the intermediate classroom: The students' view*. Unpublished masters thesis, Queen's University, Kingston, ON.

Cohen, P. A., Kulik, J. A., & Kulik, C. C. (1982). Educational outcomes of tutoring: A meta-analysis of findings. *American Educational Research Journal, 19*, 237–248.

Cohen, S. B. (1983). Assigning report card grades to the mainstreamed child. *Teaching Exceptional Children, 15*, 186–189.

Cole, D. A., Vandercook, T., & Rynders, J. (1988). Comparison of two peer interaction programs: Children with and without severe disabilities. *American Educational Research Journal, 25*, 415–439.

Coleman, M., Wheeler, L., & Webber, J. (1993). Research on interpersonal problem-solving training: A review. *Remedial and Special Education, 14*(2), 25–37.

Comber, G., Zeiderman, H., & Maistrellis, N. (1989). The Touchstones Project: Discussion classes for students of all abilities. *Educational Leadership, 49*(6), 39–42.

Connor, F. (1990). Physical education for children with autism. *Teaching Exceptional Children, 23*(1), 30–33.

Conseil superieur de l'éducation du Québec. (1977). *The education of Quebec children suffering from learning or emotional disorders*. Québec: Author.

Cook, L., & Friend, M. (1993). Educational leadership for teacher collaboration. In B. Billingsley (Ed.), *Program leadership for serving students with disabilities* (pp. 421–444). Richmond, VA: Virginia Department of Education.

Cooper, H. (1989). Synthesis of research on homework. *Educational Leadership, 47*(3), 85–91.

Cooper, H., & Nye, B. (1994). Homework for students with learning disabilities: The implications of research for policy and practice. *Journal of Learning Disabilities, 27*(8), 470–480.

Coppola, M. A. (1987). The "perfect" student: Being alert to autism. *Education Digest, L11*(9), 33–35.

Council on Interracial Books for Children. (1994). 10 quick ways to analyze children's books for racism and sexism. In *Rethinking our classrooms* (pp. 14–15). Milwaukee, WI: Rethinking Schools.

Covert, J., Williams, L., & Kennedy, W. (1991). Some perceived professional needs of beginning teachers in Newfoundland. *Alberta Journal of Educational Research, 37*, 3–17.

Cowen, E. L., Pederson, A., Babijian, H., Izzo, L. D., & Trost, M. A. (1973). Long-term follow-up of early detected vulnerable children. *Journal of Consulting and Clinical Psychology, 41*, 438–446.

Crawford, C. G. (1980). *Math without fear*. New York: New Viewpoints/Vision Books.

Cripps, S. (Spring, 1991). An examination of the role of paraprofessionals in three New Brunswick school districts. *New Brunswick Teachers' Association News*, 11–12.

Cuban, L. (1989). The "at risk" label and the problem of urban school reform. *Phi Delta Kappan, 70*, 780–801.

Cullinan, D., & Epstein, M. H. (1994). Behavior disorders. In N. Haring, L. McCormick, & T. Haring (Eds.), *Exceptional children and youth*. Columbus, OH: Merrill.

Cullinan, D., Epstein, M. H., & Lloyd, J. (1983). *Behavior disorders of children and adolescents*. Englewood Cliffs, NJ: Prentice-Hall.

Cummins, J. (1981). *Bilingualism and minority language children*. Toronto: Ontario Institute for Studies in Education.

Dalrymple, N. (1990). *Some social behaviors that students with autism need help to learn and apply in everyday situations*. Bloomington, IN: Indiana Resource Center for Autism, Institute for the Study of Developmental Disabilities.

Davidson, I., & Wiener, J. (1991). Creating educational change: The in-school team. *Exceptionality Education Canada, 1*(2), 25–44.

Davis, G. A., & Rimm, S. B. (1994). *Education of the gifted and talented* (3rd ed.). Boston: Allyn and Bacon.

Dean, A. V., Salend, S. J., & Taylor, L. (1994). *Multicultural education: A challenge for special educators*. Teaching Exceptional Children, 26(1), 40–43.

Debs, P., Hopkins, R., Laity, L., & Sloan, L. (1989). The PASSES notetaking strategy. Unpublished manuscript, Northern Illinois University, DeKalb.

Dei, G. (1994). Anti-racist education,working across differences: Introduction. *Orbit, 25*(2), 1–3).

Deluke, S. V., & Knoblock, P. (1987). Teacher behavior as preventive discipline. *Teaching Exceptional Children, 19*(4), 18–24.

Deno, S. L. (1985). Curriculum-based measurement: The emerging alternative. *Exceptional Children, 52,* 219–232.

Deno, S. L., & Fuchs, L. (1987). Developing curriculum-based measurement systems for data-based special education problem solving. *Focus on Exceptional Children, 19*(8), 1–16.

Deno, S. L., & Mirkin, P. K. (1977). *Data-based program modification: A manual.* Reston, VA: Council for Exceptional Children.

Deshler, D. D., & Graham, S. (1980). *Tape recording educational materials for secondary handicapped students.* Teaching Exceptional Children, 12, 52–54.

Deshler, D. D., Putnam, M. L., & Bulgren, J. A. (1985). Academic accommodations for adolescents with behavior and learning problems. In S. Braaten, R. B. Rutherford, & W. Evans (Eds.), *Programming for adolescents with behavioral disorders* (Vol. 2, pp. 20–30). Reston, VA: Council for Children with Behavior Disorders.

Dettmer, P., Thurston, L. P., & Dyck, N. (1993). *Consultation, collaboration, and teamwork for students with special needs.* Boston: Allyn and Bacon.

Downing, J. A. (1990). Contingency contracts: A step-by-step format. *Intervention in School and Clinic, 26,* 111–113.

Doyle, W. (1986). Classroom organization and management. In M. Wittrock (Ed.), *Handbook of research on teaching* (pp. 392–431). New York: Macmillan.

Doyle, W. (1990). Classroom management techniques. In O. C. Moles (Ed.), *Student discipline strategies.* Albany: State University of New York Press.

Drugs & Drug Abuse Education. (1994). Prevalence of any illicit drug use, 1979–1993. *Drugs & Drug Abuse Education, 25*(8), 56.

Dunn, L. M. (1968). Special education for the mildly handicapped—Is much of it justifiable? *Exceptional Children 35,* 5–22.

Duquette, C. (1996). Behaviour and procedures of secondary teachers in the integrated classroom. In J. Andrews (Ed.), *Teaching students with diverse needs: Secondary classrooms* (pp. 146–159). Scarborough: Nelson Canada.

Durlak, C. M. (1992). Preparing high school students with learning disabilities for the transition to postsecondary education: Training for self-determination. Unpublished doctoral dissertation, Northern Illinois University, DeKalb.

Durlak, C. M., Rose, E., & Bursuck, W. D. (1994). Preparing high school students with learning disabilities for the transition to postsecondary education: Teaching the skills of self-determination. *Journal of Learning Disabilities, 27*(1), 51–59.

Dworet, D., Davis, C., & Martin, J. (1996). Classroom management in the elementary school. In J. Andrews (Ed.), *Teaching students with diverse needs: Elementary classrooms* (pp. 125–151). Scarborough: Nelson Canada.

Dyson, L. (1993). Response to the presence of a child with disabilities: Parental stress and family functioning over time. *American Journal on Mental Retardation, 98,* 207–218.

Edgington, R. (1968). But he spelled it right this morning. In J. I. Arena (Ed.), *Building spelling skills in dyslexic children* (pp. 23–24). San Rafael, CA: Academic Therapy Publications.

Edyburn, D. L. (1990). Locating information about software [special issue]. *1990–1991 Back-to-School Special Education Resource Guide,* 14–15. (Available from Technology and Media Division, Council for Exceptional Children)

Einhorn, R., Hagen, C., Johnson, J., Wujek, C., & Hoffman, L. (1991). *Authentic assessment: A collaborative approach.* Flossmoor, Illinois: SMA Communication Development Project.

Ellis, E., & Lenz, B. K. (1987). A component analysis of effective learning strategies for LD students. *Learning Disabilities Focus, 2,* 94–107.

Ellis, E. S., & Sabornie, E. J. (1990). Strategy-based adaptive instruction in content-area classes: Social validity of six options. *Teacher Education and Special Education, 13*(2), 133–144.

Ellis, E., Lenz, B. K., & Sabornie, E. J. (1987). Generalization and adaptation of learning strategies to natural environments: Part 2. Research into practice. *Remedial and Special Education, 8*(2), 6–23.

Emmer, E. T., Evertson, C. M., Sanford, J. P., Clements, B. S., & Worsham, M. E. (1983). *Organizing and managing the junior high classroom.* Austin: Research and Development Center for Teacher Education, University of Texas.

Englert, C., & Mariage, T. (1991). Making students partners in the comprehension process: Organizing the reading "POSSE." *Learning Disability Quarterly, 14,* 123–138.

Englert, C. S., Raphael, T. E., Anderson, L. M., Anthony, H. M., Fear, K. L., & Gregg, S. L. (1988). A case for writing intervention: Strategies for writing informational text. *Learning Disabilities Focus, 3*(2), 98–113.

Epilepsy Ontario. (1992). *Epilepsy: A teacher's guide.* Toronto: Author.

Epilepsy Ontario. (n.d.). *A resource kit about epilepsy.* Toronto: Author.

Epstein, M. A., Shaywitz, S. E., Shaywitz, B. A., & Woolston, J. L. (1991). The boundaries of attention deficit disorder. *Journal of Learning Disabilities, 24,* 78–86.

Epstein, M. H., Kinder, D., & Bursuck, W. D. (1989). The academic status of adolescents with behavior disorders. *Behavioral Disorders, 4*(3), 157–165.

Evans, I. M., Salisbury, C. L., Palombaro, M. M., Berryman, J., & Hollowood, T. M. (1992). Peer interactions and social acceptance of elementary-age children with severe disabilities in an inclusive school. *Journal of the Association for Persons with Severe Handicaps, 17,* 205–212.

Evans, S. B. (1991). A realistic look at the research base for collaboration in special education. *Preventing School Failure, 35*(4), 10–14.

Evans, S. S., Evans, W. H., & Mercer, C. (1986). *Assessment for instruction.* Boston: Allyn and Bacon.

Evertson, C. M., Emmer, E. T., Clements, B. S., Sanford, J. P., Worsham, M. E., & Williams, E. L. (1983). *Organizing and managing the elementary school classroom.* Austin: Research and Development Center for Teacher Education, University of Texas.

Fantuzzo, J. W., King, J. A., & Heller, L. R. (1992). Effects of reciprocal peer tutoring on mathematics and school adjustment: A component analysis. *Journal of Educational Psychology, 84,* 331–339.

Federation of Women Teachers Associations of Ontario. (1996). *Antiracist resource guide.* Toronto: Author.

Felton, R. H. (1993). Effects of instruction on the decoding skills of children with phonological-processing problems. *Journal of Learning Disabilities, 26*(9), 583–589.

Fisher, C. W., Berliner, D., Filby, N., Marliave, R., Cahen, L., & Dishaw, M. (1980). Teaching behavior, academic learning time, and student achievement: An overview. In C. Denham & A. Lieberman (Eds.), *Time to learn* (pp. 7–32). Washington, DC: National Institute of Education, Department of Education.

Flores, B., Cousin, P. T., & Diaz, E. (1991). Transforming deficit myths about learning, language, and culture. *Language Arts, 68,* 369–379.

Flowers, D. L. (1993). Brain basis for dyslexia: A summary of work in progress. Journal of *Learning Disabilities, 26*(9), 575–582.

Fogarty, R. (1990). *Designs for cooperative interactions.* Palatine, IL: Skylight Publishing.

Ford, A., Davern, L., & Schnorr, R. (1990). Inclusive education: "Making sense" of the curriculum. In S. Stainback & W. Stainback (Eds.), *Curriculum considerations in inclusive classrooms: Facilitating learning for all students.* Baltimore: Brookes.

Forest, M., & Lusthaus, E. (1990). Everyone belongs with the MAPS action planning system. *Teaching Exceptional Children, 22*(2), 32–35.

Foster-Johnson, L., & Dunlap, G. (1993). Using functional assessment to develop effective, individualized inter-

ventions for challenging behaviors. *Teaching Exceptional Children, 25*(3), 44–50.

Fox, C. L. (1989). Peer acceptance of learning disabled children in the regular classroom. *Exceptional Children, 56,* 50–59.

Freagon, S., Kincaid, M., & Kaiser, N. (1990). One educational system for all, including children and youth with severe intellectual disabilities and/or multiple handicaps. *ICEC Quarterly, 39*(2), 18–26.

Freeman, B. J. (1994). Diagnosis of the syndrome of autism: Where we have been and where we are going. In F. LaRoy & J. Streng (Eds.), *A new dawn of awakening: Proceedings of the 1994 conference.* Arlington, TX: Future Education.

Friend, M., & Cook, L. (1992a). *Interactions: Collaboration skills for school professionals.* White Plains, NY: Longman.

Friend, M., & Cook, L. (1992b). The new mainstreaming: How it really works. *Instructor, 101*(7), 30–32, 34, 36.

Frith, G. H. (1982) *The role of the special education paraprofessional: An introductory text.* Springfield, IL: Charles C. Thomas.

Fuchs, D., & Fuchs, L. (1994). Inclusive schools movement and the radicalization of special education reform. *Exceptional Children, 60,* 294–309.

Fuchs, L. S., Fuchs, D., Hamlett, C., Philips, N., & Bentz, J. (1994). Classwide curriculum-based measurement: Helping general educators meet the challenge of student diversity. *Exceptional Children, 60*(6), 518–537.

Fullan, M. (1982). *The meaning of educational change.* Toronto: OISE Press.

Fullan, M., & Stiegelbauer, S. (1991). *The new meaning of educational change* (2nd ed.). New York: Teachers College Press.

Fullwood, D. (1990). *Chances and choices: Making integration work.* Sydney, AU: Paul H. Brookes Pub.

Furman, W., & Robbins, P. (1985). What's the point? Issues in the selection of treatment objectives. In B. Schneider, K. H. Rubin, & J. E. Ledingham (Eds.), *Children's peer relations: Issues in assessment and intervention* (pp. 41–54). New York: Springer-Verlag.

Gallagher, J. J., & Gallagher, S. A. (1994). *Teaching the gifted child* (4th ed.). Boston: Allyn and Bacon.

Gallegos, A. Y., & Gallegos, M. L. (1990). A student's perspective on good teaching: MICHAEL. *Intervention in School and Clinic, 26*(1), 14–15.

Garcia, G. E., & Pearson, P. D. (1994). Assessment and diversity. In L. D. Hammond (Ed.), *Review of research in education* (pp. 337–391). Washington, DC: American Educational Research Association.

Garcia-Vasquez, E., & Ehly, S. W. (1992). Peer tutoring effects on students who are perceived as not socially accepted. *Psychology in the Schools, 29,* 256–266.

Gardner, H. (1993). *Multiple intelligences: The theory in practice.* New York: Basic Books.

Gardner, R., Sainato, D. M., Cooper, J. O., Heron, T. E., Heward, W. L., Eshelman, J. W., & Grossi, T. A. (1994). *Behavior analysis in education: Focus on measurably superior instruction.* Pacific Grove, CA: Brooks/Cole.

Gelzheiser, L. M., & Meyers, J. (1990). Special and remedial education in the classroom: Theme and variations. *Journal of Reading, Writing, and Learning Disabilities, 6,* 419–436.

Germinario, V., Cervalli, J., & Ogden, E. H. (1992). *All children successful: Real answers for helping at risk elementary students.* Lancaster, PA: Technomic.

Giangreco, M. F., Dennis, R., Cloninger, C., Edelman, S., & Schattman, R. (1993). "I've counted Jon": Transformational experiences of teachers educating students with disabilities. *Exceptional Children, 59,* 359–372.

Gillberg, C. (1989). Asperger syndrome in 23 Swedish children. *Developmental Medicine and Child Neurology, 31,* 520–531.

Goldstein, A. P., Sprafkin, R. P., Gershaw, N. J., & Klein, P. (1980). *Skill-streaming the adolescent: A structured approach to teaching prosocial skills.* Champaign, IL: Research Press.

Good, T. L., & Brophy, J. (1988). *Looking into classrooms* (4th ed.). New York: Harper and Row.

Graham, S., & Freeman, S. (1986). Strategy training and teacher- vs. student-controlled study conditions: Effects on LD students' spelling performance. *Learning Disability Quarterly, 9,* 15–22.

Graham, S., & Miller, L. (1980). Handwriting research and practice: A unified approach. *Focus on Exceptional Children, 13*(2), 1–16.

Graley, J. (1994). A path to the mainstream of life: Facilitated communication/behavior/inclusion: Three interacting ingredients. In F. LaRoy & J. Streng (Eds.), *A new dawn of awakening: Proceedings of the 1994 conference.* Arlington, TX: Future Education.

Grandin, T. (1984). My experiences as an autistic child and review of selected literature. *Journal of Orthomolecular Psychiatry, 13,* 144–174.

Greenburg, D. E. (1987). *A special educator's perspective on interfacing special and general education: A review for administrators.* Reston, VA: Council for Exceptional Children.

Greenwood, C. R. (1991). Longitudinal analysis of time, engagement, and achievement in at-risk versus non-risk students. *Exceptional Children, 57,* 521–535.

Greenwood, C. R., Delquadri, J. C., & Hall, R. V. (1989). Longitudinal effects of classwide peer tutoring. *Journal of Educational Psychology, 81,* 371–383.

Greenwood, C. R., & Rieth, H. G. (1994). Current dimensions of technology-based assessment in special education. *Exceptional Children, 61*(2), 105–113.

Gresham, F.M. (1993). School-based social skills training: Implications for students with mild disabilities. *Exceptionality Education Canada, 3*(1&2), 61–78.

Griffith, D. R. (1992). Prenatal exposure to cocaine and other drugs: Developmental and educational prognoses. *Phi Delta Kappan, 74,* 30–34.

Haines, L., Sanche, R., & Robertson, G. (1993). Instruction CoPlanner: A software tool to facilitate collaborative resource teaching. *Canadian Journal of Educational Communications, 22,* 177–187.

Hallahan, D. P., & Kauffman, J. M. (1991). *Exceptional children: Introduction to special education.* Englewood Cliffs, NJ: Prentice-Hall.

Hallahan, D. P., Kauffman, J. M., & Lloyd, J. W. (1985). *Introduction to learning disabilities.* Englewood Cliffs, NJ: Prentice-Hall.

Hallenbeck, M. J., & McMaster, D. (1991). Disability simulation. *Teaching Exceptional Children, 23*(3), 12–15.

Hamre-Nietupski, S., McDonald, J., & Nietupski, J. (1992). Integrating elementary students with multiple disabilities into supported regular classes: Challenges and solutions. *Teaching Exceptional Children, 24*(3), 6–9.

Hardman, M. L., Drew, C. J., Egan, M. W., & Wolf, B. (1993). *Human exceptionality: Society, school, and family* (4th ed.). Boston: Allyn and Bacon.

Hardy, M.I., McLeod, J., Minto, H., Perkins, S.A., & Quance, W.R. (1971). *Standards for education of exceptional children in Canada: The SEECC report.* Toronto: Leonard Crainford.

Haring, N. G., & McCormick, L. (Eds.). (1986). *Exceptional children and youth* (4th ed.). Columbus, OH: Merrill.

Haring, T. G., Breen, C., Pitts-Conway, V., Lee, M., & Gaylord-Ross, R. (1987). Adolescent peer tutoring and special friend experiences. *Journal of the Association for Persons with Severe Handicaps, 12,* 280–286.

Harris, K. C., Harvey, P., Garcia, L., Innes, D., Lynn, P., Munoz, D., Sexton, K., & Stoica, R. (1987). Meeting the needs of special high school students in regular education classrooms. *Teacher Education and Special Education, 10,* 143–152.

Harris, T. (1994). Christine's inclusion: An example of peers supporting one another. In J.S. Thousand, R.A. Villa, & A.I. Nevin (Eds.), *Creativity and collaborative learning* (pp. 293–301). Baltimore, MD: Paul H. Brookes.

Harvard Graduate School of Education. (1992). *Cooperative learning: Making it work.* The Best of the Harvard Education Letter. Cambridge, MA: Author.

Haynes, N. M., & Gebreyesus, S. (1992). Cooperative learning: A case for African-American students. *School Psychology Review, 21,* 577–585.

Heath, N. (1992). Learning disabilities and depression: Research, theory, and practice. *Exceptionality Education Canada, 2*(3&4), 59–74.

Heath, N. (1996). The emotional domain: Self-concept and depression in children with learning disabilities. *Advances in Learning and Behavioral Disabilities, 10,* 47–75.

Heron, T. E., & Harris, K. C. (1993). *The educational consultant: Helping professionals, parents, and mainstreamed students* (3rd ed.). Austin, TX: Pro-Ed.

Hess, R. (1987). *Grading-credit-diploma: Accommodation practices for students with mild disabilities.* Des Moines: Iowa State Department of Education.

Hetterscheidt, J., Pott, L., Russell, K., & Tchang, J. (1992). Using the computer as a reading portfolio. *Educational Leadership, 49*(8), 73.

Hightower, A. D., Avery, R. R., & Levinson, H. R. (1988, April). *The study buddy program: A preventive intervention for 4th and 5th grades.* Paper presented at the National Association of School Psychologists annual meeting, Chicago, IL.

Hollingsworth, M. G. (1996). Computers in secondary education: Practices today, preparing for tomorrow. In J. Andrews (Ed.), *Teaching students with diverse needs: Secondary classrooms* (pp. 243–274). Scarborough: Nelson Canada.

Homme, L. (1970). *How to use contingency contracting in the classroom.* Champaign, IL: Research Press.

Hoover, K. H., & Hollingsworth, P. M. (1982). *A handbook for elementary school teachers.* Boston: Allyn and Bacon.

Horton, S. V. (1987). Study guides: A paper on curriculum modification. Unpublished manuscript, University of Washington.

Housego, B. E. J. (1990). Student teachers' feelings of preparedness to teach. *Canadian Journal of Education, 15,* 37–56.

Howell, K. M., & Morehead, M. K. (1993). *Curriculum-based evaluation for special and remedial education* (2nd ed.). Columbus, OH: Merrill.

Hughes, C. A., Ruhl, K. L., & Peterson, S. K. (1988). Teaching self-management skills. *Teaching Exceptional Children, 23*(2), 70–72.

Hull, G. A. (1989). Research on writing: Building a cognitive and social understanding of composing. In L. B. Resnick & L. E. Klopfer (Eds.), *Toward the thinking curriculum: Current cognitive research* (pp. 104–128). Pittsburgh, PA: Association for Supervision and Curriculum.

Human Resources and Labour Canada. (1993). *Leaving school.* Ottawa: Queen's Printer.

Hurt, G. D. (1991). Mild brain injury: Critical factors in vocational rehabilitation. *Journal of Rehabilitation, 57*(4), 36–40.

Hutchinson, N. L. (1986). *Instruction of representation and solution in algebraic problem solving with learning disabled adolescents.* Unpublished doctoral thesis, Simon Fraser University, Burnaby, BC.

Hutchinson, N. L. (1996). Using performance assessments to evaluate career development programs. *Guidance and Counselling, 11*(3), 3–7.

Hutchinson, N. L. (1994). Evaluating career development in school-based programs: Performance assessments. *Canadian Journal of Counselling, 28,* 326–333.

Hutchinson, N. L. (1996). Promoting social development and social acceptance in secondary school classrooms. In J. Andrews (Ed.), *Teaching students with diverse needs: Secondary classrooms* (pp. 160–180). Scarborough: Nelson Canada.

Hutchinson, N. L. (1993). Effects of cognitive strategy instruction on algebra problem solving of adolescents with learning disabilities. *Learning Disability Quarterly, 16*(1), 34–63.

Hutchinson, N. L. (in press). Creating an inclusive classroom with young adolescents in an urban school. *Exceptionality Education Canada.*

Hutchinson, N. L., & Freeman, J. (1994). *Pathways.* Scarborough, ON: Nelson Canada.

Hutchinson, N.L., & Freeman, J. G. (1994). *Pathways: Knowing about yourself, knowing about careers.* Toronto: Nelson Canada.

solving problems on the job. *Journal of Employment Counseling, 33*(1), 2–19.

Hutchinson, N. L., & Schmid, C. (1996). Perceptions of a resource teacher about programs for preschoolers with special needs and their families. *Canadian Journal of Research in Early Childhood Education, 5*(1), 73–82.

Hynd, G. W., Voeller, K. K., Hern, K. L., & Marshall, R. M. (1991). Neurobiological basis of attention-deficit hyperactivity disorder (ADHD). *School Psychology Review, 20,* 174–186.

Idol, L., Nevin, A., & Paolucci-Whitcomb, P. (1994). *Collaborative consultation* (2nd ed.). Austin, TX: Pro-Ed.

Isaacson, S. L. (1987). Effective instruction in written language. *Focus on Exceptional Children, 19*(6), 1–12.

Jarolimek, J., & Foster, C. D. (1993). *Teaching and learning in the elementary school.* New York: Macmillan.

Jaussi, K. R. (1991). Drawing the outsiders in: Deaf students in the mainstream. *Perspectives in Education and Deafness, 9*(5), 12–15.

Jayanthi, M., & Friend, M. (1992). Interpersonal problem solving: A selected literature review to guide practice. *Journal of Educational and Psychological Consultation, 3,* 147–152.

Jayanthi, M., Epstein, M. H., Polloway, E., & Bursuck, W. D. (in press). Test adaptations: A national survey of the testing practices of general education teachers. Journal of Special Education.

Jayanthi, M., Nelson, J. S., Sawyer, V., Bursuck, W. D., & Epstein, M. H. (1995). Homework-communication problems among parents, general education, and special education teachers: An exploratory study. *Remedial and Special Education, 16*(2), 102–116.

Jeffreys, M., & Gall, R. S. (1996). *The learning journey: Enhancing lifelong learning and self-determination for people with special needs.* Calgary: Detselig.

Jenkins, J. R., & Jenkins, L. M. (1981). *Cross-age and peer tutoring: Help for children with learning problems.* Reston, VA: Council for Exceptional Children.

Jenkins, J., & Jenkins, L. (1985). Peer tutoring in elementary and secondary programs. *Focus on Exceptional Children, 17*(6), 1–12.

Jenson, W. R., Sheridan, S. M., Olympia, D., & Andrews, D. (1994). Homework and students with learning disabilities and behavior disorders: A practical, parent-based approach. *Journal of Learning Disabilities, 27*(9), 538–549.

Johnson, D. W., & Johnson, R. T. (1989). Cooperative learning: What special education teachers need to know. *The Pointer, 33*(2), 5–11.

Johnson, D. W., & Johnson, R. T. (1992). *Learning together and alone: Cooperative, competitive, and individualistic learning* (3rd ed.). Englewood Cliffs, NJ: Prentice-Hall.

Johnson, D. W., & Johnson, R. T. (1994). *Learning together and alone* (4th ed.). Boston: Allyn and Bacon.

Johnson, D. W., Johnson, R. T., Holubec, E. J., & Roy, P. (1984). *Circles of learning.* Alexandria, VA: Association for Supervision and Curriculum Development.

Johnson, D. W., Johnson, R. T., & Maruyama, G. (1983). Interdependence and interpersonal attraction among heterogeneous and homogeneous individuals: A theoretical formulation and a meta-analysis of the research. *Review of Educational Research, 53*, 5–54.

Johnson, L. J., Pugach, M. C., & Hammitte, D. J. (1988). Barriers to effective special education consultation. *Remedial and Special Education, 9*(6), 41–47.

Johnson, R. T. (1992). Learning technology contexts for at risk children. In H. C. Waxman, J. W. De Felix, J. E. Anderson, & H. P. Baptiste (Eds.), *Students at risk in at risk schools.* Newbury Park, CA: Corwin Press.

Jones, K. H., & Bender, W. N. (1993). Utilization of paraprofessionals in special education: A review of the literature. *Remedial and Special Education, 14*(1), 7–14.

Jones, V., & Jones, L. (1990). *Comprehensive classroom management.* Boston: Allyn and Bacon.

Jordan, A. (1994). *Skills in collaborative consultation.* New York: Routledge.

Kagan, S. (1992). *Cooperative learning.* San Jaun Capistrano, CA: Kagan Cooperative Learning.

Kagan, S. (1990). A structural approach to cooperative learning. *Educational Leadership, 47*(4), 12–15.

Kamann, M., & Perry, N. (1994). Amalgamating support services to support integration. *Exceptionality Education Canada, 4*(3&4), 91–106.

Kameenui, E., & Simmons, D. (1991). *Designing instructional strategies: The prevention of academic learning problems.* Columbus, OH: Merrill.

Kanner, L. (1964). *A history of the care and study of the mentally retarded.* Springfield, IL: Charles C. Thomas.

Kauffman, J., & Hallahan, D. P. (Eds.). (1995). *The illusion of full inclusion: A comprehensive critique of a current special education bandwagon.* Austin, TX: PRO-ED.

Kazdin, A. E. (1977). *The token economy: A review and evaluation.* New York: Plenum.

Keating, D. P. (1990). Adolescent thinking. In S. S. Feldman & G. R. Elliott (Eds.), *At the threshold: The developing adolescent* (pp. 54–89). Boston: Harvard University Press.

Keating, D. P. (1991). Curriculum options for the developmentally advanced: A developmental alternative to gifted education. *Exceptionality Education Canada, 1*(1), 53–83.

Keefe, C., & Candler, A. (1989). LD students and word processors: Questions and answers. *Learning Disabilities Focus, 4*(2), 78–83.

Kemp, L. (1992). Responding to diversity in the urban student population. *NASSP Bulletin, 76* (546), 37–40.

Kerschner, J. R. (1990). Self-concept and IQ as predictors of remedial success in children with learning disabilities. *Journal of Learning Disabilities, 23*, 368–374.

Kindsvatter, R., Wilen, W., & Ishler, M. (1988). *Dynamics of effective teaching.* New York: Longman.

Kirby, J. (1996). *The PASS tests and phonological processing in beginning reading.* (incomplete)

Kirst, M. W. (1991). Improving children's services: Overcoming barriers, creating new opportunities. *Phi Delta Kappan, 72*, 615–618.

Klesmer, H. (1994). *ESL achievement project: Development of English as a second language achievement criteria as a function of age and length of residence in Canada.* North York, ON: North York Board of Education.

Knapp, M. S., & Shields, P. M. (1990). Reconceiving academic instruction for the children of poverty. *Phi Delta Kappan, 71*, 753–758.

Knapp, M. S., Turnbull, B. J., & Shields, P. M. (1990). New directions for educating the children of poverty. *Educational Leadership, 48*(1), 4–8.

Koorland, M. A., Monda, L. E., & Vail, C. O. (1988). Recording behavior with ease. Teaching *Exceptional Children, 21*(1), 59–61.

Koskinen, P. S., Wilson, R. M., Gambrell, L. B., & Neuman, S. B. (1993). Captioned video and vocabulary learning: An innovative practice in literacy instruction. *Reading Teacher, 47*(1), 36–43.

Kunc, N. (1984). *Ready, willing and disabled.* Toronto: Frontier College.

Kysela, G. M., McDonald, L., & Brenton-Haden, S. (1992). Family functioning and the concept of learning disability. *Exceptionality Education Canada, 2*(3&4), 143–162.

Lam, Y. L. J., & McQuarrie, N. (1989). Paraprofessionals are an administrative time bomb. *The Canadian School Executive, 9*(3), 3–6, 12.

Lamont, I. L., & Hill, J. L. (1991). Roles and responsibilities of paraprofessionals in the regular elementary classroom. *B.C. Journal of Special Education, 15*(1), 1–24.

Landfried, S. E. (1989). "Enabling" undermines responsibility in students. *Educational Leadership, 47*(3), 79–83.

Langan, J. (1982). *Reading and study skills* (2nd ed.). New York: McGraw-Hill.

Langer, J. (1984). Examining background knowledge and text comprehension. *Reading Research Quarterly, 19*, 468–481.

Lass, N.J. (1991). Adolescents' perceptions of normal and voice-disordered children. *Journal of Communication Disorders, 24*, 267–274.

Lavoie, R. (1991). *How difficult can this be? Understanding learning disabilities.* Portland, OR: Educational Productions.

Lavoie, R. D. (1989). *Mainstreaming: A collection of field-tested strategies to help make the mainstreaming classroom more successful for learning disabled children, their classmates . . . and their teachers.* Norwalk, CT: Connecticut Association for Children with Learning Disabilities.

Layman, R. (1990). *Child abuse.* Detroit, MI: Omnigraphics.

Lazarowitz, R., & Karsenty, G. (1990). Cooperative learning and students' academic achievement, process skills, learning environments, and self-esteem in tenth-grade biology classrooms. In S. Sharan (Ed.), *Cooperative learning* (pp. 123–149). New York: Praeger.

Lee, E. (1994). Taking multicultural, anti-racist education seriously. *Rethinking Schools* (Special Edition), 19–22.

Leinhardt, G., & Zigmond, N. (1988). The effects of self-questioning and story structure training on the reading comprehension of poor readers. *Learning Disabilities Research, 4*(1), 41–51.

Lenz, B. K. (1983). Using the advance organizer. *Pointer, 27*, 11–13.

Lenz, B. K., Alley, G., & Schumaker, J. B. (1987). Activating the inactive learner: Advance organizers in the secondary content classroom. *Learning Disability Quarterly, 10*, 53–67.

Lepper, M. R., Greene, D., & Nesbitt, R.E. (1973). Undermining children's intrinsic interest with extrinsic reward: A test of the overjustification hypothesis. *Journal of Personality and Social Psychology, 28*, 129–137.

Lerner, J. W. (1987). The regular education initiative: Some unanswered questions. *Learning Disabilities Focus, 3*(1), 3–7.

Lerner, J. (1993). *Learning disabilities: Theories, diagnoses, and teaching strategies* (6th ed.). Boston: Houghton Mifflin.

Lessen, E., & Bursuck, W. D. (1983). A preliminary analysis of special education referral forms for a rural school district. Unpublished data collection. Northern Illinois University, DeKalb.

Lessen, E., Sommers, M., & Bursuck, W. (1988). *Curriculum-based assessment and instructional design.* DeKalb, IL: DeKalb County Special Education Association.

Levesque, N. (1997). *Perceptions of friendships and peer groups: The school experiences of two adolescents with learning disabilities.* Unpublished masters thesis, Queen's University.

Levy, N. R., & Rosenberg, M. S. (1990). Strategies for improving the written expression of students with learning disabilities. *Learning Disabilities Forum, 16*(1), 23–30.

Lew, M., Mesch, D., Johnson, D. W., & Johnson, R. (1986). Positive interdependence, academic and collaborative-skills group contingencies, and isolated students. *American Educational Research Journal, 23*, 476–488.

Lewis, R. B. (1993). *Special education technology: Classroom applications.* Pacific Grove, CA: Brooks/Cole.

Lezak, M. D., & O'Brien, K. P. (1988). Longitudinal study of emotional, social, and physical changes after traumatic brain injury. *Journal of Learning Disabilities, 21*, 456–461.

Licht, B. G., Kistner, J. A., Ozkaragoz, T., Shapiro, S., & Clausen, L. (1985). Causal attributions of learning disabled children: Individual difference of their implications for persistence. *Journal of Educational Psychology, 77*, 208–216.

Linehan, M. F. (1992). Children who are homeless: Educational strategies for school personnel. *Phi Delta Kappan, 74*, 61–66.

Little, J. W. (1982). Norms of collegiality and experimentation: Workplace conditions of school success. *American Educational Research Journal, 19*, 325–340.

Lombardi, T. P., Odell, K. S., & Novotny, D. E. (1990). Special education and students at risk: Findings from a national study. *Remedial and Special Education, 12*(1), 56–62.

Lombardo, V. S. (1980). *Paraprofessionals in special education.* Springfield, IL: Charles C. Thomas.

Long, N. J., & Newman, R. G. (1971). Managing surface behavior of children in school. In N. J. Long, W. C. Morse, & R. G. Newman (Eds.), *Conflict in the classroom: The education of children with problems* (2nd ed.). Belmont, CA: Wadsworth.

Lord, J. (1991). *Lives in transition: The process of personal empowerment.* Kitchener, ON: Centre for Research and Education in Human Services.

Lortie, D. C. (1975). *Schoolteacher: A sociological study.* Chicago: University of Chicago Press.

Lovitt, T. C., & Horton, S. V. (1987). How to develop study guides. *Journal of Reading, Writing and Learning Disabilities, 3*, 333–343.

Lovitt, T. C., Rudsit, J., Jenkins, J., Pious, C., & Beneditti, D. (1985). Two methods of adapting science materials for learning disabled and regular seventh graders. *Learning Disability Quarterly, 8,* 275–285.

Lowell York, J., Doyle, M. E., & Kronberg, R. (1995). Module 3. *Curriculum as everything students learn in school: Individualizing learning opportunities.* Baltimore: Brookes.

Lupart, J. L. (1990). Parents and gifted education (PAGE): A program for parents of gifted children. *Agate, 4*(2), 16–20.

Lynch, E. W., Lewis, R. B., & Murphy, D. S. (1993a). Educational services for children with chronic illnesses: Perspectives of educators and families. *Exceptional Children, 59,* 210–220.

Lynch, E. W., Lewis, R. B., & Murphy, D. S. (1993b). Improving education for children with chronic illnesses. *Principal, 73*(2), 38–40.

MacArthur, C. A., & Stoddard, B. (1990, April). Teaching learning disabled students to revise: A peer editor strategy. Paper presented at the annual meeting of the American Education Research Association, Boston, MA.

MacCuspie, P.A. (1996). *Promoting acceptance of children with disabilities: From tolerance to inclusion.* Halifax: Atlantic Provinces Special Education Authority.

MacCuspie, P. A. (1993). Short-term placements: A crucial role for residential schools. *Journal of Visual Impairment and Blindness, 87*(b), 193–198.

Maclean's. (1991). *Sex, politics and dreams,* (January 7), pp. 32–36, 38.

Maheady, L., Mallette, B., & Harper, B. F. (1991). Accommodating cultural, linguistic, and academic diversity: Some peer-mediated instructional options. *Preventing School Failure, 36*(1), 28–31.

Maker, J. C. (1993). Gifted students in the regular classroom: What practices are defensible and feasible? In C. J. Maker (Ed.), *Critical issues in gifted education: Programs for the gifted in regular classrooms* (Vol. III). Austin, TX: Pro-Ed.

Male, M. (1994). *Technology for inclusion: Meeting the special needs of all students.* Boston: Allyn and Bacon.

Mandell, A. L. (1996). A question of rights: The educational placement of children with mental and physical disabilities. *Exceptionality Education Canada, 6*(1), 1–14.

Mandlebaum, L. H., & Wilson, R. (1989). Teaching listening skills. *LD Forum, 15*(1), 7–9.

Manitoba Education and Training. (August, 1989). *Special education in Manitoba: Policy and procedural guidelines.* Winnipeg: Author.

Manitoba Teachers' Society. (1990). *Report of the Task Force on the Physical and Emotional Abuse of Teachers.* Winnipeg: Author.

Marston, D. B. (1989). A curriculum-based measurement approach to assessing academic performance: What it is and why do it. In M. R. Shinn (Ed.), *Curriculum-based measurement: Assessing special children* (pp. 18–78). New York: Guilford.

Marston, D., Tindal, G., & Deno, S. (1984). Eligibility for learning disability services: A direct and repeated measurement approach. *Exceptional Children, 50,* 554–556.

Martin, D. A. (1987). Children and adolescents with traumatic brain injury: Impact on the family. *Journal of Learning Disabilities, 21,* 464–470.

Martin, J., & Sugarman, J. (1993). *Models of classroom management: Principles, applications and critical perspectives* (2nd ed.). Calgary: Detselig.

Marzola, E. S. (1987). Using manipulatives in math instruction. *Reading, Writing, and Learning Disabilities, 3,* 9–20.

Mathes, P. G., & Fuchs, L. S. (1994). The efficacy of peer tutoring in reading for students with mild disabilities: A best-evidence synthesis. *School Psychology Review, 23,* 59–80.

Matthews, D. J. (1993). Linguistic giftedness in the context of domain-specific development. *Exceptionality Education Canada, 3*(3), 1–23.

Matthews, D. J. (in press). Giftedness at adolescence: Diverse options required. *Exceptionality Education Canada.*

McBurnett, K., Lahey, B. B., & Pfiffner, L. J. (1993). Diagnosis of attention deficit disorders in DSM-IV: Scientific basis and implications for education. *Exceptional Children, 60,* 108–117.

McGookey, K. (1992). Drama, disability, and your classroom. *Teaching Exceptional Children, 24*(2), 12–14.

McInnes, J. (1987). *Networks: Weave a dream.* Scarborough: Nelson Canada.

McIntyre, T. (1992). *The behavior management handbook: Setting up effective management systems.* Boston: Allyn and Bacon.

McLeod, K., & Krugly-Smolska, E. (1997). *Multicultural education: A place to start.* Toronto: Canadian Association of Second Language Teachers.

Meichenbaum, D., & Goodman, J. (1971). Training impulsive children to talk to themselves: A means of developing self-control. *Journal of Abnormal Psychology, 77,* 115–126.

Meichenbaum, D. (1977). *Cognitive behavior modification: An integrative approach.* New York: Plenum.

Mercer, C. D. (1991). *Students with learning disabilities* (4th ed.). Columbus, OH: Merrill.

Mikkelsen, G. (1992, Spring/Summer). *Building a welcoming classroom. What's Working.* Minneapolis: Minnesota Inclusive Education Technical Assistance Program, University of Minnesota College of Education.

Miner, B. (1994). Taking multicultural, anti-racist education seriously: An interview with educator Enid Lee. In *Rethinking our classrooms* (pp. 19–22). Milwaukee, WI: Rethinking Schools.

Ministère de l'Education, Gouvernement du Québec. (April, 1992). *Educational success for all: Special education policy update.* Québec: Author.

Minow, M. (1985). Learning to live with the dilemma of difference: Bilingual and special education. *Law and Contemporary Problems, 48,* 157–211.

Miranda, A., & Guerrero, M. (1986). The funny farola. In *Adventures* (pp. 42–53). Boston: Houghton Mifflin.

Montgomery County Public Schools. (1985). *Blueprint for study strategies.* Rockville, MD: Board of Education of Montgomery County.

Moore, D. W., Readance, J. E., & Rickelman, R. (1989). *Prereading activities for content-area reading and learning* (2nd ed.). Newark, DE: International Reading Association.

Morehouse, J. A., & Albright, L. (1991). Training trends and needs of paraprofessionals in transition service delivery agencies. *Teacher Education and Special Education, 14,* 248–256.

Morgan, D. P. (1993). Substance use prevention and students with behavioral disorders: Guidelines for school professionals. *Journal of Emotional and Behavioral Disorders, 1,* 170–178.

Morris, R. J. (1985). *Behavior modification with exceptional children: Principles and practices.* Glenview, IL: Scott, Foresman.

Morse, W. C. (1987). Introduction to the special issue. *Teaching Exceptional Children, 19*(4), 4–6.

Morsink, C. V., & Lenk, L. L. (1992). The delivery of special education programs and services. *Remedial and Special Education, 13*(6), 33–43.

Napier, E. (1995). *Integrating students with special needs: Effective strategies to provide the most enabling education for all students.* Vancouver: EduServ.

Nastasi, B., & Clements, D. (1991). Research on cooperative learning: Implications for practice. *School Psychology Review, 20,* 110–131.

National Council of Teachers of Mathematics. (1990). *Mathematics for the young child.* Reston, VA: National Council of Teachers of Mathematics.

National Information Center for Children and Youth with Disabilities. (1991). The education of children and youth with special needs: What do the laws say? *NICHCY News Digest, 1*(1), 1–15.

National Information Center for Children and Youth with Disabilities. (1993). Including special education in the school community. *NICHCY News Digest, 2*(2), 1–7.

Neel, R. S., & Cessna, K. K. (1993). Behavioral intent: Instructional content for students with behavior disorders. In K. K. Cessna (Ed.), *Instructionally differentiated programming: A needs-based approach for students with behavior disorders.* Denver: Colorado Department of Education.

New Brunswick Department of Education. (1991). *Position statement on inclusive, quality education.* Fredericton: Author.

New Brunswick Department of Education. (July, 1994). *Best practices for inclusion.* Fredericton: Author.

New Brunswick Department of Education, Student Services Branch. (1994). *Teacher assistant guidelines for standards and evaluation.* Fredericton: New Brunswick Department of Education.

Newfoundland Classroom Issues Committee. (January, 1995). *Report to the Social Policy Committee of the provincial cabinet.* St. John's: Government of Newfoundland.

Northwest Territories Department of Education, Culture and Employment. (1995). *Bill 25: Education Act summary.* Yellowknife: Author.

Northwest Territories Department of Education, Culture and Employment. (1996). *Educating all our children: Departmental directive on inclusive schooling.* Yellowknife: Author.

Nova Scotia Department of Education and Culture. (1996). *Special education policy manual.* Halifax: Author.

Oakland, T. (1981). Nonbiased assessment of minority group children. *Exceptional Education Quarterly, 1*(3), 31–46.

O'Brien, J., Forest, M., Snow, J., & Hasbury, D. (1989). *Action for inclusion: How to improve schools by welcoming children with special needs into regular classrooms.* Toronto: Frontier College.

O'Brien, J., Snow, J., Forest, M., & Hasbury, D. (1989). *Action for inclusion.* Toronto: Frontier College Press.

Office for Disability Issues. (1997). *A way with words: Guidelines and appropriate terminology for the portrayal of persons with disabilities.* Ottawa: Human Resource Development Canada.

Okolo, C. M. (1993). Computers and individuals with mild disabilities. In J. Lindsey (Ed.), *Computers and exceptional individuals* (pp. 111–141). Austin, TX: Pro-Ed.

Olson, M. W., & Gee, T. C. (1991). Content reading instruction in the primary grades: Perceptions and strategies. *Reading Teacher, 45*(4), 298–307.

O'Neil, J. (1992). On tracking and individual differences: A conversation with Jeannie Oakes. *Educational Leadership, 50*(1), 18–21.

Ontario Ministry of Education. (1987). *Vision: Resource guide.* Toronto: Queen's Printer for Ontario.

Ontario Ministry of Education and Training. (1993). *Antiracism and ethnocultural equity in school boards: Guidelines for policy development and implementation.* Toronto: Author.

Ontario Ministry of Education and Training. (1995a). *Consultation to validate: Categories of exceptionalities and definitions.* Toronto: Author.

Ontario Ministry of Education and Training. (1995b). *Consultation to validate: Regulation 305 (Identification and placement of exceptional pupils)*. Toronto: Author.

Ornstein, A. C. (1990). *Strategies for effective teaching*. New York: Harper and Row.

Overton, T. (1992). *Assessment in special education*. New York: Macmillan.

Paine, S. C., Radicchi, J., Rosellini, L. C., Deutchman, L., & Darch, C. B. (1983). *Structuring your classroom for academic success*. Champaign, IL: Research Press.

Palinscar, A., & Brown, A. (1988). Teaching and practicing thinking skills to promote comprehension in the context of group problem solving. *Remedial and Special Education, 9*(1), 53–59.

Palmer, J. D. (1988). For the manager who must build a team. In W. B. Reddy (Ed.), *Team building: Blueprints for productivity and satisfaction*. Alexandria, VA: NTL Institute for Applied Behavioral Science.

Patton, J. R. (1994). Practical recommendations for using homework with students with learning disabilities. *Journal of Learning Disabilities, 27*(9), 570–578.

Patton, J. R., Payne, J. S., & Beirne-Smith, M. (1986). *Mental retardation* (2nd ed.). Columbus, OH: Merrill.

Pauk, W. (1989). *How to study in college*. Boston: Houghton Mifflin.

Paulson, F., Paulson, P., & Meyer, C. (1991). What makes a portfolio a portfolio? *Educational Leadership, 48*(5), 60–63.

Peckham, V. C. (1993). Children with cancer in the classroom. *Teaching Exceptional Children, 26*(1), 26–32.

Pendarvis, E. D., Howley, A. A., & Howley, C. B. (1990). *The abilities of gifted children*. Englewood Cliffs, NJ: Prentice-Hall.

Phillips, V., & McCullough, L. (1990). Consultation-based programming: Instituting the collaborative ethic in schools. *Exceptional Children, 56*, 291–304.

Piper, D. (1993). Students in the mainstream who face linguistic and cultural challenges. In J. Andrews & J. Lupart (Eds.), *The inclusive classroom: Educating exceptional children* (pp. 169–208). Scarborough: Nelson Canada.

Polloway, E. A., Epstein, M. H., Bursuck, W. D., Jayanthi, M., & Cumblad, C. (1994). Homework practices of general education teachers. *Journal of Learning Disabilities, 27*(8), 100–109.

Poteet, J. A., Choate, J. S., & Stewart, S. C. (1993). Performance assessment and special education: Practices and prospects. *Focus on Exceptional Children, 26*(1), 1–20.

Pratt, C., & Moreno, S. J. (1994). Including students with autism in typical school settings. In F. LaRoy & J. Streng (Eds.), *A new dawn of awakening: Proceedings of the 1994 conference*. Arlington, TX: Future Education.

Pray, B. S., Hall, C. W., & Markley, R. P. (1992). Social skills training: An analysis of social behaviors selected for individualized education programs. *Remedial and Special Education, 13*(5), 43–49.

Prigatano, G. P. (1992). Personality disturbances associated with traumatic brain injury. *Journal of Consulting and Clinical Psychology, 60*, 360–368.

Prince Edward Island Department of Education. (November, 1995). *A model of special education service delivery: Draft*. Charlottetown: Author.

Principles for fair student assessment practices for education in Canada. (1993). Edmonton: Joint Advisory Committee.

Putnam, J. (1993). *Cooperative learning and strategies for inclusion*. Toronto: Brookes.

Putnam, J. W. (1993a). *Cooperative learning and strategies for inclusion: Celebrating diversity in the classroom*. Baltimore: Brookes.

Putnam, J. W. (1993b). The process of cooperative learning. In J. W. Putnam (Ed.), *Cooperative learning and strategies for inclusion: Celebrating diversity in the classroom* (pp.15–40). Baltimore: Brookes.

Putnam, J. W., Rynders, J. E., Johnson, R. T., & Johnson, D. W. (1989). Collaborative skill instruction for promoting interactions between mentally handicapped and nonhandicapped children. *Exceptional Children, 55*, 550–557.

Putnam, L., & Wesson, C. (1990). The teacher's role in teaching content-area information. *LD Forum, 16*(1), 55–60.

Ramsey, W. L., Gabriel, L. A., McGuirk, J. F., Phillips, C. R., & Watenpaugh, T. R. (1983). *General science*. New York: Holt, Rinehart & Winston.

Raphael, T. E., Kirschner, B. W., & Englert, C. S. (1986). *Text structure instruction within process-writing classrooms. A manual for instruction* (Occasional paper No. 104). East Lansing: Michigan State University, Institute for Research on Teaching.

Ratey, J. J., Grandin, T., & Miller, A. (1992). Defense behavior and coping in an autistic savant: The story of Temple Grandin, Ph.D. *Psychiatry, 55*, 382–391.

Reetz, L., & Rasmussen, T. (1988). Arithmetic mind joggers. *Academic Therapy, 24*(1), 79–82.

Reeve, R. E. (1990). ADHD: Facts and fallacies. *Intervention in School and Clinic, 26*(2), 70–78.

Reid, R., Maag, J. W., & Vasa, S. F. (1994). Attention deficit hyperactivity disorder as a disability category: A critique. *Exceptional Children, 60*, 198–214.

Reisberg, L., & Gerlach, K. (1992). Collaboration and teaming: A guide for para-educators and the teacher. Bremerton, WA: Olympic Educational Service District #114.

Rekrut, M. D. (1994). Peer and cross-age tutoring: The lessons of research. *Journal of Reading, 37*, 356–362.

Reynolds, C. R. (1982). The problem of bias in psychological assessment. In C. R. Reynolds & T. B. Gutkin (Eds.), *The handbook of social psychology* (pp. 178–208). New York: Wiley.

Rikhye, C. H., Gothelf, C. R., & Appell, M. W. (1989). A classroom environment checklist for students. *Teaching Exceptional Children, 22*(1), 44–46.

Roberts, C. A., & Lazure, M. D. (1970). *One million children: A national study of Canadian children with emotional and learning disorders.* Toronto: Leonard Crainford.

Robichaud, O., & Enns, R. (1980). The integration issue. In M. Csapo & L. Goguen (Eds.), *Special education across Canada: Issues and concerns for the '80's* (pp. 201–214). Vancouver: Centre for Human Development and Research.

Robinson, S., & Smith, J. (1981). Listening skills: Teaching learning disabled students to be better listeners. *Focus on Exceptional Children, 13*(8), 1–15.

Rodgers-Rhyme, A., & Volpiansky, P. (1991). *PARTNERS in problem solving staff development program: Participant guide.* Madison: Wisconsin Department of Public Instruction.

Rojewski, J. W., Pollard, R. R., & Meers, G. D. (1990). Grading mainstreamed special needs students: Determining practices and attitudes of secondary vocational educators using a qualitative approach. *Remedial and Special Education, 12*(1), 7–15.

Rojewski, J. W., Pollard, R. R., & Meers, G. D. (1992). Grading secondary vocational students with disabilities. *Exceptional Children, 59*(1), 68–76.

Rosenfield, S. A. (1987). *Instructional consultation.* Hillsdale, NJ: Erlbaum.

Rosenshine, B. (1979). Content, time, and direct instruction. In P. Peterson & H. Walberg (Eds.), *Research on teaching: Concepts, findings, and implications* (pp. 28–56). Berkeley: McCutchan.

Rosenshine, B., & Meister, C. (1992). The use of scaffolds for teaching higher-level cognitive strategies. *Educational Leadership, 49,* 26–33.

Rosenshine, B., & Stevens, R. (1986). Teaching functions. In M. C. Wittrock (Ed.), *Handbook of research on teaching* (pp. 376–391). New York: Macmillan.

Ross, J. A. (1988). Improving social-environmental studies problem solving through cooperative learning. *American Education Research Journal, 25,* 573–591.

Ross, R., & Kurtz, R. (1993). Making manipulatives work: A strategy for success. *Arithmetic Teacher, 40*(5), 254–257.

Runge, A., Walker, J., & Shea, T. M. (1975). A passport to positive parent-teacher communication. *Teaching Exceptional Children, 7*(3), 91–92.

Ryan, E. B., Weed, K. A., & Short, E. J. (1986). Cognitive behavior modification: Promoting active self-regulatory learning styles. In J.K. Torgeson & B.Y.L. Wong (Eds.), *Psychological and educational perspectives on learning disabilities* (pp. 367–397). Toronto: Academic Press.

Sabornie, E. J., Kauffman, J. M., Ellis, E. S., Marshall, K. J., & Elksnin, L. K. (1988). The bi-directional and cross-categorical social status of learning disabled, behaviorally disordered, and non-handicapped adolescents. *Journal of Special Education, 21,* 39–56.

Sabornie, E. J., & Beard, G. H. (1990). Teaching social skills. *Teaching Exceptional Children, 23*(1), 35–38.

Salvia, J., & Ysseldyke, J. (1995). Assessment in special and remedial education (6th ed.). Boston: Houghton Mifflin.

Sanche, R. P., Schwier, R. A., & Haines, L. P. (1990). Teacher ratings of two inservice education programs on classroom management. *Canadian Journal of Education, 15,* 293–298.

Sapon-Shevin, M. (1992). Celebrating diversity, creating community: Curriculum that honors and builds on differences. In S. Stainback and W. Stainback (Eds.), *Curriculum considerations in inclusive classrooms: Facilitating learning for all students.* Baltimore: Brookes.

Sapon-Shevin, M. (1994). Why gifted students belong in inclusive schools. *Educational Leadership, 52*(4), 64–68, 70.

Saskatchewan Education. (April, 1996). *Special education policy manual: Draft.* Regina: Author.

Schaps, E., & Solomon, D. (1990). Schools and classrooms as caring communities. *Educational Leadership, 48*(3), 38–42.

Scheerenberger, R. C. (1983). *A history of mental retardation.* Baltimore: Brookes.

Schein, E. H. (1988). *Process consultation volume I: Its role in organization development.* Reading, MA: Addison-Wesley.

Schloss, P. J., & Smith, M. A. (1994). *Applied behavior analysis in the classroom.* Boston: Allyn and Bacon.

Schmid, C., & Hutchinson, N. L. (1994). The role of the family in programs for preschoolers with special needs: A case study of three Canadian families. Paper presented at the annual meeting of the American Educational Research Association, New Orleans, LA.

Schonert-Reichl, K.A. (1995). The friendships and peer relations of adolescents with behavioural problems. *Exceptionality Education Canada, 5*(3&4), 55–80.

Schuller, C. F. (1982). Using instructional resources and technology. In D. E. Orlosky (Ed.), *Introduction to education* (pp. 400–429). Columbus, OH: Merrill.

Schulze, K. A., Rule, S., & Innocenti, M. S. (1989). Coincidental teaching: Parents promoting social skills at home. *Teaching Exceptional Children, 21*(2), 24–27.

Schumaker, J. B., & Deshler, D. D. (1988). Implementing the Regular Education Initiative in secondary schools: A different ball game. *Journal of Learning Disabilities, 21*(1), 36–42.

Schumaker, J. B., Deshler, D. D., & Denton, P. (1984). *The learning strategies curriculum: The paraphrasing strategy.* Lawrence: University of Kansas.

Schunk, D. (1989). Self-efficacy and cognitive achievement. Implications for students with learning disabilities. *Journal of Learning Disabilities, 22*(1), 14–22.

Scruggs, T. E., & Mastropieri, M. A. (1992). Effective mainstreaming strategies for mildly handicapped students. *Elementary School Journal, 92,* 389–409.

Scruggs, T. E., Mastropieri, M. A., & Richter, L. (1985). Peer tutoring with behaviorally disordered students. *Behavioral Disorders, 13,* 283–294.

Scruggs, T., & Mastropieri, M. A. (1988). Are learning disabled students "test-wise"? A review of recent research. *Learning Disabilities Focus, 3*(2), 87–97.

Senesh, L. (1973). *The American way of life.* Chicago: Science Research Associates.

Serff, P. (1996). *A follow-up study with participants of the BreakAway Company.(?)* Unpublished masters thesis, Queen's University.

Sharan, S. (1980). Cooperative learning in small groups: Recent methods and effects on achievement, attitudes, and ethnic relations. *Review of Educational Research, 50,* 241–271.

Sharan, S., Kussell, P., Hertz-Lazarowitz, R., Bejarano, Y., Raviv, S., & Sharan, Y. (1984). *Cooperative learning in the classroom: Research in desegregated schools.* Hillsdale, NJ: Erlbaum.

Shaywitz, S. E., Escobar, M. D., Shaywitz, B. A., Fletcher, J. M., & Makuch, R. (1992). Evidence that dyslexia may represent the lower tail of a normal distribution of reading ability. *New England Journal of Medicine, 326,* 145–150.

Shea, T. M., & Bauer, A. M. (1991). *Parents and teachers of children with exceptionalities: A handbook for collaboration* (2nd ed.). Boston: Allyn and Bacon.

Shea, T. M., & Bauer, A. M. (1994). *Learners with disabilities: A social systems perspective of special education.* Madison, WI: Brown & Benchmark.

Sheinker, J., & Sheinker, A. (1989). *Meta-cognitive approach to study strategies.* Rockville, MD: Aspen.

Shepherd, J. F. (1990). *College study skills.* Boston: Houghton Mifflin.

Simich-Dudgeon, C., McCreedy, L., & Schleppegrell, M. (1988/1989). *Helping limited English proficient children communicate in the classroom: A handbook for teachers.* Washington, DC: National Clearinghouse for Bilingual Education.

Sirvis, B. (1988). Physical disabilities. In E. L. Meyen & T. M. Skrtic (Eds.), *Exceptional children and youth: An introduction* (3rd ed.). Denver. Love.

Slavin, R. E. (1994). *Cooperative learning* (2nd ed.). Boston: Allyn and Bacon.

Slavin, R. E., Madden, N. A., Dolan, L. J., Wasik, B. A., Ross, S. M., & Smith, L. J. (1994). "Whenever and wherever we choose": The replication of "Success for All." *Phi Delta Kappan, 75,* 639–647.

Smith, C. R. (1994). *Learning disabilities: The interaction of learner, task, and setting.* Boston: Allyn and Bacon.

Smith, D. D., & Luckasson, R. (1995). *Introduction to special education: Teaching in an age of challenge* (2nd ed.). Boston: Allyn and Bacon.

Smith, D. D., & Rivera, D. M. (1993). *Effective discipline* (2nd ed.). Austin, TX: Pro-Ed.

Smith, H. A. (1985). TO FOLLOW

Smith, M. A., & Mirsa, A. (1992). A comprehensive management system for students in regular classrooms. *Elementary School Journal, 92*(3), 354–371.

Smith, S. (1980). *No easy answers.* New York: Bantam Books.

Smith, W. J. (1994). *Equal educational opportunity for students with disabilities: Legislative action in Canada.* Montreal: McGill University, Office of Research on Educational Policy.

Snow, J., & Forest, M. (1987). Circles. In M. Forest (Ed.), *More education integration* (pp. 169–176). Downsview, Ontario: G. Allan Roeher Institute.

Snyder, K. (1988). RIDGES: A problem-solving math strategy. *Academic Therapy, 23*(3), 261–263.

Sobel, R., LaRaus, R., DeLeon, L. A., & Morris, H. P. (1986). *The challenge of freedom.* New York: Macmillan. Publisher of record: Glencoe Division, Macmillan/McGraw-Hill School Publishing.

Solomon, D., Watson, M., Schaps, E., Battistich, V., & Solomon, J. (1990). Cooperative learning as part of a comprehensive classroom program designed to promote prosocial development. In S. Sharan (Ed.), *Cooperative learning.* New York: Praeger.

Sontag, J. C., & Schacht, R. (1994). An ethnic comparison of parent participating and information needs in early intervention. *Exceptional Children, 60,* 422–433.

Sparks, D., & Sparks, G. M. (1984). *Effective teaching for higher achievement.* Alexandria, VA: Association for Supervision and Curriculum Development.

Sprague, J. R., & Horner, R. H. (1990). Easy does it: Preventing challenging behaviors. *Teaching Exceptional Children, 23*(1), 13–15.

Stainback, S., & Stainback, W. (1988). Educating students with severe disabilities. *Teaching Exceptional Children, 21*(1), 16–19.

Stainback, S., & Stainback, W. (1992). Schools as inclusive communities. In W. Stainback & S. Stainback (Eds.), *Controversial issues confronting special education: Divergent perspectives.* Boston: Allyn and Bacon.

Stainback, S., & Stainback, W. (1992). *Curriculum considerations in inclusive classrooms: Facilitating learning for all students.* Toronto: Brookes.

Stainback, W., Stainback, S., Etscheidt, S., & Doud, J. (1986). A nonintrusive intervention for acting-out behavior. *Teaching Exceptional Children, 19*(1), 38–41.

Stainback, W., Stainback, S., & Froyen, L. (1987). Structuring the classroom to prevent disruptive behaviors. *Teaching Exceptional Children, 19*(4), 12–16.

Stainback, S., Stainback, W., & Jackson, H. J. (1992). Toward inclusive classrooms. In S. Stainback and W. Stainback (Eds.), *Curriculum considerations in inclusive classrooms: Facilitating learning for all students.* Baltimore: Brookes.

Stainback, W., Stainback, S., & Wilkinson, A. (1992). Encouraging peer supports and friendships. *Teaching Exceptional Children, 24*(2), 6–11.

Stanley, J. C., & Benbow, C. P. (1986). Youths who reason exceptionally well mathematically. In R. J. Sternberg & J. E. Davidson (Eds.), *Conceptions of giftedness* (pp. 361-387). New York: Cambridge University Press.

Stanovich, K. E. (1986). Matthew effects in reading: Some consequences of individual differences in the acquisition of literacy. *Reading Research Quarterly, 21,* 360–407.

Stanovich, K. E. (1994). Constructivism in reading education. *The Journal of Special Education, 28,* 259–274.

Stanovich, K. E., & Stanovich, P. J. (1995). How research might inform the debate about early reading acquisition. *Journal of Research in Reading, 18*(2), 87–105.

Starlin, C. M. (1982). *Iowa monograph: On reading and writing.* Des Moines: State of Iowa, Office of Public Instruction.

Stephen, V. P., Varble, M. E., & Taitt, H. (1993). Instructional and organizational change to meet minority and at risk students' needs. *Journal of Staff Development, 14*(4), 40–43.

Stevens, L. J., & Price, M. (1992). Meeting the challenge of educating children at risk. *Phi Delta Kappan, 74,* 18–23.

Strang, J. D., & Rourke, B. P. (1985). Arithmetic disability subtypes: The neuropsychological significance of specific arithmetical impairment in childhood. In B. P. Rourke (Ed.), *Neuropsychology of learning disabilities.* New York: Guilford Press.

Stringer, J. A. (1984). *A study of training programs for Native Indian teaching assistants with emphasis on the program at Lytton.* Unpublished masters thesis, University of British Columbia, Vancouver.

Swanson, J. M., Cantwell, D., Lerner, M., McBurnett, K., Pfiffner, L., & Kotkin, R. (1992). Treatment of ADHD: Beyond medication. *Beyond Behavior, 4*(1), 13–16, 18–22.

Szetela, W., & Nicol, C. (1992). Evaluating problem solving in mathematics. *Educational Leadership, 49*(8), 42–45.

Thousand, J. S., & Villa, R. A. (1990). Strategies for educating learners with severe disabilities within their local home schools and communities. *Focus on Exceptional Children, 23*(3), 1–24.

Tindal, G. A., & Marston, D. B. (1990). *Classroom-based assessment: Evaluating instructional outcomes.* Columbus, OH: Merrill.

Torgesen, J. (1991). Learning disabilities: Historical and conceptual issues. In B. Wong (Ed.), *Learning about learning disabilities* (pp. 3–39). San Diego: Academic Press.

Toronto Board of Education. (n.d.). *Benchmarks: Standards of student achievement.* Toronto: Author.

Tower, C. B. (1989). Understanding child abuse and neglect. Boston: Allyn and Bacon.

Tozer, R., & Strickland, D. (1986). *A pictorial history of Algonquin Park.* Whitney, ON: Ontario Ministry of Natural Resources and Friends of Algonquin Park.

Tucker, B. F., & Colson, S. E. (1992). Traumatic brain injury: An overview of school re-entry. *Intervention in School and Clinic, 27,* 198–206.

Tucker, J. A. (1985). Curriculum-based assessment: An introduction. *Exceptional Children, 52,* 199–204.

Tucker, J. A. (1989). Less required energy: A response to Danielson and Bellamy. *Exceptional Children, 55,* 456–458.

Turnbull, A. P., & Turnbull, H. R. (1990). *Families, professionals, and exceptionality: A special partnership* (2nd ed.). Columbus, OH: Merrill.

Turner, L. (1996). Sightless seer 1893-1968: Edwin Albert Baker. In Humber, C. J. (Ed.), *Canadian heirloom series, Volume V, Wayfarers: Canadian achievers.* Mississauga: Heirloom Pub. Inc.

U.S. Department of Education. (1988). *Tenth annual report to Congress on the implementation of the Individuals with Disabilities Education Act.* Washington, DC: Author.

U.S. Department of Education. (1993). *Fifteenth annual report to Congress on the implementation of the Individuals with Disabilities Education Act.* Washington, DC: Author.

U.S. Department of Justice, Civil Rights Division, Coordination and Review Section. (1990). *Americans with Disabilities Act requirements: Fact sheet.* Washington, DC: Author.

Vacc, N. N., & Cannon, S. J. (1991). Cross-age tutoring in mathematics: Sixth graders helping students who are moderately handicapped. *Education and Training in Mental Retardation, 26,* 89–97.

Vacca, R. T., & Vacca, J. L. (1986). *Content area reading* (2nd ed.). Boston: Little Brown.

Valpy, M. (1993, October 23). The 40% factor. *The Globe and Mail,* pp. D1, D5.

Vandercook, T., York, J., & Forest, M. (1989). The McGill Action Planning System (MAPS): A strategy for building the vision. *Journal of the Association for Persons with Severe Handicaps, 14*(3), 205–218.

Vandervelden, M. C., & Siegel, L. S. (1997). Teaching phonological processing skills in early literacy: A developmental approach. *Learning Disability Quarterly, 20,* 63–280.

VanGundy, A. B. (1988). *Techniques of structured problem solving* (2nd ed.). New York: Van Nostrand Reinhold.

Van Riper, C., & Emerick, L. (1984). *Speech correction: An introduction to speech pathology and audiology.* Englewood Cliffs, NJ: Prentice-Hall.

Vergason, G. A., & Anderegg, M. L. (1992). Preserving the least restrictive environment. In W. Stainback & S. Stainback (Eds.), *Controversial issues confronting special education: Divergent perspectives* (pp. 45–54). Boston: Allyn and Bacon.

Villa, R. A., & Thousand, J. S. (1992). Student collaboration: An essential for curriculum delivery in the 21st century. In S. Stainback and W. Stainback (Eds.), *Curriculum considerations in inclusive classrooms: Facilitating learning for all students.* Baltimore: Brookes.

Voeltz, L. J., Hemphill, N. J., Brown, S., Kishi, G., Klein, R., Fruehling, R., Collie, J., Levy, G., & Kube, C. (1983). *The special friends program: A trainer's manual for integrated school settings.* Honolulu: University of Hawaii, Department of Special Education.

Voix, R. G. (1968). *Evaluating reading and study skills in the secondary classroom: A guide for content teachers.* Newark, DE: International Reading Association.

Voltz, D. L., & Elliott, R. N. (1990). Resource room teacher roles in promoting interaction with regular educators. *Teacher Education and Special Education, 13,* 160–166.

Waggoner, K., & Wilgosh, L. (1990). Concerns of families of children with learning disabilities. *Journal of Learning Disabilities, 23,* 97–98, 113.

Wagner, R. K. (1988). Phonological processing abilities and reading: Implications for disabled readers. *Journal of Learning Disabilities, 19,* 623–630.

Wallis, S. (1993, September). *Multicultural teaching: Meeting the challenges that arise in practice.* Curriculum Update, pp. 1–8.

Wang, M. C., Reynolds, M. C., & Walberg, H. J. (1988). Integrating the children of the second system. *Phi Delta Kappan, 70,* 248–251.

Watson, D. L., & Rangel, L. (1989). Don't forget the slow learner. *Clearinghouse, 62,* 266–268.

Watt, D., & Roessingh, H. (1994). ESL dropout: The myth of educational equity. *Alberta Journal of Educational Research, 40,* 283–296.

Webber, J., & Scheuermann, B. (1991). Accentuate the positive . . . Eliminate the negative! *Teaching Exceptional Children, 24*(1), 13–19.

Westby, C. E., & Ford, V. (1993). The role of team culture in assessment and intervention. *Journal of Educational and Psychological Consultation, 4,* 319–341.

Wheelock, A. (1992). The case for untracking. *Educational Leadership, 50*(2), 6–10.

White, A. E., & White, L. L. (1992). A collaborative model for students with mild disabilities in middle schools. *Focus on Exceptional Children, 24*(9), 1–10.

White, S., & Bond, M. R. (1992). Transition services in a large school district: Practical solutions to complex problems. *Teaching Exceptional Children, 24*(4), 44–47.

Whitmore, J. R. (1988). Gifted children at risk for learning difficulties. *Teaching Exceptional Children, 20*(4), 10–14.

Wiener, J. (1994). Social and affective impacts of full inclusion. *Exceptionality Education Canada, 4*(3&4), 107–117.

Wiener, J., & Davidson, I. (1990). The in-school team: A preventive model of service delivery in special education. *Canadian Journal of Education, 15,* 427–444.

Wiener, J., Harris, P. J., & Shirer, C. (1990). Achievement and social-behavioural correlates of peer status in LD children. *Learning Disability Quarterly, 13,* 114–127.

Wiggins, G. (1992). Creating tests worth taking. *Educational Leadership, 49*(8), 26–33.

Williams, J. N. (1986). Accommodations for secondary learning disabled/mainstreamed students on teacher-made tests. Unpublished manuscript. Wheaton, MD: Wheaton High School.

Williams, S. L., Walker, H. M., Holmes, D., Todis, B., & Fabre, T. R. (1989). Social validation of adolescent social skills by teachers and students. *Remedial and Special Education, 10*(4), 18–27, 37.

Wilson, R. J. (1990). Classroom processes in evaluating student achievement. *Alberta Journal of Educational Research, 36,* 4-17.

Wilson, R. J. (1996). *Assessing students in classrooms and schools.* Scarborough: Allyn & Bacon.

Winebrenner, S. (1992). *Teaching gifted kids in the regular classroom: Strategies and techniques every teacher can use to meet the academic needs of the gifted and talented.* Minneapolis: Free Spirit Publishing.

Winne, P, Graham, L. & Prock, L. (1993). A model of poor readers' text-based inferencing. Effects of explanatory feedback. *Reading Research Quarterly, 28,* 53-66.

Winzer, M., Rogow, S., & David, C. (1987). *Exceptional children in Canada.* Toronto: Prentice Hall.

Wisniewski, L., & Alper, S. (1994). Including students with severe disabilities in general education settings. *Remedial and Special Education, 15*(1), 4–13.

Witt, J. C., & Martens, B. K. (1988). Problems with problem-solving consultation: A re-analysis of assumptions, goals, and methods. *School Psychology Review, 17,* 211–226.

Wolfensberger, W., Nirge, B., Olshansky, S., Perske, R., & Roos, P. (1972). *The principle of normalization in human services.* Toronto: National Institute on Mental Retardation.

Wong, B. Y. L. (1996). *The ABCs of learning disabilities.* Toronto: Academic Press.

Wood, J. W., Miederhoff, J. W., & Ulschmid, B. (1989). Adapting test construction for mainstreamed social studies students. *Social Education, 53*(1), 46–49.

Wyman, S. L. (1993). *How to respond to your culturally diverse student population*. Alexandria, VA: Association for Supervision and Curriculum Development.

Yell, M. L. (1990). The use of corporal punishment, suspension, expulsion, and timeout with behaviorally disordered students in public schools: Legal considerations. *Behavioral Disorders, 15*(2), 100–109.

York, J., & Vandercook, T. (1990). Strategies for achieving an integrated education for middle school students with severe disabilities. *Remedial and Special Education, 11*(5), 6–16.

York, J., Vandercook, T., MacDonald, C., Heise-Neff, C., & Caughey, E. (1992). Feedback about integrating middle-school students with severe disabilities in general education classes. *Exceptional Children, 58*, 244–258.

York, J., Vandercook, T., & Stave, K. (1990). Recreation and leisure activities: Determining the favorites for middle school students. *Teaching Exceptional Children, 22*(4), 10–13.

Ysseldyke, J. E., & Algozzine, B. (1995). *Special education: A practical approach for teachers* (3rd ed.). Geneva, IL: Houghton Mifflin.

Ysseldyke, J., & Christensen, S. (1987). *TIES: The instructional environment scale*. Austin, TX: Pro-Ed.

Yukon Education. (1996). *Partners in education: The Yukon education act*. Whitehorse: Author.

Yukon Special Programs Branch. (1995). *Special programs services: A handbook of procedures and guidelines*. Whitehorse: Department of Education.

Zentall, S.S. (1983). Effects of psychotropic drugs on the behaviour of pre-academic children: A review. *Topics in Early Childhood Special Education, 3*, 29–39.

Zentall, S. S. (1993). Research on the educational implications of attention deficit hyperactivity disorder. *Exceptional Children, 60*, 143–153.

Name Index

Subject Index

A
Ability OnLine, 12
Absence seizures, 127-28
Academic learning time, 210
Academics
  basic skills, 26, 270-76
  cognitive and learning strategies, 26-27
  survival skills, 27, 160
Acceleration, 146-47
Accommodations. *See* Adaptations
Accountability, shared, 71
Activity reinforcers, 392
Adaptations
  age-appropriate, 32
  for autism, 134-35
  basic skills, 270-76
  bypass strategies, 29-30
  in classroom organization, 30
  in classroom teaching, 30
  for communication disorders, 151-53
  for developmental disabilities, 113-14
  for health impairments, 129-30
  in homework, 300-3
  INCLUDE approach, 23-33
  independent learning strategies, 308-39
  independent student practice, 296, 298-304
  instructional material, 303-4
  intensive instruction strategy, 31

for learning and behaviour disabilities, 164-69
for physical disabilities, 125-26
in seatwork assignments, 298-99
selection guidelines for, 28, 32
for sensory impairments, 116-19
in subject-area content instruction, 276-91
in tests, 236-37, 344-56
for traumatic brain injury, 333-36
for visual impairments, 117-19
Adapted education program, 5
See also Special education
Adaptive behaviour scales, 109
Adaptive devices. *See* Assistive technology
Administrators, 42
Advance organizers, 279-80
Advice, 75
Advocate, 46
Age-appropriate adaptations, 32
AIDS (acquired immune deficiency syndrome), 129
Alberta
  categorical approach, 14
  education reform, 12
  inclusion in special education, 13, 14
Alcohol abuse, 192-93

See Fetal alcohol syndrome (FAS)
Alternative communication, 112
Alternative teaching, 81
American Sign Language (ASL), 123
Anecdotal comments, 61
Anecdotal recording, 404-5, 408
Anger control, 171, 196
Anger Management (social-skills training package), 446
Anticipation guides, 278, 279, 280
Anti-racist education, 187-89
Anxiety, 164
Apparent intent
  identifying, 403-4
  responding to, 388-89
Asking questions, 294-96
Asperger's syndrome, 134
Assessment
  community-referenced, 248-49
  content-area, 257-62
  curriculum-based, 249, 252-54, 263, 264
  curriculum-placement, 242-43
  defined, 240
  in-depth, 241
  in initial interventions, 241
  performance-based, 365-71
  portfolio, 371-74
  program-placement, 241-42

sources of information, 243-52
See also Evaluation; Probes; Tests
Assignments
  differentiating between short- and long-term, 334
  homework, 235, 300-3
  seatwork, 298-99
Assistive technology, 226-27
  for communication, 112, 428-29
  and disability awareness, 427
  for hearing impairments, 123
  for students at risk, 194-95
  visual impairments, for students with, 119, 121
Asthma, 129
At risk. *See* Students at risk
Attention, 158-59
Attention-deficit disorder (ADD). *See* Attention-Deficit/ Hyperactivity Disorder (ADHD)
Attention-Deficit/Hyperactivity Disorder (ADHD), 19, 29
  characteristics of, 169-70
  defined, 169
  interventions for, 170-72
Attention disorder, 169
Attribution retraining, 167-68

Photo Credits